# KINGFISHER
# HISTORY
# ENCYCLOPEDIA

**KINGFISHER**
LONDON & NEW YORK

Copyright © 1999, 2022 by Macmillan Publishers International Ltd
First American edition published in 1999
This updated edition published in 2022 in the United States by Kingfisher,
120 Broadway, New York, NY 10271
Kingfisher is an imprint of Macmillan Children's Books, London.
All rights reserved.

Distributed in the U.S. and Canada by Macmillan,
120 Broadway, New York, NY 10271

LIBRARY OF CONGRESS CATALOGING-IN-PUBLICATION DATA
The Kingfisher history encyclopedia.—1st ed.
p. cm.
Includes index.
Summary: A reference guide to world history, featuring a time line,
key date boxes, and biographies of historical figures.
1. World history—Juvenile literature. [1. World history.]
I. Kingfisher Books.
D20.K558 1999
909—dc21 98-50409 CIP AC

CONTRIBUTORS
Jane Birch, Teresa Chris, Neil Grant, Ken Hills, Julian Holland,
Palden Jenkins, Elizabeth Longley, Fiona Macdonald, Hazel Martell,
Mike McGuire, Theodore Rowland-Entwhistle, Giles Sparrow
2012 edition: with thanks to Professor Ben Fortna, School of Oriental and African Studies,
University of London, U.K.

ARTWORK ARCHIVISTS
Wendy Allison, Steve Robinson

ARTISTS
Jonathan Adams, Hemesh Alles, Marion Appleton, Sue Barclay, R. Barnett, Noel Bateman,
Simon Bishop, Richard Bonson, Nick Cannan, Vanessa Card, Tony Chance, Harry Clow,
Stephen Conlin, Peter Dennis, Dave Etchell, Jeff Farrow, James Field, Ian Fish, Michael Fisher,
Eugene Fleury, Chris Forsey, Dewey Franklin, Terry Gabbey, Fred Gambino, John Gillatt,
Matthew Gore, Jeremy Gower, Neil Gower, Ray Grinaway, Allan Hardcastle, Nick Harris,
Nicholas Hewetson, Bruce Hogarth, Christian Hook, Richard Hook, Simon Huson, John James,
Peter Jarvis, John Kelly, Deborah Kindred, Adrian Lascombe, Chris Lenthall, Jason Lewis,
Chris Lyon, Kevin Maddison, Shirley Mallinson, Shane Marsh, David MacAllister, Angus McBride,
Stefan Morris, Jackie Moore, Teresa Morris, Frank Nichols, Chris D. Orr, Sharon Pallent, R. Payne,
R. Philips, Jayne Pickering, Melvyn Pickering, Malcolm Porter, Mike Posen, Mike Roffe,
Chris Rothero, David Salarya, Mike Saunders, Rodney Shackell, Rob Shone, Mark Stacey,
Paul Stangroom, Branca Surla, Smiljka Surla, Stephen Sweet, Mike Taylor, George Thompson,
Martin Wilson, David Wright, Paul Wright

ISBN: 978-0-7534-7769-4

Kingfisher books are available for special promotions and premiums. For details contact:
Special Markets Department, Macmillan, 120 Broadway, New York, NY 10271.

For more information, please visit www.kingfisherbooks.com

EU representative: 1st Floor, The Liffey Trust Centre,
117-126 Sheriff Street Upper, Dublin 1 D01 YC43

Printed in Thailand
2 4 6 8 10 9 7 5 3 1
1TR/0622/RRDTLD/UNV/128MA

MIX
Paper | Supporting
responsible forestry
FSC
www.fsc.org
FSC® C116313

# KINGFISHER
# HISTORY
# ENCYCLOPEDIA

## KINGFISHER
### LONDON & NEW YORK

# CONTENTS

# INTRODUCTION

Often, fact is stranger than fiction. The *Kingfisher History Encyclopedia* is packed full of fascinating facts and real-life stories about the people, places, and events of the past that have shaped the colorful, but still turbulent world that we know today. The causes and effects of the actions and events are explained in full, giving a vivid picture of how leaders, tyrants, artists, and scientists who lived hundreds of years ago have left a legacy that still impinges on people's lives in the twenty-first century.

Use your *Kingfisher History Encyclopedia* to discover past events and find out how people have lived their lives over the last 40,000 years—from Stone Age cave dwellers to the Anglo-Saxons, from the Aztecs and Incas of Mesoamerica to the Manchus in China, and from the American Revolution to United Nations peacekeeping.

This user-friendly encyclopedia contains many features to help you look things up easily, or just have fun browsing. The in-depth coverage of each historical period also makes the encyclopedia perfect for all your school projects and homework assignments.

The clear, informative text is accompanied by key date boxes, colorful photographs, and superb illustrations and maps. At-a-glance world maps at the beginning of each chapter highlight the major events that happened during a particular time period. These are arranged according to continent or area of the world. At the end of each of the ten chapters, there are three special feature spreads that give an overview of the arts, architecture, and science and technology of the featured time period. Finally, there is a Ready Reference section at the back of the book containing lists of names and dates for quick and easy access.

Whether you use your *Kingfisher History Encyclopedia* for homework, or just dip into it at random, it will add considerably to your understanding of the past, and will stimulate you to explore the lives of our ancestors further.

◀ Man-made structures tell us a great deal about the past. One of the largest and most famous is the Great Wall of China. Its construction was ordered by the first Qin emperor, Shi Huangdi, around 221 B.C., to keep out invaders from the north. Stretching for 4,000 mi. (6,400km), the wall was built by joining together shorter walls that had been built earlier. The wall has been rebuilt many times. Most of the wall that can be seen today was constructed during the Ming dynasty (1368–1644).

# WHAT IS HISTORY?

The word "history" comes from the ancient Greek word *histo* meaning "know this." In Greek, "I know" also meant "I have seen," and *historeo* came to mean "learn by inquiry." The Greeks thought that the only way to know something was to either see it for themselves, or ask questions about it. The Greek historian Thucydides wrote that too many people often believed the first story they heard. Ancient Greeks understood the essence of history. First, historical knowledge must be based on evidence. Second, history is not one story, but several. Third, everything must be checked for mistakes. Historians try to find out not only what happened, but why it happened.

The ancient Egyptians left administrative and religious records, using a writing system called hieroglyphics, on paper made from papyrus.

"History" has come to mean many things. It is an account of past events, in sequence of time; it is the study of events, their causes and results; and it is all that is preserved or remembered about the past. For evidence, historians use written accounts, artifacts such as weapons and tools, and spoken (oral) accounts. To remember something, people write it down, or mark it in some way. This is because events, even important ones, disappear from memory or become confused. Our lives may seem different from people's lives in the past, but some things have not changed—Roman roads are still used every day and games like chess were played centuries ago.

Documentary evidence is very important to historians. English families that have had a connection with one place stretching back over 1,000 years may find a reference to their family in the *Domesday Book*, compiled in 1086. It records who owned land, who lived there, how much it was worth, and what taxes were paid.

## LOCAL HISTORY

Oral history is a good source of local history. Listening to the recollections of older people, looking at their photographs, and sharing their memories reveals a lot about the past. Family history is a branch of local history. Photographs of family members may reach as far back as great-great-grandparents. Important family events were often recorded in the front of a family bible. Local record offices store diaries, letters, census returns, old photographs, records of large estates, school textbooks, and business accounts from firms that have long stopped trading. Church records give details of baptisms, marriages, and funerals.

Buildings often tell us a lot about the past. In the early 1600s, the great Mogul emperor Akbar was buried in this highly decorated tomb, which still stands in the city of Fatehpur Sikri in India.

## THE WORK OF HISTORIANS

The first real historian was Herodotus. He used the Greek word *historia* to mean "investigation." Although Herodotus was writing at a time when everyone believed their lives were controlled by the gods, he also looked for rational explanations and was the first person to look at the cause and effect of events. Sometimes history is written by those who play a major part in it. Julius Caesar wrote about the wars in Gaul (France), and Winston Churchill wrote about World War I and II. Not all historians witness the events they write about. Most depend on accounts and documents produced at the time. Those who write history should always be aware of any bias or prejudice in themselves and in other writers. Bias means being influenced by a particular point of view, and prejudice literally means "judging before"— before all the facts have been looked at. Historians also have to avoid the mistake of writing about the past as if all events were leading with a fixed purpose to the present.

## THE WORK OF ARCHAEOLOGISTS

Archaeology is the study of the peoples of the past by the scientific analysis of the things they leave behind. Archaeologists study objects (artifacts), features (buildings), and seeds or animal bones (ecofacts). Archaeology can tell us about societies that existed before written records were made, and add to our knowledge of civilized societies.

Archaeologists treat the things they find as clues to the lives of the people who used them. They can sometimes discover the reasons for great changes in the societies they are studying. Kathleen Kenyon, digging at the site of Jericho in 1952, found out that its walls were destroyed in biblical times, but by fire—not by the sound of trumpets! Archaeology can often present historians with evidence that makes them reexamine their views of early societies. In 1939, at Sutton Hoo in England, the remains of an Anglo-Saxon treasure ship were discovered. The artifacts found there are evidence of a society from the so-called "Dark Ages" that are far from primitive.

Since the 1950s, archaeologists have been concerned with finding general theories that explain the changes that occur in human societies. They now try to find out why farming developed in Mexico around 7000 B.C. or why the first cities grew in the Near East. Computers can be used to process the statistics and they have made this sort of study much faster and more efficient.

Artifacts such as coins, pottery, tools, and weapons are sometimes found in great abundance. Studying them can add to our knowledge of social and military history. Ecofacts, such as animal bones, skins, and

Delicate *netsuke* give an insight into Japanese life in the 1700s.

This selection of items found by archaelogists in the wreck of the ship *Mary Rose* shows us what a sailor was likely to take to sea in 1536. They include a pouch, a whistle, a comb, and a rosary.

plant seeds, help identify the jobs people did and what they ate. Pictures and paintings can also provide valuable information. We can tell a lot about what people looked like, and what they did, from cave paintings, frescoes, portraits, and pictures in stained glass.

When digging, archaeologists try to avoid damaging anything. A grid is used to locate and record the exact position, size, and condition of finds. All earth removed from a site is collected in pails and later sifted in case any small find has been missed. Accurate written records are made and each level of the site is photographed.

# THE ANCIENT WORLD

## 40,000 – 500 B.C.

This is the earliest history of humanity, as it
evolved from cave dwellers to village-dwelling
farmers to populations in towns, up to and
including the first advanced civilizations. It was
around 40,000 B.C. that humans first built their
own homes and painted pictures on the walls
of caves. It was not until around 8000 B.C.
that the first farming and trading villages were
built, and another 5,000 years—250 generations—
passed before important civilizations
appeared in Egypt and Mesopotamia.

▲ The first people lived in caves and eventually made fire by using a
bow to spin a stick against another piece of wood to create sparks.

◀ The Ancient Egyptians believed in life after death. They worshipped
many gods, including Osiris, the god of the dead, whose image is seen
here (left) with Anubis (center) and Horus (right) in a painting on the
tomb of Horemheb, who died in 1292 B.C.

3

# EARLY HUMANS 40,000–10,000 B.C.

By about 40,000 B.C., humans had spread across Africa, Europe, and Asia, and even reached Australia. The history of our species *Homo sapiens* ("wise human") had begun.

Recent discoveries of fossils and advances in genetics have shed light on human origins in Africa. However, the more we discover, the more questions are raised. Evolution seems more like a complicated puzzle than a simple timeline.

### THE HUMAN FAMILY

The term "hominid" is used to describe all great apes, extinct or modern, as well as humans and their ancestors. The word "hominin" describes the closer line of human relatives—*Ardipethecus, Paranthropus, Australopithecus,* and *Homo.* Long before humans existed, our ancestors were migrating. Early fossils of our direct ancestor *Homo erectus* ("upright human")

Early peoples shaped flints to make tools and weapons, such as scrapers, knives, and arrowheads.

This shelter, discovered in the Ukraine, was made of wood and covered with animal skins weighed down with mammoth bones. It was built to survive harsh winters.

are found not only in Africa, but as far away as China.

### THE RISE OF HOMO SAPIENS

*Homo sapiens* evolved in Africa nearly 300,000 years ago. Some humans left their homeland at a very early date, but most modern humans are probably descended from a group that left Africa about 70–60,000 years ago. Until about 28,000 years ago, humans in Europe and Asia coexisted with other less advanced hominins, such as

## THE ICE AGE

Long periods of global cold are called ice ages. Within them are cold extremes called "glacials." The last glacial began about 33,000 years ago. At this time, polar and continental ice increased, so people and animals had to adapt to extreme cold. So much water was locked up in ice that sea levels were 90 m (300ft.) lower than today. This meant migrating hunters could reach new lands.

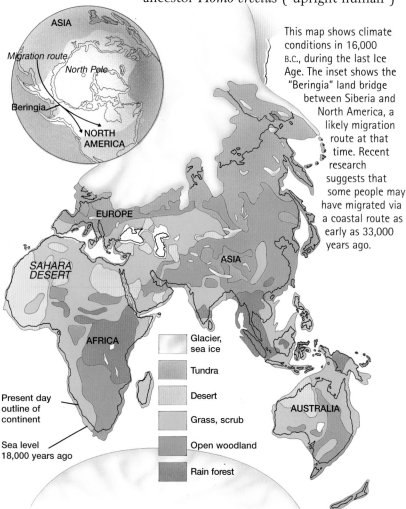

This map shows climate conditions in 16,000 B.C., during the last Ice Age. The inset shows the "Beringia" land bridge between Siberia and North America, a likely migration route at that time. Recent research suggests that some people may have migrated via a coastal route as early as 33,000 years ago.

ASIA
Migration route
North Pole
Beringia
NORTH AMERICA
EUROPE
ASIA
SAHARA DESERT
AFRICA
AUSTRALIA

Present day outline of continent

Sea level 18,000 years ago

Glacier, sea ice
Tundra
Desert
Grass, scrub
Open woodland
Rain forest

Prehistoric cave art has survived in France and Spain, the oldest possibly drawn by Neanderthals. Ancient paintings have also been found in Australia and Indonesia.

Neanderthals (*Homo neanderthalis*) and Denisovans (*Homo denisova*). Modern humans' DNA proves that there was some interbreeding between all three groups.

## LIFE IN THE STONE AGE

Early modern humans gathered berries and roots, and hunted wild animals. They lived in caves and simple shelters and made clothes of skins and fur. People made tools and weapons of stone, so the whole of this period is known in Europe and Asia as the Paleolithic or Old Stone Age. By 10,000 B.C., the climate had warmed and water levels rose. The making of tools became more precise. This was the Mesolithic or Middle Stone Age.

▲ This is a tented encampment in Eastern Europe about 25,000 years ago. Nomadic communities hunted large wild animals such as mammoths. Every part of the animal was used, for food, clothing, shelter, tools, or ornaments. This way of life demanded teamwork and cooperation.

◄ Control of fire was already of importance to *Homo Erectus*. Both Neanderthals and early humans made fires by striking sparks from a flint. Later, using friction methods such as this bow drill to light a fire were perfected.

Early Europeans made jewelry from stones, bones, ivory, shells, and teeth. It was often buried in graves.

Many big animals died out at the end of the last glacial. People could still hunt deer, hares, and wildfowl, and gather wild food, but the future would rely on farmers rather than hunters.

# THE FIRST FARMERS 10,000–4000 B.C.

**As the planet warmed, Neolithic or New Stone Age peoples learned how to domesticate animals and grow crops for food—the development of agriculture.**

People first worshiped mother-goddesses about 25,000 years ago. They believed that, like the Earth, these goddesses gave life to all living things.

Wheat and barley were crossed with grasses to breed new strains. They were used to make bread, the staple of human diet in every early civilization.

The earliest farmers settled nearly 10,000 years ago in the Fertile Crescent in the Middle East. Here people grew wheat and barley. They kept goats, sheep, pigs, and cattle that they used for meat, milk, hides, wool, and to carry things. The improvement in the design of simple tools allowed people to clear land more effectively, build villages, and stay in one place. Later, agriculture also developed in China, northwest India, Africa, and the Americas.

## DOMESTICATION

The first animal to be domesticated was the dog, as early as 12,000 B.C. Dogs were used for herding and as night guards. The horse, goat, and sheep were also domesticated. Farmers learned how to breed animals in order to change their characteristics. A number of species spread as well—chickens and pheasants, for example, originated in the Far East. Meanwhile, some animals, such as aurochs, were hunted to extinction.

Early civilizations of the Middle East grew up in the Fertile Crescent, an ideal area for farming and settled village life, for trade, and later for building towns.

## IRRIGATION

One of the most important inventions was irrigation, a system of supplying cultivated land with water. Farmers in the Fertile Crescent and Mesoamerica dug channels to carry water to their crops. Using reservoirs and sluiceways, land lying far from rivers could be made fertile. In Egypt and China, annual floods were controlled to provide irrigation. In wetter climates, drainage was also important. After many generations, some farmers started bartering goods with neighbors and travelers, leading to the growth of trade and the founding of the first towns and civilizations.

▶ Nomadic peoples followed wild herds or moved from season to season. They went where the pickings or the weather were best. They used temporary homes and simple tools. When tribes met they would trade items, hold festivals, and arrange marriages.

◀ In early villages, people thatched their houses, kept their animals in pens and pastures, and tended vegetable patches. They developed new techniques for storing food, fertilizing fields, and making tools.

6

# SUMER AND AKKAD 5000–1600 B.C.

**The first people to settle in Mesopotamia were the Sumerians more than 7,000 years ago. They built a number of independent city-states—the first civilization.**

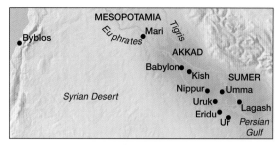

The fertile Tigris and Euphrates river valleys acted as the birthplace of trading cities, extending their influence far and wide—an attractive target for marauding warriors.

The Sumerian civilization consisted of a number of city-states—cities that were also independent nations. Some of these cities lasted for 3,000 years. They were located on important trade routes along the Tigris and Euphrates rivers. Their traders traveled to Egypt and India.

In 2360 B.C., Sargon of Akkad invaded Mesopotamia, carving out the world's first empire.

Scribes and accountants were important, and involved in all aspects of Sumerian daily life, including trade, law, and religion.

### SUMERIAN CITIES
Each city-state had fine public buildings, markets, workshops, and water systems. There was a royal palace and a *ziggurat*, on top of which was a shrine dedicated to the god of that city. Around the public buildings were houses. Beyond these lay the farmers' fields and the marshlands of the Mesopotamian rivers.

### READING AND WRITING
The Sumerians devised one of the earliest writing systems, *cuneiform*. From about 3200 B.C. they wrote on clay tablets, and scribes held a key role in their society. Thousands of tablets have survived, containing accounts, records, sacred scripts, and letters. The contents of their graves have shown that the Sumerians were wealthy and their craftspeople skilled.

### INTERNAL STRIFE
Around 2900 B.C., with city populations growing, power shifted away from the priesthoods which had been all-powerful—commerce gradually becoming more important than religion. Rivalry between different cities grew, and they fought each other for supremacy. They were also invaded by tribes from Persia, Arabia, and Turkey who wanted to share the cities' wealth and power.

### AKKAD AND UR
Eventually, the city of Akkad grew dominant. The city was led by Sargon, who created the world's first empire around 2334 B.C. His rule brought more order—but it also brought cruelty and violence. Around 2100 B.C., as Akkad declined, the city of Ur took its place, rising to prominence for a century. After its fall, Assyria and Babylon grew to dominate the area.

Reeds are still used as a building material, as in this mudhif from southern Iraq. This Mesopotamian tradition goes back to at least 3,300 B.C.

## ZIGGURATS
Built of sunbaked clay bricks, ziggurats towered impressively over the river plains. Building them demanded careful architecture and engineering. The shrine at the top was dedicated to the god of the city. Here, priest-kings performed rituals to benefit the cities and their lands and to appease the gods.

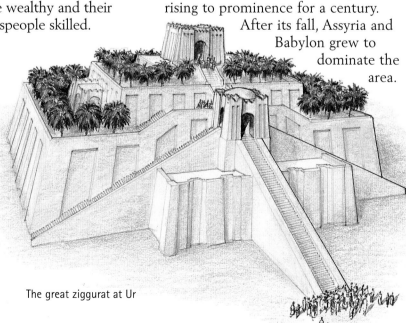

The great ziggurat at Ur

7

# ANCIENT EGYPT 4000–1800 B.C.

Ancient Egypt was surrounded by deserts, but it was green and fertile because of the Nile River. It flooded every year, depositing rich, silty soil along its banks.

The Egyptians loved to wear lucky charms. Their favorites were carved stone scarabs. The scarab beetle was sacred to the sun god, Re.

The Egyptians used the Nile for transportation and cultivated the land alongside it. They grew wheat and barley for bread and beer, and flax for linen; they raised cattle as beasts of burden. Egyptians had a highly developed religion and advanced medical, astronomical, and engineering knowledge.

### THE PHARAOHS

For most of their history, Egyptians were united in one kingdom. Administrators and priests ran everyday affairs, but the head of society was the pharaoh—a living god. People believed that ceremonies he performed kept the good will of the gods, kept the Nile flowing, and kept society in order. When the pharaoh died, his body was mummified and placed inside a stone sarcophagus in an imposing tomb, along with jewelry, clothing, furniture, and food—everything he would need for eternity. Sacred writings on the tomb walls were meant to protect him in the afterlife.

Papyrus is a stiff paper made from papyrus reeds. The Egyptians glued sheets of it together to make scrolls. Administrative and religious texts were written in hieroglyphs.

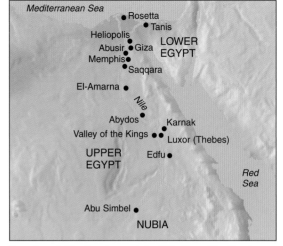

Egyptian civilization hugged the Nile River. The flood plains of the delta were rich and highly populated, though cities stretched a long way up the Nile. Riverboat transportation was important to traders.

### EGYPTIAN SOCIETY

Most people in Egypt were farmers. They gave part of their produce to the local temple as taxes. Very few people could read and write, and schooling was only for boys. Those who could write were called scribes. It was they who went on to become the priests and administrators who ran the country for the pharaoh. But at the heart of Egyptian life was communication with the gods.

## PYRAMIDS

From around 2630 B.C., Egyptians built many pyramids, the most famous being the Great Pyramid at Giza. No one knows exactly why the shape was chosen, but the scale and dimensions suggest astronomical, mathematical, and spiritual purposes. By building such great monuments, the pharaohs sought to please the gods and to leave a significant, permanent mark on history. Some of the long stone blocks above the king's Chamber weighed 60 tons, and around 2.3 million of them were used.

The Great Pyramid, the first of three pyramids at Giza and the tomb of the pharaoh Khufu, had many passageways and chambers.

Entrance

New

Underground chamber

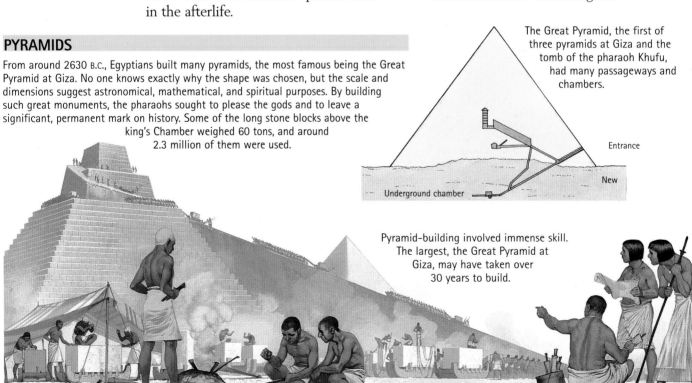

Pyramid-building involved immense skill. The largest, the Great Pyramid at Giza, may have taken over 30 years to build.

EGYPTIAN GODS

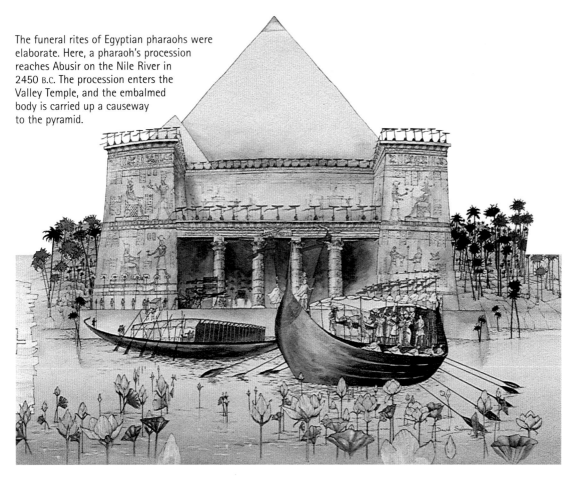

The funeral rites of Egyptian pharaohs were elaborate. Here, a pharaoh's procession reaches Abusir on the Nile River in 2450 B.C. The procession enters the Valley Temple, and the embalmed body is carried up a causeway to the pyramid.

Horus was the sky-god, and his spirit entered the living pharaoh. His eyes were the sun and the moon.

Ptah, the creator-god, invented the arts. He was the local god of the capital, Memphis.

Hathor, the goddess of love and beauty, once raised the sun up to heaven on her horns.

Isis, sister and wife of Osiris, was the mother of Horus. She had great magical powers.

Re-Horakhty, the sun-god and Horus joined together, is shown with the sun on a hawk's head.

Osiris was the god of the dead. In his realm, souls were judged for their worthiness.

Toward this end the Egyptians created remarkable works of stone carving. They built enormous pyramids and temples. Tall obelisks were cut from one block of stone. No effort or expense was spared to honor the gods—or the pharaoh, who was their living link with humanity. The Egyptians developed a way to preserve the body of their god-king, and many building projects were undertaken to provide him with a tomb for his eternal protection. In time, everyone who could afford it would have their preserved bodies placed in tombs, with treasures for the afterlife and sacred scrolls to guide them to it.

## RETURN TO GREATNESS
After the time of the first pharaohs and the pyramid builders, there was a decline that lasted for over 100 years. With no strong ruler, the people felt the gods had abandoned them. Then, around 2055, Mentuhotep II became pharaoh, brought order, and restored Egypt's greatness. This period was called the Middle Kingdom.

The pharaohs reorganized the country and again built pyramids, although not as large as those at Giza. Some of Egypt's finest art and literature was produced during the Middle Kingdom.

Egypt had been isolated from the rest of the world at this time. Ancient Egyptians were not great travelers, sailors, or conquerors, but great Middle Kingdom rulers such as Amenemhat I and Senwosret III expanded Egypt's boundaries. They built forts to protect the country, and created a strong army. They invaded countries such as Nubia to take control of gold reserves.

### KEY DATES
**3300** Growth of towns in lower Nile valley and development of hieroglyphics
**3000** Upper and Lower Egypt united
**2920** The first pharaohs
**2575** Old Kingdom, capital Memphis—high point of Egyptian civilization
**2550** The Great Pyramid is completed
**2040** Middle Kingdom—expansion and development
**1550** New Kingdom—Egypt at its largest and wealthiest

9

# MEGALITHIC EUROPE 4500–1200 B.C.

**From the New Stone Age to the early Bronze Age, huge stones called megaliths were erected in many parts of Europe, from Scotland to Malta.**

Recent archaeology has given us new insights into one of the most impressive monuments of this period, Stonehenge in southern England. It was raised from 3100 B.C. onward. Part of it was quarried in Wales, 140 mi. (225km) to the west, and had stood there as a monument before being hauled to its present location. Larger sandstone trilthons (pillars and lintels) were raised at Stonehenge over 1,500 years, aligned with the midsummer sunrise. They may have been linked to burials and rituals honoring dead ancestors, and perhaps healing. They formed part of a wider sacred landscape that extended to a larger megalithic circle at Avebury.

Stoney Littleton long barrow, near Bath in southwest England, has several small chambers that would have been used for ancestral burial purposes over a number of years.

A megalith in Portugal. No one really knows the purpose of these chambers—they were possibly built as tombs, or places for meditation or healing. They range in age from 4,000 to 6,000 years old.

The Ring of Brodgar in the Orkney Islands, off northeast Scotland, is about the same age as Stonehenge. The stones there are all tall, thin and pointed.

Lintel

Stones transported on wooden rollers

Stonehenge was built in stages over a 1,500-year period. It is thought that the stones were fitted and aligned precisely so that exact sightings could be made of sunrise and moonrise at specific times of the year.

Lever

Ramp

Upright Sarsen stones

## STONEHENGE

Stonehenge on Salisbury Plain, in England, is Europe's most elaborate ancient monument. It was laid out to mark the rising and setting points of the sun and moon, and particularly the midsummer sunrise. Some stones were probably transported great distances before being erected.

Copper ore was laboriously dug by hand in this deep mine near Salzburg in eastern Austria, around 1200 B.C. The ore was transported to the surface in sacks and crushed with heavy stone hammers.

## KEY DATES

| | |
|---|---|
| 4500 | Farming develops in western Europe |
| 4300 | First megaliths built in Brittany and Ireland |
| 3000 | Building of Stonehenge begins |
| 3200 | Stone circle building period starts |
| 2400 | Copper first comes into use in western Europe |
| 2000 | Peak of megalith building period. Stonehenge construction almost complete |

## MAINLAND EUROPE

Stone circles have been found in the west of Ireland that are even older than those in Britain. At Carnac in Brittany, in northwestern France, there is an impressive series of avenues made up of 3,000 large stones, stretching for several miles. Brittany also has many single standing stones, called menhirs. Standing stones are found all over Europe from Spain to Ireland and Scotland to Sweden.

Many burial chambers (barrows) were covered with soil to make a mound—they are found in France, Ireland, and England. There are also "quoits," made up of three vertical stones with a single large slab balanced on top.

Another remarkable collection of megalithic monuments is in Malta. Some of the oldest have walls made of massive stones. Several of the temples contain dressed stones carved with simple designs. The most remarkable Maltese monument is the Hypogeum, an underground temple carved on three levels deep into the rock.

The remains of megalithic homes have been found at Skara Brae in the Orkney Isles north of Scotland. These stone houses were engulfed in sand and preserved for thousands of years. They have helped us to reconstruct a picture of life in ancient times.

# THE INDUS VALLEY 4000–1800 B.C.

**The early peoples of the Indian subcontinent lived on the banks of the Ganges and Indus rivers. The first civilization sprang up in the Indus Valley, now in Pakistan.**

The two largest cities in the Indus Valley around 2000 B.C. were Mohenjo-Daro and Harappa, each with around 40,000 people. They were among the world's largest cities at the time. At the center of each lay an artificial mound which served as a citadel (stronghold). On this mound stood a large granary which, to the population, served as a kind of central bank. These forgotten cities were only discovered in the 1920s.

Indus seals like this were attached to bales of merchandise. They have been found not only in Mohenjo-Daro, but also as far away as Sumer. This is evidence of a wide trade network.

### CITY LAYOUT
Around the citadel the city buildings were arranged in a grid pattern—administration buildings, markets, storage areas, workshops, houses, and temples. Each house was built around a courtyard, and had rooms, a toilet, and a well. Buildings were

The climate was wetter in the Indus Valley than today. The rivers were used not only for trade and transportation, but also for irrigation of the flat lands of the valley.

made from mud bricks baked in wood-fired ovens. The citadel at Mohenjo-Daro had a bathhouse, as well as private and public baths and meeting places.

Brick-lined shafts like this are found in the courtyards of Mohenjo-Daro. They may have been wells or used for cool storage of grains and oil.

These ruins are all that remain of the 4,000-year-old city of Mohenjo-Daro.

## FARMERS AND CRAFTWORKERS

Among other crops, the farmers of the Indus Valley grew barley, wheat, cotton, melons, and dates. Elephants and water buffalo were tamed to work in the fields. The area had many skilled potters who used wheels for throwing pots—a new technology at the time. Harappans used stone tools and made knives, weapons, bowls, and figures in bronze. They had an advanced system of waste-disposal that included the building of covered drains and the installation of garbage chutes.

## THE END OF A CIVILIZATION

No one knows who the people of the Indus Valley were or where they came from. We do not understand their writing, either. The area had similarities to Sumer, but also major differences. The city dwellers traded with the cities of Sumer; they also traded with the tribespeople of India and central Asia. The Indus Valley civilization lasted 800 years, but came to an end about 3,700 years ago. No one knows why it ended, but there are various possible causes: floods; disease; a breakdown in trade, the economy, or civil order; or immigration and takeover by the Aryans who moved into India from central Asia. All trace of the cities lay buried under sand until they were rediscovered in the 1920s.

These are the excavated remains of the Great Bath at Mohenjo-Daro. The people appear to have placed great importance on hygiene and access to water. They may also have used the baths for sports and ceremonies.

▲ The storehouses at the center of the cities were very valuable to the inhabitants—they could have had religious as well as practical significance, since grain may have been regarded as sacred.

Bathhouse

City granary

◄ An artist's impression shows Mohenjo-Daro at the height of its prosperity. Unlike Sumerian cities, it was built in a grid pattern, suggesting orderly government and planning. The bathhouse had its own indoor well, and what seems to have been a granary had a sophisticated storage and ventilation system.

13

# ANCIENT CRETE 3000–1450 B.C.

**The earliest European civilization began on the island of Crete about 4,500 years ago. It is called the Minoan civilization after the legendary King Minos.**

Stories say that Minos built a labyrinth (maze) in which he kept a Minotaur, a creature with the head of a bull and the body of a man. The Minoan civilization was at its height from 2200 to 1450 B.C. The Minoans owed their prosperity to their abilities as seafarers and traders.

Crete was well placed for trading with and influencing other areas. In the end, this was the Minoans' undoing, since the Mycenaeans envied their civilization and eventually invaded.

### MINOAN CITIES

The Minoans built several large cities connected by paved roads, each of them a small city-state. At the heart of each city was a palace with a water supply, decorations, windows, and stone seats. Minoan craftsmen were renowned as potters and builders. They also made beautiful silver and gold jewelry. The capital, Knossos, had the grandest palace. It had splendid royal apartments, rooms for religious ceremonies, workshops, and a school.

Minoans were expert shipbuilders. They traveled around the Aegean Sea and to Egypt in boats like this, carrying their pottery and other craftworks far and wide.

This figure was found at Knossos. It combines the snake cult of Crete and worship of the mother-goddess. The figure itself wears the typical clothing of a Minoan woman.

The internal walls of the palace were plastered and decorated with large, magnificently painted pictures.

### DOWNFALL OF A CIVILIZATION

The Minoan civilization came to a sudden and mysterious end in about 1450 B.C. A volcanic eruption on the nearby island of Thera had already been a major disaster, overwhelming much of Crete. The end came when Knossos was invaded by the Mycenaeans who greatly admired the Minoans and took their ideas to the European mainland. In Crete lay the roots of the later Greek classical civilization.

The massive royal palace at Knossos, 500 ft. sq. (150m sq.) was several storeys high and built from wood, stone, and clay. A large courtyard was in the center. The royal apartments were on the east of the court, on the first floor.

The walls of the state rooms at Knossos were elaborately decorated. The wall painting shows the sport of bull leaping. The bull was a sacred symbol of power, and the ability to vault over its horns symbolized the mastering of its strength.

14

# THE MYCENEANS 2000–1200 B.C.

**Mycenae was a city on the southern peninsula of Greece. It was the center of the first Greek civilization, which developed after that of the Minoans in Crete.**

The ruins of the Lion Gate at Mycenae, the main entrance to the city, built around 1300BC. It was one of the few ways through the walls, which were built with huge stones and were easy to defend.

This gold mask was found in a grave in Mycenae by archaeologist Heinrich Schliemann. He thought it was Agamemnon's mask—modern scholars think it belonged to a man who lived 300 years earlier.

This beautiful gold goblet from Mycenae clearly demonstrates the skill of the local craftsworkers.

The Mycenaeans (known as Achaeans) migrated to Greece from the Balkans around 2000 B.C. Mycenaean civilization began as a series of hillside villages occupied by people speaking an ancient form of the Greek language. By about 1650 B.C., many villages had grown into fortified towns, with rich palaces and luxurious goods that rivaled those made by the highly skilled craftworkers. Mycenae consisted of about 20 city-states.

## MYCENAEAN TOMBS

Before they built fortresses and cities the Mycenaeans buried their leaders in elaborate "beehive tombs." These were built of large stone blocks, shaped to form a great dome. One tomb at Mycenae, the Treasury of Atreus, has a doorway nearly 20 ft. (6m) high, that opens into a chamber 43 ft. (13m) high and 46 ft. (14m) wide. It was once lined with bronze plates. The richness of these tombs shows that a great deal of money and effort was spent on royalty and the aristocracy. One king had as many as 400 bronzesmiths and hundreds of slaves. Wealthy Mycenaeans treasured the gold that they imported from Egypt. Skilled craftworkers made gold cups, masks, flowers, and jewelry; even their swords and armor were inlaid with gold.

## EXPANSION AND DOWNFALL

Around 1450 B.C., the Mycenaeans conquered Crete and established colonies around the Aegean Sea and on the islands of Rhodes and Cyprus. They traded throughout the Mediterranean, particularly with Phoenicia, Egypt, and Italy. However, around 1200 B.C., Mycenae fell to invading wandering raiders called the Sea Peoples. Many Mycenaeans were forced to flee to other countries.

This reconstruction shows the city of Mycenae as it probably looked at the height of its power. The royal palace on the hilltop was built on several levels.

# SHANG DYNASTY 1766–1122 B.C.

**The earliest civilizations in China from around 3200 B.C. grew up on the banks of the three largest rivers: the Huang He, Chang Jiang, and Xi Jiang.**

Shang civilization was based around the Huang He River in the north, though it also influenced central China. Later, the Zhou dynasty extended control over a larger area.

Like the people of Sumer, Egypt, and the Indus Valley, Chinese farmers relied on the country's rivers for transportation and water to grow their crops—paddy fields needed floods in springtime to help the rice grow. But the Chinese also faced two dangers: major floods and devastating raids by tribes from the north and west.

A piece of bronze Shang money, cast in the shape of a spade. This may have been made to slot into a case or sheath where several coins would be kept.

### EARLY CULTURES

The first towns appeared around 3000 B.C., during the Longshan period, around the Huang He (Yellow River) in the north. According to tradition, Huangdi, the Yellow Emperor, was the first emperor from around 2700 B.C. The first dynasty was that of the Xia (Hsia), who ruled for four centuries from 2200 B.C. Yu, its founder, is credited with taming the rivers by building dikes to stop floods, and also irrigation channels.

### THE SHANG DYNASTY

The earliest dynasty we have evidence for was the Shang, founded by Emperor Tang. The Shang ruled north China for more than 600 years. They lived in a string of cities along the Huang He, with the capital at Anyang. The city had many large palaces and temples, built mainly of carved wood. The Zhou dynasty replaced the Shang in 1122 B.C.

The Shang people grew millet, wheat, and rice, and also mulberries for feeding silkworms, from which they produced silk. They kept cattle, pigs, sheep, dogs, and chickens, and hunted deer and wild boar. The Shang used horses to draw plows, carriages, and chariots. Early in their history, they used cowrie shells as money, later switching to bronze. They were skilled in working bronze and jade, and made highly decorated practical and religious objects.

▼ Tradition says that silk was discovered by Empress Xiling Ji around 2690 B.C. She was the wife of the legendary Yellow Emperor, Huangdi, who was reputed to have brought civilization, medicine, and writing to China. The empress found that silkworms fed on mulberry leaves, so she had mulberry groves planted. Silk was spun into a fine textile that was so valued it was even used as a form of money. Silk manufacture remained a closely kept secret by the Chinese for about 3,000 years.

This is an oracle bone from the time of the Shang dynasty. Large numbers of these have been found, engraved with early Chinese pictograms (picture writing). Diviners used these to interpret the future.

16

## KEY DATES

**3000** The first Chinese towns appear, during the Longshan culture

**2700** Huangdi, the "Yellow Emperor," becomes emperor

**2200** Period of Xia dynasty—Yu is the emperor

**1766** Foundation of the Shang dynasty by Emperor Tang

**1400** Peak of the Shang period

**1122** Zhou dynasty displaces the Shang

## BRONZE

Bronze is a mixture of copper and tin, which, when polished, looks like gold. The Shang became strong through their bronze-working, since it was a hard metal with many uses in tools, household items, and weapons. Bronze was also used for adornments, artistic, and religious items. It was cast in clay molds carved with patterns. Across the world, bronze represented a technological breakthrough.

## CHINESE WRITING

Around 1600 B.C., the Shang developed the earliest forms of Chinese calligraphy—a pictorial writing in which each letter represents a whole word. The Chinese script we know today evolved from Shang writing. The Shang worshiped their ancestors, who were seen as wise guides for their way of life, and they used oracles to help them make decisions.

▼ This bronze vessel was designed during the Shang period to store large amounts of wine and was known as a *pou*. The high quality and intricate design show that by this time bronze-casting was a highly developed art. Other bronze vessels, called *jue*, with three legs and a long spout, were used for pouring wine during ceremonies. These vessels would have had a long pouring spout.

▲ The ancient Chinese cooked sacrificial food in large bronze decorated vessels like this one. It had long legs so that it could stand over a coal fire.

Shang warriors fought in cumbersome armor made of bamboo and wood, padded with cloth. Early Chinese were warlike, and tribes used to fight long feuds. Centralized states such as the Shang developed to stop the feuding between warlords.

# THE HITTITES 1600–1200 B.C.

**Around 1650 B.C., a number of small city-states were united, through warfare. The result was the rich and powerful Hittite kingdom.**

▲ This Hittite relief from Zincurli, now in modern-day Turkey, shows a man carrying a gazelle on his shoulders.

The Hittites consisted of several tribes and they spoke as many as six languages among them. One was the language of the Hatti, the original occupants of Anatolia. The Hittites were the first use iron—a metal that replaced the softer bronze.

### THE HITTITE EMPIRE
The Hittites were a warlike people. They controlled the supply of iron, and they used chariots, which gave them a great military advantage. They worshiped around 1,000 gods, chief of which was a storm-god. Early on, in 1595 B.C., they sacked Babylonia, plummeting it into a dark age. Gradually they conquered Anatolia, Syria, and the Levant (Lebanon), challenging the hold that the Assyrians and Egyptians had on the area.

The Hittite territories at their peak, around 1300 B.C. They fought with the Egyptians, Assyrians, and Phrygians, and their empire disappeared in less than a century.

◄ The Hittites carved many works of art on boulders, shaping only part of the rock and leaving the rest in its natural form. This sphinxlike gateway once guarded a Hittite settlement located at Alaca, in what is now modern Turkey.

The Hittites adopted civilized ways, such as writing, from other peoples. They also introduced the horse into the Middle East from China. Men were dominant in society, and they were rich and well traveled. The Hittites reached their peak around 1300 B.C. The Hittites survived many threats until they fell to the Sea Peoples. Finally, they were destroyed and occupied by the Phrygians, who came from the Balkans, to the north. The Hittites were never heard of again, but they had had a strong influence on their neighbors.

This Hittite rock-carved relief at Yazilikaya shows the protector-god Sharruma with the goddess Ishtar in the background. The relief was carved around 1250 B.C.

18

# BABYLON 1900–700 B.C.

**Ur's domination of Mesopotamia was followed by many invasions. Around 1894 B.C. the Babylonians replaced their rulers with a dynasty that lasted 300 years.**

The Babylonians began to dominate southern Mesopotamia under their sixth ruler, Hammurabi the Great (1780–1750 B.C.). He was a highly efficient ruler, famous for the code of laws that he laid down, and he gave the region stability after turbulent times.

Babylon became the central power of Mesopotamia. The armies of Babylonia were well-disciplined, and they conquered the city-states of Isin, Elam, and Uruk, and the strong kingdom of Mari. But Mesopotamia had no clear boundaries, making it vulnerable to attack. Trade and culture thrived for 150 years, but then the Hittites sacked Babylon in 1595 B.C.

▲ A local boundary stone from Babylon is carved with prayers that ask the gods to protect the owner's land.

▲ Hammurabi was famous for his detailed code of laws. Well known to us today is "An eye for an eye, and a tooth for a tooth," prescribing punishments for personal crimes. The laws brought all of Babylon under a uniform legal system. They protected the weak from the strong, and regulated business and land ownership.

This stela shows Shamash, the god of justice, giving Hammurabi the instruction to formulate a code of laws. Underneath are inscribed the laws that Hammurabi codified, for all to see. In this way, people were shown that the laws were given to Hammurabi by the gods.

Under Hammurabi and his successors, Babylon controlled the whole of Mesopotamia. However, it became vulnerable to invasion from the north and west.

Its cities continued for 100 years under different foreign rulers. Then, for 500 years, Babylon was overshadowed by Assyria before its next rise to greatness.

## EARLY SCIENCE

The mathematicians of Babylonia devised a system of counting based on the number 60, from which we get the number of minutes in an hour and the degrees (60 x 6) in a circle. Babylonian scholars developed early sciences and astrology from the knowledge they gained from the Sumerians.

Skilled archers helped Babylon to defend itself against the Assyrians and many other invaders—Kassites, Aramaeans, Elamites, and Hittites. Its wealth, and its location at the meeting place of roads from Asia to the Mediterranean, was envied by jealous neighbors.

# THE ASSYRIANS 1900–612 B.C.

While Babylonia ruled southern Mesopotamia, the warlike Assyrians dominated the north. Their kingdom lay in the valley of the upper Tigris River.

Ashurbanipal was the last great ruler of Assyria. A ruthless soldier, he was also a patron of the arts, building the great library at Nineveh and vast gardens stocked with plants from all over the known world.

King Adadnirari I, the country's first powerful ruler (1770–50 B.C.), enlarged the Assyrian lands and took the boastful title "King of Everything." He and his successors were fierce dictators, who did not allow individual states to be independent. Assyria grew rich through the activities of its trading families, who sold textiles and metals far and wide.

## COLLAPSE AND REBIRTH

As Assyria grew in size, rebellions by its conquered subjects increased. Eventually, Assyria fell to the Hurrians (relatives of the Hittites). The Hurrians dominated Assyria for over 250 years. As their overlordship dwindled, Assyria grew in strength again. Its next period of greatness

The Assyrian Empire grew and shrank in phases. It reached its greatest extent at the end, around 650 B.C., covering the whole of the Fertile Crescent. When Ashurbanipal died, Egypt and Babylon broke away and the empire collapsed.

lasted for 300 years. It reached its height under Tiglathpileser I (1115–1093 B.C.), who led many campaigns against neighboring lands. Assyria eventually dominated the whole region, including Babylon.

## ASHURBANIPAL'S PALACE

The Assyrian king was an absolute ruler with very active involvement in all matters of state. In his magnificent palace, Ashurbanipal, surrounded by his advisors, heard the cases presented by the people. The palace was large, with extensive gardens. As a patron of learning, the king ordered many historic records from Babylon and Sumer to be written down, and texts on mathematics, chemistry, and astronomy were produced. Literary texts such as the *Epic of Gilgamesh* and the story of the Flood, from Akkadian times, were also recorded. All of these were destroyed by invaders after Ashurbanipal's death, though many records survived.

The Assyrian king meets his courtiers and administrators.

The Assyrians believed that the winged lion from Ashurbanipal's palace could ward off evil.

Here, Assyrian workers bring in materials for the building of a new palace, supervised by their king. Oarsmen in hide-covered boats tow a raft along the Tigris.

## ASSYRIA FLOURISHES

From about 1076 B.C., Assyria and Babylonia were overrun by Aramaean tribes from Syria. But 150 years later, Ashurdan II and his successors reconquered the Assyrian Empire. The capital was moved to Nineveh, and buildings were erected and irrigation schemes undertaken. Assyrian kings expanded their lands to control all trade routes and suppress troublesome neighbors. The Assyrian Empire was at its greatest extent under Tiglathpileser III (745–727 B.C.), when it included the lands of Babylon, Syria, Palestine, Cyprus, northern Arabia, and Egypt.

## ASSYRIAN LIFE

The Assyrians were great builders and erected magnificent cities, temples, and palaces. The men wore long coatlike garments and were bearded. Women wore a sleeved tunic and a shawl over their shoulders. It was not unknown for men to sell their wives and children into slavery to pay off debts.

The Assyrians were experts at siege warfare. Their battering-rams knocked holes in city walls; then scaling ladders and mobile towers helped the men climb over. The soldiers protected themselves with large shields.

### KEY DATES

| | |
|---|---|
| 2500 | Assyrians settle the upper Tigris valley |
| 1900 | Growth of Old Assyria |
| 1680 | Assyria falls to the Hurrians (until 1400) |
| 1300–1200 | Assyrian expansion |
| 1076 | Assyria falls to the Aramaeans (until 934) |
| 730–630 | Assyrian expansion at its greatest |
| 612 | Fall of Assyria to the Babylonians and Medes |

## THE FINAL CHAPTER

The last and greatest ruler of Assyria was King Ashurbanipal. He was a scholarly king and during his reign he created a huge library in Nineveh, his capital. The ancient records of Sumer and Akkad were preserved on clay tablets, together with literature and histories, mathematics, and astronomy from ancient times. When Ashurbanipal died in 627 B.C. the Assyrian empire fell to the Babylonians and Medes.

Ishtar was the goddess of war to the Assyrians. To the Babylonians she was the mother-goddess.

# THE HEBREWS 1800–587 B.C.

**The Hebrews first settled in Palestine about 4,000 years ago. They came to Palestine from Ur, although no one knows exactly where they came from before then.**

Their name meant "the people from the other side" of the Euphrates River. Their story is told in the Bible. According to the Old Testament, the leader of the first Hebrews was Abraham, a shepherd who lived in Ur. Abraham traveled with his family first to Syria and then to Canaan (now Palestine), where they finally settled.

Solomon (965–928 B.C.) was one of the wiser kings of history and he carried out his royal duties fairly. His rule brought order and peace, and Jerusalem became one of the richest cities of the period.

After Solomon's death, Israel split into two different states, Israel and Judah—this weakened them against outside attack and led to their downfall.

### EARLY YEARS

Abraham's grandson, Jacob (also called Israel), had twelve sons. He is said to have started the twelve tribes of Israel, which were named after his sons. When famine struck Canaan, Jacob led his people to safety in Egypt. Later, they became slaves of the Egyptians until Moses led them out of Egypt and took them back to Canaan, probably around 1200 B.C. There, led by Joshua, they fought the Philistines for the right to settle and establish the land of Israel. Tradition has it that they used the sound of trumpets to bring down the walls of the city of Jericho.

### THE FIRST STATE OF ISRAEL

Around 1020 B.C., the Philistines began to threaten the Hebrews. To defend themselves, the Hebrews banded together and appointed Saul their first king. His successor, David, united all the tribes, made Jerusalem the new nation's capital, and added a number of other territories. As defensive measures, his son Solomon built several new cities and a wall around the capital. The great temple at Jerusalem was his most famous work. He was a peace-loving king.

## SOLOMON'S TEMPLE

Solomon built an impressive temple in Jerusalem, at great expense, to house the Israelites' holy treasure, the Ark of the Covenant, which contained Moses' Ten Commandments. The Temple became the focus of Jewish culture. It is said that Solomon's temple had walls inlaid with precious jewels, and that it was designed in accordance with mathematical principles learned from the Egyptians.

This panoramic painting by James Tissot (1836–1902) imagines the Exodus, the journey of the Israelites from Egypt to the land of Canaan, led by Moses.

According to the Bible, Solomon was a wise king. It is said that two women came before him with a child, each claiming to be its mother. Solomon suggested that he cut the child in two, so each mother could have half. One woman broke down and gave up her claim. Solomon recognized her as the true mother, and gave her the child. His reign marked the peak of Israel's history. After he died, his people argued and divided into two nations: Israel and Judah.

## TROUBLES AND DISPERSION

After a rebellion by the Israelites, the Assyrians captured Israel in 721 B.C., and then Judah in 683. The Jews scattered in various directions, and many were carried away to Assyria as slaves. Nebuchadnezzar of Babylon crushed a Jewish rebellion in 597 and most of the Jews were taken to Babylon. During that exile, much of the Old Testament of the Bible was written down. This was the beginning of the *diaspora*, the dispersion of the Jews, which lasted into the 1900s.

▲ This early Christian fresco from Italy shows three Hebrew captives cast into a burning fiery furnace for refusing to worship the gold statue of Nebuchadnezzar, the ruler of Babylon.

| KEY DATES | |
|---|---|
| c.1800 | Abraham and the Hebrews move to Canaan |
| c.1200 | Moses and Joshua take the Jews to Canaan |
| c.1020 | Saul becomes king of the Hebrews |
| c.1000 | David becomes king of the Hebrews |
| 965–928 | Solomon, king of Israel, reigns |
| 721 | Assyrians invade Israel, dispersing many Jews |
| 587 | Babylonians destroy Jerusalem and deport most of the Jews to Babylon |

A Jewish man blows on a *shofar*, a ram's horn fitted with a reed to amplify the sound it makes. It is possible these were used to bring down the walls of Jericho—or at least to frighten the inhabitants into opening the gates. The shofar is one of the world's oldest musical instruments, and it is blown on Jewish holy days. The woven prayer-shawl is called a *tallith*.

# EGYPT, THE NEW KINGDOM 1550–1070 B.C.

**The New Kingdom is the third major division of Egyptian history. It was a time of artistic achievement, military might, prosperity at home, and prestige abroad.**

After the Middle Kingdom, a weak and divided Egypt was dominated by the Hyksos from Canaan, for 100 years. They ruled in Lower Egypt, the north. Around 1550, an Upper Egyptian royal family rose and battled to oust the Hyksos and reunite the whole country. In 1532 they succeeded. Ahmose established the 18th dynasty and became the first pharaoh of the New Kingdom—Egypt's Golden Age.

### THE NEW KINGDOM

One of its early pharaohs, Thutmose I, conquered Palestine and the lands west of the Euphrates around 1500 B.C. During the rule of Amenhotep III, the New Kingdom, with its capital at Thebes, was rich and prosperous. Farmers and workers lived simply, but the nobility had a luxurious lifestyle. By law, men and women were equal, and women owned property. Women were able to follow one of four main professions: priestess, midwife, dancer, or mourner. Apart from the nobles, scribes and priests held the most important positions in Egyptian society.

In Ancient Egypt, the dead were embalmed and tightly wrapped in cloth, a process called mummification, so that they would "live" forever. The mummy was put inside a coffin that was often highly decorated.

### AKHENATEN

The strangest ruler was Amenhotep IV (1353–35 B.C.). He attempted to change Egyptian religion by replacing its many gods and complex traditions with worship of only one god: Aten. He changed his name to Akhenaten and built a new capital at El-Amarna, dedicated to Aten. His queen, Nefertiti, was not of royal birth and may not have been Egyptian. When Akhenaten died, the priests of the old gods regained control, and worship of Aten was discouraged. The dead king's name was removed from every monument and record. His new city was abandoned and it was as if he had never existed.

Prosperous Egyptians were buried with jewelry, pottery, and models showing activities such as baking, brewing, and fishing. These models provide vivid details about the everyday life of the Egyptians.

This solid gold mask lay over the face of Tutankhamun's mummy. His tomb was found in the Valley of the Kings in 1922, and the mummy with its sumptuous mask was revealed to stunned onlookers.

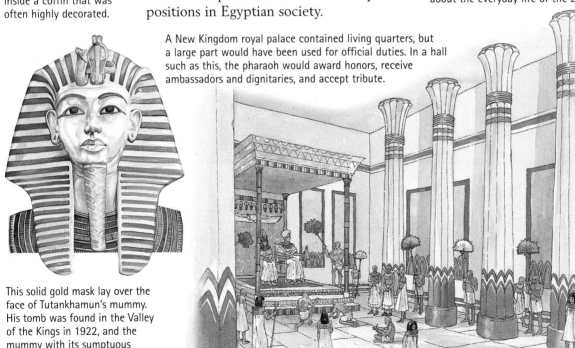

A New Kingdom royal palace contained living quarters, but a large part would have been used for official duties. In a hall such as this, the pharaoh would award honors, receive ambassadors and dignitaries, and accept tribute.

24

# THE END OF GREATNESS

Most New Kingdom rulers were buried in the Valley of the Kings, in tombs cut deeply into the rock. But robbers still broke in. Only one tomb survived, almost intact, to modern times, that of the boy-king Tutankhamen, who succeeded Akhenaten and died not yet twenty years of age. Egypt stayed powerful for a time, especially under Seti I and his son Ramses II—the Great—of the 19th dynasty (1307–1196 B.C.). Over time, rulers became weaker. Priests took control, and finally Egypt fell to a succession of foreign invaders. The Greeks conquered Egypt and ruled for around 300 years. Finally, Egypt became a Roman territory. Her monuments fell to ruins, her history and writings were forgotten.

Egyptian doctors treated their patients with a combination of medical practice and religious magic.

◀ Early Egyptian ships were flat-bottomed, suitable only for river transportation. Later they began to make larger, heavier ships with deeper, rounded bottoms that could be used for sea travel. These ships greatly increased Egypt's ability to trade goods with the lands bordering the Mediterranean Sea.

▲ Hatshepsut was the daughter of the great Thutmose I and widow of the weak Thutmose II. After her husband's death she took the throne and ruled as pharaoh in her own right. She wore male clothing and even the traditional false beard worn by the pharaohs.

◀ Kahun was an Egyptian town built of mud bricks. The houses had two levels, plus a flat roof on which people spent much of their time. Trades and crafts occupied different areas in the town, as they do in modern Eastern cities. A pyramid was connected to Kahun by a causeway. On the edge of the town was a temple.

# THE PHOENICIANS 1500–500 B.C.

**The Phoenicians were the greatest seafarers of the ancient world. They lived along a coastal strip in the Levant at the eastern end of the Mediterranean Sea.**

The Phoenicians were the first to make transparent glass like this perfume bottle, on a large scale.

▲ Phoenicians were famous for ivory carvings, like this finely detailed head.

The Phoenicians, who were merchant adventurers, lived in a string of independent city-states with good harbors in what is now Lebanon. Originally from Canaan, they were not interested in farming the land, but in seafaring, manufacturing, and trading.

## TRADE AND CRAFTS

The Phoenicians traded overland with merchants carrying valuable goods from as far away as India and China to the west. The goods were sent by sea to Egypt, Greece, Italy, and north Africa. This trade made Phoenicians prosperous and powerful. They saw the rise and fall of the Minoans and Mycenaeans, and actively helped the rise of Greece and then Rome. The Phoenicians were skilled craftworkers, making glassware, metal items, jewelry, and cloth. They also invented glass-blowing. The port of Tyre was famous for Tyrian purple dye, a rich color worn by Greeks and Romans as a sign of status.

This is how a Phoenician warship probably looked. It was a galley with a ram for attacking other ships.

## PHOENICIAN PORTS

The Phoenician ports in the Levant were Ugarit, Sidon, Byblos, and Berytus (Beirut). The main port was Tyre which, according to tradition, was founded 4,750 years ago. The city had close links with Israel. Hiram, king of Tyre, supplied King Solomon with mighty beams of Lebanon cedarwood and with craftworkers to build his great temple in Jerusalem.

▼ The Phoenician Temple of Obelisks at Byblos in the Levant, the Phoenicians' homeland. The use of this site goes back at least 4,000 years, to the same time as the Minoans.

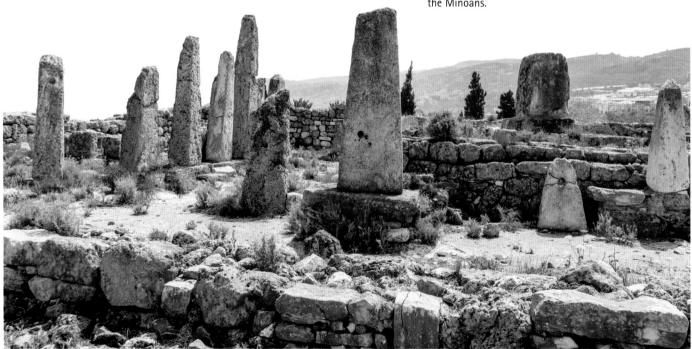

Starting in Cyprus, the Phoenicians gradually spread westward and set up many colonies around the Mediterranean. The most important was Carthage in North Africa, which became a large city. Other colonies were in Spain, Malta, Sicily, Morocco, and Sardinia. Later the Phoenicians colonized Cadiz and Tangier, founding trading posts down the coast of West Africa. Eventually, their homeland was invaded by the Babylonians around 570 B.C., so the colonies became independent, with Carthage as their chief port.

## EXPLORATION

Around 600 B.C., the Egyptians commissioned the Phoenicians to sail around the coast of Africa. This voyage took three years. Regular trade with distant countries rich in tin and silver, like Britain, started around 450 B.C. The Phoenicians' downfall came in 200–100 B.C., when Rome, which was seeking to control the Mediterranean, fought them and destroyed Carthage.

▲ The main Carthaginian deity was the warrior god, Baal Haamon, connected with fertility. This is the temple of Salambo Tophet, from around 700 B.C. where worshipers sacrificed and buried children.

◀ The Phoenicians sailed from port to port throughout the Mediterranean, trading valuable goods and transporting them for others. Here a Phoenician trading ship docks in an Egyptian city. Phoenicians did not control great areas of land as other nations sought to do, but they were nevertheless very influential. They connected the different parts of the ancient world.

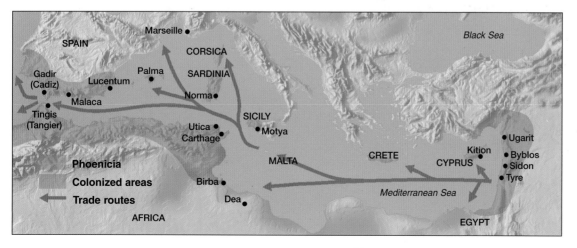

The bold sailors from the city-states of Phoenicia founded many colonies along the coasts of the Mediterranean, trading throughout that sea and venturing into the Atlantic, sailing to West Africa and Britain.

# AFRICA 6000–200 B.C.

**Although the earliest human remains have been found in Africa, not much was known until recently of the continent's history before 1500 B.C., except for Egypt.**

These are Masai women of recent times, from what is now Kenya. They are dressed in traditional ceremonial clothes.

▼ These ancient rock paintings of cows with their herders are in the Ennedi Mountains, Chad. They date from before 3500 B.C. when the Sahara was habitable grassland.

Today the Sahara forms a great desert barrier between northern and central Africa, but in about 6000 B.C. that barrier did not exist. Rock drawings and paintings show that the climate was much wetter, and that more people were able to live in the Sahara. The land began to dry up after around 3500 B.C., but desert trade towns and routes remained open, providing a link between northern and central Africa.

## NUBIA AND KUSH

Egyptian culture spread up the Nile to Nubia (now Sudan). The kingdom of Kush grew out of Nubia from 2000 B.C. onward. Kush was valuable to Egypt as a trading partner and a source of gold. Egypt conquered Kush in 1500 B.C., to secure gold deposits there but in 750 B.C. was itself conquered by the Kushites, who founded the 25th dynasty of pharaohs. Kush never had a Bronze Age, but went straight from using stone to using iron. The capital was moved from Napata, its religious center, to Meroë, because Meroë was surrounded by rich iron ore deposits.

Africa, a vast continent, has many different environments in which many diverse cultures have grown up. North Africa was dominated by Egyptian and Mediterranean cultures. South of the Sahara Desert people lived without being affected directly by them.

This meant that Kush became an important center of ironworking, supplying Egypt, Babylon, Arabia, and Ethiopia. Meroë imitated Egypt, and it preserved many Egyptian traditions for the future at a time when Egypt itself was going through cultural changes. Ethiopia was also an important, though self-contained, area of culture with religious traditions of its own.

These ruined pyramids are at Meroë, northeast of today's Khartoum. The kingdom of Meroë developed from Nubia, a kingdom once influenced by Egypt.

## CENTRAL AND SOUTHERN AFRICA

Around the Niger River lived farming tribes, with a few trading towns. Downstream, the Nok nation of Nigeria became ironworking and village-dwelling craftspeople. To the east there were the nomadic shepherds and village-dwelling people of Chad. Across central Africa, Bantu peoples were moving south from Nigeria, taking ironworking and farming with them. Southern Africa was occupied by shepherds as well as hunter-gatherers known as the Khoisan.

### KEY DATES

| | |
|---|---|
| 3000 | Desertification of the Sahara begins |
| 2750 | Farming begins in West Africa |
| 700 | Nubian kingdom of Kush flourishes |
| 600 | Growth of Nok culture, Nigeria, and Meroë |
| 200 | Djenné-Djenno, the first African city, is established |

▲ A wall painting in the tomb of Sobekhotep shows foreigners bringing tribute to the pharaoh. Here, a group of African peoples bring gifts prized by the Egyptians: from Nubia, gold in large rings; from farther south, logs of ebony and fly whisks made from giraffe's tails, and fruit and a small monkey, and, finally, a baboon.

▶ Rock paintings and relief carvings are found across much of the Sahara. This cattle-herding scene was painted on rock in the Tasili area in the central Sahara. The artist has even recorded the color patterns of the individual cows.

# THE AMERICAS 1500–350 B.C.

**Many of the first Americans may have arrived overland from Asia when the sea levels were lower. Their descendants populated the Americas over the millennia.**

A Folsom point, a type of arrowhead found at Folsom in North America, dating from 9000 B.C.

Many early Americans remained hunters, fishers, and food gatherers, but in two separate areas, new civilizations developed—in Central America, Ecuador and Peru.

### THE OLMECS OF MEXICO

In Mesoamerica, some 9,000 years ago, the Indigenous Americans settled and grew crops of Indian corn, beans, and pumpkins. Small villages sprang up in which the people made pottery and wove cloth. Out of this culture, around 1500 B.C., the first American civilization was born. The city-dwelling Olmecs built their capital at La Venta, near the Gulf of Mexico. The Olmecs built large earth and stone pyramids as centers for religious worship, and they produced huge sculptures and fine jade carvings. Many of their sculptures mix human and jaguar-like features. The Olmecs also had their own kind of writing and a sophisticated calendar system. Their neighbors, the Zapotecs and Maya, also developed advanced city civilizations.

This fine stone bowl is a magnificent example of the Chavín people's skill in stone carving. It was the work of a sculptor living in Peru 2,500 years ago.

### CIVILIZATION IN THE ANDES

The first fishing and farming villages in South America were in northern Peru. About 2,800 years ago a more advanced culture appeared, called the Chavín. The Chavín people made pottery, wove cloth on looms, built in stone, and made elaborate carvings. The largest building in their capital was three stories high. Inside was a maze of rooms, corridors, and stairs.

| KEY DATES | |
|---|---|
| 2600 | Ceremonial centers built in Peru |
| 2200 | Farming villages founded in Mexico |
| 1200 | Olmec towns and ceremonial centers built |
| 850 | Chavín culture grows |
| 600 | Earliest Maya temple-pyramids built |
| 350 | Decline of the Olmecs |

▲ This is one of eight enormous heads carved from basalt by the Olmecs; some are almost 10 ft. (3m) tall. They may represent early rulers, and each wears a distinctly different head covering.

▶ Dating from around 1200 B.C., this Olmec "altar" was probably a throne. The figure of an Olmec ruler sits in the niche underneath.

# ARYAN INDIA 1500–500 B.C.

About 3,500 years ago the Aryans, a band of tough warriors and shepherds, fled south across the Hindu Kush mountains to settle in the subcontinent of India.

Gautama Siddhartha (c.563–483 B.C.) was a prince. He saw the suffering of the people and left his family to search for truth. He later attained enlightenment, becoming known as Buddha. He taught a kinder faith that respected all living beings.

A natural disaster, maybe drought or disease, or a civil war, made the Aryans flee from their homelands in southern Russia. They spread out to Anatolia and Persia as well as India. They lived in tribal villages, probably in wooden houses, unlike the brick cities of the Indus Valley people.

### THE ARYANS IN INDIA
Aryans counted their wealth in cattle and sheep. They were not as advanced as the Indian peoples, but they were tougher. They were warriors and gamblers, beef-eaters and wine drinkers, and loved music, dancing, and chariot racing. Gradually, they settled down and adopted many of the ways of the Indigenous Indians, becoming crop growers and ironworkers. Among the crops was rice, unknown to the Aryans but already grown in the Indus Valley.

After the Aryans invaded northern India, many of the Indigenous peoples, the Dravidians and the Munda, moved to the southern and eastern parts of India.

### HINDU CULTURE
The use of the plow and irrigation systems enabled the Aryans to grow enough crops to support large towns. By 500 B.C. there were 16 major kingdoms in northern India, the most prominent being Maghada. Maghada was the birthplace of the Mauryan Empire and of two new religions—Jainism and Buddhism. The Aryans had no form of writing. Like many ancient peoples, they passed on their history and religious beliefs by word of mouth. These traditions, called the *Vedas*—the Books of Knowledge—were written down much later. The oldest of these is the *Rig-Veda*, a collection of more than 1,000 hymns, composed in their language, Sanskrit. Most of what we know about the Aryans' daily lives in ancient times comes from the *Vedas*, the ancient "old testament" of the Hindus. Unlike other faiths, Hinduism was not started by one teacher—its beliefs accumulated gradually over time.

▲ The Aryans introduced the caste system, headed by the educated Brahmin priests who ruled the country. The Kshatriyas were warriors, and the Vaisyas were traders and farmers. The darker skinned Indigenous Dravidians were servants and workers. It was impossible to change caste or marry outside it.

◄ One of the chief Hindu deities is Shiva, the transformer, who is both a creator and destroyer, the lord of change. He is depicted dancing in a halo of flames.

31

# THE FOUNDING OF ROME 753–510 B.C.

**According to tradition, the city of Rome was founded in 753 B.C. by local tribespeople who had established their camps on Rome's seven hills.**

Legends say that early Rome was ruled by local kings, of whom Romulus was the first. The citizens were Sabines and Latins, who united to form one town, thinking of themselves as Romans. They were influenced by their neighbors to the north, the Etruscans, and traders from Greece and Carthage, who brought in new ideas about culture and society.

According to legend, Rome was founded by twin brothers, Romulus and Remus, grandsons of King Numitor. The king's wicked brother Amulius put the babies in a basket to float down the Tiber River to their deaths. However, they were rescued and suckled by a she-wolf. They founded Rome, but quarreled, and Remus was killed. Romulus became the first king of Rome.

In its early days, Rome was surrounded by Etruscans, Samnites, and others. Greeks and Phoenicians also had colonies in and around Italy. As Rome expanded, it had to overcome these older societies.

## ETRUSCANS

The Etruscans, whose kingdom was called Etruria, lived in a group of city-states which emerged around 800 B.C. They were farmers, metalworkers, seafarers, and traders and liked music, games, and gambling. They were greatly influenced by the Greeks, adopting the Greek alphabet, wearing himaton (robes), and believing in Greek gods. Many of their ways were passed to the Romans, who eventually took Greek-style culture to its ultimate expression.

successive kings ruled Rome for 240 years. Kings did not have complete power—they had to contend with an assembly of nobles, who grew more influential as time passed.

## KINGS OF ROME

The kings of Rome wore togas with purple borders. In processions, the kings were preceded by standard-bearers who carried a *fasces* (a bundle of rods and an ax blade), a symbol of power representing the king's right to rule over everyone else.

Legend has it that seven

▼ This terracotta sarcophagus of an Etruscan husband and wife was made around 510 B.C. Women had more status in Etruscan society than they did among Greeks or Latins, where they were kept in the background.

An assembly had a say in electing the king and what he could do, especially in war. The kings formed armies to defend Rome. There were arguments between the kings and the patricians (the leading families). The kings represented the old ways, and urban Rome was changing. The new elite of patricians eventually overthrew the monarchy in 509 B.C., and declared Rome a republic. It was the first republic in the history of the world. The Romans did not plan to become a great imperial power—at first they wanted only to protect themselves and fight off their interfering neighbors. However, within 500 years, Rome was to become the center of the Western world, taking over from the Greeks.

| KEY DATES | |
|---|---|
| 800 | The Etruscan civilization emerges |
| 753 | Traditional date for the founding of Rome |
| 509 | Foundation of the Roman Republic |
| 400 | Decline of Etruria |

▲ The Etruscans left little writing, but their paintings were vivid. This one from a tomb shows lyre and flute players.

▲ A *fasces* was a symbol of power in Rome. The wooden rods symbolized punishment, and the ax represented life and death.

◀ Greek art and dress greatly influenced the Etruscans. The figures in the tomb of the Augurs—diviners or soothsayers—at Tarquinia, painted around 500 B.C., clearly show Greek touches.

# BABYLON REVIVED 626–539 B.C.

**Tribespeople from the west, called Chaldeans, migrated into Assyria and Babylonia from about 1100 B.C. Several Chaldeans served as kings under their Assyrian overlords.**

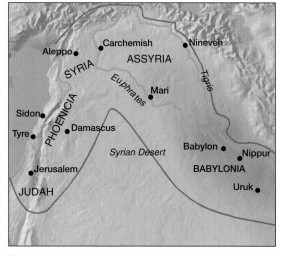

The map shows Nebuchadnezzar's Babylonian Empire at its fullest extent, controlling all of the lands known as the Fertile Crescent.

Nebuchadnezzar reigned for 43 years and his reign was marked by many military campaigns. Twice he subdued revolts in Judah, and when Phoenicia rebelled he besieged its chief port, Tyre, for thirteen years.

In 626 B.C., a Chaldean king called Nabopolassar took power, declared Babylonia independent, and threw off the Assyrian yoke. Nabopolassar then crushed the Assyrians in 612 B.C. His son Nebuchadnezzar drove the Egyptians back into Egypt and took Syria.

## NEBUCHADNEZZAR

Nebuchadnezzar was one of the most famous kings of Babylonia. He came to power in about 605 B.C. His story is told in the Bible, in the Book of Daniel. He invaded many of the former Assyrian lands and the deserts west of Babylon. Among other conquests, Nebuchadnezzar captured Jerusalem and forced thousands of Jews to live in Babylon as prisoners because they had been rebellious. He made Babylon the master of all the lands within the Fertile Crescent.

## BABYLON

Nebuchadnezzar devoted most of his time to making Babylon still more beautiful, a capital of the world. He had huge walls built around the city, and he named the main gate after the goddess Ishtar. His famous Hanging Gardens are probably mythical, but he did build a large bridge over the Euphrates River, and an enormous ziggurat, the Temple of Marduk or Bel (the "tower of Babel"). Nebuchadnezzar built himself a fine palace and he also improved the other cities. He encouraged the worship of the old god Marduk, seeking to revive Babylon's and Sumer's former greatness. Nebuchadnezzar ruled for more than 40 years, but in his later years he suffered from spells of madness.

▲ Flanked by lions and owls, the goddess Ishtar wears a crown of lunar horns. Ishtar was the chief goddess of the Babylonians.

▶ Babylon was a seafaring nation, situated on the Euphrates River. Great reed boats were built that traveled as far as India and East Africa. It was also the focus of land routes from Asia to the West.

34

## THE CITY OF BABYLON

The Greek historian, Herodotus, described Babylon as the most splendid city in the world. It was already ancient when Nebuchadnezzar rebuilt it with new temples, palaces, roads, walls, gates, and a bridge across the Euphrates. The Temple of Marduk, or Bel, a Sumerian-style ziggurat, was very tall and became known as the Tower of Babel. The Greeks regarded the Hanging Gardens as one of the wonders of the world. Babylon was a metropolis with markets and workshops selling and making everything imaginable. It supplied Greeks, Indians, Persians, and Egyptians with all kinds of goods.

This view of the city shows the Ishtar Gate on the main processional way, and the Temple of Marduk.

At this angle, the Euphrates Bridge is in the foreground and, behind it, the legendary Hanging Gardens of Babylon.

### DECLINE AND FALL

The Babylonian Empire survived for only six years after Nebuchadnezzar died. His son, Awil-Marduk (given the name of "Evil Merodach" in the Bible), reigned for three years before being assassinated. Two other kings, one of them a child, reigned for just three more years.

A Syrian prince, Nabu-Na'id, then seized power in Babylon, and tried to persuade the people to worship his own god, Sin, rather than Marduk. He made Belsharusur (Belshazzar) co-ruler.

Meanwhile, in Persia, a new young king, Cyrus II, had risen to power after taking the throne in 557 B.C. He had ambitions to take over Mesopotamia and found a Persian empire. In pursuit of this goal, he invaded Babylonia and captured the city of Babylon in 539 B.C. Nabu-Na'id was deposed and his son killed by the invading forces. Cyrus the Great, as he became known, freed the rebellious Jews who had been made captive in 586 B.C. by the young Nebuchadnezzar.

Babylonia was then ruled by the Persians for more than two relatively peaceful and stable centuries, until the time of another youthful king, Alexander the Great, who defeated the Persians and captured Babylon in 331 B.C., making it his capital.

### KEY DATES

| | |
|---|---|
| 853 | Assyria takes control of Babylon |
| 626 | Babylonians rebel against the Assyrians |
| 612 | Nineveh (Assyria) sacked by the Babylonians and the Medes |
| 604 | Nebuchadnezzar becomes king—Babylon's peak |
| 539 | Babylon conquered by Cyrus the Great of Persia |

# GREEK DARK AGE 1100–600 B.C.

**When many of the Mycenaeans fled around 1200 B.C., Greece entered its "Dark Age." This left a gap which was filled by a new people, the Dorians.**

There is no written history of this period, which lasted over 500 years. The Dorians did not have the culture or the skills of the Mycenaeans. They spoke a different kind of Greek, and they did not yet write things down.

Many of the city-dwelling Mycenaeans were scattered by wandering raiders or "Sea Peoples," and those who remained were country dwellers. The Dorians, from the Balkans, marched in and dominated Greece from 1100 B.C.

### HISTORIC SAGAS

The Dorians preserved memories of the Mycenaean age by telling long poetic sagas. When they adopted writing from the Phoenicians, they wrote down these poems. Two poems, Homer's *Iliad* and *Odyssey*, tell of the siege of Troy and one of its heroes, Odysseus. Objects found in Mycenaean graves match Homer's descriptions.

### CITY LIFE

During the Dark Age, people abandoned town life to live in tribes ruled by warlords. By 600 B.C. city life had revived and overseas colonization began. Power was held by tyrants (unelected leaders) or oligarchies (groups of leaders). Trade, population, and prosperity grew. After times of unrest around 500 B.C., some cities, such as Athens, appointed reformers to reorganize government, law, and trade. This was the beginning of Classical Greece.

Homer was a blind bard who, around 800 B.C., composed the epic poems the *Iliad* and *Odyssey*, which described people and events. He probably gathered together all the legends of Mycenae and retold them. Homer would have sung or recited his sagas to an audience. Some scholars believe his works were composed by more than one poet.

Greek warfare developed during the Dark Age. Heavily armed foot soldiers, called *hoplites*, fought in a close formation known as a *phalanx*. They fought as a unit, covering each other.

People in Greece loved listening to stories about their gods and heroes. Here, a Dorian bard is telling poetic histories to the people. The bards were not only entertainers and teachers, they also carried news of events to people.

# THE ZHOU DYNASTY 1122–221 B.C.

**The Zhou dynasty ruled China for over 800 years. They brought China a golden age—the growth of towns, trade, and early Chinese imperial culture.**

The Zhou (pronounced Chou) began as a group of wandering herders who had settled in the fertile Wei Valley in western China. They ousted the last king of the Shang dynasty, who was cruel and a drunkard. The Zhou domain was not a single kingdom, but a collection of large estates, whose rulers owed loyalty to the king. Society was divided into rich nobles, common people, and slaves. A merchant class also developed. The Zhou introduced ironworking to China, using the metal for weapons, domestic items, and farm tools such as plows. Iron made farming easier and gave Zhou soldiers an advantage in war.

These Zhou iron battle-axes from around 500 B.C. were made at the beginning of the "Period of Warring States."

### ROYAL DECLINE

After a few centuries, royal authority declined, and China entered an unstable "Springs and Autumns" period. The king held official power, though he was dictated to by the strongest lord of the time. Later, the "Period of Warring States" followed, which was dominated by warlords. During this troubled period, early classical Chinese thought took shape—this was the time of Confucius and Laozi, philosophers and sages. At this time the idea of a centralized Chinese imperial state came into being.

Confucius, Laozi, and the Buddha as a child, painted during the 1700s. They were all alive at around the same time, but it is thought that only Confucius and Laozi are likely to have met.

This picture of an archer on horseback was stamped on a clay tile, made during the Zhou dynasty.

The people living in this ancient Chinese village of the earlier Zhou period would have been isolated and self-sufficient.

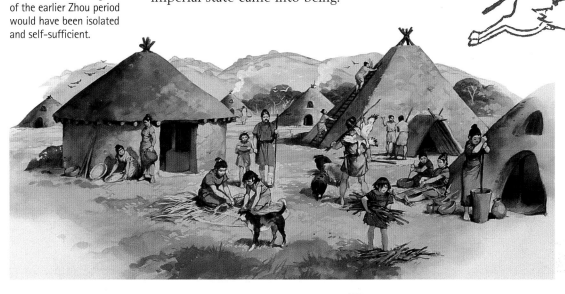

# THE PERSIAN EMPIRE 559–331 B.C.

**Iran used to be known as Persia. Its people comprised two groups, the Medes and the Persians, who migrated to Persia from central Asia about 2,800 years ago.**

Darius I (548–486 B.C.) was a great general who extended the empire east and west, reorganizing it into 20 provinces. He built good roads as well as a new royal capital at Persepolis. From Lydia in Anatolia, he introduced gold and silver money to Persia. Darius called himself *Shahanshah*, king of kings.

At first the Medes were very powerful. Then, nearly 2,550 years ago, Cyrus, the ruler of the Persians, rebelled against the Medes and seized control. Cyrus the Great made Persia the center of a mighty new empire. His capital was at Ecbatana on the Silk Road, now buried under the modern city of Hamadan.

## CONQUERING KINGS
Cyrus commanded a mighty army of cavalry and skilled archers. Taking advantage of the weaknesses of his neighbors, he conquered an empire extending from the Mediterranean to Afghanistan. His son Cambyses invaded Egypt. The Persians gained the support of their subjects by ruling fairly. Darius I eventually extended the empire into India and Greece. He also reorganized it, appointing *satraps* (governors) to each province. They paid him taxes in cereals, silver, and agricultural produce.

This frieze was carved in low relief on a thin stone at the Palace of Apadana, Persepolis. These works of art covered the walls and stairways of the palace.

## UNITING THE ANCIENT WORLD
Darius built roads and market towns to reach all parts of his huge empire, and encouraged trade by introducing a standard coinage. The Persians controlled the western end of the Silk Road from China, and all trade from India to the Mediterranean. This wealthy, cosmopolitan empire linked most of the ancient civilizations of the time. However, it relied on the strength of its rulers. Eventually, the Greeks brought the empire down and took it over.

▶ The tomb of Cyrus the Great was built at Pasargadae in Iran. Cyrus is regarded as the author of the world's first charter on human rights.

This is a Persian infantryman. The Persian army was successful because of its clever use of strategy. It covered tremendous distances during its campaigns.

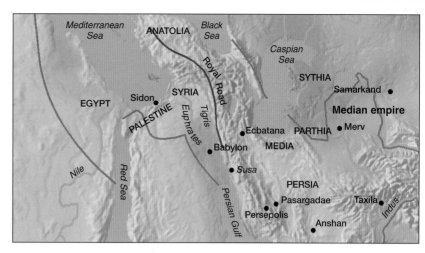

## RELIGIOUS TEACHING

In religion, the Persians followed the teachings of a Persian prophet named Zarathustra (in Greek, Zoroaster). Zoroaster had adapted the ancient Persian tribal religion, which the Persians had brought with them from central Asia. They worshiped one god, Ahura Mazda, who they believed was locked in divine battle with Ahriman (representing sleep) and Satan (representing evil).

Although Zoroastrianism did not become a world religion, it later influenced many other faiths including Christianity and still exists as Parseeism in India. Its influence can be clearly seen in the biblical Book of Revelations.

An impression from a cylinder seal, with cuneiform writing on the left, shows Darius I hunting a lion from a chariot with a bow and arrow. The winged figure overhead is an image of Ahura Mazda, main god of the Persians.

### KEY DATES

**c.850–750** The Medes and Persians migrate into Iran
**c.600** Zoroaster reforms the ancient Persian religion
**559–525** Cyrus the Great creates the Persian Empire
**521–486** Darius expands empire to its high point
**480** Greeks halt Persian expansion at Salamis
**331** Fall of Persia to Alexander the Great

This map shows the Persian Empire at its greatest extent under Darius. Susa became its administrative center and Persepolis was its center of state. The Royal Road was built to speed communications.

Darius built himself a grand palace in his new capital city of Persepolis. The staircase of the palace was carved with this procession of dignitaries in ceremonial attire.

39

# THE ARTS 25,000–500 B.C.

**Since the earliest days, humans have decorated objects, made adornments, and represented ideas in artistic ways. This is a crucial part of the development of culture.**

The early people who lived in Europe some 25,000 years ago made little clay models of goddesses and animals. These are thought to be totems or religious objects to help encourage the fertility of the land or to communicate with the spirits of the animals. Some ancient peoples painted vivid pictures deep inside caves showing animals, tribal shamans, and hunting scenes.

### ARTISTIC SKILLS

Once people started leading more settled lives, they began to make pottery and other decorated items. In China, the people of Yangshao painted pots with geometrical patterns on them. As copper and bronze replaced stone for weapons and tools, metalworkers became important, and the tools and objects they made were richly decorated. They did this not just to make them beautiful. By carving gods or sacred symbols on their tools or weapons, they believed that they would make them more effective.

This Olmec figure is carved in green jade. It represents a jaguar spirit associated with Tláloc, the god of rain and fertility.

▲ This fish from the Egyptian New Kingdom is a bottle for cosmetics. It was made around 1200 B.C. from strips of colored glass wrapped around a core. The ripples were made by drawing a point across the glass before it hardened.

▶ This elaborate game board was found in a cemetery in the Sumerian city of Ur. It is around 4,500 years old. Sadly, the rules of this game have not survived.

This delicately-carved woman's head made of ivory was found in France. It may be the world's earliest known portrait. It was carved around 20,000 B.C.

As towns and cities grew and states became wealthier, impressive temples, palaces, and other monumental buildings were decorated with carvings and paintings showing what life was like. From the frescoes of Mycenae to the Egyptian tomb paintings and from Olmec carvings to Chinese painted pottery, the art of these ancient people has given us an insight into their way of life.

The Chinese valued jade, which they saw as a pure material with which to work. They carved many objects from it, like this intricate open ring which was probably worn by a wealthy Chinese woman around 1000 B.C.

## WRITING

Writing was originally a work of art, made up of pictures representing ideas or objects. Around 1000 B.C., the Phoenicians invented the world's first alphabet. It had 22 characters; all were consonants, none were vowel sounds. The "pictograms" of ancient China represented whole words—one pictogram might mean "mountain" or "town." Modern Chinese characters still represent concepts like this, instead of sounds.

▲ A fresco is a picture painted on damp plaster, so that the paint sinks in deeply to last a long time. This fresco of dogs on a boar hunt was painted on a wall in Mycaenae, about 1500 B.C.

◄ This rock painting is from the Tasili area of the Sahara Desert. It is around 6,000 years old, a time when the Sahara was greener and supported a population of herders.

The Greeks heavily influenced Etruscan art, as can be seen in this picture painted around 500 B.C. in the Tomb of the Leopards at Tarquinia. The reclining banqueters at a funeral are asking for another jar of wine.

# ARCHITECTURE 40,000–1500 B.C.

The earliest humans lived in caves or any other natural shelter they could find. Eventually, people started making more comfortable homes and other buildings for themselves, using wood, mud, and stone.

The first bricks were shaped from mud and left to harden in the hot sun.

The houses of the New Stone Age city of Çatal Hüyük in Anatolia, Turkey, were built in 6000 B.C. They were so tightly packed that there were no streets. People walked along the rooftops.

The first buildings people made were tents of animal skins supported on wooden poles. In some places, they used mammoth bones to weight the structure down.

## MUD-BRICK HOUSES

Around 6000 B.C., people started to build homes using dried mud and wood. They covered the walls with fine plaster, on which they painted decorations with pigments taken from plants. The floors were bare, or covered with straw or animal hides. Furniture, such as as tables and beds, was also made from mud bricks.

## ROOFING MATERIAL

To keep out the weather, early people made roofs of wooden poles covered with twigs and leaves, straw or thick mats of soil known as sods. In hot climates, roofs were made flat to reflect the sun's rays, keeping the buildings cool. Houses in Jerusalem had flat roofs, each one with a parapet, or low wall, to stop visitors falling over the edge. In temperate climates, roofs were made sloping so that rainwater would run off quickly. Around 4000 B.C. some Sumerians of Mesopotamia built their homes entirely from marsh reeds. They used several layers of reeds to create large, curved roofs, but these roofs did not survive very long; they needed to be replaced every few years.

The builders of Çatal Hüyük built their houses with a framework of wooden posts and beams. They constructed the walls with mud bricks and then filled in any holes with daub—a mixture of mud and straw.

A ladder gave access to the house through the roof

Wooden poles were laid across the walls to support a flat roof

Plaster

Smooth finish of mud on outside of walls

Sunbaked mud bricks

Central hearth

Pyramids housed the bodies of Egyptian kings. The stone pyramid complex of the pharaoh Sahure at Abusir near Memphis was built in about 2450 B.C. A causeway led directly from a lake formed by the Nile floods to the mortuary temple. The body was then buried in the pyramid.

Pyramid

Causeway

Mortuary temple

## BUILDING WITH STONE

Around 3000 B.C., people in Europe, Egypt, South America, the Middle East, and China started to use stone as building material. At first they used uncut stone. Then, as metal tools were developed, they cut and shaped the stone into large, rectangular slabs. The blocks of stone were laid one on top of the other. Flat or sloping roofs spanned the walls.

Not all these early buildings were built for people to live in. Some were made for religious purposes, and others as tombs for the dead or shelters for farm animals. They include the pyramids and temples of Egypt and South America, the ziggurats of the Middle East, and monuments such as Stonehenge in Britain. Unlike those made from mud and wood, many stone buildings have survived to the present day.

The first builders used stone tools. Later builders had metal tools which were more efficient.

Around 2000 B.C. the Chinese were building houses with wooden posts and roofs of straw.

Thatch (woven straw) roof

Bare earth floor

Skara Brae, in the Orkney Islands off the coast of Scotland, was a small farming settlement with stone houses. Inside, there were stone cupboards and beds. The settlement was buried by sand at the height of a fierce storm 4,500 years ago.

## VILLAGE LIFE IN EUROPE

The first European farmers made their house walls of hurdles of woven twigs, plastered with clay to keep out the wind and rain. They often decorated the walls with colorful pigments taken from plants.

# SCIENCE AND TECHNOLOGY 25,000–500 B.C.

**The early history of the world is often divided into periods named after the materials used for the technology of the time—stone, bronze, or iron.**

The three main divisions are Stone Age, Bronze Age, and Iron Age. These divisions cover different periods of time in different parts of the world, and they represent periods of development rather than specific historic dates. For example, in Çatal Hüyük in Turkey the use of copper started around 6200 B.C., but for Indigenous Australians, the Stone Age continued almost until the present day.

## THE SPREAD OF TECHNOLOGIES

In ancient China, the Bronze Age started around 2700 B.C., and it lasted for over 2,000 years. In other places, technologies were introduced through foreign contact. In Africa, ironworking started around 800 B.C., when it was imported from Egypt, leading them out of the Stone Age. One of the most significant inventions was the wheel, first used by the Sumerians more than 5,000 years ago; it needed flat surfaces such as roads to run on. Boats were important, powered by paddles or poles, then oars and sails—these were the best means of travel, and many early civilizations depended on rivers and boats for transportation.

The first tools were made of any available hard stone. Flint made a greater variety possible, allowing the making of sharper edges. A knife-like blade, a borer, and a sharp point are shown here.

Early humans of around 40,000 years ago used implements of wood, bone, and stone. They knew how to prepare animal skins for clothes and shelters and how to shape objects into useful tools.

## MAKING LIFE EASIER

Many farming, domestic, and military implements were needed. They ranged from needles and eating utensils, pots and furniture, spades and saws, to swords and battering rams—all invented to meet different needs over the centuries. Each of them made life easier and better. These objects allowed urban civilizations to come into being and flourish.

▼ ▶ The first boats were dugouts, made from a single tree trunk. Later, more complex boats were made, such as the coracle, made of animal skins fixed over a wooden frame. These were first built around 6,000 years ago in Britain.

Coracle

Dugout

▲ A reconstruction of a loom from Iron Age Europe of around 500 B.C. It was used for weaving colored woolen threads into cloth. The vertical threads, weighed down with clay loomweights, were moved back and forth while a shuttle was passed between them to bind the threads together as a woven material. Such cloth was a great step forward from the use of skins.

No one knows when the wheel was invented. It was probably first made from a sliced log, or it might have developed from potters' wheels. Carts were certainly in use in Sumer more than 5,000 years ago. These carried large loads over longer distances. From the cart came an important weapon of war, the chariot, which speeded up battle charges. The wheel was also used as a pulley to lift heavy loads. New forms of woodworking allowed the building of lighter wheels, and metals made stronger axles.

## FROM ABACUS TO COMPUTER

All of the technologies in use today have their roots in this prehistoric period. In modern times we use computers, but counting systems, such as the abacus, were invented thousands of years ago.

## WHEN IT HAPPENED

| | |
|---|---|
| c.8500 B.C. | Arrowheads first made in North America |
| c.8000 B.C. | First farming in Mesopotamia |
| c.3000 B.C. | The wheel is used on chariots in Mesopotamia |
| c.2700 B.C. | Chinese start making bronze and weaving silk |
| c.2500 B.C. | Bricks are first used for building in the Indus Valley |
| c.1500 B.C. | Iron is smelted by the Hittites in the Middle East |

▲ This bronze bucket and highly decorated ax head were made in Europe around 600 B.C.

Early smelters used bellows to heat a fire to a temperature where a metal such as copper would melt into liquid. This was then poured into molds. When cooled, the metal product would be finished with polishing and sharpening. Later, copper and tin were mixed to make the much harder bronze.

An iron dagger with its sheath from ancient Europe, and a Roman scythe and nails. Nails made woodworking much easier and quicker.

# THE CLASSICAL WORLD

## 499 B.C.–A.D. 500

This was the great age of ancient Greece and Rome. These two extraordinary civilizations were responsible for shaping much of the world we live in today. By about 100 B.C., the ancient world was dominated by four empires. Rome was already the most powerful, stretching from Europe to North Africa. In the Far East, the Han dynasty controlled almost all of what is now China, and the Middle East was ruled by the Sassanids. In India, the Gupta family held power. But, by about A.D. 450, these four empires had collapsed.

▲ Sages and philosophers traditionally influenced Chinese society, but they came under attack during the modernizing Qin period.

◄ The Temple of Olympian Zeus in Athens, Greece, was begun in the 500s B.C., but not completed until the 100s B.C.

# CLASSICAL GREECE 600–337 B.C.

**Ancient Greece was made up of independent city-states, each with its own laws and customs. Here, the Greeks created a new society with new ideas.**

The Aegean Sea was well placed for the founding of a maritime civilization, with cities dotted along both coastlines, and easy access to the Mediterranean Sea.

▲ Athens led the way in the development of richly painted pottery.

Each city-state or *polis* grew up on the plains, and the mountains around them provided natural limits and defenses. Citizens built high, strong walls around their cities, and an *acropolis* (citadel) was erected on a high place inside the walls. At the heart of each city was the *agora*, a large open space used for meetings and markets.

## CITIES AND COLONIES

The two most important city-states were Athens and Sparta. There were many other cities, such as Corinth, Chalcis, Miletos, Smyrna, and Eretria, each with its own way of life, customs, and forms of government. The city-states expanded to build colonies northward on the Black Sea, in Cyrenaica on the coast of north Africa (Libya), Sicily, southern Italy, and even as far away as the southern coasts of France and Spain. Greek city-states were very competitive with each other.

## GREEK CULTURE

The Greeks created a new society with new ideas. They fought hard for their freedom, especially against the Persians who threatened Greece. Being traders, sailors, and adventurers, the Greeks influenced many faraway cultures. Philosophers, doctors, and scientists taught a new way of thinking, based on observation and discussion. Old rural traditions died off as the cities grew to dominate the countryside. New art, architecture, and sciences were created.

▶ Here, the traders of a Greek colonizing expedition, around 500 B.C., draw their ships up onto the beach to start business. The newly built walled city would contain a marketplace, temples, law courts, and government offices as well as houses, workshops, and defenses.

◀ At the battle of Salamis, c. 480 B.C., 380 Greek ships, called *triremes*, faced a Persian force of 1,200 ships. The more mobile triremes drove the Persians into a confused huddle. Persian defeats on land and at sea led them to withdraw from Greece.

## EDUCATION

The sons of freemen were sent to school, and girls were taught weaving and household skills by their mothers. Starting at the age of six or seven, the boys learned reading, writing, dancing, music, and athletics. They wrote on wax tablets, using a stick called a *stylus*.

◄ Here, Greek children study a number of subjects with their tutors.

▼ This painting shows a schoolboy being tested by one of his tutors.

## DISUNITY BETWEEN CITY-STATES

Athens, Sparta, and other city-states united to fight off Persian invasions for 60 years, and triumphed at the battles of Marathon and Salamis around 480 B.C. However, from 431 B.C. they spent more than 25 years fighting each other in the Peloponnesian War because Sparta feared the growth of Athenian power. The independent Greek cities, therefore, never united as one country. This disunity resulted in their defeat in 338 B.C. by Philip II of Macedon, father of Alexander the Great, at the Battle of Chaeronia.

### KEY DATES

| | |
|---|---|
| 800s | The first city-states founded in Greece |
| 594 | Reform of the Athenian constitution |
| 540s | Persians conquer Ionia (eastern Aegean) |
| 480 | Persian invasion ends |
| 431–404 | Peloponnesian Wars: Athens against Sparta |
| 404 | Athens falls to Sparta |
| 371 | Sparta declines—Thebes now main city-state |
| 338 | Philip of Macedon conquers Greece |

▲ A silver four-drachma "owl" piece was the most common coin in the ancient Greek world. Issued in Athens, one side carried a picture of Athena, goddess of wisdom and patron and protector of Athens. The other side carried a picture of an owl, Athena's symbol, carrying an olive branch.

◄ Greek philosophers have had a great impact on history, and their works are still studied today. The freethinking atmosphere in Athens stimulated questioning and discussion on many different subjects. Herodotus and Thucydides were famous Greek historians, and Plato, Socrates, and Aristotle were philosophers and scientists.

# GREEK CITY-STATES 600–337 B.C.

**There were many Greek city-states. Athens and Sparta were the leading cities, constantly fighting each other to dominate Greece.**

Athens and Sparta had very different beliefs and ways of life. Athens was a busy, cosmopolitan trading city run by public debate and decision making—a center for new ideas and trade from all over the known world. Athens became great through prosperity and invention. Sparta was steered by its two kings, and had a very strictly ruled and militaristic society. Sparta threatened Athens' leadership with a well-trained and superior army. Athens was the birthplace of democracy under the reformers Kleisthenes (around 500 B.C.) and Pericles (around 460 B.C.). Voting was enjoyed by freemen, but not by women, foreigners, or slaves. By 400 B.C. it was the leading city-state, controlling the seas and a number of colonies abroad. Many cities paid tribute to Athens for protection and trade advantages. Its statesmen, soldiers, writers, architects, philosophers, artists, and mathematicians had a wide influence.

The sculpted head of a Greek goddess. The Greeks made their gods look very human, introducing realism into their art. In later centuries, this artistic realism reached as far as India and Japan, where statues of the Buddha were also made in a realistic style.

Greek theaters were built so that everyone could see the stage and hear the actors. Greek plays often had a strong moral message, and many Greek dramas survive to this day.

Cities such as Corinth, Thebes, Samos, and Byzantium also made up the culture now known as classical Greece. Being smaller than Athens and Sparta, they often had to ally themselves with each other to survive—sometimes switching sides. Each made its own special contribution to Greek culture.

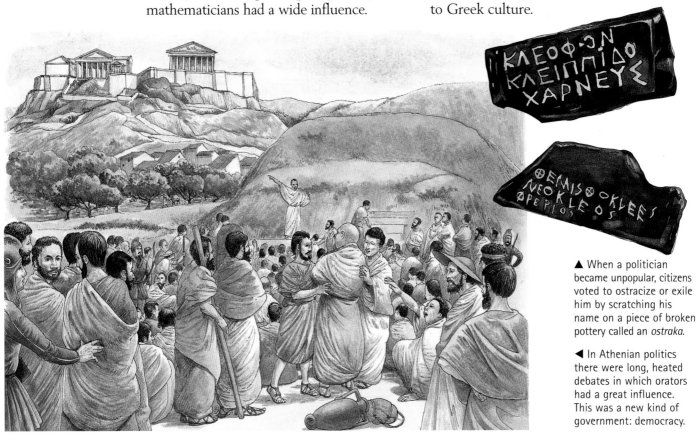

▲ When a politician became unpopular, citizens voted to ostracize or exile him by scratching his name on a piece of broken pottery called an *ostraka*.

◄ In Athenian politics there were long, heated debates in which orators had a great influence. This was a new kind of government: democracy.

The Acropolis in Athens was first built as a fort. Around 400 B.C. it was transformed into a complex of spectacular shrines and temples.

## SPARTA

Sparta had a large army, and life for the Spartans was much harsher than for civilized, cultured Athenians. Spartans were renowned for their strength, dedication, and courage. Sparta relied on a vast population of land slaves called *helots* to provide food. A helot rebellion in 464 B.C. lasted for 20 long years, until the Spartans created an army to control the slaves—the first dictatorial "police state." Spartan life was tough from birth onward: babies who were weak or sick were left to die on the mountainside. Boys were given strenuous training in military skills and sports from the age of seven until they were 20, when they became citizens. Then they joined the army. Even when married, Spartans ate and slept in communal barracks until they were 30 years old.

▼ In this Greek agricultural scene, a shepherd is guarding his sheep, pigs are being herded, olives are being pressed, and the oil is being sold to a merchant.

▲ Greek city houses were built around a courtyard with a large kitchen. Flat roofs provided extra living space in the summer.

# ALEXANDER THE GREAT 336–323 B.C.

**After the end of the disastrous Peloponnesian War, the age of Spartan domination did not last long. By 359 B.C. Philip of Macedon controlled all of Greece.**

Alexander was one of the greatest generals of all time. In 13 years, he united Greece, Egypt, and Babylon, spreading Greek ("hellenistic") ideas and customs far and wide.

Philip of Macedon was assassinated in 336 B.C., shortly after he had invaded Greece. His son Alexander was only 20 years old when he became king. He set out to destroy the Persian threat to Greece—and to gain Persia's wealth.

His first campaign in 334 B.C. gave him control of Asia Minor, and he quickly took Syria and Egypt. By 331 B.C., Persia had fallen and Alexander had taken Babylon. He then embarked on a program of exporting Greek culture and city building to the lands the Greeks invaded. He was a modernizer, and many people welcomed, or at least accepted, the Greeks. Alexander then marched to central Asia and India. In India, his soldiers refused to go farther. They withdrew to Babylon, Alexander's

Alexander founded many new cities, the greatest of which was Alexandria in Egypt. Its imposing lighthouse, the Pharos, at around 330 ft. (100m), was one of the seven wonders of the ancient world.

new capital. In 323 B.C., at the age of 32, Alexander suddenly died of fever. His generals were left to battle for shares of the Greek Macedonia Empire, which now stretched from Egypt to India.

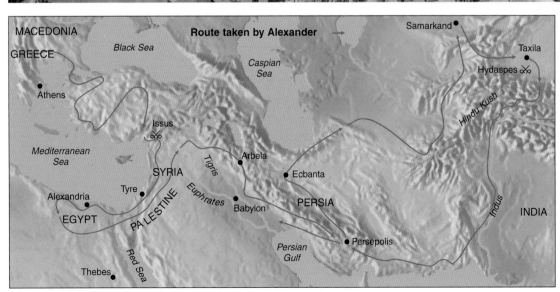

Route taken by Alexander

▲ This Greek painting shows Alexander beating the Persian king, Darius, at the battle of Issus, in Syria, in 333 B.C. Alexander eventually took over the whole Persian Empire.

◄ In just a few years, Alexander's troops marched many thousands of miles, building new cities, peopling them with Greeks, and modernizing whole countries with Greek ideas and trade. Babylon became the new capital of the Greek Empire.

# INDIA: THE MAURYAN EMPIRE 321–233 B.C.

**The Mauryan Empire was founded by Chandragupta. It extended from Bengal to the Hindu Kush and united all the lands of northern India.**

Asoka said, "All people are my children." He set out to create a kind of heaven on Earth in Mauryan India.

Chandragupta took power in Maghada in 321 B.C., and within ten years he had invaded most of northern India. He was a good organizer, and India became prosperous under his influence. His son Bindusara (293–268 B.C.) extended the empire far into southern India.

### ASOKA THE EMPIRE BUILDER

Chandragupta's grandson, Asoka (268–233 B.C.), was the greatest Mauryan ruler. He enlarged the empire, which was inhabited by peoples of more than 60 different beliefs and languages. Asoka was a Hindu, but he adopted Buddhism after seeing a particularly horrific battle. He adopted the Buddhist moral rules of good conduct and nonviolence and brought peace, culture, dignity, and prosperity to his subjects. He built up the religion from a small sect, and sent out missionaries as far as Indonesia, central Asia, and Egypt. He had many stone pillars erected around India, covered with moral and religious guidelines for his people. Asoka was one of history's fairest monarchs.

◄ The lion capital at Sarnath, erected by Asoka, has been adopted by modern India as one of its national column on which it stood marked the place where Buddha preached.

The Mauryans made sure that there was plenty of food available by developing large irrigation and farming schemes across India, such as these rice paddies in the Ganges Valley of northern India.

### MAURYAN LIFE

On a practical level, Asoka tried to improve the conditions of his people. He had reservoirs and irrigation systems built and wells dug, and he set up rest houses at regular intervals along the roads of the empire, to encourage travel and trade and to bring together all its different regions into one system. Asoka also employed a large secret police to help him run his diverse empire. Although Asoka tried to unite the empire, under his rule religious differences between Hindus, Buddhists, and others actually became more distinct. After his death the Mauryan Empire soon became weak and India fragmented into small kingdoms.

The Great Stupa at Sanchi, in India, was built later than the Mauryan period. This elaborate temple was an expression of the rich Buddhist culture that Asoka had established.

# CHINA: THE QIN DYNASTY 221–206 B.C.

**The warlike Qin tribes of western China conquered their neighbors from 350 B.C. onward. By 221 B.C. they had built the empire from which China takes its name.**

King Zheng of Qin (pronounced "*Chin*") united most of China in just ten years, ending the Warring States period. He changed his name to Shi Huangdi (meaning "First Emperor") and founded the first imperial dynasty of China.

▲ The ancient Chinese were great inventors. They invented the wheelbarrow, which they used to carry both goods and people in the 2nd century B.C.— Europe only adopted it 1,000 years later.

### IMPERIAL CHINA

Shi Huangdi reorganized the government, bringing everything under central control. He standardized all weights and measures, Chinese writing, and even the width of wagon wheels; he made laws and institutions in the Qin tradition, and introduced a single currency. He was a ruthless modernizer, abolishing the powers of the feudal aristocracy and sending out administrators to run the regions. He built roads and canals, and improved farming with irrigation and drainage schemes. To protect China from barbarians, construction began on the Great Wall, much of which still exists today. He established imperial traditions that remained consistent through different dynastic periods over 2,000 years. In 221 B.C., Shi Huangdi destroyed many traditional literary works, including those of Confucius, and even executed 400 scholars, to ensure modernization.

▲ Sages and philosophers traditionally influenced Chinese society and government and also played a religious role. As preservers of knowledge, they came under attack during the modernizing Qin period.

For the first time, China was united. The Qin built the Great Wall to protect it from tribes from the north. The Qin capital was Xianyang on the upper Yellow River, the area where the Qin originated.

### THE MANDATE OF HEAVEN

Shi Huangdi was a warrior who used cavalry rather than chariots. He was used to being obeyed, and some of his actions made him very unpopular. Yet he commanded respect and achieved results, and he used his power to make changes quickly and to unite China. He also had principles. He believed that the emperor had been given the "mandate of heaven" by the gods, and that he must earn the support of the gods by governing well. This principle meant that the emperor could also be deposed if he misgoverned the country.

▶ Life was bustling in a typical Qin town of a few thousand people, with its market, buildings, and defenses.

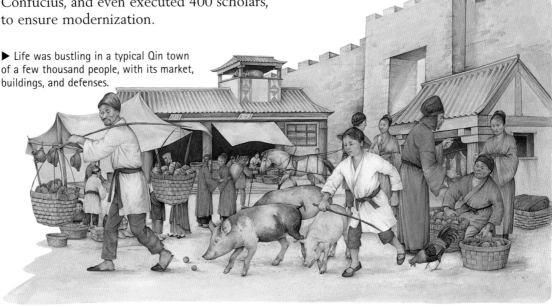

## KEY DATES

| | |
|---|---|
| 350s | Qin becomes a militaristic state |
| 315 | Qin becomes the leading state in China |
| 256 | Qin annexes the state of Zhou (Luoyang) |
| 230 | King Qin Zheng begins to unify China by force |
| 221 | Qin dynasty unites the country for the first time in one empire |
| 214 | To protect China from Hun raids, construction of the Great Wall begins |
| 212 | Shi Hunagdi burns all historical documents, books are banned, and Chinese script standardized |
| 209–202 | Civil war between competing warlords |
| 202 | Founding of the Han dynasty by Liu Bang |

◀ This bronze statue is a fantastic fire-breathing, winged animal from Chinese mythology. The Chinese also made creatures like this in jade.

## THE QIN LEGACY

Shi Huangdi died in 210 B.C., and four years later the Qin dynasty was overthrown because the changes and laws they made were too harsh. A civil war broke out. The idea of a united empire, however, had become fixed in the minds of the people. An ordinary man, named Liu Bang, who had become a Qin official, founded a new dynasty and, as a result, gained popular support. The Han dynasty was to rule for 400 years, on the basis that Shi Huangdi had established.

◀ Shi Huangdi's tomb housed his body and possessions for use in the afterlife. It also contained 7,000 larger-than-life terracotta soldiers. Each face was realistic and may have represented the actual faces of a specific soldier.

## THE GREAT WALL OF CHINA

The Qin used large numbers of forced laborers to build much of the Great Wall. It was 1,400 mi. (2,250km) long and built from packed earth and rubble. Stone, bricks, and mortar were added later. The scale of this operation shows how important it was to the Chinese to keep the raiding tribes of the north out. These tribes preyed on Chinese security and prosperity, and China suffered greatly before the wall was built and the raiders beaten off.

The Great Wall, now more than 2,200 years old, is a popular tourist attraction today. When it was built, it protected civilized China from the devastating raids carried out by the Huns (Xiongnu) and other tribes from the north.

# AFRICA 500 B.C.–A.D. 500

**Most of Africa was unaffected by outside influences. In West Africa, new nations were being formed, and migration was changing southern Africa.**

The introduction of the camel to the Sahara brought major changes around 100 B.C. Caravans were able to cross the desert carrying gold, ivory, gums, spices, and slaves. Trading towns became established in West Africa: Djenné-Djeno, Niani, Yelwa, and Nok were on rivers or at the edges of deserts and rain forests. These towns were the capitals of the first budding African states. North–south trade passed through Meroë and Aksum, bypassing the Sahara into the regions now known as Chad, Rwanda, and Kenya.

▲ This terracotta head from Nok is a fine example of sculpture that flourished from 400 B.C. to A.D. 200.

Africa had four main centers of cultural growth: Aksum (Ethiopia), the Berber north African coast, negro West Africa, and the developing Bantu areas farther south.

## AKSUM

Meroë collapsed in 350 B.C., and Aksum, on the Red Sea coast of Ethiopia, grew rich exporting ivory, precious stones, and perfumes to Arabia, Greece, and Rome, reaching its peak in A.D. 350. Around that time its king, Ezana, adopted Christianity. Cities and great monoliths were built. Aksum thrived until A.D. 1000.

## BANTU EXPANSION

Farming, Bantu-speaking people from Nigeria gradually migrated south and east, and by A.D. 500 they had occupied central and southern Africa, leaving the rain forests to the pygmies and the Kalahari Desert to the Khoisan bushmen. On Africa's east coast the Bantu had started to trade with Greeks and Romans.

▼ Greek trading missions on the east African coast bought medicinal herbs, aromatic gums, jewels, and gold from the Bantu-speaking tribespeople of the hinterlands.

▲ To smelt iron, iron ore was put into an earthen furnace. Bellows were then used to raise its temperature to extract metal from the ore.

▲ The leaders of Aksum were very religious. They built tall monoliths like this at places of importance, such as over royal tombs.

# JUDEA 600 B.C.–A.D. 135

**Since their 60-year exile in Babylon, from 597 B.C., the Jews, with their different religious beliefs, had grown further apart from their Near-Eastern neighbors.**

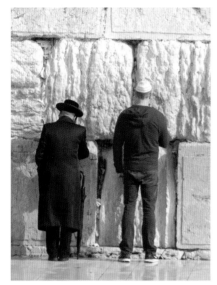

▲ The Western Wall in Jerusalem is at the site of the Temple that was destroyed by the Romans in A.D. 70.

The Jews worshiped one god, Yahweh, built synagogues, and observed strict religious laws. On returning from exile in Babylon in 538 B.C., they emphasized Jewish law and beliefs, and set themselves apart from non-Jews, or Gentiles. Palestine was under Greek rule and many Jews fought to stop their influence destroying Jewish traditions.

### ROMAN PALESTINE

After Greek rule, Judea was independent for nearly 80 years before being conquered by Rome. The Romans appointed Herod as king of Judea in 37 B.C. Jewish people were free to travel and trade, and many left to settle elsewhere. When Pontius Pilate

The *menorah*, a Jewish ceremonial candlestick, was shaped by Moses to signify the seven days of Creation. One stood in the Temple at Jerusalem.

became Judea's Roman governor in A.D. 26, life became hard for the Jews. They loathed the Romans and their taxes. After much rebelliousness, the Romans forced the Jews to leave Judea in A.D. 135.

▼ The ancient fortress of Masada is where besieged Jewish rebels committed suicide in A.D. 73 rather than surrender to the Romans.

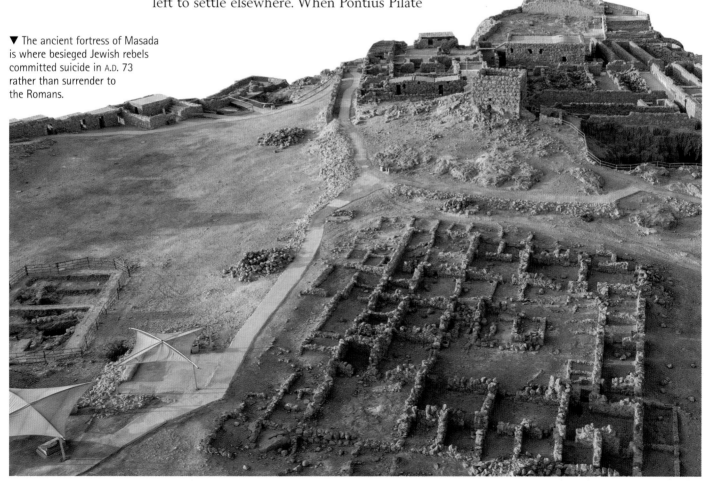

# THE ROMAN REPUBLIC 509–27 B.C.

**Rome was by now run by patricians (the ruling class). They sought to expand Rome's interests, first in Italy and later throughout the Mediterranean.**

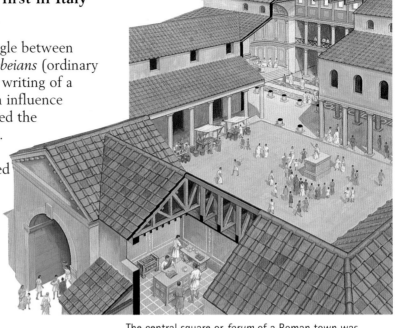

The central square or *forum* of a Roman town was where people met each other, announcements were made, markets were held, and where the town hall, treasury, and law courts were located.

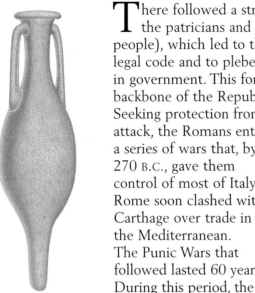

Jars like this *amphora* were used to store and transport olive oil and wine throughout the Roman Empire.

The Colosseum in Rome, an enormous stadium, was used for gladiatorial contests, sports, and the gory killing of animals, captured enemies, and slaves.

There followed a struggle between the patricians and *plebeians* (ordinary people), which led to the writing of a legal code and to plebeian influence in government. This formed the backbone of the Republic. Seeking protection from attack, the Romans entered a series of wars that, by 270 B.C., gave them control of most of Italy. Rome soon clashed with Carthage over trade in the Mediterranean. The Punic Wars that followed lasted 60 years. During this period, the Carthaginian emperor, Hannibal, led his army across the Alps to invade Italy. After a series of victories by Hannibal, the brilliant Roman general, Scipio, set off to Africa to attack Carthage. This forced Hannibal back to Carthage, where he was finally defeated by Scipio. The Romans soon established new cities, building order and prosperity and giving conquered peoples a form of Roman citizenship if they cooperated. By 44 B.C. the Romans ruled Spain, France, Europe south of the Danube, Anatolia, and northern Africa, dominating the Mediterranean. In less than 200 years, the Romans had become the controlling force in the West.

## THE END OF THE REPUBLIC

In 100 B.C., friction grew between the patricians and plebeians. The army was opened up to landless citizens, who were rewarded for their services with land and status in the colonies. Power struggles between generals ended in civil war, and, in 44 B.C., Julius Caesar became dictator for life. Alarmed Republicans assassinated him, and the Republic soon ended.

Vital to the growing empire was the system of roads built to speed up trade, mail delivery, and troop movements. On the right, a water-carrying aqueduct is being built over a road.

## THE PUNIC WARS

Expanding their influence, the Romans came up against the Phoenicians in Carthage. The Punic Wars (264–241 and 218–202 B.C.) began over a fight for Sicily, but grew to threaten the great cities of Rome and Carthage. The Carthaginian general, Hannibal, nearly won, after invading Italy from the Alps. The Roman general, Scipio Africanus, avoided a head-on battle, instead attacking Spain in 206 and then Carthage itself in 202 B.C. The Phoenicians lost everything, and the Romans then dominated the Mediterranean Sea and its trade.

Hannibal's army marched from Spain, over the Alps, and into Italy. It was so formidable that the Romans avoided confronting it. They attacked Carthage instead, and forced Hannibal to rush back to defend it.

The Carthaginians used African elephants to frighten the Roman troops. When they crossed the Alps, most of the elephants died.

Hannibal was a brilliant strategist and a modest man who carried out maneuvers no one believed could work. The Romans beat him only by outwitting his strategy.

# THE ROMAN EMPIRE 27 B.C.–A.D. 475

**After Julius Caesar's death in 44 B.C., Romans preferred dictatorship to chaos. Octavian, his successor, gradually took control. He became the first emperor.**

Octavian was Caesar's nephew. He was an able politician, getting himself elected as Consul (president) year after year. He called himself *princeps* ("first citizen"), not king. Renamed Augustus ("imposing one"), he reorganized the government and empire and imposed peace. Under him, trade extended as far as East Africa, India, and China, and the empire's towns, roads, and territories grew ever larger.

Julius Caesar was a ruthless and ambitious general and politician who conquered the Celts of Gaul and later became Rome's first dictator for life—an appointment that angered Republicans and led to Caesar's murder.

Heavily armed Roman legionaries: a *centurion* (officer) with a *ballista* (catapult), a legionary (soldier), and a standard-bearer.

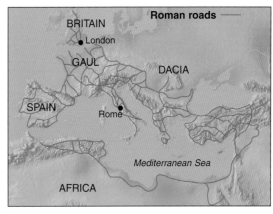

The Roman Empire dominated most of the Western world, uniting it into one economic system, under one goverment.

## ROMAN EMPERORS

Emperors relied more on the army than on the Roman people for support. Patricians no longer had great power. Many had moved to rich country estates and the far provinces. Most of the Roman emperors chose their successors; some unpopular or controversial ones were deposed by soldiers. In A.D. 68–69, four emperors were deposed in one year. From A.D. 100, Rome was ruled by strong emperors—Trajan, Hadrian, Antoninus, and Marcus Aurelius—most of whom were not actually Roman. By A.D. 117 the empire had grown too large and Rome's soldiers could no longer be paid with booty, slaves, and land taken in conquest. The burden on Rome grew.

When attacking a fortress, legionnaires would form a protective shield like this—a *testudo* (tortoise), that advanced slowly under fire from stones and arrows.

## THE ROMAN ARMY

Soldiers joined the army to gain rewards of promotion, land, or power—especially if they were not Roman. This meant that soldiers dominated the empire and its colonies, becoming landowners and the ruling class. The army was very international, often hiring barbarians as mercenaries. Legions fought in such faraway places as Scotland, Morocco, and Arabia. Roads, forts, and border walls were built to maintain security.

A permanent Roman army camp was like a miniature city, with all the services necessary to support a legion—the troops were, after all, far from their homes in other parts of the empire. These military bases were located in the areas that were most in need of permanent protection.

## THE ROMAN EMPIRE

The final conquests, in the century following Augustus, had been in Britain, Syria, Palestine, and Egypt. The Jews and Britons had been difficult to beat, and the Parthians impossible. However, most of the conquered peoples adapted. People in Gaul, North Africa, Syria, Britain, and Hungary adopted Roman ways and thought of themselves as Roman citizens. Running a huge empire was difficult, and it was united by business, not religious or ethnic ties. Provincial peoples were allowed to get on with their lives, as long as they obeyed the rules set by the Romans.

The Appian Way, a major road from Rome to the southeast coast, was built in 312 B.C. Soldiers, traders, and travelers could now travel along it very quickly.

### KEY DATES

| | |
|---|---|
| 509 B.C. | Roman republic founded |
| 496 | Romans defeat Latins at Battle of Lake Regillus |
| 493 | Roman-Latin alliance forms the Latin League, which fights the Etruscans |
| 390 | Rome sacked by Celts |
| 306 | Romans defeat Etruscans |
| 300s | Romans expand to dominate Italy |
| 264–202 | Punic Wars and the fall of Carthage |
| 146 | Rome takes Greece |
| 50s | Caesar conquers Gaul |
| 49–31 | Civil War between competing generals |
| 27 B.C. | Octavian: end of republic, growth of empire |
| A.D. 160 | Plague and crisis cut population and trade |
| 212 | Roman citizenship granted to all inhabitants of the empire |
| 286 | Diocletian divides and reorganizes the empire |
| 324 | Founding of Constantinople |
| 370 | Barbarian attacks on the empire |
| 410 | The Visigoths sack Rome—rapid decline of the city results |
| 476 | Fall of the last emperor, Romulus Augustus |

# ROMAN LIFE 509 B.C.–A.D. 475

**The Romans did not really invent many things to advance their civilization—they took what had already been invented and developed it further.**

▲ Everyday objects like this key were handmade in specialized workshops.

▲ The Romans used olive oil to fill lamps to light their homes.

The Roman way of life became known as *Romanitas*—everything that had to do with being a citizen of the empire. It was not just an empire—it was a system, a single market, and a union of different lands, sharing a developed way of life.

## THE POWER OF THE PEOPLE

The Greeks created democracy and the Romans took it further. Democracy meant government by patricians, the ruling class, although plebeians (ordinary people) had some influence in elections. Slaves—mostly non-Roman—had no power at all. Roman democracy worked well for a time, but in the end it was misused. It was replaced by the rule of an emperor.

## THE SENATE

The Republic was ruled by an elected Senate, a group of patricians who selected two consuls each year to act as presidents. These presidents were advised by the Senate. Later, Roman soldiers gained greater power than the ordinary people, and the consuls became military dictators. After the death of Augustus, Rome was ruled by a succession of emperors who held absolute power.

## URBAN LIFE

At its peak, Rome's population was about one million. Alexandria and Antioch were home to 100,000 inhabitants each. Other Roman cities had 10,000–50,000 inhabitants. Each city was carefully laid out with its official buildings and public squares, baths, a stadium, markets, workshops, and storehouses, as well as living quarters for each social class.

▲ A Roman emperor wore a toga, or cloak, over a long tunic. Beside him stands his young slave.

▲ Slaves did the fetching and carrying, both in the city and on farms in the country.

## A ROMAN TOWN

The Romans were superb builders. They built roads across the countryside and walls around their towns for protection. People went to the public baths to wash, relax, and meet friends. There were temples dedicated to gods and goddesses. Business was done in the forum, originally the city's marketplace.

## KEY DATES

| | |
|---|---|
| 200 B.C. | Growth of classical Roman art, architecture, and literature |
| 103 | Revolt by slaves in Rome |
| 91 | War between Rome and Italian cities |
| 88 | Civil war in Rome |
| c.30 B.C. | The poet Virgil and the historian Livy at work |
| A.D. 64 | Start of persecution of Christians in Rome, under Nero |
| 100 | The empire reaches its greatest extent |
| 160 | Thousands of Roman citizens die from the plague |
| 200 | The empire's road system is completed |
| 260 | Beginning of barbarian incursions |
| 313 | Constantine decrees religious tolerance |
| 410 | Fall of the empire in the west |

The Romans used chariots drawn by horses for races and fast travel. Races were held in sports arenas. Goods were carried in carts drawn by strong, heavy oxen.

## THE COUNTRYSIDE

As Roman life developed, farms were bought and reorganized by rich city-dwellers or awarded to soldiers as estates. Tenants, peasants, and slaves did the work, growing produce for sale in the cities. Large quantities of food and materials were transported from the farms to Rome and other cities. In addition, the legions required feeding, so the country estates were prepared for large-scale and profitable food production.

## EVERYDAY LIFE

Life in Rome was in many ways similar to city life today. High-rise houses, traffic problems, shopping, waste disposal, hustle, and bustle were all common features. Rome was also a meeting place for people from all over the empire, and the people communicated in the common tongues, Latin and Greek. It was a money economy and a very complex society with different classes, belief systems, and several different religions.

## A COUNTRY VILLA

Wealthy Romans lived in large town houses. They also had grand villas in the country. Some villas were run as large farms. The owner and his family could enjoy a comfortable house and garden, with a heating system to keep them warm in the winter. Many large farms used slave labor to grow highly profitable crops of grain or olives, or to raise sheep and goats for milk, meat, and hides.

# THE CELTS 500 B.C.–A.D. 43

**The Greeks and Romans regarded their neighbors to the west and north as barbarians. In reality, these Iron Age peoples had a rich and enduring culture.**

Across mainland Europe, tribal territories stretched from Germany eastward along the River Danube, westward into Belgium and France, and southward through the Alps into northern Italy. The Greeks called the inhabitants *Keltoi* or *Galatai*. The Romans called them *Celtae* or *Galli* (Gauls).

### IRON AGE EUROPE
In Spain, local customs were intermixed with those of the Gauls, creating a "Celtiberian" culture. The peoples of Britain and Ireland (Britons, Picts, and Gaels) were part of the Celtic world too, thanks to ancient settlement and trading links with mainland Europe. These European tribes had many differences and were rarely united, but all were referred to as "Celts" by later historians. They did share related languages. Some of these died out long ago, but others evolved into languages still spoken today: Irish, Scottish Gaelic, Manx, Welsh, Cornish, and Breton.

An aristocratic class included chieftains, local kings and queens, and druids, who acted as priests and lawmakers. Ordinary villagers worked as farmers and smiths. There were fortified towns called *oppida*. Elsewhere, hillforts served as trading centres and meeting places.

This bull appears on a silver ceremonial cauldron, which was found at Gundestrup, in Denmark. It was probably made in Thrace, between about 150 and 1 B.C.

### A CELTIC VISION
An intricate, swirling style of art known as "La Tène" spread far and wide. The Celts excelled at crafts and working in gold, bronze, and iron. Their designs often featured plants and animals, reflecting their religious beliefs about nature, gods, and goddesses.

▲ This fine bronze shield facing is decorated in the La Tène style. It was found in the River Thames in London, U.K., and dates from the 2nd to 1st century B.C. It may have been thrown into the river as an offering to the gods.

▲ Vertcingetorix, a king and chieftain of the Arverni tribe, united the Gauls against Rome. He was defeated at Alesia in 52 B.C.

▶ A Celtic chieftain and his household feast in their timbered hall, while listening to the poetic songs of a bard.

In the west of Gaul, Britain, and Ireland, roundhouses were made of timber and thatch, with wattle-and-daub (or sometimes stone) walls. Smoke floated out through the thatched roof, but rain was unable to seep in. The sleeping space was around the inside of the walls, and cooking and washing took place around the central hearth.

▼ Cernunnos, the stag-god, was worshipped across the Celtic world, and appears here on the Gundestrup cauldron. Caldrons were believed to have magical powers.

## WARS AND INVASIONS

The Gauls sacked Rome in about 387 B.C., attacked Greece in 279 B.C. and even reached Galatia (in Anatolia). They were famed as fierce warriors, but by 52 B.C., they had been conquered by the military might of Rome. Julius Caesar also invaded southeastern Britain in 55–54 B.C., but the main conquest of Britain began in A.D. 43. Rome failed to control the far north and never invaded Ireland, but most of Britain, Gaul—and the other Celtic lands—remained in the Roman empire until the 400s A.D. By then, Germanic invaders and settlers were already sweeping across western Europe—the Anglo-Saxons, Franks, Goths, and Vandals.

Boudicca was queen of the Iceni, a tribe of eastern Britain (present-day Norfolk). She led a rebellion against the occupying Romans in A.D. 60, in which 70,000–80,000 Romans were killed and London was burned down. She is said to have died or committed suicide after she was defeated.

65

# CHINA: THE HAN DYNASTY 206 B.C.–A.D 220

**The Han was the first long-lasting dynasty of united imperial China. Han China enjoyed stability and greatness and was a fine example of civilization.**

For 400 years from 206 B.C. to A.D. 220, China was ruled by emperors of the Han dynasty. They were more lenient and stable than the Qin, and practiced fair Confucian principles of law and administration.

### THE EARLY HAN

The dynasty was founded by Liu Bang, a commoner who was popular because he relaxed the harsh laws, cut taxes, and favored the people. The capital was Chang'an, which, after 100 years, became the world's largest city. It was at the end of the Silk Road along which China traded with Persia and Rome. Han China saw itself as the "Middle Kingdom," the center of the world. There was a great flowering of culture, wealth, and learning. At this time, Han China was as large and developed as the extensive Roman Empire. The Han developed a system of administration by highly educated officials. People who wanted to work as public officials had to take an examination on the writings of Confucius.

▲ A ceramic horse and rider made in Han China around 80 B.C. Stirrups were not introduced into China until around A.D. 300.

▼ Here, Chinese soldiers of the Han period engage in battle. Lacking stirrups, the horsemen on both sides were easily knocked to the ground during fighting at close quarters.

This bronze model of a prosperous man in his carriage was found in the tomb of the Han general, Wuwei. It was probably made around A.D. 100.

### THE MARTIAL EMPEROR

Wu Di, the "Martial Emperor," reigned for 55 years from 141 B.C. He added part of central Asia, Korea, and much of southern China to his empire. At great expense, he beat back the Xiongnu (Huns) of Mongolia, who often raided China. He improved the mandarin administration, built schools, canals, cities, and buildings, and encouraged foreign contact. Buddhism was introduced to China during this high point in the country's long history.

▲ The emperor's many representatives were always treated with great respect. The speedy transportation of officials from one place to another was helped by stations where fresh horses were provided.

◄ Emperor Guangwu declared himself ruler and ruled from A.D. 25-57.

## WANG MANG

During the following century, the Han grew weak, while the nobles grew ever stronger. A courtier, Wang Mang, rebelled, took power, and ruled from A.D. 9–23. He introduced many changes and reforms, favoring the people against landowners and nobles, and reforming land rights and the judicial system. Eventually the nobles overthrew Wang Mang, and the Han dynasty was restored.

## THE LATER HAN

The Han produced exquisite objects of wood, lacquer, and silk. They also replaced many of the writings that had been destroyed by the Qin. Chinese inventors were far ahead of the rest of the world. Their invention of paper took centuries to reach the West. Many of the cities they built were large and elegant. However, the population had grown, and rebellions among landless and poor peasants became frequent. Barbarians again attacked the borders, and warlords took over the army. The last Han emperor gave up his throne in A.D. 220 and the empire fell apart.

City streets in Han China were crowded. The muddy roads were full of carts, chariots, and traders. Craftsmen, letter writers, storytellers, and astrologers also plied their trade noisily in the open air.

# CHRISTIANITY A.D. 30–400

**Around the time that Jesus of Nazareth was born there were many faiths and sects in the Roman Empire. Within 400 years, Christianity became dominant.**

The Jewish people believed that a Messiah (savior) would be born to lead them. At the time that Jesus of Nazareth was born, Judea was suffering under Roman rule. At about the age of 30, Jesus began publicly teaching, and it is said that he performed many miracles, such as healing. The Jewish authorities accused him of blasphemy and he was tried before the Roman governor, Pontius Pilate. He was crucified, but his followers reported seeing him alive after his death.

The Chi-Rho symbol, or labarum, was adopted by early Christians. Its P and X are the first two letters in the Greek spelling of Christ. The symbol Chi-Rho itself is a short form of the word *chreston*, or "good omen."

## A CHURCH IS BORN

This "resurrection" formed the basis of a new faith, breaking with old Jewish traditions and founded by Jesus' closest disciples, the apostles. It gradually spread among both exiled Jews and non-Jews throughout the Roman world. Early followers—especially Paul—taught that Christianity was open to anyone who chose to be baptized. By A.D. 300, it had spread to Egypt, Aksum, Syria, Armenia, Anatolia, Greece, Rome, France, Britain, and India.

The Essenes were a Jewish sect. Their abandoned scrolls, found in a cave at Qumran near the Dead Sea, in 1947, included one which deals with the Messiah and what was to happen after he appeared.

Christians kept their faith quietly, because the Roman authorities often persecuted them, and caused many of them to go into hiding. Many died a painful death in the arena. In Egypt, a group of Christians withdrew to the desert to live as hermits. They were the first Christian monks.

A painting of Jesus as he was portrayed in the first centuries after his death.

## JESUS OF NAZARETH

Jesus was born in Bethlehem, in Judea. Around the age of 12, in discussions with learned rabbis at the temple, Jesus showed himself to be special. Nothing more is known about his life until he was around 30 years of age. He then began a public life of teaching. Jesus attracted large crowds. He used parables—stories that taught lessons by example. Love and respect for others was at the heart of his teaching. Three years after he began his mission, the Romans put him to death.

### KEY DATES

| | |
|---|---|
| 3 B.C. | Probable year of the birth of Jesus of Nazareth, in Bethlehem |
| 30 | Approximate date of the crucifixion of Jesus Christ |
| 45–64 | The missions of Paul to Greece, Anatolia, and Rome |
| 65–100 | The Christian Gospels are written |
| 180 | Foundation of early Church institutions |
| 249–311 | Periodic persecutions of Christians in the Roman Empire |
| 269 | St. Anthony establishes Christian monasticism in Egypt |
| 313 | Emperor Constantine recognizes the Christian church |
| 325 | Church doctrine formalized |
| 337 | Constantine is baptized on his deathbed |

## STATE RELIGION

Religious persecution in the Roman Empire was halted when Emperor Constantine recognized Christianity in A.D. 313. Later it became the official state religion. Constantine called the first council of all bishops, at Nicaea, urging them to resolve their differences and write down one doctrine—the Nicene Creed. Politically, he saw the Church as a way of bringing new life to his empire. His actions defined Christianity, greatly affecting Europe and, eventually, most of the rest of the world. It also meant that the ideas of some teachers were outlawed as "heresies," and this led to the disappearance of many aspects of the faith. It also led to death or exile for those who disagreed with the doctrine. The Gnostic, Celtic, and Nestorian churches were examples of branches that eventually died out—although the Nestorians journeyed to Persia and as far as China to prevent this.

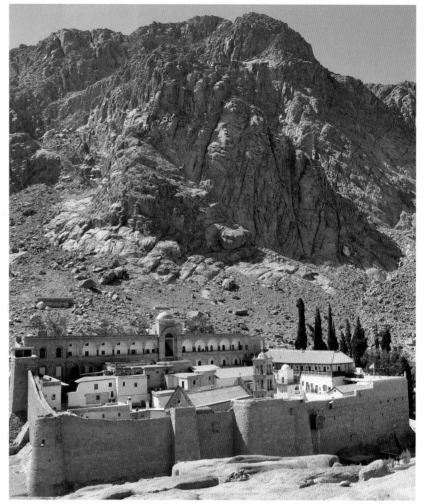

In the A.D. 300s , an Egyptian Christian, Anthony, traveled to the Sinai desert and began the monastic tradition. St. Catherine's monastery, at the base of Mt. Sinai, is one of the oldest monasteries in the area.

Constantine changed the church from a sect into a powerful institution. Legend has it that he adopted the Christian symbol after being told in a dream to paint it on his soldiers' shields before a crucial battle outside Rome in A.D. 312—a battle he won.

# PARTHIANS AND SASSANIDS 238 B.C.–A.D. 637

The Parthians were Asiatic nomads who had moved south into Persia around 1000 B.C. About 300 B.C., the Parni tribe, later to become their rulers, joined them.

The Parthians and the Parni lived in northern Iran under Persian and then Greek Seleucid rule. The head of the Parni became the Seleucid governor of Parthia. Then, in 238 B.C., he declared independence and made himself high king over a number of local chiefs in the land. The Parthians adopted existing local ways of doing things (Greek, Persian, Babylonian), rather than inventing their own, although in time they adopted more and more Persian customs. Parthia grew prosperous through Silk Road trade from China.

Shapur I became the Persian shah (emperor) in A.D. 242. Two years later he shocked the Romans by defeating them. Shapur was the greatest of the Sassanid shahs and ruled for 30 years.

The Parthians were famous for horseback fighting. They would gallop away from the enemy as if fleeing, and then turn and shoot backward at their pursuers. This led to the term "Parthian shot."

## RISE AND FALL OF THE PARTHIANS

The greatest Parthian leaders were two brothers, both called Mithradates. Little is known of Parthia, except that the Parthians conquered Babylonia and Bactria (Afghanistan) and were friendly with Han China. They fought the Romans regularly, stopping the Roman expansion eastward. Their army was strong and well-organized. Famous for horseback fighting, they swept into battle at great speed, behind a hail of arrows, and were able to quickly overwhelm all armed opposition.

## THE RISE OF THE SASSANIDS

The Parthian wars with Rome were costly and unpopular. After 450 years of superiority in Persia, they became a spent force. In A.D. 225, this made it possible for a local king named Ardashir to overthrow the Parthians. Ardashir ruled over a Persian dynasty, the Sassanids. He made the Parsee faith (Zoroastrianism) into the state religion of Persia. This was a new idea, later copied by Constantine of Rome. Ardashir led the Persians into a new period of greatness.

Around A.D. 275, Shapur I built a wonderful palace at Ctesiphon in Babylonia, of which only these ruins remain. Ctesiphon became a wealthy city and a major center for the area, communicating with the West and with China.

70

## SHAPUR I OF PERSIA

The Sassanid shahs (emperors) wanted to carry on in the ancient traditions of old Persia, and they also wanted to reclaim the lands Darius had once ruled before they were conquered by Alexander the Great. Their court at Ctesiphon (near Babylon) became the focus for a brilliant culture, and the wealthy empire became Rome's greatest rival. Shapur I was an outstanding Sassanid ruler. He fought the Romans and even captured the Roman emperor Valerian, and had him killed. Shapur conquered Armenia, Syria, Bactria, and Sogdiana (Afghanistan), and the Indus Valley (Pakistan). At home, Shapur sponsored a cultural flowering of Persia that centered on Zoroastrian religious ideas. In 480, Persia suffered a religious revolt and the invasion of hordes of Huns from Mongolia. After these problems were dealt with, Shah Khosru II conquered Egypt and Byzantium. However, he was killed, a civil war broke out, weakening Persia. Sassanid Persia collapsed when the newly inspired Muslim Arabs conquered the area in 637, eventually converting the Persians to Islam.

| KEY DATES | |
|---|---|
| 238 B.C. | Parthian Arsaces I declares independence from Seleucia |
| 141 | Mithradates invades Mesopotamia |
| 53 | Parthians destroy the Roman army in Syria |
| A.D. 225 | Sassanids overthrow the Parthians |
| 240–272 | Shapur I—Sassanid Persia at its high point |
| 480s | Hun invasions of eastern Persia |
| 616 | Khosru II conquers Egypt |
| 637 | Persia falls to the Muslim Arabs |

Parthian and Sassanid wealth came through trade on the Silk Road which passed through Parthia from China to the West. This carved life-size figure of Hercules was placed by the Silk Road to guard the route.

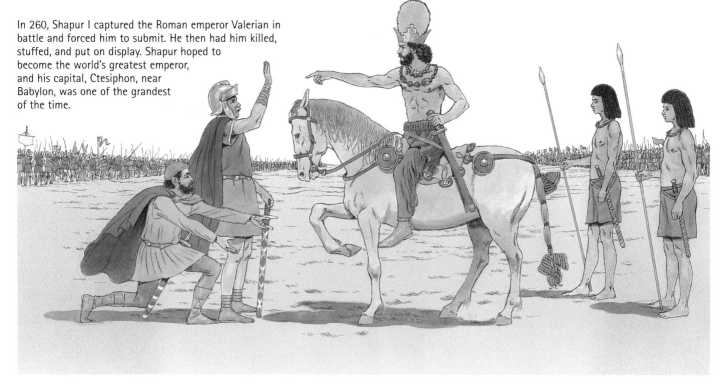

In 260, Shapur I captured the Roman emperor Valerian in battle and forced him to submit. He then had him killed, stuffed, and put on display. Shapur hoped to become the world's greatest emperor, and his capital, Ctesiphon, near Babylon, was one of the grandest of the time.

# THE AMERICAS 500 B.C.–A.D. 500

**During this period there were many different cultures in the Americas. By A.D. 100, the city-state of Teotihuacán had grown to dominate Mexico.**

An eagle's claw cut from a sheet of mica (a flat, glassy mineral that forms rock) by the Hopewell Indians of Ohio in around A.D. 200.

E xcept for visits by Pacific Polynesians to Peru during the A.D. 300s, the Americas were isolated from the rest of the world. Even so, Teotihuacán, dominated by its enormous Pyramid of the Sun, was the world's fifth largest city, with 200,000 people.

## NORTH AMERICA
Several cultural groups existed here. The nomadic, buffalo-hunting Plains tribes occupied the Midwest, and the woodland tribal nations lived in the Northeast. In the Mississippi Valley, the copper-working, trading Hopewell culture was in decline by A.D. 500. In the Southwest, the village-dwelling, corn-growing Hohokam and Mogollon peoples were thriving. On the West Coast and in the North, simpler hunting, fishing, and food-gathering societies such as the Makah and Inuit flourished.

### THE GREAT SERPENT MOUND

No one knows exactly who built the Great Serpent Mound. It is possible that it was the Adena Indians, predecessors to the Hopewell culture. It was built in what is now Ohio, somewhere between 1000 B.C. and A.D. 700. This mound, some 1,300 ft. (400m) long, may have been a ceremonial center depicting the cosmic serpent (a symbol of the life force in nature) eating the cosmic egg. This would probably have symbolized the eternal cycle of death and rebirth, or represented the incarnation of the life force.

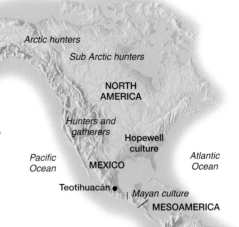

There were many different cultures in the Americas. Apart from the urban civilizations, such as Teotihuacán, there were many simpler cultures scattered throughout the region.

## MESOAMERICA
The Olmecs (1200–300 B.C.) and the Zapotecs (1400–400 B.C.) were the earliest civilizations in Mexico. The Zapotecs were noted for their learning and were the first Americans to develop writing (800 B.C.). They also had a mathematical calendar system, which they later taught to the Maya and the people of Teotihuacán.

A carved stone sculpture from Teotihuacán. Surprisingly unwarlike, this city nevertheless had a great influence on all other neighboring cultures—especially through its crafts and other goods.

## TEOTIHUACÁN

As the Olmecs and Zapotecs declined, the city-state of Teotihuacán, founded around 200 B.C., grew to dominate Mexico by A.D. 100. At its height 600 years later, Teotihuacán was larger than ancient Rome. It was built in a planned grid system, with impressive temple complexes and pyramids, many craft workshops, trading markets, and foreign residents' quarters. It was the largest trading city in the Americas, linking and supplying North and South America. Teotihuacán influenced other Mexican cultures such as the Maya, and it imported materials from as far away as the Great Lakes and Colombia. It was surrounded by other cities, but it was unusually peaceful. It mysteriously declined around A.D. 600, although the Aztecs carried its heritage on into later times.

## SOUTH AMERICA

In Peru, the state of Moche, at its peak around A.D. 300, made fine pottery, textiles, and metalwork. Farther south, the city of Tiwanaku, 12,200 ft. (3,660m) above sea level beside Lake Titicaca in the Andes, was inhabited by 40,000 people and featured enormous stone temples and palaces. Founded around 300 B.C., the city reached its golden age around A.D. 500.

This is one of the stone stepped Mayan pyramids at Tikal, Guatemala. At the top of the steps stands a temple. Around 300 B.C. (possibly even earlier), the Maya began building huge temple complexes. The one at El Mirador covers over 6 sq. mi. (16 sq km.)

### KEY DATES

**350 B.C.** Earliest Maya city-states appear
**300 B.C.** Tiwanaku, Peru, founded (peak A.D. 500, abandoned 1000)
**200 B.C.** Teotihuacán founded (peak A.D. 500)
**200 B.C.** Moche culture, coastal Ecuador (peak A.D. 300, conquered 700)
**100 B.C.** Hopewell culture (peak A.D. 300, ended 800)
**A.D. 300** Beginning of Classical period of Maya civilization (until 800)
**300** Mogollon culture, North America
**400** Hohokam culture, North America (until 1450)

A shell carving of a priest or official who served at Palenque, one of the main ceremonial centers of the Mayan civilization.

# THE GUPTA DYNASTY A.D. 320–510

**The Guptas became emperors of northern India in A.D. 320 and remained in power for 200 years. The stage was set for them by a people called the Kushans.**

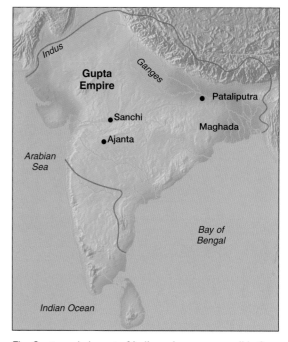

The Kushans were Greek-influenced Asian nomads in Bactria (now northern Afghanistan). They founded a kingdom there in A.D. 25, then moved north into Turkestan and farther south into Afghanistan and India, dominating the area by A.D. 100. Their greatest king was Kanishka (100-130), a Buddhist who supported social tolerance and the arts. Controlling most land trade across Asia, the wealthy Kushans gave stability to Asian trade. Around 240, however, Shapur of Persia took much of their land, and they never recovered.

The Guptas were minor princes in Maghada. Chandragupta I married a Maghada princess and became king in 320. He started the Gupta tradition of aiding the arts and religions and helped develop Indian society.

Krishna ("the first wise man") is one of the ten incarnations of the god Vishnu. He is associated with love and wisdom, and is featured in the *Mahabharata* and *Bhagavad Gita*, two great Hindu holy books.

The Guptas ruled most of India and were responsible for its golden age. Their capital, Pataliputra, was one of the largest cities in the world at that time.

## THE GUPTA MAHARAJAHS

Chandragupta's son Samudragupta continued in his father's footsteps. Ruling from 335 for 45 years, he expanded Gupta rule by force and diplomacy across northern India and into southeastern India. His own son Chandragupta II (380-414) took Gupta India to its high point, one of the greatest times of Indian history. Skandagupta (455-467) beat off an invasion of India by Huns from central Asia. However, the Gupta Empire had been ruled through a loose arrangement of local *rajahs* (kings) under the Gupta *maharajah* (emperor), and after Skandagupta died, many local kingdoms broke away. By 510, the Guptas had been beaten by another wave of Hun invaders, and India broke up into *rajputs* (small kingdoms). An alliance of these rajputs beat off the Huns again in 528. India remained divided for 650 years, except for a period when Sri Harsha, a religious rajah of Kanauj (606-647), succeeded in uniting northern India for 40 years.

This shrine to the teachings of the Buddha was carved from rock about 1,500 years ago, in Cave 27 at Ajanta. This vast site is a treasure store of Indian art.

## AJANTA CAVES

The Ajanta caves were rediscovered by a group of British officers on a tiger hunt in 1819. The 29 caves near Bombay were created by Buddhist monks between 200 B.C. and A.D. 650, using hammers and chisels. They were built as a monastic retreat, and the walls were covered with fine paintings that depict stories from the life of the Buddha. There were also many sculptures. The caves mark the peak of the religious culture of India, in which yoga and meditation were fully developed. Not far away, at Ellora, other caves contain art from the Hindu, Buddhist, and Jain religious traditions which, during the tolerant Gupta period, thrived happily alongside one another.

▲ The elaborately carved Chaitya Hall in the Ajanta caves complex was used as a temple and a hall for meditation and philosophical debates.

◄ A wall painting from Ajanta shows musicians and dancers entertaining the royal household. Actors, magicians, acrobats, and wrestlers would also have taken part in this entertainment.

## GUPTA CULTURE

The Gupta maharajahs succeeded one another as good and strong rulers. Copying Asoka, they set up monuments inscribed with religious texts all over India. They built new villages and towns, putting Hindu brahmins (priests) in charge. Agriculture and trade flourished. Indians migrated as far as Indonesia, and Buddhism spread to China. Both Hindu and Buddhist cultures developed. The Hindu sacred epics, the *Mahabarata* and the *Ramayana*, were written at this time. Kalidasa, India's great poet and dramatist, wrote about love, adventure, and the beauty of nature. The Buddhist university at Nalanda had an impressive 30,000 students. This was India's golden age, its classical era of music, dance, sculpture, art, and literature.

The Buddhist Wheel of Life. The eight main spokes represent the eight different states of being that Buddhists identify in the cycle of reincarnation of souls—only one of which is waking daily life.

### KEY DATES

A.D. **75–100** The Kushan invasion of India
**100–130** Kanishka—the peak of the Kushan period
**320–335** Rule by Chandragupta I (founder of the Gupta Empire)
**335–380** Rule by Samudragupta (conquers northern and eastern India)
**380–414** Rule by Chandragupta II (Gupta Empire at its peak)
**470s** Decline of the Gupta Empire
**505** Gupta Empire ends

# THE DECLINE OF ROME A.D. 200–476

**In 165, a plague swept through the Roman Empire and dramatically reduced the population. Rome's subsequent decline lasted three hundred years.**

The plague lasted for two years and was followed from 180 by the rule of the mad emperor Commodus, uprisings in Africa and Britain, and a succession of quickly toppled and inadequate emperors. The government at home was falling apart, and Rome was in chaos.

The emperor Diocletian created a *tetrarchy* (rule of four) to administer the two halves of the empire. The tetrarchy consisted of two emperors helped by two lieutenants.

## PROVINCIAL CHANGES

Power shifted to the provinces where the people wanted to keep their Roman status. The Parthians in the east and the British in the north created trouble, and a new force was appearing: the barbarians. Marcomanni, Goths, Franks, Alemanni, and Vandals were pressing in, and in 260–272 the Romans had to abandon Hungary and Bavaria to them. Parts of the empire such as Gaul, Britain, and Syria, were becoming separate and the Roman economy was also declining.

From 250–550 the Romans were constantly battling with Germanic and Asiatic barbarians, who sought to join the empire, to raid it for booty, or to bring it down.

## THE EMPIRE DIVIDES

In 284, the emperor Diocletian decided that the empire was too large for one man to rule and divided it into two, the Greek-speaking East and the Latin-speaking West. He appointed a co-emperor called Maximilian to rule the western half. The army was reorganized and enlarged to 500,000 men, and taxes were changed to pay for it. Provinces were reorganized to make them more governable. Romanitas was promoted by emphasizing the emperor's divine authority.

The vast empire grew too large and complex to rule, so Diocletian divided it. This meant that the rich East was not inclined to help the embattled West, so the West ground to a halt. High taxation levels meant that many Romans cared little—it was cheaper to live without the empire.

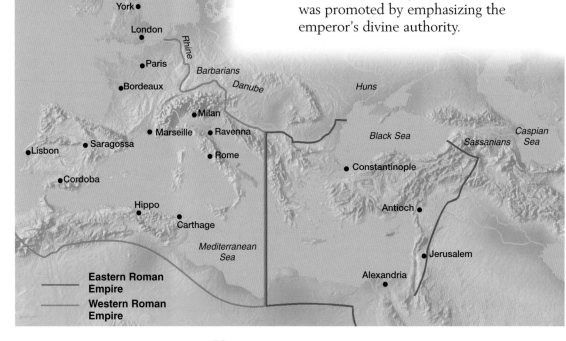

Eastern Roman Empire

Western Roman Empire

Hadrian's Wall — York — London — Paris — Bordeaux — Lisbon — Saragossa — Cordoba — Marseille — Milan — Ravenna — Rome — Hippo — Carthage — Constantinople — Antioch — Jerusalem — Alexandria — Black Sea — Caspian Sea — Sassanians — Huns — Barbarians — Rhine — Danube — Mediterranean Sea

Constantine ruled as emperor from 312 to 337.

## CONSTANTINE

Constantine saw himself as the savior of the Roman Empire. He decided to use the growing strength of Christianity to build a new culture in the empire. Calling bishops to a number of councils, he made them settle church doctrine and become organized. He favored the Christians, whom he considered to be less corrupt and self-seeking than the Romans. However, he was not a Christian himself until he converted on his deathbed. He was the last strong emperor of the Roman Empire. By moving the capital to Constantinople and founding the Byzantine Empire, however, he also weakened the West and hastened Rome's eventual downfall. The Roman Catholic church continued to be a cultural and religious force in the West long after Rome fell.

▲ Constantine's arch in Rome was built to bring back a spirit of victory and supremacy to Rome, after a century of many disappointments. However, Rome's real achievements at the time were not as great as the arch was meant to suggest.

◀ A detail from the arch of Constantine shows Roman soldiers besieging the town of Verona in 312. This battle was part of Constantine's war against his coemperor Maxentius. The arch was dedicated in 315.

## THE END OF THE EMPIRE

Emperor Constantine tried to revive the empire. He favored and promoted Christians, built churches, and held church councils, making Christianity a state religion. In 330 he moved the capital to Byzantium, calling it Constantinople. This city became as grand as Rome, and the west grew weaker and poorer. The western half of the empire, under attack by the barbarians, collapsed after Rome was sacked in 410 and 455. The last emperor was deposed by the Goths in 476. Following this, the western empire was replaced by a number of Germanic kingdoms. The empire in the East, known as the Byzantine Empire, lasted until 1453. Though many Roman ways were adopted by the barbarians, the western Roman Empire was at an end.

| KEY DATES | |
|---|---|
| 165–167 | Plague sweeps through the Roman Empire |
| 167–180 | The Marcomanni Wars against the first barbarians |
| 250 | Emperor worship made compulsory under Decius |
| 250–270 | Barbarians attack the empire from the north |
| 276 | Emperor Tacitus killed by his troops |
| 286 | Diocletian divides the empire in two and rules eastern empire; Maximilian rules western |
| 324 | Constantinople founded as the new imperial capital |
| 370 | Arrival of Huns in Europe: Germans seek refuge in empire |
| 378–415 | The Visigoths rebel and ravage the empire |
| 406 | Roman withdrawal from Britain, Gaul, and Iberia |
| 410 | The Visigoths sack Rome |
| 441 | The Huns defeat the Romans |
| 476 | Death of the last Roman emperor |

Emperor Justinian ruled as emperor from 527–565. He continued the fight against the barbarians.

# THE BARBARIANS A.D. 1–450

**The term barbarian means "outsider"—and Romans thought them to be uncivilized. They lived in small farming communities and were ferocious warriors.**

A map showing the complex movements of the main barbarian tribes around 370–450, as they occupied different parts of the western Roman Empire.

An ornate bronze brooch, commonly used by barbarians to fasten their cloaks, is an example of the fine craftsmanship of these people. This piece of jewelry was made around 400 in a style that was fashionable in Denmark and later in Saxon England.

The Germans living in southern Sweden and northern Germany moved south and pushed the Celts west. The Romans tried to control the Germans and were seriously beaten by them in A.D. 9. The Romans traded with some friendly German tribes, and recruited some into the Roman army. Some tribes, such as the Franks, Alemanni, and Goths raided the empire in 260–270, and the Romans had to make peace and settle them.

## THE HUNS

The Huns (Xiongnu) had been evicted from Mongolia by the Chinese. They swept into Europe, settling in Hungary around 370. The German tribes panicked, pushing into the empire for safety. The Romans settled many of them, though the Vandals in Greece rebelled, and by 410 they sacked Rome itself. From 440–450, the Huns ravaged Greece, Germany, and Gaul, destroying everything. An alliance of Romans and Germans defeated them, but the empire was then in decline. After Attila the Hun attacked northern Italy, the western empire finally broke down.

## THE NEW EUROPEANS

As Rome collapsed, barbarians settled in Germany, Italy, Spain, Britain, and France, gradually adopting many Roman customs. By 800, the Frankish king Charlemagne ruled an empire spanning Germany and France. The Visigoths settled in Spain, and the Vandals took Carthage. The Huns retreated to Romania and the Ukraine. The Lombards settled in Italy and founded a strong kingdom under King Odoacer. The Burgundians settled in eastern France, and the Saxons and Jutes took England.

A scene based on a Roman tomb carving from around 200 shows Roman soldiers in a fierce battle with German barbarians.

This relief from the obelisk of Theodosius was erected in Constantinople in 390. The stone carvings show the emperor receiving the submission of the barbarian peoples. Theodosius was the last emperor of a united Roman Empire (379–395), and an enthusiastic Christian. He was of barbarian blood, born of Germans who had joined the Roman Empire.

▼ A painting from the 1460s imagines the scene in 549, when an Ostrogoth king called Totila captured the Italian city of Perugia after a long siege.

## ATTILA THE HUN

Attila became king of the Huns (Xiongnu) in 433. He set up a new Hun homeland in Hungary after they had massacred, looted, and taken slaves throughout eastern Europe (433–441). The Huns then devastated the Balkans and Greece (447–450), forcing the Romans to pay gold to save Constantinople. The Huns later invaded Gaul and northern Italy, but they were beaten by a combined Roman and Visigoth army. In 453, Attila took a German wife and died suddenly in bed, possibly from poisoning. Attila was a military genius and a great Hun leader. When he died, the Huns migrated eastward to the Ukraine and caused no more trouble in the West.

◀ Attila the Hun was highly respected, mainly because no one could beat him and his soldiers. When he died, the Huns fell.

### KEY DATES

| | |
|---|---|
| 70 B.C. | Germanic people occupy parts of Gaul |
| 56 | Julius Caesar sends the Germans out of Gaul |
| A.D. 9 | German rebellion against the Romans |
| 200 | Germans form a confederation |
| 260 | Barbarians move into the Roman Empire |
| 367 | Scots, Picts, and Saxons attack Roman Britain |
| 451–454 | Huns devastate Gaul and northern Italy |

# JAPAN 300 B.C.–A.D. 800

**Japan is one of the oldest nations in the world. People have been living there from around 30,000 B.C. Classical Japan took shape from around 300 B.C.**

In ancient times, Japan was occupied by the Ainu people. The Ainu were unique, and not related to any other tribe. Today's Japanese people moved onto the islands in prehistoric times, from Korea and Manchuria on the mainland. They forced the Ainu onto the northernmost island, Hokkaido.

### THE YAYOI

Around 300 B.C., the Yayoi were beginning the rise that would make them Japan's predominant tribe. They introduced bronze and iron and also rice and barley from Korea and China. They shaped Japanese culture and the Shinto religion, in which nature spirits (*kami*) and tribal ancestors were worshiped. Tradition says that Jimmu, the legendary first emperor (*tenno*), great-grandson of Ameratsu, "Goddess of the Sun," appeared in 660 B.C. In fact, if he existed at all, it was probably several hundred years after this.

The Ainu, or Ezo, did not look like modern-day Japanese—they had lighter complexions and much more hair, like these two tribal elders. The Ainu had no written language, and, because they were looked down on by the Japanese, there are few records of their history.

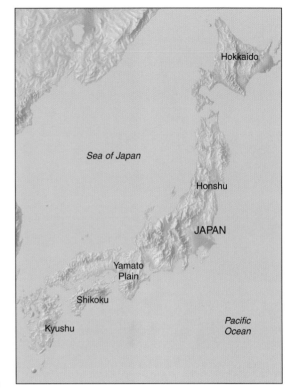

Japan is made up of four main islands, and the biggest, Honshu, has always been the dominant one. In early times, the indigenous Ainu people were squeezed out of Honshu and north onto the island of Hokkaido.

### THE YAMATO

Around A.D. 167, an elderly priestess called Himiko of the Yamato tribe became ruler. She used her religious influence to unite about 30 of the Japanese tribes. Himiko sent ambassadors to China, and from that time Chinese culture and, later, Buddhism, influenced the Japanese. The Yamato increased in power during the A.D. 200s. Today's Japanese emperors can trace their ancestry to the Yamato, who claimed descent from the sun goddess. During this period, until 646, much of Japan was united as one state, and it invaded southern Korea. With the establishment of Buddhism during the 500s, Shinto was threatened. Around 600, Prince Shotoku reformed the Yamato state, centralizing it in the Chinese style and reducing the power of the tribal lords. Temples and towns were built, and there was great cultural development. The 700s saw Japan's golden age. Rivalry between Shinto and Buddhism was also resolved by merging both into a common Japanese religious culture.

A painted scroll from the A.D. 300s shows a Yamato court lady being dressed by her servant. The boxes are for cosmetics.

80

# THE SHINTO RELIGION

Shinto is the ancient nature religion of Japan. Its mythology was written down in the 700s, in the *Kojiki* and the *Nihongi*. Shinto worshipers believed in the power of natural energies and spirits, or kami. Shinto priests sought to please the spirits, attracting their support and protection. In Shinto, it is believed that all life began in a cosmic egg that formed in the primordial chaos. The egg separated and became the gods (kamis), and the union of two kamis brought the Earth into being, with Japan as their special home. The sun goddess also came from this marriage, and the emperor was thought to descend from her. Many influences entered Shinto from Buddhism, and both religions coexisted throughout Japanese history, although there were periods of rivalry.

▶ This is a reconstruction of a Shinto shrine at Izumo, an area known for its places of Shinto worship. The priests held ceremonies of renewal and purification there at special times of the year to appeal to the kami to send them bumper crops and give the people good health and fertility.

▲ Shinto priests were originally tribal shamans. In later times, their traditions, dress, and temples became more formal, in response to the challenge from Buddhism.

▶ This is the main gate of the Shinto Kasuga shrine at Nara. These gates not only served the usual purpose, they also marked the energy lines along which the spirits traveled to reach the temple, which was carefully placed in a special location.

## THE NARA PERIOD

A permanent capital was established at Nara around 710. Gradually, the emperor became a ceremonial figure, serving as the representative of the gods. Government was controlled by officials and monks and there were greater political struggles. In 794, the emperor moved the capital to Heian (Kyoto), where a new phase of Japanese history began. Japan had developed from a tribal land to become a strong state. Little has been recorded about the life of ordinary people, because records were only kept about the imperial court and temples.

| KEY DATES | |
|---|---|
| 300 B.C. | Beginning of the Yayoi culture |
| A.D. 239 | Queen Himiko sends an embassy to China |
| 300 | The Yamato period—farming, towns, ironworking |
| 366 | The Japanese invade southern Korea (until 562) |
| 552 | Full introduction of Buddhism |
| 593–622 | Prince Shotoku creates a Chinese-style centralized state |
| 646 | Yamato period ends |
| 710 | Nara becomes permanent capital (the Nara period) |
| 794 | Emperor Kammu moves his court to Heian (Kyoto) |

In Shinto, small clay figures were used as totems to bring good fortune to places or to the souls of the dead in the afterlife.

# THE MAYA 300 B.C.–A.D. 800

**The Maya lived in what is now southern Mexico and Guatemala. They created a civilization that was at its peak while the Roman Empire was crumbling.**

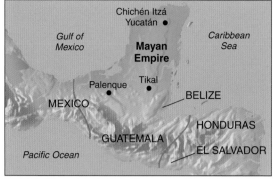

The Mayan heartland moved from the south in early times to the center around Tikal. After A.D. 800 the Maya lived in the north of Yucatán.

The Maya existed as far back as 2000 B.C. Over the centuries, by draining marshy land and building irrigation systems, they became successful farmers, able to support a large population. In the early phase, from 300 B.C. to A.D. 300, they built many cities in Guatemala, Belize, and southern Yucatán, each with its own character and artistic style. Their cities had temple pyramids, a fortified palace, marketplaces, workshops, and living quarters.

### MAYAN CLASS SYSTEM

The Maya had a class system: the nobles, priests, rulers, officials, and their servants lived in the cities while ordinary people lived on the land, going into the cities for markets and religious festivals. There was an alphabet of 800 hieroglyphs, and the Maya studied advanced mathematics, astronomy, and calendar systems. As in ancient Greece, each city was an independent city-state, and there was feuding between them, usually to demand tribute and take prisoners. Around A.D. 230, a violent volcanic eruption blew apart Mount Ilopango in the south, and covered a large area with ash. The southern cities had to be abandoned, and this marked the end of the "pre-classic" period of Mayan civilization.

The engraved figures found in Mayan ruins often show richly dressed people, such as this priest with his ornate headdress. He appears to be holding a knife in his left hand.

### THE CLASSIC PERIOD

Between 300 and 800, Mayan civilization reached its peak. Many new cities were built in Yucatán. The dominant city was Tikal, although Palenque, Yaxchilán, Copán, and Calakmul were also important.

▲ The Maya wrote in hieroglyphs (picture writing), which are found carved on huge stone monuments and written in books made of bark paper.

◄ The Maya played a ball game which may have had religious importance to them as a kind of oracle. In vast courts they bounced a solid rubber ball back and forth using their hips, thighs, and elbows, aiming for a hoop in the side wall. The ball probably represented the sun.

The Maya were skilled craftspeople, making stone sculptures, jade carvings, decorated pottery, paintings, advanced tools, and gold and copper objects. They built roads and shipping lanes to encourage trade. Their mathematical system counted in 20s, and used three symbols: a bar for "five," a dot for "one," and a shell for "zero."

## HUMAN SACRIFICE

The Maya practiced blood sacrifice. They viewed this life and the afterlife as equal worlds, and killing people for religious purposes, to please the gods and ancestors and to bring fertility and prosperity, was an acceptable thing to do. In later times, ambitious building projects meant that peasants had to supply ever more food and labor, and hostage-taking wars to capture sacrificial victims drastically cut the population. The agricultural system collapsed, and with it the cities. By 950, most central Mayan cities lay in ruins—though a later phase followed. Mayan peoples still live in Central America.

These were the four kinds of people at the top of the Mayan social pyramid: an official, a warrior, a noble, and a priest.

## MAYAN CITIES

In the early days of Mayan city building, the largest city was El Mirador, founded in 150 B.C., and had a population of 80,000 people by A.D. 100. It was abandoned around A.D. 150. Tikal, ruled by its king Stormy Sky, later became the largest city, with some 100,000 people around 450. Most cities were impressive and planned in grids. They were built around the ceremonial centers, and often oriented to astronomical events such as the rising and setting points of the sun. The religious basis of Mayan cities and their use of pyramids resembled that of the ancient Egyptians 2,000 years earlier.

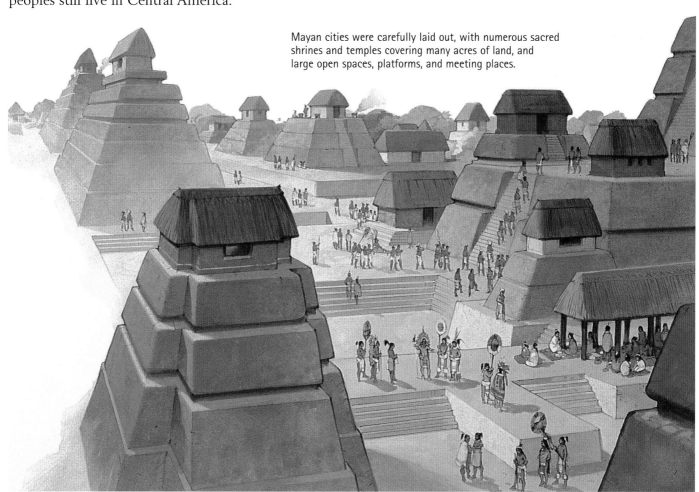

Mayan cities were carefully laid out, with numerous sacred shrines and temples covering many acres of land, and large open spaces, platforms, and meeting places.

# THE POLYNESIANS 2000 B.C.–A.D. 1000

**The Polynesians were a unique people of the Pacific islands. They were remarkable sailors, venturing far into the Pacific Ocean in search of new homelands.**

A carved effigy of the god Tangaroa Upao Vahu, the first of the Polynesian gods. Polynesians believed that Tangaroa created the world and brought them to it from the heavens.

In their mythology, the Polynesians say they came from the heavens, through a mystical land often thought to be Hawaii. Historians and language experts believe they may originate in Taiwan, migrating in open canoes to the Philippines around 3000 B.C., then to the Bismarck archipelago off New Guinea around 2000 B.C. They carried with them pigs, dogs, and chickens, as well as fruit and vegetables (coconuts, taros, yams, breadfruit, and bananas). From these people, the Lapita culture developed. Its people used shells to make tools and they also made pottery which had intricate and beautiful patterns.

## POLYNESIAN TRAVELS

The Polynesians developed large oceangoing canoes that could be sailed or paddled at great speed. They made use of the winds and ocean currents to help them on their way. These were stabilized boats, built with outriggers or doubled up like catamarans, so that they could withstand the wind and waves of the open sea. With these boats they were able to move between the many island groups of the Pacific.

### KEY DATES

| | |
|---|---|
| 2000 B.C. | Growth of the Lapita culture in Melanesia |
| 1300 B.C. | Migration to the "Polynesian triangle" around Fiji |
| 200 B.C. | Migration to Tahiti and the Marquesas |
| A.D. 300 | Migration to Rapa Nui—visits to America |
| 400 | Migration to the Hawaiian islands |
| 850 | Occupation of Aotearoa—birth of the Maori culture |

## MIGRATION

The Polynesians embarked on planned journeys of discovery. They were great navigators, and had advanced knowledge of the stars, ocean currents, winds, and wildlife. Around 1300–1000 B.C. the Polynesians moved to New Caledonia, Vanuatu, Fiji, Samoa, and Tonga, and then to Tahiti and the Marquesas Islands by 200 B.C. They reached Easter Island by A.D. 300, and Hawaii by 400. Some of them migrated to Aotearoa (New Zealand) by 1300s, where they settled and became known as the Maori. On the islands they bred animals and used the vegetables and fruit they carried to plant new crops that are now found throughout the islands.

These are two of the main types of oceangoing Polynesian canoes. On the left, the outrigger canoe, with carrying racks, would have been useful for island hopping; the double canoe, with shelters and a larger capacity, would have been valuable for longer journeys.

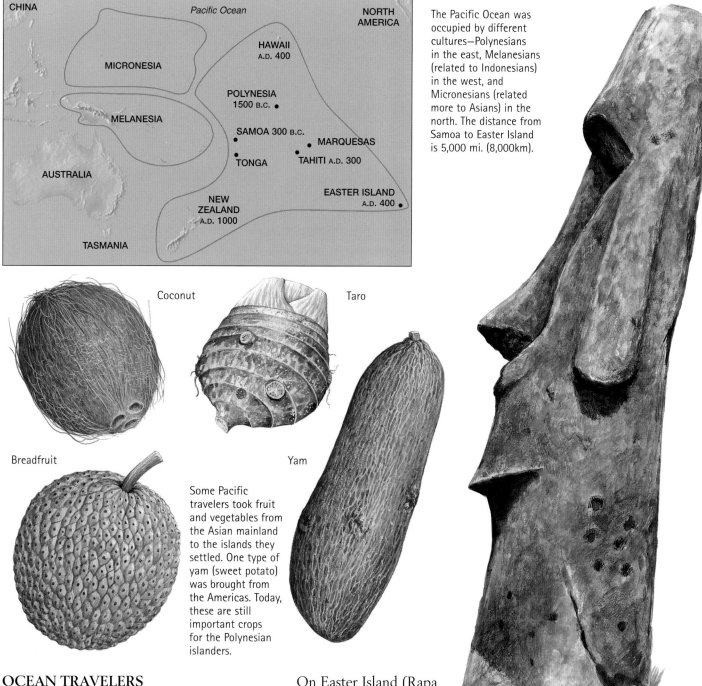

CHINA
Pacific Ocean
NORTH AMERICA
MICRONESIA
HAWAII A.D. 400
POLYNESIA 1500 B.C.
MELANESIA
SAMOA 300 B.C.
MARQUESAS
TONGA
TAHITI A.D. 300
AUSTRALIA
EASTER ISLAND A.D. 400
NEW ZEALAND A.D. 1000
TASMANIA

The Pacific Ocean was occupied by different cultures—Polynesians in the east, Melanesians (related to Indonesians) in the west, and Micronesians (related more to Asians) in the north. The distance from Samoa to Easter Island is 5,000 mi. (8,000km).

Coconut

Taro

Breadfruit

Yam

Some Pacific travelers took fruit and vegetables from the Asian mainland to the islands they settled. One type of yam (sweet potato) was brought from the Americas. Today, these are still important crops for the Polynesian islanders.

## OCEAN TRAVELERS

The Polynesian exploration and settlement of the Pacific Ocean is one of the greatest maritime expansions in history. They crossed thousands of miles of open sea in their explorations and migrations. On the Pacific islands, they lived in tribal societies ruled by chiefs, and they became experts in wood carving. They were isolated from Asia and Indonesia, where towns and nations were developing. It was only when European explorers such as Captain Cook arrived in the region in the 1700s that they began to be influenced by outsiders.

On Easter Island (Rapa Nui) there are over 900 moai, unique stone sculptures measuring up to 40 ft. (12 m). They are believed to have been erected between 1250 and 1500, and may have represented the spirits of ancestors guarding the community. Theories that the ancient way of life suffered a collapse because of habitat destruction are now challenged. Meanwhile, in Aotearoa, the Maori developed their own separate tribal culture, growing in number to 250,000 and splitting into village farmers and warrior societies.

Carved from soft volcanic rock, each one of these enormous 900 heads on Easter Island (Rapa Nui) weighs more than 50 tonnes. The statues were placed at *ahu* sites—areas in the open air intended for religious worshippers. About 200 years ago, most of the Rapa Nui statues were pushed face down—no one knows why.

85

# THE ARTS 500 B.C.–A.D. 500

During this period, the arts were developed increasingly for their own sake, and less for the religious, royal, or traditional purposes of previous millennia.

This pot was made in Roman Britain around A.D. 200, the time of Britain's first "industrial revolution." It shows a gladiator yielding in combat and asking for mercy.

The arts were gradually being developed to express creativity and decorate houses, streets, and everyday objects. The wealth accumulated by empires and urban traders was used to sponsor and support artists, leading to major advances in artistic creation. There was more realism—the Greeks and Romans made statues and paintings which directly and accurately represented people and life around them in a new way. In Greece, the finest art was produced in the classical period, and this reached its height about 400–300 B.C. Through the campaigns of Alexander the Great, Greek ideas about artistic realism reached as far as India; and the spread of Buddhism took them farther east to China, Japan, and southeast Asia. Roman artists copied the work of the Greeks, and developed their own, sometimes harshly realistic style.

Throughout the empires of this period, the houses of the rich were decorated with bright paintings on the walls, statues, reliefs, and mosaics. Buildings were adorned with elaborate carvings and paintings. In Africa and the Americas, artistic styles developed separately from elsewhere, and China too had its own styles, which were unique.

This figure of the goddess Aphrodite, now known as the Venus de Milo, was sculpted in 130 B.C. by Alexandros of Antioch in the Greek style. Though a goddess, she is portrayed as a person in realistic form, showing human feelings or "pathos."

◄ This vase was owned by a man named Leandros, whose name is written across the top. The vase itself, in the shape of the head of an African woman, may be from one of the Greek colonies in northern Africa.

◄ This intricate brooch of gilded bronze and garnets was made by an Ostrogoth in Spain in the late A.D. 400s. The eagle may have symbolized the spirit, with the eight calendar points of the year at the center.

A sculpture from the tomb of a Roman blacksmith, shows his assistant using a bellows to heat up metals in a furnace, the smith at his anvil, and the tools of his trade.

▲ This head from a shrine at Taxila in present-day Pakistan was fashioned in the Greek style, although it is Buddhist in origin.

## THE EMERGENCE OF NEW IDEAS

In Mexico, writing was composed of pictures rather than letters, mixing ideas with artistic expression. The Chinese made objects from wood coated with lacquer, and they also painted on silk. During the same period, the Greeks pioneered the theater, portraying real-life situations. They were the first to represent moods and emotions in their art. Since creativity is natural to humans, every culture, whether simple or sophisticated, had its own art forms, carved in wood or stone, written or painted on papyrus or bark, sewn into clothing and tapestries, or cast in metals. New ideas emerged through the arts, and during this important period many different styles were established, some continuing up to the present day.

◀ These Chinese cranes from the late Zhou dynasty (around 300 B.C.), were coated with lacquer, a natural varnish, which was painted on in layers, and set until it became hard. Cranes were seen as the bringers of good news and grace.

A pottery model of a watchtower made in later Han China around A.D. 100. Such towers were built to guard noblemen's estates from unwanted visitors—they may also have had religious significance.

A copper raven made by the Hopewell people of eastern North America around 100 B.C. The Hopewell controlled rich reserves of very pure copper, which they exported as far as Mexico.

This Mayan stone carving shows a shaman in ceremonial dress entering a mystical world.

# ARCHITECTURE 500 B.C.–A.D. 500

**The growth of empires and cities led to the construction of many public buildings. The most magnificent were the ones for state and religious use.**

In the cities of the developed world of the time, buildings were constructed from stone for strength and durability, and often faced with a decorative stone such as marble to make them look impressive. They were built by hand, although tools and devices such as scaffolding had been developed that made construction of large buildings and sophisticated arches possible. Many buildings today are not much more advanced than they were 2,000 years ago. The Greeks were skilled architects. The study of mathematics helped them design well-proportioned buildings that suited their surroundings. By 300 B.C., the Greeks had also developed town planning, designing whole cities in detail and arranging the streets in a grid pattern. The city builders of Mesoamerica also used urban planning. In other places, cities evolved from their former origins as villages, forts, harbors, or road junctions with a more random pattern of design.

Greek, Roman, Indian, and Chinese builders had virtually the same hand tools used today. These included saws, chisels, pincers, planes, and hammers.

The Parthenon in Athens, completed in 432 B.C., was one of the finest of all Greek temples. The columns were developed from the idea of tree-trunk supports. Stone-dressing became an advanced art, and complex scaffolding was used to allow the building of enormous structures.

The Romans developed a technique to build vaulted passageways. They found that one vault could cross another and still support a heavy building on top.

## ROMAN DEVELOPMENTS

The Romans adopted many Greek ideas, but also discovered new techniques. One was how to make concrete in around 200 B.C. At first they used it in foundations, but soon it was also used in the construction of walls and huge domed roofs. They also developed arches for buildings, bridges, and aqueducts. By A.D. 200, Roman cities had apartment buildings, called *insulae*, that were four or five stories high. Roman cities were a foretaste of the densely packed cities of today—Rome had an enormous traffic problem.

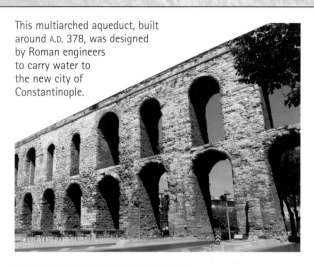

This multiarched aqueduct, built around A.D. 378, was designed by Roman engineers to carry water to the new city of Constantinople.

## LARGE-SCALE BUILDING

Engineering works became much more ambitious and sophisticated. Paved, drained, and raised roads were built in the Roman Empire, Persia, India, China, and Mexico. They allowed much faster transportation and the use of carts to carry bigger loads. Water was channeled into canals or along raised aqueducts to supply the cities. In Mesoamerica, enormous pyramids and other structures were built in impressively large religious centers. All this engineering work involved the assembling and organization of large numbers of people, as well as food supplies and building materials. Architects, surveyors, and engineers were in demand, to select materials and supervise construction. This represented a tremendous growth in practical skills, as well as knowledge of mathematics and engineering principles.

The specialized construction trades that we know today developed from this time. All over the world, building techniques improved gradually, even in simpler societies and villages—although their use of wood, which rots and falls apart, means that few traces of their buildings remain. In cold climates, new methods of dealing with cold and damp were developed. In hot climates, cool and shady buildings were built, with arches, good light, and ventilation. The Maya built high pyramids to be able to reach above the tree level of the jungles around them. Construction principles remain the same today.

These are the ruins of Gaochang, a city built by the Han Chinese on the Silk Road to the West. The Silk Road cities were rich and cosmopolitan, and accommodated travelers from many different lands.

Mayan pyramids were built without cranes and bulldozers. Millions of blocks of stone were prepared and erected, and when building the upper parts, everything was carried up by hand. This must have been a work of tremendous coordination.

# SCIENCE AND TECHNOLOGY 500 B.C.–A.D. 500

**Rapid progress was made in China and Europe because of greater investment, more sophisticated ideas, and larger-scale projects.**

The wealth and security found in the growing empires meant that great advances could be made. Some advances were made as solutions to practical problems or as the result of newly available materials. Others were made by urban people who had the leisure to study. The Greek philosopher Aristotle (384–322 B.C.) is considered to be one of the founders of Western science. He, and several other scientists, philosophers, geographers, and doctors of his time, pioneered a rational approach to the world, based on observation. They questioned how and why things worked the way they did. China, too, was the source of many inventions, from gunpowder to magnetic compasses and calculators (abacuses).

The abacus was widely used in China at the beginning of this period. It was an early calculator that allowed the computation of difficult sums. Modern computers became faster only in the early 1980s.

In acupuncture, the Chinese used the tips of needles to stimulate nerves to treat illnesses. This chart shows the parts of the body where the needles are placed. Acupuncture is still practiced today and has become widely used in the West in modern times.

The Archimedes screw is a device for lifting water from one level to another. It takes its name from the Greek inventor Archimedes (287–212 B.C.) who lived in Syracuse on the island of Sicily.

Papermaking was first developed in Han China around A.D. 105, and paper documents soon became common. It took over 1,000 years for papermaking to reach Europe.

## A TIME OF PROGRESS

All cultures had their scientists, doctors and researchers—they were distancing themselves from the past and adopting new ideas. Businessmen were interested in investing in these ideas to make money. Knowledge and sophisticated technologies were gradually improving: new strains of plants, new medicines, mathematical systems, ways of piping water, recording information, and forging metals were developed. This was a time of progress that slowed down as the world became more insecure from the A.D. 300s onward.

## WHEN IT HAPPENED

**450 B.C.** In Nigeria, people of the Nok culture smelt iron in furnaces

**250 B.C.** Greek mathematician and inventor Archimedes active

**200 B.C.** The Romans first use concrete

**10 B.C.** The Romans start using cranes in construction

**A.D. 78** Zhang Heng, inventor of the seismograph, is born in China

**100** Paper-making invented in Han China

**127** Ptolemy (Egypt) writes about music, astronomy, mathematics, and geography

**270** Magnetic compass used in China

A Greek doctor examines a young patient. The Greeks adopted a scientific approach to medicine and made extensive studies of human anatomy. They laid the foundations of Western medicine.

This coin-operated machine was used to sell sacred water at a Greek temple. A falling coin triggered the mechanism to release a measure of the sacred water into a container.

A specially built kiln for firing large numbers of pots. Though styles varied, kilns were found in every culture.

This cubit rule and curved calipers were used by Han scientists in China to accurately measure the width and thickness of objects.

This Roman water mill was built around A.D. 100. The waterwheel's rotation was transferred through wooden shafts and gearwheels to the millstones which ground the grain. Large mills had six or more waterwheels arranged in a line along a riverbank. Waterwheels were also used in China to raise water from rivers into irrigation channels to water the fields.

# EARLY MIDDLE AGES

## 501–1100

This period used to be called the Dark Ages because historians thought that civilization ended when the western Roman Empire fell. Many people now call these years the Early Middle Ages because they mark the start of the period that separates ancient and modern history. The former Roman Empire split into two: the western part peopled by farmers, skilled metalworkers, and shipbuilders; the eastern part became the Byzantine Empire. The Chinese and Arabs still led the way in science and technology. Major religions, such as Buddhism, Christianity, and Islam were spread either by trade or by warfare.

▲ Most art in early medieval Europe was inspired by religious beliefs. This fine ivory carving from Germany shows Christ in Majesty.

◀ This Mayan stone carving from the 900s was found in the ruins of the city of Chichén-Itzá on the Yucatán Peninsula of Mexico.

93

# THE BYZANTINE EMPIRE 476–1453

**Byzantium inherited the eastern half of the Roman Empire, surviving nearly a thousand years until, finally, it was taken over by the Ottoman Turks.**

Justinian ruled Byzantium for 38 years with his wife Theodora. They were lawmakers and reformers, and they restored the empire's power and lands. They gave shape to the sophisticated culture of Byzantium, building great churches and acting as patrons of art and literature.

▼ Byzantium was often under attack. Its navy had a secret weapon invented by Kallinikos in 677 called "Greek Fire," a mixture that burst into flames when it touched water. It was made from lime, sulfur, and petroleum.

Constantinople, the eastern Roman capital, had been built by Emperor Constantine on the site of the ancient Greek port of Byzantium. When the Roman Empire collapsed in 476, the city became the capital of the new Byzantine Empire. The edges of the Roman Empire's territories had been captured by barbarians, so the early emperors of Byzantium, Anastasius (491–518) and Justinian (527–565), fought to reclaim Rome's former territories. During Justinian's long reign, he sent able generals—Belisarius, Narses, and Liberius—to add North Africa, much of Italy, and southern Spain to its list of reclaimed territories. However, many of these gains were soon lost under his successors.

A revival followed when Emperor Heraclius (610–641) reorganized the empire and brought state and church closer together. He beat back the Sassanid Persians, who had occupied Syria, Palestine, and Egypt. Under his rule, Constantinople became a rich center of learning, high culture, and religion. The city was well placed for controlling trade between Asia and Europe. The empire produced gold, grain, olives, silk, and wine, which were traded for spices, precious stones, furs, and ivory from Asia and Africa.

Centered on the strategic city of Constantinople, Byzantium controlled east-west trade and for long periods dominated the Mediterranean Sea and the Black Sea.

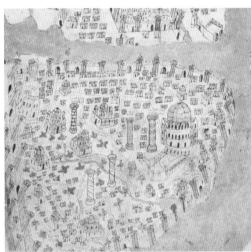

▲ This pictorial map shows Constantinople in 1422, not long before it fell to the Ottomans. It became a Muslim city, and was renamed Istanbul in 1453.

94

This classic Byzantine Orthodox mosaic is on the inside of a church dome in Ravenna, Italy. It shows Jesus being baptized by John the Baptist. The presence of the god of the Jordan River identifies the place of the baptism.

The Byzantines made elaborate crosses, icons, caskets, and other sacred relics. These became an important part of life in the Orthodox Church.

▼ Saint Sophia, the Church of the Holy Wisdom, was built in Constantinople for Justinian around 530. It took 10,000 people to construct it. Today, it is a mosque.

## KEY DATES

| | |
|---|---|
| 476 | Fall of the last Roman emperor in the west |
| 491–518 | Emperor Anastasius in Constantinople |
| 527–565 | Emperor Justinian's generals reconquer former territories |
| 610–641 | Emperor Heraclius expands Byzantium |
| 633–640 | Arabs take Syria, Egypt, and North Africa |
| 679 | Bulgars overrun Balkan territories |
| 976–1026 | Basil II rebuilds the empire |
| 1071 | Seljuk Turks take Anatolia |
| 1204–61 | Norman Crusaders capture Constantinople |
| 1453 | Fall of Byzantium to the Ottoman Turks |

The Byzantine basilica of St. Apollinare was built near Ravenna in Italy during the 500s. In this period, Byzantine architecture was gradually steering away from the old Roman styles.

The Byzantine Empire declined during the 700s—the Arabs twice tried to take Constantinople itself. However, under Basil II (976–1025), the empire flourished again. Then, soon after Basil died, Anatolia was lost to the Turks, and the empire again declined. It was taken over by the Crusaders for 50 years during the 1200s, but it was reclaimed again by Michael VIII in 1261. Finally, the city of Constantinople was taken by the Ottoman Turks in 1453. The sophisticated Byzantine culture had been the most lively and creative in Europe, and the Orthodox faith had spread as far as Russia and eastern Europe.

# CHRISTIAN MONASTICISM 269–1216

**To escape the busy city of Alexandria, a group of Christians formed a community in the Egyptian desert. This marked the beginning of the monastic tradition.**

▲ Monks and nuns led simple lives, studying, praying, and caring for the sick.

In the first 200 years of Christianity, some Christians had lived as hermits on remote islands or in deserts, spending their time in prayer. In 269, an Egyptian hermit, Anthony of Thebes, brought several hermits together to form a community— the first monastery. This idea spread to other countries, where other monasteries and convents were established. Some of these communities were linked by a shared set of guidelines. The most famous was the rule of St. Benedict, founder of the Monte Cassino monastery in Italy, around 529. In the Benedictine order, monks worked and worshiped together.

A page from the *Book of Durrow*, written and illustrated around 675 by Irish monks. Beautifully decorated manuscripts were meticulously produced by hand.

By 900, other orders had appeared. The Cluniacs in France followed strict rules of poverty and chastity, reacting against growing corruption in the Church. The Cistercians, founded around 1115, were even stricter, with some monks spending all their time in prayer and administration while "lay" brothers did the heavy work. St. Francis of Assisi founded the Franciscans to preach and care for the poor, and St. Dominic founded an order devoted to preaching and teaching.

An early monastery was like a village, with a church or abbey at its center. There were also kitchens, stables, living quarters, and gardens, as well as a library and hospital. Well-organized monasteries contributed much to ordinary society in return for tithes—money, land, or livestock given for the support of the Church and clergy.

Many monasteries had schools and libraries where specially trained monks copied out books by hand. Some learned monks wrote new books on history, medicine, and philosophy, as well as religious doctrine.

## MONASTERIES AND SOCIETY

Life in a monastery was spent praying, sleeping, and working. Each monk or nun received food, a room or cell, and a habit, or clothing, and they were provided for all their lives. This was more than most ordinary people had, so there was no shortage of new members. Although monks and nuns lived apart from the world, monasteries still played an important role in everyday life.

## SEATS OF LEARNING

The best way to get an education was by joining a monastery. Monasteries had libraries of classical and biblical texts—the basis for much of the learning of the time. Great works were written by monks such as the Venerable Bede, famous for his history of England, completed in 731. Some monks stayed in monasteries, and some became parish priests, while others became clerks to kings and bishops. Most monasteries provided shelter for travelers and pilgrims. They also cared for the poor and treated the sick, with medicines made with herbs from the monastery gardens.

| KEY DATES | |
|---|---|
| 269 | St. Anthony founds the first monastic community in Egypt |
| c.540 | St. Benedict writes his Benedictine monastic rule |
| c.930 | Cluniac monastic reform movement |
| c.960 | Byzantine Orthodox monastic orders set up |
| 1054 | Orthodox and Catholic churches split apart |
| 1115 | Founding of Cistercian monastery of Clairvaux |
| 1209 | Franciscan order receives papal approval |
| 1216 | Dominican order founded |

▲ The *Book of Kells* is a book of Gospels begun on the island of Iona off the coast of Scotland and completed in Ireland. The pages were illuminated (decorated) in the Celtic style between 650 and 690. This page shows Christ with four angels.

◄ The Venerable Bede was a monk who lived in Jarrow in northeast England. He is known as the "father of English history" because he wrote *The Ecclesiastical History of the English People*. Bede was the first historian to date events from the time of the birth of Jesus—most other writers of the time related dates to reigns or notable events.

# SUI AND TANG CHINA 589–907

**The Sui dynasty reunited China after 370 years of division, but it lasted only 30 years. It was followed by the Tang dynasty, which lasted nearly 300 years.**

The Tang people believed that dragons symbolized the energies of the Earth and that all things should be in harmony with one another. These beliefs even influenced their thinking about building practices.

From the fall of the Han to the rise of the Sui, China was divided into three kingdoms—Wei in the north, Shu in the west, and Wu in the south. There was constant warfare, as well as nomad invasions from Mongolia and Tibet. Many towns were ruined, and the population fell. Devastation in the north led to migrations southward, making the south more politically important. During this time, Buddhism became more widespread in China, bringing in many foreign ideas. Finally, in 581, Yang Jian, a general from Wei, overthrew his rulers and founded the Sui dynasty. By 589 he had unified China.

### SUI DYNASTY

Yang Jian renamed himself Emperor Wen. Before he came to power, taxes were high and people were drafted into the army for long periods of time. As emperor, he cut taxes and abolished compulsory military service, governing firmly from his capital, Chang'an. He also encouraged the development of agriculture by setting up irrigation schemes and redistributing land. All these things helped make the country wealthy.

China grew in size during the Tang period. It expanded into central Asia, and many large projects were started, such as the canal system and irrigation schemes.

The second Sui emperor was Yangdi. Under Yangdi's rule, China's Grand Canal was rebuilt so that it linked the main rivers of China. He also had palaces and pleasure parks built. The money for them was raised by ordering people to pay ten years' tax in advance. The peasants rebelled and, in 618, Yangdi was killed.

### TANG DYNASTY

The second Tang emperor, Taizong (626–649), reorganized government, cut taxes, and redistributed land. The reorganization of this united empire was far in advance of anything found

Rice paddies need controlled watering and large-scale drainage works. The Tang dynasty created conditions in which such large-scale projects became possible.

in other parts of the world. This stable period marked the beginning of nearly 300 years which promoted Chinese excellence in the arts, science, and technology. Between 640 and 660, Tang China expanded into central Asia, seeking to keep troublesome nomads from controlling the Silk Road. The Chinese went as far as modern-day Korea, Afghanistan, and Thailand. After Taizong's time, a rebellion by An Lushan in Beijing in 755 challenged Tang rule, and the Tang never fully recovered. Imperial rule became a formality, and power shifted to regional governors and courtiers. The Tibetans also defeated the Chinese in central Asia and there were more rebellions during the 800s. By 907 the Tang dynasty had collapsed and there followed a period of civil wars that lasted until 960.

This wall painting from a tomb shows the Tang princess Yong Tai, who was forced to commit suicide at the age of 17 for criticizing her grandmother, Empress Yu. In China, obeying and submitting to one's parents and elders was considered to be very important.

## THE GRAND CANAL

Started by the Sui and completed by the Tang, the Grand Canal was an enormous undertaking. It stretched over 500 mi. (800km) from the Huang He River to the Yangzi, and linked the major cities and capitals of the north with the rice-growing and craft-producing areas of the south. Road travel from north to south was difficult, and sea travel was hampered by typhoons and pirates. The canal allowed safe, long-distance, freight-carrying transportation, to bind China's northern and central regions closer together.

These ceramic ornaments are examples of the foreign animals that would have been seen in the Tang capital, Chang'an. The camel carried silk, and the horse, larger than the Chinese variety, originated in central Asia. Chang'an lay at the Chinese end of the Silk Road and was the world's largest city, with two million people.

| KEY DATES | |
|---|---|
| 589 | Yang Jian unites China, founding Sui dynasty |
| 602–610 | Military actions in Taiwan, Vietnam, Korea, and central Asia |
| 618 | Tang dynasty founded by Li Yuan |
| 626–649 | Emperor Taizong—expansion of Tang China |
| 640–660 | Chinese expansion in central Asia and Korea |
| 755–763 | An Lushan's rebellion—Tang power declines |
| 870s | Major peasant rebellions throughout China |
| 907 | Tang dynasty collapses |

# ISLAM 622–750

**Islam established itself very quickly and influenced many other civilizations. Within 150 years it had grown into a huge empire guided by religious principles.**

▲ This is a Muslim portrayal of the Archangel Gabriel (Jizreel). Gabriel is recognized by Muslims as the messenger of Allah to the prophet Muhammad.

The prophet Muhammad, who founded the religion called Islam, was born in Mecca in 570. At the time, the Arab peoples worshiped many different gods. Muhammad became a successful, widely-traveled trader, and was influenced by the Judeo-Christian belief in just one God. When he was 40 years old, his life changed: he saw the Archangel Gabriel in a series of visions. Muhammad then wrote down the *Koran*, the Muslim holy book, under dictation from Gabriel. He was instructed to teach about prayer, purification, and *Allah*, the one God. The word *Islam* means "surrender to Allah."

When Muhammad started teaching, the rulers of Mecca felt threatened by his ideas. Muhammad and his followers had to flee to Medina in 622 and the Muslim calendar counts its dates from this flight— the *Hegira*. In Medina, Muhammad organized a Muslim society, building a mosque. His following grew quickly— many Arabs were poor and Islam preached a fairer society. In 630, Muhammad recaptured Mecca and became its ruler. He kept nonbelievers out and banned idol-worship. Muhammad died in 632.

▼ The Dome of the Rock, the important Muslim shrine known as Qubbat as Sahra, in Jerusalem was completed in 691 on the site of Solomon's Temple. It was built where Muhammad had experienced an important vision in a dream. Decorated with complex geometrical patterns, this mosque shows an early Islamic architectural style.

This page from the *Koran* was written in early Arabic lettering style during the 800s. One aspect of the new Islamic culture was its artistic and cultural creativity.

## ISLAMIC EXPANSION

The new Muslim *caliph* (leader), called for a *jihad*, or holy war. Within ten years, under Caliph Umar, the Arabs conquered Syria and Palestine (defeating the Byzantines), Mesopotamia and Persia (bringing down the Sassanids), as well as Egypt and Libya. After the death of Caliph Uthman, there were disputes between his successor, Muawiya, and Ali, Muhammad's son-in-law. Ali's murder in 661 led Muslims to split permanently into two factions—the Sunnis, and the Shiites, who were followers of Ali.

▲ Muslims traveled widely, as explorers and traders, and carried ideas about Islam with them. Their faith decreed that they should make at least one pilgrimage to Mecca.

◀ At the battle of Yarmuk, in Syria, in 636, Muslim forces defeated a Byzantine army twice their size. This was a major loss for Byzantium, and the Muslims captured Syria and Palestine, the most prosperous part of the Byzantine Empire. They took Jerusalem and established the beginnings of a large empire.

▼ Arabic knowledge of medicine, healing, and surgical technique was well advanced for this time. This picture shows doctors setting a broken limb.

## THE UMAYYAD DYNASTY

In 661, the Arabs established a capital at Damascus, and Muawiya became the first Umayyad caliph. Territorial expansion followed—Muslim armies invaded central Asia, Afghanistan, Armenia, northern Africa, and Spain. They twice attacked Constantinople, without success. When they invaded Europe, they were defeated by the Franks in France in 732 and had to retreat. The Umayyads organized their empire in the Byzantine style. They were tolerant and did not force conversion to Islam. Many people converted because Muslims were seen as genuine liberators, bringing an end to the old order, establishing clear laws, and increasing trade. Arabic became a universal language across Islam, except in Persia which was mainly Shiite and retained its distinct culture. This common language helped ideas and knowledge to spread quickly from one place to another.

| KEY DATES | |
|---|---|
| 610 | Muhammad experiences his first vision |
| 622 | The *Hegira*—the flight from Mecca to Medina—takes place |
| 630 | Muhammed takes Mecca and forms an Islamic state |
| 636–642 | Muslims take Palestine, Syria, Persia, and Egypt |
| 656–661 | Caliphate of Ali—dispute between factions |
| 661–680 | Founding of Umayyad dynasty |
| 711 | Arabs invade Spain |
| 732 | Franks defeat the Arabs at Poitiers, France |
| 750 | Umayyad dynasty overthrown by the Abbasids |

▲ Arabs were good astronomers. The astrolabe allowed them to navigate at sea—and in the desert.

◀ The Arabs sailed in *dhows*. These wooden boats had large triangular sails and carried cargo and passengers.

# PERSECUTION OF THE JEWS 70–1300

**After rebelling against Roman rule, the Jewish people went into exile. Toleration in their new lands was often followed by severe persecution.**

▲ The *Magen David* (Star of David), is an ancient symbol. It first appeared as a symbol of Judaism around 960 B.C.

▼ A rabbi teaches his pupil "Hillel's Golden Rule" during the late 1300s in Germany. There was a strong emphasis on education to preserve Jewish culture and to ensure survival.

During A.D. 66–73, the Jews of Judea fought against their Roman rulers. The Romans massacred many, and in A.D. 70, destroyed the Great Temple of Jerusalem. Jews were barred from entering Jerusalem under penalty of death. In A.D. 116, Jewish rebellions in Roman-controlled Egypt, Cyrene, and Cyprus were also crushed. There was continual unrest in Judea. During the Second Jewish Revolt, A.D. 132–135, hundreds of thousands of Jews were massacred or sold as slaves. Jerusalem was razed to the ground and the Romans built a new city on the site, naming it Aelia Capitolina. On the mount where the Great Temple had stood was a new temple, dedicated to Jupiter. Survivors were driven from Judea to join established communities in Babylon, Anatolia, Greece, and northern

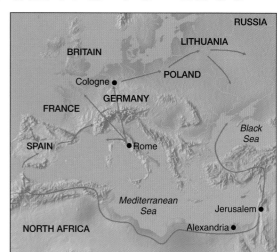

The arrows show the approximate movement of Jewish people during the *Diaspora* (dispersal) and the early stages of persecution during the 1100s.

Africa. The *Diaspora*, or dispersal of the Jewish people, that began with the Babylonian exile in 586 B.C., grew in momentum.

After Constantine, Christian Romans became increasingly intolerant. They expected Jews to become Christians, and in the 400s downgraded their citizenship. Some Jews moved even farther away, to Germany and Spain. They established small, close communities in cities, keeping to their own traditions and maintaining contact through international networks. As a result, the two great Jewish traditions arose—the Ashkenazic Jews in Germany, whose popular language is Yiddish, and the Sephardic Jews, whose language is Ladino.

In the Near East, Spain, and northern Africa, Jewish communities prospered. Under Islamic rule, they enjoyed security and protection from their enemies.

102

# EUROPEAN ANTI-SEMITISM

In medieval Europe, Jews could not own property or join armies. Instead, they became skilled craftworkers, doctors, and traders. Eventually they were allowed to be moneylenders, which was forbidden to Christians, who considered lending money for interest a sin. Kings and traders protected the Jews who provided this service. Ordinary people, however, resented what they saw as affluence during generally hard times.

By 1100, the Crusades had begun, and feelings towards non-Christians had hardened. Across Europe, people turned against some Jews, and forced them to live in particular areas of cities called "ghettos." Many others were persecuted or expelled from their homes. Thousands of Jews were killed during the Crusades (1092–1215). Jews were also expelled from England in 1290 and from France in 1306. Many fled from Spain and Germany to eastern European countries.

| KEY DATES | |
|---|---|
| 66–132 | Jewish revolts and the Roman expulsion of the Jews |
| 700s | Jews find refuge in the new Arabic Empire |
| 1100s | Persecutions in France and Germany |
| 1189 | Jewish massacre in York, England |
| 1215 | Lateran Council allows Jews to lend money |
| 1280 | Early Jewish ghetto in Morocco |
| 1290 | Expulsion of Jews from England |

▲ In medieval times, Jewish moneylenders were heavily involved in financing the economic growth of Europe, particularly in Venice and Genoa in Italy.

▼ Crusaders massacred Jews at Metx in 1096. There were outbreaks of violence against the Jews in France and Germany at this time, as many Christians blamed the Jews for the death of Jesus Christ.

This English medieval manuscript shows violence against Jews. Persecution was common in many parts of Europe, because many Christians blamed the Jews for the death of Jesus Christ.

# NORTH AMERICA 500–1492

The first North American towns appeared in the Mississippi valley during the 700s. In Colorado, the Anasazi were building villages called *pueblos*.

Across North America there were very different cultures, ranging from town dwellers along the Mississippi and Ohio Rivers to self-sufficient, village-dwelling people on the Pacific coast and the nomadic tribes of the Plains.

The first true North American towns appeared along the Mississippi and Ohio Rivers. Now known as the Temple Mound culture, each town had a central plaza with up to 20 rectangular earth mounds around it. On top of these were temples for the dead. A palisade (wooden wall) surrounded the plaza. Outside, up to 10,000 people lived in longhouses with adobe (dried mud) walls and thatched roofs. The people traded along the rivers, possibly taking copper from Wisconsin to Mexico. They hunted for meat and were also farmers. They grew corn, sunflowers, beans, and pumpkins. They made war with tribes such as the Algonquin and first used bows and arrows around 800. The Temple Mound culture reached its peak during the 1100s, but mysteriously disappeared by 1450. Elsewhere, permanent village cultures were developing. The Woodland Americans of the east were farmers, hunters, and traders.

▲ The Iroquois were a confederation of hunting tribes who lived in the woodlands of what is now New York State. They lived in village communities, gathering food, hunting, and trading with other tribes.

The Plains Tribes, who were usually nomadic buffalo hunters, began building riverside farming villages around 900. On the Pacific coast, there were many food-collecting, hunting, and fishing peoples. Some of them already lived in permanent villages and had well-developed societies. In the far north, the hunting Inuit were even trading with Vikings around 1000. The Cree, Chippewa, and Algonquin tribes of Canada lived their lives close to nature and had little contact with foreigners and traders.

▲ The Sioux or Dakota peoples followed the buffalo herds as they migrated across the midwestern plains. The Sioux *tepees* were built of buffalo skins draped around a framework of sloping poles. They could be dismantled easily and carried by the Sioux as they traveled.

The Mohawk lived in longhouses in permanent villages in what is now New England. Villages were surrounded by a ditch and stockade for protection. The Mohawk grew food in plots around their houses, and hunted for meat and skins.

## PUEBLO CULTURES

In the Southwest, several cultures thrived between 700 and 1300. These were the Anasazi, Hohokam, and Mogollon, the predecessors to today's Hopi. They were trader-farmers living in small towns. After 700, these people moved from pit houses—large roofed-over holes—into large, multistory communal buildings, some housing up to 250 people. They used irrigation systems and relied on "skywatchers"—knowledgeable shamans who predicted the rains. By 1300, these unique cultures had disappeared.

| KEY DATES | |
|---|---|
| 300 | Growth of Anasazi, Mogollon, Hohokam cultures |
| 800 | Agricultural growth in many cultures |
| 800 | Founding of the first Mississippi towns |
| 1000–1200 | Southwestern and Mississippi cultures at their peak |
| 1300 | Decline of Anasazi, Mogollon, and Hohokam cultures |
| 1450 | Mississippi towns depopulated |
| 1500 | Europeans arrive on East coast |

## THE ANASAZI PEOPLE

*Anasazi*, a Navajo word, means "ancient ones who are not us." The Anasazi grew corn, beans, squash, and cotton, and lived in *pueblos* (tribal towns) with unique buildings nestling high up in canyons. They were known for their pottery, textiles, and artwork. Around Chaco Canyon, a network of 125 villages was linked by 250 mi. (400km) of roads. The Anasazi had advanced shamanic religious rituals, with large tribal trance dances. They had unique knowledge and legends, and constructed underground ceremonial chambers called *kivas*.

◄ Religious ceremonies played an important role in pueblo life. These masked men are performing a ceremony to make rain fall on the desert so that their crops will grow.

▼ The Cliff Palace, sheltering under a cliff at Mesa Verde, Colorado, was built by the Anasazi. It housed around 250 people, who lived as a closely knit community. In front of the ruined palace are ceremonial *kivas* (without their roofs), which were originally used for religious purposes.

# BULGARS AND SLAVS 600–1453

Bulgaria and Kyiv had a significant influence on eastern Europe. Their adoption of Orthodox Christianity affected both their peoples and the Orthodox church.

Vladimir, Grand Prince of Kyiv (c.956–1015), interviewed Catholic and Orthodox Christians, Muslims, and Jews, and opted for the Orthodox faith, probably for political as much as religious advantages. Vladimir was the youngest son of Grand Prince Svyatoslav, who brought down the Khazars. Vladimir conducted campaigns to secure Kyiv's territories.

The Bulgars were the descendants of the Huns, who settled beside the Volga River in Russia, and reached the height of their power around 650. Then the Khazars from lower down the Volga destroyed their kingdom. As a result, many Bulgars migrated to the Danube area, dominating the local Slavs and founding a Bulgar state. Byzantium took action against them, especially when the Bulgars killed their emperor in battle in 811. In the 860s, two missionaries, Cyril and Methodius, were sent to convert the Bulgars and draw them into Byzantium's influence. This helped, but the quarrels did not end until the Bulgars were beaten in 1014. To punish them, Basil II had 14,000 Bulgars blinded, and the Bulgar khan died of shock.

During the mid-800s, Cyril and his brother Methodius devised the Cyrillic alphabet, based on Greek letters, for use in writing the Slavonic languages.

## ORTHODOX DIPLOMACY

In Byzantium, the state and the church were closely linked. Religious and diplomatic missions were sent out and, in this way, Byzantium converted the Bulgars to Christianity. Catholic Rome and Orthodox Constantinople competed for influence in eastern Europe. Kyiv adopted the Orthodox beliefs, and a Russian Orthodox culture was born there. Cyrillic lettering, still used today by Russians and Bulgarians, was invented by Cyril the missionary and his brother Methodius. By the time Byzantium fell in 1453, Russia had become the home of Orthodoxy.

When the Bulgars killed the Byzantine emperor Nicephorus in 811, they made his skull into a goblet to take to their khan, Krum. The Byzantine emperors called the Bulgar khans *czars*—a name that was adopted later by Russian rulers.

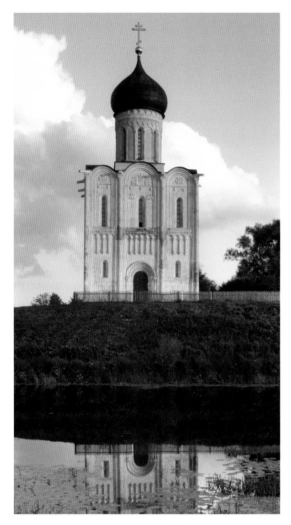

The Church of Intercession, an example of early Orthodox church construction in Russia, was built at Bogolyubovo in 1165.

## THE RISE AND FALL OF KYIV

The Slavs came from what is now Belarus. The first states in Russia were Slavic, and led by Swedish Viking traders (*Ros*, or "oarsmen"). The greatest Rus leader was Rurik, who founded Novgorod, Smolensk, and Kyiv. The Vikings traded with Baghdad and Constantinople, and Kyiv grew rich as a trading city. The Vikings considered themselves a superior class, mixing only gradually with the Slavs. In 988, the Kyivan prince Vladimir converted to Christianity, marrying a Byzantine princess. He then made the nobility and people adopt Christianity. This brought Kyiv new trade, culture, and respectability abroad. Under Jaroslav the Wise (1019–54) Kyiv was a center of splendor and influence that rivaled Constantinople, with diplomatic connections across Europe.

Churches were built, and the first Russian laws were written, as well as the first works of Russian art and literature. Kyiv was on the steppes (plains) of the Ukraine, and vulnerable to nomadic warriors such as the Pechenegi who threatened, and the Polovtsy who sacked, the city. After Jaroslav died, the state of Kyiv broke up, and the Russians retreated into safer northern areas. Here a new Russia was being established, centered around the growing city of Moscow.

A central theme of Orthodox culture was the icon, or holy image, which was believed to have spiritual and healing powers. Icon painting spread from Byzantium, through Kyiv, into later Russian culture.

▶ This helmet from the 1200s belonged to the prince of a small principality called Suzdal, once part of Kyivan Russia.

107

# THE CAROLINGIANS 751–843

The Carolingian dynasty established a rich and powerful empire in Europe. Its founders were the were the former Germanic "barbarians" known as the Franks.

Charlemagne's empire unified most of western Europe. Its capital, Aachen, lay not far from the capital of today's European Union in Brussels.

The Franks had settled in what is now Belgium and northern France. Their leader, Clovis (481–511), of the Merovingian dynasty, established a capital at Paris. Clovis became a Christian and earned Rome's support. He united the Frankish tribes, defeated the Gauls, the Alemanni (a confederation of Germans), and the Visigoths, and created a kingdom resembling today's France. His sons consolidated this, but quarrels broke out. Power fell to Charles Martel, who led the Franks against the invading Muslims at Poitiers in 732. Charles founded the Carolingian dynasty, and in 751, under his son Pepin, the Carolingians replaced the Merovingians as Frankish rulers. In 768, Pepin's sons, Carloman and Charlemagne, inherited his kingdom. Carloman died in 771, and Charlemagne took full control.

This gold image of Charlemagne, inset with precious stones and known as a reliquary, was made in Germany around 1350, to hold parts of Charlemagne's skull.

He first conquered the rest of France, and then what is now Germany, Italy, and the Netherlands, creating an enormous European empire. In central Europe he quelled the Saxons and the Avars, forcing them both to accept Christianity.

## CHARLEMAGNE'S CORONATION

Obtaining the blessing of the Church gave a nation greater respectability. For the pope, Charlemagne's grand coronation in 800 was a political move against Constantinople—there was now a Christian empire in the West as well as in the East. Charlemagne offered to marry the Byzantine empress Irene, but this was unacceptable to many people. Missions were sent to Charlemagne from Persia and the Baghdad Caliphate, as well as from the rulers of Europe. Had Charlemagne's empire remained intact, European history might have been very different.

Pope Leo III crowned Charlemagne Holy Roman emperor in 800.

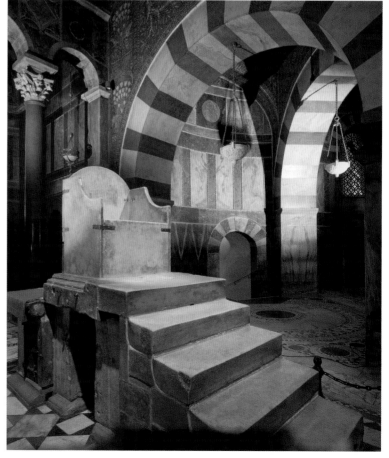

Holy Roman emperors were crowned in the Palatine Chapel, Aachen.

## THE CAROLINGIAN RENAISSANCE

Charlemagne supported the Roman church, favoring its influence in his kingdom. In return, in 800, the pope crowned Charlemagne as the first Holy Roman emperor. Charlemagne was a lawmaker and founded schools, cathedrals, and monasteries run by Irish, British, and Italian monks. He also invited scholars, scribes, architects, and philosophers to his court. His capital at Aachen became the chief center of learning in western Christendom. Charlemagne died in 814. His successor Louis the Pious ruled successfully but, on his death in 843, the empire was divided between his three sons. The empire later became two countries: Germany and France. The Carolingians ruled Germany until 911 and France until 987.

◄ Charlemagne was a great military leader who, once he had invaded lands, tried to improve conditions and encourage the poor to improve their standard of living.

BEATISSIMO PAPAE DAMASO
bIERONIMUS

▲ The Carolingian Renaissance inspired this ivory carving of Christ in Majesty in 850–875. The Aachen scholars created a new script called *minuscule*, with clear, rounded letters, but Charlemagne never learned to write.

### KEY DATES

| | |
|---|---|
| 486–510 | France united by Merovingian king, Clovis |
| 732 | Charles Martel beats the Arabs at Poitiers |
| 751 | Pepin, the first Carolingian king |
| 768 | Charlemagne becomes Carolingian king |
| 782 | Charlemagne defeats the Saxons |
| 790s | Charlemagne defeats the Avars in Austria |
| 800 | Pope crowns Charlemagne |
| 814 | Charlemagne dies |
| 843 | Carolingian Empire divided into three |

# THE ABBASID DYNASTY 750–1258

**During the 500 years of rule by the Abbasid dynasty, the Islamic Empire was unified, its culture flourished, and Baghdad became one of the world's greatest cities.**

The stories for *The Thousand and One Nights* came from many different countries, including India, Syria, and Egypt. The stories feature Ali Baba, Sinbad the Sailor, and Aladdin.

In 750, there were disagreements between the Arabs as well as dissent among the invaded peoples. The Umayyads were overthrown by the Abbasid family who then ruled the Islamic world for 500 years. The Abbasids were descended from Muhammad's uncle, al-Abbas. Under al-Mansur, their first caliph, they moved their capital to the new city of Baghdad in 762, and adopted many Persian and Greek traditions. Their most famous ruler was Harun al-Rashid (786–809), the fifth caliph. From 791 until 806, he fought a long war with the Byzantine Empire, which he eventually won. Parts of the empire sought independence, but Harun al-Rashid managed to suppress them. In spite of these wars he found time to encourage learning and the arts, bringing together Persian, Greek, Arab, and Indian influences. Baghdad became a world center for astronomy, mathematics, geography, medicine, law, and philosophy. The court in Baghdad was the setting for much of *The Thousand and One Nights*, a book still enjoyed today. Under later caliphs, various provinces became independent, but they still followed Islam, its law, and culture. The Abbasid caliphs increasingly lost power and became spiritual figureheads. The Muslim empire separated into emirates, whose fortunes rose and fell at different times. Yet the Muslim world acted as one civilization with many different centers.

When Harun al-Rashid became caliph in 786, he ended a decade of uncertainty and rivalry in the Islamic Empire.

This elaborately decorated tile, made in Persia during the 1100s, shows that Islamic art in the Abbasid period which was very rich and sophisticated.

This decorated Persian bowl was made during the Abbasid dynasty. It shows how Muslim artists created new styles with intricate designs.

People came to the Abbasid court in Baghdad from all over the empire, even from as far away as central Asia and Spain.

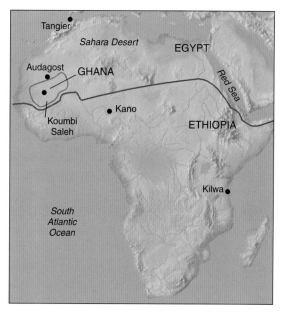

Ghana grew rich on gold, making it the first African nation. Its capital, Koumbi Saleh, was very cosmopolitan. Gold was transported north to Morocco, Tunisia, the Nile, and Arabia.

# GHANA 700–1240

**Ghana was the first truly African state. Most Africans still lived in tribal village societies, but Ghana, a center of the gold trade, opened up new possibilities.**

The medieval kingdom of Ghana lay farther north, inland from today's nation of Ghana. Its roots lay in the 300s, when the African Soninke tribes were ruled by the Maga, a Berber clan from Morocco. The Berbers had mastered transsaharan camel travel, and traded salt for gold from the Soninke. When the Arabic Muslims invaded northern Africa there was an upsurge in the gold trade, and by 700, Ghana was rich and important as a trading center. In 770, the Soninke ousted the Maga, and built a nation under Kaya Maghan Sisse, who became Soninke king around 790. Ghana's capital was the city of Koumbi Saleh, where Africans and Berbers met and traded. During the 800s, Arab traders described Ghana as "the land of gold." The gold came from Ashanti and Senegal to the south and west, and trade routes led north and east to Morocco, Libya, and Aksum, and so on to Europe and Asia.

Prester John was a legendary king who was said to rule over a Christian empire in the Asia or Africa.

Ghana reached its peak during the 900s, controlling both the gold and salt trades. Other goods that passed through Ghana included woolen cloth and luxury items from Europe, and leather goods and slaves from the south. In 990, Ghana took over the neighboring Berber kingdom of Audagost—making Ghana 500 mi. (800km) across. In 1076, it fell to the Almoravids, a puritanical Berber Muslim sect. The Almoravids ruled Morocco and Spain, but they fell in 1147, and power returned to Ghana until, in 1240, the country became part of a new African nation, Mali.

Berber and Arab traders transported goods hundreds of miles across the Sahara Desert with camel caravans. Without traders, Ghana and its successors, Mali and Songhai, would not have become rich nations.

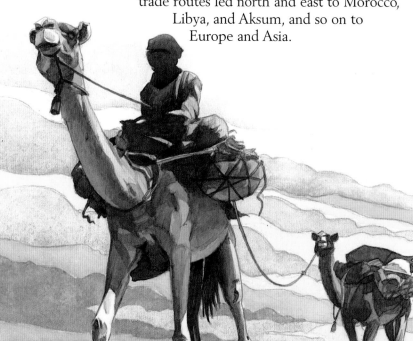

# FUJIWARA JAPAN 800–1200

**During the late 800s, the Fujiwara clan became the rulers of Japan on behalf of the emperor. During the Fujiwara period, art and literature flourished in Japan.**

Japanese horses were dressed with many ornaments on their harnesses. This horse bell would probably have been worn on the horse's hindquarters.

From the early 300s, Japan had been ruled by an emperor. If an emperor died while his eldest son was still young, a regent, usually someone in the emperor's family, was chosen to rule until the new emperor grew up. In the 800s the Fujiwara clan gained importance at the Japanese court when Fujiwara Yoshifusa's daughter married the emperor. By tradition, children were brought up by their mother's family, and so the Fujiwaras brought up the next emperor.

An illustration from the *The Tale of Genji*, a novel about the complexities of Fujiwara court life. It was written by Lady Murasaki Shikibu, a lady-in-waiting to the empress.

This meant that Fujiwara Yoshifusa was the first regent from outside the imperial family, marking the start of the Fujiwara period. More Fujiwara daughters were married to future emperors and the Fujiwara family grew powerful. Soon, every emperor had a permanent Fujiwara regent, who controlled the running of the country while the emperor spent his time on religious and court matters. For 300 years, the Fujiwara family dominated Japan.

Court life was very formal, with rules for everything. This man is reading a letter. Even the color of the letter paper and the way it was folded were considered important.

The Great Torii Gate, at Itsukushima or Miyajima-Shrine Island was built during the 800s. It is part of a classic Shinto shrine. The torii stood as a kind of divider, to separate the sacred areas of the temple from the nonreligious parts.

## FUJIWARA CULTURE

During the Fujiwara period Japanese art and literature flourished. This happened at the imperial court in Kyoto, among nobles on their estates, and in the temples, so ordinary people saw little of it. The rich and powerful were very insulated from the rest of society. Great works of art were painted, and literature was written in a new style—notably, Lady Murasaki Shikibu's classic *The Tale of Genji*. Until that time, the Japanese had tended to imitate Chinese styles. Clans favored by the Fujiwaras prospered. Then other clans, largely of military families, began to grow more powerful, and the provinces and clan estates started to act increasingly on their own behalf. They fought among themselves until the Fujiwaras could no longer control the country. During the 1100s, there were many rebellions until, finally, the Gempei civil war broke out in 1180, and the Fujiwara were replaced by the powerful Minamoto shoguns.

This clay figure of a protector-god stood outside Shinto temples to protect them from demons. The clothing worn by this figure is typical of a Japanese warrior of the 700s.

### KEY DATES

| | |
|---|---|
| 794 | Japanese court moves to a new capital at Heian (Kyoto) |
| 858 | Fujiwara Yoshifusa becomes regent |
| 930 | Fujiwara gain full dominance: economic reforms |
| c.1000 | Peak of artistic and literary expression in Japan |
| 1180–85 | Gempei civil war: rise of the Minamoto shoguns |

This is a jikido, or refectory, a hall where Buddhist monks used to live and take their meals. It is part of the To-ji Buddhist temple complex, which was founded in 796 to give sacred protection to the city now known as Kyoto. Japanese buildings were usually made of wood, which was safer if there was an earthquake. Sadly, many fine wooden buildings were destroyed by fire instead.

# MAGYARS AND BOHEMIANS 896–1273

During this period, central Europe had no real nations. Bohemia and Poland were Slavic heartlands, and Hungary was occupied by Asiatic Magyars.

▲ Duke Wenceslas, prince of Bohemia in the 920s, tried to modernize his country and convert it to Christianity. He was famous for his charity and fairness. His pagan brother, Boleslav, opposed him and had him killed in 929. Later, Wenceslas was made a saint, and he is the patron saint of Czech Republic.

▼ The Magyars rode strong Asiatic horses, and they could cover long distances very quickly. This helped them become the scourge of Europe for 55 years, raiding Germany, France, and Italy, weakening many states and killing many people.

The Magyars were Asian horse-riding nomads from the steppes (plains) of today's Kazakstan. Seeking a new homeland, they raided central Europe and, under prince Arpad in the late 800s, they occupied Hungary. Just 25,000 Magyars defeated all the Slavs by using speed and shock tactics. Then they started raiding Germany, Italy, and France for slaves and riches. For decades, they sacked monasteries and ruined farms, torturing and killing people in the process. They were so fast, they could be attacked only when weighed down with their booty. Eventually, the German emperor Otto I defeated them in 955. Under Prince Geiza (972–997) the Magyars made peace, adopted Christianity, and settled down as nobles ruling the Slavs. In 1000, Pope Sylvester II crowned Stephen I Magyar king of Hungary. Stephen's reign brought peace and prosperity—he was later canonized. By 1200, Hungary was a strong nation. But in 1241 the Mongols swept in, devasting the country just as the Magyars had once done.

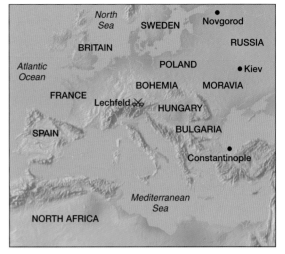

▲ In the forests of central Europe, various new states developed among the Slavonic tribes from about 800 to the late 1200s: Hungary, Bohemia and Moravia (now the Czech Republic), and Poland.

▲ Prince Arpad led his people from Asia into Europe, founding the Magyar Arpad dynasty and the nation of Hungary. This is his statue in Budapest, the Magyar capital, which straddles the River Danube.

## POLAND

The Polish tribes were united by Miesko I around 960, and became Christian. His son Boleslav Chrobry tried to unite all Slavic lands, including Bohemia, Moravia, and Kiev, but later the Poles had to retreat. Though the church and German influences brought the Poles together, the provinces were disunited, and this weakness was to prove significant when other countries tried to take parts of Poland.

## MORAVIA AND BOHEMIA

Northwest of Hungary and southwest of Poland were the Slavonic states of Moravia and Bohemia (now the Czech Republic). Moravia was established by Duke Moymir in 830, who freed it from Carolingian domination. During the 800s, Bohemia was part of the Moravian Empire. The Germans tried to reclaim Bohemia from the Moravians, but there was a Slav revolt in 874. Moravia was reunited under Sviatopluk, who made peace and expanded the country. In 906, the Magyars destroyed Moravia.

Meanwhile, around Prague, a new Bohemian state was developing. One national character of this time was Duke ("good king") Wenceslas, noted for his charity. Bohemia took over Moravia in 1029, gaining recognition from the Holy Roman Empire by 1086. Many German traders moved in, and expanded the local economy. The peak of Bohemian power came under Ottokar II, who took over Austria in 1251. He lost it to Rudolf the Hapsburg in 1273. Bohemia was overrun by the Germans in 1300, but it remained a distinct country linked with Moravia.

▲ King Stephen, later canonized, receives the crown of Hungary from Pope Sylvester II, making him Apostolic King. This alliance helped Hungary become respectable, and it helped the pope gain influence in central Europe.

▼ Each country has its national hero. For Hungary, it is St. Stephen. This statue of Stephen on his horse was erected in 1902.

This crown was given to King Stephen by Pope Sylvester in 1000. The symbolic effect of such crownings was to give a nation recognition and to bind it into the European order of the time.

### KEY DATES

| | |
|---|---|
| 830 | Moymir establishes the Moravian state |
| 896–907 | Prince Arpad, leader of the Magyars |
| 906 | Moravia falls to the Magyars |
| 920 | Wenceslas tries to modernize Bohemia |
| 955 | Defeat of the Magyars, ending Magyar raids on Europe |
| 960 | Unification of Poland under Miesko I |
| 997–1038 | St. Stephen, king of Hungary |
| 1241 | Collapse of Hungary after Mongol raids |
| 1260 | Peak of Bohemian power and prosperity |
| 1308 | Bohemia and Moravia come under German control |

# ANGLO-SAXON ENGLAND c.600–1066

**The arrival of the Angles, Saxons, and Jutes in England during the 400s and 500s created a new people, the English, and eventually the kingdom of England.**

The Angles buried their kings, with their possessions, in ships, to take them to the afterlife. This gold clasp comes from a famous burial ship of the 600s, discovered at Sutton Hoo, in eastern England.

Vortigern, the British high king, hired German mercenaries, but failed to pay them. In revenge, they set out to conquer Britain. Settlers soon followed, beaching their boats and wading ashore with cattle and sheep.

The Romans left Britain around 410. There was a brief revival of power for the now romanized British. In 446, the British high king, Vortigern, invited Germanic Saxons from the Rhineland to enter Britain as mercenaries to support in his struggle with the Picts. The Saxons gained a foothold in the southeast, but were held off between 500 and 539, by the now legendary British leader Arthur. After a battle in 552, the Saxons started taking over southern and central England. Many Britons were killed or lost their lands; many emigrated to Wales, Cornwall, Ireland, Scotland, Brittany, and northwest Spain.

## THE BIRTH OF ENGLAND

In the wake of the Germanic invaders, many of their countrymen emigrated to England. During the 500s and 600s, they slowly populated the country. British towns, villages, and farms were abandoned, and the Celtic Christian church retreated with them. The Germans brought new farming and ownership patterns, and their pagan tribal groupings gradually took the shape of kingdoms. Seven kingdoms were eventually formed: East Anglia, Mercia, and Northumbria (ruled by the Angles); Essex, Sussex, and Wessex (ruled by the Saxons); and Kent (ruled by the Jutes).

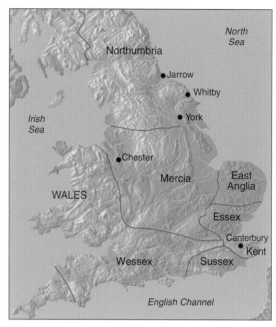

England was divided into seven kingdoms. From 878 Northumbria, East Anglia, and much of Mercia came under Viking control and formed the Danelaw.

In 597, the pope sent Augustine to convert the English. These converts coexisted with the pagans, but there were disputes with Celtic Christians. These were settled at the Synod of Whitby in 664, where the Celts agreed to submit to papal authority. The seven kingdoms often fought to claim the title "Bretwalda" (lord of Britain). In the 600s, the Northumbrian kings Edwin, Oswald, and Oswy, and in the 700s, the Mercian kings Ethelbald and Offa, gained supremacy. Egbert of Wessex was the first king of a united England, in 829.

116

▼ King Alfred the Great was one of England's Great leaders. He created laws based on justice and encouraged education.

## STRUGGLES FOR POWER

In 789, the first Vikings appeared in England, and by the middle of the 800s they had started to settle. When Alfred the Great was king of Wessex in 871, the Vikings were threatening to overrun his kingdom. Alfred fought nine battles against them in one year alone. He finally defeated them in 878 and made them sign the Treaty of Wedmore. which divided England in two—the Saxon west and Danelaw in the east. Alfred was a lawmaker, a scholar, and a just king. In his time, texts were translated into early English, and *The Anglo-Saxon Chronicle*, an important history book, was begun. By 940, Danelaw had been won back from the Danes. England was reunified under Edgar (959–75), but in 1013 the Danes returned, and England was ruled until 1035 by the Danish king, Canute the Great. There was better cooperation between the Danes and Saxons under Edward the Confessor. In 1066, Harold II, having just fought invading Norwegians in Yorkshire, was beaten by invading Normans, under Duke William.

▲ The Ruthwell Cross, carved in a Celtic style by Saxon monks during the 700s, was richly decorated with scenes from the Gospels.

### KEY DATES

| | |
|---|---|
| 446 | Arrival of Jutish mercenaries led by Hengist and Horsa |
| 560 onward | Large-scale immigration of English Saxons |
| 597 | Augustine arrives to convert English Saxons |
| 793 | Viking raid on Lindisfarne monastery |
| 870 onward | Immigration of the Danes into Danelaw |
| 871–99 | Alfred the Great crowned king of Wessex |
| 1013 | The Danes conquer all of England |
| 1066 | The Normans, led by Duke William, conquer England |

▼ Anglo-Saxon society had three classes— thanes or nobles, churls or freemen, and serfs or slaves. In this picture, serfs are harvesting barley.

# THE HOLY ROMAN EMPIRE 962–1440

**Otto I became king of Germany in 936. He wanted to revive the old Roman Empire and was crowned as the first Holy Roman emperor by the pope in 962.**

The Holy Roman Empire was neither particularly holy, nor Roman. Founded by Charlemagne in 800, it was concerned with the power of kings and it was German. After Charlemagne's death the Carolingian Empire gradually broke up, and France and Germany were separated. In Germany, a high king was elected as an overlord so that he could bind together the many independently ruling dukes, counts, and bishops. The first of these overlords was Conrad I of Franconia, elected in 911. Later, the ambitious Otto I (936–973) wanted to revive the Roman Empire. Otto brought stability by uniting all of the rulers who owed him allegiance and by defeating the Magyars.

Otto I was on the throne of Germany for 37 years. He made the Holy Roman Empire a great and lasting institution by uniting his country's regional rulers and making them cooperate with him.

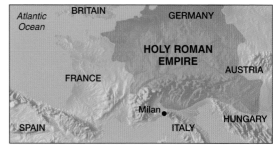

The Holy Roman Empire united all of the German-speaking peoples and extended its power into Italy, both to protect and to try to control the popes.

Otto conquered Bohemia, Austria, and northern Italy. After 25 years, he had the pope crown him Emperor Augustus, founding an imperial tradition that lasted 850 years until 1806. His empire became a revived Holy Roman Empire.

The Holy Roman emperor had the right to be crowned by the pope in Rome. Many popes and emperors disagreed over questions of power and authority, and this led to problems because each side wanted to interfere in the other's affairs.

Henry IV went to see the pope at Canossa, in January 1077, to settle a dispute over power. Pope Gregory VII kept him waiting outside in a snowstorm for three days before forgiving him and removing the ban of excommunication.

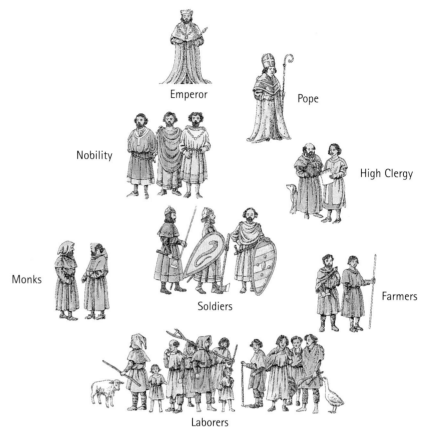

Emperor

Pope

Nobility

High Clergy

Monks

Soldiers

Farmers

Laborers

## POPES AND EMPERORS

Several popes wanted help in ruling Christian Europe but often came into conflict with the emperors. Catholics had to obey the pope, so he was powerful. Popes wanted to choose emperors, and emperors wanted to choose popes and control Church affairs. Finally, Emperor Henry IV and Pope Gregory VII clashed— in 1075, Gregory said Henry had no right to choose bishops. In revenge, Henry said that Gregory was no longer pope. Gregory excommunicated him, which meant that Henry was no longer recognized by the Christian Church and his subjects did not have to obey him. In 1077, Henry asked to be forgiven. The quarrel over choosing bishops was finally settled in 1122, but there were more disputes, which led to a gradual separation of church and state.

| KEY DATES | |
|---|---|
| 911 | Conrad I of Franconia is elected German king |
| 936–973 | Otto I strengthens the Holy Roman Empire |
| 955 | Otto I defeats the Magyars |
| 1056–1106 | Henry IV in conflict with the pope |
| 1122 | Concordat of Worms: an agreement between emperor and pope |
| 1200 | Peak of the political power of the Roman Catholic Church |
| 1300 | Popes lose political power |
| 1440 | Holy Roman Empire passes to the Austrian Hapsburg dynasty |

▲ Noblemen usually supported the emperor against the pope, but sometimes they rebelled. Soldiers usually supported the nobles, who gave them land; and peasant laborers were employed by soldiers and nobles. Similarly, monks supported clerics, who supported the pope. These were "feudal" relationships, where a person gave allegiance and taxes in return for protection, land, or rights. Everyone was bound into feudal relationships throughout society.

In 1100, the pope and the Holy Roman emperor signed an agreement at St. Peter's Cathedral, in Worms, in southwestern Germany. The agreement ended a long-running dispute over who was responsible for the appointment of bishops.

119

# CAPETIAN FRANCE 987–1328

In France, the Carolingian dynasty was followed by the Capetians in 987. Founded by Hugh Capet, the dynasty's aim was to unite France as a proud nation.

The dynasty founded by Hugh Capet died out in 1328. Monarchs of the later French royal houses of Valois and Bourbon claimed indirect descent from him.

Capet was the nickname given to Hugh Capet, the dynasty's founder, because of the short cape he wore when he was a lay abbot. As Duke of Francia, he had been the chief vassal of the last Carolingian king, and was himself elected French king. His position was not very strong: from Paris, he ruled northern France, but the dukes of Normandy, Burgundy, and Aquitaine were nearly as powerful as he was.

## THE MAKING OF FRANCE

The aim of the Capetians was to unite France and build it up as a proud and prosperous nation. Capetian influence and French nationalistic feeling grew under Louis the Fat (1108–37), who made alliances with Church leaders against the Germans and the English.

When Hugh Capet came to power, France was split into large dukedoms. Marriages and shifting political alliances meant that France was kept divided for some time. The Capetians' aim was to unite France under one rule.

Unlike the kings, the dukes were more interested in the fortunes of their own dynasties than those of France as a whole. Marriage alliances allowed land to pass out of central control, and this was to become a problem.

The Oratory of St Michel d'Aiguilhe is an imposing structure in Burgundy. This part of France was ruled by the mighty dukes of Burgundy, against whose power the Capetian kings could not complete.

The coronation of Hugh Capet, as imagined by an artist in an illuminated manuscript from the 1300s.

# FRENCH AND NORMANS

In 1152, King Louis VII's wife, Eleanor of Aquitaine, divorced him—he was away on Crusades too often. She then married Henry II, the French-Norman king of England, putting Aquitaine under Norman rule. France was then split into two halves, and this led to conflict. By 1214, the French had regained some of the Norman land, and by 1226, Louis VIII had strengthened France greatly. This process was continued by Louis IX (St. Louis), who conquered the south and overcame several rebellious nobles. However, the dukes still held much power, and the Normans exploited this. They wanted to control France. The question of Norman power in France was not resolved and, after the Capetians fell in 1328, a century of war began between the English and French. The Capetians had given France nationhood and stability, but this had taken some time to achieve.

Hugh Capet's monogram, a special symbol made from overlapping letters. Monograms were often used as official markers on coins or as a seal on documents.

## ABBEYS AND CATHEDRALS

In medieval times there were two major employers: the kings and the Church. Many churches, monasteries, and cathedrals were built during the 1100s and 1200s, but not only for religious reasons. The building stimulated the economy, provided employment, and symbolized greatness, stability, and wealth. Also, the Church acted as a European religious overlord to kings, and it was in the interest of kings to attract the favor of the pope. The new churches of the time were symbols of progress and prosperity as well as places of worship.

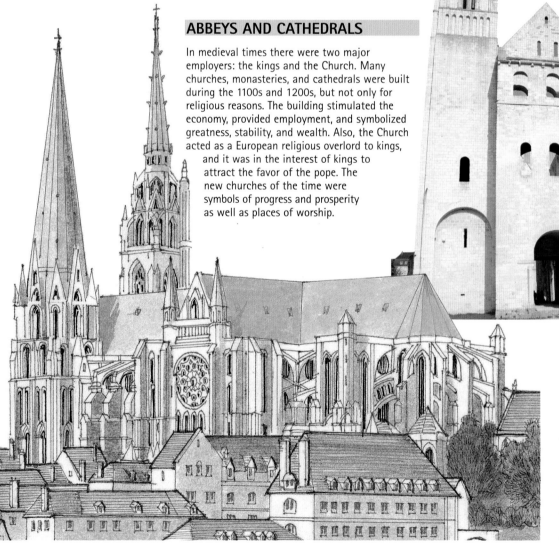

Jumièges Abbey was built around 1040 as part of a drive by the Capetians to make France into an influential kingdom supported by the pope.

The Capetians made France stable and wealthy. One result of this was the building of great cathedrals such as Chartres. Construction began in 1195, and it took 35 years to complete.

121

# THE AMERICAS 500–1200

In Mesoamerica, the Toltecs came into prominence following the destruction of Teotihuacán. Meanwhile, in South America two new civilizations were developing.

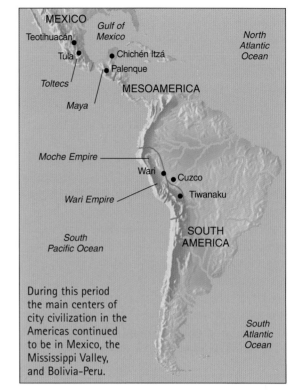

During this period the main centers of city civilization in the Americas continued to be in Mexico, the Mississippi Valley, and Bolivia-Peru.

By 600, Teotihuacán was in decline, and around 750 it was burned to the ground, possibly by tribes from the north. Various peoples tried to assume control, and around 900, the Toltecs established a capital at Tula. It became the center of a military state and trading network that reached from Colorado to Colombia. In 1000, far away in Yucatán, a faction of the Toltecs invaded the Mayan Empire, expanding the northern Mayan city of Chichén Itzá. The Toltec Empire came to an end in 1168, when it was overrun, and Tula was destroyed. Soon afterward, the Aztecs moved into the area.

## THE LATER MAYA

Many Mayan cities were abandoned around 800, although some still flourished in northern Yucatán from 900 onward. Around 1000, Yucatán was invaded by Toltecs, who stayed there until 1221, building a copy of Tula at Chichén Itzá. Warrior chiefs took power from the priests, and caused crafts such as pottery, art, and literature to decline in quality.

The Toltecs were very militaristic. Their temples were guarded by stone statues of warriors such as this one from Tula.

The Toltecs were beaten by the Maya from Mayapán, whose Cocom dynasty dominated Yucatán for 200 years until civil war broke out in 1480. The Spanish arrived during the 1500s, but the last Maya city-state, Tayasal, did not fall until 1697.

## THE PYRAMIDS OF ETOWAH

Etowah was one of the towns of the Mississippian culture in North America. This city culture spread far beyond the Mississippi valley—Etowah was near today's Atlanta, and famous as a source of mica, a transparent form of rock which could be split into fine sheets, like glass. The Etowans used tools of copper and stone, and built earthen pyramids with temples or the palaces of their chiefs on top. Their cities often had 10,000–20,000 inhabitants. They traded with Mexico and the Great Lakes area, and they made items to trade with the village-dwelling tribes of North America.

## TIWANAKU AND WARI

Civilization in South America was based in two places. One was at Tiwanaku, a large temple-city 12,000 ft. (3660m) above sea level near Lake Titicaca in Bolivia. Between 600 and 1000, it had a population of 100,000. The people of Tiwanaku made distinctive pottery and jewelry, massive stone dry-stack walls, and enormous temple-stones. They created a string of towns stretching to the coast and into the Brazilian rain forests. The other civilization was Wari, which included remnants of several earlier local cultures such as Nazca and Moche. This was a powerful military empire, covering over half of modern Peru. Wari and Tiwanaku may have followed the same religion, but Wari was militaristic and Tiwanaku was peaceful. The two empires prospered until about 1000, when they were both abandoned, possibly because of drought.

▲ This is one of the many massive carved stone figures of Tiwanaku, erected around 700. Tiwanaku, near the southern edge of Lake Titicaca, was ruled by a priesthood according to religious principles. The city had several large temples.

This pottery image of a god from Wari, decorated with corn, was probably honored by farmers to help grow their crops.

This bowl from the Mimbres people of the southwest had a hole made in it to "kill" the bowl. It was then buried with its owner.

▲ This earring from Wari is made of stone inlaid with bone and shell. The Wari people also made beautiful jewelry and small objects out of gold.

### KEY DATES

| | |
|---|---|
| 600 | Teotihuacán is sacked and burned |
| 800 | Toltec migration into central Mexico |
| 900 | Toltecs establish a city-state at Tula |
| 1000 | Tiwanaku and Wari abandoned |
| 1168 | Tula destroyed |
| 1200 | Building of the Mississippian temple-cities |
| 1200 | Rise of the Aztecs and the Incas |

◄ The sun god Viracocha was carved on the Gateway of the Sun at Tiwanaku around 600. This giant gateway opened into the Kalasasaya, the largest of the city's building areas and the main temple.

# THE VIKINGS c.600–1000

**The Vikings have a reputation as raiders and violent warriors. But they were also traders and settlers, whose impact on European history has been great and lasting.**

During the 700s, the Vikings began to venture from their homelands in Norway, Denmark, and Sweden in search of adventure, treasure, and better farmland. They made excellent wooden ships that could sail on rough seas and up rivers, and landed easily on beaches. At first they raided rich monasteries and coastal towns, and later they sailed up the Rhine, Seine, and Loire rivers to attack inland cities. Local rulers bought them off with silver and gold. Not all Vikings were raiders. Many were farmers looking for new land or traders seeking business. They were first-class sailors and traders, and ventured as far as Constantinople and Baghdad in search of conquest or trade.

Viking coins minted in the 800s were made of real silver or gold, so the coins themselves were actually worth the value they represented.

Viking men and women wore everyday clothes that were both practical and fashionable. Their gold and silver jewelry was sometimes broken up and used as money.

## VIKING LONGSHIPS

The Vikings built superb boats, with sturdy keels acting as frames, which made the ships faster and more seaworthy. The boats were capable of being sailed or rowed. They could also be hauled by teams of men across land when necessary—even being dragged long distances overland in Russia, to get from one river to another. They could be beached easily without the need for a harbor. A dragon's head on the bow was intended to scare off evil spirits, sea monsters, and enemies.

Vikings believed that brave warriors went to Valhalla, the hall of the god Odin, when they died. High-ranking Vikings might be buried in ceremonial ships, or in graves marked by stones in the shape of a ship.

## VIKING TRADERS AND SETTLERS

In Britain, the Vikings settled mainly in northern and eastern England, northern Scotland, the Isle of Man, and Ireland. In Ireland they destroyed many monasteries and founded the first towns. In France, the Vikings settled in Normandy, which had been given to them by the French king in 911 to discourage their raiding. In 1066, as Normans, they invaded England, and in the early 1070s, southern Italy, and Sicily. Vikings also settled in Iceland, and some sailed on to Greenland and North America. Others entered the Mediterranean, raiding southern France, Spain, and Byzantium. Beaten back by the Byzantines, Vikings sold them their services as traders and warriors instead. Swedish Vikings took over the Baltic Sea, and built trading towns such as Visby, Novgorod, and Kiev. Sailing down Russia's rivers, they met Bulgar, Khazar, Byzantine, and Arab traders. By 1000 the Vikings had settled down, and their Nordic homelands became Christian nations. They had an enormous effect on the future of northern Europe: they established trading routes and towns; founded Russia, greatly influenced Holland, Poland, Britain, France, and Ireland; and weakened the Carolingian Empire. Their descendants, the Normans, were influential in Europe and led the Crusades. Because of the Viking raiders, people had to rely on local feudal lords, and exchanged work, produce, and fighting men for protection. Gradually, Europe became more disunited, fighting grew frequent, and gaps grew between the rich and poor.

▲ The Vikings were skilled metalworkers. This is a die, used for stamping a pattern onto hot metal. It shows two shamans with weapons, poised for ritual animal sacrifice.

▼ The Viking town called Hedeby, now in Germany was well known for its craftworkers and traders. Hedeby was one of the ports from which the Vikings sailed far and wide.

# THE NORMANS c.800–c.1200

**The Normans were descendants of Vikings who had settled in France. They became very powerful, conquering England and lands in southern Europe.**

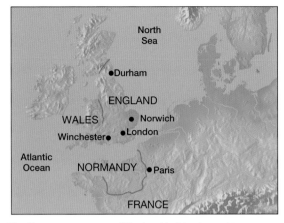

The Norman conquest of England led in the end to centuries of alliances, disputes and wars between England and the kingdom of France.

William the Conqueror, Duke of Normandy, was king of England from 1066 to 1087.

Viking armies besieged Paris in 845 and in 886–886. In 911, the Viking chieftain Hrólfr (or Rollo) was awarded a large tract of land ("Normandy") in return for an agreement to protect Paris. The Normans (from "Northmen") adopted the French language and rapidly wielded influence farther afield.

## NORMANS IN BRITAIN AND IRELAND

The English king Edward the Confessor died in 1066. The new king, Harold Godwinson, was immediately faced with rival claims to the throne. His first challenge came from the king of Norway, Harald Hardrada, whom he defeated and killed at the Battle of Stamford Bridge. Harold hurried south where, three days later, William, the Duke of Normandy, landed an army. Harold was killed at the Battle of Hastings and William was crowned King of England on Christmas Day, 1066. In the first four years, he faced many rebellions, which were brutally suppressed. William's supporters were rewarded with land, and became a new ruling class, speaking Norman French.

The government was centralized and, to help with taxation, a register of land and wealth—the Domesday Book—was ordered. The Norman military relied on fast-moving soldiers on horseback, the predecessors of medieval knights, and conquered lands were guarded by castles. At first, these were wooden towers on mounds, surrounded by palisades (the "motte-and-bailey" design). These were soon replaced by keeps and towers of stone. The Normans failed to take Scotland, but occupied parts of South Wales. Semi-independent Norman "marcher lords" controlled the Welsh borders. A Cambro-Norman nobleman, Richard de Clare ("Strongbow"), began the Norman invasion of Ireland.

▲ William the Conqueror was succeeded by two of his sons. William II ruled from 1087–1100, Henry from 1100–1135. They established firm Norman rule, but it collapsed under the next king, Stephen, who died in 1154.

▶ The Bayeux Tapestry was made to commemorate the Norman invasion of England in 1066. Halley's Comet, shown clearly on the tapestry, came close to the Earth in that year, and it was taken as an omen that the invasion was justified.

## NORMANS ACROSS EUROPE

The Normans were also busy elsewhere in Europe. Around 1060, Norman soldiers under Robert Guiscard invaded Sicily and southern Italy, to support the pope against the Byzantines and Arabs. As a result, they were favored by the pope and often protected him. In the 1200s, they became leaders of the Crusades. Through political marriages, and by serving as knights, papal agents, bishops, and royal courtiers, Norman lords formed a feudal network which became very influential across Europe in the 1200s. In these feudal relationships, a noble who pledged allegiance and gave military support to a king was rewarded with lands and titles. These nobles then ruled estates and provinces, demanding loyalty of their followers and in exchange rewarding them with lands and positions of power. And so feudalism that started in France became established throughout Europe.

To honor ancient traditions, local law courts were often held outdoors. The lord of the manor was the judge. This court, or assize, held in 1072, met to decide whether some lands belonged to the Bishop of Bayeux, in Normandy, or to Canterbury Cathedral.

## THE FEUDAL SYSTEM

Under the feudal system, people held land in exchange for services. It developed during the 700s under the Franks and was introduced to England by the Normans. In exchange for receiving estates and titles, Norman nobles paid taxes to the king, provided knights, and raised armies. Nobles gave their knights land in exchange for military service and taxes. A knight had to have *villeins* (peasant workers) to manage his land. The villeins lived in villages near the manor house. In exchange for a farm or house, they worked for the lord of the manor, paying him in crops or money.

Stories about heroic knights and courtly love between lords and ladies were very popular in Norman England.

# THE SELJUK TURKS 1037–1243

**The Seljuks invaded the Middle East from 1037 onward, ending Arabian domination of the Islamic world and opening the way for the Ottomans.**

The Seljuks streamed down from Bokhara to Baghdad, and later, westward into Anatolia, almost as far as Constantinople. Anatolia (Turkey) then became Muslim.

This minaret at the Jami mosque in Simnan, Iran, shows typical Seljuk patterns in its elaborate brickwork. The Seljuks became Muslims around 970, and considered themselves defenders of the Islamic faith.

The Turks were originally a family of tribes living in Turkestan, central Asia. They split up during the 500s, and spread to Russia, China, India, and Persia. Some Turks abandoned the nomad life to become administrators and mercenary warriors. They served the Abbasids, Fatimids, and others, and sometimes rose to high office. Turks such as the Seljuks, Ottomans, Mamluks, Bulgars, and Khazars soon began to have great influence. They also joined forces with the Mongols. The Turkish cities of Samarkand and Bokhara grew wealthy and cultured in Islamic times.

## SELJUK EXPANSION

To the east of the Caspian Sea lived a Turkic group called the Ghuzz, or Turkomans. The Seljuk broke away from the Ghuzz in 950, moving south and west. The Abbasid caliph in Baghdad was having difficulties, and he asked the Seljuks for their help. Led by Tughril Beg, the Seljuks invaded Persia and occupied Baghdad by 1055. The Abbasid caliph appointed Tughril as sultan under him—in effect, he gave the Abbasid Empire to the Seljuks. In this way, the Seljuks rose from being a simple nomadic tribe to rulers of the Islamic world. Alp Arslan, Tughril's nephew, became

sultan in 1063. He took Syria and Armenia and raided Anatolia. In 1071, the Byzantine emperor fought back. Alp Arslan hired Norman and Turkish mercenaries and marched into Armenia. The armies met at Manzikert. The Seljuks won because they pretended to be defeated and ran away. When the Byzantines pursued them, they turned around and badly defeated the Byzantine army. The Seljuks captured the Byzantine emperor and held him for ransom. This victory laid the foundation of what later became the Ottoman Empire. Alp Arslan was a compassionate leader and ruled the empire well. With his blessing, many Turkomans and Seljuks moved into Anatolia.

Like most nomads from the Asian steppes, the Seljuks were great horsemen. Using the new invention of stirrups, they could stay on horseback and fire arrows accurately in battle. This picture shows them defeating the Byzantines at the battle of Manzikert.

## MALIK SHAH

The Seljuk Empire reached its greatest power under the rule of Alp Arslan's son, Malik Shah (1072–92). He was a patron of the sciences and the arts and built fine mosques in his capital, Isfahan. His minister, Nizam al-Mulk, was respected as a statesman. During this time, Seljuks took over Anatolia (Turkey) completely, and founded the Sultanate of Rum right next to Constantinople. On Malik Shah's death, the Seljuk Empire broke up into small states, and a variety of Seljuk, Mamluk, and Kurdish sultanates continued through the 1300s, all under the eye of the Abbasid caliph in Baghdad. Then, in 1220, the Mongols overran the area, finally occupying Baghdad in 1258.

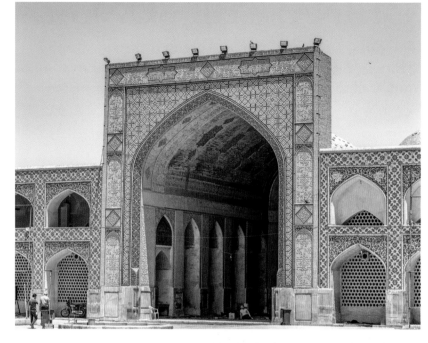

▲ The Jameh or Friday mosque was built in Isfahan, Persia, in the Seljuk style. The Seljuks were great patrons of learning, architecture, and culture.

| KEY DATES | |
|---|---|
| 950 | The Seljuks break away from the Ghuzz Turks |
| 1038 | Seljuks conquer Khorasan (Afghanistan) |
| 1055 | Seljuks conquer Baghdad |
| 1071 | Seljuks defeat the Byzantines at Manzikert |
| 1072 | Peak of the Seljuk Empire |
| 1081 | Founding of the Seljuk sultanate of Rum |
| 1092 | Death of Malik Shah—Seljuk Empire breaks up |
| 1243 | Mongol invasions: Seljuks become Mongol vassals |
| 1258 | Mongols destroy the Abbasid caliphate |

▲ These fine tiles are from the Karatay Madrassa, a domed school in Konya, Turkey. It was built in 1251, under the rule of Seljuk sultans. Today, the building is a museum of ceramics and tiles.

◄ Though the Seljuks brought new life to the Abbasid Empire, life in the Muslim world went on very much as before. This scene shows what a souk, or indoor trading hall, in Baghdad, would have looked like during the 1100s.

# CHINA: THE SONG DYNASTY 960–1279

**The Song (or Sung) dynasty created the third united Chinese Empire. This was a time of great innovation and took China into a long period of cultural eminence.**

The seven-storey Longhua Pagoda in Shanghai was built in 977 at the start of the Song dynasty.

After the Tang dynasty fell in 907, China became fragmented. In the Huang He Valley, five emperors tried to start new dynasties over 53 years. None succeeded until Song Taizu took power in 960, founding the Song dynasty. He brought the many warlords and armies under control, and by both military and diplomatic means began to reunify China. This took 16 years and was completed by his brother, Song Taizong, the second Song emperor, in 979.

### THE NORTHERN SONG PERIOD

Now surrounded by other states, China under the Song was smaller than in Tang times. In the northwest was Xixia, which was Tibetan; in the northeast was Liao, ruled by Mongol Khitans; in the southeast was Nan Chao, a Thai state; and in the south was Annam, a Vietnamese kingdom. The Song emperors worked hard to make peace with all of them.

Until the Jin invaded the north in 1127, the Song ruled all of China. They were then forced to move south where they prospered for another 150 years until the Mongols invaded.

Agriculture expanded and the population grew—especially in the south, which was now wealthy and important. By the end of the Song period there were probably around 100 million people living in China.

▼ Song artists often painted landscapes with small central features in them. This example of landscape painting from the Song period called "Old Trees, Level Distance."

This stoneware vase with a peony flower design is typical of the porcelain of the Song period. Europe didn't master porcelain-making techniques for many centuries.

"A Buddhist Temple in the Mountains" was painted by Li Cheng during the 900s.

## THE SOUTHERN SONG PERIOD

In 1068, the prime minister, Wang Anshi, reformed the government. He simplified the tax system and reduced the size of the huge army. Although these cuts saved money, they also made invasion easier. In 1127, northern China was attacked by the Jin, and the Song capital, Kaifeng, was lost. The Song withdrew to Hangzhou, south of the Yangtze, and the north was then ruled by the Jin until Kublai Khan's Mongols took over in 1234. Hangzhou became a large, beautiful city, with canals, parks, and fine buildings. The Southern Song lasted until 1279, when southern China was overrun by the Mongols.

The Song period saw great prosperity and advancement in new technologies, arts, and literature. They invented gunpowder rockets, clocks, movable-type printing, paddle-wheel boats, magnetic compasses, and waterpowered machinery. Landscape painting, fine porcelain, poetry, and theater flourished. Banking and trade became important, towns grew large, and new crops were introduced. Song China could have become even greater, had it not been brought down by the Mongol invaders.

### KEY DATES

| | |
|---|---|
| 907 | Fall of the Tang dynasty |
| 960 | Song Taizu founds the Song dynasty |
| 979 | Song Taizong completes unification of China |
| 1000 | Culture and the economy thrive in China |
| 1068–86 | Wang Anshi's reforms |
| 1127 | The Jin take northern China: the Song retreat to Hangzhou |
| 1234 | The Mongols conquer northern China, ousting the Jin |
| 1279 | The Mongols conquer southern China: Song period ends |

## CHINESE PORCELAIN

Throughout the world, pottery had been made of clay that produced a chunky and rough finish. Around 900, the Song dynasty Chinese invented porcelain, which was made from kaolin, a fine white clay. Their craftworkers made smooth and delicate porcelain which, when used with special glazes and painting styles, could be beautifully decorated—making each piece a work of art. During this period, Chinese emperors even had factories built to make porcelain specially for their palaces. Porcelain production soon became an enormous industry in China.

Song emperors had ceramic factories built to supply fine porcelain.

This porcelain wine vessel, standing inside a warmer, was used for making mulled wine.

131

# THE ARTS 501–1100

**During this period, most artistic expression was for religious purposes. But religious authorities did encourage the development of arts, music, and crafts.**

Churches, mosques, and temples attracted the finest craftworkers and musicians. Religious feeling encouraged them to stretch their talents to create delicate, elaborate works. Gifted people were usually educated by religious authorities. Ordinary people bore many hardships, but religion allowed them to think of higher matters and pray for better times, at least in the afterlife. Even tough, warlike rulers often had a gentle, religious side to them, and they brought artists, musicians, poets, and thinkers to their courts, turning a court into a cultural center. This earned a ruler not only God's approval, but also that of society and learned scholars.

▲ Alfred the Great of Wessex was very religious. This was the top of a bookmark that he may have had made for a priest to keep his place when reading the Bible. The words around the edge say "Alfred had me made."

▼ For the ship-burials of their chieftains, the Vikings created elaborate decorations carved in wood or inlaid with metals. Vikings were not just warriors, but also skilled craftworkers and lovers of fine objects.

Monastic scribes illuminated their lettering with religious pictures, using red lead, gold, silver, and special inks. Some scribes would spend years on each book using styles that showed Greek, Roman, Egyptian, Celtic, and German influences.

Temples, churches, and mosques were wealthy and used the arts to communicate religious stories and ideas. At this time most people could not read or write, and in many areas religious ceremonies were performed in foreign languages. So pictures, music, carvings, mosaics, and architecture were all used for teaching and raising people's spirits. Each culture developed its own artistic, musical, and literary style.

A picture of St. Mark from the Irish *Book of Kells* shows Celtic knotwork and spirals mixed with early Christian styles from Rome, Egypt, and Byzantium.

Byzantine churches were decorated with mosaics and holy pictures called icons. In Europe's monasteries, monks spent long hours copying books by hand. They illuminated, or decorated, the capital letters of texts and borders of pages with detailed designs. Muslims specialized in calligraphy, or beautiful handwriting, and in making elaborate geometrical patterns on their buildings. Buddhists in Asia painted stories of the life of the Buddha. In Tang and Song China, they painted and carved new kinds of landscape art and natural images. In Mexico, manuscripts, stone carvings, and murals, or wall paintings, were common.

▲ A Byzantine mosaic inside the dome of the Arian Baptistry in Ravenna, Italy, shows Jesus being baptized by John the Baptist. The twelve Apostles, each carrying a crown, are depicted around him. Each individual figure in the painting is a work of art in itself.

◀ Under Islamic law, artists were not allowed to paint pictures of people or animals—this was thought to be idolatry, the worship of idols. As a result, artists used calligraphy and decorated texts with geometric designs and flowing patterns of leaves and flowers.

During the Song dynasty, fine porcelain was also made for export. This special pale green bowl, with a celadon glaze, was said to crack or change color if poison was put into it, and was much valued by vulnerable leaders.

# ARCHITECTURE 501–1100

**Building styles varied throughout the world, ranging from simple structures in remote villages to grand architectural works in cities and empires.**

Climate and availability of building materials were major factors. In hot, humid climates, buildings were made to keep people cool and shaded, while in cold climates they needed to offer protection from wind, rain, snow, and chill. Where trees were plentiful, buildings were made entirely of wood. This was especially true in northern Europe and Japan. Even the first castles were built of wood, although many were later replaced using more durable stone. In warmer climates sunbaked bricks, or adobe, were used. Bricks and stone were more difficult to work with, but the builders of churches, mosques, and palaces often used them, hoping to leave a lasting mark on history. With advances in building techniques, architectural styles became more complex, frequently featuring arches, lofty roofs, and domes. Minarets, pagodas, and church spires became

Motte and bailey castles were common all over western Europe. If attacked, villagers could shelter within the castle. But the village itself was still vulnerable to burning and looting.

In later castles of the Middle Ages, outer walls were built to enclose settlements, sometimes around whole towns. The Normans were masters of castle-building—but the Japanese, Arabs, and Maya were also skilled in the art.

▲ Muslims built minarets beside mosques so that the *muezzin*, or caller, could climb them to call the people to prayer. The design of these minarets, and of the cupolas, or onion-shaped domes, on top of the mosques themselves, is typical of Muslim architecture.

▶ Villages like this Saxon one in England, with its central hall and a stockade, were common across the world. Different materials and styles were used, but the structure and layout were usually the same.

The Church of Hagia Sophia ("Holy Wisdom") in Constantinople was built during the early 500s. An immense work of Byzantine architecture, it was later converted into a mosque by the Ottomans.

▲ Norman builders had only simple equipment to help them build great cathedrals and castles. Their methods were often ingenious, and they were very skilled. Building methods like those used by the Normans did not change fundamentally for nearly 1,000 years, until the introduction of steel and concrete.

▶ Supporting the great weight of the roof, the pillars and arches of Durham cathedral in England have a typical Norman, or "Romanesque," style, which developed around 1100. Not only beautiful in shape, these lofty, light-filled buildings were also well built and have stood for many hundreds of years.

taller, and their shapes more graceful.

Fortifications were made taller and bulkier. By 1000, fine buildings for traders, markets, and trade guilds were also appearing. Cities, such as Hangzhou, Teotihuacán, Cordoba, and Kanauj were built on a grand scale. A more secular, or nonreligious, style was slowly emerging, establishing designs to be followed by architects in later times. However, the majority of people still lived in simple structures. American tepees, European log cabins, Arabic tents, and Indonesian longhouses, built quickly with simple materials, more than satisfied their inhabitants' needs. They were probably often more comfortable to live in than drafty stone castles or grand palaces.

In Aotearoa (New Zealand), the Maoris constructed wooden buildings. They were carved with stone tools, and they often added carved bone, colorful shells, and stones for special features, such as the eyes of their gods.

# SCIENCE AND TECHNOLOGY 501–1100

**During this period, the world's greatest inventors and scientists were Chinese and Arab. Europeans were far behind, and Americans mainly copied their ancestors.**

Many advances in science and technology were made independently by the Chinese and the Arabs. However, there was contact between them, so they also learned from each other. The Arabs were influenced by many new ideas from India and Persia; for example, the use of the number zero and the decimal counting system came from India. While all cultures across the world knew about herbal medicines and their uses, the Chinese and the Arabs were the most advanced. Arab doctors wrote medical books which were studied by both Chinese and Europeans. The Chinese understood how vaccination worked—this arose from their knowledge of acupuncture. They made magnetic compasses that could be used for navigation at sea and in the desert, and they invented gunpowder for fireworks and as a signaling device. It was the Europeans, several centuries later, who first used it in guns. Chinese ships, called junks, were the world's largest, and only the Vikings could match their seamanship.

The Arabs further developed the technical knowledge of ancient Greece, Persia, and India. They built machines like this, which raised water using the power produced by the falling water, the animal's movement, and the gears.

The Chinese invented paddle-wheel riverboats, and they designed large wooden machines for making cloth, irrigating fields, and lifting heavy weights. They also invented wood-block printing, dyes, paints and paintbrushes, and developed new types of vegetables.

▲ The inventor Su Song built this clock tower in 1090, at Kaifeng, the Song capital. It was powered by water dripping onto a wheel. A gong sounded to mark the hours.

▲ Grain crops were cut with a scythe (right). Using a flail (left), the grain was separated from the husks by tossing it up into the air where the lighter chaff blew away.

▶ Charcoal was used as a fuel in metal smelting. Wood was roasted in a smoldering, smothered fire. It slowly dried out, leaving charcoal behind.

◀ During this period the Arabs made significant advances in the use of medicine. In this illustration from an Arabic manuscript of the 1100s, a doctor and an apothecary—a pharmacist or druggist—are making an herbal medicine which they could use to counteract the effects of poisons.

## BOOKS AND IDEAS

One of the greatest advances during this period was printing. From the 500s, the Chinese had used wooden blocks, or woodcuts, that were carved to print a whole page. They soon progressed to using movable type for individual letters, so that pages could be made up and printed quickly in large quantities. In the mid-700s, the Chinese technique of papermaking was passed on to the Arabs, who later passed it to Europe. The Arabs were skilled in astronomy and mathematics, and they drew the most accurate maps available at the time. The Muslim cities of Fez, Cairo, Baghdad, Cordoba, and Samarkand were home to the world's first universities. However, these developments did not result in a technological revolution, because the pace of development had slowed down in China and the Muslim world by 1100.

▶ The Arabs were great astronomers. They invented the astrolabe, which measured the angles of stars to the horizon, for use in navigation and star charts. This one dates from the 11th century.

## WHEN IT HAPPENED

**593** Woodblocks used for printing in China
**595** Decimal counting used in India
**700** Waterwheels to drive mills in Europe
**700** Major advances in chemistry in Baghdad
**751** Technique of papermaking spreads from China to the Muslim world
**810** Algebra invented in Persia; Arabs adopt decimals
**868** Earliest known printed book is produced in China
**900** Arabic advances in astronomy
**900** Chinese develop porcelain

▲ The Chinese made compasses from magnetized metal and stone. The figure on top of this one always pointed to the south.

◀ The Chinese used fireworks in religious ceremonies. They made fireworks that could operate from big dragonlike kites high up in the sky.

# HIGH MIDDLE AGES

## 1101–1460

During the Middle Ages, empires rose and fell around the world. Many wars were undertaken in the name of religion. In Europe, alliances were made and quickly broken and a sense of nationalism began to grow. European traders ventured as far afield as China, camel caravans trudged across the Sahara and Venetian ships sailed the Mediterranean Sea with their goods. These were times of faith and fortune, of war and torture, famine and wealth.

By the end of the Middle Ages, learning had become a possibility for everyone who could read.

▲ The Krak des Chevaliers, in what is now Syria, was the largest and strongest castle built by the crusaders. It was garrisoned by 2,000 men, but finally fell to the Saracens in 1271.

◄ This splendid castle was painted for a prayer book of the Duc de Berry in 1412–16. The book was called *Les Très Riches Heures* ("The Very Rich Hours") and it captures the spirit of France in the high Middle Ages.

# THE CRUSADES 1095–1291

**Palestine became the center of a struggle for political and religious power when the pope called for a crusade to free the Holy Land from Muslim control.**

To Christians and Muslims, Palestine was the Holy Land, a place of pilgrimage for hundreds of years. After the Arabs conquered Palestine in 637, Christian pilgrims were still able to visit Jerusalem safely, but this changed with the arrival of the Seljuk Turks. In 1095, Pope Urban II called on Christians to free Palestine from Muslim rule. Knights and ordinary people set out, led by Peter the Hermit and Walter the Penniless. Most of them never reached Palestine, and the rest became a wild, hungry mob. In 1099, a well-disciplined Crusader army recaptured Jerusalem, massacring its inhabitants. They established four so-called Latin States, or kingdoms in Palestine and Syria. At first the Saracens, as the Crusaders called the Seljuk Turks, left the Crusader kingdoms alone. Some of the heads of the Christian

At first the Crusaders traveled overland from France and Italy to Palestine, but, to avoid having to fight the Seljuk Turks in Anatolia, they started to go by sea from Venice.

kingdoms behaved badly toward the Muslims. In 1187, Saladin (Salah ad-Din), the Kurdish sultan of Egypt, defeated the Christians at Hattin and recovered Jerusalem. In 1191, England's Richard I ("the Lionheart") led an army to the Holy Land. He took Cyprus and the city of Acre, which had been under siege by Christian forces, but he was unable to recapture Jerusalem. He and Saladin signed a treaty sharing the Holy Land, including Jerusalem—the Christians founded a "Second Kingdom" of the holy city with its heart at Acre. The fourth Crusade began in 1202,

The Crusaders wore heavy armor and rode large stallions, and the Muslims, called Saracens, wore light armor and rode mares. Both armies were formidable looking, but the Saracens were more mobile.

The Crusaders built Norman-style castles in Palestine and Syria. The Krak des Chevaliers in Syria, built by the Knights Hospitallers, was besieged by the Muslims in 1271. They eventually starved the Crusaders into surrender.

Saladin (c.1137–1193), a pious leader, led his people in a *jihad* or holy war against the Crusaders.

Richard I of England (1157–1199), known as the Lionheart (on the right), led an army of knights to the Holy Land in 1191, on the third Crusade. They failed to recapture Jerusalem, but Richard was able to secure a five-year peace treaty with Saladin. This allowed European pilgrims to visit the holy places again. On his return to England, in 1192, he was captured by Leopold of Austria and then Henry VI, the Holy Roman emperor, who held Richard for ransom for about a year. He finally reached England in 1194.

but the Crusaders were unable to pay Venice for transportation. So, in exchange for transport, they agreed to loot Christian Constantinople. In 1212, up to 50,000 children from France and Germany set off for Palestine, but most of them died of hunger or became slaves—this is known as the Children's Crusade. The fifth Crusade to Egypt failed; the last three crusades (1218–1272) were also unsuccessful. In 1291, Palestine was finally conquered by the sultan of Egypt.

▲ Louis IX, of France (1226–1270), was deeply religious. He led the Seventh Crusade (1248) and was captured. He also led the Eighth, but died of plague.

### KEY DATES

| | |
|---|---|
| 1096–99 | First Crusade takes Palestine and Syria |
| 1187 | Saladin wins back Jerusalem |
| 1189–92 | Third Crusade |
| 1202–04 | Fourth Crusade loots Constantinople |
| 1212 | Children's Crusade—a tragic failure |
| 1218–21 | Fifth Crusade—a failure |
| 1228–29 | Sixth Crusade—partly successful |
| 1291 | Acre is lost—the last Crusades |

▼ At the decisive battle of Hattin in 1187, Saladin tricked the Crusaders onto a hill on a hot day. While the Crusaders roasted in their metal armor, he surrounded and defeated them. Saladin then went on to win back Jerusalem.

# KNIGHTHOOD 1100–1400

**Mounted troops became a social elite, referred to in English as "knights." These were drawn from the upper classes, including nobility and royalty.**

In return for lands, lordships, and power, nobles did military service for their kings. They were wealthy enough to have large horses, armor, and attendants (squires). Often the younger sons of nobles became knights to gain riches or honors, because the eldest son usually inherited his father's estates. Knights were particularly important in the Crusades. Some went on crusades to gain power and lands; others went for sincere religious reasons and to protect pilgrims. But knighthood was not just about fighting. A knight was expected to be cultured, fair, and honorable, to help the weak, and protect the poor. This was known as chivalry; unfortunately, many knights did not live up to these high ideals.

The crossed legs of this carved effigy on the tomb of a Norman knight show that he had been on a crusade to the Holy Land.

## KEY DATES

| | |
|---|---|
| 1095 | Pope Urban II calls for the Crusades |
| 1113 | Knights Hospitallers founded |
| 1118 | Knights Templars founded |
| 1208 | Albigensian Crusade against the Cathars |
| 1227 | Teutonic Crusades against pagan Lithuania |
| 1291 | End of the Crusades in Palestine |
| 1312 | Knights Templars dissolved by the French king |

A squire kneels to help his master arm himself for battle. Plate armor made from steel was not introduced until the 1300s. Before that, knights wore chain mail.

## THE LIFE OF A KNIGHT

A boy began his training around the age of seven, becoming a page in the household of a knight or nobleman. By 14, he became a squire, who served at table, helped his master put on his armor, and accompanied him into battle. Later, if he performed his duties well, he was also made a knight. Knights practiced their skills in mock battles called tournaments. In these, most knights carried a scarf or glove from a lady, to show they were fighting on her behalf. Richard I of England and Louis IX of France were famous for their support of the romantic ideals of chivalry. In the Crusades, some knights took monastic vows of chastity and poverty, and joined the Templars, Hospitallers, or Teutonic Knights. The Knights Templars were so trusted that they carried people's money for them. As a result, the Templars became bankers and were very powerful in Europe. However, by 1312, the Templars were abolished for malpractices, such as dishonesty in business and heresy.

Two important Crusader orders of knights were the Knights Templars (left) and the Knights of St. John, or Hospitallers (right). The Hospitallers set up a hospital for pilgrims in Jerusalem, and the Templars guarded the original site of the Temple in Jerusalem.

◄ The tradition of the troubadours started in southern France just before 1100. These minstrel-poets sang songs of romantic love, chivalry, and religion.

▲ Axes, pikes, and swords were the main weapons that knights used during the Crusades.

▼ In tournaments, knights jousted against each other to show their knightly skills and bravery. Although they used blunt swords and lances, knights were often killed or maimed. Mock sieges and assaults on castles were also staged.

In 1227, the German Teutonic Knights were sent to colonize Prussia (now Lithuania). Other knights were sent on missions within Europe—such as the Albigensian Crusade sent by the pope to subdue the Cathars. The Cathars were Christians living in southwestern France who disagreed with the pope.

From the 1300s, knighthood became more of a royal honor than a military role. Some knights performed worthy tasks, helping people in difficulty and bringing justice; other knights sought power or wealth for themselves. Knights often argued, which was one reason why the Crusades eventually failed.

# HENRY OF ANJOU 1154–1189

**Henry of Anjou became Henry II, the first Plantagenet king of England, in 1154. With his lands in France he became one of the most powerful rulers in Europe.**

Henry II (1133–89) was a man of great humor but he also had a violent temper. Through his strong rule, he brought a period of peace and prosperity to both England and France.

Eleanor of Aquitaine (1122-1204) was one of the most powerful and remarkable women of the Middle Ages.

▲▶ Thomas à Becket (c.1118–70), Henry's chancellor, became Archbishop of Canterbury in 1162. He frequently opposed the king, and in 1170, was murdered in Canterbury Cathedral (right). This was a mistake that Henry much regretted.

Henry of Anjou was William the Conqueror's great-grandson. His mother, Matilda, was the widow of the Holy Roman emperor Henry V, who had died in 1125. She was the daughter of Henry I of England, who named her his heir after his sons had died. Henry I also wanted to strengthen his hold on Normandy, so, in 1128, he had Matilda marry Count Geoffrey of Anjou in France. In 1127, Henry had forced the English nobles to accept a woman as heir to the thrones of England and Normandy, but they were now furious that Matilda had married into a French royal house. When Henry died in 1135, the Church and the nobility split, and most threw their support behind Matilda's cousin Stephen as king. Civil war broke out in 1139, but in the end, Stephen remained king. He was later forced to make Matilda and Geoffrey's son, Henry of Anjou, his heir.

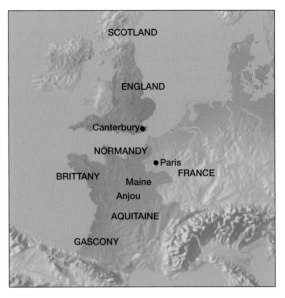

Thanks to inheritance and marriage, Henry II of England's rule extended from the Scottish borders to southwestern France, an area known as the Angevin empire.

When Henry of Anjou became Henry II of England at the age of 21, he inherited the French provinces of Anjou, Maine, and Touraine from his father, and Normandy and Brittany from his mother. In 1152, he married Eleanor, the abandoned wife of the French king Louis VII, thus gaining Aquitaine. As a result of this, he ruled England and two thirds of France.

## HENRY AND BECKET

Henry was an energetic ruler and traveled widely throughout his kingdom. He was well educated and cultured, and his court at Chinon in France was attended by many erudite scholars and troubadours (minstrels). Henry brought his nobles firmly under control, improved the laws of England, and forced the Scots and Welsh to obey him. When Norman nobles took control in Ireland, he subdued them and made himself king of Ireland in 1172. Henry chose capable ministers, among them Thomas à Becket, who became his chancellor. When Henry made him Archbishop of Canterbury, Becket began to assert the rights of the Church. After years of quarrels, Henry is said to have exclaimed, "Who will rid me of this turbulent priest?" Four knights took him at his word and killed Becket. Henry later did penance for this crime.

◀ Eleanor of Aquitaine died in 1204. Her tomb in the abbey church at Frontrevault, in western France, lies next to that of one of her sons, Richard I. Her husband, Henry II, who died in 1189, lies nearby.

## LIFE IN A CASTLE

Castles were large buildings that were cold and drafty to live in. They were military fortresses that also housed the lord's soldiers and servants. Towns soon grew outside the castle walls. In the lord's dwellings, the lady's servants lived in the top room, where linen and clothes were stored. Under this was the master bedroom, where the lord and lady slept. Below this was the *solar*, the lord's private living room, and on the ground floor were the great hall and a secure storeroom for the master's weapons and valuables.

▲ After the murder of Becket, the pope demanded that Henry do penance and be flogged. This was done, and Henry expressed his regrets. He was later pardoned.

Henry's empire was a family possession, not a country, and he planned to divide it among his four sons. They squabbled over this and then revolted against him. Two of them died, leaving Richard (the Lionheart) and John. Richard became king of England in 1189, and was followed after his death in 1199 by John. Henry had been a great and creative king, who had set up English common law, but he died in 1189, feeling that his life had been a failure. After his death, his sons lost most of his French lands, and the new order that Henry had built in England soon disintegrated.

### KEY DATES

| | |
|---|---|
| 1122 | Eleanor of Aquitaine is born |
| 1133 | Henry of Anjou born |
| 1139 | Eleanor of Aquitaine marries Louis VII of France; marriage later annulled |
| 1152 | Henry marries Eleanor of Aquitaine |
| 1154 | Henry becomes king of England |
| 1157 | Submission of the king of Scotland |
| 1162 | Thomas à Becket becomes Archbishop of Canterbury |
| 1166–76 | Legal reforms in England |
| 1170 | Murder of Thomas à Becket |
| 1171 | Henry becomes king of Ireland |
| 1173 | Thomas à Becket made a saint |
| 1174 | Rebellions by Henry's sons |
| 1189 | Henry dies in France |

# IRELAND 700–1350

**This period of Irish history saw increasingly permanent domination by foreigners, following invasions first by the Vikings and then by the English.**

▲ Strongbow, or Richard de Clare (c. 1130–1176) invaded Ireland from Pembroke, in Wales. He became king of Leinster.

▼ MacMurrough Kavanagh, king of Leinster, rides to make peace with the Earl of Gloucester during the Norman invasions.

Ireland was inhabited mainly by Gaelic Celts who lived in about 150 *tuath* or tribes. They frequently feuded and warred, which became a hindrance to Ireland's prosperity. Then, in 432, a man arrived who changed the course of Irish history— St. Patrick. He traveled around Ireland converting Irish chiefs to Christianity and preaching peace. By 600, Ireland had become one of Europe's main Christian centers, and Irish monks preached all across Europe. In 795, the Vikings invaded the island, and for the next 40 years raided and destroyed monasteries. By 840, they began to settle, founding towns such as Dublin, Waterford, Cork, and Limerick. From these, they traded and mixed with the Irish people, adopting many of their customs.

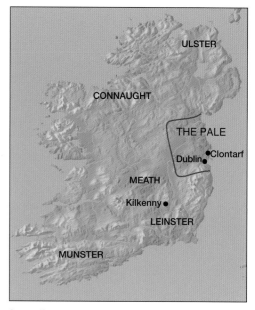

In medieval times, there were five kingdoms in Ireland. All that was left of direct Norman rule was a small area around Dublin called the Pale.

The rest of Ireland was still traditionally Irish. By now, the five largest kingdoms were Ulster, Leinster, Munster, Connaught, and Meath. In 976, Brian Boru, king of Munster, set about invading his neighbors. By 1011, he dominated Ireland, but on his death other local kings fought to be high king. The last strong high king was Turlough O'Connor of Connaught. After he died in 1156, two kings became rivals. One of these, Dermot MacMurrough of Leinster, asked for help from the Normans in England.

## THE COMING OF THE ENGLISH

The Earl of Pembroke, or "Strongbow," supported Dermot MacMurrough in return for marrying his daughter and inheriting Leinster. In 1170, Strongbow and other Norman nobles invaded, seizing Irish lands for themselves. This alarmed the king of England, Henry II, who proclaimed himself overlord of Ireland. Many Irish, fearing chaos, supported him and the Norman nobles submitted. Like the Vikings before them, many Normans soon adopted the customs of the Irish. However, in 1366, Lionel, Edward III's son and governor of Ireland, ordered the Irish-Norman families to stop speaking Gaelic and marrying Irish women. This demand was not accepted, and the Irish-Normans now looked upon the English as interfering foreigners. By the late 1400s English rule existed only in the Dublin area, called "the English Pale."

| KEY DATES | |
|---|---|
| 432 | St. Patrick introduces Christianity to Ireland |
| 795 | The start of Viking raids—destruction of Irish monasteries |
| 840 | Vikings settle, establishing coastal trading towns |
| 1014 | Brian Boru, king of Munster, defeats Vikings at the Battle of Clontarf |
| 1148 | Richard de Clare becomes Earl of Pembroke |
| 1166 | Rory O'Connor becomes first king of Ireland since 1014 |
| 1170 | Norman invasion of Ireland led by Richard de Clare |
| 1171 | Richard de Clare becomes king of Leinster; Henry II annexes Ireland |
| 1366 | Irish-Normans revolt against English orders banning Gaelic and mixed marriages |
| 1530s | Henry VIII reimposes English control |

During the unsuccessful English campaigns in Ireland, between 1367 and 1400, ships had to carry provisions across the Irish Sea to the English troops.

▼ On the Rock of Cashel, in County Tipperary, site of royal fortifications since the 300s, stand the ruins of St. Patrick's Cathedral. Given to the Church in 1101, the cross (far left) is where the kings of Munster were traditionally crowned.

# SHOGUNS AND SAMURAI 1200–1500

**The shoguns were generals who acted as governmental dictators, and the samurai were Japanese knights. They both dominated Japan for almost 700 years.**

A samurai's main weapons were a bow made of boxwood or bamboo and one or two single-edged swords. Samurai were strictly trained from childhood, following a code called *bushido*—the warrior's way.

The Fujiwara family had held power in Japan for 300 years since the 800s. However, their influence broke down when local dissent spread and when they ran out of daughters, the traditional brides of the emperor. For a time, some of the former emperors ruled. Then the Taira clan took over briefly until a rival clan, the Minamoto, rallied under Minamoto Yoritomo and seized power. Yoritomo assumed the title *sei-i tai shogun*, which means "barbarian-conquering great general." In 1192, he set up the Kamakura shogunate, through which he ruled Japan from his estate, Kamakura, near Edo (Tokyo). His powers were unlimited. From that time on, shoguns ruled Japan as military dictators until 1868. When Yoritomo died in 1199, the Hojo family, a branch of the Taira clan, became regents to the shoguns, and held power in an unofficial capacity until the Kamakura shogunate ended in 1333.

Minamoto Yoritomo (1147–1199) was an ambitious nobleman who saw his chance in the chaos that followed the breakdown of the power of the Fujiwara. Yoritomo ruthlessly crushed his enemies, including many of his own family. He set up the shogunate, a rigid feudal system that affected the whole country with him—the first shogun—as its head.

Japanese government was complicated. The emperor was a ceremonial figure to whom everyone bowed down, but the shogun had the real power. The regents to the emperors and shoguns also had influence, as did the *daimyos* or lords, who jostled for position at court and frequently battled over land. As a result, a class of warriors, or *samurai*, developed, who fought for the daimyos.

Samurai had elaborate decorated armor and many rituals. They were not only warriors who followed the code of *bushido*—the observance of very rigid rules that affected everything they did—but also had to be trained in the arts and religion.

▶ During the 1100s, Zen, a branch of Buddhism, spread from China to Japan. It had simple but strict rules, which the samurai followed. Buddhist shrines, like this gateway, were also built in the Chinese style.

As with European knights and Muslim warriors, religion and war were very closely connected for a samurai. He took a long time dressing and arming himself for battle, with strict rules of cleanliness and ritual.

## KNIGHTS OF JAPAN

The samurai were knights who were prepared to fight to the death for their daimyos, to whom they swore undying loyalty. Like the European knight, a samurai believed in truth and honor, and had a strict code of conduct called *bushido*. Before combat, a samurai would shout his name and those of his ancestors, and boast of his heroic deeds. In battle he fought hand to hand, often using two swords at once. If defeated or captured by his enemy, he had to commit ritual suicide (*hara-kiri*) in order to save face. At times, rivalry between samurai was destructive.

In 1333, the Ashikaga clan overthrew the Kamakura shogunate and the emperor, putting a new emperor in power. He appointed them as shoguns, this time in Kyoto. However, there was frequent samurai fighting between daimyos. This increased until the Onin civil war broke out, lasting from 1467–77, and Japan split into nearly 400 clan-states. The Kyoto emperors became powerless and impoverished. Despite this, trade and culture grew in Japan, centered on the daimyo estates. For ordinary people, the daimyo wars brought high taxes, insecurity, and disruption to their lives.

## THE SAMURAI IN BATTLE

Samurai battles were very ritualistic. They involved prayer and posturing (making oneself look strong) beforehand, with shouting and noisemaking using rattles and gongs to frighten the enemy. Individual samurai would undertake duels and contests. Often, battles were like a dance or a ceremonial game of chess. However, samurai warfare was deadly once they joined in full battle. During the Ashikaga period (1338–1573), much of the fighting deteriorated into meaningless squabbles for honor and plots of land.

149

# EUROPEAN TRADE 1100–1450

**Trade and industry rapidly grew to provide services for rising populations. Merchants and bankers thrived and found new influence from meeting society's needs.**

The early Middle Ages was a time of growth for Europe. The population was increasing, and more land was cultivated to grow food. This led to surplus produce for trading. Towns grew larger, with regular trade fairs at places like Troyes, Lyon, Kiev, Antwerp, Frankfurt, Leipzig, London, and Krakow. River links and shipping routes were busier. Instead of exchanging goods (bartering), money was used, and increasingly, people went into business for profit. Jewish traders, Knights Templars, and certain business families specialized in moneylending and the safekeeping of valuables. Italy was the richest part of Europe. Venice and Genoa were large independent seaports and banking centers, buying spices, silks, and other luxuries from the East. Goods from Asia came through Constantinople, Egypt, and Syria, and from Africa through Tunisia and Morocco. They were traded for cloth, furs, hides, iron, linen, timber, silver, and slaves.

The perils of travel in medieval times are shown in this drawing of a highwayman stealing a traveler's money. Highwaymen often lay in wait for their victims at roadsides.

In a medieval town, markets were usually held once a week. Livestock, food, metals, cloth, leather, and woodwork were all sold there, and people met to discuss local affairs.

In the 1100s, cities and ports grew along trade routes in Europe. Italian merchants attended fairs such as that at Troyes to buy Flemish cloth and sell Asian goods.

Most of Europe's money was silver, but the Asian countries traded in gold. This caused problems, so the Templars, Jewish traders, and Italian merchants invented banking, with bills of exchange and "promissory notes" that could be used instead of cash. Industries grew in the Rhineland (Germany), northern France, Flanders, and England, importing materials like copper, alum, wool, and charcoal, and exporting goods and clothes.

# THE GROWTH OF COMMERCE

A new class of merchants and skilled craftworkers appeared. Merchants grew rich through buying and selling, but they also risked loss because of highway robbery or piracy on the high seas where cargoes and fortunes could be lost. Trading companies, cities, and organizations like the Hanseatic League in the Baltic Sea worked together to protect trade, and opened offices in ports and marketplaces. To protect their trade, the Venetians and Genoese became Mediterranean naval powers. Around 1350, in Genoa, insurance services were offered, to protect traders against loss and bankruptcy. Banking families such as the Fuggers in Augsburg, Germany, and the Medicis in Florence, Italy, grew in wealth and influence. A new commercial order was developing, and kings, nobles, and clerics slowly lost power as they grew dependent on merchants and indebted to bankers. Soon, this new class began to influence the decisions of kings.

In Europe, posthouses and taverns were built along main roads. They provided refreshments, a place to stay, and a change of horse for merchants, pilgrims, and other travelers.

## THE HANSEATIC LEAGUE

In 1241, two German towns, Hamburg and Lübeck, set up a *Hansa* or trading association, which developed into the Hanseatic League in 1260, and involved many former Viking towns. They carried food and raw materials from eastern Europe in exchange for manufactured goods from the west. The Hanseatic League dominated trade between England, Scandinavia, Germany, and Russia during the 1300s.

The seal of Danzig, one of the leading Hansa towns.

Hanseatic merchants used these sturdy ships to carry goods between Baltic and Atlantic ports. They established warehouses, customs, banking systems, and defensive structures.

# VENICE 1100–1500

**During medieval times, the city-state of Venice dominated most of the trade between Europe, Asia, and Africa—becoming rich and powerful in the process.**

Venice had been founded in Roman times by the Veneti, a Romanized tribe that withdrew to the marshes to avoid raids by the Celts, Hannibal, and others. Their town was built on stilts and piles driven into the mud, with canals between the built-up islands they had constructed. There was no land to farm, so the early Venetians fished in the sea. Gradually, their small boats began to venture farther afield to trade. By 1100, Venice had become a very wealthy place, and its rich traders were living in sumptuous palaces. Protected by the sea, the city did not have to spend time and money on the building of elaborate fortifications. Its ships sailed around the Mediterranean, trading with the Byzantines and Arabs, who themselves traded with Russia, Asia, and Africa. Imported goods were sent overland into Europe. The cosmopolitan population of Venice—Jews, Germans, French, Italians, and Arabs—introduced many new ideas.

▲ Four bronze horses, dating from around 300 B.C., were seized by the Venetians at the sack of Constantinople in 1204, during the fourth Crusade. The Crusades allowed Venice to grow even richer and more influential.

Venice was originally built on stilts and piles driven into the mud of a marsh. Between the built-up islands were canals which can be seen in this bird's-eye view and map of the city from the 1500s.

St. Mark's Cathedral was built to house the relics of St. Mark as well as other treasures which the Venetians had looted from Alexandria and Constantinople.

## GROWTH OF VENETIAN POWER

During the 1100s, the Venetians expanded their influence by taking an active part in the Crusades. As the power of Byzantium declined, Venice took over its trade, and used several well-placed islands like Corfu and Crete as ports. After fighting off its great Italian rival, Genoa, during the 1300s, Venetian ships dominated all trading and cargo transportation between Europe and the East, and reached the height of its power during the 1400s. Venice did not own much land, but it controlled so much business that its silver dinars and gold ducats were used everywhere as money.

VENETIE MD

Like other places in medieval Italy, Venice was a city-state and largely independent. Its rulers were called doges, from the Latin word *dux*, which means "leader." Doges were elected for life and came from the most powerful families in Venice. They had almost absolute power over the government, the army, and the Church. But, after 1140, they lost most of their powers, which were transferred to a Great Council.

▲ The *Lion of St. Mark* was commissioned from the Venetian painter Vittore Carpaccio in 1516. The lion has been Venice's emblem for centuries.

◄ Convoys of ships sailed to the Levant to buy cotton, silk, and porcelain from China, spices from Zanzibar and Indonesia, and gems and ivory from Burma. Venice was famous for its lace and glassware.

### KEY DATES

| | |
|---|---|
| 726 | First doge is elected |
| 800s | The rise of Venice as a trading port |
| 1081 | Venetians gain trade privileges in Byzantium |
| 1090s | Arab dominance of Mediterranean trade ends |
| 1192 | Venice transports Crusaders to Constantinople by ship |
| 1381 | Venice defeats Genoa, to dominate all trade |
| 1400s | The economic center of Europe shifts north |

Venetian banks lent money and underwrote contracts, guaranteeing payment if things went wrong. Banks encouraged trade, but their interest rates were high.

# CHARTER AND PARLIAMENT 1215–1485

In England, in the 1200s, there was a growing struggle between the kings and the lords. The absolute power of kings was being questioned by those they ruled.

King John of England, the youngest son of Henry II, was given to violent outbursts of temper. Not surprisingly, he soon angered his barons in English-ruled Anjou and Poitiers, and he lost those lands to France. In England, he taxed his barons heavily and ruled so harshly that they rebelled. The barons threatened John, and demanded that he recognize their traditional rights and obey the law.

King John (1199–1216), quarrelled with his nobles, who turned against him, and forced him to sign the Magna Carta.

This is the great seal of King John, affixed to the bottom of the Magna Carta. John's seal showed his consent, and so turned the charter into the law of the land.

### THE MAGNA CARTA

In 1215, the barons met King John in a meadow called Runnymede, beside the Thames River. There, they forced him to put his seal on the Magna Carta, or "great charter." This document covered many important areas, including weights and measures, the powers of sheriffs, and the legal rights of freemen and boroughs (towns). The king agreed to obey the law himself, and he was not allowed to raise taxes without the agreement of his Great Council of nobles. No sooner had John agreed to the charter than he went back on his word. A civil war broke out, but John soon died, leaving the throne to his young son who became Henry III. The charter was reissued, and in 1225, it became the law of England. Henry III was incompetent and he spent large sums of money, so the barons banded together again, this time led by Simon de Montfort. They forced Henry to agree to consult the Great Council in all major matters. Like his father, Henry III went back on the deal, but de Montfort defeated him in battle at Lewes in 1264. Simon de Montfort and the Council then ruled England in Henry's name.

In 1215, John was forced to put his seal on the Magna Carta at Runnymede. John did not actually sign the charter, and possibly could not even write.

## THE POWER OF PARLIAMENT

In 1265, Simon de Montfort called a new Parliament of two chambers, the House of Lords (previously the Great Council of nobles and bishops,) and the House of Commons. The House of Commons was made up of two knights from every shire and two people (burgesses) who represented each borough. Later, Edward I (1272–1307), a successful ruler, reformed England's law and administration; he created a Model Parliament which included even more representatives from the country. However, the king still held power. In 1388, there was a major clash and the "Merciless" Parliament removed some of King Richard II's rights.

As time went on, Parliament's powers gradually grew. The House of Commons slowly gained greater power, although it was mostly the richer classes that were represented in Parliament. Full-scale democracy only arrived in the 1900s.

| KEY DATES | |
| --- | --- |
| 1215 | King John reluctantly affixes his seal to the Magna Carta |
| 1216 | King John dies. His nine-year-old son, Henry III, becomes king |
| 1225 | The Magna Carta becomes the law of England |
| 1227 | Henry III, now aged 20, begins to rule |
| 1258 | Council of nobles set up |
| 1265 | Simon de Montfort's Parliament is called |
| 1272 | Edward I becomes king of England |
| 1295 | Edward I's Model Parliament |
| 1307 | Edward II becomes king of England |
| 1388 | The "Merciless" Parliament (against Richard II) |

▶ Simon de Montfort (c.1208–1265) was a Norman baron who became Earl of Leicester. In 1264–65 he virtually ruled the country on behalf of the king.

▲ Henry III, is pictured here at his coronation in 1216. He ruled for 55 years. He lost much of his power as king because he was not a good ruler. He was more interested in the arts and in building churches.

Queen

King

Bishop  Lord  Lady  Knight  Merchant  Nun

Peasant

These were the different social classes of the time, in order of power from the king downward. The largest number of people were peasants, who had no power at all. Some lords and priests treated them fairly, allowing them to voice their concerns, but this was rare.

# MALI AND ETHIOPIA 1240–1500

**In West Africa, the Mali Empire grew powerful by controlling the gold trade. In the east, the Christian empire of Ethiopia was isolated by the spread of Islam.**

Mali had important links with the Muslim world. The Great Mosque at Timbuktu was designed by As-Saheli, an Egyptian.

In 1240, Sundiata Keita, the ruler of the small Malinke kingdom in West Africa, brought about the collapse of the nation of Ghana, and established a new nation called Mali. He set up a well organized state that possessed fertile farmlands beside the Niger River. Under Sundiata's rule, Mali controlled the gold trade and became rich and powerful. Many of the camel caravan routes across the Sahara Desert led to Mali's fine cities, such as Koumbi Saleh, Djenné, and Timbuktu.

Mali's trading cities exported ivory, gold, and slaves to the Muslim world, and to Venice and Genoa in Europe. In exchange, they imported salt, cloth, ceramics, glass, horses, and luxuries. Timbuktu and Djenné became centers of scholarship, where different peoples and faiths mingled. Timbuktu had a university and 100 schools. Mali reached the height of its power, and also became Muslim, under Sundiata's grandson Mansa Musa (1307–37). He made a pilgrimage to Mecca in 1324, taking 500 slaves and 90 camels loaded with gold. In 1325, Mali overpowered Songhay, lower down the Niger River, but in 1464 Songhay's ruler declared independence. Mali's decline had begun in 1350, and by 1500, it had been conquered by Songhay.

Timbuktu was a prosperous city on the Niger River. It was the destination of many caravan routes across the Sahara and had schools, a university, mosques, and markets.

This is part of a 14th-century Catalan map of northwest Africa that shows major towns and trading routes, and features Mansa Musa, the great ruler of Mali.

## THE GREAT MOSQUE AT DJENNÉ

During the 1100s, when Mali was founded and Islam was adopted, Mansa Musa ordered a mosque built in the ancient city of Djenné a center for the gold trade. The present Great Mosque, finished in 1907, was built of mud brick in the traditional style.

## THE FOUNDING OF ETHIOPIA

In East Africa, the old nation of Aksum had collapsed around 1000. Ethiopia (Abyssinia) was founded by the Jewish Zagwe dynasty around 1137. Most Ethiopians practiced Coptic Christianity. Their church was cut off by the spread of Islam, but there was contact with Christianity through an Ethiopian monastery in Jerusalem. Lalibela became emperor in 1190, moved the capital from Aksum and built a new one at the holy city of Roha, later renamed Lalibela in his honor.

In 1270, Yekuno Amlak founded the Solomonic dynasty—they claimed descent from Solomon and the Queen of Sheba. Ethiopia expanded its borders into the mountains of East Africa, taking in many tribes. It was a unique country, untouched by others for a long time, isolated from the rest of the world by its mountain location. However, having been at its strongest during the 1300s and 1400s, it was plagued by internal discord in the 1500s. In medieval Europe, Ethiopia was regarded as a mysterious Christian kingdom, with a mythical king called Prester John. The very last emperor of Ethiopia, Haile Selassie, who ruled from 1930 to 1974 was a descendant of Yekuno.

The Ethiopians built cross-shaped churches, carved and hollowed out of solid rock. Both of these pictures are of the Church of St. George at the holy city of Lalibela, one of 11 such churches built in the 1200s.

| KEY DATES | |
|---|---|
| 1137 | Founding of Ethiopia by the Zagwe dynasty |
| 1190s | Lalibela built as the capital of Ethiopia |
| 1240 | Sundiata Keita founds the state of Mali |
| 1270 | Yekuno Amlak founds the Solomonic dynasty; Ethiopia expands |
| 1307–37 | Mansa Musa, Mali's greatest ruler |
| 1350 | Mali goes into slow decline |
| 1300s–1400s | High point of Ethiopian culture |
| c.1500 | Songhay overwhelms Mali |

157

# BENIN AND ZIMBABWE 1100–1480

**Benin was an advanced kingdom in the tropical forests of West Africa. Zimbabwe was a gold-mining centre in the high grasslands of southeast Africa.**

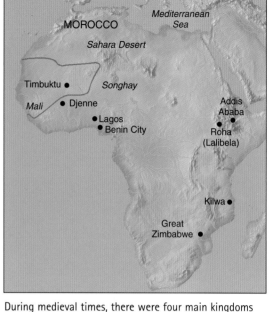

During medieval times, there were four main kingdoms that flourished in Africa: Mali (later overwhelmed by Songhay), Ethiopia, Benin, and Zimbabwe.

Benin was situated in what is now southeastern Nigeria. It was the longest lasting of the forest kingdoms of rain-forested West Africa. Its capital, Benin City, was founded in about A.D. 900 and was at its most prosperous during the 1400s. The city had wide streets lined with large wooden houses and was enclosed by walls 25 mi. (40km) long. The palace of the *oba* (king) was richly decorated with bronze plaques and carvings. The city's busy traders dealt in cloth, ivory, metals (especially bronze), palm oil, and pepper. Benin was famous for its art, especially sculptures using pottery, ivory, or brass.

This ivory mask is thought to be of Idia, the mother of Esigie, an *oba* or king of Benin in the 16th century. The oba would have hung it around the waist on ceremonial occasions.

▶ This Benin bronze shows an oba seated on his throne, with two subjects. kneeling before him. Benin craftsmen cast "bronzes" (most were actually brass) by the "lost wax" process. A wax model was carved, then covered with clay to make a mould. The wax would be melted away, and molten bronze would be poured into the mould. Many copies could then be made using this process.

Benin flourished under the leadership of Oba Eware the Great, who ruled from 1440 to 1473. He modernized and expanded Benin. Usually, warring African states made slaves of their prisoners, but Benin avoided this—so when the Portuguese began buying slaves from West Africa in the 1500s, Benin did not join in the slave trade. This protected it from European colonialization until 1897.

Many of the peoples of West Africa lived in tribal villages, herding animals and growing crops. The grasslands of central Africa (shown here) were very different environments from the tropical forests of the west.

158

## ZIMBABWE

Zimbabwe grew prosperous from its large reserves of copper and gold. Dug from over one thousand mines, much of it was bought by Arab traders on the east coast from the 900s onward. They built the only towns in southern Africa, and Zimbabwe is best known for its walled palace city, Great Zimbabwe, built between 1100 and 1400. However, little is known of the Zimbabweans. They were not great warriors, so Zimbabwe did not expand its borders by military means.

Around 1450, Zimbabwe was absorbed into the Shona kingdom of Rozvi (Mwenemutapa), named after a line of strong kings. This warrior kingdom took control of most of what is now Zimbabwe and Mozambique. It continued to trade gold and copper with the Arabs and grew rich from this. This changed when the Portuguese settlers tried to gain control of the mines. Rozvi fought against this for some time, but by 1629, the mines had fallen under Portuguese control. Nevertheless, Rozvi survived until the 1830s.

This is a bronze head of an *oni*, or king, of Ife, from the 1300s. He is wearing the headdress of a sea god. Ife was a kingdom that once bordered Benin.

### GREAT ZIMBABWE

Modern Zimbabwe is named after the walled city of Great Zimbabwe. The massive stone structures are thought to have been built by the Gokomere culture, ancestors of the Shona people, between the 11th and 14th centuries. A *zimbabwe* is a stone-built enclosure, of which there were many in southeast Africa, but this was the largest and grandest.

▲ The ruins of the Great Enclosure can be seen today on the 60-acre (24ha) site of Great Zimbabwe.

# RELIGION IN THE MIDDLE AGES 1100–1500

**In the Middle Ages, religious institutions worldwide had grown powerful and influential. This brought enormous benefits, but also led to corruption.**

St. Francis of Assisi (1182–1226) founded the Order of Franciscan Friars in 1210. Two years later, he founded the Poor Clares, an order for women.

By 1200, even the newest religion, Islam, was 500 years old. Religions had become major institutions, and were established in the traditions of every country. In many places, everyday life had become difficult—there was poverty and hardship, and those not suffering from these often experienced corruption and crime. Many religious people began to feel that it might be beneficial to withdraw from the world and worship God by becoming hermits, monks, and nuns. This made monastic communities attractive. In Europe, China, and Tibet, monastic traditions, with their strict rules and simple lifestyles, grew strong. Monasteries provided the local community with health care, education, employment, and refuge. They encouraged pilgrimages and provided a positive influence during troubled times.

St. Francis devoted himself to helping the poor and sick. He also loved nature and was said to talk to animals. He was well known for his compassion and for caring for small creatures. He was made a saint two years after his death.

During the early Middle Ages, thousands of churches were built all over Europe. They contained no pews or benches—people had to stand during services—although there were ledges that the old and infirm could lean on.

This is the Church of St. Peter in Rome as it looked in the Middle Ages. Built in Roman times in 325, it became the pope's headquarters, until it was demolished in 1506 and replaced by a much grander Renaissance church.

## RELIGIOUS POWER

The priesthood was influential in politics as well as religion. In Europe, there was rivalry between popes and kings, priests, and lords—and even between competing popes. The Church became corrupt—priestly posts and the forgiveness of sins could be bought. In Islam, there was no priesthood, but there were many different Muslim groups

In Mayan and Toltec Mexico, priests were all-powerful, and demanded blood sacrifice of their people. Worldwide, many people had a simple faith, but no real religious education. In Europe, religion was taught in Latin, and in India it was taught in Sanskrit—languages that most people did not understand. Pilgrimage was important—Muslims went to Mecca, Christians to Rome and Jerusalem, and Buddhists and Hindus to holy mountains and temples. Many people could not improve their lives, so they prayed for a better life in heaven (Christians, Muslims, and the Maya), or in their next life (Hindus and Buddhists). Around the world great temples, cathedrals, churches, and mosques were built—some of the finest architecture of the time.

The Great Mosque at Cordoba in Muslim Spain was one of the most elegant buildings ever erected. Over a thousand pillars held up the roof—this made the interior light and airy, an important feature of buildings in hot climates.

▲ Mosques were built in many countries, from Africa to India—even in parts of China. These are the ruins of the mosque at Kilwa, a Muslim city-state off the coast of East Africa that traded with Zimbabwe.

▼ The monastery of Likir was founded in the Ladakh region of the Himalayas in 1065. Its religious leaders, called *lamas*, followed a form of Buddhism, which spread into Tibet, Mongolia, and Siberia.

◄ Quetzalcóatl was a god honored by the Toltecs, the Maya, and the Aztecs. He was the god associated with civilization and learning, and with the spiritual protection of the priesthood.

## RELIGION AND CULTURE

During the Middle Ages, great religious thinkers were at work. Scholars such as Meister Eckhart in Germany, Thomas Aquinas in Italy, Maimonides and Ibn Arabi in Egypt, Marpa the Translator in Tibet, Ramanuja in India, and Dogen in Japan shaped the ideas of the age. Religion became a part of everyday life, affecting the arts and sciences, medicine, government, and society. It formed the heart of the world's many cultures. But there was a growing gap between what people believed and what they practiced. Some thought it was all right to pray on holy days and break the rules the rest of the time. Some temples and churches became so rich and corrupt that many people began to question their faith.

# THE MONGOL EMPIRE 1206–1405

**The Mongols created the largest empire in history. Their presence was felt strongly in China, Russia, and in the Islamic world, but their empire did not last long.**

Genghis Khan (c.1162–1227) was a great leader, general, and organizer. During one campaign, his army traveled at breakneck speed—275 mi. (440km) in just three days. He died after falling from a horse.

In 1180, a 13-year-old boy was made leader of his tribe when his father was poisoned. The boy was named Temujin, and his tribe, the Yakka Mongols, were a warlike nomadic people in Mongolia. Two thirds of the tribe promptly deserted him, but Temujin soon reunited them and went on to take over other Mongol tribes. In 1206, at a meeting of the *khans* (chiefs), Temujin was hailed as Genghis Khan, "Emperor of All Men." He promised that future generations of Mongols would lead lives of luxury. Genghis Khan began a career of conquest, by training a ruthless, fast-moving, and well disciplined army. His hordes terrified their opponents, killing anyone who did not surrender or change sides. In a series of outstanding campaigns, Genghis Khan conquered Turkestan, northern China, and Korea, then swung westward to overrun Afghanistan, Persia, and parts of Russia. Part of his success came from the fact that his opponents were not united.

In battle, the Mongols were unstoppable. Their bows fired farther than any had before, their horses were fast, and their tactics tricked many of their opponents.

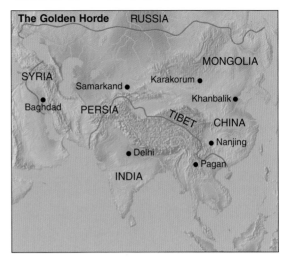

At its greatest extent, in the 1200s, during the reign of Kublai Khan, the Mongol Empire extended from the Pacific Ocean to the Black Sea.

## MONGOL EXPANSION

After Genghis died, Ogodai and Möngke Khan conquered Armenia, Tibet, more of China, and then ravaged eastern Europe. Ghengis's grandson, Kublai Khan, completed the conquest of China. He made himself first emperor of the Yuan dynasty (1271–1368). Some aspects of Mongol rule were good—they gave women status, encouraged scholars, respected different religions, and helped trade. They opened the Asian Silk Roads to East-West travelers. Other aspects were not so good—their ruthless armies destroyed cities and massacred many. However, the Song in southern China were able to resist them for 20 years before they fell, and the Delhi Sultanate stopped them from invading India. By 1260, Mongol expansion had ended.

The Mongols were a nomadic people from the plains of Mongolia who lived in portable *yurts*—large, round tents made of hides or cloth. They herded cattle, sheep, goats, and horses. Even when they invaded cities, their army stayed outside in yurt encampments.

## THE RISE OF TIMUR

From 1275, a Venetian merchant named Marco Polo spent 17 years at the court of Kublai Khan. His stories gave Europeans their first picture of China and its wealth. After Kublai Khan's death in 1294, the mighty Mongol Empire began to break up. Some khans, such as the Chagatais in Turkestan, the Ilkhans in Persia, and the Golden Horde in southern Russia, kept smaller empires for themselves. Cruel though the Mongols were, none was as barbarous as the great Mongol-Turkish ruler of Samarkand, Tamerlane, or Timur (1336–1405). His army went on the rampage between 1361 and 1405, and brutally overran Persia, Armenia, Georgia, Mesopotamia, Azerbaijan, and the Golden Horde.

Despite his cruel reputation, Tamerlane was a great patron of the arts, astronomy, and architecture in Samarkand. Generally, however, the Mongols left no lasting mark on the world, except for the destruction they brought. China and Russia became poor, the Muslim world was in turmoil, and European countries like Poland and Serbia suffered greatly. After Tamerlane's death in 1405, the Mongol reign of terror was over, except in Russia and Turkestan.

In battle, the Mongols wore light armor made of leather and iron. They were so fast and ruthless that most of their opponents gave up in fear. Large silk flags streamed behind them. Anyone who opposed them was destined to die.

## MONGOL SPORTS

The Mongols loved horseriding, wrestling, and archery. The great khans encouraged sport as a way of developing battle skills and discovering talented soldiers. There were many sports contests, and military promotion could be gained from success in these. Participating in sports also fostered teamwork, which was one of the Mongols' greatest strengths.

From an early age, Mongol boys practiced archery and wrestling.

The Mongols adopted the ancient Persian game of polo.

# AZTECS AND INCAS 1100–1500

Two great civilizations were founded in the Americas within about a hundred years of each other: the Inca Empire in Peru and the Aztec Empire in Mexico.

The Aztec and Inca empires developed independently of each other in North and South America. By the beginning of the 1500s, they had both expanded and had great influence over their regions.

The Aztec god Huitzilopochtli was sometimes depicted as a snake. This image is made of wood, and covered with jade stones.

Legends say that the Aztec people originally came from northern Mexico. Then, in 1168, on the instructions of their god Huitzilopochtli (often depicted as a snake), they began to migrate southward. They eventually settled in the valley of Mexico, where they set up farming communities. Around 1325, during a time of warfare, they moved to a safe site on an island in Lake Texcoco. This is the site of present-day Mexico City.

The Great Temple lay at the heart of the island city of Tenochtitlan. On top of the pyramid were shrines to the gods Tláloc and Huitzilopochtli. The monument in front of it was dedicated to Quetzalcóatl.

▼ Tenochtitlan lay in the center of Lake Texcoco and was linked to the mainland by causeways. A network of canals threaded through the city.

## THE CITY OF TENOCHTITLAN

The Aztecs created garden-islands in Lake Texcoco on which to grow food. They also started to build a great city, called Tenochtitlan. It was easily defended, since it could be reached only by the causeways (raised roads) that the Aztecs had built across the lake. The Aztecs traded throughout Mexico, and their men served in the armies of other cities in return for payment. Under their great leader, Itzcóatl who ruled from 1427–40, they began to conquer these neighboring cities, eventually building up the Aztec Empire which, by 1500, stretched coast to coast.

## THE INCA EMPIRE

According to tradition, Manco Capac and his sister, Mama Ocllo, were the first rulers of the Incas around 1200. They called themselves "the Children of the Sun." The Incas lived in a valley high in the Andes mountains, in what is now Peru. There they built a city called Cusco, and others such as Machu Picchu. *Cusco* means "navel" or "center of the world." For 200 years, the Incas lived there, isolated from the rest of the world. However, under Pachacutec, a brilliant general and their emperor from 1438 to 1471, the Incas began a time of conquest. By 1500, they had created an extensive empire.

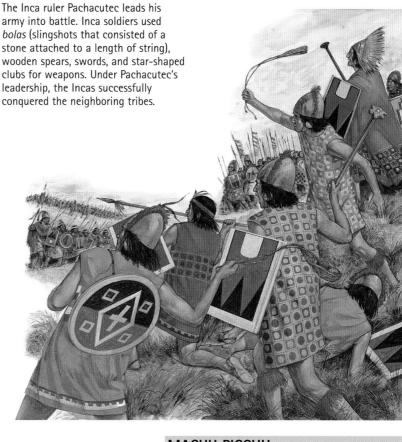

The Inca ruler Pachacutec leads his army into battle. Inca soldiers used *bolas* (slingshots that consisted of a stone attached to a length of string), wooden spears, swords, and star-shaped clubs for weapons. Under Pachacutec's leadership, the Incas successfully conquered the neighboring tribes.

Gold, silver, and precious stones were used to craft beautiful objects for noble families. The objects also played a role in religious rituals.

## MACHU PICCHU

Machu Picchu was a remarkable Inca mountaintop city that was so well concealed that it was only rediscovered in 1911. High in the Andes, the city was one of the last strongholds of the Incas against the invading Spaniards. It was built using stones that fit together precisely, without mortar. Machu Picchu was a spiritual center, with an astronomical observatory and temples.

# MEDIEVAL EXPLORERS 1270–1490

**In the Middle Ages, many bold men made long, and often dangerous, journeys to distant lands. These new contacts improved trade and spread political influence.**

▲ Prince Henry the Navigator (1394–1460) was responsible for the port city of Ceuta in Morocco. This led to his fascination with ships. He sponsored expeditions and the work that led to a new ship, the caravel. He encouraged more precise mapmaking and seafaring instruments. The sailors he trained were the first Europeans to undertake long sea voyages. Soon the Portuguese opened up new routes around Africa to India and the Far East.

The first medieval explorers were the Vikings, who went as far as America, Morocco, and Baghdad. The first account of central Asia was written by a Franciscan friar, John of Pian del Carpine, who visited the Mongol khan on behalf of Pope Innocent IV in 1245. The best known European traveler was Marco Polo, a young Venetian who journeyed to meet Kublai Khan in China and remained there for many years. Returning in 1295, he composed a vivid account of his travels.

Between 1325 and 1350, Ibn Battuta, a Moroccan lawyer, traveled to Russia, central Asia, India, southern China, and Africa, writing detailed descriptions of his travels. Admiral Zheng He was sent by the Chinese Ming emperor Yongle on seven naval expeditions between 1405 and 1433. His fleet sailed to Indonesia, India, Persia, Mecca, and East Africa, establishing diplomatic relations and extending China's political influence over maritime Asia. Zheng He took back gifts to the emperor, including spices and exotic animals.

Camel caravans took Muslim travelers and traders across the deserts of Africa and Asia, making them some of the most traveled people of the medieval period.

## PRINCE HENRY THE NAVIGATOR

Henry was a son of the king of Portugal. At the age of 21, he discovered treasures in Morocco that had been carried overland from Songhai and Senegal in West Africa. He was curious to know if these places could be reached by sea. So, after about 1420, Henry paid Portuguese sailors to explore the coast of Africa. Encouraged by their discoveries, he built a school of navigation at Sagres in Portugal, to train sailors for further voyages of discovery.

Kublai Khan sent Marco Polo on various journeys, including to the Chinese borders of Tibet. Polo told of how they burned bamboo on their campfire, which caused loud crackling noises that terrified the horses. However, the noise also scared off wild animals.

The incredible journeys of medieval travelers covered thousands of miles. The greatest of these travelers were Marco Polo, Ibn Battuta, and Zheng He.

Marco Polo first visited China with his father, a Venetian trader. He stayed there longer, playing an active role in the court of Kublai Khan. He was even sent on missions for the khan around China and to Pagan in Burma.

Marco Polo was away from Venice for 25 years. His overland journey to China took four years, and the return journey by sea from China to Persia, then overland, took three. He acted as a regional governor and ambassador for the khan while in China. The khan welcomed many foreigners, and he found Europeans to be very unusual, exotic visitors.

By the time Prince Henry died in 1460, Portuguese explorers had reached what is now Sierra Leone. Henry's work inspired later Portuguese explorers to sail farther down the coast of West Africa, seeking a sea route to India and the Far East. The world was now on the verge of a great expansion of international contact. The Chinese could have been the first international travelers, but its emperors preferred isolation, and traders were discouraged from travel. Muslims had also traveled far and wide, though by 1500 they had lost their urge to expand further. Meanwhile, the Europeans were about to change their inward-looking policies and seek new horizons.

▲ Ibn Battuta (1304–68) was a lifelong traveler from North Africa who wrote lengthy accounts of his journeys. He traveled to Africa and Russia, to Morocco and India, and by sea to southern China. His stories were the most accurate and useful of all the accounts written by medieval travelers.

◄ Admiral Zheng He's fleet of huge oceangoing junks were specially built for his expeditions. On his first voyage, his fleet consisted of 62 of these ships.

# THE HUNDRED YEARS' WAR 1337–1453

**The Hundred Years' War was a series of short, costly wars in which the English kings tried to dominate France, but met great resistance.**

John of Gaunt (1340–1399) was one of the sons of Edward III. As regent (1377–1386) for his nephew Richard II, he was the most powerful man in England.

In 1328, Charles IV of France died. The French barons gave the throne to his cousin, Philip VI, but Charles's nephew, Edward III of England, challenged him. Philip confiscated Edward's French lands, and in 1337 war broke out. At the start of the conflict, which actually lasted 116 years, the English defeated a French fleet in the English Channel at Sluys, then invaded France, winning a major battle at Crécy, and capturing Calais. Both sides ran out of money and had to agree to a truce, which lasted from 1347 until 1355. In 1355, a fresh English invasion took place, led by Edward's heir, Edward, whose nickname was the Black Prince. He won a resounding victory at Poitiers. The Treaty of Brétigny in 1360 gave England large parts of France. But a new campaign followed, and England lost most of her French possessions.

The English longbow (left) shot farther and faster than ever before. The French crossbow (right) was easier to load and fire than a longbow, but much slower. Large numbers of Welsh archers were deployed by the English in the Hundred Years' War.

In the late 1360s, both were inherited by children—Charles VI of France and Richard II of England. Richard's uncle, John of Gaunt (for Ghent in Belgium, his birthplace), ruled for him. In 1396, Richard II married Charles VI's daughter, Isabelle, and a 20-year truce was agreed.

▲ Edward, (1330–1376), Prince of Wales, father of Richard II, wore black armor and so was later called "the Black Prince."

▶ Edward III, (1312–1377) invaded France in 1346. His army of 10,000 defeated a French army twice its size at Crécy. The English easily outshot the French crossbows.

## BATTLE OF AGINCOURT

The Battle of Agincourt in 1415 was a notable English victory. Henry V commanded about 900 men-at-arms and 3,000 archers. The French had at least three times as many heavily armed troops, but they were badly led and organized.

## THE END OF A COSTLY WAR

After a long truce the war began again in 1415. Henry V (1387–1422), England's adventurous king, revived his country's claim to the French throne. England still held Calais and parts of Bordeaux. Henry captured Harfleur in Normandy and heavily defeated the French at Agincourt. Henry then occupied much of northern France. Charles VI made him heir to the French throne in 1420. He also married Charles's daughter, Catherine of Valois. Henry died just 15 months later, leaving the throne to his infant son, Henry VI. Charles VI died soon after.

In support of the claim, Henry's uncle, John, Duke of Bedford, besieged Orléans. The French forces, led by a 17-year-old peasant girl, Joan of Arc, successfully defended the town. Joan claimed she saw visions and heard voices telling her to free France. She escorted the new but uncrowned king, Charles VII, to Reims to be crowned. However, Joan was soon defeated at Paris and captured by the Burgundians. They sold her to the English, who burned her as a witch. Sporadic fighting went on for some years afterward. The French recaptured their lands by 1453, ending the war. Only Calais remained English. This had been a kings' war—but it was the people who had paid the price.

### KEY DATES

E = English victory, F = French victory
| | |
|---|---|
| 1340 | Battle of Sluys (E), at sea |
| 1346 | Battle of Crécy (E) |
| 1347 | Battle of Calais (E) |
| 1356 | Battle of Poitiers (E) |
| 1372 | Battle of La Rochelle (F), at sea |
| 1415 | Battle of Agincourt (E) |
| 1428 | Battle of Orléans (F) |
| 1450 | Battle of Formigny (F) |
| 1451 | Battle of Bordeaux (F) |

At the age of 17, Joan of Arc (1412–1431) led the French against the English, during France's darkest hour. The English accused her of being a witch, because she claimed she had visions and heard voices telling her to drive the English out of France.

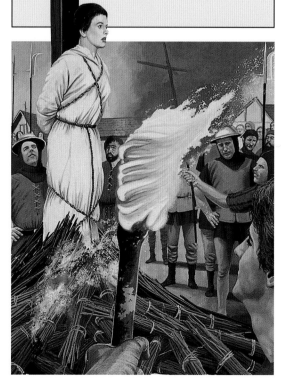

Joan of Arc was burned at the stake in 1431. Five hundred years later, in 1920, she was made a saint.

# THE BLACK DEATH 1347–1351

**The Black Death was one of the worst disasters in history. It resulted in the death of around a third of the population of the Middle East and Europe.**

The Black Death was carried by fleas on rats. It may have spread from an area in southern China or Southeast Asia.

Rats were common in houses, ships, and food storerooms, so the disease spread rapidly through the population.

In the art of the time, the Black Death was depicted as a skeleton riding furiously on horseback.

The Black Death killed about 25 million people in Europe alone, and probably millions more in Asia. It began as bubonic plague. Its name comes from spots of blood under the skin that turned black and from swellings (buboes) in the groin and armpits. Most victims died horribly, shortly after symptoms appeared. Bubonic plague was transmitted to humans by fleas on rats—it could not be passed from person to person. But if pneumonia developed in a plague victim, the infection became pneumonic plague, which could be passed on to another person. It was highly contagious, spread rapidly, and most victims died.

The disease was carried from southern China or Burma, through central Asia, along the Silk Road to Baghdad and the Crimea. In 1347, it arrived by ship at Genoa, in Italy, and spread to Paris and London in 1348, and Scandinavia and Russia in 1349. No one was safe from it.

European towns were filthy, with rubbish, rats, and human excrement in the streets. Human waste was thrown out of windows and trodden underfoot. The lack of basic hygiene was the reason that the plague spread so fast.

## THE IMMEDIATE EFFECTS

The Black Death devastated whole regions: houses stood empty, villages and towns were abandoned, and people in some trades and even some entire areas were completely wiped out. Baghdad and Mecca were emptied. Doctors, priests, and the people who buried the plague victims also died. In the end, fields were littered with unburied corpses. Society and the economy in Europe began to disintegrate.

▶ The Black Death spread through Europe from Genoa. Some areas, including Ireland and parts of France lost 10 percent of their population. Other areas, including northern Italy, eastern England, and Norway, lost as much as 50 percent.

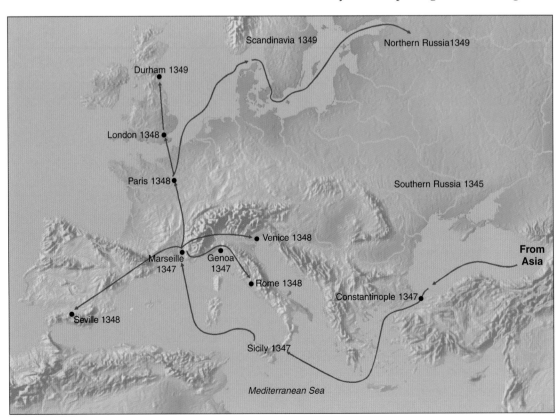

Scandinavia 1349
Northern Russia 1349
Durham 1349
London 1348
Paris 1348
Southern Russia 1345
Venice 1348
Marseille 1347
Genoa 1347
Rome 1348
Constantinople 1347
**From Asia**
Seville 1348
Sicily 1347
*Mediterranean Sea*

## THE LONG-TERM EFFECTS

The Black Death destroyed many people's faith in God. To them it appeared to have no logic, killing good as well as bad people. Farms were abandoned and churches were empty. Until the onset of the Black Death, Europe usually had a surplus of labor and low wages, but the shortage of workers now made wages soar. Many country people began moving into the empty towns, working for actual money for the first time. The already weak feudal system collapsed. There were revolts. Europe and the Muslim world were in shock. Over the next 100 years, many things changed. The medieval period was making way for a new, more questioning, world.

People burned the clothes of the dead to try to stop the plague from spreading. This didn't work because the disease was caused by fleas living on rats that were found everywhere at the time.

▲ It was important to remove infected bodies quickly, even when people were still bewailing the loss of their loved ones. Criers went around the streets calling "Bring out your dead!"

◀ At night, plague carts were loaded with corpses to be taken away and buried. The Black Death spread quickly in towns because of the crowded housing conditions and lack of hygiene. Even isolated monasteries did not escape since the disease was carried there by infected people pleading for help.

171

# CHINA: THE MING DYNASTY 1368–1644

**After a long campaign, the Mongols were driven out of China. There then followed 150 years of peace and prosperity under the Ming dynasty.**

Emperor Hongwu (1328–1398) reorganized the administration of China and set up colleges for training mandarins (civil servants). Candidates for these posts had to pass examinations in literature and philosophy.

Kublai Khan was a great Chinese emperor, but he was a foreigner. When he died in 1294, he was followed by a series of feeble Yuan emperors, famines, and much hardship. The last Yuan emperor, Shundi, or Toghon Temür, was a bad ruler. The Chinese people were tired of being ruled harshly by foreigners. They found a Chinese ruler in Zhu Yuanzhang, who had been a monk and, during bad times, a beggar. As a rebel bandit chief, he had a ready-made army. He also proved to be an excellent general.

After a 13-year campaign, he captured Beijing, drove the Mongols back to Mongolia, and became emperor in 1368. He founded the Ming ("bright") dynasty, and took the name Hongwu ("very warlike"). He moved the capital south to the fortified city of Nanjing. Hongwu ruled China for 30 years as a dictator, guarding against Mongol incursions and restoring order and prosperity to his country.

▼ In Beijing, the Ming emperor Yongle built the Forbidden City, which only the emperor and his household were allowed to use. This is a typical building inside the imperial complex.

Art, literature, and ceramics had developed during the Song and the Yuan dynasties. This vase demonstrates another period of excellence in the arts under the Ming.

Hongwu left his throne to a grandson, Jianwen (born Zhu Yunwen), but he was overthrown four years later by his uncle Zhu Di, who became Emperor Yongle (pronounced *Yong-lay*) in 1403.

# PEACE UNDER THE MING

China grew great again under Yongle, who was emperor from 1403 to 1424. Roads, towns, and canals were rebuilt, and when he moved to Beijing, he built the great halls, palaces, and temples of the Forbidden City. Learning and the arts flourished. Trade and industry were encouraged, and, unusually, China looked outward, exporting goods and spreading Chinese influence abroad. The Muslim admiral Zheng He was sent on long voyages to India, the Middle East, and Africa. After Yongle's reign, however, China lost interest in other countries. Many Chinese settled in Southeast Asia, and became involved with the growing "China trade." Government administration was improved and, apart from problems with piracy and Mongol attacks, flourished for a century.

From 1517 onward, the Portuguese and other Europeans arrived on the coast, trading mainly in Guangzhou (Canton). In the late 1500s, there was a series of emperors who were disliked and wasteful, and there were attacks on the borders. Trade declined, corruption and banditry grew, and there was famine and rebellion. In 1592, the Japanese invaded neighboring Korea, thereby threatening the security of China. Rebels eventually took over much of China, and in 1644, the Ming dynasty finally fell.

Gardening and landscaping developed into a very special art form in China and Japan. Water was an important ingredient in this exquisite Chinese ornamental garden.

| KEY DATES | |
|---|---|
| 1353–54 | The Black Death breaks out across China |
| 1368 | The Ming dynasty is founded by Zhu Yuanzhang |
| 1403–24 | The reign of Ming Emperor Yongle |
| 1517 | Arrival of the first European traders in southern China |
| 1552–55 | Major attacks on shipping by pirates off the coast of China |
| 1582 | Growing corruption and decline |
| 1592 | The Japanese invade Korea, threatening China's security |
| 1644 | Fall of the Ming dynasty |

This brush holder, from the Ming period, is skilfully carved from elephant ivory. Carving in ivory became popular during the Ming dynasty, despite the dwindling elephant population in China.

Landscape painting also became a highly developed art form under the Ming. This Ming landscape painting of a mountain scene is by celebrated artist Shen Zhou (1427–1509).

# CONSTANTINOPLE 1204–1453

**The Byzantine Empire lasted 1,000 years. The Ottoman Turks eventually reached the doorstep of Constantinople, and had taken over the city by 1453.**

The Byzantine basilica of St. Sophia in Constantinople was turned into a mosque after the Ottoman takeover in 1453. The minarets were added at this time.

Byzantium had one major city—Constantinople. In the later centuries of its dominance, foreign powers moved ever closer to the city, and Byzantine territory was much reduced. The Byzantines were slowly losing heart. In 1204, Frankish and Norman Crusaders had taken the city, renaming it "the Latin Empire." The Greek Byzantines regained it in 1261, but but it never did recover. A series of civil wars also weakened the empire.

### THE OTTOMAN TURKS

Around 1070, before the Crusaders arrived, the Seljuk Turks had entered Anatolia, where they founded the sultanate of Rum. The Mongols destroyed it around 1240, and by 1280 the Ottoman Turks had started settling southeast of Constantinople. The Ottomans built up their empire quickly. They encircled the city and crossed into Europe, where, in 1361, they took Adrianople, making it their capital. Tamberlane defeated them in 1402, but from 1430 onward the Ottomans continued their expansion into Europe.

The Ottomans were in control of most of Greece, Bosnia, Albania, and Bulgaria by 1450, and tried to conquer Hungary. All that was left of the Byzantine Empire was Constantinople itself. In 1453, the Turks, led by Mehmet II, made a final assault on the city. The last Byzantine emperor, Constantine XI, had 10,000 men whereas Mehmet had between 100,000 and 150,000. The Turks even dragged 70 of their ships overland, bypassing Constantinople's outer sea defenses, to attack by surprise. Protected by strong walls, the Byzantines held out for 54 days until finally Mehmet's best troops overran the city, ending the Byzantine Empire.

A *janissary*, here in ceremonial dress, was an elite soldier of the Ottoman army. The first janissaries were young Christian prisoners of war whose life was spared if they converted to Islam and fought for the Turks.

Teams of oxen and thousands of soldiers dragged 70 small galleys of Mehmet II's fleet over a neck of land into an unprotected stretch of sea near Constantinople. They were able to bypass the Byzantine sea defenses and besiege the city.

Mehmet II was one of the most successful Ottoman sultans. He was well educated, built many public buildings, and repopulated Istanbul with people from all parts of his empire.

## A NEW BREED OF MUSLIMS

The Byzantine Empire had given birth to an outstanding medieval culture. Its decline was slow. It changed from a great power into a small country possessing a long history, but with little future. The Ottoman Turks, replacing the Byzantines, wanted to be involved in Europe. Many of their administrators were captured Europeans. The Ottomans were a new breed of Muslims who came from the East yet looked West. They occupied the traditional territory of the Byzantine Empire—the Balkans, the Black Sea, Anatolia, and Syria, and also invaded other lands. After Mehmet and his army overran Constantinople in 1453, the name of the city was changed to Istanbul, but life continued as before. However, the Muslims were now much closer to Europe, which caused the Europeans concern.

▲ This fresco from the Moldovita monastery in Romania, depicts the Ottoman siege of Constantinople in 1453, the final hour of Byzantine Empire's 1,000-year history.

▼ Castles were strategically built to guard the Bosphorus, the narrow sea route that connected the Black Sea with the Mediterranean.

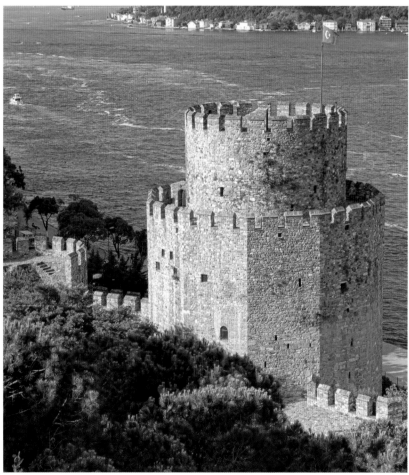

### KEY DATES

| | |
|---|---|
| 1071 | The Seljuks defeat the Byzantines, occupying Anatolia |
| 1204 | Crusaders capture Constantinople |
| 1243 | The Mongols destroy the Seljuk sultanate of Rum |
| 1261 | Byzantines retake Constantinople |
| 1280 | The Ottomans in Anatolia move close to Constantinople |
| 1389 | Ottomans defeat the Serbs in Kosovo |
| 1391 | Ottomans defeat European Crusaders in Romania |
| 1453 | The final fall of Constantinople |

# THE KHMER EMPIRE 802–1440

**The Khmer Empire was created in 802, when the Khmer people were united by Jayavarman II. It reached its peak under Suryavarman I and Suryavarman II.**

Around 400, the Khmer had created a state called Chen-la which was at its strongest around 700 under Jayavarman I. Previously Hindu, the Khmer adopted Buddhism during this time. Chen-la declined, and, after a brief occupation by the Javanese, a new Khmer state was created in 802 by Rajah Jayavarman II. He was a "god-king" or *devarajah* (like the Tibetan Dalai Lama today). He ruled from a city called Angkor Thom, near a lake called Tonle Sap. The Khmers wrote books on paper, palm leaves, and vellum. Fire, rot, and termites have long since destroyed them, but it is possible to learn about the Khmers from Chinese histories, and from the many carvings in the ruins of Angkor Thom ("great city") and Angkor Wat ("great temple") nearby.

The Khmer lived in what is now Cambodia. Their armies conquered many of the surrounding lands, dominating mainland Southeast Asia during the 1100s.

The building of Angkor Thom, originally called Yasodharapura, was started just before 900. The richly decorated temple complex of Angkor Wat was built between 1113 and 1150.

▼ Angkor Wat, a huge temple complex built of red sandstone, was surrounded by walls and a moat 590 ft. (180m) wide and 2.5 mi. (4km) long. The temple had three main enclosures (representing the outer world) surrounding an inner holy shrine.

The temple complex of Angkor Wat was richly decorated with many carved sandstone figures. The temple was abandoned in the 15th century and was brought to the attention of the wider world in the 19th century.

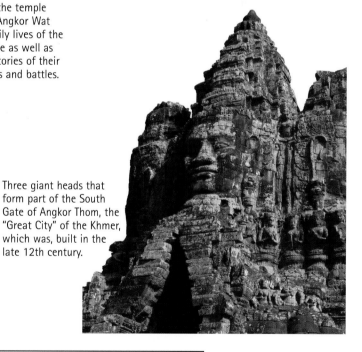

▲ Many of the temple carvings at Angkor Wat show the daily lives of the Khmer people as well as telling the stories of their sacred myths and battles.

The Khmer armies, which may have included hundreds of war elephants, fought many battles and conquered most of the surrounding lands, including Thailand and Champa (southern Vietnam). The empire reached its peak between 1010 and 1150, under Suryavarman I and Suryavarman II. During the 1200s, the people grew tired of serving the devarajahs through forced labor, and Khmer life began to break down. In 1444, invading Thai armies forced the Khmer to abandon Angkor. From then on, Cambodia was dominated by the Thai kingdom of Siam.

Three giant heads that form part of the South Gate of Angkor Thom, the "Great City" of the Khmer, which was, built in the late 12th century.

## KHMER DAILY LIFE

The Khmer were builders, craftworkers, fishermen, farmers, and warriors. Many lived in houses perched on stilts around Tonle Sap. Their main food was rice, and their special irrigation systems produced three crops a year. The kings were still Hindus, but most of the population was Buddhist. They held elaborate religious ceremonies in connection with the seasons of the year. They traded with India and Java, and also with China, bartering spices and rhinoceros horn for porcelain and lacquerware. The royal women of the court wore skirts, leaving the upper part of the body bare. They were encouraged to study law, astrology, and languages. Men wore only a loose loin covering.

| KEY DATES | |
|---|---|
| c.400 | Founding of Chen-la, after the fall of Funan |
| c.700 | Chen-la reaches its peak of development |
| 802 | Jayavarman II founds the Khmer nation by uniting the people |
| 880s | The Khmer conquer the Mon and Thai peoples |
| 900 | Angkor Thom founded |
| 1050–1150 | The Khmer Empire at its high point under Suryavarman I and Suryavarman II |
| 1113–50 | Angkor Wat is built |
| c.1215 | Death of last Angkor king, Jayavarman VII; empire starts to fall into decline |
| 1444 | Angkor abandoned after Thai invasions led by Ayutthaya |

These heavenly dancers were carved on one of the walls at Angkor Wat in about 1200.

# THE ARTS 1101–1460

This was a period of consolidation and improvement in the arts. The sense of invention and creativity of the early Middle Ages was developed further and refined.

During the late Middle Ages, artistic creativity around the world was blossoming. Medieval arts and music had developed, refining the styles and techniques created in the previous 500 years. There were now grander institutions, such as the Church, requiring artistic works, and there was a growing number of patrons—rich people who bought works of art and sponsored artists.

The arts of the Tang and the Song in China reached new heights of refinement in the Yuan and Ming periods. Ceramics, literature, music, theater, landscape painting and gardening, lacquerware, and sculpture all flourished.

Each noble family in Europe had its own coat of arms. Heraldry used many different symbols to tell a story about the family's history and aims.

This enamel reliquary was made in Limoges, France, in the 1180s. It depicts the murder of St Thomas à Becket in Canterbury, England in 1170.

In Japan, local styles replaced the imported Chinese styles which had been adopted earlier. In comparison, the Toltecs and Aztecs took on and adapted earlier styles from Teotihuacán and the Maya. Islamic art, now a long-standing tradition, was modernized by different schools of thought in Spain, Morocco, Egypt, and Samarkand. In Europe, most art and music was created for the Church, including stained glass, tapestry, and choral music. During the 1300s and 1400s, some artists, working privately, began to paint pictures in a realistic style.

▼ During the Ming dynasty, the Chinese made ornamental blue-and-white pottery in the imperial factories. Later, many pieces were exported to Europe.

◄ Stained-glass windows were made from pieces of colored glass, joined together with strips of lead. This window in Chartres Cathedral, France, depicts the life of St Nicholas and was made in 1220–1225.

▼ These two Aztec women are making cloth. One is spinning raw cotton into yarn for the other to weave on a backstrap loom. One end was tied to the woman's belt.

▼ In Europe there was a tradition of street theater at markets and festivals. Popular plays were performed on the back of a wagon, or on a makeshift stage.

In Europe, there were mystery plays based on the Bible or on traditional myths, and poems about heroes such as Charlemagne and King Arthur. Geoffrey Chaucer wrote about courtly love and ordinary people. Books were available to a wider public as they began to be written in local languages, rather than in Latin.

◄ Wooden furniture and wall panels were often carved with scenes from stories. This scene is from *The Pardoner's Tale* by Geoffrey Chaucer from his great *Canterbury Tales*. It shows Death teaching a lesson to three men.

◄ The temple complex at Angkor Wat, in present-day Cambodia, was built during the peak of the Khmer Empire in the 1100s. Its sandstone walls were carved with pictures of the Khmer people, their daily lives, myths, and battles. This wall depicts the army of King Suryavarman II on the march.

# ARCHITECTURE 1101–1460

Throughout the world, remarkable craftsmanship and technical advances led to the construction of imposing and elegant buildings during the Middle Ages.

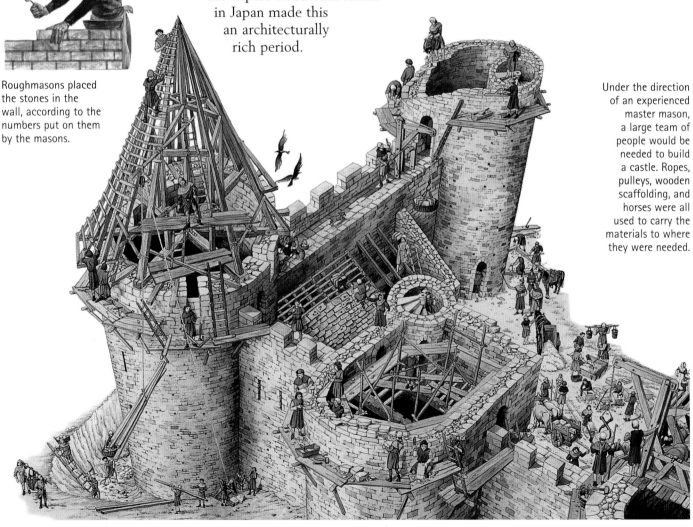

Freemasons, or masons, were skilled and valued workers. They cut and shaped stones accurately for use in building.

Roughmasons placed the stones in the wall, according to the numbers put on them by the masons.

Most people in Europe built houses with wood because it was cheap and plentiful. Unfortunately, it caught fire easily and tended to rot. Therefore, important buildings were constructed in stone. Castles and city walls were built with thick, well-laid stones. Cathedrals were designed in a new Gothic style. Instead of the rounded arches and sturdy pillars of the older Romanesque style, they had pointed arches, slender pillars, and high stained-glass windows. Worldwide, buildings were becoming finer in shape and less bulky. The carved decorations of Khmer temples, the roofs of Ming palaces, and temples in China, and the expert woodwork found in Japan made this an architecturally rich period.

Most castle walls had slots called loopholes. They were narrow on the outside and wide on the inside, letting the archers shoot out, but attackers could not shoot in.

## MUSLIM ARCHITECTURE

The arrival of the Ottoman Turks in the Muslim world brought a new lease on life to Islamic architecture. Earlier Islamic styles gave way to Seljuk and Persian influences, different from earlier styles in detail and shape. The newest Muslim architecture came from Turkey, Morocco, Afghanistan, and Samarkand, where arches, domes, pillars, and mosaics were developed.

Under the direction of an experienced master mason, a large team of people would be needed to build a castle. Ropes, pulleys, wooden scaffolding, and horses were all used to carry the materials to where they were needed.

Gothic-style cathedrals were taller and lighter than earlier ones. They were built according to carefully worked out engineering principles, and they took years to build.

Timur, the last great Mongol leader, was buried in a beautiful jade-covered vault in Samarkand. This is one of the finest examples of Islamic art from this period.

In South America, high in the Andes, the Inca city of Machu Picchu was a remarkable feat of engineering. Here, the Incas built high walls of massive stones which fit together so exactly that not even an earthquake could move them. The city still stands today. The Tibetans built monasteries clinging to precipitous Himalayan mountainsides—such as the Potala in Lhasa. During the 1200s, the Ethiopians carved Christian churches out of solid rock, making them safe from any form of attack. These rock-cut churches still survive, as do many other grand buildings around the world from this period.

Stonecutters left their own special marks to identify their work. Some of them also carved the faces of people they knew on the gargoyles and other decorations around the churches they built.

In India and Southeast Asia, stonecutting was at a peak of development during this period. This ornately carved stone gate guarded the entrance to a temple in Orissa, India.

# Science and Technology 1101–1460

**The spread of knowledge from China and Muslim countries led to a new fascination with learning that swept through Europe in the Middle Ages.**

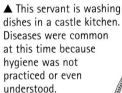

Eyeglasses for farsighted people were first worn in about 1285. Those for nearsighted people were not invented until around 1430.

The Chinese, the Indians, and the Arabs were still ahead of the rest of the world in science and technology. Crusaders returning to Europe from Palestine brought with them Arabic knowledge of medicine, technology, astronomy, and mathematics. The city-states of Venice and Genoa, exposed to Asian influences through trade, often received these ideas first. The great Italian mathematician, Fibonacci, based his work on knowledge gleaned from Arabic texts. In England, Roger Bacon, one of the earliest Western scientists, based his ideas of reflection and refraction on works brought in from Muslim Spain and Egypt.

## PRINTING

Knowledge of papermaking spread to Europe from Arabia at the end of this period. The Koreans and Chinese had also invented movable-type printing, and this was later developed in Europe, setting off a revolution in knowledge. But for most of this period, all books were still written by hand, and most people in Europe could not read.

▲ This servant is washing dishes in a castle kitchen. Diseases were common at this time because hygiene was not practiced or even understood.

The great Mongol emperor of China, Kublai Khan, founded the Institute of Muslim Astronomy in Beijing in the 1200s, to observe important planetary events. China had a special government astronomy department.

## ADVANCES IN CHINA

Chinese writing and education was very advanced, and Chinese medicine, mathematics, and other sciences were already well developed. The government administrators, called mandarins, were actually required to be scholarly. This helped the progress of Chinese sciences and technologies. The Mongols also brought foreign ideas with them, which would later benefit Ming China.

This is a special Aztec calendar stone that uses their system of 20-day months. Each year had 18 months, as well as a final five unlucky days (*nemontemi*) The figure in the center is the sun god Tonatiuh.

Monks distilled alcohol (aqua vitae—the water of life) from wine to make alcoholic beverages. Fermented cereals were used to make whiskey.

Waterpowered wheels were used to drive simple machinery such as the hammer used in ironworking (shown here). This process made metalworking much easier.

## THE SPREAD OF KNOWLEDGE

There was a new spirit of inquiry in the air. The Arabs learned from the East, and the Europeans learned from the Arabs. When the first Westerners, such as the Venetian Marco Polo, went East, they took European ideas with them. More knowledge from ancient Greece came to Europe after the fall of the Byzantine Empire, when many scholars fled from Constantinople to Italy. When Admiral Zheng He sailed from China to India, Arabia, and Africa, his fleets carried scholars and collectors to gather items and information from the places they visited.

◀▲ Early medieval books were entirely handmade. Scribes wrote on sheets of parchment which were bound together with wooden boards. This made books rare and expensive.

Once people started printing with movable type, books could be produced more quickly and efficiently. Although this made books cheaper, only the rich could afford them or knew how to read.

The Chinese were skilled ironworkers. A group of workers can be seen here forging a large ship's anchor in the 1300s.

## WHEN IT HAPPENED

**1100** Returning Crusaders bring Arabic knowledge back to Europe
**1202** Fibonacci, an Italian mathematician, writes about Hindu-Arabic numbering
**1260** Englishman Roger Bacon describes the laws of reflection and refraction
**1275** First human dissection carried out
**1397** Movable type produced in Korea

# THE RENAISSANCE

## 1461–1600

Renaissance means "rebirth." In the late
Middle Ages, there was a revival of interest
in humanism and Greeks and Romans works.
During the Renaissance, this developed into a
burst of intellectual energy and scholarship, in
art, architecture, music, drama, literature, and
the sciences. The Europeans' discovery of the
Americas expanded their horizons, but also led
to an invasion of this New World, slavery, the
beginnings of colonialism, empire building,
and capitalist economics. This was our
entry into the modern world.

▲ The Inca celebrated two festivals of the sun. One was in June,
the other in December. The emperor led the ceremonies, attended
by officials from all over the empire, in the great square at Cusco.

◄ This is a detail from "Madonna of the Magnificat," painted by
Italian Renaissance artist Sandro Botticelli in 1465.

# THE AZTECS 1430–1520

**During the 1400s, the Aztecs dominated Mexico from the wondrous city of Tenochtitlan, dominated by pyramids, on an island in the middle of a lake.**

The Aztecs had started to expand in 1430, under the emperor Itzcóatl, and by 1500, they controlled a large empire in Mexico. Tenochtitlan had a population of about 300,000, and was at its most powerful, under Montezuma II (also known as Moctezuma II). In order to feed everyone, food was grown on artificial islands, or *chinampas*, built up in Lake Texcoco, in the middle of which the city stood. Conquered lands provided corn, beans, and cocoa, cotton cloth, and gold, silver, and jade for Aztec craftworkers. Traders bought turquoise from the Pueblo Indians in the north, and from the south came brightly colored feathers, which were used to make elaborately decorated capes, fans, headdresses, and shields. Aztec society was organized along military lines. All young men served in the army from the age of 17 to 22. Some stayed longer than this, because even a peasant could rise to be an army commander if he was good enough.

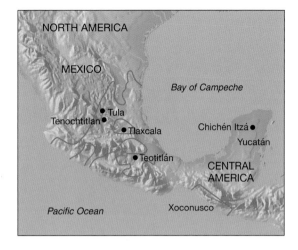

The Aztecs dominated the center of Mexico from coast to coast, including several cities. They also influenced much wider areas to the north and south.

## HUMAN SACRIFICES

One of the main tasks of the army was to take many prisoners of war. The prisoners were sacrificed in Tenochtitlan, at the huge pyramid-temples in the middle of the city. Religious blood sacrifice was important to the Aztecs who sacrificed to many different gods. All of these gods were believed to need a great deal of human blood—especially the god of war, Huitzilopochtli. This armed aggression and human sacrifice gradually turned the Aztecs' neighbors against them.

▲ Priests were powerful in Aztec society. They did not marry, and they were responsible for conducting all of the many ceremonies in the Aztec 260-day calendar. They also carried out human sacrifices, using knives with blades made from very sharp stone, such as chalcedony, flint, or obsidian.

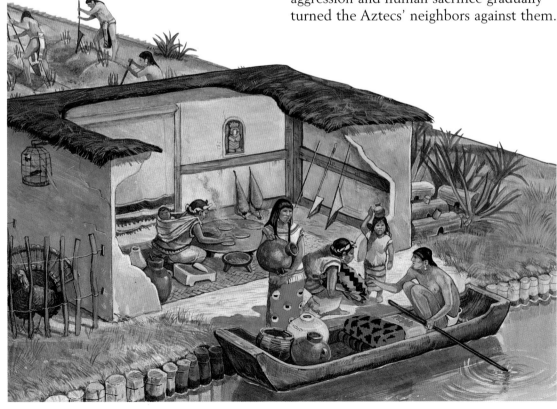

► Ordinary Aztecs lived in huts with thatched roofs. They ate pancakes made from cornmeal, with spicy bean and vegetable fillings, very like Mexican tortillas today.

This ceremonial headdress from the 1500s is made mainly of quetzal feathers. Parrot feathers in brown, crimson, white, and blue were also used.

## RISE AND FALL OF THE AZTECS

The Aztecs traded far and wide around Mexico, into what is now the United States, and south to Colombia. They sold high-value items made by craftworkers—clothing, jewelry, and household and ceremonial items. They also exacted tribute—payments made by cities to keep the Aztecs from invading them. The capital, Tenochtitlan, was one of the world's best-planned cities. The streets and canals were laid out in a grid pattern on its lake island, and arranged around a huge ceremonial area of pyramids, temples, palaces, and gardens. Three wide causeways linked the city to the mainland. But the Aztecs' greed for sacrificial victims meant that, when the Spanish arrived in 1519, their neighboring societies helped them conquer the Aztecs by the following year.

▲ The emperor was treated like a god, and he could be spoken to only by priests and nobles. Ordinary people had to keep their eyes down when the ruler traveled through the capital.

◀ This terracotta statue bears the hideously grinning skull face of the Aztec god of death. The Aztecs used human skulls to make masks. They encrusted them with turquoise and seashells and lined them inside with red leather.

▼ Three long causeways linked Tenochtitlan to the mainland. Traders traveled far and wide from the city, and some of them acted as spies for the emperor. The causeways were also a good defense for the city. When the Spanish arrived, it was trickery and disease, not direct attack, that helped them overcome the Aztecs.

187

# THE INCA EMPIRE 1438–1533

**For a century, the Incas ruled a vast, well-organized, mountaintop empire, high in the Andes in South America. Their empire was obliterated by the Spanish.**

This golden pendant made by the Incas has markings showing mathematical patterns. These had a religious and calendrical significance for the Incas.

The Inca ruler was known as the *Sapa Inca*. He was believed to be descended from Inti, the sun god, who gave him the right to rule. He was also worshiped as a god himself. The Sapa Inca ran the country from Cusco, thought to be Inti's home. Royal officials oversaw and directed everything in all parts of the empire. They looked after the affairs of the cities, and made sure the factories and workshops that produced pottery, textiles, and decorative metal objects, as well as the farms, were all working efficiently. Writing was unknown to the Incas, so they kept all their records on *quipus*. These were cords with knots tied in them to convey information, such as records of population and taxes. At its greatest period in 1525, the empire stretched for 2,200 mi. (3,500km). The cities, towns, and villages were all linked by a network of roads. Communication was provided by relay runners.

The Incas were skillful engineers. Their vast empire was linked by stone-covered roads that crisscrossed the high mountains of the Andes, which form the backbone of South America.

## INCA EXPANSION

When Pachacuti became the Sapa Inca in 1438, he began to expand his lands around Cusco. In 1450, he conquered the Titicaca basin; and in 1463, he went to war against the Lupaca and Colla tribes. Under his son Tupac Inca Yupanqui's command, the Inca army defeated the neighboring Chimu Empire in 1466, and Tupac Inca Yupanqui continued to expand the empire after he became the tenth Sapa Inca in 1471. During the next 15 years, he conquered lands far to the south, and later took control of lands to the north and west.

▲ A *quipu* was a length of string, or cord, from which several strings hung. These were in different colors, and each had knots in it. "Quipu" comes from the word for knot. By its style, color, and position, each knot was a valuable piece of information, usually a number. The Incas would hold up the long cord at the top and "read" the information in the downward rows.

▶ The Incas cut terraces into the Andes with wooden tools. Alpacas and llamas grazed on higher ground, and the Incas grew corn, pumpkins, quinoa, and fruit lower down.

# RISE AND FALL OF THE INCAS

The Incas reached a very high level of technology and organization, and came up with ingenious ways of farming on steep slopes, and building bridges, roads, and towns high in the mountains.

Tupac Inca Yupanqui built many of these roads and towns. His son, Huayna Capac, the Sapa Inca from 1493, further expanded the empire, building a second capital at Quito. When he died in 1525, the empire was divided between his sons: Huascar ruled the south, and Atahualpa the north. This division led to civil war just before the Spanish landed in 1532. The invaders took advantage of the road system while the Incas argued among themselves, and the Spanish were able to destroy the empire by 1533.

| KEY DATES | |
|---|---|
| 1200 | Manco Capac establishes the Inca dynasty and capital of Cusco |
| 1350 | Local expansion of the Incas under Mayta Capa |
| 1438 | Pachacuti becomes the Sapa Inca |
| 1450 | Pachacuti greatly enlarges the Inca Empire |
| 1466 | Tupac Inca overruns the Chimu Empire |
| 1485 | Tupac Inca conquers Chile and Peru |
| 1493 | Quito becomes the second capital |
| 1525 | Huayna Capa dies, and civil war breaks out between Cusco and Quito |
| 1532 | The Spanish invade the Inca Empire |
| 1533 | The Spanish destroy the Inca Empire |

▲ Two main roads ran the length of the empire. They were connected with every town and village by smaller roads. Goods were carried by trains of llamas. Quipus were delivered by relay runners.

▲ Relay runners carried official messages and packages throughout the empire. Each runner ran about 1 mi. (1.5km) before the next one took over. To make sure of a quick changeover, a runner announced his approach by blowing on a conch shell.

◀ Each year, the Incas would celebrate the Great Festival of the sun, to give thanks for the growth of crops and the continuation of life, and to pray for blessings in the future—not unlike the Christian festival of Easter.

# THE RECONQUEST OF SPAIN 1469–1516

The reconquest of Muslim-ruled Spain by the Spanish began during the 1100s. The country was fully reunited 300 years later, under Ferdinand and Isabella.

▲ Ferdinand (1452–1516) succeeded to the throne of Aragon. He was a tough politician and ruled Spain together with his wife, Isabella.

▲ Isabella (1451–1504) inherited the kingdom of Castile. She and her husband, Ferdinand, eventually became rulers of all Spain.

After the fall of the Roman Empire, Spain had been ruled by the Visigoths for 300 years. Then came the invading Berbers (Moors) from northern Africa in 711, establishing a Muslim caliphate which lasted from 756 until 1031. At this time, Christians in the north of Spain started pushing southward. They started a *reconquista* (reconquest) which, by 1235, had limited the Muslims to Granada in the south of the country.

However, Catholic Spain was divided into several countries—León, Castile, Navarre, and Aragon. In the 1400s, León had joined with Castile, making Castile and Aragon the two largest. The first step toward finally uniting Spain was made in 1469 when Ferdinand, heir to Aragon, married Isabella of Castile. When the king of Castile died in 1474, Isabella and Ferdinand succeeded him as joint rulers of his kingdom. Five years later, Ferdinand inherited Aragon and made Isabella joint ruler of Aragon as well.

▼ The Christian armies of Aragon and Castile defeated the Moors in 1492, and the Moors were driven back to North Africa where they were shown no mercy.

Spain was divided for much of the 1400s, though the uniting of Aragon and Castile in 1479 made the eventual union of Spain almost inevitable.

## THE SPANISH INQUISITION

Many Muslims and Jews had converted to Christianity and stayed in Spain, making a great contribution to its culture. But their success was resented. The king and queen decided that all non-Christians should leave Spain. They wanted to find those who had "converted" but still followed the old religion secretly. Spain used religion as a political weapon. The pope gave permission for an Inquisition, a court that investigated heresy, but the Spanish misused the power and imprisoned, tortured, and killed thousands of people.

## THE REUNIFICATION OF SPAIN

In 1492, fourteen years after the Spanish Inquisition began, Moorish Granada was recaptured by Aragon and Castile. Many Muslims and Jews were expelled or forcibly converted—as many as 200,000 Jews left the country. This persecution resulted in many skilled and able people moving away to France, Germany, and the Ottoman Empire.

In the same year, Ferdinand and Isabella sponsored the voyage of Christopher Columbus—they were seeking a sea route to India and China, but instead found the Americas. This began a period of Spanish conquest that brought about the downfall of the Aztecs, Maya, and Incas.

Ferdinand and Isabella had five daughters, one of whom, Catherine of Aragon, married Henry VIII of England. But Ferdinand and Isabella had no son, and descent passed through their daughter Joanna. When Isabella died in 1504, Ferdinand acted as regent for the young Joanna. In 1515, Navarre joined Castile, and Ferdinand finally became king of a united Spain. Joanna's son, Charles V, eventually became the Hapsburg emperor, the most powerful ruler in Europe. Under his rule, Spain experienced its golden age.

A map of the world based on Ptolemy's *Geographia*, shows how the world was thought to look in 1486, before world exploration by Europeans really began.

▲ Boabdil, the last Moorish emir of Granada, leaves the city after the conquest by Aragon and Castile in 1492, ending a long era of Muslim rule in Spain.

### KEY DATES

| | |
|---|---|
| 1248 | The Christians reconquer most of Spain |
| 1469 | The marriage of Ferdinand and Isabella |
| 1474 | Isabella inherits Castile |
| 1478 | The Spanish Inquisition is established |
| 1479 | Aragon and Castile are united |
| 1492 | The conquest of Granada—end of Muslim rule in southern Spain. Christopher Columbus' expedition to India is financed by Isabella |
| 1504 | Isabella dies |
| 1515 | Navarre joins Castile—Spain is finally united |
| 1516 | Ferdinand dies |

▲ During the Spanish Inquisition, books that were written by people suspected of heresy were burned. This painting by Pedro Berruguete not only celebrates the Catholic victory in Spain, but also vividly illustrates the power of the Inquisition.

# THE RENAISSANCE 1450–1600

**The Renaissance was a bridge from medieval to modern culture. It was a revolutionary period in the arts and sciences that eventually changed the whole world.**

Developed in the 1440s, Gutenberg's printing press with movable type made books available to people throughout Europe for the first time.

Renaissance architects copied the elegant styles of Ancient Greece and Rome for buildings such as the Tempietto in Rome.

During the 14th century, life in Europe had been affected by wars, peasant revolts, and the Black Death. The old order was dying, and people were seeking something new. In medieval times, the Church had dominated the arts, education, and learning. People had accepted what they were told without asking questions. Then, in the 1300s, Italian scholars began to take an interest in the writings of the ancient Greeks and Romans—ideas that passed into Europe from the Byzantine empire and the Arab world. This interest grew when, in 1397, Manuel Chrysoloras, a scholar from Constantinople, became the first professor of Greek at the University of Florence in northern Italy. Scholars became fascinated by the questions that ancient philosophers dealt with. From these studies grew a belief system called *humanism*. Suddenly people, not God, were considered responsible for choosing the course of their lives. After the fall of the Byzantine Empire and Muslim Spain in the 1400s, many scholars moved to Italy and northwestern Europe, taking many old manuscripts and ideas with them.

▼ Sandro Botticelli (1445–1510) was an Italian artist famous for his religious and mythological paintings, such as "The Adoration of the Kings." He was sponsored by the influential Medici family of Florence.

During the Renaissance, the ideal person was the "universal" man or woman. This was someone who was educated to be skillful in a variety of subjects including literature, painting, science, music, and philosophy.

## THE PEAK OF THE RENAISSANCE

The Renaissance affected art and science, architecture and sculpture. Ideas became more realistic, more human, and less dominated by religion. Paintings and statues were more lifelike, music explored new feelings, and books asked real-life questions. Rich families such as the Medicis and the Borgias in Italy and the burghers of Holland became patrons of the arts and sciences. Printed books helped to spread new ideas. The Italian Renaissance peaked in Venice and Florence, matched by a Northern Renaissance in Antwerp and Haarlem. People looked closely at the world, made detailed scientific observations, collected exotic objects, and considered new ideas.

## THE NEW SPIRIT OF INQUIRY

Some people studied plants and animals. Others investigated astronomy and geology. Sometimes their findings brought them into conflict with the Church. When Nicolaus Copernicus (1473–1543) realized that the Earth moved around the sun, he dared not publish his views until he was actually on his deathbed. He feared the reaction of the Church, which continued to insist that the Earth stood at the center of the universe.

This new spirit of inquiry and interest in humanity eventually led some people to question the authority of the Church. Thinkers such as Jan Hus in Bohemia and John Wycliffe in England began to question the Church openly. People's own opinions became more important— rulers and the Church could no longer do just as they pleased.

## THE BIRTH OF A MODERN WORLD

Demand for change led to advances in science and art, and even caused some people to set sail for unexplored lands. New universities encouraged new ideas. Money and trade also became significant. Foods and products such as coffee, sugar, tobacco, potatoes, pineapples, porcelain, and cotton were imported to Europe from Africa, America, India, and China.

No longer bound to the land by feudalism, people began to move around. Many of them went to cities to seek their fortune. Northwestern Europe grew in importance, and power shifted slowly from the nobles and clerics to the bankers and politicians. These changes marked the beginning of a modern world that was to develop rapidly over the next 400 years.

The Dutch scholar and humanist Desiderius Erasmus (1467–1536), was critical of the Catholic Church and, later, of the Reformers, especially Luther.

## EVERYDAY LIFE IN FLORENCE

Florence, in Italy, was one of the great centers of Renaissance learning and art. Lorenzo de' Medici became joint ruler of the city with his brother Giuliano, in 1469, and was a powerful patron to many writers, artists, and scientists. The city grew rich from trade and commerce, its people wore fine clothes, and its streets thronged with skilled craftspeople.

# ITALY 1460–1530

**During this period, Italy was divided into small states. This made for great variation—some states were progressive while others were more conservative.**

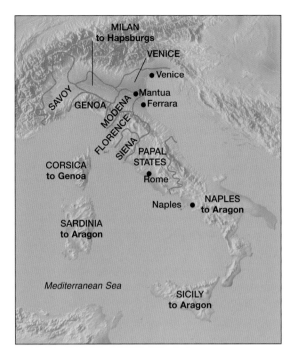

During the Middle Ages, much of Italy was controlled by the Holy Roman Empire. Following a power struggle between emperors and popes, many cities formed their own independent states.

To further the ambitions of her father, Rodrigo, (Pope Alexander VI), Lucrezia Borgia (1480–1519) was married three times. With her third husband, the Duke of Ferrara, she became a great patron of the arts. Their court became a magnet for artists and writers. She is also known for her devotion to causes involving children and education.

Many Italian states, such as Florence, Venice, and Rome, were really large cities. Others were ruled by dukes, as in Mantua, Milan, Urbino, and Ferrara. Most of these states were ruled by families who had grown rich from trade and commerce in the late Middle Ages.

The most powerful family of the time was the Medici family of Florence. They had made a great fortune during the 1300s through banking and moneylending. The best known of the Medicis is Lorenzo, who became joint ruler of Florence with his brother in 1469. He was a cunning statesman and banker as well as a patron of writers, artists, philosophers, and scientists. He was eager to promote his family and saw his second son become pope. Under Lorenzo's influence, Florence became one of the most beautiful and prosperous cities in Italy, and a center of the Renaissance. Lorenzo helped make the form of Italian spoken in Florence into the language of the whole country.

Another family, the Borgias, sought power through the Church and the military. Two Borgias became pope. One of them, Rodrigo, schemed to help his children. When he died, the family's power collapsed.

## LORENZO DE' MEDICI

In 1469, when he was 20 years old, Lorenzo became joint ruler of Florence with his brother Giuliano. He was the grandson of Cosimo de' Medici, who was the second Medici to hold power in Florence. Lorenzo's brother was killed in a plot by a rival family in 1478. Lorenzo did everything he could to further his family's interests—his second son Giovanni became Pope Leo X—and to build a large gathering of scholars and creative people. He was the first patron of the artist Michelangelo. He maintained and expanded the family traditions of banking and government.

▼ The Medici villa at Florence was built in 1480 for Lorenzo the Magnificent by Renaissance architect Giuliano da Sangallo.

Lorenzo de' Medici (1449–1492)—"The Magnificent" – ruled Florence from 1478 to 1492.

◄ The magnificent city of Florence was at the height of its powers during the late 1400s. Ruled by the Medicis, it became home to many great artists, architects, writers, and scientists of the Renaissance. Florence also became one of Europe's main business and banking centers.

The Sforzas were a great family of Milan. Ludovico Sforza (1452–1508), was a man of taste, but also one with ruthless ambition. He ruled as regent for his nephew, the duke of Milan, but made himself the real center of power. He made alliances with Rodrigo Borgia and married a daughter of the powerful d'Este family, from Ferrara. Ludovico's court attracted great artists from all fields, among them Leonardo da Vinci.

Families like the Medicis represented "new money," with new values and ideas. They paid for exploration, centers of learning, public works, and new, imported products. People traveled to Italy to learn new ideas, which were taken back to other parts of Europe, and Europeans flocked to Florence, Venice, and Milan to gain support for their own ideas. Although future centers of modern development were to be in northwestern Europe, much of the energy of the early Renaissance came from the city-states of Italy.

◄ Raphael was influenced by the work of Da Vinci and Michelangelo in Florence. This is his "Deposition of Christ," which he painted in 1507 at the age of 24. The following year Pope Julius II asked him to do a major work in the Vatican in Rome.

► Wealthy Renaissance people enjoyed a very comfortable life. In addition to palaces or large city residences, many had country villas where they welcomed groups of visitors. They would spend time hunting, holding parties, discussing literature, and writing poetry.

# EUROPEAN EXPLORERS 1460–1600

**During the second half of the 1400s, European sailors and navigators planned voyages which would take them far beyond the limits of the world they knew.**

In 1488, Bartholomeu Dias (1450–1500) sailed around Africa's Cape of Good Hope in a terrible storm—thereafter it was feared as the "Cape of Storms."

Vasco da Gama (1469–1525) rounded the Cape of Good Hope in 1497, and sailed up the east coast of Africa. With the help of an Indian sailor, he then crossed the Indian Ocean to Calicut in India, returning home with a cargo of spices. He went back to India to defend Portuguese interests and was made viceroy of India in 1524.

The urge to explore was partly a result of a new interest in the world, encouraged by the Renaissance; but the main intention was to bypass the Islamic world in order to set up new trading links with India and the Far East, the source of spices and other luxuries. Until the fall of the Byzantine Empire in 1453, spices were brought overland to Constantinople and then carried across the Mediterranean to Europe. In spite of their expense, spices were essential. The only way to preserve meat was by salting it. Adding spices helped hide the salty taste, and they also concealed the taste of meat which had spoiled despite being salted.

The Portuguese had set up harbors and forts along the west coast of Africa, trading with the Africans in gold, ivory, and silver. Gradually, they sailed farther south, and in 1488, Bartholomeu Dias sailed around the tip of southern Africa—pushed by a fierce gale. His frightened, exhausted crew refused to go any farther. Nine years later, Dias helped Vasco da Gama plan a voyage around the Cape of Good Hope to Calicut in India.

A sailor's personal property from the year 1536, salvaged from the wreck of Henry VIII's flagship, the *Mary Rose*. It includes a pouch, a whistle, a rosary, and a comb.

Vasco da Gama was followed by Pedro Cabral who returned from India with a cargo of pepper. This encouraged other navigators to try to sail farther east. In 1517, the Portuguese had reached China, and nearly 30 years later they had arrived in Japan. The Portuguese were driven not only by trading possibilities, but also by a determination to spread Christianity to the peoples of the East.

▶ Vasco da Gama's small ships were a development of the traditional caravel, with its triangular lateen sail. His ships had both square and lateen sails, making them more maneuverable and adaptable on the seas.

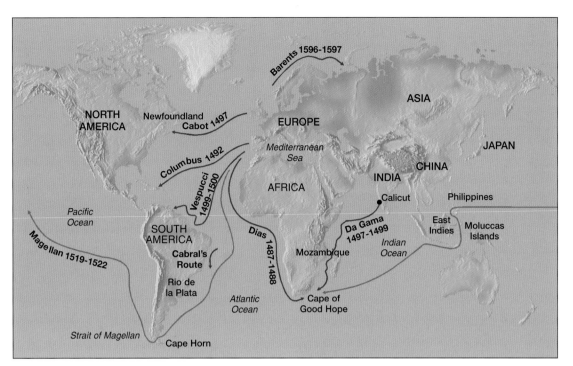

◄ Navigators from Europe tried many routes to reach the Spice Islands, the Moluccas. They discovered more than they expected, opening up new routes and laying the foundations of future empires.

▲ Although Portuguese by birth, Ferdinand Magellan (1480–1521) sailed for Spain. He led the first expedition to sail around the world, and gave the Pacific Ocean its name.

## WESTWARD EXPLORATION

While the Portuguese sailed east, the Spanish sailed west. In 1492, Columbus found the West Indies. Amerigo Vespucci reached South America in 1499, but didn't realize until his voyage of 1501 that he had found a new continent. In 1497, John Cabot, a Venetian sponsored by England's Henry VII, discovered Newfoundland. In 1535, Jacques Cartier sailed up the St. Lawrence River, claiming the area for France. Ferdinand Magellan rounded South America in 1519. He died in the Philippines, but part of his crew returned to Spain in 1522—the first explorers to sail around the world.

## CHRISTOPHER COLUMBUS

In 1492, Queen Isabella sponsored Christopher Columbus, a navigator from Genoa in Italy, to find a western route to India. It is possible that he knew of America from Viking tales he had heard in Iceland. Most people believed the world was much smaller than it really was. When Columbus reached a group of islands across the Atlantic, he called them the West Indies. They were in fact the islands of the Caribbean. Columbus made three more voyages there, but it is not known whether he really knew if they were America or Asia.

▲ Christopher Columbus (1451–1506) first went to sea at the age of fourteen. He was shipwrecked and washed up on the coast of Portugal.

◄ When Christopher Columbus and his crew landed on Guanahani in the Bahamas, he claimed it for Spain.

# THE SONGHAY EMPIRE 1460–1603

**Songhay replaced and enlarged the state of Mali. During the 1200s, Mali itself had replaced Ghana as the dominant gold-trading nation of West Africa.**

The city of Timbuktu, a center of trade and learning, was brutally captured by Sonni Ali of Songhai in 1468.

When Europeans arrived in Africa in the 1460s, the continent had many states and kingdoms. Tradition has Songhay founded in the 600s by a Berber Christian called al-Yaman, beside the Niger River. By 1200, the rulers moved to Gao, farther up the Niger, where they converted to Islam. Songhay became part of Mali in 1325, after Gao was captured by Mansa Muse, the Muslim emperor of Mali. In 1464, Sonni Ali made Songhay independent again and expanded its territory, taking over Mali, including Timbuktu and Djenné. Songhay became rich and powerful, dominating West Africa. Sonni Ali was cruel and immoral, and persecuted religious people. He drowned in 1492, and in 1493, Askia Mohammed I founded a new dynasty. Under his leadership, Songhay grew, trading gold, first with the Arabs, then with the Portuguese. Askia was a good ruler—he respected religious beliefs and rebuilt Songhay's society. Timbuktu again became an international center of learning.

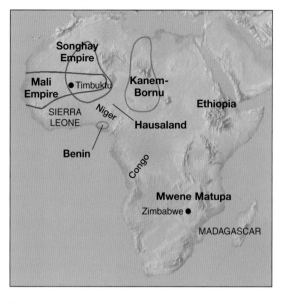

Early European explorers who settled on the coasts of Africa knew nothing about its rich interior. Songhay traded its gold and slaves for luxury goods and salt.

## THE DECLINE OF SONGHAY

In 1528, Askia Mohammed I was deposed by his son, and a succession of weak and corrupt rulers followed. Songhay grew weaker, and finally fell to the Moroccans in 1591. Songhay was not the only state in West Africa. To the east was Kanem–Bornu, an African empire which grew around Lake Chad. By 1100, it had become a center of Muslim civilization, reaching its peak under Idris Aloma, who came to power in 1571 and ruled until 1603.

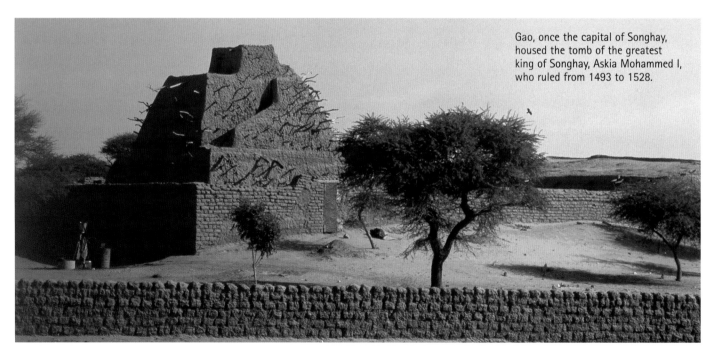

Gao, once the capital of Songhay, housed the tomb of the greatest king of Songhay, Askia Mohammed I, who ruled from 1493 to 1528.

# SAFAVID PERSIA 1500–1722

At the beginning of the 1500s, Persia regained
independence under the Safavid dynasty. Persia soon
became one of the leading cultures of the world.

▲ This fragment of a
military standard from
Safavid Persia was used in
ceremonies to honor those
who had been killed in
battle. It was made
of precious metals and
richly inlaid with
precious stones.

Persians had been prominent in the
Abbasid Empire since 642, and then
again under the Seljuks and Mongol
Ilkhans. After a period of disorder, the
Safavid dynasty came to power after the
they captured the city of Tabriz in 1501,
making Persia independent. Their leader
was Ismail I who had himself crowned
*shah*, or ruler. The name "Safavid" came
from Ismail's ancestor Safi od-Din, a Sufi
holy man who lived around 1300. By
1508, Ismail controlled all of Persia and
most of Mesopotamia. He established
Shiite Islam as the state religion. Doctrinal
differences, together with disputes over
land, led to a long series of Muslim
religious wars between the Shiite Safavids
and the Sunni Ottomans. They started in
1514 when the Ottoman sultan, Selim
I, invaded western Persia. Under the
Safavids, Persia developed its own identity
after centuries of foreign domination, and
the powerful dynasty lasted for 200 years.

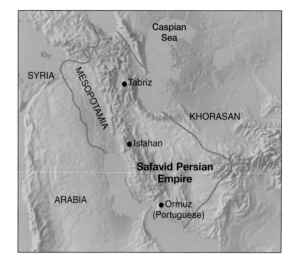

Under the Safavids, Persia again became independent
and a major power in the region. They made friends and
traded with the Portuguese, though they were troubled
by the Ottomans to the west and the Turks to the east.

Safavid Persia was continually under
pressure from Ottomans in the west
and Uzbeks in the east, until the reign
of Abbas I who made peace and created
a cultural renaissance in Persia. After his
death in 1629, a series of weak shahs
followed, and the Safavids were brought
down by invading Afghans in 1722.

## ABBAS THE GREAT

The Safavid dynasty reached its peak under Shah Abbas
the Great (1571–1629), who ruled from 1587. A good
military leader, he made peace with the Ottomans and
drove the Uzbek Turks out of eastern Iran. He moved his
capital to Isfahan and made it into one of the world's
finest cities, with a magnificent palace and mosque.
Covered bazaars (markets) surrounded the main square,
trees and streams flanked the market square, and a central
avenue had gardens on both sides. Abbas the Great set in
motion a revival of Persian culture, creating lasting friendly
relations with Europe, and entertaining foreign visitors.

◀ This Persian painting
shows Abbas receiving
guests in his palace.

▲ Abbas built the mosque at
Isfahan, and decorated it with
complex geometric patterns.

# TUDOR ENGLAND 1485–1603

**During the Tudor period, England grew great and powerful. It forged a strong new identity, broke its ties with Rome, and sowed the seeds of an imperial future.**

Henry Tudor (1457–1509) came to power in 1485.

Henry VIII (1491–1547) brought about great changes in England.

The Tudors, a Welsh family, rose to power after the confusion of a long civil war, the Wars of the Roses (1455–1485). The first Tudor king, Henry VII, banned private armies and put down any nobles who opposed him. He enriched his own finances and those of the nation. In 1509, when the young Henry VIII became king, England was an important power in Europe. Henry married Catherine of Aragon, daughter of Spain's Ferdinand and Isabella, and spent 15 years as a pleasure-seeking Renaissance-style ruler, while Thomas Wolsey ran the government. After wars against France and Scotland Henry became more politically aware. In 1521, he wrote a treatise attacking Luther, and the pope gave him the title Defender of the Faith. He had only one living child, Mary, and Henry wanted a male heir, so

Henry VIII loved banquets. He was well-educated, played several musical instruments, and wrote songs. He also enjoyed lively discussions on religion, art, and politics.

he asked the pope's permission to divorce Catherine. He was refused. At this time, new religious ideas and demands for Church reform were common, so Henry broke with Rome and made himself head of the Church in England.

## DISSOLUTION OF THE MONASTERIES

Between 1536 and 1540, Henry closed 800 monasteries. He turned 10,000 monks and nuns out and sold or gave away their lands. He did this to break the power of Rome in England, and to raise money. He founded the Protestant Church of England, though he was not enthusiastically Protestant—Protestantism really developed under Elizabeth I.

Henry VIII rebuilt the English navy, and his pride and joy was the *Mary Rose*. In 1536, he went to Portsmouth to watch it sail. However, the ship's balance was affected by the 700 sailors on deck, and it capsized and sank.

Henry married six times, and during his reign, strengthened English control of Wales and Ireland, established a large navy, and planned various colonial and commercial ventures. He was succeeded in 1547 by his only son, Edward VI (1537–1553) who died at the age of sixteen. During his reign, the Church of England grew stronger. Edward was followed by his half-sister, Mary I (1516–1558). Devoutly religious, she tried to restore England to Catholicism.

## THE FIRST ELIZABETHANS

When Mary died, her sister Elizabeth I came to the throne. Elizabeth was hard-working, popular, and intelligent. She refused to marry, and she made her own decisions. The Catholic Mary, Queen of Scots, Elizabeth's cousin, was found guilty of plotting against her, but Elizabeth resisted pressure to have her executed for many years. Elizabeth aided European Protestants and sent out English pirates against Spanish ships. She made a settlement between English Catholics and Protestants, and fought a war with Spain, defeating the Spanish Armada. England began to develop overseas ventures, and at home its industries and economy grew. This was Shakespeare's time, when English culture and society flowered, laying the foundations for a powerful empire.

Elizabeth I (1533–1603) became queen of England and Ireland in 1558. She ruled for 45 years and, due to her active involvement in government, England went through a period of stability, as well as cultural and economic expansion.

## MARY, QUEEN OF SCOTS 1542–1587

Mary Stuart became queen of Scotland in 1542 when she was only a week old. Her father, James V, was the nephew of Henry VIII, and this encouraged the Catholic Mary to claim the English throne. She was educated in France and married the heir to the French throne in 1558. After his death in 1560, Mary returned to Scotland where she proved unpopular. She abdicated and fled to England in 1568. As a focus for Catholic dissent against Elizabeth, Mary became involved in plots and was imprisoned in Fotheringay Castle, where she was executed in 1587 on a charge of treason.

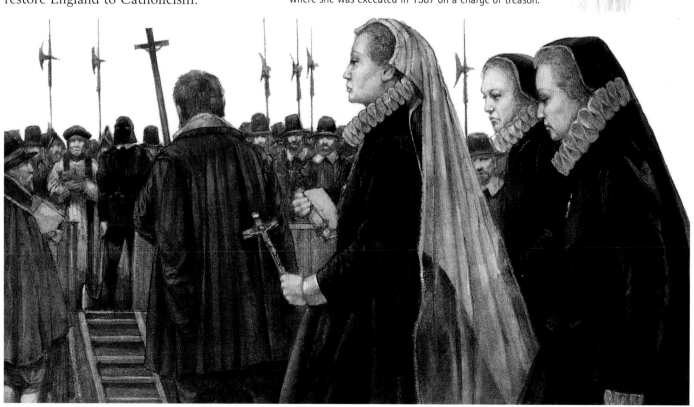

# THE PORTUGUESE EMPIRE 1520–1600

**Portuguese seafarers and traders paved the way for European colonialism around the world. At its height, their trading empire spanned the whole globe.**

This ornamental African mask from Benin is carved from ivory. It shows a queen mother, or *iyoba*, of Benin. Her headdress is made up of images of Portuguese merchants.

The Portuguese were the leading seafaring explorers of Europe. They had long been fishermen, accustomed to the high seas. Henry the Navigator began the training of sailors in the mid-1400s, and sent ships down the west coast of Africa. There were large profits at stake in the trade of exotic goods. Portuguese explorers reached the East Indies (Indonesia) in the early 1500s, following the Muslim trade routes to the Moluccas (Spice Islands), which were rich in the spices such as cinnamon, cloves, and nutmeg, that Europe wanted. To control this valuable trade, the Portuguese conquered the Moluccas and seized many of the best-placed ports on the Indian Ocean. They also visited China. Because Portuguese traders needed to sail around Africa in order to return to Lisbon, forts were set up at various places along the African coast to supply and protect the ships.

▲ The Portuguese were the first Europeans to trade with West African countries. This brass plaque from Benin shows Portuguese men symbolically holding up the pillars supporting the palace of the oba (king) of Benin.

▼ The Portuguese Empire at its greatest extent in about 1600 was far-flung, but very profitable. Trading posts and ports to service ships were positioned in strategic locations along the major trade routes.

▲ In the 1500s, Benin craftspeople carved items such as this ivory saltcellar, for export to Europe. Around the base are figures of Portuguese noblemen.

A ILHA E CIDADE DE GOA METROPOLITANA DA INDIA E PARTES ORIENTAIS QVE ESTA EN 15 GRAOS DA BANDA DO NORTE.

## THE START OF THE SLAVE TRADE

From Africa, the Portuguese bought gold and slaves to work on their sugar plantations. The first ones were on the African island of Sâo Tomé, but the sugar was inferior and the market collapsed. Problems grew. In the 1570s, a slave named Amador led a major revolt. Raids by pirates were a continuing threat. Sâo Tomé became only a place where slaves were loaded onto ships bound for Brazil—and so the transatlantic slave trade began.

At its height in the 1500s, the Portuguese Empire did not possess large areas of colonial land like the Spanish, but they did hold well-placed, valuable trading posts and plantations. These included Angola and Mozambique, the islands of Cape Verde, Madeira, and the Azores; the bases of Ormuz (Persia), Goa and Calicut (India), and Colombo (Sri Lanka); and trading posts in the Far East, such as Macao (China), the Celebes, Java, and Malacca.

| KEY DATES | |
|---|---|
| 1419 | The Portuguese reach Madeira |
| 1471 | The Portuguese reach Asante and Benin |
| 1488 | Dias rounds the Cape of Good Hope |
| 1498 | Vasco da Gama reaches India |
| 1500 | Cabral explores the coast of Brazil |
| 1505–20 | Asian trading posts founded in Goa and Malacca |
| 1520 | Magellan discovers the Moluccas (Spice Islands) |
| 1530 | First Portuguese colony established in Brazil |
| 1534 | First African slaves are brought to Brazil |

The port of Goa in India was an important trading link in the Portuguese Empire. It is shown here in a map made in 1595 by a Portuguese–Dutch engraver, Johannes Baptista van Doetechum the Younger.

Before the Portuguese arrived in the Moluccas, its rulers enjoyed high profits from the lucrative spice trade. Under Portuguese rule the local rulers were bypassed. Spices from the Moluccas included cloves, nutmeg, pepper, cinnamon, and ginger.

# THE REFORMATION 1520–1618

**During the Reformation, a new kind of Christianity, with many new groups and sects, developed. This led to social divisions and eventually war across Europe.**

John Calvin (1509–1564) was born in France and was originally named Jean Chauvin. He was a strict Protestant and believed that God had already ordained the future and that only those chosen by God (the Elect) would be saved.

Europe suffered a series of violent religious civil wars. There were many massacres, and people accused of being heretics were burned at the stake.

By the early 1500s, the new ideas of the Renaissance led some people to challenge the teachings of the Roman Catholic Church. The way its leaders ran the Church was strongly criticized. Priests, monks, and nuns no longer led lives of poverty, celibacy, and simplicity, and popes and bishops were too interested in money and power. People sought Church reform. This became known as "the Reformation." It had started quietly over 100 years before, but gained momentum in 1517 when Martin Luther, a German priest, nailed a list of 95 statements (theses) to the church door at Wittenberg, criticizing the role of the Church. Luther hated the sale of "indulgences"—the forgiveness of sins in exchange for money. He hoped that his list would lead to healthy debate, but he was accused of heresy (going against Church beliefs), and excommunicated from the Catholic Church in 1521.

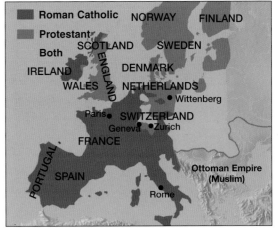

The Reformation in the 1500s meant that Europe was divided roughly north–south over religious beliefs— Protestant to the north and Roman Catholic to the south. This division also happened within individual countries such as France, and later led to civil war.

## THE EARLY PROTESTANTS

Luther had gained support in Germany and Switzerland, setting up his own Lutheran church. Other groups, such as Quakers, Anabaptists, Mennonites, and Moravian Hussites did the same. After a conference in 1529, they were all called Protestants. Ulrich Zwingli led the Reformation in Switzerland. His views were more extreme, and this led to a civil war in which Zwingli was killed. He was followed by John Calvin, who gained followers in France, Germany, and Holland. He established the Reformation in Switzerland and influenced John Knox, who took the Reformation to Scotland. Some groups pooled all their property to form communities, taking over whole towns.

▲ Martin Luther (1483–1546) believed that people are saved by faith alone, not by buying indulgences. He wanted faith to be based on the Bible, not on corrupt religious traditions. He believed that church services should be in the local language, not Latin. The cartoon on the right shows the devil dictating Luther's sermons to him.

The Council of Trent met three times between 1545 and 1563. It began a major reform within the the Catholic Church and sought to stop the spread of Protestantism.

▲ The Catholic Church used pictures for teaching, and this 1470 woodcut from Germany shows a good Catholic on his deathbed, being given the last rites.

▼ Julius II, pope from 1503 to 1513, was concerned with politics, and was a great patron of the arts. Popes after him were forced to reform the Church from within.

## THE COUNTER-REFORMATION

In 1522, Pope Adrian VI admitted there were many problems in the Roman Catholic Church, but following his death, nothing more was done until 1534, when Paul III became pope. This was the year Henry VIII of England broke away from Rome. Paul began to reform the Church in a movement known as the Counter-Reformation. He began by encouraging the preaching and missionary work of an Italian order of friars called the Capuchins. Six years later, he approved the founding of the Society of Jesus, or Jesuits, which had been started by Ignatius Loyola, to spread Catholicism. He also called together a group known as the Council of Trent, in 1545, to decide on further Church reforms. The council enforced vows of poverty and set up Church colleges (seminaries) to educate monks, nuns, and priests. All this led to a revival of Catholic faith and active opposition to the Protestants.

However, the religious dispute in Europe grew into a political one when Philip II of Spain tried to restore Catholicism in England, France, and Holland by force. Other rulers took sides. Civil war erupted in France, and Protestant Holland revolted against Spanish domination. Eventually, the Thirty Years' War broke out in 1618.

| KEY DATES | |
|---|---|
| 1517 | Luther's 95 Theses, announced at Wittenberg, Germany |
| 1522 | Luther's Bible is published in German |
| 1523 | Zwingli's Program of Reform established in Switzerland |
| 1530s | Protestant social movements and revolts in Germany |
| 1534 | England separates from the Roman Church |
| 1540s | Calvin establishes Protestant church in Geneva |
| 1545 | The first Council of Trent—the Counter-Reformation begins |
| 1562–98 | The Huguenot Wars in France |
| 1566 | Calvinist church founded in the Netherlands |
| 1580s | Increase of tension between European rulers |
| 1618 | Outbreak of the Thirty Years' War (until 1648) |

# THE OTTOMAN EMPIRE 1453–1600

**Following the taking of Constantinople in 1453, the Ottoman Empire soon became a force to be reckoned with in the Middle East and around the Mediterranean.**

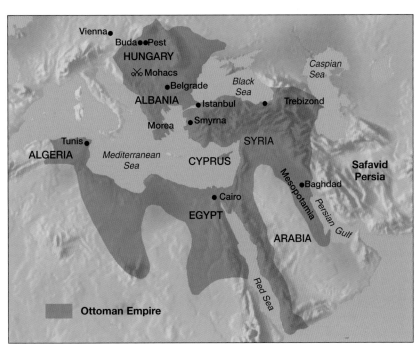

▲ The Ottoman *spahi*, or cavalry knights were given land in return for military service, and became a local ruling class across the empire.

▼ By 1566, the Ottoman Empire stretched into three continents. Süleyman had built up a strong navy and won control of the Mediterranean. He also dominated the Red Sea and Persian Gulf.

When Constantinople fell to Mehmet II in 1453, the Ottoman Empire began its golden age. The former Byzantine capital became known as Istanbul, and became the center of an enormous empire, which at its peak, stretched from Algeria to Persia and Hungary to Arabia. The empire was founded by Osman I in 1301, and by 1389, it had extended into Europe. The Mongols halted its expansion for a while, but, after takingConstantinople, Mehmet II quickly conquered 12 kingdoms and 200 cities in Anatolia and the Balkans. Then Selim I gained Syria, Arabia, and Egypt between 1512 and 1520.

## SÜLEYMAN THE MAGNIFICENT

Süleyman the Magnificent ruled for 46 years from 1520. He conquered Belgrade and Hungary, but failed in his siege of Vienna, the capital of the Holy Roman Empire. He later took Mesopotamia, Armenia, and the Caucasus region. The Ottomans gained control of the eastern Mediterranean and Black Sea (thereby dominating Venetian and Genoan trade), and also North Africa and the Ukraine.

Women in the Ottoman Empire led a secluded life. Outside their home they had to wear a veil and could only meet men from their own families.

To his own people, Süleyman was known as *Qanuni*, the Lawgiver, because he reformed the Ottoman administration and the legal system. He gave shape to the Ottoman Empire, enriching everything from architecture to courtly life. He was a poet, scholar, and patron of the arts, and he rebuilt much of Istanbul.

Europeans called him Süleyman the Magnificent because of the splendor of his court and his military victories in Europe. These included a series of campaigns in which he captured Belgrade in Serbia in 1521, and threw the Crusader Knights of St. John out of Rhodes in 1522. His greatest victory was at Mohacs in Hungary in 1526; his siege of Vienna in 1529 threatened the heart of Europe; and he took the Muslim holy city of Mecca in 1538. Meanwhile, the Turkish fleet, under the former corsair Barbarossa (Khayr ad-Din Pasha), attacked and ravaged the coasts of Spain, Italy, and Greece.

Map labels: Vienna • Buda •• Pest, HUNGARY, ✂ Mohacs, • Belgrade, ALBANIA, • Istanbul, Morea, • Smyrna, Tunis •, ALGERIA, *Mediterranean Sea*, *Black Sea*, *Caspian Sea*, • Trebizond, SYRIA, CYPRUS, Safavid Persia, • Baghdad, Mesopotamia, Persian Gulf, • Cairo, EGYPT, ARABIA, Red Sea

■ Ottoman Empire

Süleyman the Magnificent (1494–1566), became sultan in 1520 and turned the Ottoman Empire into a vast and rich Sunni Muslim empire straddling three continents.

## MUSLIM WARS

Süleyman waged three campaigns in the east against the Safavid Empire of Persia. This was a war between Muslims—between the Sunni Ottomans and the Shiite Persians. Süleyman took Baghdad, but the eastern border of the empire was never secure. The wars between the two empires lasted throughout the 1500s and diverted Ottoman attention so that they did not advance further into Europe.

## THE START OF A SLOW DECLINE

When Süleyman died, his son Selim II became sultan. Selim led a life of leisure, while his ministers and generals ran the empire. The Ottomans themselves were not many in number. They relied on taking Russian and North African slaves, and drafting one in five boys from their European territories, to train them as administrators and soldiers. Ordinary people were left alone as long as they were obedient and paid taxes, and no one was forcibly converted to Islam. The Ottomans relied on Greeks, Armenians, Venetians, and other foreigners as traders, making the Ottoman Empire international in character. However, by 1600, the empire had begun a long, slow decline.

▲ Süleyman's greatest victory was at the battle of Mohacs in 1526 where he crushed the Hungarian army. His army overwhelmed an alliance of central European nations and killed the king of Bohemia.

▼ Süleyman's failure to capture Vienna, the capital of the Holy Roman Empire in 1529 prevented him from moving farther into Germany and central Europe. Ottoman advances halted there. The use of cannons was a fairly recent development in warfare.

| KEY DATES | |
|---|---|
| 1453 | The Ottomans take Constantinople |
| c.1460 | Greece, Serbia, and Bosnia taken |
| 1512–20 | Selim I takes Syria, Arabia, and Egypt |
| 1522 | Süleyman takes Rhodes from the Knights of St. John |
| 1526 | Battle of Mohacs: Hungary taken |
| 1529 | Siege of Vienna (failed) |
| 1534 | Süleyman takes Baghdad and Armenia |
| 1538 | Süleyman takes the holy city of Mecca |
| 1540s onward | The flowering of Ottoman culture |
| 1566 | Death of Süleyman, the Ottoman Empire passes its peak |

# INDIA: THE MOGULS 1504–1605

**The Islamic world was changing. India, a divided subcontinent, was invaded by the Moguls. They established a strong Empire in the north of India.**

▲ Babur (1483–1530), born in Turkestan, was the first Mogul emperor in India. He died in Agra.

Babur, a descendant of Genghis Khan and Tamerlane, led a tribe in Turkestan called the Moguls—the name Mogul is a variation of the word "Mongol." Driven out by the Uzbeks, they invaded Kabul in Afghanistan in 1504. Then they set their sights on India, a patchwork of often-warring Hindu and Muslim states. After an experimental attack in 1519, 12,000 Moguls swept through the Khyber Pass into India in 1526, invading the Delhi sultanate, the greatest power in India.

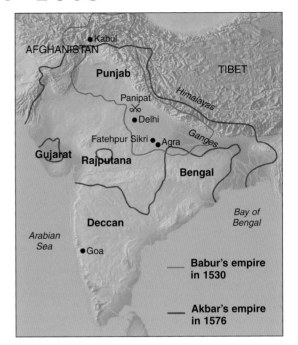

Babur's empire in 1530

Akbar's empire in 1576

Expanding outward from Delhi, the Mogul Empire grew to cover all of northern India and much of central India. Although it was Muslim-ruled, it accommodated the many faiths and cultures of India.

Babur and his followers were Muslims. When they invaded India, the Ottoman Empire supplied them with guns and soldiers. Babur's troops also rode swift horses which easily outmaneuvered the Indians' slower elephants. This helped them defeat a much larger Indian army at a battle in which the sultan of Delhi was killed. After this victory, Babur made Delhi his capital. When Babur died in 1530, his son Humayun became ruler.

◀ A splendid miniature painting in the Mogul style shows Babur recognizing his son, Humayun, as his heir.

▲ Babur had a full-scale account of India written. It details the nature, people, and customs of his empire.

Humayun invaded western India, but in 1540, the Surs chased out the Moguls, forcing them back into Persia. Humayun returned in 1555, overcame the Surs, and moved back to Delhi. A year later, before he was able to win back the whole empire, Humayun was killed in an accident.

## AKBAR EXPANDS THE EMPIRE

Humayun's succesor was Babur's grandson, Akbar. He became emperor at the age of 13 and ruled until his death in 1605. Akbar was a great military leader and wise ruler. His army pushed west into Gujarat and east into Bengal—the richest province in northern India. It produced rice and silk, which provided Akbar with his main source of income. By 1576, Akbar controlled all of northern India.

Although Akbar was a Muslim, many of his subjects were Hindus, and to keep the peace, he married a Hindu princess. He believed in religious tolerance, bringing the Hindus into the government and encouraging their overseas trade. He set up a well-organized empire with professional administrators.

## MOGUL GREATNESS

During this period, India traded profitably with Africa, the Ottomans, Europe, and the Far East. By this time, the Portuguese had trading posts and ports in India. The country also had the world's largest textile industry. Akbar welcomed Christian Jesuits and Persian artists to his court, and he tried unsuccessfully to create a new religion for India. He built schools for children as well as a new capital city at Fatehpur Sikri. The city combined Muslim and Hindu styles of architecture.

| KEY DATES | |
|---|---|
| 1504 | The Moguls seize Kabul |
| 1526 | Delhi becomes the Mogul capital in India |
| 1556 | Akbar the Great, the greatest Mogul emperor, begins reign |
| 1571 | Fatehpur Sikri becomes the new capital |
| 1605 | Jahangir becomes Mogul emperor (Nur Jahan rules 1611–22) |
| 1628 | Shah Jahan, Mogul emperor |
| 1658 | Aurangzeb, the last great Mogul emperor |
| 1707 | Beginning of the decline of the Moguls |
| 1803 | The fall of the last Mogul stronghold to the English |

# AKBAR, THE THIRD MOGUL EMPEROR

Akbar inherited the Mogul Empire at the age of 13, and he ruled for nearly 50 years. He invaded Rajasthan, Gujarat, Bengal, Kashmir, and the Deccan to rule most of India. He taxed farming peasants less, encouraged traders, and introduced a very efficient government and military service. This served later Mogul emperors and their people well. Though Akbar could not read, he welcomed scholars of all religions, artists, and foreign travelers to his court. His greatest success was in making peace with the Hindu majority of the Indian population, ending many Hindu–Muslim conflicts.

▲ Akbar (1542–1605) believed in religious toleration. His own beliefs included ideas from different religions. In 1575, he set up a center for the study of religion through the exchange of ideas. Akbar found, however, that the scholars were not as broad-minded as he had hoped—each one argued without really listening to anyone else's point of view.

◀ Although some local rulers rebelled against Akbar's rule, they were soon defeated. Here, the rebel Bahadur Khan is shown yielding to Akbar.

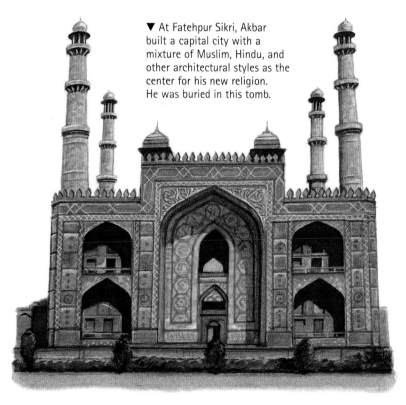

▼ At Fatehpur Sikri, Akbar built a capital city with a mixture of Muslim, Hindu, and other architectural styles as the center for his new religion. He was buried in this tomb.

# THE CONQUISTADORES 1519–1550

**The Spanish conquistadores were soldiers and adventurers who invaded the Americas. In doing so, they destroyed the great Aztec and Inca civilizations.**

Hernán Cortés (1485–1547) returned to Spain where he died in poverty.

Francisco Pizarro (c.1475–1541) marched on the Incas in 1532. He was murdered in Lima.

Soon after the navigators had found the Americas, Spanish adventurers, known as *conquistadores* (conquerors), followed them. After conquering many Caribbean islands, they explored the American mainland, hoping to find treasure. In 1519, about 500 Spanish soldiers, led by Hernán Cortés, reached the Aztec city of Tenochtitlan, where, at first, they were welcomed. It is thought that the Aztec emperor, Montezuma II, believed that Cortés was the god Quetzalcóatl, whose return he had been awaiting. The Spanish tricked and captured Montezuma, and Cortés ruled in his place. When Cortés left, the Aztecs rebelled and defeated the remaining Spanish. With the help of an interpreter, Cortés then won the support of the neighboring tribes who had been conquered by the Aztecs. In 1521, he returned to Tenochtitlan with an indigenous army and destroyed the city.

At first Montezuma welcomed Cortés to Tenochtitlan, showering him with gifts. This goodwill died when the Spanish seized power. Most of the Aztecs soon died of diseases brought by the foreigners.

## THE END OF THE INCA EMPIRE

Another conquistador, Francisco Pizarro, landed in Peru in 1532, seeking to conquer the Incas. An Inca civil war was already in progress between Huascar and Atahualpa, the sons of Huayna Capac. Atahualpa killed Huascar with the help of the Spanish, but Pizarro then had Atahualpa executed. The Incas soon surrendered, and by 1533 their vast empire was in Spanish hands.

## THE CAPTURE OF ATAHUALPA

In 1532, Pizarro, with only 159 men against a large Inca army, kidnapped the Inca leader, Atahualpa. He was a god to the Incas, which, to them, made Pizarro more powerful than the gods. The Incas soon yielded, and Atahualpa was executed. Like the Aztecs, the Incas were tricked into submission, and a whole civilization died.

# THE SPANISH EMPIRE 1533–1600

**Spain's occupation of large areas of the Americas brought harsh conditions and disease to the Indigenous Americans. By 1600, Spain had the largest empire.**

After the fall of the Aztecs and Incas, the king of Spain added their territories to his empire. The Aztec Empire became the Viceroyalty of New Spain in 1533. Later in the 1500s, it also included parts of California, Arizona, and New Mexico. The land of the Incas became the Viceroyalty of Peru. Many people from Spain emigrated to live in this new Spanish Empire. The colonies were ruled by the Council of the Indies, based in Spain. The colonial Spaniards treated the Indigenous Americans cruelly, and they were forced to mine silver and work as slaves. Millions died because they had no resistance to European diseases such as measles and smallpox. The colonists were followed by Spanish missionaries, who destroyed temples and idols and set up churches in their place, trying to convert the Indigenous Americans.

The Spanish Empire continued to expand under the reign of Philip II (1556–1598). Most of the Philippine Islands were conquered in 1571. Then, in 1578, King Sebastian of Portugal was killed in Morocco. Philip was his closest relative, so he inherited the Portuguese Empire. By 1600, the Spanish had the world's largest empire, but they were losing power. Philip's opposition to the Protestants in Europe led to expensive wars that used up the gold and silver from the Americas.

The conquistadores were followed by missionaries, who tried to convert the Indigenous Americans—by force, if necessary. They destroyed their temples and made the people build churches in their place.

The Spanish forced the Indigenous Americans to mine gold and silver, which was then sent back to Spain. The harsh conditions and new diseases brought by the Spanish decimated the population of Mexico, which fell from 25 million in 1500 to just one million in 1600.

▲ The Spanish took new foods, such as pineapples, tomatoes, potatoes, cocoa, peppers, and sunflowers back to Europe.

▶ The Spanish Empire was large and yielded vast wealth, especially from gold and silver mined in Mexico and Peru.

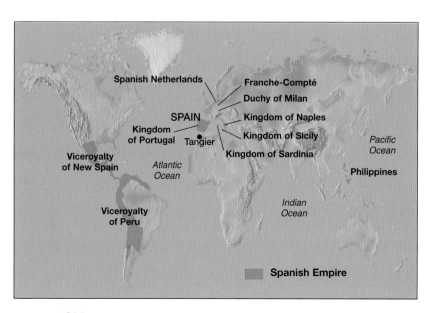

Spanish Netherlands
Franche-Compté
Duchy of Milan
SPAIN
Kingdom of Portugal
Tangier
Kingdom of Naples
Kingdom of Sicily
Kingdom of Sardinia
Viceroyalty of New Spain
Atlantic Ocean
Pacific Ocean
Philippines
Viceroyalty of Peru
Indian Ocean

Spanish Empire

# THE HAPSBURGS 1273–1556

**The Hapsburg family came from Habichtsburg in Switzerland. They dominated European politics for more than 600 years, from the 1200s until 1914.**

▲ Charles V (1500–1558) became king of Spain in 1516 and Holy Roman emperor in 1519. In 1553, he gave the imperial crown to his brother, and two years later gave his kingdoms (Spain, the Netherlands, the Americas) to his son Philip.

▼ After Charles V's death, the Austrian Hapsburgs ruled the Holy Roman Empire. The Spanish Hapsburgs ruled Spain, the Netherlands, parts of Italy, and Latin America.

The Hapsburg family took its name from their castle in Switzerland—Habichtsburg, or "Hawk's Castle." By 1200, the Hapsburg lands were in Austria. After 1438, the Holy Roman emperor was almost always a Hapsburg. In the late 1400s, Maximilian I (1459–1519) expanded Hapsburg influence by advantageous marriages. His son, Philip of Burgundy (1478–1506), married Joanna, a daughter of Ferdinand and Isabella of Spain. Their son, Charles V, was to be the most powerful Hapsburg of all.

When Philip died in 1506, Charles inherited Burgundy and the Netherlands. In 1516, Ferdinand of Spain left him Spain and Naples, and in 1519 he inherited the Holy Roman Empire from Maximilian. This led to rivalry with Francis I of France, and their countries were at war for most of Charles's reign. A devout Catholic, Charles did not like the spread of Protestantism. He called two diets, or assemblies, to reconcile the differences with the Lutherans, but both failed. In 1546, he took up arms against some of them—the League of Schmalkalden.

Rudolf I (1218–1291) was elected king of Germany in 1273, and became the first Hapsburg Holy Roman emperor, although never officially crowned. The title, Holy Roman emperor, remained in the Hapsburg family until 1806.

Charles defeated the League in 1547, but later had to agree to their demands. By 1556, he had spent much of Spain's wealth fruitlessly, and was exhausted by war. He retired to a monastery, after dividing his lands between his son Philip (who gained Spain, the Netherlands, and the American colonies) and his brother, Ferdinand (who gained Austria and the Holy Roman crown).

The double-headed eagle was the emblem of the Holy Roman Empire. The power of the emperors decreased in the 1500s, as some of the German states became more powerful.

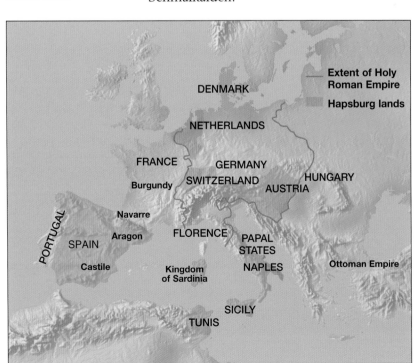

Extent of Holy Roman Empire

Hapsburg lands

DENMARK

NETHERLANDS

FRANCE

Burgundy  GERMANY
SWITZERLAND  AUSTRIA  HUNGARY

Navarre

PORTUGAL

Aragon  FLORENCE  PAPAL STATES

SPAIN

Castile  Kingdom of Sardinia  NAPLES  Ottoman Empire

SICILY

TUNIS

### KEY DATES

| | |
|---|---|
| 1020 | Habichtsburg, the family home, is built |
| 1459–1519 | Maximilian I expands Hapsburg influence |
| 1506 | Charles V inherits Burgundy and the Netherlands |
| 1516 | Charles V inherits Spain and Naples |
| 1519–56 | Charles V, Holy Roman emperor |
| 1546 | War between the Hapsburgs and the Protestants |
| 1618–48 | Thirty Years' War between the Catholics and the Protestants |

# THE SPANISH ARMADA 1588

**The Armada was sent by Europe's most powerful country to invade an increasingly ambitious England. Its failure led to 300 years of English rule on the seas.**

▲ Francis Drake (1543–1596) was a pirate and adventurer. After raiding gold from Spanish galleons in the Caribbean, he was made first a captain and later an admiral, and helped defeat the Spanish Armada. In 1580, he was the first Englishman to sail around the world—on his ship, the *Golden Hind*.

Philip II ruled Spain and its empire from 1556 to 1598. His strong Catholic beliefs provoked revolts in Holland and Spain, led to war with the Ottomans and England, and sucked Spain into the French Wars of Religion. His absolute rule and military activities left Spain economically ruined, despite the gold and silver Spain received from the Americas. Spain did not like England. Elizabeth I had turned down Philip II's marriage proposal. British pirates often raided Spanish colonies and fleets. Worst of all, England was Protestant.

In 1588, Philip sent the Armada from Lisbon to attack England. Its 130 galleons carried 8,000 sailors and 19,000 soldiers. Delayed by storms, the Armada was sighted and harassed by the English as far as Calais, where it was due to meet

It was important for Elizabeth I to defeat the Armada. She did not like her brother-in-law Philip II, and she had ambitions for England, helped by England's victory.

another Spanish fleet that did not arrive.

During the night, the English caused havoc by sending in fireships, and then pounding the escaping ships with gunfire. A strong wind blew the remaining ships into the North Sea. The Armada sailed around Scotland, and only half of the ships finally returned to Spain. This was an enormous setback for the Spanish.

▲ Philip II (1527–1598) ruled Spain from 1556 until his death. He believed that he had a mission to win worldwide power for Spain and the Roman Catholic Church. He married Mary Tudor (Mary I) of England.

▶ Philip II sent his Armada against England in August 1588. The Spanish had larger ships, but the English ships were faster and more maneuverable. The defeat of the Armada meant the end of Spain as a great naval power.

# FRENCH WARS OF RELIGION 1562–1600

**The spread of the Protestant faith led to problems in some parts of Europe—nowhere more so than in France, which suffered from 36 years of bloody civil wars.**

▲ Catherine de' Medici (1519–1589) was the daughter of Lorenzo de' Medici and wife of Henry II of France. She ruled France as regent for her young son Charles IX.

Many French people had become Protestant Calvinists. The majority remained Catholic, but Protestants (called Huguenots) were influential, since many were prosperous traders and craftspeople. At first they were tolerated, but the nobility (especially the Catholic Guise family) and foreign powers, who were competing for influence, complicated matters. In 1560, the new king, Charles IX, was only ten. The country was ruled by his mother, Catherine de' Medici, who supported the Catholics. In 1562, the Guises massacred many Huguenots. For the next 36 years, a series of civil wars took place. In 1572, Catherine plotted a massacre of leading Huguenots and, on St. Bartholomew's Day, after 3,000 Huguenots were killed in Paris, thousands more were killed throughout France.

◄ Henry of Navarre, a Protestant, married into the royal Valois family, but he was imprisoned by the Catholics. He eventually became Henry IV and ruled from 1589 to 1610.

In 1598, Henry IV of France signed the Edict of Nantes, granting the Huguenots freedom of worship and a place in French society. This ended the French Wars of Religion.

Moderate people were horrified at this bloody massacre, and conflict now grew between extremists and moderates as well as between Catholics and Huguenots. In 1574, Henry III (1551–1589), another of Catherine de' Medici's sons, became king. He was also influenced by his mother, and civil war continued. In 1576, Henry made a settlement between all sides. This was known as the Edict of Beaulieu, but it failed to stop the turmoil.

In 1572, Henry of Guise persuaded Catherine de' Medici to allow the murder of a Huguenot admiral. In the events that followed, many thousands more were killed.

## THE WAR OF THE THREE HENRYS

In the same year as the Edict of Beaulieu, an extremist Catholic group, led by Henry of Guise, was formed to oppose the settlement, and the religious difficulties increased. The Catholics, allied with Spain and other Catholic countries, tried to block the Huguenot Henry of Navarre from inheriting the throne. This led to the War of the Three Henrys, involving King Henry III, the Huguenot Henry of Navarre, and the Catholic Henry of Guise. Henry III lost control, and war broke out. Henry of Guise tried to take the throne and, in 1585, he banned the Protestant religion. In 1589, Henry III had Henry of Guise murdered. However, Henry III was then assassinated by a fanatical monk.

Henry of Navarre became King Henry IV of France, and to calm things, he decided to convert to Catholicism in 1593. The Huguenot Wars finally ended in 1598 with the Edict of Nantes, which allowed religious freedom and equality to all. There was to be more trouble in the 1600s, however, and by the 1680s, many Huguenots had left France for their own safety.

▲ In France and the rest of Europe, it was common for Protestants to be accused of heresy. The punishment for this crime was usually to be burned alive at the stake. The soul of the heretic was supposed to burn and be sent down to hell.

◄ Many Huguenots were skilled traders, craftspeople, and educated townspeople. It was important for France to keep them, since they ran many industries and professions. After 1685, many of them left France for other countries or the colonies, taking their skills and wealth with them.

| KEY DATES | |
|---|---|
| 1533 | Catherine de' Medici marries Henry II of France |
| 1559 | Henry II dies and is succeeded by his son Francis II who dies after a year; Catherine de Medici is regent |
| 1560 | Charles IX becomes king, at the age of 10; Catherine again acts as regent |
| 1562 | The Massacre of Vassy marks the beginning of the Huguenot Wars |
| 1570 | Peace and limited rights are agreed for the Huguenots |
| 1572 | The Massacre of St. Bartholomew's Day |
| 1574 | The moderate Henry III becomes king |
| 1576 | Edict of Beaulieu—a pact that imposes tolerance of the Huguenots |
| 1585–89 | War of the Three Henrys |
| 1589 | Henry of Navarre becomes king of France |
| 1593 | Henry of Navarre (Henry IV) converts to Catholicism |
| 1598 | The Edict of Nantes grants religious freedom and equality to all |

# RUSSIA 1462–1613

**During this period, Russia grew from a collection of small principalities into a great country. Its isolation ended, allowing it to play a major role in history.**

▲ Ivan III (1440–1505) was the first ruler of all Russia. He made Moscow his capital. By the time he died from alcoholism, he had set Russia on a new course.

▲ Ivan III adopted the Byzantine symbol of the double-headed eagle as his own emblem—both Byzantium and Russia looked east and west.

After the decline of Kyiv around 1060, Russia survived as an assortment of separate small principalities such as Novgorod, Smolensk, Kyiv, and Vladimir. This suddenly changed when the Mongols, under Batu Khan, invaded in 1238. They burned Moscow and damaged Kyiv. The Khanate of the Golden Horde (or Tartars) dominated Russia by demanding tribute in money and soldiers, and the Russians cooperated to avoid trouble. (In the 1300s, Kyiv was absorbed into Lithuania for a time.)

In 1263, Moscow had a new ruler, Prince Daniel, who gradually expanded its territories. Slowly, Moscow began to dominate the other Russian states. In 1380, the Muscovites defeated the Golden Horde, although the Tartars carried on raiding Moscow and demanding tribute until 1480, when Ivan III finally defeated them. Ivan III, or Ivan the Great, came to the throne of Moscow in 1462. He expanded Moscow and gave it a sense of pride, introduced a legal code, and declared himself "ruler of all Russia." In 1472, he married Sophia, the niece of the last Byzantine emperor, and appointed himself as the protector of the Eastern Orthodox Church, calling Moscow "the third Rome."

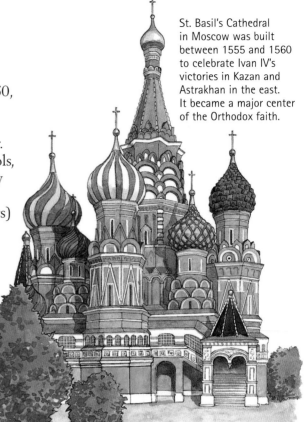

St. Basil's Cathedral in Moscow was built between 1555 and 1560 to celebrate Ivan IV's victories in Kazan and Astrakhan in the east. It became a major center of the Orthodox faith.

By 1480, Ivan III had brought Novgorod and other cities under his control. He rebuilt Moscow's famous *Kremlin* (citadel). When he died in 1505, he was succeeded by his son Vasili III, who ruled until 1533. Vasili III was succeeded in turn by Ivan IV, his three-year-old son.

▼ The boyars of Russia had been independent until Ivan the Terrible brought them under his control. They then joined the growing trade with the West in fur, timber, and other raw materials.

## IVAN THE TERRIBLE

Ivan IV, or "Ivan the Terrible," was the Grand Prince of Moscow from 1533 to 1584. He was crowned as the first *czar* (emperor) in 1547. His harsh upbringing left him with a violent and unpredictable character, but his nickname meant "awe-inspiring" rather than "terrible." He improved the legal system as well as reforming trading links with England and other European countries—Russia had until then been isolated. He captured Kazan and Astrakhan from the Tartars, pushing on toward Siberia. Ivan reduced the power of the boyars (the nobility) by instituting a kind of secret police, to bring the country under stronger control. He set many patterns for the future, and established strong central control by the czars. In 1581, in a fit of anger, he killed his son and heir Ivan, and so was succeeded by his second son, Fyodor, who was not seen as a strong leader.

## THE ROMANOV CZARS

After Ivan IV died in 1584, Boris Godunov ruled as regent until Fyodor died in 1598. Boris made himself czar, despite opposition from the boyars. He promoted foreign trade and defeated the Swedes, who sought to invade Russia. When he died in 1605, Russia entered eight years of civil war, as rival forces fought for the throne. Eventually, Ivan IV's great-nephew Mikhail Romanov (1596–1645) gained the throne in 1613. He was czar for thirty years, founding the Romanov dynasty, which ruled until 1917.

▲ The Kremlin was the center of Moscow. It was actually a fort and many palaces, churches, and cathedrals were rebuilt within the protection of its walls by Ivan III. It became the symbol of the centralized power of the czars.

◄ Fyodor I, son of Ivan the Terrible, ruled Russia from 1584 to 1598. He was a weak and sickly man. His brother-in-law Boris Godunov held the real power and became czar on Fyodor's death.

Ivan IV (1530-1584) was a strong ruler who truly set the course of Russia's expansion. Known as the Ivan the Terrible, he had a formidable personality.

### KEY DATES

| | |
|---|---|
| 1238 | Invasion of Russia by the Mongols |
| 1263 | Moscow begins to grow larger |
| 1462–1505 | Ivan III, the Great, strengthens Moscow |
| 1472 | Ivan III appoints himself protector of the Eastern Orthodox Church |
| 1480 | End of Tartar dominance of Russia |
| 1505–33 | Vasili III is ruler |
| 1533–84 | Ivan IV, the Terrible, expands Russia |
| 1584–98 | Fyodor is czar and Boris Godunov regent |
| 1598–1605 | Boris Godunov rules as czar |
| 1605–13 | Civil war between rival boyars |
| 1613 | Mikhail Romanov, first of the Romanovs, becomes czar |

# DUTCH INDEPENDENCE 1477–1648

**The Netherlands was a fast-developing Protestant area with a promising future, but ruled by Catholic Spain. The Dutch wanted to control their own affairs.**

William of Orange (1533–1584)—"the Silent"—became Spanish governor of part of the Netherlands in 1559. He disagreed with Philip II's treatment of the Protestants and turned against Spain. He led the Dutch Revolt from 1567 to 1572, and in 1573 became a Calvinist. Philip offered a reward for his death. In 1584, having escaped one assassination attempt, he was killed by a fanatical Catholic, Balthasar Gérards.

After the collapse of Charlemagne's empire in the 800s, the Netherlands, made up of 17 provinces in what is now Belgium, Luxembourg, and the Netherlands, were very fragmented since they belonged to various ruling families. In the 1300s and 1400s, the dukes of Burgundy, Philip the Bold and John the Fearless, acquired Flanders (Belgium) and the Netherlands. These lands stayed under Burgundy's control until Charles V, inheritor of Burgundian lands and a member of the Hapsburg dynasty, made them a Spanish possession in 1516. This did not suit the people of the Netherlands, since most of them were Protestant. The fight for independence started when Charles's son Philip II became king of Spain in 1556. He resisted the Protestant tide and tried to take complete control. He sent the Duke of Alba as governor to the Netherlands with orders to use terror, if necessary, to crush any opposition.

The Duke of Alba executed two leaders of the independence

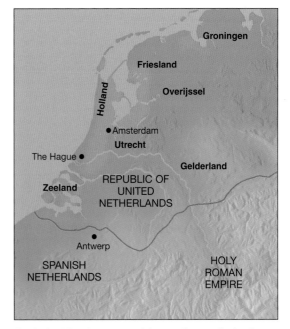

The United Provinces grew richer as the marshy land was drained and developed. As a Protestant country with growing trade and industry, independence from Spain, an old-fashioned imperial power, became necessary.

movement, and this resulted in the Dutch Revolts—led by William of Orange. The more ruthless the Duke of Alba became, the more the opposition grew. There were public executions, towns were pillaged, and whole populations were massacred. The Dutch used many guerrilla tactics, such as the flooding of the lowlands, to halt the Spanish advance. In 1576, Spanish troops sacked Antwerp, one of Europe's richest ports, and ended its prosperity.

▲ A cartoon of the time shows the aristocratic Duke of Alba trying to stamp out heresy in the Netherlands by trampling on the bodies of executed Protestants.

▶ In 1573, a Protestant alliance known as the "Sea Beggars" managed to capture the Dutch town of Geertruidenberg from its Catholic garrison and Spanish officers.

## STRUGGLE AND INDEPENDENCE

Many merchants and bankers moved to Amsterdam, rebuilding it into a fine city defended by canals and a growing navy. They developed modern trade, banking, and industry, becoming one of Europe's main Protestant centers. Spain brought the Catholic southern provinces (Belgium) back under its control, but in 1581, seven Protestant northern provinces declared themselves independent. Fortunately for them, Spain was busy fighting France, England, and the Ottomans, and so was unable to stop the Dutch.

This struggle for independence was a religious war and a fight between modern Dutch town-dwelling burghers and the traditional Spanish royal hierarchy. Led by William of Orange, the Dutch declared the Republic of the United Netherlands. A truce followed in 1609, but it was not until 1648 that Spain officially recognized Dutch independence.

▶ A 16th-century map of Amsterdam, an important center for trade. Goods were transported around the city along the canals.

| KEY DATES | |
|---|---|
| 1477 | The Netherlands become a Hapsburg possession |
| 1516 | The Spanish take control of the Netherlands |
| 1568 | The Dutch Revolt begins |
| 1576 | The sack of Antwerp—a turning point |
| 1581 | The Northern Provinces declare independence |
| 1609 | Truce—the Dutch effectively win the war |
| 1648 | Dutch independence fully recognized |

▲ The Duke of Alba, Spanish governor of the Netherlands, was ordered to punish the rebels. In 1567 he set up a tribunal, which became known as the "Council of Troubles." Many of the accused were executed or exiled.

219

# NORTH AMERICA 1460–1600

**North America was a land of many different peoples, each with their own traditions, way of life, and culture. The arrival of the Europeans was disastrous for them.**

▲ The tribes of the Iroquois wore masks during important tribal ceremonies. The masks represented the spirits of mythological creatures.

When the Europeans first arrived in America in the 1500s, there were millions of Indigenous Americans, in hundreds of tribes and many nations. They did not believe that they owned the land but thought that it was held in common for the entire tribe. Each tribe had its own customs, language, and way of life, according to where it lived. For example, on the Plains where wild animals such as buffalo were plentiful, the Cheyenne and Pawnee lived a nomadic lifestyle, hunting and trapping. Hunters on the Plains sometimes camouflaged themselves in animal skins when they went in search of prey. The animals they caught provided them with meat, and also with skins for clothing and shelters. Tribes who lived on the coast or by lakes made wooden canoes and fished for their food. Other tribes were village-dwelling farmers, who grew crops, herded animals, and hunted and fished.

▲ The French explorer Jacques Cartier (1491–1557) sailed up the St. Lawrence River in what is now Canada, and claimed the area for France. One of his men drew this map of the Huron town of Hochelaga—now the city of Montreal.

▶ The Miami tribe of Ohio made clothing from hides and furs. Skins were cleaned and stretched, then cut and sewn into garments and moccasins. Women did most of the domestic work and crop-growing, but they also held power in tribal decision-making.

Some Indigenous Americans built totems to the spirits of nature, often with an eagle at the top to represent the farseeing powers of Great Spirit.

In the Southwest, people living in villages, called *pueblos*, grew crops of corn, squash, and beans by building dams to irrigate the dry land. They had roads, complex societies with strong religious traditions, and they traded with the Aztecs and other Indigenous peoples.

Along the Mississippi River, an advanced city civilization had thrived, although it was in decline from 1450 onward. The Mississippians supplied Indigenous American tribes with tools, cloth, valuables, and goods brought from far away.

People on the east coast lived by farming corn, beans, and tobacco in plots around their villages, and they engaged in local trade and barter. In the Northeast, Indigenous American fields and clearings reminded European settlers of home—with the result that the region gained the name "New England." Many tribes were part of confederations or nations related by blood, tradition, or political agreements. Sometimes disagreements between tribes led to war.

▲ The people of the northeastern woodlands made decorated moccasins and ceremonial pipes which were used to celebrate special occasions.

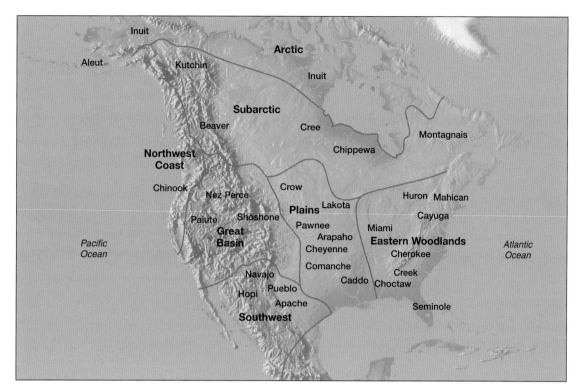

The Indigenous peoples were very diverse. The map shows where the main tribes of Indigenous Americans lived in 1500, before Europeans arrived and started driving them off their lands. At this time there were about six million Indigenous North Americans. These numbers fell drastically as the colonists spread west across the continent.

▼ The Chippewa lived in wigwams made of bent branches and covered with an outer layer of skins or birchbark to fend off the winter cold.

## THE ARRIVAL OF THE EUROPEANS

Like the Aztecs and the Incas, none of the Indigenous American tribes had horses or wheeled transportation before the Europeans arrived. Their knowledge of metal was limited, and most of their tools were made from wood or stone. Their weapons were bows and arrows, slingshots, and spears. At first, some tribes were friendly to the Europeans, and even helped them survive. But things changed disastrously for the Indigenous peoples when more aggressive European settlers arrived. Whole villages of Indigenous Americans died from European diseases such as smallpox and the measles. Others were killed in disputes, and the rest were driven off their lands.

▶ The nomadic Plains Indians lived in *tepees*. In the evenings, stories were told, both to entertain and to pass on the history, customs, laws, and ways of the tribe. They also held tribal councils to settle disputes and decide the tribe's future.

221

# JAPAN AND CHINA 1467–1644

**After first welcoming the Europeans, the Japanese began to see dangers in foreign influence. Meanwhile, in China, the Ming dynasty was losing control.**

In 1467, civil war broke out among the great feudal lords of Japan. The emperor had lost most of his power, and even the shogun had very little influence over the running of the country. For more than 100 years, private armies of samurai fought each other in the struggle to dominate Japan. During these civil wars, Europeans began to visit the country. The first to arrive were Portuguese sailors, in 1542. Seven years later, a Spanish Jesuit missionary, Francis Xavier, began trying to convert the Japanese to Christianity. Other traders and missionaries followed and were welcomed at first.

As well as introducing a new religion to Japan, the Europeans also brought firearms with them. Some samurai looked down on these, believing they were the weapons of cowards, but others quickly saw their advantages in battle. One samurai, Oda Nobunaga (1534–1582), equipped his men with muskets (guns) and with their help, captured Kyoto, the capital, in 1568.

Jesuit missionaries entered China in the 1500s with the emperor's permission. They converted tens of thousands to Christianity.

Hideyoshi (1536–1598) broke the traditional power of the feudal lords and the Buddhist temples, but his plans to build a Japanese Empire failed.

## STRUGGLE AND CIVIL WAR

Nobunaga was wounded and later committed suicide, but his work was continued by Hideyoshi, who became Kampaku, or chief imperial minister, in 1585. He planned a great Japanese Empire that would include China. Hideyoshi invaded Korea in 1592 and 1597, but failed to conquer it. He died in Korea. Hideyoshi had appointed Tokugawa Ieyasu (1543–1616) as his son's guardian, but a power struggle broke out. Ieyasu defeated his rivals at the battle of Sekigahara in 1600. He became the first shogun of the Tokugawa dynasty in 1603. Hideyoshi and Ieyasu took strong central control of Japan and its trading, banning foreigners, Christianity, and overseas travel.

## BATTLE OF NAGASHINO

At the battle of Nagashino in 1575, Oda Nobunaga armed his 3,000 men with muskets bought from the Portuguese. They defeated a much larger force of mounted samurai, who were armed with the traditional weapons of swords and bows and arrows. This was a turning point in Japan—the beginning of modern times in which European influences played a part. The Japanese tried to control these influences, banning Christians and foreign traders. But the Europeans sided with certain lords in southern Japan, and European goods and ideas crept in.

## MING CHINA

By 1500, the Ming dynasty was weakening.
The emperor stopped Chinese ships from
sailing beyond coastal waters, but allowed
foreign ships to visit China. Japanese
pirates were also attacking the coast,
making these waters dangerous for sailors.
In 1517, European traders arrived, and in
1557, the Portuguese were permitted to
settle in Macao. Some Jesuit priests were
allowed into Beijing.

Defeating Mongol invasions and the
Japanese invasion of Korea destabilized
China. Famines, rising taxes, and official
corruption led to unrest. In 1641, rebels
took over parts of China, and in 1644,
the Manchus from the north were called
in to help drive out the rebels in Beijing.
The Manchus, taking advantage of this
chaos, took over and set up their own
Qing dynasty of emperors.

### KEY DATES

| 1517 | Portuguese traders first arrive in China |
| 1542 | Mongol invasion of China |
| 1549 | First Jesuit mission to Japan |
| 1568 | Nobunaga takes Kyoto and central Japan |
| 1582 | Corruption breaks out in the Ming government |
| 1590 | Hideyoshi gains control of northern and eastern Japan |
| 1592–98 | Japanese invasions of Korea |
| 1641 | Rebels take over parts of China |
| 1644 | Manchus take over Beijing: the Ming dynasty falls |

◀ To protect themselves from Japanese pirates, the Chinese developed floating mines (water bombs). This idea eventually reached the West.

▶ The Japanese Tea Ceremony is called *cha-no-yu*. It was brought to Japan by Buddhist monks from China, but the ceremony spread beyond the monasteries in the 1400s. The great teamaster Sen Rikyu laid down the rules for the ceremony in the 1500s.

Hideyoshi built many castles in Japan. He built this particular castle, Himeji, in 1577 to act as his headquarters during the civil wars between rival samurai.

# ART AND ARCHITECTURE 1461–1600

**The Asian empires of the Ottomans, the Safavids and the Moghuls saw a blossoming of the arts. The "Renaissance" in Europe was a surge of creativity.**

The Gothic architecture of France's high Middle Ages, with its soaring cathedral spires and flying buttresses, was now out of fashion. Italian architects such as Andrea Palladio (1508–80) were inspired by the classical temples of ancient Greece and Rome. Palaces and grand houses replaced the draughty castles of the Middle Ages, whose massive walls could be knocked down easily by cannon balls.

### THE DIVINE AND THE HUMAN

The artists Leonardo da Vinci (1452–1519), Michelangelo (1475–1564), and Raphael (1483–1520) were geniuses at the forefront of the Renaissance. Michelangelo painted the ceiling of the Sistine Chapel in Rome, and the Roman Catholic Church was a great patron of the arts. However, as with the ancient Greeks and Romans, the realistic presentation of the human form and its anatomy was of central concern. As well as religious art, Renaissance artists were inspired by classical myths, portraits, and landscapes.

The Incas did not have the potter's wheel, but they made beautiful ceramics. They also worked in gold and silver and wove richly patterned textiles.

In Europe, organs and harpsichords were popular instruments. A pipe organ was played by one person, while another operated the bellows to blow air through the pipes.

◀ Islamic religious art did not depict human or animal forms, believing that creation of life was the preserve of God alone. This led to forms of intricate ornamentation that were abstract or very stylized.

▶ This is a detail from the entrance to the Lotfollah Mosque in the Safavid capital of Isfahan, Persia. It is an intricate style of artwork that was also used in Moghul India.

The original Globe Theatre in London, UK, was built in 1599. It was associated with the English playwright and poet William Shakespeare (1564–1616).

▶ The massive dome of the cathedral in Florence, Italy, was designed by Filippo Brunelleschi (1377–1446) and completed in 1436. It broke with the medieval architectural tradition and was a technological masterpiece. Florence was the birthplace of the Renaissance.

## IN NORTHERN EUROPE

Northern European art was rooted in detailed realism at this time, and artists such as the German Albrecht Dürer (1471–1528) traveled to Rome. The Protestant Reformation from 1517 marked an increased interest in secular art. The German Hans Holbein the Younger (1497–1543) is remembered for his fine portraits, many painted for the Tudor royal court in England.

The development of printing presses in the Renaissance transformed art and literature alike, making them more readily available to ordinary people. Printing also revolutionized the world of music, as notation no longer had to be copied out or learned by ear. New instruments became popular, such as the viol da gamba, lute, harpsichord, and organ.

## THE WIDER WORLD

The fall of Constantinople to the Ottoman Turks in 1453 is sometimes said to mark the end of the Middle Ages. The Ottoman empire's greatest architect was Mimar Sinan (c. 1490–1588), a great builder of mosques, schools, public baths, aqueducts, and palaces. Decorative arts included ceramics, splendid textiles and carpets. In Safavid Persia, the rule (1587–1629) of Shah Abbas saw the creation of a beautiful new capital at Isfahan, and marked a golden age in both architecture and arts. This was also a remarkable period in Moghul India.

At this time, the cultural diversity of the world and its regions was still very marked. This began to change with the brutal European conquest of the Americas (the "New World") from the 1500s and the destruction of indigenous cultures. A globalized economy and cultural values imposed by Europeans became dominant in many parts of the modern world.

The Golden Temple was built in Amritsar, India, to serve as the spiritual center for the new Sikh religion. Sikhism had developed in the Punjab during the Moghul period of religious tolerance.

# SCIENCE AND TECHNOLOGY 1461–1600

**In contrast to the rest of the world, a new spirit of inquiry was awakening in Europe. This gave birth to a growing revolution in science and technology.**

By 1500, windmills had become more advanced, and were used for grinding grain and pumping water. The Dutch used them to drain and reclaim the wetlands of the Netherlands.

In much of the world, research and development of new ideas and technologies was slowing down. Ming China was in decline and becoming isolated, and India, Persia, and the Ottoman Empire were not as inventive as they had been previously. However, when European travelers arrived on their shores, Asians were interested in the new ideas and inventions—guns, astronomical knowledge, clocks, new tools, and shipbuilding methods—that they brought with them. The Koreans invented ironclad ships, based on the ideas brought in by a Dutch visitor. Meanwhile, Indigenous American cultures, before the European settlers arrived and destroyed them, tended to adapt and improve the technologies of their forefathers. Both the Aztecs and the Incas fully exploited these improvements when building their great cities.

An astrolabe

A backstaff

A magnetic compass

▲ Long sea journeys required improved navigational aids for calculating position and direction. The astrolabe was Arabic and, with the backstaff, was used to figure out a ship's latitude. The compass, first used by the Chinese in the 1100s, was used to keep a ship on course.

▶ The Italian Leonardo da Vinci was both an artist and an inventive genius. Among his many designs are these sketches for making flying machines. Although in practice they did not work, and it was not until 1902 that humans could fly, his work pointed the way to the future.

## A REVOLUTION IN EUROPE

The revival of learning in Europe during the 1400s and 1500s led people to start observing the world around them. They explored and experimented to find out how things really were, rather than just accepting what they were told by the Church. Sometimes this led to clashes with the Church, as was the case with Galileo in 1615, after he had invented thermometers, telescopes, and developed ideas about gravity, mathematics, and astronomy. Many outstanding ideas and inventions were produced at this time. The first successful watch was invented in 1504, and the microscope in 1590. People studied the structure of the human body, and in 1543, Andreas Vesalius published some of the first accurate descriptions of human anatomy.

Tycho Brahe (1546–1601) carefully mapped and studied the heavenly bodies. The king of Denmark had an observatory built for him on the island of Hveen, complete with instruments, library, laboratory, and living quarters. The telescope had not yet been invented, but Brahe established the positions of 777 stars by naked-eye observation.

Although the pace of development had slowed considerably, the Chinese still produced beautiful porcelain. This Ming porcelain vase, with a peacock, was made in the 15th century.

Traditional medieval ideas about alchemy, astrology, geometry, and herbal medicine also thrived, led by such thinkers as Paracelsus, Kepler, and Nostradamus. Scientific and exploring societies were founded. Some inventors such as Leonardo da Vinci were even thinking about airplanes, helicopters, and submarines. This flourishing of genius in Europe marked the beginning of a scientific and technological revolution, which was to continue into the future. It laid the foundations for today's modern world.

▼ During the Renaissance, scholars began to study mathematical theory. This was essential for their scientific experiments.

## WHEN IT HAPPENED

**1492** Martin Behaim makes the first globe
**1504** Peter Heinlein invents the watch
**1512** Nicolaus Copernicus suggests that the Earth moves around the sun.
**1518** Royal College of Physicians founded in London
**1528** First manual on surgery is published
**1540** Michael Servetus discovers the circulation of the blood
**1546** Mapmaker Gerardus Mercator identifies the Earth's magnetic poles
**1600** William Gilbert writes about magnetism and electricity

# TRADE AND EMPIRE

## 1601–1707

The Europeans were now beginning to take over the world. The biggest impact was in the Americas. British and French settlers occupied the east coast of North America, and Spanish *conquistadores* had already taken over Mexico and South America. European trading posts were now dotted around the world—only Japan kept them out. In Europe, this century brought a tragic mixture of wars, revolution, and devastation, as well as enormous growth and progress in the sciences and arts.

▲ In 1620, a ship called the *Mayflower* sailed from Plymouth in England, carrying pilgrims to a new life in North America.

◀ The Taj Mahal, near Agra in India, was built in the 1600s by Shah Jehan as a mausoleum for his wife, Mumtaz Mahal.

229

# JAPAN IN ISOLATION 1603–1716

**The Tokugawa shoguns brought stability to Japan after years of chaos. Fearing disruptive influences from foreigners, they sealed Japan from the outside world.**

Shinto religious traditions remained strong under the Tokugawas, but the role of the temples in politics and the economy was reduced.

In 1603, Tokugawa Ieyasu (1543–1616), head of a powerful family, became shogun—largely by political maneuvering and military force. Edo (later renamed Tokyo), the small fishing village that had been his headquarters, became his capital. Here, Ieyasu began to build what became the world's largest castle. He retired in 1605, and made his son Hidetada shogun. But Ieyasu continued to control the government until his death.

Ieyasu thought that there were two threats to Japan: the violent rivalry between *daimyos* (lords) that had caused great instability, and the growing foreign influence. He placed the daimyos under constant watch in Edo and kept them so busy organizing—and paying for—the building of the palace there, that they had no time to make trouble and no money for soldiers.

▲ There were important technical and cultural advances in Japan during this time. However, because of Japan's "closed door" policy to foreigners, these advances were not seen by the outside world. These exquisite Japanese porcelain figures date from this period.

▶ Nijo Castle in Kyoto was built in the 1600s for the Tokugawa Bakufu, the ambassador to the emperor. Even though the emperor was by now largely powerless, it was still important for the shogun to remain on friendly terms with him.

Japan is a fertile and well-populated country, with many valleys and plains separated by mountains. These geographical extremes made it difficult to unify during this period.

JAPAN
Hokkaido
Honshu
Edo ●
● Kyoto
● Nagasaki
● Deshima

When the foreign missionaries and traders began to involve themselves in Japanese politics, Ieyasu realized that their ideas could lead to more violence. For the sake of harmony, the shogun placed restrictions on them. The strongest Christian influence was in Nagasaki. In 1638, after a revolt there, the shogun had 37,000 converts killed, and banned Christianity.

## JAPAN BECOMES PROSPEROUS

Following the rebellion by Japanese Christians in Nagasaki, only a few Dutch and Chinese traders were allowed into Japan. Japanese people were not allowed to go abroad, and those who lived away from the country were not allowed to return. Christian priests were ordered to leave or be killed, and their churches were torn down. Japanese Christians were executed. Life became strictly regulated, and the country was sealed off from outside influences. Tokugawa rule gave Japan almost 250 years of peace.

Japan grew more prosperous because it now operated as one country. Merchants and farmers were encouraged to expand their businesses, and traditional *daimyos* and samurai warriors lost their positions and grew poor. Like Europe, Japan was changing from a feudal society into a trading economy. Cities and towns grew larger, and the population expanded greatly during the 1600s and 1700s. Though Japanese society still kept its strict rules of behavior, people were becoming better educated.

There were temporary setbacks to Japan's growth during this period. In 1684, the fifth Tokugawa shogun, Tsunayoshi, introduced some reforms inspired by Buddhist scholars of the 1100s. They were not popular. In 1703, the capital, Edo (Tokyo), was destroyed by an earthquake and fire. However, in 1716, a reforming shogun, Yoshimune, came to power and Japan's isolation from the rest of the world began to break down.

▲ The Tosho-gu Temple at Nikko, built during the 1600s, was dedicated to Ieyasu, who, after his death, was looked on as a saint.

◄ Sumo wrestling began in 1624. It was encouraged as an alternative to samurai warriors killing each other. Wrestlers were selected when young. They trained for many years.

◄ The Dutch were permitted to occupy the island of Deshima in Nagasaki Bay as a trading base. A few ships were allowed to visit each year, exchanging foreign goods for Japanese silks and other products. The Dutch were not allowed to cross onto the Japanese mainland.

### KEY DATES

| | |
|---|---|
| 1603 | Ieyasu founds the Tokugawa Shogunate |
| 1609 | Small Dutch trading base established on the island of Deshima in Nagasaki Bay |
| 1612 | Persecution of Nagasaki Christians begins |
| 1637 | Portuguese traders banned and expelled |
| 1637–3 | The Shimabara Rebellion in Nagasaki |
| 1684 | Hardship after Tokugawa Tsunayoshi's reforms |
| 1703 | Edo (Tokyo) destroyed by earthquake and fire |
| 1716 | Yoshimune, a reformer, comes to power |

# THE STUARTS 1603–1649

**The Stuart dynasty came from Scotland. In England, they faced a complicated political situation that led to six years of civil war and the downfall of a king.**

James I (1566-1625) was an intelligent king who did his best in a difficult situation, and during his time, England and Scotland moved closer to being united. He was not popular. He believed in divine right, which claimed that a ruler could do as he wished and was responsible only to God.

Queen Elizabeth I, the last Tudor monarch of England, died in 1603 without an heir. James VI of Scotland, son of Mary, Queen of Scots, succeeded her as James I of England. James was descended from Henry VIII's sister and Elizabeth's aunt, Margaret Tudor, who had married the Scottish king, James IV, in 1503. His family, the Stuarts, had ruled Scotland since 1371.

England and Scotland now had the same king, but they still remained separate countries. James dreamed of uniting them, but many English and Scottish people were opposed to this. He tried to make peace between Catholics, Anglicans, and Puritans. The Puritans were extreme Protestants who wished to abolish church ceremony and music, bishops, church hierarchies, and other "popish" traditions. James angered them by refusing to go as far as they wanted. But he ordered a new translation of the Bible, the King James Bible, to try to bring Christians together.

As England's prosperity grew under Tudor and Stuart rule, many towns were renewed. They were not planned, but rebuilt along existing winding streets.

### JAMES THE SPENDER

James made peace with Catholic Spain to try and ease tensions between European Catholics and Protestants, and Britain was at peace for 20 years. But in 1624 James was drawn into the Thirty Years' War in Germany on the Protestant side, supporting his son-in-law, Frederick. James fell deeply into debt. The cost of running the country was growing and James himself was a lavish spender. He believed Parliament should obey him without question and grant whatever he asked for. But Parliament and the king's ministers had grown stronger in Tudor times, and he clashed with them when his demands for money were refused.

### THE GUNPOWDER PLOT

Catholics in England were frustrated by Protestant intolerance toward them, and, although James I tried to please everyone, opinions pulled in conflicting directions. Some Catholics saw violence as the only way to gain toleration for Catholicism, though many disliked this idea. A small group plotted to kill both the king and parliamentarians by blowing up Parliament during its ceremonial opening on November 5, 1605. One of the conspirators was Guy Fawkes, who was discovered guarding barrels of gunpowder in the cellars of Parliament. He and the other plotters were arrested, tortured, and put to death. After this, attitudes toward Catholics hardened.

The King James Bible, or Authorized Version, published in 1611, was carefully translated under James I's guidance, in order to serve as the one Bible for Anglicans, Puritans, and Catholics. It was admired because of the beauty of its language, and has survived to this day. It is still used in some churches.

| KEY DATES | |
|---|---|
| 1603 | James I becomes king of England |
| 1605 | The Gunpowder Plot to blow up Parliament |
| 1608 | James disagrees with Parliament over money |
| 1621 | James again disagrees with Parliament |
| 1625 | Charles I becomes king |
| 1629 | Charles closes Parliament |
| 1637 | Charles's court splits after a crisis |
| 1640 | Charles recalls Parliament—clashes follow |
| 1642 | The English Civil War begins |
| 1649 | Charles I is executed by parliamentarians |

Charles left London and raised an army. He was defeated in 1646, and handed power to Parliament, but he then escaped to continue the Civil War. Finally, Charles was recaptured, brought to trial, and executed in 1649. For 12 years following the English Civil War, England had no king.

▼ During Tudor and Stuart times, the wealthy gained more power and influence. However, disagreements increased between the different groups, especially over money, business, and religious matters.

## CHARLES I

James I tried to please everyone. He was unpopular in England because he made mistakes, and because he was Scottish and his Danish wife, Anne, was Catholic. His belief in the rights of the king was also disliked. When he died in 1625, his son Charles became king and inherited his lack of popularity.

Charles I (1600–1649) also disliked parliamentary interference, and handled situations badly. People took sides and supported either the king or Parliament. This became a battle between traditional and modern ideas. When, in 1629, Parliament refused to give Charles more money and allow him to rule in his own way, he sent the parliamentarians home and tried to govern without them.

Charles ruled without Parliament for eleven years, but his court and ministers were divided over many important questions. Charles also angered the Scots, who thought he had become too English, and lost their support. Parliament, called back in 1640, united against him. It tried to limit his powers and suppress his supporters. In 1642, Charles tried to arrest five parliamentary leaders, but Parliament, including the nobility, opposed him fiercely.

# EARLY AMERICAN SETTLERS 1607–1650

**When the first Europeans arrived, the Indigenous Americans were unsure about them. Little did they know that these settlers would come in their millions.**

The Plymouth Colony settlers were hardy, but not farmers. They would have starved if an Indigenous American named Squanto had not made friends with them and showed them how to survive by growing corn and catching fish.

For a century after John Cabot discovered Newfoundland in 1497, most Europeans regarded North America as unimportant. They did not appreciate its potential, and saw little economic value there. Their main interests were in finding a sea route to Asia and acquiring easy riches by raiding Spanish galleons laden with gold in the Caribbean. Early explorers returned home without finding the gold, exotic cities, and sea passages to Asia that they had sought. Both Cartier's French colony at Quebec (1534–1541) and Raleigh's English colony at Roanoke (1584–1590) failed. However, a Spanish settlement founded in 1565 at St. Augustine in Florida survived. Only in 1607–1608, when new colonies were founded at Quebec and Jamestown, did the Europeans realize that the new lands might be valuable. From 1600 onward, many Europeans, wishing to escape religious strife and war at home, sailed to North America to start a new life.

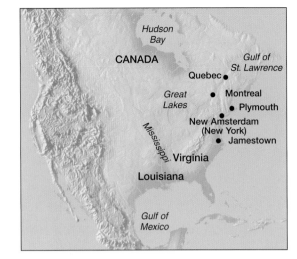

The place names of modern northeast America show that most of the successful early European settlers came from either England or France.

The first successful English colony, founded in 1607 at Jamestown, Virginia, was almost wiped out by disease, hunger, and troubles with the Indigenous Americans, but it survived. The colony's leader, John Smith, wrote a book that attracted even more settlers.

▲ A group of Puritans landed at Plymouth, Massachusetts, in 1620. Known as the Pilgrim Fathers, they are regarded as the founders of modern America—a new nation founded on the principles of liberty and justice.

▶ The *Mayflower* carried 102 Puritan colonists and 47 crew members in cramped conditions. Escaping from religious persecution, they set out from Plymouth, England, in 1620 and landed near Cape Cod. There they founded a small settlement which they also named Plymouth.

▲ When the Puritans landed in America in 1620 they knew nothing about living in this new wilderness. Food ran short, and many of the settlers died from disease and exposure. Nearly half of them died during the first winter, and only 54 were still alive the following spring.

## THE NEW AMERICANS

English colonist John Rolfe introduced tobacco growing to the settlers in 1612. The crop earned them money and Jamestown prospered. As the demand for tobacco increased, the tobacco growers needed more land, which they took from the native people. This struggle for land led to bitter wars between colonists and the Indigenous Americans. The arrival in Massachusetts of the Pilgrims in 1620 marked a turning point—they had come to stay, and to live according to Puritan principles. In 1625, the Dutch established a colony on Manhattan Island, today's New York City. French colonists also arrived, settling north of the St. Lawrence River in what is now Canada.

Fur trading, particularly in beaver skins, became profitable because of the high demand in Europe. From the 1630s onward, more Puritan refugees and migrants from England arrived. They had no hope of return, and, though life was hard, the New England colonies thrived.

| KEY DATES | |
|---|---|
| 1492 | Columbus arrives in the Americas |
| 1497 | Cabot lands in Newfoundland |
| 1513 | Spanish Ponce de León explores Florida |
| 1540 | Coronado (Spanish) enters New Mexico |
| 1534–41 | Cartier (French) explores the St. Lawrence |
| 1584–90 | Raleigh's English Roanoke colony (fails) |
| 1607 | Jamestown, Virginia (English), founded |
| 1608 | Champlain establishes Quebec and New France |
| 1620 | Arrival of the Pilgrims in New England |
| 1625 | Dutch settle in New Amsterdam (New York) |

By 1700, there were about 400,000 Europeans in North America, and the New England colonies were well established. Whole communities had moved there from Europe, and before long they were self-supporting. Harvard College was founded near Boston in 1636.

235

# THE SWEDISH EMPIRE 1560–1721

**Sweden's greatest king, Gustavus Adolphus, and his reforming chancellor, Axel Oxenstierna, made Sweden into a great, modern Protestant power.**

Gustavus Adolphus (1594–1632) was a brave and inspiring leader, and he governed Sweden well. He made a modernized state with impressive cities, industries, and a strong army. He ruled for 21 years from 1611.

▲ Count Axel Oxenstierna (1583–1654) was Sweden's chancellor for 42 years from 1612. He was a great reformer. After Gustavus Adolphus' death, Oxenstierna ran the country for a further 22 years under Queen Christina. He master-minded Sweden's growth into a modern Protestant power.

▶ Gustavus Adolphus led his army to victory against the Catholic League at the Battle of Breitenfeld in 1631. The Thirty Years' War, which lasted until 1648, devastated large areas of Europe.

In 1520, Sweden, led by King Gustavus Vasa, rebelled against Denmark and gained independence. The Swedes then started to break the dominance of the Hanseatic League over the Baltic Sea region. Although Sweden was sparsely populated, it had a strong government and a growing trade with England and Holland. The Swedes fought in Estonia, eventually conquering the country by 1582. In later campaigns they gained Karelia, east of Finland, and Lapland in the north.

Gustavus Adolphus was born in 1594. He became king of Sweden in 1611, at the age of 17. He was to become Sweden's greatest king. A devout and educated Protestant, he spoke many languages. He had Sweden's towns rebuilt, and its industries flourished. Its frontline army was only 40,000 strong, but Gustavus made it the best in Europe. By 1629, he had defeated the armies of Denmark, Russia, and Poland, making Sweden the leading military power in northern Europe.

Gustavus Adolphus built a great fleet and made Sweden the dominant Baltic state. His flagship, the *Vasa*, however, capsized and sank on its maiden voyage in 1628.

Gustavus' fellow Protestant princes in Germany faced defeat in the Thirty Years' War. If Germany became Catholic, then Sweden would be isolated, so Gustavus Adolphus declared war on Emperor Ferdinand II of Austria. In July 1630, Gustavus landed an army in Germany. In 1631, at Breitenfeld near Leipzig, the Swedes defeated the emperor's army.

## SWEDEN'S ERA

In the spring of 1632, the Swedish army occupied Munich and advanced against Vienna, Ferdinand's capital. At the battle of Lützen, the emperor's forces retreated in disorder, but Gustavus died in battle. There was a temporary setback in 1634 when the Swedes were defeated at the battle of Nördlingen. Their fortunes soon turned when they defeated the Catholics at Jankau in 1645. In 1655, they entered Poland, and in 1658 took southern Sweden from the Danes. Under Charles XII, they overcame the Danes, Russians, Poles, and Saxons. But in 1709 they ventured too far—into the Ukraine. Tired and far from home, they were defeated by the Russians and, by 1721, all Swedish gains south of the Baltic and in Russia had been lost.

### KEY DATES

| | |
|---|---|
| 1520 | Sweden gains independence from Denmark |
| 1523–60 | Gustavus Vasa modernizes Sweden |
| 1580 | Sweden conquers Estonia |
| 1611–32 | Gustavus Adolphus reigns as king of Sweden |
| 1620s | Sweden becomes the leading northern power |
| 1630–34 | Sweden successful in the Thirty Years' War |
| 1643–45 | Swedish victories against Denmark and Austria |
| 1697–1708 | Many Swedish victories throughout Europe |
| 1709 | Swedes defeated by the Russians |
| 1721 | Sweden in retreat—the end of its period of dominance |

▲ Tidö Castle in Sweden was built around 1620. During this period, Sweden developed from a simple agricultural nation into a great European power.

▶ Gustavus Adolphus equipped his army with new guns which could be easily transported by the soldiers. Through their extensive knowledge of mining, the Swedes had become masters in metallurgy and the use of explosives. They applied this knowledge to war.

## THE BATTLE OF LÜTZEN

The Swedes fought alongside the Protestant Germans against the Catholic forces of imperial Austria at Lützen. The Catholic army was much larger, and the Protestant attack was delayed by foggy conditions. But good tactics and bravery helped the Protestants break through and rout the Catholics. Gustavus Adolphus, who always led his troops from the front, was killed. However, his fellow general, Bernard, Duke of Saxe Weimar, kept fighting, and after a full day's battle, the Catholics fled in chaos.

# THE THIRTY YEARS' WAR 1618–1648

**The Thirty Years' War was the world's first modern war. Starting as a religious conflict between Catholics and Protestants, it ended as a fight for power in Europe.**

Frederick (1596–1632), the "Winter King" of Bohemia, was the son-in-law of England's James I.

Ferdinand II of Austria (1578–1637) was a Catholic. He tried to impose his religion on all his subjects.

In 1618, tensions exploded in Bohemia between Catholics and Protestants, and between the Hapsburgs and other royal houses. Ferdinand II, the Holy Roman emperor, had inherited the Bohemian throne in 1617 and two years later, in 1619, the Austrian throne. Until that time, the Hapsburgs had been neutral in matters of religion. Bohemia had long been Protestant, but Ferdinand was Catholic, and he unwisely forced Bohemia to become Catholic. This resulted in the Bohemians revolting against him.

In 1619, the German rulers who elected the Holy Roman emperor met at Prague. They deposed Ferdinand II as king of Bohemia and made Frederick, a Protestant, king in his place. This resulted in a series of wars, fought mainly in Germany, which eventually involved most of Europe for the next thirty years.

At first, the Catholics won most of the battles, with Spanish Hapsburg help and money. In 1625, the Danes joined the Protestants, but to no avail. The Catholics had two outstanding generals, Count Wallenstein and Count Tilly, whose troops fought well, and by 1629, the Protestant allies were in trouble.

The use of guns and cannons increased the destruction and cost of the war. The matchlock musket was improved by the Swedes to make it lighter and faster to reload.

## SWEDEN ENTERS THE WAR

Frederick fled and a Catholic prince, Maximilian of Bavaria, was appointed king of Bohemia. The struggle then moved northward. Led by Wallenstein, the emperor's army defeated the Danes and overran northern Germany. It seemed that nothing could stop Ferdinand from forcing Germany to become Catholic until, in 1630, Protestant Gustavus Adolphus of Sweden entered the war. He took back northern Germany, soundly defeating the Catholics in battles at Breitenfeld and Lützen. But the battles took their toll. Tilly was killed at Breitenfeld, and Gustavus Adolphus died at Lützen.

## THE DEFENESTRATION OF PRAGUE

In Prague, in 1618, a group of Bohemian Protestant nobles met with representatives of the Catholic Hapsburg emperor. Their arguments became so heated that the Bohemians threw the emperor's men out of a window—in other words, defenestrated them—of Hradčany Castle, the Hapsburg stronghold. This violent action is known as the "Defenestration of Prague" and sparked the Thirty Years' War.

The French entered the war in 1635, a year after the Swedes were beaten at Nördlingen. The French minister Cardinal Richelieu already supported the Protestants because he opposed the ambitious Hapsburgs. The same year, the German Protestant princes withdrew from the war, bankrupt and defeated. Many alliances switched, and the conflict grew even more complicated. The French advanced into Catholic Bavaria to overcome the Spanish Hapsburgs and Sweden defeated the Austrian Hapsburgs. When the French and Swedes were poised to take over Bavaria and threaten Austria, the Hapsburg emperor asked for peace.

## THE RESULTS OF THE WAR

During this long war, large guns and mercenary troops had been used. This had been expensive and caused great devastation. Troops looted whole areas of Germany and at times even switched sides. Germany was ruined, and the Netherlands and Switzerland gained independence; however, France, Sweden, and Holland grew stronger. Some states gained land and others lost it. One German state, Brandenburg–Prussia, grew stronger and was to become even more important. The Hapsburgs lost their power, and the Holy Roman Empire grew weaker. Germany broke down into 300 small states. Many European governments became secular, which meant that they no longer forced religious beliefs on their subjects. The Peace of Westphalia, which ended the war, was the first major European treaty of modern times.

▲ One of the worst events of the Thirty Years' War was the destruction of the German city of Magdeburg by the Catholics under Count Tilly in 1631. Until then, Tilly had been highly respected across Europe.

▶ The Catholic Count Albrecht Wallenstein (1583–1634) was an outstanding general. He became rich from the war, and tried to build his own empire in northern Germany. This made him very unpopular with the emperor, and eventually led to his downfall.

▼ Wallenstein and his men were murdered at Eger in Germany in 1634, when it was discovered that he was using the war as a way of creating power for himself.

### KEY DATES

| | |
|---|---|
| 1618–20 | Bohemian revolt against Austria |
| 1625–27 | Denmark joins the Protestants |
| 1629 | Protestant Germans losing the war |
| 1630 | Gustavus Adolphus of Sweden joins the war, overrunning northern Germany |
| 1631 | Tilly storms and destroys Magdeburg |
| 1631–32 | Protestant victories at Breitenfeld and Lützen |
| 1634 | Protestants are defeated at Nördlingen. Count Wallenstein is murdered |
| 1635 | Protestant Germans make peace—France joins the war |
| 1645 | French and Swedish victories in Germany |
| 1648 | The Peace of Westphalia treaty ends the war |

# FRANCE AND RICHELIEU 1624–1661

**Louis XIII became king at the age of nine. He later appointed as his chief minister the man who was to make France the leading nation in Europe.**

The clothing of the French nobility was elaborate. Wigs, hats, and clothes were a sign of status. This was a French army officer's clothing when on campaign.

Marie de Médicis (1573–1642) was queen of France, then regent to her son Louis XIII. She clung to power, but was banished in 1617. Richelieu helped her make peace with her son in 1620. But when she tried to replace Louis in 1630, she was permanently exiled to Brussels.

In 1624, Louis XIII of France appointed Cardinal Richelieu as his chief minister. They worked together for eighteen years. Richelieu's ambition was to unify France into one centrally ruled country and make it great. Regional dukes held a lot of power, so he set out to reduce their influence. In 1628, he also dealt harshly with the troublesome French Protestant Huguenots. Richelieu was disliked by Catholic leaders, nobles, and judges because he stopped many of their privileges, and the high taxes he levied caused mass revolts. He believed in strong control, and used force to get his way.

Abroad, Austria and Spain were the main threats to France. The Hapsburgs ruled both countries and, if they joined forces, France would be vulnerable. By 1631, during the Thirty Years' War, Hapsburg Austria controlled most of Germany and threatened to dominate Europe.

## CARDINAL RICHELIEU

Armand du Plessis, the Duke of Richelieu (1585–1642), became a bishop in 1607 and a cardinal in 1622. He entered the council of the regent, Marie de Médicis, in 1616, and became chief minister in 1624. Richelieu believed in absolutism—the right of the king to do what he wanted. He believed the king was responsible to God, not to the Church, the nobility, or the people. Richelieu used spies effectively and suppressed all opposition. He trained his successor, Cardinal Mazarin, who continued Richelieu's policies and ruled as regent for the young Louis XIV until 1661. In many European countries, this was a time when chief ministers were very powerful.

Louis XIII (1601-1643) was the son of Henry IV and the second king of the Bourbon line. He became king as a boy in 1610 and assumed power in 1617. He was very influenced by Cardinal Richelieu, but he outlasted Richelieu by one year, and left the throne to his young son, Louis XIV.

La Rochelle was the stronghold of the Protestant Huguenots, who had developed their own army and navy. Richelieu besieged the port in 1628 and broke their power. In this painting, Louis XIII is depicted visiting the scene of the siege in October of that year.

## FRANCE BECOMES STRONGER

To weaken Austria, Richelieu paid Sweden, the Netherlands, and Denmark to fight a common enemy, the Hapsburgs. In 1635, France declared war on Spain (which ruled Belgium and Burgundy). The fighting went on until 1648 and outlasted Richelieu, but his plans succeeded. He tried to extend France to what he thought were its natural frontiers—the Pyrenees in the southwest and the Rhine in the east.

When Richelieu died in 1642, his follower Cardinal Mazarin continued his policies. France replaced Spain as Europe's greatest power. A revolt by the French nobility, called the Fronde, was put down in 1653. When Louis XIV came to the throne he was only five, and Mazarin ruled as regent. By the end of Mazarin's life, in 1661, France had changed greatly. It had grown larger, stronger, and richer; its armies had become the finest in Europe, and Louis XIV was to be its greatest king.

▶ The royal flag of the ruling Bourbon kings of France acted as the French flag until 1790, the time of the French Revolution.

▼ Richelieu allowed the Protestant Huguenots religious freedom, but he fought to break their political and military power. This grisly massacre of Huguenots was initiated by Richelieu.

241

# DECLINE OF SPAIN 1598–1700

**After a century of greatness, Spain went through a long, slow decline that arose from its refusal to recognize the changing times, and its failure to adapt to them.**

Philip III (1578–1621) became king of Spain, but his real interests were religious, not political. During his reign, Spain began to lose its place in the world as a great European and colonial power.

▼ Wealth from the New World was not just spent on wars. Philip II had built the magnificent palace at El Escorial, near Madrid, at the end of the 1500s. Its library housed a priceless collection of Greek, Latin, and Arabic manuscripts.

When Philip III became king of Spain in 1598, his country was bankrupt. The Spanish army was outdated, and the government was corrupt and incompetent. Spain had amassed great riches from the Americas, but their value had decreased because Europe was by now flooded with Spanish gold and silver.

The opportunity to make easy fortunes had rotted Spanish society, and sensible ways of making money, such as promoting and developing trade, education, and crafts, had been ignored. Yet Spain's empire was still the largest in the world, consisting of most of South and Central America and a large part of North America, as well as the Philippines and settlements in Asia and Africa. Philip had no interest in politics, and Spain was run by his ministers. The first of these, the Duke of Lerma, used his position to make himself very rich. His greatest mistake was expelling the Moriscos in 1606.

The most famous Spanish author at this time was Miguel de Cervantes (1547–1616), who wrote *Don Quixote*. The book tells the story of a foolish landowner who sees himself as a brave knight and has a series of amusing adventures with his squire, the peasant Sancho Panza.

The Moriscos were Muslim Moors who had stayed in Spain and converted to Christianity. Lerma suspected that they were plotting against the government. However, the Moriscos were extremely hardworking and skilled, and Spain could not afford to lose them.

At this time, the Roman Catholic Church was more powerful even than the king or his ministers. Through the Inquisition it supervised and controlled every aspect of Spanish life. Religious issues were considered to be more important than any economic interests, and the nation grew steadily poorer.

## THE END OF THE HAPSBURGS

In 1621, Philip III was succeeded by his son Philip IV. His reign was disastrous. The Spanish support of the Catholic cause in the Thirty Years' War and the wars against Richelieu's France had all proved very costly, and Spain had gained little. By now the flow of treasure from America had dwindled. At home, a revolt in Catalonia plunged Spain further into debt. In December 1640, a mass rising in Portugal ended its union with Spain, leading to further losses. However, fighting continued and Spain did not recognize Portugal's independence until 1668.

Philip IV was followed in 1665 by his four-year-old son, Charles II, the last Hapsburg king of Spain. When Charles grew up he failed to produce an heir and was succeeded by Philip of Anjou, grandson of France's Louis XIV.

Philip V introduced a new order into Spain, but the country was now no longer a great power. A European war was fought over who should rule Spain— the Hapsburgs or the French Bourbons. The result, in 1713, was that Spain lost its possessions in Italy, as well as Gibraltar and Belgium. The Hapsburg dynasty lost Spain to the Bourbons.

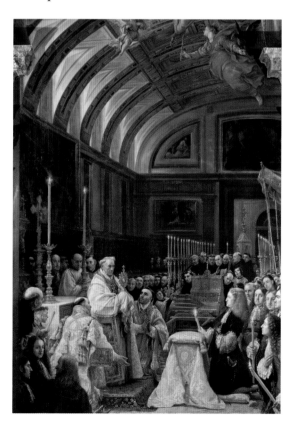

This painting shows Charles II receiving Holy Communion at El Escorial, with a pomp and splendor that was at odds with the reality of a country in decline.

## SPANISH DECLINE

Spain had experienced one century of brilliance and wealth, and one century of decline. It had failed to recognize the new order in northern Europe, with the great economic development led by Protestants. The Catholic order in Spain had failed to modernize itself, and tried to keep power in the hands of nobles, bishops, and kings. As a result, Spain failed to develop after its spectacular growth around 1492, and by 1700 other European countries had surpassed it.

Charles II, who was king for 35 years until his death in 1700, was depicted in paintings as a grand monarch, but his reign was not successful. He failed to produce an heir and was the last Hapsburg king of Spain.

| KEY DATES | |
|---|---|
| 1598 | Spain loses war with France after interfering in French affairs |
| 1598–1621 | Philip III is king of Spain |
| 1606 | Expulsion of the Moriscos from Spain |
| 1621–48 | Spain loses the Netherlands |
| 1621–65 | Philip IV is king of Spain |
| 1640 | Portugal and its empire separate from Spain |
| 1648 | Spain finally accepts Dutch independence |
| 1665–1700 | Charles II reigns as the last Spanish Hapsburg king |
| 1701–13 | The War of the Spanish Succession— Spain loses possessions in Italy, Belgium, and Gibraltar |
| 1700–46 | Philip V is the first Bourbon king of Spain |

# EAST INDIA COMPANIES 1600–1700

**The East India Companies were powerful trading organizations set up by the English, Dutch, and French to protect their business interests in southeastern Asia.**

The ships of the East India Companies, first used for trading, were also converted into warships for use against pirates, Asians, and ships from other companies.

In 1600, the English East India Company was formed in London. Its purpose was to unite the English traders doing business in southeastern Asia. There was cut-throat competition for trade in this area which had first been controlled by the Spaniards and the Portuguese. During the 1600s, the contest for this lucrative trade with the East was between the Dutch, English, and French.

The Netherlands followed England and set up a Dutch East India Company in 1602, with its headquarters in Amsterdam and also at Batavia (Jakarta) on the island of Java. The French formed their own East India company later, in 1664.

These organizations became immensely powerful. Trading was only one of their activities—they also had a political influence. They armed their ships to fight at sea and maintained private armies. The East India companies set up military as well as trading bases and made treaties with local rulers around them. They waged war on neighboring nations and on each other. In many ways they behaved like independent states.

In the 1600s, many European travelers visited India. Through them, knowledge of the impressive history and culture of India began to reach Europe.

The English lost the contest to control the spice trade in the East Indies to the Dutch. India then became the center of English activities, and by 1700, they had sole trading rights in India, with a number of key ports, notably Calcutta, Madras, and Bombay. The Dutch had ports on the Cape in South Africa, in Persia, Ceylon, Malaya, and Japan, and also dominated the Spice Islands (now Indonesia). The French were less successful in their attempt to dominate India. Many private fortunes were made. Sailors and traders often died of disease or fighting. Some made homes in Asia, founding European centers in India, Southeast Asia, and China.

▲ In 1652, the Dutch founded a base at the Cape of Good Hope (Cape Town) as a staging post for ships on the long voyage from Europe to the Far East. This later became a Dutch colony.

▶ The English colony of Madras (modern Chennai) was a major port for exporting cotton goods. It was also the center of a region noted for making cloth with brightly colored designs.

# THE DUTCH EMPIRE 1660–1664

**The Dutch Empire was founded on worldwide trade. During the 1600s, their huge merchant fleet helped the Dutch to become a powerful trading nation.**

Amsterdam was the center of European banking in the 1600s. A bank was founded there in 1609 that deposited and loaned money to finance trade.

▲ Peter Stuyvesant (c. 1610–1672) was the harsh governor of the New Netherland colony in North America from 1647 to 1664. He was against religious freedom. He was hated both by the Indigenous Americans and the colonists. In 1664, they surrendered without a fight to a small English fleet.

▼ From 1619 Batavia, on the site of modern Jakarta, became the center of world trade in spices such as cloves, nutmeg, and pepper. Immense wealth flowed back to the Netherlands through the Dutch East India Company.

By 1600, Amsterdam was Europe's busiest port, with warehouses, banks, and trading houses, as well as a large fleet of ships. Frustrated by their exclusion from South America by the Spanish and Portuguese, the Dutch headed for the Far East. They founded an East India Company for their traders. They took control of trade from the Spice Islands or "East Indies," seizing Java and the Moluccas from the Portuguese.

The Dutch East India Company established its headquarters at Batavia (Jakarta) on the island of Java (now part of Indonesia) in 1619. The company maintained an army and a powerful fleet of ships that drove the English and the Portuguese out of the East Indies and seized Ceylon, the port of Malacca, and several ports in India. The company even set up a trading post in Japan—the only Europeans allowed to do so.

In 1652, the Dutch occupied the Cape of Good Hope on the southern tip of Africa, as a midway point on the long journey from the Far East to Europe. From there, Dutch ships were able to take the shortest route to the East Indies, straight across the Indian Ocean.

## EXPANSION AND CONTRACTION

The huge merchant fleet of the Netherlands was also busy elsewhere. In 1621, the Dutch West India Company was founded across the Atlantic. By 1623, 800 Dutch ships were engaged in the Caribbean, trading in sugar, tobacco, animal hides, and slaves. The company established a colony in Guiana, and they captured Curaçao. For a while, they controlled northeastern Brazil.

In North America, the company founded the colony of New Netherland along the Hudson River in 1624. From there they exported furs, timber, and other goods bought from Indigenous Americans.

Eventually, the Dutch lost their naval supremacy to the English and their empire suffered. They lost Ceylon, Malacca, and the Cape to the English, and were left with just their Southeast Asian empire.

# ENGLISH CIVIL WAR 1642–1660

**The English Civil War was fought between supporters of the king and supporters of Parliament. For five years the country was run by a dictator, Oliver Cromwell.**

▲ Charles I (1600–1649) came to the throne of England in 1625, the same year that he married Henrietta Maria of France. His belief in the divine right of the king first led to clashes with Parliament and eventually to the English Civil War.

▲ Oliver Cromwell (1599–1658) went to college in Cambridge and studied law in London. He was first elected to Parliament in 1628, representing Cambridge. He recruited and trained Parliament's New Model Army. He was a strict Puritan and believed that God had chosen him to perform His will.

The English Civil War was fought between supporters of King Charles I and supporters of Parliament. Like his father, James I, Charles believed in divine right, claiming that his right to rule came directly from God. This belief put Charles at odds with Parliament.

Charles became king in 1625 and immediately began to quarrel with Parliament over his right to imprison people who opposed him over religion, and taxes. In 1629, he dissolved Parliament, and, for 11 years, tried to rule alone.

In 1637, Charles attempted to impose the Anglican form of public worship on the Scots. The Presbyterian Scots rebelled, raising an army that, in 1640, occupied part of northern England. Charles recalled Parliament to ask for money to put down the rebellion by the Scots, but Parliament demanded reforms. Civil war broke out after Charles tried to arrest his five leading parliamentary opponents. In 1642, fighting broke out all over the country between Royalists (supporters of the king), known as Cavaliers, and supporters of Parliament, known as Roundheads.

■ Parliament's Headquarters

▲ Royalist Headquarters

▲ During the Civil War, the west and north generally supported the king, and the south and east supported Parliament, though there were local divisions across the country. The first major battle took place at Edgehill in 1642; the last at Worcester in 1651.

The king made Oxford his capital, and his forces at first held the advantage. However, Parliament secured the support of the Scottish army, and in the long run, proved superior, for it had the money to maintain a professional army. This New Model Army led by Sir Thomas Fairfax decisively defeated Charles's forces at Naseby in 1645. The king surrendered in 1646, after Oxford fell to the Roundheads.

Roundheads

Cavalier

▶ The king's Cavalier forces were crushingly defeated by the New Model Army of the Roundheads at the battle of Naseby in 1645. This was the decisive victory for Parliamentary forces during the English Civil War.

Charles was imprisoned on the Isle of Wight, where he plotted to start the war again with Scottish help. A second phase of fighting broke out, with Royalist risings and a failed invasion attempt by the Scots. In 1648, parliamentarians who still respected the king were removed from Parliament by Oliver Cromwell. The remaining Rump Parliament, as it was called, found Charles guilty of treason and executed him in 1649.

## OLIVER CROMWELL

After Charles' execution, Parliament abolished the monarchy, and England became a Commonwealth. Parliament governed the country, but had an ongoing struggle with the army. In 1653, Oliver Cromwell emerged as a strong leader and ruled the country as Lord Protector. Cromwell clashed with some parliamentarians and was forced to govern with the help of army generals. He fought a war with the Dutch over trade and control of the seas, took control of Ireland, and planned colonial expansion.

His dictatorship was not universally popular because of his use of force and high taxes he imposed. But he introduced education reforms and gave more equality to the people. In 1658, Cromwell died and was succeeded by his son Richard. He was not an effective ruler and the army removed him. The English people wanted a king again, and in 1660, the son of Charles I took the throne as Charles II.

## THE TRIAL OF CHARLES I

Charles was unpopular because he married a Catholic. He also imposed high taxes to pay for wars that people did not want, as well as trying to limit the powers of Parliament—he dissolved it for 11 years. At his trial and execution, he behaved with great dignity, and this won him some sympathy. At his execution, Charles put on an extra shirt so that people would not think that, when he shivered from the cold, he was shivering with fear. His body was secretly buried by his supporters at Windsor Castle.

◀ The seal of the House of Commons depicts the Commonwealth Parliament in session in 1651.

▼ Shortly after the end of the Civil War, there were two disasters in London. The first was the Great Plague, which arrived from Europe, and killed about 20 percent of London's population in 1665. Then, in 1666, the Great Fire destroyed most of the city.

# CHINA: THE QING DYNASTY 1644–1770

**The Qing dynasty was founded by the Manchus, a Siberian people who lived in Manchuria. The Qing dynasty would rule China from 1644 to 1911.**

The Manchus came to conquer China from lands lying north of the Great Wall. During the Manchu period, the size and population of China grew, and the troublesome Mongols were finally defeated.

This intricate gold flower-shaped brooch was made during the Qing period and was exported to Europe.

▼ A 19th-century painting of a tea shop in China. During the Qing dynasty China exported large amounts of goods to Europe, including porcelain, silk, cotton, and tea. Chinese art, furnishings, and lacquer work became the height of fashion.

The Ming dynasty of emperors had ruled China since 1368. But heavy taxation had made their rule unpopular and rebellions broke out all over the country. The last Ming emperor, Chongzhen, hanged himself as peasant rebels overran his capital, Beijing. In the confusion that followed, the Manchu chieftain Dorgon led an army south from Manchuria. He occupied Beijing and set up the Qing ("pure") dynasty. His nephew Shunzhi was the first Qing emperor.

Resistance to the Manchus continued in China's southern provinces, and 40 years went by before all of China submitted to their rule. The Manchus lived separately from the Chinese in closed-off areas. Marriage between Chinese and Manchus was forbidden. Chinese men were even compelled to wear their long hair in *queues* (pigtails) to show that they were inferior to the Manchus.

However, both Chinese and Manchus were employed as civil servants to run the empire. As time passed, the Manchus adopted Chinese customs and were eventually accepted. They were few in number, so they had to be careful not to be too excessive in their treatment of the Chinese. They brought new life and efficiency to the country without disturbing the nation's customs.

## A RICH AND POWERFUL EMPIRE

At first China prospered under Qing rule. The empire grew and trade increased, particularly with Europe. Chinese silk and porcelain were considered the finest in the world, and their cotton goods were inexpensive and of high quality. Huge quantities of Chinese tea were sold abroad when tea drinking became fashionable in Europe in the 1700s.

The empire became so rich and powerful that its rulers were able to treat the rest of the world with contempt. Under Emperor Kangxi's rule (1661–1722), foreign traders were forced to kneel whenever his commands were read out. The Manchus also forced several nations into vassal status, including Tibet, Annam (now Vietnam), Burma, Mongolia, and Turkestan, making the Chinese Empire the world's largest at the time. They made a deal with the Russians over land and trade.

Early on, there were some rebellions in southeast China and among ethnic minorities, who protested against Chinese people moving into their areas. But, on the whole, the Qing period brought peace, prosperity, and security to China. The population grew dramatically from 100 million in 1650 to 300 million in 1800, and Chinese (Han) people spread out to the west and southwest of China. In the late 1700s, however, corruption and decline began to set in.

▲ Tibet (Xizang) was ruled by a Buddhist leader called the Dalai Lama. The third Dalai Lama rebuilt the Potala monastery in Lhasa, the capital, as his residence in 1645. The Dalai Lamas came under the influence of the Mongols, but the Qing army invaded and by the mid-1700s, Tibet was part of the Chinese Empire.

◄ Porcelain vessels from the mid-17th century saw new colors and glazes introduced, such as turquoise.

◄ The Chinese silk industry employed thousands of workers, especially women, to weave silk into cloth on looms. Silk cloth was made for use in China and for export to Europe. Cotton was also imported and then made into cloth for export. The weavers of the port of Suzhou were particularly famous for their silks.

### KEY DATES

| | |
|---|---|
| 1644 | The Manchus found the Qing dynasty in Beijing |
| 1644–60 | Manchu forces conquer most of China |
| 1661 | The island of Taiwan is captured from the Dutch by supporters of the defeated Ming; Kangxi becomes second Qing emperor |
| 1674–81 | Rebellions in the south, soon suppressed |
| 1683 | Manchu forces capture the island of Taiwan from supporters of defeated Ming |
| 1689 | Russians swap Siberian land for trade in China |
| 1696 | The Manchus defeat the Mongols in Mongolia |
| 1717–20 | War against the Mongols to control Tibet |
| 1750s | Chinese invade Tibet and Turkestan |
| 1760s | Chinese invade Burma, making it a vassal state |

# THE SUN KING 1643–1715

**Louis XIV was determined to make France a great nation. The whole life of France revolved around him and he became the most powerful ruler in Europe.**

Louis XIV (1638–1715) became king in 1643 at the age of five. His mother, Anne of Austria, ruled as regent on his behalf for eight years until 1651. In 1648, the people of Paris, burdened for many years by heavy taxes, rose in revolt. Louis was forced to flee the city. The revolt, called the Fronde, collapsed in 1653. Louis decided this would never happen again and, in 1661, at the age of 22, took control. He turned France into an absolute state, ruled solely by the king. In 1665, Louis appointed Jean Colbert as his Controller-General of Finance. Colbert made France the best-run country in Europe. He reorganized taxes and reformed laws. New industries were set up. He had roads, canals, and bridges built, and he greatly expanded the French navy and merchant fleet. Louis and the royal family moved into a magnificent new palace at Versailles in 1682. Heads of the noble families of France were also made to live there so that Louis could keep an eye on them.

In 1667 Louis XIV defeated the Spanish army near the Bruges canal, during an invasion of what is now Belgium. He went on to fight the Dutch.

As Louis grew older, he came under the influence of others and became more rigid, especially in his religious beliefs. Conflict developed. In 1685, he revoked the Edict of Nantes, and no longer showed tolerance toward the Huguenots.

To Louis, France's natural boundaries were the Alps, the Pyrenees, and the Rhine. He plunged France into war to expand it to these borders. The French army became the largest, most formidable fighting force in Europe. But Louis lost most of the land he had gained. He left his grandson and heir, Louis XV, a country under rigid control and nearly bankrupt from war.

▲ Louis XIV wanted France to be a great cultural center. He helped develop the arts, including ballet. In 1661, he set up the Royal Academy of Dance. Here the king himself dances as the sun god Apollo in *The Ballet of the Night* in 1653—an event that lasted an incredible twelve hours. It is because of this performance that Louis came to be called the Sun King.

▶ Louis built the most magnificent palace in Europe at Versailles, near Paris. It took 36,000 workers 47 years to complete. The king and court were waited on by 15,000 guards, courtiers, and attendants.

# DECLINE OF MOGUL INDIA 1605–1707

**After the death of Akbar the Great, the Mogul Empire began to decline. The warlike Marathas and the British eventually caused its disintegration.**

Mumtaz Mahal was Shah Jahan's favorite wife. She died in childbirth in 1629, after 19 years of marriage. The magnificent Taj Mahal, a masterpiece of Mogul architecture, was built in memory of her.

Akbar, the founder of the Mogul Empire in India, died in 1605. His son Jahangir (1569–1627) succeeded him, but was not interested in ruling. He preferred the company of painters and poets, so he lavished his energies and money on constructing splendid buildings and elaborate gardens. Meanwhile, his beautiful, ambitious wife, Nur Jahan, ruled the country. Shah Jahan (1592–1666) succeeded his father Jahangir as emperor in 1628. He extended the empire, and by 1636, he had conquered the Deccan in central India. His end was tragic. In 1657, he fell ill, and his four sons quarreled over his succession. Aurangzeb (1618–1707), the third son, imprisoned his father, killed his brothers, and seized the throne.

Shah Jahan conquered the Deccan in central India and rebuilt Delhi as the capital of the Mogul Empire. Imprisoned by his son in 1657, he died in captivity.

Aurangzeb conquered much of the rest of India, but he could not overcome the warlike Marathas on the west coast. He was a fanatical Muslim. Most of his subjects were Hindus, and he persecuted them without mercy. Opposition to him grew. The Marathas overran the Deccan, and revolts broke out across India. After Aurangzeb died in 1707, the empire began to break up. The 1700s saw many wars, and the provincial governors (*nawabs*) became more independent. The Marathas and the British began to take over the Mogul lands.

## TAJ MAHAL

Shah Jahan built the Taj Mahal near Agra as a tomb for Mumtaz Mahal ("Chosen One of the Palace"). The beautiful building was made of white marble inlaid with patterns of semiprecious stones, and took 11 years to build. The whole complex took a total of 22 years to complete.

| KEY DATES | |
|---|---|
| 1605 | Jahangir, emperor for 23 years |
| 1608 | The English arrive in India |
| 1611–22 | Nur Jahan, Jahangir's wife, rules |
| 1628 | Shah Jahan, emperor for 30 years |
| 1658 | Aurangzeb, last great Moghul, 49 years |
| 1660s | Rise of the Marathas, the Moghuls' opponents |
| 1707 | Beginning of decline of the Moghuls |

# THE OTTOMAN EMPIRE 1602–1783

**After the reign of Süleyman the Magnificent, the Ottoman Empire entered a long and slow decline. Nevertheless, the empire survived until 1923.**

Sultan Osman II (1603–1622) ruled from 1618. He was young, strict, and fond of archery. He restricted the power of the Janissaries (senior army officers), but they took over, had him killed, and replaced him with Mustafa I.

In 1565, Süleyman the Magnificent decided to invade Malta, occupied at the time by the Crusader Knights of St. John. Although the Turks greatly outnumbered the Knights, their invasion was not successful, and they had to withdraw after several months. Süleyman died in 1566. In 1571, when the Ottomans tried to invade Venetian-ruled Cyprus, their invasion force was destroyed by a combined fleet from the navies of Venice, Spain, and the Papal States, at Lepanto off the coast of Greece. In 1602, a long and costly war broke out with Safavid Persia, with no gain. Plagues and economic crises also hit Istanbul. Once-profitable trade routes linking Asia, Africa, and Europe were bypassed as new sea routes around Africa and land routes through Siberia opened.

## THE EMPIRE FADES

The Thirty Years' War in Europe gave the Ottomans some peace. But when, in 1656, they tried to invade Crete, the Venetians blocked the Dardanelles (the narrow sea passage from the Mediterranean to the Black Sea), threatening Istanbul itself. This caused panic, and the sultan, Ibrahim, was deposed by army officers. A new grand vizier (chief minister), Mehmet Kuprili, took charge. He reformed the economy and army, and Ottoman fortunes revived.

The next vizier, Kara Mustafa, tried to invade Hapsburg Vienna for a second time in 1683. The defenders of Vienna held out for two months until an army of Germans and Poles arrived to defeat the Turks. The Austrians invaded Hungary, the Venetians took part of Greece, and the Russians threatened Azov in the Ukraine. Another vizier, Mustafa Kuprili, took office in 1690. He managed to drive back the Austrians, but he was killed in 1691. During the 1690s, the Ottomans finally lost Hungary and Azov. Their European empire was saved only because Austria went to war with France.

▲ Sultan Mustafa I (1591–1639) ruled twice —between 1617–1618 and again between 1622–1623.

▶ The Ottoman Empire was still large, but it was slowly falling apart at the seams as its prosperity dwindled.

Ottoman Empire

Ottoman territories lost

## THE EMPIRE SHRINKS

Between 1710 and 1720, the Ottomans regained Azov and Greece, but they lost Serbia and parts of Armenia. They also lost control of most of northern Africa—Algeria, Tunisia, and Libya. Officially, these countries were still Ottoman, but were actually independent. In 1736, the Russians attacked again, and by 1783, they had taken the Crimea and most of the Ukraine—the Ottomans no longer controlled the Black Sea. In Anatolia, local chiefs were rebelling, and in Istanbul, people were worried about the future.

The Ottoman Empire was still strong, but it had lost much of its trade and wealth. The progress made in the early days of the Ottoman Empire in religion, the arts, and social advances, slowed. The Ottomans' only friends, the Moguls, were also in decline, while the Europeans were advancing rapidly. But the Ottoman Empire was not yet finished.

▶ This 17th-century Ottoman miniature shows the Sultan Ahmed and his attendants visiting the Topkapi Palace, Hagia Sophia and the Blue Mosque. To keep the sultans separate from politics and the people, they were looked after lavishly. The authority of the sultans was finally weakened by a series of bloody contests for power among the ruling families.

▼ The siege of Vienna in 1683 marked the farthest point of the Ottoman Turks' advance into Europe. The defenders of Vienna held out for two months, just long enough for a slow-moving army of Germans and Poles to arrive. The Turks were utterly defeated in a 15-hour battle on September 12, 1683.

# THE AGE OF REASON 1600–1750

**By the mid-1600s, the ideas of the Renaissance had spread through most of Europe. New discoveries were being made about the world and human beings.**

▲ New ideas in science and philosophy were debated in salons such as that of Ninon de Lenclos (1620–1705). Such salons were the breeding-ground for the Age of Reason in Europe.

▲ John Locke (1632–1704) was an English philosopher who examined the nature and scope of human understanding.

Within a few hundred years, the people of Europe had witnessed great changes. Ships were now traveling to far-off lands, bringing back goods and knowledge from other cultures. Europe had become a money-based economy, with new and larger cities and towns. Literature, theater, and opera had made great strides. Kings and nobles lived on elegant estates, isolated from the rest of the population. Ministers and civil servants controlled governments. New thinkers had introduced radical ideas.

Life was now very different for everyone, rich and poor. People began to question and doubt the truth of many commonly held ideas. The words of the Bible and the philosophers of ancient Greece no longer satisfied everyone. Many people began to believe in their ability to think things out for themselves. At the same time, new discoveries were being made about the world and the heavens, and about other countries and human beings. There was an urge to examine, research, experiment, and discuss anything and everything, to cross a new frontier of scientific inquiry. This revolution in scientific methods and ways of thinking became known as the Age of Reason.

Sir Isaac Newton (1642–1727) produced a reflector telescope that sharpened and magnified the vision of distant stars. Astronomy became a more accurate science.

Travelers went to Japan, Armenia, Mexico, Arabia, and Africa, to explore and report back on what they found. New medicines (as well as diseases) arrived from far-off lands. Doctors began opening corpses to study the body's organs and their functions. Botanists collected and started to classify plants; chemists experimented with compounds. During the 1600s, telescopes, barometers, pendulum clocks, calculating machines, and air pumps were all invented.

## THE ROYAL OBSERVATORY

The Royal Greenwich Observatory was founded by Charles II, himself an astronomer, and was built by Christopher Wren in 1675. The first Astronomer Royal was John Flamsteed, a noted astronomer of the time. The observatory was built to produce accurate star charts and tables of planetary motion for sailors. Greenwich became a center for the study of time. Greenwich Mean Time, the world's time standard, was established in 1880. For centuries, Greenwich was a leading observatory— until London's pollution and electric streetlighting in the 1900s made it necessary to move its astronomical work to other, less polluted places in England.

254

## LOGIC AND NEW IDEAS

Mathematicians such as Leibnitz and Descartes worked with geometry and calculus. Galileo and Newton studied gravity, and Kepler worked on planetary motion. Tycho Brahe cataloged the stars; Snellius, Huygens, and Grimaldi researched the behavior of light; and Boyle studied gases. Mechanical objects followed a logic that made sense, and this logic was also applied to human society and politics. Francis Bacon developed the idea of the perfect state. Others wrote about government, the rights of people, and the "contract" between rulers and ruled.

New institutions grew up where these ideas could be discussed. Cardinal Richelieu's Académie Française was founded in 1635. Early members of the Royal Society in England were the chemist Robert Boyle, the physicist Isaac Newton, the diarist Samuel Pepys, and the architect Christopher Wren. In the new smoke-filled coffeehouses and teahouses around Europe, people were talking to each other as never before. A new, nonreligious, "rational" way of seeing things took shape. The work of René Descartes, Isaac Newton, Francis Bacon, Galileo, and many others formed the foundation for today's knowledge of the world.

▼ The first orrery was built in 1700 to demonstrate the movements of the planets around the sun, and moons around the planets. A handle turns the planets.

▲ In 1652, the first coffeehouse was opened in London. People discussed business and politics and exchanged information. The most famous was Lloyd's coffeehouse, which served people who insured shipping.

▲ Until the 1600s, the Church forbade people to cut open human corpses for study. This painting by Rembrandt shows a doctor giving an anatomy lesson.

▲ Galileo Galilei (1564–1642) was an astronomer, mathematician, and physicist. He offended the Catholic Church by teaching that the Earth revolves around the sun.

### KEY DATES

| | |
|---|---|
| 1608 | Hans Lippershey, a Dutch optician, invents the first telescope |
| 1609 | Galileo studies the heavens; Kepler formulates Laws of Planetary Motion |
| 1628 | Harvey discovers blood circulation |
| 1635 | Académie Française founded |
| 1637 | Descartes' Analytical Geometry explained |
| 1644 | Evangelista Torricelli, an Italian scientist, publishes his theory on the barometer |
| 1647 | Pascal invents an adding machine |
| 1657 | Huygens builds a pendulum clock |
| 1660 | A barometer is used to forecast the weather |
| 1666 | Newton formulates Laws of Gravitation |
| 1673 | Leibnitz invents a calculating machine |
| 1705 | Edmund Halley predicts return of comet in 1758 |
| 1735 | Carl Linnaeus classifies plants and animals |
| 1742 | Anders Celsius devises Celsius scale of temperature |

▲ Galileo's early telescopes were primitive, but they helped him discover four of Jupiter's moons.

# SLAVERY AND PIRATES 1517–1810

**The early development of many colonies in the Americas was carried out by pirates, the owners of sugar plantations, and millions of African slaves.**

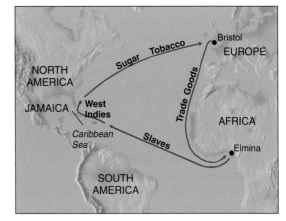

From ports such as Bristol, finished goods were shipped for sale in West Africa. Once the goods had been sold in Africa, the ship would be loaded with slaves to take to the West Indies. The final leg of the voyage would bring a cargo of sugar back to Europe.

Within a hundred years of Columbus' landing in 1492, most of the native peoples of the Caribbean islands, the Arawaks and Caribs, were dead as a result of European mistreatment and diseases. By the early 1600s, the Caribbean was a battleground. The Spanish, French, English, and Dutch all fought for the islands they called the West Indies. Some islands changed hands several times in a fierce contest for trade and for land to establish European colonies.

English, French, and Dutch privateers became pirates to make their fortune. They were often sponsored by their governments, since they caused trouble for the Spanish, captured islands, established settlements, and made good profits. Some were later sent out as admirals or colonial governors. Francis Drake sailed around the world between 1577 and 1580, raided Spanish ships, and returned home rich. Captain Kidd was enlisted to help control pirates, but joined them instead. Edward Teach (Blackbeard) and Captain Morgan raided Spanish settlements and galleons in the Caribbean. They paved the way for the establishment of colonies. The Spanish lost gold to the pirates, but this did not stop them from colonizing the Americas.

## THE SLAVE TRADE

In Europe, tea and coffee were becoming fashionable, and this led to a huge demand for sugar to sweeten them. Sugar grew well in the climate of the West Indies, but its cultivation needed many workers. Local labor could not be found, because many of the original islanders had died, and so the colonists imported slaves from West Africa.

Europeans saw nothing wrong with using Africans as slaves. They were bought cheaply, crammed into ships, and then sold to plantation owners. Two thirds of them died, either on the voyage or from disease, harsh treatment, and overwork. Even so, by 1800, there were nine million African slaves in the Americas.

▲ West Africa was rich in gold. Arabs called the area "Guinea" and Europeans borrowed the word. In 1663, a guinea coin of Guinea gold was issued by order of Charles I.

▲ Newly captured slaves were chained together by the neck or feet. Iron collars stopped the slaves from running away.

▲ Iron manacles (handcuffs) that could not be opened without special tools were used to hold slaves' arms together.

▶ Whole families and villages of Africans were shipped to the Americas as slaves. Many did not survive the journey. West Africa, the Congo, and Angola lost much of their populations.

▲ Slaves harvested the sugarcane on plantations in the Caribbean. Landowners grew wealthy. They often returned to Europe where they lived well, and left their plantations in the hands of managers.

## THE TRIANGLE OF TRADE

The European-owned sugar plantations in the Caribbean were often very large. They had warehouses, boatyards, churches, slave quarters, and the landowner's grand house. A triangle of trade developed, taking finished goods from Europe to West Africa, slaves from West Africa to the Americas (the Middle Passage), and plantation products back to Europe. The profitable markets in Europe for sugar, tobacco, oils, and other products were exploited. Piracy, plantations, and slavery were driven by the urge for profit. Slavery continued into the 1800s. Most of today's African–Americans are the descendants of slave ancestors.

▶ For centuries, people had been enslaved as a result of conflicts, and often bought and sold. On the eastern African coast, Arabs traded slaves and, when the Portuguese arrived, they used enslaved people on their colonies.

## HENRY MORGAN

Welsh Captain Morgan (1635–1688), pirate, was the scourge of the Caribbean between the 1660s and 1680s. He organized fleets of buccaneers, attacked Spanish galleons in midocean, and seized their treasures. Much of the booty went to England, to reward investors who sponsored his voyages. He captured Porto Bello in 1668, sacked Maracaibo in 1669, and took Panama in 1671. Later, he was knighted for his services against the Spanish, and was made lieutenant governor of Jamaica in 1674. He died in 1688, aged 53. Buccaneers like Morgan helped England's economy to prosper.

257

# AFRICAN STATES 1550–1700

In the 1600s, Africa was a patchwork of different peoples and kingdoms. Each had its own customs, form of government, language, and gods.

Gao, Katsina, and Kano adopted the Muslim faith, brought to West Africa across the Sahara by the Arabs. The coastal kingdoms kept their own religions. Much of northeast Africa was under Ottoman control.

The West African kingdom of Benin is famous for its bronzes. This ram's head was made in the 1600s for a chief, who would have worn it on his belt.

During this period, the nations of Africa were developing rapidly. If the Europeans had not arrived, the African nations would probably have advanced their cultures much farther. Although Europeans did not have a great influence until the 1800s, they bought gold, exotic items, and slaves, and sold guns, cloth, tools, and finished goods. By doing so, traditional African trade and society were changed. Some areas, such as West Africa, lost many people to slavery. Social divisions increased as chieftains and traders made profitable deals with the Europeans. Some chiefs even sold their own people into slavery.

The largest African state was Songhay. European traders on the coast took the gold and slave trade away from Songhay, and its wealth collapsed. In 1591, a Moroccan army crossed the Sahara and invaded the country. South of the Sahara, new states had emerged, including Mossi, the city-states of Hausaland, and Kanem-Bornu, and Darfur. These Muslim states traded with the Ottomans and Arabs.

In the east, Christian Ethiopia was surrounded by Muslim countries. Muslims in some parts of the country rebelled, ravaging Ethiopia. The Portuguese arrived and drove out the Muslims in 1543, and Ethiopia was left in peace. Along the east and west coasts, the Portuguese built forts and slave depots. These attracted Africans to the coasts and encouraged chiefs to grow rich by joining in the slave trade.

▲ This Ashanti helmet was decorated with gold animal horns and charms. Europeans were unable to buy slaves with gold from the Ashanti because they had all they needed. Instead they paid for them with guns that increased Ashanti military power.

▶ The Portuguese built forts around the shores of Africa. This pictorial map, made in 1558, shows the coast of West Africa.

## DAHOMEY AND ASHANTI

A number of states occupied the forest zone along the west African coast. In 1625, a new kingdom called Allada was founded by King Akaba. Between 1645 and 1685, it merged with two other kingdoms to become Dahomey. This new state grew wealthy from the gold and slave trades. Dahomey was overrun in 1747 by Yorubas from Oyo (now in Nigeria). Dahomey became notorious to Europeans because, when its chief died, thousands of slaves were sacrificed so they could accompany him to the afterlife.

West of Dahomey lay Ashanti. In 1689, Osei Tutu founded the powerful Ashanti confederacy and built its capital at Kumasi. It grew wealthy from trade in cola nuts, gold, and slaves. The important Portuguese-controlled fort and trading post at Elmira in Ashanti was taken over by the Dutch in 1637.

Africa provided the slaves needed to work the rapidly growing plantations in the Americas. Millions were shipped across the Atlantic. Many died either during slave wars between African states to capture slaves or on the terrible voyage across the Atlantic ocean—the Middle Passage. To lose such an enormous number of its people was a catastrophe for Africa.

▲ A tribal celebration in the kingdom of Loango in the Congo region in 1686. After the arrival of the Europeans, tribal security and unity gradually gave way to increased social distrust and control by greedy chiefs.

▶ A European trader offers brandy to the chief of the Alcaty tribe, in Senegal, West Africa, in exchange for water, around 1690.

| KEY DATES | |
|---|---|
| 1570 | Rise of Kanem-Bornu as a major nation |
| 1575 | Portuguese first settle in Angola |
| 1588 | The English Guinea Company is founded |
| 1600 | Mwenemutapa at its zenith |
| 1625 | New kingdom of Allada set up by King Akaba |
| 1637 | Dutch drive Portuguese from the Gold Coast |
| 1652 | Dutch East India Company founds Cape Town |
| 1660s | Rise of Bambara kingdoms in West Africa |
| 1685 | Founding of Dahomey from three kingdoms |
| 1689 | Osei Tutu founds the Ashanti Empire |
| 1701 | Military expansion of Ashanti by Osei Tutu |

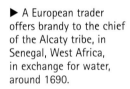

◀ Here an *oba* (ruler) of Benin rides in a procession of his people. Once the richest state in West Africa, by 1700, the kingdom of Benin was on the wane. It was overwhelmed by the growing strength of the Yoruba people and the kingdom of Oyo.

# IRELAND 1540–1800

**English Protestant rule in Ireland was finally and forcibly imposed during the 1600s. There was resistance, but this was brutally crushed by the English.**

The Irish never relented to English rule. Henry II of England had conquered most of Ireland in 1171, and for the next 400 years English monarchs had struggled to maintain their authority there. Relations became more strained as time passed. The problem was mainly religious. The Irish were Catholic and the English had become Protestant. Irish priests encouraged rebellion by teaching that the English were heretics with no rightful authority over Ireland. But the English took strong measures to keep the Irish under their control. They dissolved many old monasteries and sold the land to families who supported their rule. The Irish reacted with frequent revolts. In 1556, Mary I sent troops into central Ireland to forcibly remove some of the native Irish and give their land to English settlers.

▲ James Butler, the Duke of Ormonde (1610–1688), governed Ireland for Charles I of England.

▼ In 1649, the fortified town of Drogheda was beseiged by Parliamentary forces under Cromwell.

## PLANTATIONS AND REVOLT

The established hold of the English was further extended in 1580. English colonists were promised wealth and opportunity, and they quickly developed the land and new towns. But their colony was destroyed in 1598 by an Irish attack. A revolt broke out in Ulster, a purely Irish area, but was suppressed by 1603. The English started a settler colony (plantation) there, mostly with Puritan Scots settlers, strengthened by fortified towns such as Londonderry. Some Irish fought back, but many left. By the mid-1600s, the Catholics of Ulster were outnumbered by Protestants.

In 1642, an Irish uprising began, and thousands of Protestant settlers were killed. Engaged in the English Civil War, Cromwell did not tackle the uprising until 1649. He arrived with a large army and crushed the Irish with a brutality that has never been forgiven. Local people were moved to poor land in the west of the country, and English soldiers were given the land to settle. Catholics now owned less than half the land in Ireland.

## HARSH PROTESTANT RULE

Irish hopes were briefly raised when Catholic James II became king of England. His daughter married William of Orange from Holland, commander of a grand alliance of countries fighting France. William became king of England in 1688. James, the "Old Pretender" escaped to Ireland. Eventually James's army (the Jacobites) met William's at the battle of the Boyne in 1690, and William triumphed.

This series of events marked a turning point in Irish history. Harsh laws were introduced that banned Catholics from owning guns. They were also forbidden to be involved in politics, to hold land, to receive education, and even to own large horses. Catholics converting to the Protestant faith were given land taken from those that remained Catholic. Communities broke apart, with some Irish accepting their lot, others resisting, and yet more leaving the country. But, while the 1700s were relatively peaceful, new trouble was brewing. When Wolfe Tone led a rebellion in the 1790s, many Irish people were killed, a French invasion was fought off, and the rebellion cruelly crushed. However, the English were forced to realize that the Irish Catholics were there to stay.

▲ This map of Ireland was made by a Frenchman in 1635. Fourteen years later, Cromwell arrived with a large army and brutally suppressed an uprising against English rule. Many Irish people were moved to poor land in the west.

### KEY DATES

| | |
|---|---|
| 1556 | Mary I starts Protestant plantations in Ireland |
| 1580 | Further plantation settlements established |
| 1598 | Revolts across Ireland, especially in Ulster |
| 1642 | Irish uprising against English control |
| 1649 | Cromwell's suppression of the Irish revolt |
| 1690 | Battle of the Boyne—a Protestant victory |
| 1798 | Wolfe Tone's nationalist rebellion |

▲ Being Catholic, James II was the great hope of the Irish Catholics. However, European power politics became caught up in the Irish question, and the English, under William III, had to defeat James.

## THE BATTLE OF THE BOYNE

This decisive battle took place near Drogheda in 1690. The army of the recently deposed James II, last of the Stuart kings, was outnumbered by the Protestant army of William III. When William's troops crossed the Boyne River, James's troops fled. James went into exile in France, and William's rule in England was strengthened by the victory.

# RUSSIAN EXPANSION 1613–1725

**At the beginning of Peter the Great's reign, Russia was a backward state. Peter began the process that turned Russia into one of the world's superpowers.**

Peter the Great (1672–1725) is here portrayed as a cat.

In 1682, at the age of ten, Peter I, known as Peter the Great, became joint czar of Russia with his half-brother Ivan V. Their half-sister Sophia Alekseyevna ruled as regent while they were young. Ivan was feebleminded, which Peter found very frustrating. In 1689, Peter seized complete control. At the beginning of his reign, Russia was a relatively backward state compared with the countries of western Europe. Peter's ambition was to make Russia a great European power.

◄ Peter encouraged fine craftsmanship. He gave this jeweled cup to his son Alexis in 1694. He could also be cruel. In 1718, he imprisoned and tortured Alexis to death.

► Czar Peter had enormous energy and was constantly at work making laws, drilling troops, planning towns, building ships, and even extracting teeth. He was careful with money, and gave most of his income to the state. He died after diving into the Neva River in the winter to rescue some drowning sailors.

The boyars had been Russia's ruling class since the 900s. When Peter returned from Europe, he abolished their powers. He made them cut off their beards as part of his plan to modernize Russia.

## RUSSIA LOOKS WESTWARD

Russia was a vast and potentially wealthy country. Its explorers were pushing east into Siberia. The Ural Mountains, rich in minerals, had been opened up, bringing new resources. Peter wanted to shift Russia's focus away from the East, and to make it look westward. This involved reducing the power of the boyars (nobles). The boyars had been the hereditary ruling class in Russia for 700 years, and they wanted to preserve tradition and further their own interests.

Peter realized that Russia would remain in isolation until it secured an outlet to the West, either through the Baltic, which was dominated by Sweden, or the Black Sea, which was dominated by the Ottomans. Russia had no ports except Archangel in the far north, which was frozen solid during the winter months.

To gain a warm-water port, Peter set out to conquer coastal territory. He captured Azov on the Black Sea from the Ottomans (though he later lost it again). In 1700, he went to war against Sweden, defeating Charles XII at Poltava in the Ukraine. In the peace treaty that followed he gained Estonia and Livonia. This gave him the foothold he needed on the Baltic coast.

## PETER AND THE WEST

Peter centralized the government, and brought the Orthodox Church under state control. He changed the role of the nobility, and required them to serve him.

In 1697, Peter began an 18-month tour of western Europe, especially Holland and England, seeking to learn the ways and skills of the West. He traveled widely, disguised as an ordinary citizen, and visited factories, hospitals, almshouses (houses for the poor), and museums. To learn the art of shipbuilding, Peter worked as a carpenter in various European shipyards. Subsequently, he hired hundreds of the craftsmen and technicians to teach their skills to the Russian people.

On his return to Russia, Peter created a new civil service organized along European lines, and made his courtiers adopt Western dress and manners. He built factories, canals, and roads, and founded new industries. He improved the army and built a navy, and founded St. Petersburg as his new capital.

Although Peter was very enthusiastic, he could also be forceful and cruel, which lost him support. Peter's plan was only half-complete when he died in 1725, but he had started a process that was later to turn Russia into one of the superpowers of the modern world.

▲ When Peter the Great visited England, few knew that he was the czar of Russia. He was an inquisitive man and questioned everyone he met. He enjoyed the practical aspects of woodworking and shipbuilding.

▼ Peter the Great brought many European architects and craftspeople to build his grand new capital at St. Petersburg. It was designed in the new Baroque style which was spreading across Europe. He is shown here discussing the plans with an architect in 1703.

◄ In spite of Peter's many reforms, Russian peasants continued to live in poverty. They often starved during the long, harsh Russian winters.

# THE GREAT NORTHERN WAR 1700–1721

**Following a war between Sweden and other northern European countries, Sweden lost most of its empire, and Russia became the leading power in the Baltic.**

This painting shows King Charles XI of Sweden (1655–1697) and his family. The future Charles XII (1682–1718) is held by his mother, Queen Eleonora.

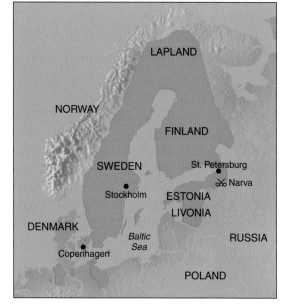

This map shows the Swedish Empire at its greatest extent in 1660. Sweden was the largest military power in northern Europe and was in an ideal position to invade Russia in 1708.

The Great Northern War was fought between Sweden and other northern European powers, led by Peter the Great of Russia. At stake was control of the Baltic Sea and the lands around it. In 1700, Sweden was attacked by Denmark, Saxony, Poland, and Russia. Sweden's Charles XII was only 18, and his enemies hoped to take advantage of his inexperience. But Charles proved to be a born leader. He defeated the Russians at Narva in Estonia, forcing Saxony, Poland, and Denmark out of the war and putting a new king on the Polish throne. Eight years later, Charles invaded Russia. But the bitter winter of 1708–1709 set in, and the Russians retreated, destroying everything as they went. The Swedes ran short of food, and struggled against repeated Russian attacks. By the spring, Charles's army was just half its original size.

At the battle of Poltava in June 1709, the Russians beat the Swedes, and Charles fled to Turkey. He returned to Sweden in 1714, and beat off a Danish invasion in 1716. He invaded Norway and was killed there in 1718. Without Charles, and exhausted by 20 years of fighting, the Swedes agreed peace terms in 1721.

▲ Czar Peter the Great ruled Russia from 1682 until 1725. He was a great modernizer, who made Russia look westward to Europe. The Great Northern War ended with Russia in a much stronger position.

▶ The Battle of Poltava, near Kiev, in the Ukraine, in 1709, brought Sweden's power and dominance in the region to an end. Peter the Great's army was larger and better equipped, and the Swedes were tired, hungry, and far from home.

# THE SPANISH SUCCESSION 1701–1713

**When Charles II of Spain died in 1700 he left no heir. The question of who should succeed him led to the War of the Spanish Succession.**

▲ John Churchill, Duke of Marlborough (1650–1722), commander of the allied forces, won great battles at Blenheim, Ramillies, Oudenarde, and Malplaquet.

▲ Prince Eugene of Savoy (1663–1736) fought the Turks at the siege of Vienna in 1683. By 1701, he had become commander-in-chief of the Austrian forces and fought at the battles of Blenheim and Oudenarde.

The French Bourbons and the Austrian Hapsburgs both claimed the Spanish throne. Before Charles II died in 1700, they had signed an agreement dividing his empire. But Charles's will left his lands to Philip of Anjou, the grandson of Louis XIV of France. Louis ignored his earlier agreement with the Hapsburgs, and chose to back Philip instead. But an alliance between France and Spain was not acceptable to every country in Europe.

By 1701, western Europe was at war. Organized by William III of England, England, the Netherlands, most German states, and Austria formed a grand alliance against France. In 1704, a French army was overwhelmed at Blenheim by a combined force under the Duke of Marlborough. He won three more victories over the French in the Spanish Netherlands. In 1706, an Austrian army under Prince Eugene of Savoy drove the French from Italy.

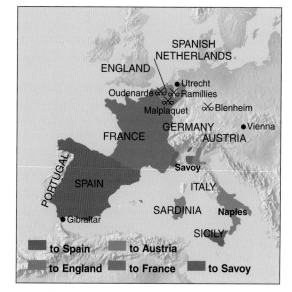

At the Treaty of Utrecht in 1713, France retained her frontiers. Austria took the Spanish Netherlands and Naples, England gained Gibraltar and Newfoundland. Philip V remained king of Spain.

The allies then invaded Spain, but the French forces pushed them out again, leaving Louis' grandson Philip V on the Spanish throne. The long war had exhausted both sides and, in 1713, a peace treaty was signed at Utrecht.

## THE BATTLE OF BLENHEIM

In 1704, the Battle of Blenheim was fought in Bavaria among four armies and several nations. The French and Bavarians were marching on Vienna. The armies of Marlborough and Eugene intercepted them at Blenheim, and in the ensuing battle, 12,000 allies and 30,000 French and Bavarians were killed. However, it was a victory for Marlborough and Eugene, and Vienna was saved.

# COLONIAL AMERICA 1600–1700

**Settlers were arriving on the North American continent in large numbers. These European peoples shaped the character of future life in the "New World."**

▲ William Penn (1644–1718) was a wealthy Quaker who founded Pennsylvania in 1681. He set out to welcome people who had suffered religious persecution and hardship.

The French and Spanish made up the majority of the early European settlers, but they were later overtaken by the English and Germans. The majority were Protestants who had suffered persecution. Within 20 years of the first Puritans arriving, there were 20,000 English people living in Massachusetts. The colony developed rapidly, with Boston as its capital. Some of these colonists moved to Rhode Island because they disliked Puritan religious restrictions.

In 1625, at the mouth of the Hudson River, New York had started out as a Dutch colony. When the English took over in 1664, English, German, and a variety of other nationalities settled there. It soon grew into a large cosmopolitan city of traders and craftspeople. Farther down the coast in 1681, in repayment of a debt, the English king gave Pennsylvania to a group of Quakers led by William Penn. Penn was a religious idealist and dreamed of a "holy experiment"—a new society. He helped poor people from Europe settle in the colony. Many English, Scottish, Welsh, Irish, and German settlers moved there to start a new life.

▼ The Quaker Society of Friends was founded in England in the mid-1600s. They were Puritans and disliked priestly control of the Church. Quakers, including women, were encouraged to preach and speak out.

Settlers worked hard to build a new life. This is a small family farm in Maryland (previously New Sweden). The family kept cattle, pigs, and chickens and grew wheat, vegetables, tobacco, and cotton.

Farther south, the Carolinas and Virginia grew in size after the English Civil War, when King Charles II granted land there to his royalist supporters. They established profitable plantations growing tobacco, cotton, rice, and indigo. The settlers imported slaves from Africa to work the land from 1619 onward. Soon the majority of the people were slaves.

The Puritans of New England had a high regard for education. In 1636, the Massachusetts government founded Harvard College in Cambridge.

## PIONEERING SETTLERS

In the southwest, Spanish–Mexican pioneers pushed up into New Mexico, and built a capital at Santa Fe in 1609. This was a colony of forts, mines, and trading posts. With Florida also in their hands, the Spanish might have taken all of North America, but Spain lost its control over the seas and they missed their chance. The French had settled around the St. Lawrence, the Great Lakes, and the Mississippi. As colonists, traders, fur-trappers, and pioneers, they were few in number. By 1700, there were 12 English colonies along the Atlantic coast, with some 250,000 English compared to only 20,000 French. Germans, Dutch, Swedes, Bohemians, Lithuanians, and other nationalities all found homes in different areas. The new America was being built by hardworking, ordinary people rather than distant European governments.

## INDIGENOUS PEOPLES

At first, the Indigenous Americans and European settlers both gained from mixing together and in some cases, coexisting peacefully. But as more settlers arrived, native lands were seized. There were several atrocities, and native distrust of and resistance to the settlers grew. Local conflicts arose, leading to war in the 1670s. The settlers won, and native resistance declined. Some indigenous peoples were actively driven from their homelands. As European takeover became certain, a gradual tide of indigenous migrations began.

▼ The first elected representatives of the colony of Virginia, together with its governor and council, met in 1619 at Jamestown to make the laws.

▼ Fur was an important commodity that the settlers exported to Europe. Here, two French fur traders meet Indigenous Americans near Lake Superior.

## SALEM WITCH TRIAL

In 1692, several young girls in the town of Salem, Massachusetts, claimed that they had been bewitched by a West Indian slave, named Tituba. Most people of the time believed in witchcraft and the Puritans of Salem took fright. This led to the trial and execution of 14 women and 6 men accused of witchcraft. Several people died in prison, and 150 more awaited trial. Eventually, the madness was stopped by the governor, William Phips, and by a respected Congregational preacher, Increase Mather.

# ART AND ARCHITECTURE 1601–1707

**The modern world took shape in the 1600s. Advances in science and technology, European colonization overseas, and new wealth affected all forms of art.**

Town-houses in Amsterdam were built of brick and finely carved stonework. The shortage of building land meant that the Dutch built tall houses close together.

The austere classical lines of early Renaissance architecture evolved into a more flamboyant and exuberant style, designed to show off the wealth and power of the ruling elite, the clergy and newly rich traders, in palaces, townhouses, churches, and gardens. This style of grand design began in France and Italy and spread through Europe. It was called baroque. In the 1700s, it evolved into the rococo style, using extreme ornamentation and theatrical effects.

Molière (1622-1673) wrote plays to entertain the court of Louis XIV of France. Best known are his comedies, which laugh at human failings such as stinginess and snobbishness. Some said he couldn't take anything seriously. Both the Church and people who were powerful in society saw this as dangerous.

## THE MASTER PAINTERS

Artists during the 17th century were masters of realism, of light and darkness, and color. It was in this period that landscape painting became popular in Europe.

In the Netherlands, Peter Paul Rubens (1577–1640) was an artist in the baroque style, dramatic, and bold. He lived mostly in Antwerp, but traveled widely, painting altarpieces, court portraits, and scenes from classical mythlogy. Anthony van Dyck (1599–1641) was a Flemish painter who became portraitist to the royal court of Charles I in London. Spanish painter Diego Velázquez (1599–1660) was another baroque artist and the leading painter at the court of King Philip IV of Spain. Dutch artist Rembrandt van Rijn (1606–1669) does not really fit into the baroque mood. A master of both print and paint, he is remembered for his biblical scenes, portraits of leading citizens of the Dutch Republic and for a moving series of self-portraits.

Kabuki drama was developed in Japan in the 1600s. It was extremely formal, combining dialogue, songs, music, and dance. Men took all the parts in the plays, many of which are still performed in Japan today.

The Blue Mosque in Istanbul was designed by Mehmet Agha (pupil of the great Turkish architect Sinan) and built between 1606 and 1616. The complex, with its fine domes and courtyards, included a college, hospital, and libraries.

◀ This is "David Slaying Goliath" by Giovanni Bernini (1598–1680), who was the leading Italian sculptor and architect of his day. Bernini designed and decorated churches, chapels, and monuments, as well as the tombs of eight of the popes.

▲ "Belshazzar's Feast" was painted by the Dutch artist Rembrandt van Rijn (1606–1669). It shows the last king of Babylon seeing a vision at a banquet. In it, Belshazzar foresaw his own death and the fall of his empire. This exotic and magical theme illustrates the growing interest in unconventional ideas in the late 1600s.

## BEYOND EUROPE

In China, during the early Qing dynasty, there were highly skilled traditional painters, but also some who broke away to create more individual, informal art, such as the Buddhist monk Shitao (1542–1707). Free brush work was used to capture the natural world of plants and animals. In the early Edo period, in Japan, there was a high literacy rate and new devolopments in printing technique with fine woodblock art. The Rinpa school of art was founded at Kyoto in 1615.

▶ In about 1637, Antony van Dyck painted this portrait of Princess Mary, daughter of King Charles I of England. About six years old, she wears an apron over a dress in the adult style, with a pearl necklace.

# SCIENCE AND TECHNOLOGY 1601–1707

In the 1600s, scientists began to understand how nature worked and how they might control it. They made discoveries that led to great advances in technology.

▲ Early industrial machines, such as this screw press, made it much easier to handle large quantities of materials.

▼ Jethro Tull (1674–1741), a prosperous English farmer and student of agricultural methods, invented the seed drill in 1701. The drill sowed seed evenly in straight lines that allowed weeding between each row. It was the first farm machine.

In the early 1600s, Francis Bacon, the great English philosopher, saw science as a study of God's creation by means of experimentation. In this way he forced a path between the religious beliefs of the past and the rise of reason and scientific inquiry. This century was an age of intellectual activity with science at its core. Until then, most thinkers rejected ideas if they broke with accepted religious beliefs. In the Age of Reason, unusual ideas and new information became acceptable. All the conclusions drawn from them were to be tested by experiment and observation.

Scientists now specialized in particular subjects. Notable breakthroughs were made by Robert Boyle in chemistry, William Harvey in medicine, and Sir Isaac Newton in physics and mathematics. Newton's idea that everything in heaven and on Earth could be understood by reason gave science a new, almost religious meaning. Meetings of scientists became popular in the 1640s. Academies, such as the Royal Society in London and the Royal Academy in Paris, were given royal patronage by the 1660s and led the way for the next 200 years.

The French philosopher René Descartes (1596–1650) argued that only ideas that could be proven by evidence or reasoning were true. This diagram illustrates his theory about the coordination of the senses.

All across Europe, new scientific ideas led to a flood of practical inventions. These were sought after by sailors, traders, generals, and kings, and there was a great deal of money to be made. Mechanical devices such as clocks, pumps, orreries, cannons, textile machines, and engineering tools were developed—sometimes by solitary geniuses, with little support.

▲ In Italy, Galileo investigated pendulums in the 1600s. The first pendulum clock was made by Dutchman Christiaan Huygens in 1656. This is an early Swiss version.

▼ Indian soldiers of the 1600s fought their battles dressed in coats of thick, quilted cloth. The cloth was tough enough to deflect the edge of a sword, but still allowed the wearer to move easily.

Thermometer     Barometer

The microscope, thermometer, and barometer all came into widespread use in the 1600s. They helped scientists carry out experiments more accurately.

Microscope

▼ Firearms such as these kept monarchs safely on their thrones. Only kings could afford to equip their armies with them. As a result, many kings grew too powerful to be overthrown by rebel subjects.

## SCIENTIFIC ADVANCES

For the first time, heat could be accurately measured with the newly invented thermometer. Advances in mathematics kept pace with those in science. The invention of calculus, logarithms, and the slide rule enabled scientists to make detailed calculations to support their theories. Electricity was first identified by William Gilbert in 1600, but it was not until the 1800s that it was put to practical use. More great breakthroughs in steam engines, textile looms, and other machinery were to come in the 1700s. All this arose out of the ideas of the Renaissance and the research of the Age of Reason, which, as each century moved forward, laid the foundations of science and technology.

## WHEN IT HAPPENED

**1608** Lippershey invents the telescope
**1609** Drebbel makes the first thermostat
**1644** Torricelli presents the barometer
**1650** Von Guericke invents the air pump
**1654** The first accurate thermometer used
**1660** Royal Society is founded in London
**1666** Royal Academy is founded in Paris
**1668** Newton invents reflecting telescope
**1687** Newton's Theory of Gravitation
**1705** Edmund Halley predicts the return of Halley's comet in 1758

Double-barreled, wheel-lock pistol

Flemish matchlock

# REVOLUTION AND INDEPENDENCE

## 1708–1835

The 1700s are often called "the century of revolutions." Between 1708 and 1835, there were revolutions against governments and growing colonial power in many parts of the world—some were successful, some were not. Political revolutions happened because people were dissatisfied with the way their countries were run. There were also revolutions in farming techniques, and industry, in science, technology, and medicine, in transportation, and in the arts—especially literature.

▲ The Jacobite Rebellion against Hanoverian rule in England ended at the Battle of Culloden in 1746, when the Jacobites were defeated by English troops led by the king's son, the Duke of Cumberland.

◄ Generals Rochambeau and Washington give orders for the attack at the siege of Yorktown during the American Revolution in 1781.

273

# AUSTRIA AND PRUSSIA 1711–1786

**The Austrian Empire was by now passing its peak, and Brandenburg–Prussia was growing stronger. They both sought to dominate the other states of Germany.**

Maria Theresa (1717– 1780) was Hapsburg empress from 1740. She slowly improved conditions in the Austrian Empire with the help of well-chosen ministers, and reformed local government, education, and the army.

Charles VI, Archduke of Austria, became Holy Roman Emperor in 1711. This made him the most powerful man in Europe, and added the lands of the Holy Roman Empire to Austrian territory. After he died in 1740, three men claimed that they, not Charles's daughter Maria Theresa, should be crowned. The rivals were Charles of Bavaria, Philip V of Spain, and Augustus of Saxony.

The situation became more complicated as other European states got involved. The War of the Austrian Succession (1740–1748) began when the Prussians invaded the Austrian province of Silesia. Prussia was supported by France, Bavaria, Saxony, Sardinia, and Spain. But Britain, Hungary, and the Netherlands backed Maria Theresa. In the end, Maria Theresa kept her throne, but Austria was weakened, and Prussia kept Silesia. The balance of power in Germany shifted to Prussia, and the Holy Roman Empire declined. Over a century later, in 1870, it was Prussia which united Germany, and Austria was left out.

The enormous Schönbrunn Palace in Vienna, built between 1696 and 1730, is a grand example of decorative Rococo architecture.

## BRANDENBURG–PRUSSIA

The Hohenzollern dynasty of Brandenburg inherited Prussia in 1618. By 1700, Brandenburg–wPrussia had become a leading Protestant power, with Berlin as its capital. Its electors (rulers who were entitled to vote for a Holy Roman emperor) built an efficient government and helped its industries thrive. Prussia's rise to power began under Frederick William I. He reigned from 1713 to 1740 and built up the army. His successor, Frederick the Great, used the army to challenge Austria, France, and Russia. During his reign, he doubled the size of Prussia, improved its business and industry, and made it a cultural center of the Enlightenment. Over the next 100 years, Prussia gained more lands, and increasingly dominated Poland and northern Germany.

Frederick the Great (1712-1786) became King of Prussia in 1740. He was stern, brave, and ambitious. Under his leadership, Prussia became a strong nation. He established religious tolerance in Prussia and freed his serfs. But many men died as a result of the wars he entered.

In the Battle of Fontenoy in Belgium, in 1745, France had a major victory over Austria and its allies. In this painting, the French king Louis XV, points to the victor of the battle, Marshal de Saxe.

# SCOTLAND: THE JACOBITES 1701–1746

**During the early 1700s, the grievances of the Scottish people and Stuart claims to the English throne led to two fateful and bloody Scottish rebellions.**

Charles Edward Stuart (1720–1788), or "Bonnie Prince Charlie" was half-Scottish, half-Polish, and raised in Rome. He led a rebellion in Scotland and was beaten at the Battle of Culloden in 1746.

▲ Flora Macdonald (1722–1790) was the daughter of a laird who worked with the English, but she supported Bonnie Prince Charlie and helped him escape, disguised as her maid.

Scottish Highlanders, many of whom were Catholic, felt threatened by Mary, daughter of James II, and the Dutch and Protestant William III on the throne. They actively supported the return of a Scottish Stuart. To control such sentiment, the English tried to break down the Highland clan system. The lairds (clan chiefs) were forced to live in Edinburgh or London. As a result, they needed more money. They raised rents and cleared people from the highlands so that they could create large areas of farmland to increase production. Family feeling in the clans broke down, and relatives just became tenants, without any clan rights.

When Mary's sister Queen Anne died in 1714, her German cousin, George of Hanover, became king. He was the great-grandson of James I and a Protestant, but a foreigner. Some people felt that the Scottish James Stuart (1688–1766), son of James II, had a better claim. Many Scottish people were also unhappy about being joined with England in the "United Kingdom" in 1707.

The Jacobites supported James Stuart. They planned rebellions both in England and Scotland, but these failed. James returned from France in 1715, but it was too late; 26 soldiers were executed and 700 sent to the West Indies as punishment. In 1745, there was another uprising. James's son, popularly known as "Bonnie Prince Charlie," or the Young Pretender, landed secretly in Scotland. He overran Scotland, then invaded England. They got only as far south as Derby. In 1746, the Jacobites were cruelly defeated at the Battle of Culloden.

Bonnie Prince Charlie fled, and returned to France in disguise. The English gained control of the Highlands, and their revenge was severe. Highland lairds were executed and clansfolk disarmed. Until 1782, they were forbidden to wear kilts or play bagpipes. Over the years, clan lands were forcibly cleared of people to make way for grazing sheep, in order to earn money by supplying wool to the woolen mills of England. Clansfolk were sent to live in the cities, Northern Ireland, and the colonies.

▼ The Jacobite army gathered at the head of Loch Shiel on August 19, 1745. The Glenfinnan Monument is a tribute to the clansmen who died in the rebellion.

▲ The Jacobites were beaten at Culloden by English troops led by the Duke of Cumberland. He had all the wounded killed, and the others were chased and punished.

275

# AGRICULTURAL REVOLUTION 1650–1800

**During the 1700s, the landscape changed dramatically in parts of Europe as profitable new farming methods were introduced.**

In many villages, the poor were forced to leave their homes to clear space for the new enclosed fields and modern farming methods.

Europrean farming methods had not changed for centuries. But by 1700, landowners, botanists, and breeders, particularly in England, were discussing better ways of running farms and growing crops. Scientists did research into animal breeding, land management, and raising crops. Cities and industries were rapidly growing larger, and there was more money to be made in farming. As profits rose, landowners studied and experimented even more. All this led to an agricultural revolution.

New plows were designed, and in 1701, the English farmer Jethro Tull (1674–1741) invented the horse-drawn seed drill, which allowed the mechanized planting of seeds in rows for ease of weeding. By rotating crops, soil fertility was increased, and by careful breeding, animals were improved. These methods all required financial investment and larger farms.

The rural landscape changed greatly during the 1700s. In many parts of England, land had been farmed in large, open medieval fields. Villagers rented strips of these fields, where they worked alongside their neighbors. This system provided enough food to keep people alive, but it did not produce a surplus to sell to town dwellers for profit.

This cartoon shows a farm worker carrying all the tools he needed to use on the new farms of the 1700s.

▲ Jethro Tull was an English pioneer of scientific farming. He invented a horse-drawn seed-drill in 1701. It sowed seeds in neat rows. He also designed a horse-drawn hoe. His writings had a great influence across Europe and in North America.

▶ English farmer Robert Bakewell (1725–95) who introduced new breeding methods to improve the quality of sheep and cattle. He was one of the first farmers to breed animals just for meat.

The first meeting of the Royal Agricultural Society of England took place on July 17, 1839 in Oxford. The meetings were held each year to show pedigree animals and discuss new machinery and farming methods.

## THE ACTS OF ENCLOSURE

Landlords decided that their fields could be farmed more efficiently if they were enclosed. Hedges and walls were built across fields, to create smaller units that were easier to work. The Acts of Enclosure, passed by Parliament between 1759 and 1801, also meant that common grazing land was enclosed. In total, 7,400,000 acres (3 million ha) of English land were enclosed during the Agricultural Revolution.

Many tenants lost their livelihoods, and had to move to towns. Rich landlords established enormous estates with grand houses. Their farms grew large, and some estates were redesigned as beautiful parkland by landscape gardeners like Lancelot ("Capability") Brown. This was all supported by the government, which itself was made up of landowners. But it brought hardship to ordinary farmers.

▲ Experimental breeding of farm animals produced new, improved strains, such as this Old English breed of pig.

### KEY DATES

| | |
|---|---|
| 1701 | Jethro Tull invents seed drill for faster planting |
| 1730 | Lord Townshend introduces the system of four-crop rotation |
| 1737 | Linnaeus develops a system of plant classification |
| 1754 | Charles Bonnet publishes a study of the food value of various crops |
| 1804 | Swiss scientist Saussure explains how plants grow |

Growing the same crop every year eventually weakens the soil. Using crop rotation increases soil fertility, especially if clover is sown every fourth year. This enriches the soil and lets it rest. Crops planted in the next three years grow better.

# INDUSTRY: EARLY REVOLUTION 1708–1815

**The Industrial Revolution began in Britain in the cotton industry. It brought a wealth of change—a rapid growth of cities, mines, canals, and factories.**

The cotton gin was patented by American Eli Whitney (1765–1825), in 1794. It removed seeds and impurities from cotton fibers.

▲ The first multireel thread-spinning machine, the spinning jenny, was invented by James Hargreaves (1720–1778) in 1764.

▼ This is a flax mill from around 1800, where flax fibers were spun and woven into linen.

During the early 1700s, most people made goods in a traditional way, usually by hand, at home or in small workshops. The men were carpenters, blacksmiths, and weavers. Others were farm laborers, who worked on the land to grow crops to feed their families. Women worked at home, looking after the animals, cleaning sheep fleeces, and spinning wool into yarn for clothes. The Industrial Revolution changed all this. Many people began to move into towns to work for wages where employers were starting larger-scale production to increase profit.

The Industrial Revolution began in Britain in the textile industry. Machines, powered by waterwheels, speeded up the spinning, weaving, and finishing of cloth. Larger mills and factories were built. New towns sprang up in areas such as Yorkshire and Staffordshire in England, and the Ruhr Valley in Germany. Industrial cities such as Newcastle, Lille, Leipzig, and Rotterdam expanded rapidly. A network of canals was built to transport goods efficiently. Soon, steam engines were developed. Newcomen built a steam engine in 1712 for pumping water from mines, but it was not until 1774 that James Watt and Matthew Boulton built engines to power machines. In 1709, Abraham Darby began to smelt iron in a blast furnace using coke.

The fantail windmill was invented by Edmund Lee in 1745. The top rotated, steered by the fantail, so that the sails always turned toward the wind. It was used to pump water and grind grain.

Britain became known as the "workshop of the world." The Industrial Revolution began there because, unlike much of Europe, it was not ravaged by war. It had plentiful supplies of iron ore and coal; it was quick to develop a canal system; it had plenty of cheap labor (because of enclosures of farmland); and plenty of money was available from colonial profits.

The first steam engine, built by Thomas Newcomen (1663–1729) in 1712, pumped water out of mines. Later designs were used to power factories.

## KEY DATES

**1709** Abraham Darby invents blast furnace
**1712** Newcomen builds a steam engine for use in mines
**1730** John Kay introduces mechanical textile machines
**1759** Wedgwood's porcelain factory opens
**1764** Hargreaves invents spinning jenny
**1769** Thomas Arkwright invents a water-powered spinning machine
**1769** Nicolas Cugnot builds a steam-powered vehicle for the French army
**1773** Arkwright builds his first spinning mill (factory)
**1794** Eli Whitney patents the cotton gin
**1807** Robert Fulton's steamboat makes first trip

## BRITAIN'S INDUSTRY BOOMS

By 1815, Britain's output of coal, textiles, and metals was equal to that of the rest of Europe. It had taken a century to reach that point. Tremendous social changes took place as people moved from the country to the towns—families and villages broke up, and workers were exploited by powerful factory owners. Many children died working in mines and mills. A new class of rich industrialists gradually evolved, as well as managers and professionals. London became the financial capital of Europe. Manufactured products were exported around the world, and raw materials such as silk, cotton, and timber were carried to new ports such as Liverpool and Glasgow, then taken inland by canal.

The Agricultural and early Industrial revolutions went hand in hand. The factories supplied new machines and tools to farmers, and farmers became more like businessmen who sold their products to growing populations in the towns. The personal relationships of local country life and local trade gave way to financial deals, middlemen, and contracts. The "dark, satanic mills" commented on by the poet William Blake were taking over.

The invention of the steam engine allowed railroads to be built to transport coal from mines to factories. In 1812, John Blenkinsop (1783–1831) designed steam rack locomotives that were used on the Middleton Railway in England.

# INDIA AND CHANGE 1707–1835

**During the 1700s, Moghul India was devastated by wars and European interference. France and Britain competed in looting the country's wealth.**

Robert Clive (1725–1774) was an administrator and soldier for the British East India Company in the 1750s and 1760s. By winning key battles against the French and Indians, and by diplomacy and bribery, he strengthened the British hold on India.

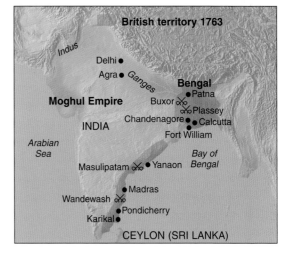

War in Europe between Britain and France spread overseas. Several major battles involving French, British, and Indian troops took place in India from 1756 to 1763.

In 1707, the Moghul emperor Aurangzeb died. During his long reign he had spent many years trying to maintain power and hold the empire together. The religious tolerance that his predecessor Akbar had once encouraged had broken down. After Aurangzeb's death, India began a century of war as different groups tried to gain control. Local rulers, who were entrusted by Moghul emperors with responsibility for the protection of distant states, built up their own private kingdoms in Oudh, Hyderabad, and Bengal instead. In western India and the Punjab, rebellions were organized by the Hindu Maratha states and Sikh princes.

From 1740 to 1760, the Hindu Marathas conquered central India, taking over most of the Moghul lands. But their attempt to take over the Moghul Empire in 1761 was thwarted by invading Afghans.

In 1739, the Persians under Nadir Shah invaded the north and sacked Delhi, the Moghul capital, killing 30,000 people. The Sikhs of the Punjab had established virtual independence by 1762. The Nizam of Hyderabad took various lands in central and southern India. India was in chaos.

▲ As governor general of the French East India Company, Joseph-François, Marquis de Dupleix (1697–1763) built up a *sepoy* (native Indian) army and challenged British interests in southern India. The appointment of Robert Clive as commander of British troops finally defeated the French plans.

▶ A royal procession to Golkonda, near Hyderabad, in about 1775. The eighteenth century saw wars and uprisings as the British East India Company took effective control over much of India.

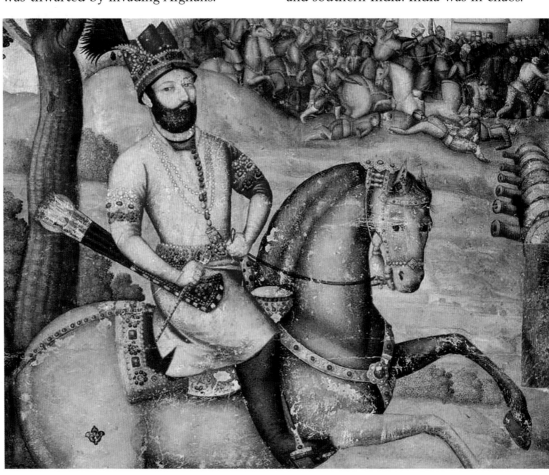

## THE BRITISH TAKEOVER

The fragile Moghul Empire was also threatened by ambitious Europeans. The British and French East India Companies had acquired vast possessions in India, centered on their profitable trading posts. They made alliances with discontented Indian leaders, using a mixture of diplomacy, bribes, and bullying. The French were given Moghul land in southern India by the *Nawab* (local ruler) of Hyderabad, in return for military support. The British allied with the Marathas and Mysore. The British general, Robert Clive, fought and defeated the French in 1752. Then, in 1756, the ruler of Bengal seized the British base in Calcutta. The following year, the British victory at Plassey gained them Bengal. By 1761, the British had seized the French base at Pondicherry, and ended the French influence in India.

During the next hundred years, the British East India Company gained ever-larger territories, or forced independent states to obey them. It was only in 1858 that the Indian Raj, the company's rule in India, was taken over by the British government. Queen Victoria was made empress of India.

## INDIA'S DOWNFALL

From 1707 to 1858, India went through a period of war and upheaval, followed by a gradual takeover by the British. In the early 1800s, the British overcame the Marathas and invaded central India, Sindh, and the Punjab (now part of Pakistan and India). Christian missionaries were allowed in from 1813, roads were built, and a new class of English-educated Indians emerged to help run the vast country. There were many small independent states, but they survived only if they obeyed the British. India was not united, but it was under British control.

Robert Clive met Mir Jafar, a Moghul general, in 1757, and offered him money and other advantages if he changed sides. Mir Jafar's support helped the British win

▲ Ivory carving is an ancient Indian art form. This ivory comb, made in Mysore, in the 1700s, shows Lakshmi, the goddess of good fortune and prosperity.

◀ The city of Bombay (now Mumbai) was known as the gateway to India. A center of shipbuilding as well as trade, it became one of the most important ports in British India.

# THE SEVEN YEARS' WAR 1756–1763

**The Seven Years' War was a battle between the European powers for continental dominance, and for control at sea and of overseas colonies.**

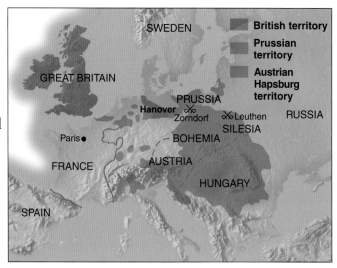

The Seven Years' War involved many nations, each with its own aims. Prussia and Britain gained the most. Prussia kept Silesia, and Britain gained greater control of Canada, India, and the seas.

▲ William Pitt, the 1st Earl of Chatham (1708–1778) was British secretary of state from 1756 to 1761. He directed the British involvement in the Seven Years' War with a sharp sense of strategy.

▼ In 1759 a British-German alliance defeated France and Saxony at Minden, in northern Germany. The Seven Years' War divided Europe and spread to North America and India.

During much of the 1700s, Austria, Prussia, Russia, and France each wanted to take control of Europe. This was unfinished business left over from the War of the Austrian Succession, which ended in 1748. But none of the European powers was strong enough to win on its own, so they made alliances. As a result, there was an uneasy balance of power.

Austria, France, Sweden, Russia, and Spain were opposed to Prussia, Britain, and Hanover. Austria wanted to recapture Silesia from Prussia, and England and France were already fighting over their Indian and Canadian colonies. But wars were expensive in time, money, weapons, and lives, and they drained the warring states' resources. Fighting started in 1756 and lasted for seven years. At first, it seemed as if the Austrians and French would win.

Then the British, under secretary of state William Pitt ("Pitt the Elder"), joined the Prussians. Prussian victories in 1757 at the battles of Rossbach (against France), Leuthen (against Austria), and Zorndorf (against Russia), along with British success against the French at Plassey in India and in Quebec, restored the balance of power.

## HOW THE WAR ENDED

In 1759, a British–Prussian army defeated the French at Minden in Germany, and the British navy defeated the French fleet at Quiberon Bay, northwest France. In 1760, the British took Montreal in Canada. Then, in 1761, William Pitt was forced to resign because his policies were unpopular with other politicians. Elizabeth, the czarina of Russia died in 1762, and the new czar, Peter III, withdrew Russia from the war. However, this did not bring an end to the hostilities. What actually ended it was the expense and destruction it brought to all sides as they ran out of money and military materials.

▼ The Battle of Zorndorf was fought between the Russians and the Prussians in 1758. The battle was fierce, and neither side really won, but Prussia benefited most, since it fended off a Russian invasion.

Ministers and diplomats now controlled governments and, after prolonged deprivation, many countries preferred to talk rather than make war. In the Treaty of Paris in 1763, it was agreed that Britain would get French lands in Canada and India, and the Prussians would keep the rich province of Silesia.

| KEY DATES | |
|---|---|
| 1740–48 | War of the Austrian Succession |
| 1756 | The Seven Years' War breaks out |
| 1757 | Battle of Plassey—British control of India grows |
| 1757–58 | Prussia battles for survival—victories at battles of Rossbach and Leuthen |
| 1759 | British gains in Canada and at sea; Battle of Minden—British–Prussian victory |
| 1760 | British take Montreal, Canada |
| 1762 | Russia withdraws from the war |
| 1763 | Treaty of Paris ends the war |

▲ In the Battle of Quiberon Bay, off Brittany in November 1759, the British navy defeated the French and, from then on, dominated the high seas.

▲ This medal was made in honor of the alliance forged at Versailles in 1756 between Austria and France.

# NORTH AMERICA 1675–1791

**The mid-1700s saw a conflict for control of North America between settlers and the Indigenous Americans, and between the English and the French.**

Joseph Brant, also known as Thayendanegea, (1742–1807), was a Mohawk. He was befriended by an English official, who gave him an English name and education. Brant fought with the British when he was just 13, and became a captain in 1775. He later visited London and was received at the British court.

French and British colonists had been fighting for many years. First came King Philip's War (1675–1676), in which the New England Wampanoag tribes rose up against the settlers. The Wampanoag lost, but not before killing 10 percent of the adult males in Massachusetts. King William's War (1689–1697), between English and French settlers, did not achieve much. In Queen Anne's War (1702–1713), the English took Acadia (Nova Scotia) and destroyed Spanish St. Augustine in Florida. Finally, in King George's War (1744–1748), the British captured Louisbourg, a French fort, but it was returned in 1748 in exchange for Madras in India.

These wars were all related to European conflicts. Each side had one long-term aim: they wanted to control North America. Each side was helped by Indigenous Americans, who fought in all the wars, hoping to receive support in their own disputes with colonists in return. But the Indigenous Americans generally lost out to the settlers, who did not respect them. For example, between 1730 and 1755, the Shawnee and Delaware peoples were forced from their lands.

European possessions in North America at the beginning of the Seven Years' War in 1756. By the end of the war in 1763, Britain controlled most of France's lands.

## PONTIAC'S REBELLION

In 1763, there was an indigenous uprising. Pontiac (1720–1769) was chief of the Ottawa and of a confederacy of Algonquin tribes. To drive the British out, the tribes attacked places from the Great Lakes to Virginia. Some 200 settlers were killed. The British retaliated, and in 1766, Pontiac made peace. He was assassinated in Illinois in 1769 by a British-paid Indigenous American.

## CAPTURE OF ACADIA

Acadia, or Nova Scotia, was claimed by the French in 1603 and settled by them. Britain also claimed it, and attacked it several times during the 1600s. Finally, they captured it in 1710, though the French held on to nearby Cape Breton Island. In the late 1750s, the British threw out 10,000 of the Acadians. Many went to Louisiana, settling around the mouth of the Mississippi, where they became known as Cajuns. Nova Scotia was then populated by Scottish people, many of whom had lost their lands in the Highland Clearances.

The British taking of Quebec in 1759 meant the beginning of the end of New France. The battle took place in the fields outside the city. The British and French generals, James Wolfe (1727–1759) and the Marquis de Montcalm (1712–1759), both died during the fighting.

## CANADA

The French and Indian War (part of the Seven Years' War) was fought from 1754. French colonists had settled in the Ohio Valley, and the British claimed it for themselves, so the French built a chain of forts and refused to leave. The French won some important battles in 1755 (Fort Duquesne) and 1756 (Fort Oswego). But the British captured Acadia in 1755, Quebec in 1759, and Montreal in 1760. The Treaty of Paris in 1763 gave Britain many former French colonies, and New France became British. Britain now controlled all of the lands east of the Mississippi River, and some French lands were given to Spain in exchange for Florida, which became British.

After the American Revolution, many colonists loyal to the crown, but with strong feelings about freedom, moved north to Canada. So, in 1791, the British Constitutional Act split Quebec into English-speaking Upper Canada (Ontario) and French-speaking Lower Canada (Quebec). The Act set up a government with an elected body in each of the two provinces. The British hoped that this would satisfy the growing demand for a government in which people felt they had a say. The French were also guaranteed continuing freedom of religion.

Through the death of General Montcalm near Quebec in 1759, the French lost their military leadership, and thus lost control of Canada.

### KEY DATES

**1675–76** King Philip's War
**1686–97** King William's War
**1710** Acadia taken by the English
**1739–41** The British fight Spanish Florida
**1744–48** King George's War
**1754–63** French and Indian War
**1760** British gain control of Canada
**1763–66** Pontiac's Rebellion
**1775** American Revolution begins

In 1775, Ethan Allen (1738–1789) and the Green Mountain Boys attacked the British garrison at Fort Ticonderoga. This was the first colonial victory in the American Revolution.

# TRADE WITH CHINA 1700–1830

**Trade with China was profitable, but the government there did not want "barbarian" influences introduced. European merchants looked for other ways to trade.**

Qianlong (1711–1795) ruled China for 60 years from 1735. He was a philosopher-emperor who supported the arts, wrote poetry, and created libraries.

Throughout the 1700s, Chinese silk, cotton, tea, lacquerware, and porcelain were highly prized in Europe. They were expensive and in short supply. Merchants from Portugal, Britain, Italy, and the Netherlands tried to expand trade with China. But the powerful Chinese emperors, who controlled all contact between their people and foreigners, were simply not interested. Qianlong (Ch'ien-lung), emperor for 60 years, was a scholar and traditionalist who had no time for "barbarians." The Europeans' problem was that they had to pay for everything in silver, because Chinese traders were not allowed to exchange foreign for Chinese goods. Also, Europeans were permitted to trade only in Guangzhou (Canton), where they were penned up in "factories" (fortified warehouses), and forced to trade through Chinese intermediaries. European traders were competitive, and fought to get the best Chinese goods and to ship them to Europe quickly to fetch the highest prices.

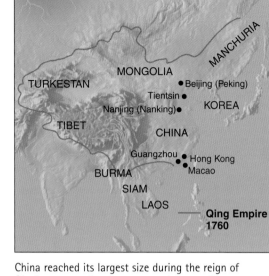

China reached its largest size during the reign of Qianlong, spreading into central Asia and Tibet—but this expansion was expensive and brought few benefits except keeping out the British and the Russians.

## THE OPIUM TRADE

Opium had long been used in China for medicinal purposes. Since European merchants were looking for other ways to trade, they established links with Chinese drug dealers, and sold them vast quantities of opium (5,000 barrels every year by the 1820s), from countries such as Burma. In return, they received precious Chinese goods for Europe. The trade grew steadily in the late 1700s, and the Qing government tried to stop it. By the 1830s, opium use was spreading through China, making people lazy, harming society and the economy, and costing China dearly.

▲ These Chinese maps from around 1800 show China, the "Middle Kingdom," sitting at the center of the world. At the time, China was isolated—but the world was knocking at its door.

▶ In 1793, the British diplomat Lord Macartney visited the Chinese emperor to encourage trade relations. Such relations were rejected, so people resorted to illegal deals. China and Britain had little respect for each other.

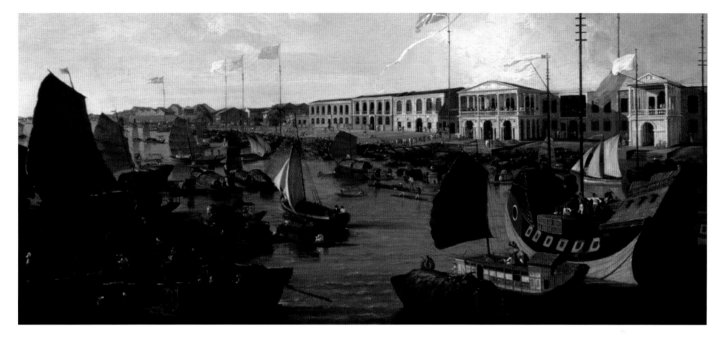

## THE QING DYNASTY

The Qing emperors were not keen to develop trade because they had urgent problems at home. Years of peace and prosperity had led to huge growth in the population (400 million by 1800), and there were now food shortages. Taxes were high, corruption was growing, and the population was moving from place to place.

The Qing rulers became very conservative, remote, and stubborn. As as result, there were protests and uprisings, often organized by secret societies with political ambitions. The White Lotus sect caused a peasant rebellion which lasted from 1795 to 1804. The effect of this was to weaken people's respect for the Qing dynasty. Foreigners—Russians, Japanese, Tibetans, and other ethnic minorities, as well as the Europeans—were also nibbling at China's edges.

## EUROPEAN INTERVENTION

The Qing emperors believed that China was the center of the world—"the Middle Kingdom, surrounded by barbarians." When a British ambassador traveled to Beijing in 1793, Qianlong refused to discuss trade. From then on, foreigners decided to get their way by other means, and the opium trade increased. By 1800, life was oppressive for many Chinese. They were heavily taxed, and Heshen, a corrupt official, had gained power. Smoking opium provided an escape for many. In 1839, when the Chinese tried to stop the trade, the British went to war. Even control of the world tea supply was almost at an end. During the 1840s, Scotsman Robert Fortune stole several tea plants in China, took them to India, and set up rival plantations.

▲ The foreign trading stations or "factories" at Guangzhou were the only places where trading with China was permitted. Europeans could not travel outside their compound, and they could trade only during certain months.

▲ The Temple of Heaven was rebuilt in 1751 during Qianlong's reign. The wooden prayer hall was enormous and highly decorated, and the roof was covered with blue ceramic tiles.

◄ Macao was a Portuguese colony on a peninsula not far from Guangzhou. It had been established in 1557, with imperial permission, and it was a center for Chinese and Japanese trade.

# THE AGE OF LOGIC 1700–1789

**The pursuit of logic and reason during the 1600s gave rise to further new social and political ideas in the 1700s. This is often called "The Enlightenment."**

▲ Voltaire (1694–1778) was one of France's greatest thinkers and authors. He wrote poetry, plays, philosophical works, and the novel *Candide*. His openly critical attitude meant that he fell out of favor with the French court.

▼ An imaginary portrait by the British artist and poet William Blake (1757–1827). It shows Sir Isaac Newton calculating how the universe is held together by the law of gravitation.

The German philosopher Immanuel Kant wrote "Dare to know! Have the courage to use your own intelligence!" People were no longer interested in traditional beliefs. The scientific research of the 1600s had begun a widespread process of examination and exploration of the world and, as a result, in the 1700s great encyclopedias were published that recorded this knowledge.

Between 1751 and 1772, Denis Diderot compiled the 28-volume *Encyclopedia*, with 200 contributors. In 1755, Samuel Johnson published his *Dictionary of the English Language*, and the *Encyclopedia Britannica* was published between 1768 and 1771.

The Enlightenment also represented a search for happiness, justice, and knowledge, in music, romance, travel, philosophy, and politics. Many absolute rulers and powerful landowners enjoyed new ideas, but they feared the consequences of ordinary people reading and talking about them. Such ideas would soon lead to revolutions.

This cartoon of Thomas Paine (1737–1809) shows him as a champion of liberty. Paine supported and provided many of the ideas which lay behind both the American and French revolutions.

### THE SPREAD OF IDEAS

The Enlightenment was led by philosophers such as Kant and Voltaire, the economist Adam Smith, the composers Haydn and Mozart, and political thinkers such as Rousseau, Locke, and Paine. Voltaire was a French writer who criticized intolerance, and rewrote the history of the world, as well as writing dramas and essays that commented on society and politics. Adam Smith, a Scottish economist, described the workings of modern economies and free markets. The French political thinker, Jean-Jacques Rousseau, wrote about social equality and democracy. Thomas Paine, a British-born revolutionary writer who visited America and France, wrote *The Rights of Man* which strongly influenced popular ideas.

It was also a time when people began to find things out by scientific experiment and observation. During this period, the basics of modern chemistry were established, and advances were also made in biology. These developments would help scientists in the future. Literature became more realistic as the first modern novels appeared. More people than ever could read, so new ideas spread more rapidly.

◀ The French philosophers and encyclopedists, Voltaire (with his hand up), Diderot, Abbe, Maury, Condorcet, and others, meet for dinner. In addition to compiling the *Encyclopedia*, they became the mouthpiece and focus for radical social ideas, and they criticized the *ancien régime* (the old order) for its conservative and authoritarian ways.

In a Europe battered by war, heavy taxes, inequalities, and oppressive governments, freethinking and freedom-seeking aspirations were becoming more prevalent. The first result of this bid for freedom occurred outside Europe, in the colonies of North America. Unexpectedly, a revolution was brewing there, which would encourage another revolution in France and further radical changes across the continent of Europe.

▶ Denis Diderot (1713–1784) was the editor of the *Encyclopedia*, published between 1751 and 1772. The 28 volumes included 17 books of text and 11 books of pictures. Each volume was censored by the publishers if they did not agree with his views.

Jean-Jacques Rousseau (1712–1778) was another of France's leading Enlightenment thinkers. In 1762, he wrote *The Social Contract* in which he emphasized the rights of people. In his novel *Émile*, he proposed a new theory of education.

## KEY DATES

| | |
|---|---|
| 1721 | J. S. Bach composes Brandenburg Concertos |
| 1730 | Peak of Rococo architecture |
| 1743 | American Philosophical Society founded |
| 1749 | Fielding's novel *Tom Jones* published |
| 1750s | Capability Brown, landscape artist, at work |
| 1751 | Publication of the *Encyclopedia* starts |
| 1752 | Benjamin Franklin identifies electricity |
| 1760s | Rousseau at work in France |
| 1768 | Royal Academy of Arts founded in England |
| 1770s | Goethe, German poet and dramatist, at work |
| 1776 | American Declaration of Independence |
| 1780s | Mozart and Haydn, composers, at work |
| 1781 | Kant's *Critique of Pure Reason* written |
| 1790s | French Revolution takes place |
| 1807 | Abolition of slavery in England |

# AFRICA 1700–1830

**Africa was now strongly affected by its increasing trade with Europeans and Arabs. Many African kingdoms grew strong and rich as a result.**

▲ Shaka Zulu (1787–1828) became Zulu leader in 1816. He taught them battle skills and expanded their lands in southeastern Africa.

In the north, the Ottoman Empire, which controlled Egypt, continued to decline. The Ashanti people on the west coast grew increasingly rich by selling slaves. In the southeast, the Portuguese were slowly building up a colony in Mozambique. The lands of the east coast (now Kenya) were ruled from Oman, a kingdom to the north, on the Arabian Sea. At the southern tip, the Cape of Good Hope, Dutch settlers began to explore the inland territory.

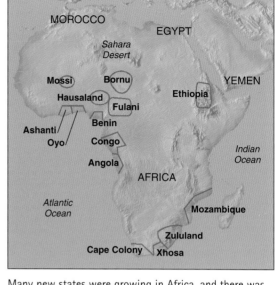

Many new states were growing in Africa, and there was much movement of peoples. Europeans and Arabs had small coastal colonies, but their influence inland was mainly felt through trade, rather than invasion.

Zulu warriors were armed with stabbing spears known as *assegai*. They wore battle headdresses and ornamental shields to frighten their enemies and also to recognize each other in battle.

## NEW AFRICAN STATES

During the 1700s, an average of 35,000 slaves each year were being sent from western Africa to the Americas. But, by the end of the century, the British were having second thoughts, and in 1787, they established Sierra Leone as a refuge for freed slaves. In 1822, Liberia was founded for freed slaves from the United States. Most European countries stopped trading in slaves in the early 1800s, but Portugal continued until 1882.

The Yao and Nyamwezi empires in eastern Africa virtually emptied that area to provide slaves. Ashanti and Oyo dominated the West African slave trade into the 1800s, then they started selling timber, ivory, hides, gold, and beeswax to the Europeans instead. This changed the West African farming practice of growing cash crops for export. Meanwhile, in eastern Africa, slaves continued to be sent by the Omani Arabs to Arabia and India.

The Zulu nation in southern Africa, led by King Shaka, fought constantly with its neighbors. The bloodshed was so great that the years from 1818 to 1828 became known as *mfecane*, or the time of troubles. There were migrations from the Sudan, the Tutsi moved into Rwanda, and the Masai into Kenya from farther north.

## AFRICAN MUSLIM STATES

On the southern edge of the Sahara, there was an Islamic revival. Many Muslims expected a *mahdi*, or savior, to appear, and various African caliphs, moved by this possibility, founded new, well-organized states such as Sokoto, Mossi, Tukulor, and Samori in inland West Africa. In Egypt, Mehmet Ali Pasha took control from the Mamluks in 1811, modernized the country, and invaded Sudan in the 1820s.

Africa was changing rapidly. Most of it still belonged to Africans, but they were not united against their common threat, the Arabs and Europeans. As a result, Africa was vulnerable.

▲ In 1809, the Hausa city of Kano in northern Nigeria was captured by the Muslim leader Usman dan Fodio, of the Hausa kingdom of Gobir. The Hausa cities converted to Islam, and became part of an Afro-Islamic state called the Sokoto Caliphate.

Mehmet Ali Pasha (1769–1849) was the Ottoman governor of Egypt, but he made Egypt virtually independent of the Ottomans and invaded the lands up the Nile River in Sudan, making Egypt the leading power in the eastern Mediterranean. He ruled Egypt from 1805 to 1848.

## MASSACRE OF THE MAMLUKS

The Mamluks were originally slaves, captured in the 800s by Muslim armies in the Caucasus and Russia. They were mostly Cossacks and Chechens by origin, trained to serve as soldiers and administrators in Egypt. By 1200, they had become palace guards and ministers. They then overthrew the sultan and ruled Egypt from 1249 to 1517. When the Ottomans took Egypt, the Mamluks became the ruling class under the Ottomans. As Ottoman power declined in the 1700s, they regained power in Egypt. After Mehmet Ali Pasha conquered the Mamluks in 1811 and took control of Egypt, he invited all the surviving Mamluk commanders to a banquet in Cairo where he had them massacred.

291

# MODERNIZING RUSSIA 1730–1796

**The rulers who followed Peter the Great continued his strategy of westernization and expansion, making Russia into a great European power.**

Peter III (1728–1762) was czar for half a year. A grandson of Peter the Great, he did not have the character to be czar, and he was not liked. Czarina Elizabeth forced him to marry Catherine.

▼ Winter was often a good time to travel in Russia, because the snow made progress faster. Catherine the Great traveled in an enclosed sled drawn by horses.

When Peter the Great died in 1725, his wife became Czarina Catherine I. However, she died after only a few years. Anna Ivanovna ruled for ten years from 1730, continuing Peter's pro-Western policies, and welcoming many foreigners at court. The Russian people themselves suffered. The czarina's court in St. Petersburg cared more about music, poetry, and wars against the Ottomans or the Europeans, than about the welfare of the peasants.

From 1741, Peter's daughter, Elizabeth (1709–1762), made Russia even more westward-looking and industrial, and she declared war on Prussia in the Seven Years' War. In 1745, she forced her son Peter, the heir to the Russian throne, to marry Catherine, who was from a poor but noble Prussian family. The marriage was not a happy one. When Elizabeth died in 1762, Peter III ruled briefly.

Catherine the Great (1729–1796) ruled Russia for 34 years. Other European leaders respected Catherine for her achievements in foreign policy, but feared her power.

Extent of Russian territory 1762

SWEDEN — Archangel
Baltic Sea — St. Petersburg — Moscow — RUSSIA
Siberia
EUROPE
Black Sea — Caspian Sea
Ottoman Empire
MONGOLIA
CHINA
INDIA

## CATHERINE THE GREAT

Peter III was a weak man, and Catherine despised him. Six months after his coronation, he was deposed and murdered. Catherine declared herself empress and ruled in his place. Although she was intelligent and cultured, she carried her private ruthlessness into public life.

To support Catherine's wars and her lavish court, Russia was drained of wealth in tax and young men. She planned to improve education and social conditions, but there were few educated officials to carry out these plans. So she asked the nobility for help, and gave them extra powers. This made the peasants' situation even worse, and led to Pugachev's Rebellion in 1773–1774. Rebels took the city of Kazan, and promised to abolish tax, serfdom, landlords, and military service. But Pugachev was brutally crushed.

◄ From the 1500s to the 1700s, the Russian Empire had more than doubled in size. During Catherine's reign, it gained ports on the coasts of the Baltic and Black seas.

## FOREIGN POLICY

Catherine's appointment of a reform commission in the 1760s failed, so she chose autocratic rule, and divided the country into regions, each ruled by nobles. Then she left the nobles to take care of Russia's internal affairs.

Her claim to greatness comes from the way she expanded Russia's lands. This strategy of expansion was masterminded by two ministers, Count Alexander Suvarov and Grigori Potemkin. In the north and west, new lands were won from Sweden in 1790. Most of Poland was seized when it was partitioned (divided). These gains gave Russia important seaports on the Baltic coast.

In the south, Russia took Azov from the Ottomans, then the Crimea, and, by 1792, the whole northern shore of the Black Sea. The Ottomans no longer controlled the Black Sea and Russia built up a powerful navy. To the east, Russia's gradual development of Siberia was also stepped up.

But Catherine was very cruel. Courtiers were flogged, and peasants who dared to complain about their situation were punished. Many poor people faced starvation, yet Catherine continued to collect heavy taxes to pay for her wars and extravagant lifestyle.

▲ Life at the Russian court was rich and elegant, sheltered from reality, and out of touch. In contrast, the peasants lived in poverty.

| KEY DATES |
| --- |
| **1741** Elizabeth becomes czarina |
| **1756–63** Russia joins the Seven Years' War |
| **1762** Catherine the Great becomes czarina |
| **1772** First partition of Poland |
| **1783** Russia annexes the Crimea |
| **1792** Russia gains Black Sea coast |
| **1793–95** Second and Third partitions of Poland |
| **1796** Death of Catherine the Great |

▶ This painting of the inside of the Winter Palace in St. Petersburg shows how impressive life in St. Petersburg was. Tropical plants thrived indoors, while people sometimes froze to death just outside the palace.

# EXPLORATION IN OCEANIA 1642–1820

**The exploration of Oceania came about quite late compared with other parts of the world. It was pioneered by Tasman, Cook, and other explorers.**

Between 1768 and 1779, the navigator Captain James Cook (1728–1779) made three voyages of discovery to the Pacific. In 1770, he landed at Botany Bay and claimed Australia for Britain.

Jean-François La Pérouse (1741–1788) was sent by Louis XVI to sail around the world on a scientific expedition. He traveled the oceans with a crew of scientists, charting, observing, and collecting samples while visiting Canada, Siberia, and Australia. His ships disappeared in 1788.

During the 1600s, Dutch seamen explored the southern Pacific and Indian oceans. By the 1620s, they had found the northern and western coast of Australia, naming it "New Holland."

In 1642, the Dutchman Abel Tasman (1603–1659) discovered the island of Tasmania. He had sailed from Mauritius and traveled so far south that he did not sight Australia. Farther to the east, Tasman reached the south island of New Zealand. After a fight with its Maori inhabitants, he returned to Batavia in the Dutch East Indies, and discovered Tonga and Fiji on the way. The next year, he sailed along the northern coast of Australia.

In 1688 and 1699, the English navigator William Dampier (1652–1715) explored the western and northwestern coastline of Australia. These explorers proved that Australia was an island, but they did not settle there. The Pacific remained largely unknown since it was too distant and too poor to attract European trading interest.

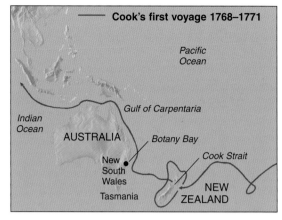

Cook's first voyage 1768–1771

Pacific Ocean

Indian Ocean

Gulf of Carpentaria

AUSTRALIA

Botany Bay

New South Wales

Cook Strait

Tasmania

NEW ZEALAND

On Cook's first voyage, he sailed from the tip of South America to New Zealand and proved that there was no large continent in between as many people thought.

The first scientific exploration of these southern lands was undertaken by Captain James Cook, who made three voyages. The first voyage (1768–1771) took him around New Zealand. Then he landed at Botany Bay in Australia, claiming it for Britain. On his second voyage (1772–1775), he explored many Pacific islands and Antarctica. On his last voyage, started in 1776, he visited New Zealand, Tonga, Tahiti, and finally Hawaii, where he was killed in a quarrel with the islanders.

## THE VOYAGES OF CAPTAIN COOK

Captain Cook was commissioned to sail to Tahiti to observe the passage of Venus in front of the sun. After this, he was secretly sent south to chart New Zealand and Australia for the British government. On his second voyage, he was the first explorer to visit the Antarctic, but he was driven back by pack ice. Cook discovered the value of carrying vegetables and fruit for his sailors, so preventing scurvy (caused by lack of Vitamin C). He also took well-trained artists with him because he was determined that the findings should be scientifically recorded. He died in Hawaii, in 1779, while on his third voyage.

# INDIGENOUS PEOPLES

The "new" lands explored by Cook had been inhabited for hundreds of years. The Indigenous peoples of New Zealand and Australia lived according to ancient traditions. Understandably, they were wary of Cook and his men—the first Europeans that they had ever seen.

The Indigenous people of Australia had lived there for thousands of years, spread out over a vast continent. They lived by foraging, hunting, and farming, and using their advanced knowledge of nature. The settlers did not recognize the rights of the Indigenous people to their own land, and set about destroying their culture. Many were killed.

The Maoris, it is thought, had sailed to Aotearoa (New Zealand) from Polynesia around 1300, and were farmers, warriors, and village dwellers. They resisted the efforts of the Europeans to move into their land.

The first settlers in Australia arrived in 1788. They were convicts who had been transported there from Britain as punishment. Free settlers started to arrive in 1793. In New Zealand, whalers, hunters, and traders were soon followed by missionaries. Many of the early settlers came from Scotland, Ireland, and Wales. The settlers introduced diseases that often killed the local peoples.

## KEY DATES

| | |
|---|---|
| 1642–44 | Tasman's voyages to Tasmania and New Zealand |
| 1688/1699 | Dampier explores western and northwestern coastline of Australia |
| 1766–68 | Bougainville discovers Polynesia and Melanesia |
| 1768–71 | Cook's first voyage |
| 1772–75 | Cook's second voyage |
| 1776–79 | Cook's third voyage |
| 1829 | Britain annexes all of Australia |
| 1840 | Britain claims New Zealand |

▲ The Maoris were skilled sailors and craftworkers who decorated their canoes with elaborate religious carvings. When Cook arrived, there were about 100,000 Maoris in New Zealand. Many were killed in later wars against British settlers and troops.

In 1779, while on his third voyage to the Pacific, Captain Cook was killed in a skirmish with Hawaiians over the theft of a boat. Initially, the British had been welcome, but after this event, his crews had to sail home without their captain.

# JAPAN AND SOUTHEAST ASIA 1603–1826

**Europeans were gradually making headway into Asia, as they sought to dominate trade. During the 1700s, these trade links turned into political battles.**

Sword guards protect the hand during fighting. This decorative Japanese sword guard dates from the 1700s.

Since 1603, Japan had been dominated by the Tokugawa shoguns, who ran the country very strictly, isolated from other lands. But they also brought peace and security. The country prospered under their rule. The population grew from 20 to 30 million in 150 years, and the output of farmers increased greatly. Towns flourished, and with them trade and the merchant classes. Skilled craftworkers made beautiful goods, especially clothes and fabrics in colored silks. Many Japanese people received a good education.

But Japan also had problems. Many Japanese had left the land, crowding into the cities, and the samurai class had fallen into debt. Heavy taxes led to riots, and many minor crimes were punished by death. In the 1740s, the enlightened shogun Yoshimune (1684–1751) lifted many harsh laws and allowed European books into the country. But the 1760s brought famine, earthquakes, and frequent uprisings, and an anti-shogun movement developed.

A small number of Dutch traders were the only foreigners allowed into Japan. They were treated scornfully, but they made so much money that they put up with the insults.

The Japanese had very advanced ideas about cleanliness and hygiene. Public baths were very popular and socially acceptable in Japan.

## SOUTHEAST ASIA

In Southeast Asia, there was no such ban on traders. Arabic and European spice traders had visited the area since medieval times, and later, Europeans had established trading posts. The Dutch dominated the area, controlling Java and creating trading posts on many of the islands. Several Muslim-dominated states in the East Indies were either friendly with or under the control of the Dutch.

During the 1700s, trade links turned into political battles. The British were gaining more interest in the area. In 1762, they forced the Spanish to give up their monopoly over the sea route to Latin America. In 1786, they took control of Penang in Malaya, and in 1795, they took the port of Malacca from the Dutch.

▲ Men below samurai rank were not allowed to wear jewelry. *Netsuke* figures in wood or ivory were used to attach things like tobacco pouches to the *obi* (sash) of their robes. Netsuke have become prized art objects.

▶ This Japanese print shows Minamoto Yoshitsune, a famous shogun of the 1100s, leaping from one boat to another. He continued to be popular long after his death, and many stories sprang up about his exploits.

During the Napoleonic Wars, the British occupied Batavia, the Dutch capital in Java. Later, they returned it, after the Dutch recognized their control of Malaya. The British established Singapore as a free port in 1819, giving special privileges to their own traders. This became a crucial stopover port for Chinese trade, and it quickly turned into the region's main commercial center. Goods from Britain and India traveled east, and goods from China and the East Indies went west.

## LOCAL WARS

European nations became involved in wars between the Southeast Asian states. They used these local conflicts to settle European disputes among themselves. The British, French, and Dutch all fought in Siam (today's Thailand) at different times, though Siam remained independent. From 1824 to 1826, an Anglo-Burmese war flared up after Burma (today's Myanmar) supported Britain's enemies, who lived close to the rich British-ruled lands of Bengal. The Europeans did not colonize mainland Southeast Asia, but they gradually made these countries dependent on them. By 1820, the Europeans had a very strong hold on Southeast Asia.

▲ The Dutch had a "factory," or trading post, at Desima Island near Nagasaki in southern Japan. This was the only foreign trading post allowed in the country. There, the Dutch exported silks and other fine Japanese products in exchange for silver.

◄ Sir Thomas Stamford Raffles (1781–1826) founded the British colonial port of Singapore in 1819. He worked hard to increase British power in Southeast Asia, and Singapore soon became the business center of the region.

## THE CAPTURE OF YANGON (RANGOON)

In 1824, the British commander, Sir Archibald Campbell, led 11,000 soldiers on a river journey of 400 mi. (640km) to capture the capital of Burma, Rangoon (today's Yangon, in Myanmar). The raid was the result of a border dispute and a desire to reduce France's influence in the region.

# THE BIRTH OF THE U.S.A. 1763–1789

**People in the Thirteen Colonies in America were dissatisfied with British rule. They fought for their independence, and a new nation was born.**

George Washington (1732–1799) was an officer in the British army and a wealthy landowner. He was made commander in chief of the new American army, fighting the British. In 1789, he became the first president of the United States.

At the end of the Seven Years' War in 1763, both the British government in London and the English colonists in America felt satisfied. They had defeated France and gained territory from them in Canada, as well as land as far west as the Mississippi River. With the French threat gone, the colonists no longer needed the British to defend them.

But the British wanted to govern the old French territories and collect higher taxes to pay for soldiers to defend these newly won lands, so they raised taxes in the 13 colonies. Local colonial assemblies argued that it was unfair for Britain to tax the American colonies, since they had no say in running the British government. They said "taxation without representation is tyranny." The colonies decided to ban all British imports. On July 4, 1776, representatives from all 13 colonies adopted the Declaration of Independence, claiming the right to rule themselves.

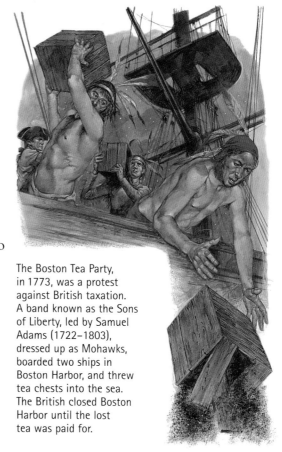

The Boston Tea Party, in 1773, was a protest against British taxation. A band known as the Sons of Liberty, led by Samuel Adams (1722–1803), dressed up as Mohawks, boarded two ships in Boston Harbor, and threw tea chests into the sea. The British closed Boston Harbor until the lost tea was paid for.

▲ The British soldiers were well-drilled professionals, while the Americans were mostly volunteers. But the Americans were highly motivated because they felt strongly about their cause. On the left is a uniformed British grenadier, and on the right is an American revolutionary soldier.

At the Battle of Bunker Hill, near Boston, in 1775, the British lost twice as many men as the Americans. It took three uphill assaults for the British to win.

## INDEPENDENCE

Guided by the ideas of Thomas Jefferson, and influenced by the Enlightenment, the American Declaration of Independence stated: "We hold these truths to be self-evident, that all men are created equal, that they are endowed by their Creator with certain inalienable Rights, that among these are Life, Liberty, and the Pursuit of Happiness."

The American Revolution had begun in 1775. At first the British were successful, despite the problems of fighting nearly 3,000 mi. (5,000km) from home. But the Americans had an advantage because they were fighting on home territory, and they believed in their cause. Six years after the conflict began, the British army surrendered at Yorktown, Virginia, having been defeated by Washington's troops. Britain eventually recognized American independence in the Treaty of Paris in 1783.

| KEY DATES | |
|---|---|
| 1763 | End of the Seven Years' War; British troops sent to North America |
| 1764 | Sugar Act taxes imported molasses |
| 1765 | Stamp Act adds tax on documents |
| 1775 | American Revolution begins; Battle of Bunker Hill takes place |
| 1776 | Declaration of Independence |
| 1781 | British army surrenders at Yorktown |
| 1783 | Britain recognizes American independence |
| 1787 | Draft American Constitution drawn up |
| 1789 | American Constitution becomes law; George Washington becomes first president |
| 1791 | Bill of Rights is adopted |

## THE U.S. CONSTITUTION

At first, the United States of America was run by the governing body that was set up during the Revolution, the Continental Congress, under the laws called the Articles of Confederation. But the Congress was weak. It was little more than an assembly of representatives from the states and could only make decisions that affected all of the states. It could borrow money, for example, but could not collect taxes from the states to raise money to repay the loan.

Some thought a whole new system of government that would unite the states into a nation was needed. In May 1787, at the Constitutional Convention in Philadelphia, they designed this system. They decided to have a president, elected every four years. He would rule with the help of a Congress (consisting of a House of Representatives and a Senate, made up of representatives from every state), and a Supreme Court.

In addition, each of the states would have an elected assembly, and run their state government as they liked. A system of checks and balances would make sure that neither the president, the Congress, nor the Supreme Court would be allowed to control the federal government.

Finally, many people worried that the Constitution did not protect all the rights they had fought so hard for. So, in 1791, ten amendments were added to the Constitution. They are the Bill of Rights.

▼ The draft Constitution was worked out at the Constitutional Convention in Philadelphia in 1787. Fifty-five delegates attended, 39 signed the document. Copies were sent to each state to be agreed by its leaders.

▲ A Liberty Medal was made to mark the victory of the Americans over the British in 1781.

▲ The Liberty Bell in Philadelphia symbolizes American independence.

▲ Thomas Jefferson (1743–1826) became the third president in 1801. He was a political leader whose ideas greatly affected American politics.

# THE FRENCH REVOLUTION 1789–1799

**In 1789, the discontented people of France overthrew their king, demanding freedom and equality. The revolution that followed changed France forever.**

Marie Antoinette (1755–1793) was Louis XVI's Austrian wife. The people thought she was arrogant and extravagant.

Louis XVI (1754–1793) became king in 1774. He was shy and not a strong ruler. His wrong decisions led to the Revolution.

The French Revolution had been building up for years. It was caused by bad government and enormous differences between the rich and the poor, and encouraged by new Enlightenment ideas about people's rights, and influenced by the American Revolution.

In the 1700s, France was in crisis. Food was scarce, prices were high, and the government was facing bankruptcy. To get more money, Louis XVI could either borrow it or raise state taxes. But first he needed approval and support from a traditional assembly, the Estates-General, which had not met for 175 years.

At the assembly, the representatives of the professional classes rebelled against the nobles and clergy. They took an oath to start a new National Assembly and demand reform. They wrote a new constitution that abolished the old order, nationalized Church lands, and reorganized local government. Louis sent troops to try and dismiss the Assembly.

When the citizens of Paris heard this, they rebelled. On July 14, 1789, a mob stormed the Bastille, the king's prison in Paris. The riot marked the beginning of a bloody revolution in which the rebels demanded "Liberty, Equality, Fraternity."

▲ Maximilien Robespierre (1758–1794) became the leader of a revolutionary group called the Jacobins in 1793. He was the head of the Committee of Public Safety and backed the execution of the king and queen. Executions grew so frequent that this time was known as the Reign of Terror. Robespierre may not have been responsible for this, but he did make enemies. In 1794, he was accused of treason and executed.

► On July 14, 1789, the people of Paris stormed the Bastille, a prison where many popular leaders had been imprisoned by the king. This was the real outbreak of the Revolution.

## THE STRUGGLE FOR POWER

In 1791, Louis XVI fled, but was captured and imprisoned. In 1792, the monarchy was abolished, and the following year, Louis and his wife were tried and executed. By this time, the revolutionary government was at war with most other European states, who were afraid that revolution might spread to their countries.

Predictably, chaos broke out, and there was a struggle for power. The new revolutionary government began rounding up its rivals, royalist or popular, calling them "enemies of the revolution." There was a political battle between two groups, the Jacobins and Girondins, which the Jacobins won. They then dominated a new ruling body, called the Committee of Public Safety. The committee mobilized French armies against foreign invasion, and from September 1793 to July 1794, they executed all who opposed them in what is known as the Reign of Terror.

During the Terror, around 18,000 people were guillotined. Soon, one man, Robespierre, wielded dictatorial power. Even he was not safe, and in 1794, he was accused of treason and executed.

## THE DIRECTORY

A new constitution was written in 1795 and a weak government, called The Directory, was formed. War had already broken out, and French revolutionary armies had conquered the Netherlands and south Germany. A young general, Napoleon Bonaparte, took over the army, and invaded Italy, Switzerland, and Egypt. The Directory came to rely on him. He grew popular and powerful. In 1799, he removed the Directory and took control.

The so-called *sans culottes* (named because they did not wear knee-length pants, like the middle class and aristrocracy), preserved public order in the streets during the Reign of Terror. Many people lost their lives as a result of the hatred of the *sans culottes*.

| KEY DATES | |
|---|---|
| 1788 | Estates-General called to a meeting |
| 1789 | National Assembly and storming of the Bastille; Declaration of the Rights of Man |
| 1791 | The New Constitution and Legislative Assembly |
| 1792 | The Revolutionary Wars and French Republic |
| 1793–94 | The Reign of Terror |
| 1794 | Robespierre's dictatorship; Holland invaded |
| 1795–99 | The Directory rules France |
| 1796 | Napoleon becomes chief army commander |
| 1799 | Napoleon takes power |

## THE REIGN OF TERROR

After Louis XVI had been executed in 1793, the Committee started to attack and execute anyone suspected of opposing the revolution. A Tribunal was set up to bring "enemies of the revolution" to trial, but these trials were often hurried and unfair. Aristocrats, royalists, priests, and any suspected people went to the guillotine. Once Robespierre had rid himself of rivals in the Committee of Public Safety, he ruled alone for a short time, until he too was sent to the guillotine in July 1794. The Reign of Terror then ended.

Here, people celebrate the end of the Reign of Terror by dancing around a tree decorated with rosettes in red, white, and blue, the national colors.

# THE NAPOLEONIC WARS 1797–1815

Restoring order after the French Revolution, Napoleon attempted to change Europe. But Britain was among those that stood against him and Napoleon was exiled.

▲ In this 1803 cartoon, Napoleon is shown straddling the world while the comparatively tiny John Bull (representing Britain) tries to fight him off alone.

▲ Napoleon wanted to create a society based on skill rather than on noble birth. To encourage achievement he founded the Legion of Honor in 1802 "for outstanding service to the state." Members of the Legion received a medal and a pension for the remainder of their lives.

Napoleon was born in Corsica, the second son of an Italian lawyer. As a young man, he had joined the French army, and his courage and quick thinking led to rapid promotion. At the age of 24, he became a general. He led a number of successful campaigns, capturing northern Italy in 1797. The new government, the Directory, feared his popularity and power. They offered Napoleon the job of invading Britain, but he suggested invading Egypt to disrupt Britain's trade route to India. In 1789, he did invade Egypt, but his plan failed after the British, led by Lord Nelson, destroyed his fleet.

In 1799, Napoleon returned to France and seized control. He dismissed the government, and appointed three consuls (officials), to run the country. He made himself first consul, and ruled for 15 years. In 1804, he crowned himself emperor.

Napoleon introduced many lasting reforms that brought new laws, a better educational system, a reorganized government, and a new national bank.

In 1799, Napoleon (1769–1821), already a war hero, took over the government by force. Many disagreed, but France was in disorder and Napoleon became first consul.

He was a brilliant general, who moved his troops quickly and using new battle tactics. He also had a very large army, because Robespierre had introduced a draft system in which all adult men were forced to serve. The army numbered 750,000 soldiers in 1799, and another two million men joined up between 1803 and 1815. Napoleon used this massive force to try to conquer Europe.

## THE BATTLE OF MARENGO

One of Napoleon's many military successes, the Battle of Marengo was fought against the Austrians in Italy in 1800. Napoleon was a brilliant leader, inspiring his troops with speeches, "leading from the front," and using very innovative tactics. He modernized warfare, used cannons and large armies, and outwitted his opponents. His control of Europe pushed many countries into the modern world.

# THE NAPOLEONIC WARS

Napoleon defeated Austria and Russia at Austerlitz in 1805, Prussia at Jena in 1806, and Russia faced a second defeat at Friedland in 1807. Napoleon created new republics allied to France and ruled by placing his relatives in positions of power. He also created Europe-wide laws and governments— known as the Continental System.

In 1805, Britain won a major sea battle against France at Trafalgar in Spain. The British admiral, Horatio Nelson (1758–1805) died, but his victory saved Britain from invasion. In 1808, Napoleon invaded Spain. This began the Peninsular Wars in which Britain supported Spain and Portugal.

The British sent troops led by the Duke of Wellington to Spain. There, he won battles at Salamanca (1812) and Vittoria (1813), pushing the French out of Spain.

Napoleon's disastrous invasion of Russia in 1812 left over 500,000 French dead of cold or hunger, or killed. In 1813, he was also crushed at Leipzig by a combined European force, led by the Prussian general, von Blücher. Finally, in 1814, France was invaded, and Napoleon was exiled. He escaped and was defeated by Wellington and von Blücher at Waterloo in Belgium. He died in exile on the remote South Atlantic island of St. Helena in 1821.

| KEY DATES | |
|---|---|
| 1796–97 | Napoleon invades Italy |
| 1798 | Campaign in Egypt |
| 1799 | Napoleon takes over French government |
| 1804 | Napoleon crowns himself emperor |
| 1805 | Battle of Austerlitz against Austria and Russia; Battle of Trafalgar—British sea victory |
| 1807 | Peace of Tilsit with Russia and Prussia |
| 1812 | Russian campaign |
| 1813 | Napoleon loses Battle of Leipzig; Spain freed at Battle of Vittoria |
| 1814 | France invaded; Napoleon exiled to Elba |
| 1815 | Napoleon's last battle, at Waterloo |

▲ Napoleon believed Russia had allied with Britain, so he invaded. When his army reached Moscow, the Russians had already burned it down. Eventually, the winter took its toll. Napoleon entered Russia with 510,000 men— butleft with only 10,000.

The Battle of Waterloo in Belgium, in 1815, was closely fought. It was Napoleon's last battle, fought against Wellington of Britain and von Blücher of Prussia.

▲ Irish-born Arthur Wellesley, Duke of Wellington (1769– 1852), fought Napoleon's armies in Spain where it took four years to push out the French. Wellington was involved in the Congress of Vienna after the Napoleonic Wars. A national hero, he became prime minister of Britain in 1828.

# THE END OF SLAVERY 1792–1888

**The European colonies in the Americas depended heavily on slave labor. But by the mid-1700s, many people were questioning the morality of this.**

William Wilberforce (1759–1833) was the member of Parliament for Hull, a busy slave trading port. The trade horrified him. He and other humanitarian Christians campaigned against the slave trade from 1788 onward.

Throughout the 1700s, Britain, France, and Spain grew rich on taxes and profits from their colonies. Much of this wealth was created by slave labor. Denmark, Sweden, Prussia, Holland, and Genoa (Piedmont) also traded in slaves. Africans were sold to Europeans by slave dealers and local rulers, who saw slave trading as a means of punishing criminals, getting rid of enemies, disposing of captives, and getting rich. Nobody knows how many slaves were sold in all, but historians have estimated that 45 million slaves were shipped between 1450 and 1870, although only 15 million survived— many died on the voyage across the Atlantic. Many Europeans disapproved of the slave trade, but they believed it was the only way to supply labor to colonial plantations.

However, some protested, saying it was against God's law and human decency. Rousseau, a French philosopher, wrote in *The Social Contract*, in 1762, "Man is born free, but everywhere he is in chains." His writings inspired the revolutions in America and France, and individual freedom became regarded as a social right, not a gift from a king. Rousseau's ideas also inspired people to fight on behalf of others who were unable to help themselves. Politicians, clergy, and ordinary people began to think how they might help the slaves. But moral arguments did not have as much force as the profits that slavery generated.

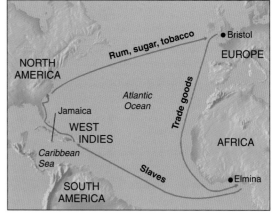

Before abolition, slave ships followed a triangular Atlantic sailing route, taking goods to Africa, slaves to the Americas, and products such as sugar back to Europe.

## ENDING THE SLAVE TRADE

Between 1777 and 1804, slavery was made illegal in the northern United States. Denmark withdrew from the slave trade in 1792, and Britain in 1807. But slave smuggling continued. The British navy clamped down on slave trading from 1815, but slavery was still legal elsewhere. A slave revolt in the French colony of Santo Domingo in 1791–1793 led to abolition by France but, in 1803, they made slavery legal again. In 1831, a slave uprising in Virginia led by Nat Turner led to harsh laws and increased support for slavery among white southerners.

▲ Some slaves escaped from plantations and set up their own villages in remote areas. In 1739, a group of escaped Jamaican slaves, called the "Maroons," rebelled against the British.

▶ Conditions on slave ships were appalling and unhealthy, and many slaves died. Slaves were stacked on dark shelves and floors in the holds of ships, hardly able to move.

## PHILANTHROPY

In Britain, Thomas Clarkson (1760–1846) and William Wilberforce had led an antislavery campaign, which resulted in the abolition of slave trading in 1807. However, slaves were not actually freed for some time. Wilberforce died just before all of the slaves in British hands were freed. Europeans had by now grown disgusted with slavery, and the British navy blocked slave-trading ships.

Slavery continued in Cuba, Costa Rica, Brazil, and the southern United States. The plantations had been built on slave labor. There was a thriving market in Europe for cheap, slave-grown cotton and tobacco, and plantation owners were reluctant to change.

In the U.S., the northern states supported freeing the slaves, but the situation in the South grew worse. Nat Turner's 1831 revolt in Virginia led to new laws designed to control the slaves. Slavery finally ended in the United States in 1863, in Cuba in 1886, and in Brazil in 1888. The Arabic slave trade in Africa ended in 1873.

◀ The leader of the Virginia slave revolt of 1831, Nat Turner (1800–1831), killed his master and 60 whites, and encouraged 75 slaves to revolt. Their revolt lasted for some weeks. He and his followers were eventually captured, tried, and hanged.

▲ The economy of the southern states relied on black slave labor. Cotton picking was one of the slaves' main jobs. The cotton was profitably exported to supply the cotton mills of industrial Europe.

### KEY DATES

| | |
|---|---|
| 1517 | Regular slave trading started by Spain |
| 1592 | British slave trading begins |
| 1739 | Jamaican "Maroon" slave revolt |
| 1760s | Slave trading at its peak |
| 1791–1804 | Santo Domingo slave revolt |
| 1792 | Danish slave trade abolished |
| 1807 | British slave trade abolished |
| 1834 | Slavery abolished in British colonies |
| 1865 | 13th Amendment abolishes slavery in U.S. |
| 1888 | Slavery abolished in Brazil |

## THE SLAVES' REVOLT IN SANTO DOMINGO

The French Revolution spread to French colonies overseas. In 1791, the National Assembly in Paris decided to give the vote to slaves in Santo Domingo (now Haiti) in the Caribbean. Plantation owners refused to obey. When they heard this, about 100,000 slaves rebelled. Many slave owners were killed, houses destroyed, and sugar and coffee plantations set on fire. Napoleon sent troops to the island and there was a long civil war led by Toussaint l'Ouverture (1746–1803), an ex-slave who declared himself ruler of the island in 1801.

# THE BRITISH IN INDIA 1774–1858

**The hold on India by the British East India Company gradually grew stronger. The British came to dominate Indian society, becoming its ruling caste.**

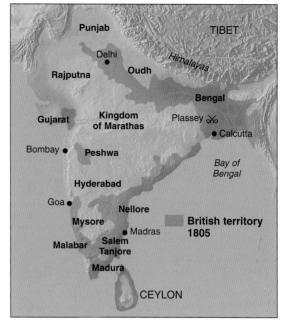

By 1805, the British controlled the rich clothmaking districts of Bengal in northeastern India, as well as the prosperous coastal lands in the south.

B y 1750, the British East India Company controlled the very profitable trade between Britain, India, and the Far East. Its officials were skillful businessmen who had built up a knowledge of Indian affairs, especially through the Indians they employed. They made friends with Indian princes, and struck bargains with both the friends and the enemies of the declining Mogul rulers. Many British people in India lived like princes themselves. By working for the East India Company many became very rich. Some of these "nabobs" (from the word *nawab*, for local ruler or rich man) built fine houses; they were designed by British architects, and furnished with luxuries from England, India, and the colonies. In Calcutta, they held horse races, tea parties, and dances. Gradually, wives and families arrived to share this way of life and a community developed.

However, some British people were attracted to Indian art, culture, and architecture, even wearing Indian clothes, at least at home. They learned Indian languages and studied Indian religions and writings. They took Indian ideas back to Britain when they went home.

This mechanical toy, called "Tipu's Tiger," shows a tiger devouring a European. It was made for Tipu Sahib of Mysore. Between 1767 and 1799, with French support, Mysore tried to resist British control of its lands.

▲ Tipu Sahib (1749–1799) of Mysore owned an ivory chess set which was made up of pieces with Indian princes and men on one side, and East India Company administrators and soldiers on the other.

▶ At first, the British mixed easily with Indians. Here, the Scottish governor Sir David Ochterlony smokes a water pipe at an Indian musical performance.

## BRITISH EXPANSION

By 1780, the East India Company controlled many of the more prosperous parts of India, but in 1784, the British government decided to stop it from expanding any further—a policy the company's managers were not happy about. Around 1800, the British were frightened by Napoleon's ambition to build an empire in India, and the government changed its policy. From 1803 to 1818, the company fought the Marathas, who ruled central India, and broke their power. In many cases, they took a soft approach, and used trade to favor certain Indian states, stationing troops there "for their protection."

The company fought in Burma, where the local rulers threatened Bengal, as well as on the Northwest Frontier and in Afghanistan, where they feared Russian influence. Between 1843 and 1849, they annexed Sind and the Punjab. Whenever a dynasty failed, or if a state was weakly governed, the company moved in. During the 1830s, the company's governor had arrogantly overruled local traditions, and brought in missionaries to convert Indians to Christianity. The company built roads, railroads, and buildings, and expanded British businesses. They insisted on using English as the language of education and business. As a result, Indian opposition gradually grew stronger.

## THE INDIAN MUTINY

Trouble broke out among the *sepoys*, the Indian soldiers in the company's army. Sparked by a terrible famine, a mutiny started in 1857. Several towns, including the capital, Delhi, were captured by the sepoys, and British men, women, and children were massacred. The mutiny was suppressed violently by British troops. Each side now became suspicious of the other side. The British started to live a more separate life, and Indians were "kept in their place." The British government took control of the East India Company in 1858, and closed it down. While India was perhaps the richest and most developed European colony of all, the British had to work very hard to control it.

Some Indian rajahs and princes made friends with the British and gained many advantages as a result. To be protected by British soldiers guaranteed a prince's power, and the British gained from the deal by having easy influence and trade in a prince's state, without having to govern it.

## HOMES FOR NABOBS

Nabobs were officers of the East India Company who had made fortunes in India. Many nabobs had themselves grown up in tough conditions, and had gone to India to escape hard times, seek a fortune, or build a new life. They worked hard, risking their lives through war or disease. They lived in conditions that reflected the opulence of Indian rulers and combined them with the trappings of the British aristocracy. When the nabobs returned to Britain, some built mansions influenced by Indian design such as Sezincote House.

# REVOLT IN LATIN AMERICA 1808–1825

**While Europe was fighting the Napoleonic Wars, the settlers of Latin America grew restless, and an independence movement gathered strength.**

▲ Simón Bolívar drove the Spanish from Colombia and Venezuela, and joined with San Martín to free Peru. He became president of Gran Colombia, but he could not stop its breakup in 1830 and resigned.

▲ José de San Martín was a revolutionary who joined the Argentinean independence movement. He marched his troops over the Andes to Chile, liberating it in 1818. In 1820, he took Lima, Peru.

Ever since Portugal and Spain had divided the New World between them in 1494, they had both ruled vast colonies in North, Central, and South America. For centuries, the colonies had suffered from distant European rule. In 1807–1808, Napoleon had marched into Portugal and Spain, and they became a battleground, as British, Spanish, and Portuguese troops fought against French soldiers. This period of confusion gave the colonies their chance. They began their fight for independence in 1808, refusing to accept Napoleon's brother Joseph as the new Spanish king, and their ruler.

## INDEPENDENCE

Argentina declared itself free of Spanish rule in 1810, followed by Paraguay in 1811. Mexico became independent from Spain in 1821, as did Peru, and Brazil finally broke free from Portugal in 1822. Venezuela finally gained its independence in 1830. The independence movement in South America owed a great deal to two energetic leaders, Simón Bolívar (1783–1830) and José de San Martín (1778–1850), both of whom were inspired by the ideas of the French Revolution.

▼ Simón Bolívar's revolutionary troops won an important victory over the Spanish colonial government of Peru at Ayacucho in 1824. This was the final decisive battle of the Latin American wars of independence.

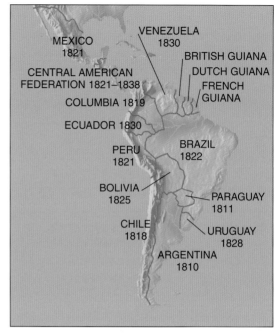

Between 1808 and 1830, 13 former colonies in South America won their independence. However, wealthy colonial settlers still owned most of the land and governed it for their own profit.

In 1819, Bolívar and other Venezuelan aristocrats defeated the Spanish in New Granada (Colombia) and Peru. In 1824, Bolívar met up with San Martín, who had marched across the Andes to liberate Chile. In 1826, Bolívar proclaimed the Republic of Gran Colombia (Venezuela, Colombia, Ecuador, and Panama), but the republic later broke up. In 1825, Upper Peru took the name of Bolivia in his honor. Both Bolívar and San Martín had fought under very difficult conditions. But, in spite of independence, conditions did not really improve, because power was still held by the plantation owners.

# UNREST IN BRITAIN 1811–1832

**In the new industrial society of mills and machines, British workers were badly treated. They demanded better pay and improved working conditions.**

Working conditions in factories were appalling. Women and children often worked for 12 hours every day, in dangerous jobs, for pitiful wages. Many workers died young.

The years of peace following the end of the Napoleonic Wars were a time of discontent. There was unemployment, and high food prices. The British government feared the growing trade union movement (workers who bargained for better working conditions), and in 1800, unions were made illegal. Life in industrial towns was grim, with poor housing, frequent accidents, and disease. But events abroad had shown British workers that they had a right to make their voices heard. They demanded improved working conditions and pay, as well as a say in government.

However, not all the protesters wanted change. From 1811 to 1813, craftsmen known as Luddites (after their leader, Ned Ludd) smashed new machinery in factories in northern England. They feared they would lose their jobs to machines. Six years later, a group of workers known as Blanketeers, wrapped in the woolen cloth they wove, marched from Manchester to London to ask the Prince Regent for his support.

Many people were destitute and not used to living in cities. Some turned to drinking gin to drown their sorrows. This engraving by William Hogarth, made in 1751, was called "Gin Lane."

Limited trade union activity was permitted from 1824. Many people campaigned for "one man, one vote." In 1832, the law was changed to reform election to Parliament, but it was still only men who owned property that were allowed to vote.

▲ This Luddite protester is dressed in women's clothes as a disguise. The Luddites were skilled craftworkers who opposed the introduction of new machinery that replaced their jobs. They were active from 1811 to 1813.

▶ The Peterloo Massacre took place in St. Peter's Fields, in Manchester, England, in 1819. Soldiers charged into a crowd of unarmed men and women who had gathered to listen to Henry Hunt, a famous campaigner for political change. Eleven people were killed and more than 400 injured.

# WESTWARD MIGRATION 1776–1845

**After independence, the fledgling United States started to develop rapidly. New immigrants spread westward, and took the lands of the Indigenous Americans.**

▲ Meriwether Lewis was commissioned by President Jefferson to explore the West with William Clark.

▲ William Clark, traveling with Lewis, reached the west coast in Oregon in 1805 and returned to report on their findings the next year.

In the early 1800s, the United States was still small and very much affected by European politics. During the Napoleonic Wars, Britain took control of the seas and blocked most sea traffic between Napoleonic Europe and the United States. This meant that Napoleon could not protect French Louisiana. Since the French controlled trade on the Mississippi River, the Americans held discussions with them. Napoleon decided to sell them Louisiana for $15 million. The Louisiana Purchase more than doubled United States territory.

### THE WAR OF 1812

The British blockade of Europe was disastrous for American trade. In 1812, the United States declared war on Britain. The Americans tried to invade Canada, but without success. They won a few battles on the Great Lakes, and the British burned down Washington, D.C., the new capital. Little progress was made, and, weary of war, they signed a treaty in 1814 that returned all territories. The British blockade was lifted, because the Napoleonic Wars were ending, and the United States was able to restore its trade and economy.

Daniel Boone (1734–1820) was held captive by a group of Shawnee fighters. As a test of courage, he was forced to run the gauntlet between two rows of fierce warriors.

### MIGRANTS AND SETTLERS

Settlers flocked to the United States after its independence in 1776. They came from all over Europe, seeking a new life in this land that seemed to promise freedom. The American population was around four million in 1803, but by 1861 it was 31 million. The first arrivals settled in the northeastern states, but as their numbers grew, they moved south and west.

The United States was like a new empire, rich in land and resources. Suddenly, the back country of the former eastern colonies became the new frontier. By 1820, this frontier crossed the Mississippi River. However, for Indigenous Americans, American expansion meant hardship, and the settlers' prosperity and liberty became poverty and confinement for them.

The Lewis and Clark expedition left St. Louis in 1804 and spent the winter in the Dakotas before crossing the Rocky Mountains to Oregon in 1805. Sacajawea, a woman of the Shoshone tribe, traveled with the expedition and helped them communicate with other Indigenous Americans they encountered.

## THE TRAIL OF TEARS

The Indigenous Americans had been promised that their traditional lands would become available for white settlement only with their permission. But the Northwest Ordinance Act, in 1787, paved the way for westward expansion—a direct threat to the tribal lands. Indigenous Americans decided to confront the white settlers. A series of wars followed in the early 1800s.

In 1830, Congress passed the Indian Removal Act. This led to great suffering. The Five Civilized Tribes—the Cherokee, Chickasaw, Choctaw, Creek, and Seminole—refused to leave their lands and be placed in a so-called Indian Territory. The Cherokee won a Supreme Court decision to stay on their lands, but President Jackson ignored it. In 1838–1839, the army moved the five tribes 800 mi. (1280km) west to Oklahoma. Thousands of helpless, betrayed Indigenous Americans died of hunger and exhaustion on what has become known as the Trail of Tears.  As the new country grew, more settlers arrived, looking for new land—always at the expense of the Indigenous Americans. New migrant trails such as the Cumberland Road from Baltimore to St. Louis opened. Lewis and Clark headed farther west. The army protected settlers and the government passed laws protecting their land claims.

Settlers on the trail to the American West faced many changes. They came from all over Europe, and hoped to make a new life in what they called "the land of the free."

The U.S. economy grew, and this benefited the growing towns in the east, where industries and businesses were located. The east was the backbone of the United States, and the west its empire. A new state could join the Union when it had a population of 60,000, and by 1821, there were 23 states in the Union.

▲ Andrew Jackson (1767–1845), was president from 1829 to 1837. He fought in the War of 1812 and invaded Florida in 1818 in a war against the Seminoles. He believed in developing the frontier in the west, encouraging settlers, and supporting them against the Indigenous Americans.

### KEY DATES

| | |
|---|---|
| 1783 | British withdrawal from the Thirteen Colonies |
| 1803 | Louisiana Purchase from France |
| 1805 | Explorers Lewis and Clark reach the Pacific |
| 1812–14 | The War of 1812 against Britain |
| 1819 | Spain gives Florida to the United States |
| 1820 | Settler frontier reaches the Mississippi River |
| 1830 | Indian Removal Act allows their legal eviction; Chief Black Hawk leads a war against settlers |
| 1838–39 | The Cherokee "Trail of Tears" to Oklahoma |
| 1845 | The United States annexes Texas |

## BATTLE OF LAKE ERIE

The Battle of Lake Erie was fought between British troops and the small American navy in September, 1813. The Americans won the battle, led by Oliver Perry (1785–1819), here shown rowing through the battle to another American vessel after his own ship had been sunk. He then announced, "We have met the enemy, and they are ours."

# THE ARTS 1708–1835

**Increased trade and travel in the 1700s opened Europe up to new influences. This happened at a time when Europe was reaching new cultural peaks of its own.**

Jane Austen (1775–1817) was the daughter of an English clergyman. She wrote six novels that commented on the society and manners of her time. Her novels, including *Emma*, *Sense and Sensibility*, and *Pride and Prejudice* are still read and enjoyed today.

In terms of power and innovation, Europeans now enjoyed worldwide dominance. European ideas and standards were entering other cultures, and the European style of moneymaking and trade affected far distant lands. Yet this trade also brought exotic, fresh influences into Europe.

Oriental china, African carvings, and Indian cotton goods arrived in Europe. Ideas, inspiration, and knowledge were drawn from the Far East, and from the new cultures of the Americas.

Painters, designers, and craftspeople found fresh inspiration in other countries and combined them with their own. European ceramics adopted Chinese styles, and textile designs featured Indian patterns. Many people welcomed these changes, but many others remained untouched by them or simply ignored the growing trend toward modernization.

Scenes from the four seasons decorate this elaborate German ornamental shield from the 1700s. It shows a romantic interest in nature that was common at the time. Small, round shields like this were called bucklers.

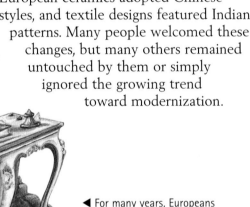

◀ For many years, Europeans tried to copy the techniques used by Chinese porcelain makers. This figure was made in the Meissen factory near Dresden in 1765.

The musical genius Wolfgang Amadeus Mozart (1756–1791) was already famous at the age of six, after playing for Maria Theresa, the empress of Austria.

▲ This is a clavichord from the 1720s. It produces a clear, light, delicate sound. German composer Johann Sebastian Bach wrote many pieces of music especially for the clavichord.

◀ *The Great Wave of Kanagawa*, a famous Japanese color woodblock print made by Hokusai (1760–1849) in 1831. It graphically records a *tsunami* (tidal wave) that had hit Japan just before that date.

▲ This Japanese *netsuke* object demonstrates the fine, detailed skills of Japanese carvers of the 1700s.

The 1700s saw great achievements in art of all kinds. In China, jade carving showed great skill. In Japan, woodblock printing grew more advanced, and *haiku* poetry became popular.

## EUROPEAN CULTURE

In Europe, three major influences were at work. The rich upper classes built extravagant mansions and opera houses, and paid artists large sums for portraits and records of scenes and events. In cities, pamphlets, coffeehouses, and street life bred a new popular culture. In the factories, new mass-produced products changed the designs and uses of everyday items, making them available to the growing populace. Society was changing, and so were its tastes.

In Europe, the composers Handel, Beethoven, Haydn, and Schubert wrote brilliant orchestral works. Constable, Ingres, Goya, and other painters were the famous artists of the day. Novelists, essayists, journalists, and publishers introduced new styles of writing. Neoclassical poets aimed for elegance, and the Romantics chose bold, emotional styles. In the theater, ballet developed and operas attracted enthusiastic audiences who demanded realistic plots and characters.

▲ This Chinese carved jade pot from the 1700s was made during the Manchu period to hold brushes that were used in calligraphy (decorative writing).

▼ This painting by French artist Jacques Louis David (1748–1825) shows the Tennis Court Oath, one of the key events that sparked the French Revolution in 1789. Only 100 years later, important historical events would be recorded by photography.

# ARCHITECTURE 1708–1835

**The year 1800 marked a turning point in architecture. Traditional styles gave way to more modern buildings constructed using new technologies.**

In 1784, the British government introduced a tax on windows. In order to save money, many people, especially the rich, blocked up some of their windows.

Across the world, most cultures by now referred back to tradition to define their architecture—inventiveness and creativity were not at their height, except in Europe. Yet, even in Europe and North America, architectural innovations tended to imitate earlier styles such as those of Greece and Rome, or to adopt exotic styles copied from the colonies, especially India.

Two main influences were at work in European architecture. First, the growth of country estates and townhouses, where grand architecture with large windows was the fashion. Second, the influence of new industries, for which large factories and cities were built. European and American cities grew, and with this came new building styles, such as Georgian architecture in England and the Palladian style in the United States.

The outside of the Royal Pavilion, in Brighton, England, was completely redesigned in 1818 by the fashionable English architect John Nash (1752–1835) for the Prince Regent, the future George IV. He based his designs on Indian architecture, but added many extravagant ideas of his own. The interior design and furniture show clear Chinese and Japanese influences.

An urge to try out new industrial techniques led architects to design new types of buildings, using new materials. In 1779, cast iron was first used to construct a bridge over the Severn River in England. This trend toward the use of new materials was to flower during the Victorian period in the 1800s.

▼ In southern Africa, the Zulus lived in stockaded settlements gathered around a central cattle pen, or *kraal*. The huts were built with wooden poles covered with matting and straw. There was one for each wife of the man who built the kraal, plus some for storing grain.

▲ The building of the English city of Bath, near the port of Bristol, was financed with profits from the colonies and the slave trade. John Wood the Elder (1705–1754) was responsible for much of its design. The Royal Crescent is a group of 30 houses built in the late 1700s from plans by his son, John Wood the Younger. He was strongly influenced by classical Greek designs.

Russian settlers moved eastward into the vast lands of Siberia. Peasant houses were made of raw timber from the forests, built cheaply and easily in traditional, simple styles. They were decorated with local designs. Similar construction methods were used by early settlers in the American West for their log cabins.

In many parts of the world traditional designs using local materials remained popular. Settlers were building housing in the new territories of the United States and Russia, and in the growing European colonies in India, Africa, and South America. In most cases, this was practical, basic, and traditional. But the governors, bosses, and plantation owners also built grand houses to remind everyone of their wealth and status.

▶ In the southern states, plantation owners, many of them descended from rich Europeans, built impressive Greek-style mansions. This emphasized their superiority in a society where, in many places, the majority of people were black slaves.

The first cast-iron bridge in the world was built across the Severn River in England in 1779. The builders used the same methods of construction that they used for wooden buildings because they were not sure how cast iron would behave.

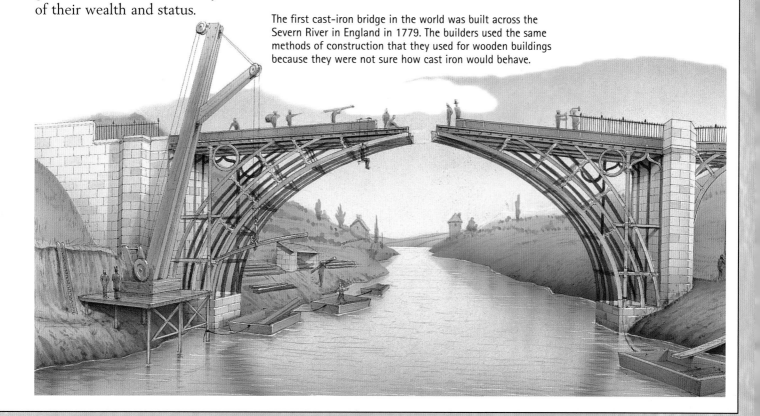

# SCIENCE AND TECHNOLOGY 1708–1835

In Europe, major breakthroughs were being made in science and technology. New machines and processes brought revolutionary changes to people's lives.

There were many developments in science and technology, particularly in Europe, during this period. Discoveries were of two kinds: theoretical and practical. Throughout the 1700s, mathematicians, scientists, and philosophers researched, discussed, and published their investigations into how the world worked, while engineers and inventors developed new and successful machines and processes.

The latest theories inspired greater invention, and more technology encouraged theoretical scientists to make further discoveries in medicine, biology, mechanics, physics, and chemistry. By 1800, the new machines had brought revolutionary changes—to the workplace, transportation and communications, and eventually to the home.

Some of these inventions simply made it easier to produce things on a large scale—such as textile machines and foundries, which produced large quantities of cloth and metal objects quickly and cheaply. But some inventions brought completely new possibilities—such as the first batteries, steamboats, and locomotives. It would take decades for some of these inventions to make a big impact on the world. Yet their creation, and the sheer amount of imagination and risk-taking involved, marked the beginning of a modern, global, technologically-based economy of the kind that we live in today.

Lady Mary Wortley Montagu (1689–1762) pioneered vaccination against smallpox, which killed thousands every year. However, it was originally the Ottomans who discovered it.

▲ In 1800, Alessandro Volta (1745–1827) designed the first electric battery, the Voltaic pile. This was the beginning of a century during which electrical technology was developed.

▶ The metric system was introduced in France in 1795. It used liters to measure liquids, grams and kilograms for weight, and meters for length, with the number 10 as the standard scale. Napoleon introduced this system to the European countries that he conquered.

▲ In 1763, John Harrison (1693–1776) won a prize from the British government for inventing the marine chronometer. This accurate clock meant that for the first time sailors could measure their exact position at sea.

▲ Claude Chappe (1763–1805) devised a system for sending messages, using semaphore signals and relay towers. The French used Chappe's system until 1850.

Paddle steamships like these were used to carry goods along rivers in the 1800s. Robert Fulton (1765–1815) built the first successful commercial steamboat, the *Clermont*. It made its first trip in 1807 and was used on the Hudson River in New York State. Although one crossed the Atlantic Ocean in 1819, long sea journeys did not suit this type of ship.

▲ The English scientist Michael Faraday (1791–1867) invented the first dynamo in 1831. It produced a small, steady supply of electric current.

## WHEN IT HAPPENED

**1752** Benjamin Franklin identifies electricity in an experiment with lightning

**1769** James Watt's steam engine patented

**1796** Edward Jenner gives first smallpox vaccination

**1800** Volta's electrical battery

**1803** Gas lighting introduced

**1804** Trevithick's steam locomotive invented

**1807** Launch of Fulton's steamboat

**1831** Faraday's electric dynamo invented

◄ In 1801, the French inventor Joseph-Marie Jacquard (1752–1834) designed the first automatic pattern loom. It used punched cards to control the design. This was a very early kind of computer programming.

▲ In 1815, Humphrey Davy (1778–1829) devised a safety lamp for use in mines. It warned miners of the presence of firedamp, an explosive gas made up of methane and air. The lamp saved many lives.

◄ George Stephenson (1781–1848) designed the *Rocket* and won a competition in 1829 to find the fastest locomotive for the Liverpool and Manchester Railway, the world's first all-steam public railroad.

# UNIFICATION AND COLONIZATION

## 1836–1913

The world map changed dramatically during this period—new nations were formed and some were unified. Africa was carved up by nations seeking new colonies, and China's power was fractured. There were more revolutions in Europe. The United States, Canada, and Russia expanded to the farthest frontiers of their countries. Railroads, telegraph wires, and steamships suddenly made the world seem smaller. New cities such as New York, Buenos Aires, Johannesburg, Bombay, and Shanghai became centers in a new global order.

▲ The coming of the railroad opened up North America, but also led to the first national strike. The strike spread along the railroad, from coast to coast, uniting the workers in their fight for decent wages.

◀ During the Second Boer War in South Africa, the Boers (Dutch settlers) were finally defeated by the British in 1902.

# INDUSTRIAL REVOLUTION 1836–1913

**The continuing revolution in industry was shaping a new world. The rapid growth of opportunities for employers and workers also brought exploitation and injustice.**

Jobs in factories, such as textile mills, often required skill rather than strength. This gave women a chance to earn a living wage, both in the towns of the New England states and in the north of Britain.

Many children worked in mines and factories, but this was banned in most countries by 1900.

The British inventor Isambard Kingdom Brunel (1806–1859) built railroads, bridges, tunnels, train stations, ports, and the world's largest ship.

During the 1700s, many people in Britain worked at home, usually producing goods by hand. There were also many farmers and farm laborers who worked on the land to grow crops to feed their families. By the middle of the 1800s, all this had changed. Many British people now lived in towns and worked in enormous factories, or in stores, offices, railroads, and other businesses designed to serve the inhabitants of these industrial centers. Leading the world, British inventors continued to develop revolutionary new machines that performed traditional tasks such as spinning and weaving much faster than they could be done by hand. Machines were also used to make iron and steel. These metals were, in turn, used to make more machines, weapons, and tools.

▼ New factories were built near rivers or canals and railroads This meant that raw materials could be delivered, and finished goods taken away. Houses for workers were often built close to the factory.

Four factors brought about the change: coal mining, a canal system, capital (money), and cheap labor. Coal was used to smelt iron and steel and to make steam to power the new machines. Barges carried raw materials and finished goods along the canals. The profits from Britain's colonies gave businessmen the money to invest. And badly paid farmworkers flocked to the towns for better paid work.

# BUSINESS BOOM

New coal mines were dug to supply coal for steam engines and coke for ironworks. By the mid-1800s, Britain's canal and rail systems linked all the major industrial cities. The new machines made goods faster and more cheaply. Factory and mine owners made huge profits, some of which they spent on more machines, so creating new jobs. Investors saved small amounts of money in banks. The banks then lent large amounts to industrialists. This developing capitalist system raised money to build factories, offices, and houses.

For many workers, life in the factories and mines was hard and dangerous. Men, women, and children worked 12 or more hours a day, often for low wages. Many workers were killed or injured by unsafe machinery before new safety laws were enforced. Towns grew rapidly and without any real planning, leaving some areas without drains or clean water. Diseases such as cholera (from dirty water) became common and killed thousands of people.

In time, laws to shorten working hours and prohibit child labor were introduced. Trade unions, at first banned, campaigned for better pay and conditions for workers. Reformers won better working conditions, and schooling for all children. Slums were cleared and new laws were brought in to control factories and houses.

The arrival of the railroad opened up North America but also led to the Great Strike of 1877. Protests by more than 100,000 workers stopped the trains.

▶ A big step forward in steelmaking was made by Henry Bessemer (1813–1898). In a Bessemer Converter, hot air was blasted through melted iron to convert it into steel. Steel was stronger and more useful than iron, but before Bessemer's invention in 1856, it was very expensive to make.

▼ In 1842, James Nasmyth (1808–1890) invented the steam hammer, used to make parts for the new steamships.

## KEY DATES

| | |
|---|---|
| 1838 | Brunel builds the steamship *Great Western* |
| 1842 | James Nasmyth invents first steam hammer |
| 1865 | George Pullman invents railroad sleeping car |
| 1869 | George Westinghouse invents air brake; Suez Canal completed, easing travel to India |
| 1886 | Samuel Gompers sets up American Federation of Labor |
| 1893 | Frank Sprague invents electric trolley |
| 1900 | United States and Germany both overtake Britain's steel production |

# TEXAS AND MEXICO 1835–1848

**Gaining independence from Spain in 1821, Mexico soon found itself in conflict with Texas over land ownership. The conflict led to war.**

The land that the Texans and the Mexicans fought over lay between the Rio Grande and the Red River. In 1848, a treaty gave the United States large tracts of land.

Sam Houston (1793–1863) was twice elected president of the Republic of Texas. He became governor of the state in 1859.

▲ A late 19th-century illustration shows the Aztec symbol for Mexico—a proud eagle perched on a cactus. Mexico's vast territories shrank after the United States gradually annexed the northern areas in the mid-1800s.

► Davy Crockett (1786–1836) was one of the defenders of the Alamo, a mission in San Antonio. In 1836, 186 men held out against the 5,000 strong Mexican army of General Santa Anna. Only two women and two children survived. Other defenders killed were Jim Bowie and William Travis. In the end, they ran out of ammunition and had to use their guns as clubs.

At the time Mexico gained its independence, its borders stretched much farther north and covered many areas now in the southern United States. Many U. S. citizens settled in Texas, which belonged to Mexico. In 1835, Texas declared its independence. The Texans appointed Sam Houston as their military commander. He captured the town of San Antonio. His opponent, the Mexican General Santa Anna, then led a large Mexican army into Texas to crush the rebellion. He laid siege to the Alamo, a mission in the center of San Antonio, and won the town back. Davy Crockett was one of the defenders of the Alamo, which was sometimes used as a fort. It became a symbol of Texan resistance during the war against Mexico.

Santa Anna was later defeated by Houston's forces at the battle of San Jacinto in 1836. Texas then became independent, and was known as the Lone Star Republic. After a few years of independence, the people of Texas voted to join the United States. In 1845, Texas became the 28th state. Clashes between Texans and Mexicans continued as Texas tried to increase its territory.

## WAR AND PEACE

President James Polk (1795–1849) sent troops to the Rio Grande, invading land still claimed by Mexico. The Mexicans resisted, and the Mexican–American War broke out. U.S. troops captured the capital, Mexico City, in 1847, and the Mexicans surrendered. The treaty of Guadalupe–Hidalgo, in 1848, gave the United States huge new territories, including the modern states of California, Nevada, Utah, Arizona, and some of New Mexico, as well as Texas.

# SOUTH AFRICA 1814–1910

**South Africa saw enormous struggles for power and territory in the 1800s as the British, the Boers, and the Zulus all competed with each other.**

Cecil Rhodes (1853–1902) was prime minister of the Cape Colony from 1890 to 1895 and sought to unite all of Africa under British rule.

▲ Cetshwayo (1826–1884) was king of the Zulus from 1873 to 1879. He led his people in the Zulu battles against the British.

In 1836, the Cape Colony at the southern tip of Africa was ruled by the British. Descendants of the original Dutch settlers, known as Boers (literally "farmers"), disliked British rule. The Boers left the Cape Colony and set out on the Great Trek. They traveled northward to the areas now known as KwaZulu-Natal and the Free State and defeated the African people who lived there. The British took over the Boer republic of KwaZulu-Natal in 1843, but they gave independence to the Transvaal and the Free State. A three-way struggle developed, with the British against the Zulus and both groups against the Boers.

In the Zulu war of 1879, the Zulus defeated the British at Isandlwana but lost to them at Rourke's Drift and Kambula. The Zulus were organized into *impis* (regiments) and fought bravely before their defeat. In 1880, the British tried to take over the Transvaal, and the First Boer War broke out. The Boers defeated the British, and the Transvaal remained independent.

Although only armed with simple weapons such as spears and knobkerries (round-headed clubs), the Zulus were often successful in inflicting heavy losses on their opponents.

## CECIL RHODES

The prime minister of the Cape Colony at that time was Cecil Rhodes. He wanted to create a British Empire in Africa that would stretch from Cape Town to Cairo in Egypt. Rhodes planned the Jameson Raid, which was designed to overthrow the Boer government of the Transvaal. The raid failed, and in 1899, the Second Boer War broke out. Although the Boers won some of the early battles, such as Spion Kop, they were defeated by the British in 1902.

The Treaty of Vereeniging was signed in May 1902, and the Boer republics became part of the British Empire in exchange for a guarantee of self-government. In 1907, this promise was honored, and they joined KwaZulu-Natal and the Cape Colony as the founding provinces of the Union of South Africa in 1910.

▲ The Great Trek is an important event in Boer history. A group of Boers left the Cape Colony with all their belongings loaded onto wagons and traveled northward into African territories.

# THE OPIUM WARS 1830–1864

**European merchants used the addictive power of opium to gain important trading links with China— a country that wished to remain closed to foreigners.**

An engraving showing a Chinese opium smoker. The sale and smoking of opium had been banned in China from the early 1700s, by order of the emperor.

The Chinese had almost no contact with the rest of the world for centuries. Many European merchants were eager to trade, especially in the rare Chinese silks and porcelain that were so popular in Europe. However, the Chinese government allowed trading to take place at only one port, Guangzhou (Canton). To get around this problem, foreign traders began to smuggle the drug opium into the country, so that the Chinese would trade their precious goods in exchange for the drug. The Chinese government tried to stop this. In 1839, Chinese officials, under the orders of Lin Zexu, the Chinese high commissioner of Guangzhou, visited British warehouses where they seized and burned up to 20,000 chests of opium.

The British would not tolerate what they saw as the confiscation of private property. In response, they sent warships that threatened the Chinese and besieged the port. The Chinese refused to pay compensation, banned trade with Britain, and fired on the British forces. Thus started the First Opium War (1839–1842) fought by the Chinese and the British.

Ships, like this British merchant ship in Lintin (now Nei Lingding) Harbor, in 1834, would have carried quantities of opium. Foreign merchants traded the drug for the precious goods that were so greatly desired by customers in Europe.

Hong Kong Island became a British colony in 1842. It soon grew into a center of trade. In 1860, the Kowloon Peninsula was added, and in 1898, the British gained the New Territories on a 99-year lease.

## TREATY OF NANJING

The war was one-sided. The British had superior forces, and they bombarded Guangzhou and captured Hong Kong from the Chinese. When this first war was over, the British forced the Chinese to sign the Treaty of Nanjing (Nanking), which opened up Chinese ports to Britain. China also had to pay compensation and give the island of Hong Kong to the British.

Britain's aggressive approach to the Chinese owed a great deal to the British foreign secretary Henry Temple, 3rd Viscount Palmerston. He was always ready to use force in what he saw as the defense of British interests overseas. In this, and later treaties, the Chinese were forced to give in to European demands. The Chinese, however, continued to fear that foreign trade meant that the country would come under foreign influence.

## SOCIAL UNREST

Trouble, largely promoted by the British, erupted again in the mid-1850s and resulted in the Second Opium War (1856–1860). This war was also eventually won by the British and it ended with another treaty. The Treaty of Tianjin (Tientsin) was signed in 1858, and it forced the Chinese to open even more ports to trade with European merchants. Other countries, including France and the United States, also signed treaties, which gained their citizens special rights and increased Western influence in China. Eager traders and missionaries rushed in.

At the same time, the huge Chinese Empire was gradually breaking down. The ruling Qing dynasty was faced with rebellions started by starving peasants. The Taiping Rebellion (1851–1864) was begun by people who wanted the land to be divided equally among ordinary people. The foreign powers helped to crush the rebellion because they wanted the Qing dynasty to continue so that the treaties would be honored.

| KEY DATES |
|---|
| **1839** Chinese officials destroy British opium stocks; Outbreak of First Opium War |
| **1842** Chinese sign the Treaty of Nanjing; Hong Kong island becomes British territory |
| **1844** Treaty of Wanghia with the United States |
| **1851** The Taiping Rebellion breaks out |
| **1856** Outbreak of Second Opium War |
| **1858** Chinese sign the Treaty of Tientsin |
| **1898** Britain obtains 99-year lease on New Territories |

▲ Britain's vastly superior navy could easily destroy Chinese junks during the opium wars.

▼ The Taiping Rebellion (1851–1864) was crushed by the Chinese with help from foreign powers who wanted Qing rule to continue.

# EUROPE: YEAR OF REVOLUTION 1848

**In 1848, protests broke out all over Europe. They demonstrated how unhappy people were with how they were governed.**

▲ Giuseppe Mazzini (1805–1872), seen here in prison, was a tireless campaigner for democracy and the unification of Italy.

The reasons for many of these rebellions were similar to those that sparked the French Revolution. One of the main factors was that people in many countries in Europe began to feel that they should have a say in their own government. In response to the rebellions and violent protests, many rulers just ignored the pleas of their people and tried to restore older systems of government, but the events of 1848 showed that change was inevitable.

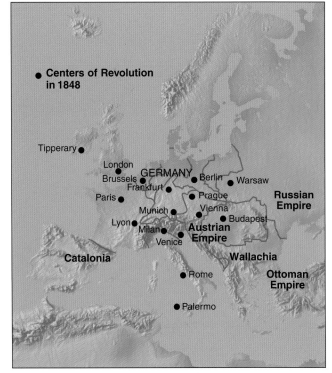

• Centers of Revolution in 1848

Tipperary
London
Brussels
GERMANY
Berlin
Warsaw
Frankfurt
Paris
Prague
Russian Empire
Munich
Vienna
Lyon
Budapest
Milan
Austrian Empire
Venice
Catalonia
Wallachia
Rome
Ottoman Empire
Palermo

Revolution in Europe had been simmering since 1815, and in 1848, most European countries experienced rebellions. The map above shows where the most serious outbreaks were.

▲ Paris revolutionaries demanding "Bread or Death" stormed government buildings in Paris. They overthrew the king, Louis-Philippe, and declared a republic with Louis Napoleon, nephew of Napoleon Bonaparte, as "prince president."

One powerful reason for the revolutions of 1848 was nationalism—the desire of people who spoke the same language to form their own independent nations. Nationalism was especially strong in Italy and Germany, which were divided into many small states, and in parts of the Austrian Empire. Other rebellions were led by people who wanted cheaper food, or changes in laws that would give land to working people.

▶ The People's Charter, drafted by William Lovett (1800–1877) in 1838, demanded political reforms, including votes for all men. It gave its name to the Chartist movement. The last and biggest Chartist demonstration took place in London, in 1848.

326

## CHARTISM

In some countries, people were demanding the right to vote. This was one of the reforms that the Chartist movement in Britain wanted. The People's Charter was first published there in May 1838. A petition said to have 1,200,000 signatures on it was handed in to Parliament in June 1839, but was rejected a month later. By February 1848, and following the revolution in France, a final petition was formed. When it was complete it was said to have over 3,000,000 names on it. On April 10, 1848 a mass march traveled across London to the Houses of Parliament to present the petition. Again, it was rejected, and Chartism lost its momentum.

Recent changes had made rebellion easier. More people were now able to read and newspapers told them what was happening in other countries. Few police forces existed, so troops had to be used against rioters. Most of the revolts of 1848 failed in their immediate demands, but over the next few years, nationalist feeling grew stronger, and many governments began to see that democratic reforms would soon be necessary.

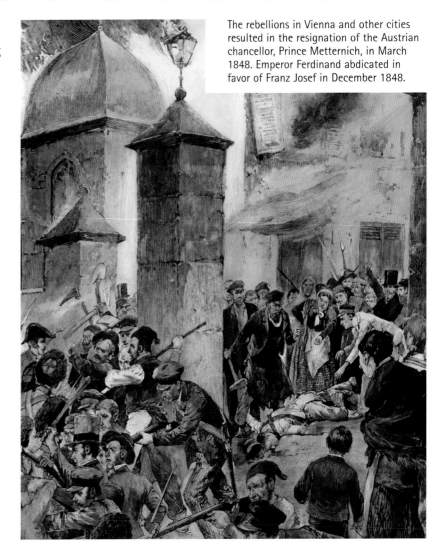

The rebellions in Vienna and other cities resulted in the resignation of the Austrian chancellor, Prince Metternich, in March 1848. Emperor Ferdinand abdicated in favor of Franz Josef in December 1848.

▼ Frankfurt, in Germany, also witnessed street fighting and rebellion. The people did succeed in forcing a change in their country's leadership. Peasants were given rights and protection and Germany's first freely elected parliament was established.

## REVOLUTION IN EUROPE

In France, the Second Republic was founded with Louis Napoleon, nephew of Napoleon Bonaparte, as "prince president." In the Italian states, revolts were widespread, but were crushed by the end of the year. The Austrian chancellor, Prince Metternich, was forced to flee, and the emperor abdicated in favor of Franz Josef.

There were uprisings in Berlin, Vienna, Prague, Budapest, Catalonia, Wallachia, Poland, and Britain. In Germany, the National Assembly met in Frankfurt, and in the Netherlands, a new constitution was introduced.

In London, the *Communist Manifesto*, written by Karl Marx and Friedrich Engels, was published. Elsewhere, the armies and peasants remained loyal to their monarchs. Revolts were crushed in Prussia and Italy, but there were some reforms.

# NEW ZEALAND 1792–1907

**Having been the sole occupants of New Zealand since the 1300s, the Maori people suddenly found themselves in competition for land.**

Whalers were among the first European settlers in New Zealand and the surrounding islands of the Pacific Ocean.

The first people to inhabit New Zealand were the Maoris, who had begun to settle in the early 14th century, having arrived from other Pacific islands in their seagoing canoes. They settled mainly along the coast and rivers of North Island, but also established communities on South Island in smaller numbers. From the end of the 1700s, more and more settlements and trading posts were being established by missionaries and whalers, despite the objections of the Maoris. By the 1830s, the growing number of European settlers on New Zealand's North Island was beginning to cause problems. The settlers needed large areas of land to graze sheep. The Maoris, on the other hand, grew crops in addition to fishing and hunting, and they welcomed trade.

Maori folklore says that the North Island of New Zealand was created by the Maori hero Maui. They believed that all land should be held in trust for the next generation, so selling land went against their tradition. This is why they did not want to sell land to the Europeans settlers.

▼ Before the arrival of the Europeans, the Maoris had no outside enemies, but different tribal groups were often at war with each other. The tribes usually lived in fortified villages, such as this one in the Bay of Islands.

Ko Tauwaki, chief of the Tukanu tribe of the Maori people. Maori folklore says that the North Island of New Zealand was created by the legendary hero Maui.

## BRITISH SOVEREIGNTY

By the 1830s, the Maori numbers had been reduced by the diseases that the Europeans accidentally introduced. Both the settlers and the Maoris wanted the British to provide strong laws and they appealed to Britain for help.

In 1840, a representative of the British government, together with 50 Maori chiefs, signed the Treaty of Waitangi. The treaty set out that if the Maoris gave control of New Zealand to the British Empire and accepted Queen Victoria as their sovereign, the British would protect all Maori land ownership rights. Under this agreement, New Zealand also became a dependency of New South Wales in Australia. The Europeans continued to take Maori land. Many thought they had bought it legally. But because there were two versions of the treaty, the Maoris thought that they had only agreed to give the British "governorship." There were several violent Maori uprisings between 1845 and 1847.

The ceremony of *ongi*, or pressing of noses, is practiced by Maori women at Taranaki on the west coast of New Zealand's North Island. The peak of Mount Egmont (Taranaki) can be seen in the distance.

## KEY DATES

| | |
|---|---|
| 1790s | First European settlers arrived, often whalers |
| 1839 | New Zealand Company established in London |
| 1840 | Treaty of Waitangi signed by British and Maoris |
| 1841 | New Zealand becomes separate Crown colony |
| 1845 | First serious unrest breaks out among Maoris |
| 1860 | Full-scale war breaks out |
| 1871 | Peace permanently established |
| 1882 | First refrigerated ships allow export of meat |
| 1907 | New Zealand becomes a dominion within the British Empire |

## MAORI WARS

In 1860, war broke out between the Maoris and the colonists. Although they fought bravely, the Maoris were forced to retreat to the mountains. Peace was established in 1871. In 1907, New Zealand became a dominion of the British Empire. New Zealand prospered, and the numbers of Maoris began to grow again.

▲ Maori tribal groups often fought each other. Maori warriors decorated their faces with elaborate tattoos to identify each other in battle.

◀ Maori uprisings occurred between 1845 and 1847, and again between 1860 and 1870. After that date, the colonial settlers made concessions and a lasting peace was established.

# THE CRIMEAN WAR 1853–1856

One of the few wars between European nations in this period took place in the Crimea. It was sparked off by a struggle for the territory of the old Ottoman Empire.

Most of the fighting during the war took place in the Crimean Peninsula, which projects southward from Russia into the Black Sea.

The Crimean War was originally a conflict between Russia and Turkey. The Russians felt that the Muslim Turks had failed to deal fairly with Christians in their Balkan territories or in the question of access to holy places in Palestine. In addition, the Russians also wanted access for their warships through the Black Sea via the Bosphorus and the Dardanelles. Negotiations between Turkey and Russia broke down, and the Turks, encouraged by the French, declared war on Russia. Russia then won the naval battle of Sinope, in the Black Sea, in 1853. Britain and France were concerned that Russia wanted to expand into the collapsing Ottoman Empire. They accordingly sent their fleets into the Black Sea to protect Turkish coasts, and quickly became Turkey's allies.

A defenseless Turkey is caught up in the merciless grip of Russia; Russia was seen as the main aggressor in the buildup to the Crimean War.

Florence Nightingale (1820– 1910) founded the first training school for nurses in London in 1860. This was a direct response to the terrible sights she and other nurses had seen while serving in the Crimea. Some 4,600 British soldiers died in battle, and a further 17,500 died of disease.

Russia also had quarrels with France, mainly to do with commercial and religious rivalry. The Turks were anxious to get rid of the strong Russian influence in their Balkan territories of Moldavia and Wallachia.

## CHARGE OF THE LIGHT BRIGADE

During the Battle of Balaklava on October 25, 1854, the British Light Brigade was ordered to charge an enemy position. The battle was won by the British, but because of the confusion of their officers, nearly 250 of the 673 men in the Light Brigade were killed or wounded during this misjudged engagement. The commanders thought that they were charging an isolated enemy outpost, but they were in fact charging a heavily fortified position.

The Battle of the Alma River in September 1854 was one of the earliest encounters of the war. It was a clear victory for the Allied forces over Russia.

## KEY DATES

| | | |
|---|---|---|
| May | 1853 | Russians occupy Moldavia and Wallachia |
| Oct. | 1853 | Turkey declares war on Russia |
| Mar. | 1854 | France and Britain declare war on Russia |
| Sept. | 1854 | Allies win Battle of the Alma River |
| Oct. | 1854 | Siege of Sevastopol begins; Battle of Balaklava and Charge of the Light Brigade |
| Nov. | 1854 | Russians heavily defeated at Inkerman |
| Sept. | 1855 | Fall of Sevastopol |
| Feb. | 1856 | Fighting stops |
| Mar. | 1856 | Treaty of Paris signed |

## THE ALLIES

Anxious to put a check on Russia's plans for expansion, Britain joined France in declaring war on Russia toward the end of March 1854. They were also supported by actual forces from Piedmont–Sardinia, and were politically supported by Austria. The allied armies fought a bloody battle at the Alma River, and, in October, laid siege to the town of Sevastopol. Attempts by the Russians to relieve the siege led to the battle of Balaklava, with the disastrous charge of the Light Brigade, followed by the battle of Inkerman in early November. All three of these major engagements were won by the Allies. Although they were partially successful in recapturing Sevastopol, they were unable to take the dockside area, and it was not until September 1855 that Sevastopol finally fell. The Russians were held back because a lack of railroads prevented supplies and reinforcements from getting through. The war ended with the Treaty of Paris on March 30, 1856.

The Crimean War marked the first time that the public was kept informed about the war by photographs and reports sent back by telegraph. Perhaps the most influential newspaperman was W. H. Russell of *The Times* in London—the first "war correspondent." Because of these reports in the British press, the war became notorious for the general level of incompetence shown by political leaders, and led, in January 1855, to the fall of the British government.

◀ The bombardment of Sevastopol by the Royal Navy in October 1854 was not enough to retake the whole town, and it was not until September 1855 that it finally fell.

▼ The Grenadier Guards fought at the battle of Inkerman in November 1854. There were many casualties of this Allied victory, but cholera and frostbite took a far greater toll than the Russian forces.

# JAPAN 1853–1913

**Under the Tokugawas, Japan had been closed to foreigners for more than 200 years. In the early 1800s, it began to experience Western influence.**

After 1868, the Meiji government improved educational standards and modernized the Japanese economy.

▲ U.S. Commodore Matthew Perry (1794–1858) is known as the man who opened up Japan to trade with the rest of the world. In 1853, he sailed to Japan, and in 1854, signed the Treaty of Kanagawa with the Japanese.

▶ This Japanese woodblock print shows Yokohama Harbor in the late 1800s. Following the Treaty of Kanagawa, the Japanese agreed to open ports to trade with the United States and several European countries.

During the first half of the 1600s, Japan's rulers decided that contact with the West must end. In particular, they feared that Christian missionaries might bring European armies to invade Japan. They therefore banned almost all foreigners from entering Japan and the Japanese from leaving their own country. As a result, people in the West were unable to appreciate the great beauty of the Japanese art of this period until the mid-to-late 1800s. In 1853, Millard Fillmore (1800–1874), the 13th President of the United States, sent four warships, under the command of Commodore Matthew Perry, on an important journey to Japan designed to bring about the opening of trade there.

The warships anchored in Tokyo Bay. The threat of American naval power helped Commodore Perry persuade the Japanese to resume trading with the West. The Japanese were impressed by Perry's steamships and by the other machinery he showed them. The two countries went on to sign the Treaty of Kanagawa a year later, in 1854, in which they opened two ports to American trade.

The ships of Commodore Perry's fleet were the first steamships that the Japanese had ever seen. They realized that they would be unable to beat them.

Soon, similar treaties had been signed with Britain, the Netherlands, and Russia. The Tokugawa were criticized by their opponents for allowing these treaties to be signed, and for many other problems they could not solve.

## RESTORATION OF THE EMPEROR

People were tired of the near total isolation that the Tokugawa family had imposed for so long. In 1868, the Tokugawa were finally overthrown and the emperor, Mutsuhito, was restored as ruler (the Meiji Restoration). Now that their country had opened up to the West, the Japanese began to modernize.

Although the Japanese wanted to keep some of their own traditions, they were also eager to learn from the industrial nations of the West. They changed and adapted both their government and their schools. Improved education meant that by 1914 the Japanese were among the best-educated people in the world. They began to import machines and introduced new industries such as cotton manufacture. Many Japanese people adopted European fashions in music and clothes. At the same time, foreigners gradually learned to respect Japanese success and culture.

With industrialization, the Japanese soon began to expand their country. They tried to take over Korea, which led to a war with China in 1894. Japan also fought Russia over this issue in 1904–1905 and finally annexed Korea in 1910. This helped make Japan the most powerful nation in its region. By 1913, Japan had become an industrial power of great importance—the first country in Asia to make such advances.

▲ Russian soldiers flee after the Battle of Mukden, in northeast China, in which the Japanese won a decisive victory in March 1905.

▼ In May 1905, Japan's fleet, led by Admiral Togo, annihilated the Russian fleet. This led to the Treaty of Portsmouth and gave the Japanese control over Korea.

# AMERICAN CIVIL WAR 1861–1865

**By the mid-1800s, the United States was badly divided. The North and South strongly disagreed about questions of states' rights and ownership of slaves.**

Ulysses S. Grant (1822–1885) was appointed commander of the Union forces in 1863. He was a tough and determined general.

Robert E. Lee (1807–1870) was in the U.S. army when civil war broke out. He resigned, and first advised, then took command of, the Confederate troops.

In 1850, the North had almost all of the manufacturing industries, thriving cities, and a growing railroad system. The South was a land of farms, and of large cotton and tobacco plantations that relied on slave labor. Slavery had long been banned in the northern states.

This division caused hostility between North and South. The Kansas–Nebraska Act (1854) gave new states the right to choose whether or not they allowed slavery. The Compromise of 1850 helped northern states protect the rights of runaway slaves—the South felt threatened.

The southern states were sure that the economy of the South would be ruined if the slaves were freed. Furthermore, the southern states believed that they had the right to make their own laws without interference from the federal government.

In 1860, Abraham Lincoln (1809–1865) was elected president. He belonged to the Republican Party, which opposed slavery, although he himself was not an abolitionist. Many southern states refused to live under such a government, and led

Union soldier

Confederate soldier

Union soldiers wore the blue uniform of the U.S. army. The Confederates usually wore gray.

by Jefferson Davis (1808–1889), they announced in December 1860 that they were seceding from (leaving) the Union and forming the Confederate States of America. The United States government declared they had no right to do this.

## BATTLE OF GETTYSBURG

The Battle of Gettysburg (July 1–3, 1863) was a turning point in the Civil War. The battle was the bloodiest ever fought on American soil, but was an important Union victory by General George Meade. He stopped an invasion of the North by General Robert E. Lee's Confederate army. From this point onward, the South's chances of winning the war declined.

◄ This shows the division of the United States at the beginning of the Civil War. Eleven of the 34 states made up the Confederacy. Most of the battles were fought in the east and southeast.

▲ The Battle of Spotsylvania, Virginia, in May 1864, was one of the many Union victories of the Civil War. In all, more than 600,000 soldiers died on both sides in the conflict.

## THE TWO SIDES

The North (Union), made up of 23 states, had more men, more money, and more industry than the South. The North also controlled the navy and started a naval blockade that prevented the South from receiving help or supplies from abroad. The 11 states of the South (the Confederacy) were much weaker, but they had the benefit of good generals and a great fighting spirit. Civil war broke out on April 12, 1861 when the forces of the South opened fire on Fort Sumter in South Carolina. The Confederates won a number of victories early in the war.

The South won the first battles in 1861, including Fredericksburg and Chancellorsville, but the turning point in the struggle came in July 1863, when the North won the biggest battle of the war, at Gettysburg. The Union forces, under the command of General George Meade, stopped an invasion of the North by General Robert E. Lee's Confederate army. Each side had over 20,000 soldiers killed or wounded.

Union flag

Confederate flag

During the Civil War, the Confederates rejected the Stars and Stripes and adopted their own flag.

For the first time in history, railroads played a vital part in warfare by moving troops, ammunition, and supplies swiftly over great distances.

Harriet Tubman (1820–1913) was an escaped slave who made trips through southern territory, helping slaves escape.

335

# THE END OF THE CIVIL WAR 1865

**Slavery was completely abolished in the United States in 1865, with the 13th Amendment to the Constitution. The country was reunited, but new problems emerged.**

General Lee's presentation sword was not handed over during the surrender ceremony, as was customary. Instead, it remained by his side.

In 1864, despite Lee's skillful tactics, General Grant captured Richmond, the capital of the South. General Sherman marched through Georgia and the other southern states, capturing Atlanta. He followed this victory with a "march to the sea," during which he destroyed towns and farms. Short of men, money, weapons, and food, Lee surrendered on April 9, 1865, ending the Civil War. More than 600,000 soldiers had died, many from diseases such as typhoid and dysentery. Five days later, Abraham Lincoln was assassinated.

The Civil War settled two important questions. First, it confirmed that the United States of America was a single nation and that no state had the right to break away. Second, it brought slavery in the southern states to an end. After the Civil War, arguments raged over how the South should be "reconstructed." Ideas included the opening of schools and the building of railroads. Abraham Lincoln's successor, Andrew Johnson (1808–1875), a Democrat, wanted better conditions for Black Americans. The Republicans wanted a harsher policy, and it was they who won the argument in the end.

General Lee surrendered to General Grant at Appomattox Court House, Virginia, on April 9, 1865. His men were outnumbered, exhausted, and starving.

The people of the South resisted most aspects of Reconstruction. Many former slaves who had fought on the Union side returned home expecting more freedom in the South. However, the Ku Klux Klan and other racist organizations began a campaign of murder and terrorism in 1866 that tried to stop Black Americans from enjoying civil rights. Northern troops withdrew, Reconstruction ended, and the Democrats took over the South.

Abraham Lincoln (1809–1865) was the 16th President of the United States. Many people believe he was the greatest of all of the presidents. "Honest Abe" was known for his integrity and the force of his arguments.

## THE GETTYSBURG ADDRESS

In November 1863, President Lincoln was invited to make a "few appropriate remarks" at the dedication of a national cemetery at Gettysburg. His speech lasted about two minutes and is today regarded as a masterpiece. Abraham Lincoln summed up the central issue of the war—the survival of a nation dedicated to freedom.

# CANADA 1763–1913

**The peace terms of 1763 effectively gave Canada over to British rule. In 1791, the British Constitutional Act split Canada into British-and French-speaking territories.**

▲ Louis Joseph Papineau (1786–1871) was a French–Canadian politician. He led the French-speaking Canadians' demand for reform and equality.

▲ William Lyon Mackenzie (1795–1861) was a member of Canada's Reform Party. He wanted Canada to have more freedom from British rule. He led the 1837 rebellion in Upper Canada.

Opposition to British rule in Canada grew during the 1830s. Rebellions broke out in both Upper and Lower Canada in 1837, led by William Lyon Mackenzie and Louis Papineau respectively. The rebels wanted self-government and, although they had some support, the most influential people in the colonies did not agree with them. The rebels were soon defeated by British troops. The British government sent Lord Durham to Canada to investigate the causes of the rebellions. His report said that Upper and Lower Canada should be united and should have control over their own affairs.

The 1840 Act of Union united the two colonies, which became known as the Province of Canada. However, many Canadians still felt that these reforms did not go far enough. This was partly because the Canadians were concerned that the United States might invade if Canada looked weak. In 1867, the British North America Act was passed, and Canada became self-governing. The act united four Canadian provinces in a dominion. The French Canadians of Quebec were promised equality, and French and English became the official languages.

Winnipeg, a center of the fur trade, was still a small town in 1870. In that year, the settlement became the capital of the province of Manitoba.

## WESTERN TERRITORIES

The vast lands to the west, which belonged to the Hudson's Bay Company, later also became part of Canada. The Northwest Territories joined the dominion in 1870, and the Yukon Territory in 1898. The Yukon had been the location of a gold rush in 1896, which led to tens of thousands of hopeful prospectors making their way over the Rocky Mountains to the goldfields and, they hoped, great wealth. Completion of the Canadian Pacific Railway in 1885 united the country. Unlike the American railroads, it formed one continuous system from the St. Lawrence River to the Pacific Ocean.

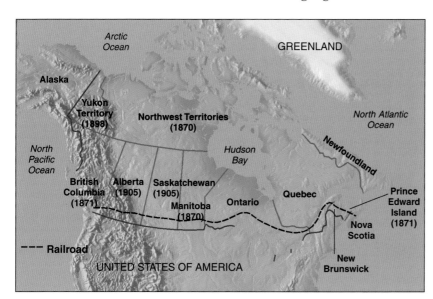

Arctic Ocean

GREENLAND

Alaska

Yukon Territory (1898)

Northwest Territories (1870)

North Atlantic Ocean

North Pacific Ocean

Hudson Bay

Newfoundland

British Columbia (1871)

Alberta (1905)

Saskatchewan (1905)

Manitoba (1870)

Ontario

Quebec

Prince Edward Island (1871)

Nova Scotia

New Brunswick

--- Railroad

UNITED STATES OF AMERICA

◄ The British North America Act of 1867 united the provinces of Nova Scotia, New Brunswick, Ontario (formerly Upper Canada), and Quebec (Lower Canada) in the Dominion of Canada.

▲ The last spike of the Canadian Pacific Railway was driven in at Eagle Pass, British Columbia, on November 7, 1885. A five-month journey now took just five days.

# ITALY 1833–1878

**The birth of the Italian nation was brought about with the help of an aristocrat, Count Camillo Cavour, and a man of the people, Giuseppe Garibaldi.**

Victor Emmanuel II (1820–1878) was the popular king of Piedmont-Sardinia. He eventually became king of all Italy.

▼ Piedmont–Sardinia took the lead in uniting Italy in 1859–1860. Nice and Savoy were given to France in 1860.

In the early 1800s, Italy was made up of a number of small states. Apart from the Kingdom of Piedmont–Sardinia and Rome, which was ruled by the pope, these states were governed by foreign countries. In the 1830s, an independence movement known as the *Risorgimento* ("resurrection") began to grow. In 1848, many revolutions against foreign rule broke out, but they were quickly suppressed. In 1849, Victor Emmanuel II became king of Piedmont–Sardinia (a northern state in the Piedmont region, which also ruled the island of Sardinia), and made Turin his capital. He was a very popular man, at least in part because he restricted the powers of the clergy, who were less well-regarded in the north than in the south. He was known as "the cavalier king."

The rebellion in Venice in 1848 was one of the last in Italy to hold out. Severely weakened by hunger and disease, the people of Venice gave up in August 1849.

## SKILLFUL POLITICIAN

Count Camillo Cavour, an Italian aristocrat with very liberal views, became the chief minister of the Kingdom of Piedmont–Sardinia in 1852. He made an alliance with France in 1858. Together, they defeated the Austrians in 1859. Austria ceded Lombardy to France who then handed it to Piedmont in exchange for Savoy and Nice. Most of northern Italy then joined with Piedmont–Sardinia.

In 1860, rebellion broke out in southern Italy, which was part of the Kingdom of the Two Sicilies. Giuseppe Garibaldi led a revolt and conquered the kingdom. His men were known as "red shirts" because of their dress, and faithfully followed their romantic and patriotic leader. It took them a mere three months to conquer all of Sicily.

Cavour was now very concerned that Garibaldi, and his seemingly unstoppable men, would attack Rome, which might in turn lead Austria or France to come to the aid of the pope. Cavour invaded the Papal States (but not Rome) and then marched his army south. Garibaldi's forces had taken Naples, and Cavour, being careful to go around Rome itself, finally met up with him.

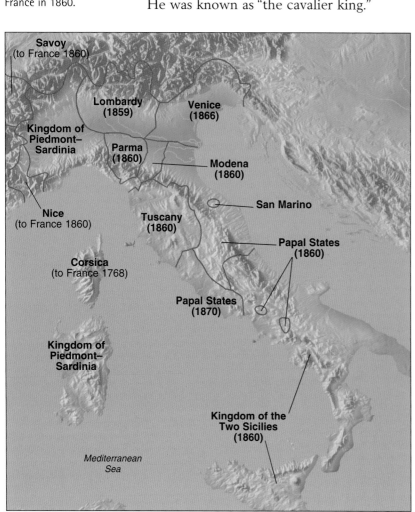

Savoy (to France 1860)

Lombardy (1859)

Venice (1866)

Kingdom of Piedmont–Sardinia

Parma (1860)

Modena (1860)

San Marino

Nice (to France 1860)

Tuscany (1860)

Papal States (1860)

Corsica (to France 1768)

Papal States (1870)

Kingdom of Piedmont–Sardinia

Kingdom of the Two Sicilies (1860)

Mediterranean Sea

Giuseppe Garibaldi (1807–1882) was a patriot who fought against foreign rule in Italy. With his "red shirts," he conquered the kingdom of the Two Sicilies in 1860, and it became part of the Kingdom of Italy.

Count Camillo Cavour (1810–1861) was the politician who made most of the plans for a unified Italy. He was also able to harness the talents of Giuseppe Garibaldi to help his own plans.

▼ A meeting between Victor Emmanuel II and Garibaldi at Teano, northeast of Naples, in 1860 eventually led to the unification of Italy.

## AGREEMENT AND UNITY

Count Cavour reached a detailed agreement with Garibaldi and his red-shirt soldiers that allowed the Kingdom of Piedmont–Sardinia to take over Sicily, Naples, and the Papal States. In February 1861, the first national parliament was held in Turin and, one month later, Victor Emmanuel II was proclaimed king of all Italy.

Two small areas were not included. Venice was still part of the Austrian Empire and Rome was ruled by the pope but occupied by France. Venice was given to Italy after Austria was defeated in the Austro–Prussian War (1866). In Rome, Pope Pius IX was totally unwilling to bend to what he still saw as a northern king. The Franco–Prussian War of 1870 forced the French to withdraw their garrison in Rome for other duties, and the Italian army immediately took over Rome. The city then became the capital of Italy. Pope Pius would not negotiate and thought of himself as a prisoner in the Vatican until he died in 1878. The people of Rome wanted unity and so it was that the ruling house of Piedmont–Sardinia reigned over a totally united country.

### KEY DATES

| | |
|---|---|
| 1830s | Mazzini founds the "Young Italy" movement |
| 1848 | Revolutions break out in Europe |
| 1849 | Victor Emmanuel II–King of Piedmont-Sardinia |
| 1852 | Cavour–chief minister of Piedmont-Sardinia |
| 1859 | Piedmont-Sardinia and France defeat Austrians |
| 1860 | Garibaldi and his army conquer Sicily |
| 1861 | First national Italian parliament held |
| 1870 | Rome joins greater Italy |

# GERMANY 1848–1871

**In the second half of the 1800s, the military might of France was overtaken by a German state, Prussia. A new and powerful Germany emerged.**

The diplomatic skills of Otto von Bismarck (1815–1898), prime minister of Prussia, kept his enemies isolated.

▲ Napoleon III (1808–1873) became emperor of France in 1852. He was captured at the Battle of Sedan during the Franco-Prussian War and sent into exile in 1871.

After the failure of the revolutions of 1848, the German Confederation, made up of over 40 states, stayed as disunited as it had been for centuries. The two strongest states, Austria and Prussia, jostled for power over all of Germany. Although weaker at first, Prussia's trade and industry grew in the 1850s. Its increasing strength was supported by the king of Prussia and his new prime minister, Otto von Bismarck.

Austria and Prussia went to war against Denmark over control of the duchies of Schleswig and Holstein. Although both duchies belonged to the royal family of Denmark, many Germans lived there. Denmark was defeated, and both duchies now came under German control. But Austria and Prussia soon clashed over how they should be administered.

## WHO WOULD LEAD GERMANY?

In 1866, Bismarck dissolved the German Confederation, and Austria declared war on Prussia, confident of victory. They had, however, not taken sufficient account of the skill and strength of the Prussian army. The Prussian forces swept through the Austrian territory at an alarming speed. The power of the Austrian Hapsburg Empire was forever weakened when they were defeated on July 3, 1866 at the Battle of Sadowa. Bismarck then set up the North German Confederation, with Prussia as the most powerful member.

The Peace of Prague was an excellent example of the skillful diplomacy and statesmanship of Bismarck. He knew that it would be dangerous to humble Austria, and he wanted to make an ally and not an enemy. Accordingly, the Hapsburgs only lost the two duchies, which they did not really want anyway, and Venice. Prussia did, however, make huge gains within the rest of Germany.

▶ In September 1870, during the Franco–Prussian War, the Prussian army laid siege to Paris. Rather than make a full assault on the city, the Prussians simply surrounded it and waited. The poor were soon facing starvation, and the wealthy were reduced to eating the animals from the Tuileries Zoo. Peace came in May 1871.

## THE BATTLE OF SEDAN

The Battle of Sedan, in northern France, on September 1–2, 1870, was the scene of an unequal conflict between Prussian forces and the French. The French forces were outnumbered two to one. Although Leboeuf, the French war minister, had claimed that the French preparation was total, once the battle began, it was found that not all of the French riflemen even had a rifle. Surrounded and unable to break out, Napoleon III, along with 85,000 French troops, was forced to surrender.

## THE FRANCO–PRUSSIAN WAR

The French emperor, Napoleon III, a poorly supported, ill-advised leader, felt threatened by Prussia's increasing power. He demanded Germany hand over some of its territory to balance out the Prussian gains. Bismarck ignored this demand, and Napoleon's threats only served to bring the previously reluctant southern German states behind Prussia.

Bismarck provoked the French when he altered the report of a conversation between the Prussian king and the French ambassador so that it looked like an insult to France. When the document, the "Ems Telegram," was published in 1870, Napoleon III was furious and declared war. In the Franco–Prussian War, Prussia defeated France in 1871 and took over Alsace and Lorraine. The remaining German states also joined in 1871. Bismarck then formed the German Second Reich, with the king of Prussia (William I) as emperor.

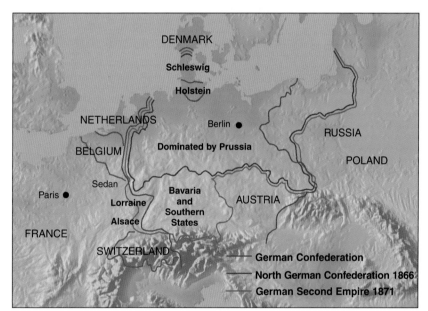

▲ The North German Confederation, dominated by Prussia, was formed in 1867. It was a union of states in which the members kept their own governments, but military and foreign policy was decided by a federal government.

### KEY DATES

| | |
|---|---|
| 1852 | Napoleon III becomes emperor of France |
| 1862 | Bismarck becomes Prussian prime minister |
| 1864 | Danish plans to take over Schleswig-Holstein |
| 1866 | Schleswig-Holstein taken over by Prussia |
| 1867 | North German Confederation formed |
| 1870 | Outbreak of the Franco–Prussian War |
| 1870 | French defeat at the Battle of Sedan, Napoleon III captured |
| 1870 | Prussian siege of Paris begins |
| 1871 | Franco-Prussian War ends at Peace of Frankfurt |
| 1871 | Second German Reich proclaimed at Versailles |
| 1873 | Napoleon III dies in exile |

◄ This image shows the keys of Paris being given to Wilhelm I by General Jules Trochu, the president of France, in 1871.

# SCRAMBLE FOR AFRICA 1880–1912

**With their greater wealth and technology, the major European powers were able to conquer large parts of the world. They claimed the territory as their own.**

Dr. David Livingstone, lost while seeking the source of the Nile, had a historic meeting with Welsh-born American journalist H. M. Stanley by Lake Tanganyika in 1871.

This cartoon shows the German eagle, poised to take as much of Africa as it can. Germany was just one of many European powers seeking new lands.

▼ During the latter part of the 1800s, rivalry between the different European powers played a large part in the scramble for Africa.

Toward the end of the 1800s, the European powers ceased to squabble among themselves for territories and trade within Europe itself. With the sudden emergence of the new force of Germany under the political control of Otto von Bismarck, all European nations looked farther afield for economic gain. Rival European nations now rushed to carve out their respective colonies in Africa. This process became known as the "scramble for Africa."

Britain and France undoubtedly led the scramble, but Germany, Belgium, and Italy were very close behind. Numerous conflicts flared up between Britain and France over colonies in West Africa. Where Britain had been happy to control a relatively small number of coastal towns and ports, by the end of the century they had taken over all of what is now Ghana and Nigeria, and effectively controlled Sierra Leone and The Gambia.

## THE SUEZ CANAL

Opened in 1869, the Suez Canal cut the sea journey between Britain and India from three months to three weeks. The Khedive of Egypt was in financial difficulties, and the British bought his half of the shares in the Suez Canal in 1875.

Relations between Britain and France worsened when the British occupied Egypt in 1882 to protect their interests during a local uprising against the Europeans. In 1885, General Gordon and many British soldiers were killed when the Mahdi, the leader in Sudan, took Khartoum on the White Nile. The Italians invaded Eritrea (now part of Ethiopia), and King Leopold of the Belgians took over the Congo.

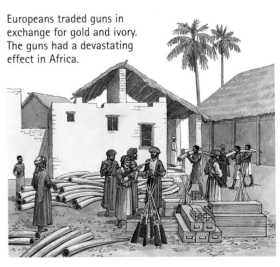

Europeans traded guns in exchange for gold and ivory. The guns had a devastating effect in Africa.

# CONSTANT EXPANSION

The scramble for Africa became a formal process at a conference in Berlin in 1884. The rival European countries cut up Africa like a cake. Only Liberia and Ethiopia, which held off an Italian invasion, remained independent. The colonization of Africa had a number of effects on Africans. The Europeans took no notice of the different African nations and tribal boundaries when the new borders were drawn. They brought new forms of government to Africa, but few Africans could vote. Profits from the colonies went back to Europe, and European colonists often took the best farmland.

| KEY DATES | |
|---|---|
| 1869 | Suez Canal opens to shipping |
| 1871 | Stanley meets Livingstone at Lake Tanganyika |
| 1876 | Leopold II of Belgium takes over the Congo |
| 1882 | British occupy Egypt to protect the Suez Canal |
| 1884 | European nations meet in Berlin to divide Africa among themselves |
| 1885 | The Mahdi besieges Khartoum |
| 1898 | British defeat the Mahdi's troops at Omdurman |
| 1893 | The French take Timbuktu, Mali, West Africa |
| 1899 | British–Egyptian rule of Sudan |
| 1912 | The African National Congress (ANC) forms in South Africa |

▲ The French conquest of Mali in West Africa was symbolized by the raising of the French flag in Timbuktu in 1893. Their advance along the Niger River was held up by the resistance of the local people, the Mande.

◀ Designed by French engineer Ferdinand de Lesseps (1805–1894), the Suez Canal considerably reduced the journey from Britain to India, and helped trade goods reach England more quickly. In 1875, the British, under the leadership of Disraeli, heard that the Khedive (viceroy) of Egypt faced bankruptcy, and they bought his share of the canal for £4 million.

# IRELAND 1800–1913

**Ireland went through a period of great suffering when disease struck the potato, the staple food of the poor. At least a million people died, and a million emigrated.**

Daniel O'Connell (1775–1847) was a fighter for the rights of Catholic people in Britain. He was the first Irish Catholic to be elected to the British Parliament. He served from 1829 to 1847.

▲ Irish tenant farmers were ruined when the potato blight struck in 1845. The harvest was poor and they could not pay their rent. Many of the farmers and their families starved to death.

Most of the people of Ireland made a living by farming small plots of rented land or working on large estates for Anglo–Irish landlords. They were desperately poor and depended on potatoes, which were cheap, to feed large families. In 1845 and 1846, potato blight, a type of fungus, spread rapidly across the land, turning the potatoes black, diseased, and inedible. Famine relief, paid for by charities and public fund-raising, was too little and came too late. The government system for the relief of property was badly planned and run, and it broke down under the pressure.

The authorities believed that the food supply would adjust itself to meet the demand, and they opposed the distribution of free food until it was too late. Efforts to bring down the price of wheat by repealing the Corn Laws also came too late. Because landlords evicted tenants who could not pay their rent, entire families were left to starve to death by the side of the road.

On May 6, 1882, in Phoenix Park in Dublin, Lord Frederick Cavendish, the Irish chief secretary, and T.H. Burke, his undersecretary, were stabbed to death by Irish Nationalists. Five were later hanged for this offense.

## IRISH EMIGRATION

To escape the famine, hundreds of thousands of Irish people emigrated, mostly to the British mainland, but great numbers also went to the United States and Canada. Blight also hit potato crops in Britain and other countries. But only in Ireland did it have such disastrous consequences, including the shadow it was to cast over Irish–British relations in future generations.

▶ Most Irish people lived a hard life with little food and comfort. Their homes were usually not very different from the barns in which their Anglo–Irish landlords kept their cattle.

During the potato famine, many Irish people had to choose between possible starvation or leaving their country. About one million people starved to death and another million emigrated over the next five years, mostly to England, Scotland, and Wales, as well as the United States. A typhoid epidemic in 1846–1847 is thought to have killed another 350,000 Irish people.

Charles Stewart Parnell was leader of the Irish Parliamentary Party in the British Parliament. He led the struggle for Irish home rule and supported the Land League, which wanted land to be given to Irish farmers.

The Irish Republican Brotherhood, or Fenians, was founded in 1858 by James Stephens (1825–1901). It was an organization that wanted to set up an Irish republic.

▼ The Fenians sometimes resorted to acts of violence in Britain. In 1867, they attacked a police van in Manchester to rescue some of their members.

## IRISH LEADERS

The demands of Irish politicians, particularly Charles Parnell (1846–1891), became increasing vocal in the British Parliament. Parnell had entered Parliament in 1875, and became president of the Irish Land League in 1879. His party demanded rent reductions and resisted the evictions of tenant farmers. The Irish politicians, and the strength of public feeling among the Irish, led to some law reforms, especially relating to land ownership rights.

However, these reforms were not enough to keep the Irish happy with British rule. Almost all of the Irish wanted home rule, or self-government. After the failure of both the 1886 and 1893 Home Rule Bills, the British Parliament finally passed the third Home Rule Bill in 1912—but it was not put into operation because of the outbreak of World War I, in 1914.

### KEY DATES

| | |
|---|---|
| 1801 | Irish Parliament abolished by the British |
| 1829 | Daniel O'Connell enters the British Parliament |
| 1845 | First potato blight leads to widespread famine |
| 1846 | Second potato blight causes worse famine |
| 1846 | Typhoid epidemic kills 350,000 Irish people |
| 1875 | Charles Parnell enters the British Parliament |
| 1879 | Parnell becomes president of the Land League |
| 1912 | Third Home Rule Bill passed, but not enacted |

# SOUTHEAST ASIA 1800–1913

**Southeast Asia was dominated by the Dutch, French, and British in the late 1800s. They grew rich on the profits from crops grown by local people.**

In Malaya, the British ruled through the local sultans. This beautiful mural of the tree of life comes from a family home in Sarawak, now part of Malaysia.

The merchant ships of the British East India Company were known as East Indiamen.

Southeast Asia was colonized by Europeans who set up plantations that were worked by the native population. The French colony of Indochina included Cambodia, Laos, and Vietnam. The French gradually conquered the area during the 1800s, despite local resistance. In Annam, the emperor, Ham Nghi, waged a guerrilla war until 1888.

The Dutch had been established in Indonesia since the 1620s. They had already taken over Indonesian trade, and from 1830, they also took over agriculture. The peasant farmers were forced to grow the crops the Dutch wanted, especially coffee and indigo (a plant from which a blue dye was made). By 1900, a nationalist movement was growing in Indonesia itself. The Indonesians made efforts to improve education and to regain some control over their business and trade.

Faced with Burmese expansion at the end of the 1700s, the British colonized Burma (Myanmar) and the Malay Peninsula during the 1800s because they wanted to protect India, which they regarded as the most valuable part of their empire. The Burmese resisted British rule in a series

Ox-pulled wagons containing tea chests at Colombo, in Ceylon (now Sri Lanka), in 1905. This mill belonged to tea merchant Thomas Lipton (1848–1931).

of bloody wars between 1824 and 1885, but by 1886, Britain controlled the whole country and made it into a province of India. It was not until 1937 that Burma was separated from India and regained some independence.

In Malaya, the situation was calmer because of British rule through the local sultans. During the early part of the 1800s, the British East India Company had set up trading posts; in 1826, Singapore, Malacca, and Penang were united to form the Straits Settlements.

▲ Indonesian princes and Dutch colonists benefited from the profits made by growing cash crops on the islands. For ordinary Indonesians, this way of life meant great hardship.

▶ Boat Quai, Singapore, in 1890. Hundreds of small boats were used to transport goods from ships to the warehouses.

## BRITISH INFLUENCE

In later years, the British went on to become responsible for other states in the Malay Peninsula and formed the Federated Malay States in 1896, with the capital at Kuala Lumpur. Demand for rubber grew rapidly in the 1800s, but the only source of supply was South America. Rubber seeds were collected in Brazil and shipped to Kew Gardens, in London, where they were raised. In 1877, 2,000 young plants were shipped and distributed to countries such as Ceylon (Sri Lanka), Malaysia, and Indonesia, where the plants flourished.

By the 1880s, British engineers, surveyors, and architects were helping to build railroads, roads, bridges, factories, and government buildings in Southeast Asia. They drew on the experience gained from the Industrial Revolution in Britain. Banking and investment were geared toward financing the empire by trading raw materials from the colonies for homemade manufactured goods.

The British also figured out how to improve the techniques used for mining the large deposits of tin and other precious metals that had been discovered in Malaya and other countries. Toward the end of the 1800s, many people went to live and work in Southeast Asia as traders, soldiers, engineers, diplomats, and government administrators.

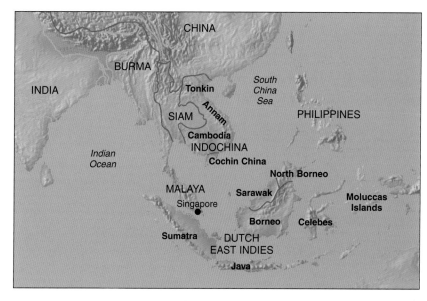

| KEY DATES | |
|---|---|
| 1813 | East India Company's trade monopoly ends |
| 1819 | Thomas Raffles of the East India Company founds Singapore as a free port |
| 1824 | British and Dutch interests settled by treaty |
| 1859 | French forces capture the citadel in Saigon |
| 1867 | Singapore and the Straits Settlements apply to be a Crown colony |
| 1877 | Brazilian rubber plants, grown in Kew Gardens, in London, exported to Southeast Asia |
| 1884–1885 | Chinese-French War |
| 1885 | At the Treaty of Tientsin (Tianjin) China recognizes French rule over Annam and Tonkin |
| 1886 | British annexe Upper Burma |
| 1887 | Union of Indochina formed from Vietnam, Cambodia, and Laos |
| 1898 | U.S.A. takes Philippines from the Spanish |

▲ Southeast Asia was dominated by three European powers in the late 1800s—the French, British, and Dutch controlled every country except Siam (Thailand).

▼ British forces attack Rangoon (now Yangon) in 1824, during the First Burma War. Burma (Myanmar) was defeated with great loss of life. It was forced to pay the British large amounts of money. After two further wars, Burma became part of the British Empire, in 1885.

# THE BRITISH EMPIRE 1815–1913

**During the 1800s, the British extended and consolidated their empire. Britain took over more land than any other nation in history.**

Soldiers from the countries that were part of the British Empire were frequently used to make sure that British power and influence continued and expanded.

▲ When William IV died in 1837, the English crown passed to his niece, Victoria (1819–1901), who was just 18 years old. When Victoria died, her reign had lasted 63 years, the longest in British history until that of her great-great-granddaughter, Elizabeth II.

▼ Between 1870 and 1913, the British Empire expanded further to take in land in Africa and Southeast Asia. This provided jobs for many British people. At its height, it included a quarter of the world's land and people.

At its height, during the reign of Queen Victoria, the British Empire included a quarter of the world's land and people. From the end of the Napoleonic Wars in 1815 to the start of World War I in 1914, Britain acquired so many new colonies that the empire stretched around the world. Britain was able to control this vast empire by its domination of the seas and world trade routes. Throughout the 1800s, British naval strength was unbeatable, and its boats constantly patrolled countries that belonged to the empire.

Because the empire covered both hemispheres it was known as "the empire on which the sun never sets." Colonies in the Caribbean, Africa, Asia, Australasia, and the Pacific were ruled from London, and were all united under the British monarch. Strategic harbors such as Gibraltar, Hong Kong, Singapore, and Aden came into British hands. Vital trade routes such as the Cape route to India, or the Suez Canal (via Egypt) to the spice and rubber plantations of Southeast Asia were also controlled by Britain.

## RAW MATERIALS

The empire provided the British with raw materials for manufacturing, and British demand for colonial products such as silk, spices, rubber, cotton, tea, coffee, and sugar led to the gradual takeover of many countries. Several countries became colonies when the British government acquired a bankrupt trading company. India was an example of a country where the British had come to trade and stayed to rule. It was the most prized colony in the empire. In 1850, India was still under the rule of the British East India Company. After the rebellion, of 1857, India was placed under the rule of the British government, whose policies were more cautious. British officials left control of local affairs to the Indian princes.

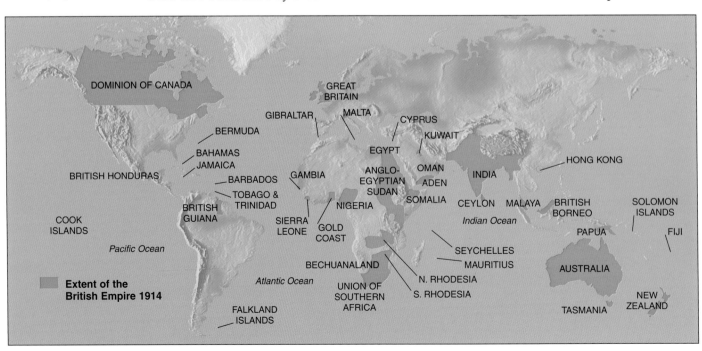

DOMINION OF CANADA
GREAT BRITAIN
GIBRALTAR
MALTA
CYPRUS
BERMUDA
KUWAIT
BAHAMAS
EGYPT
JAMAICA
HONG KONG
BRITISH HONDURAS
GAMBIA
ANGLO-EGYPTIAN SUDAN
OMAN
INDIA
BARBADOS
ADEN
TOBAGO & TRINIDAD
SOMALIA
BRITISH GUIANA
NIGERIA
CEYLON
MALAYA
BRITISH BORNEO
SOLOMON ISLANDS
COOK ISLANDS
SIERRA LEONE
GOLD COAST
Indian Ocean
PAPUA
FIJI
Pacific Ocean
SEYCHELLES
BECHUANALAND
MAURITIUS
AUSTRALIA
**Extent of the British Empire 1914**
Atlantic Ocean
UNION OF SOUTHERN AFRICA
N. RHODESIA
S. RHODESIA
NEW ZEALAND
FALKLAND ISLANDS
TASMANIA

## CONSOLIDATION

The British took over Egypt in 1883 to guard the Suez Canal and the route to India. After a rebellion in the south of Egypt led by a religious leader, the Mahdi, Britain entered Sudan in 1898. The British set up trade links throughout the empire by appointing an agent in every port. They organized local produce for export and markets for British imports. The British navy protected their interests and kept the sea routes safe for shipping.

British influence extended into mainland settlements in Central and South America, and into China where it had trading outposts. Queen Victoria, herself empress of India since 1876, was a keen supporter of a foreign policy that pursued colonial expansion and upheld the empire. As more British people emigrated to countries within the empire, these lands were given more freedom to govern themselves. Many colonies, notably Canada, Australia, and South Africa, became dominions rather than colonies and were allowed self-government.

### KEY DATES

| | |
|---|---|
| 1824 | Penal colony established in Brisbane, Australia |
| 1829 | Britain claims West Australia |
| 1837 | Victoria becomes queen of the United Kingdom |
| 1850 | Australian Colonies Government Act gives limited independence to Australia |
| 1852 | New Zealand is granted a constitution |
| 1857 | Indian mutiny against British rule begins |
| 1867 | British North American Act grants home rule to Canada |
| 1875 | Britain buys controlling interest in Suez Canal |
| 1876 | Queen Victoria becomes empress of India |
| 1884 | Britain annexes southeastern New Guinea |
| 1890 | Zanzibar becomes a British protectorate |
| 1901 | New South Wales, Queensland, Victoria, South Australia, Western Australia, and Tasmania become the Commonwealth of Australia; Queen Victoria dies |
| 1907 | Dominion of New Zealand is founded |

## END OF EMPIRE

Toward the end of the 1800s, some colonies began to break away from British rule. Home rule was granted to Canada in 1867, and independence to Australia in 1901. Both countries became dominions although they remained part of the British Empire. The gradual loosening of ties with the British Empire reflected the fact that Britain had ceased to be the leading industrial nation in the world. Germany and the United States had overtaken it, with France and Russia close behind.

The British government passed the Australian Colonies Government Act in 1850. This gave limited independence to the country. In 1901, the colonies of New South Wales, Queensland, Victoria, South Australia, Western Australia, and Tasmania became the Commonwealth of Australia.

◄ This cartoon from the 1800s shows the imperial lion rowing its cubs (the colonies) to a gathering celebrating 60 years of Victoria's rule.

▼ In 1897, Victoria celebrated her Diamond Jubilee. The guests of honor included Indian princes, African chiefs, Pacific Islanders, and Chinese from Hong Kong.

# THE PLAINS WARS 1849–1913

The plains of the American Midwest had once seemed vast and endless. In the 1800s, they became the scene of a struggle for land ownership.

▲ The Pawnee were one of the Plains tribes. They lived by hunting buffalo.

▲ General George Custer (1839–1876) died in the Battle of the Little Bighorn.

▲ Sitting Bull (1831–1890) was a Dakota (Sioux) medicine man and war chief.

Many groups of Indigenous Americans lived on the Great Plains of the American West and had done so for thousands of years. This vast area stretched from the Mississippi River in the east to the Rocky Mountains in the west, and from Canada in the north to Texas in the south. Until the 1600s, many Plains tribes were farmers. They grew corn, beans, and other food, but they also hunted buffalo, on foot, using bows and arrows. Their way of life on the plains began to change during the 1600s when the Spanish introduced the horse.

With horses, the Indigenous Americans could easily follow the buffalo. The buffalo not only provided them with meat, but also with tools and weapons fashioned from the animals' bones, and tepees and clothing made with the skins. Some of the larger tribes of Indigenous Americans became known as the Plains tribes. Early white settlers forced some tribes to move west from their original homelands east of the Mississippi River.

## WAGONS TO THE WEST

After the Civil War, the land between the Mississippi River and the Rocky Mountains was thought of as a wilderness of plains and mountains. The government encouraged pioneers to migrate westward. Settlers traveled west together in wagon trains for protection on the long journey across plains, rivers, and mountains, which could take up to eight months.

Indigenous Americans depended on buffalo for their food, clothing, and shelter. Many buffalo were also killed to supply meat to workers laying track for the railroads.

## SETTLERS MOVE WEST

The government encouraged people to migrate westward. Under the Homestead Act of 1862, a family could have 160 acres (65ha) for a small fee, as long as they did not sell the land for five years. More land was given to those who made improvements by drilling wells or planting trees. The Act encouraged farmers to move into and settle on the Great Plains.

The government also encouraged the building of railroads, which carried people into unsettled regions. It gave land to the railroads so generously that many lines were built simply to obtain land. By 1869, the Union Pacific Railroad was finished—connecting America from coast to coast.

## STRUGGLE FOR SURVIVAL

The expansion of the railroads soon changed the face of the United States. They brought even more settlers to the Indigenous American homelands. The two cultures came into conflict. Local Indigenous American chiefs made land agreements with the settlers, without realizing that they were signing away their rights. The settlers' idea of private property meant nothing to the Indigenous Americans. They thought they could continue to hunt on the land. Many bought guns and attacked the settlers' homesteads, their wagon trains, and the railroads.

Between 1860 and 1885, the number of buffalo was reduced—largely by white hunters—from 15 million to only 2,000. Starting in 1866, a series of wars took place. The goal was to claim land for white settlers. To do this, the Indigenous Americans were driven onto reservations, or destroyed if they resisted. President Rutherford B. Hayes (1822–1893) said, in 1893, "Many, if not most, of our Indian wars had their origin in broken promises and acts of injustice." By then, it was too late—the few survivors of the Plains tribes had been forced onto the poor quality land of the reservations.

▲ Virginia City in Nevada began in 1859 when gold and silver were found. By 1876, it was a large town, but when the gold and silver ran out, it became a ghost town.

▲ In 1848, gold was discovered at Sutter's Mill, in California, and the gold rush started. By 1855, San Francisco's population had grown from 800 to 50,000.

The Indigenous Americans were used to hunting and did not want to be farmers. They were not allowed to become American citizens and had few civil rights. Fierce battles with soldiers resulted in the deaths of thousands of Indigenous Americans. The last battle was at Wounded Knee in South Dakota, in 1890, when soldiers slaughtered 200 Sioux. Soon, all the tribes were moved onto reservations, and the Indigenous American way of life was changed forever.

▲ The possibility of making their fortune attracted people of many nationalities to the American goldfields. Thousands of Chinese people traveled to California in the 1850s and the 1870s to work as laborers.

◄ In a dispute about mining rights in the Black Hills, the U.S. government went to war against Indigenous American peoples in Montana. In June 1876 a force of the 7th Cavalry commanded by George Armstrong Custer was surrounded and destroyed near the Little Bighorn river by warriors of the Lakota, Arapaho, and Northern Cheyenne.

351

# THE BOXER REBELLION 1900

**Under the weak Manchu government, the Chinese Empire appeared to be breaking up. Discontent at Western influence led to the Boxer Rebellion in 1900.**

The last emperor of China was Puyi (1906–1967). He became emperor at the age of two and lost the throne when he was six.

## KEY DATES

**1898** The Hundred Days of Reform end when Empress Cixi comes to power. Britain gains Hong Kong on a 99-year lease from China.
**1900** Foreign embassies in Beijing are besieged by Boxer rebels. American, Japanese, and European troops end the rebellion. The empress flees Beijing.
**1905** Sun Yatsen founds a group that becomes known as the Chinese Nationalist Party, or Guomindang.
**1911** The army backs a nationalist rebellion. Manchu rule ends, and a republic is declared. Sun Yatsen becomes provisional president.

Much of the Chinese Empire under the weak and corrupt Manchu government was dominated by competing European powers. Many powerful groups struggled to preserve the country from Westerners, but the Chinese recognized that they would have to copy Western ways and set up new industries.

In 1898, the reformers gained power for a brief time. New laws were passed to turn China into a modern state. They sought to change the civil service and to deal with the day-to-day problems rather than rely on ancient and outdated texts. They founded a university in Beijing and started to reform the army. But the "Hundred Days of Reform" ended when the dowager empress, Cixi regained power. Many reformers were executed.

In 1900, a revolt began in northern China against all foreigners, but especially Christians. It was led by a secret organization—the Society of Harmonious Fists, or "Boxers." They were secretly supported by the Manchu government.

## THE END OF THE MANCHUS

In 1900, the Boxers attacked the European embassies in Beijing. They killed many Europeans, especially missionaries, as well as Chinese Christians. They held a number of embassies under siege for two months. An international force was set up, made up of American, British, French, German, Japanese, and Russian soldiers. An earlier, smaller, less well-equipped unit was unable to take Beijing, but in the summer, a second force successfully freed the embassies.

Having crushed the rebellion, the Chinese government was unable to prevent foreign interference. They were obliged to punish officials thought to be involved, to pay an indemnity payment, and to allow foreign troops into the embassies. Educated Chinese began to plot the overthrow of the Manchu regime.

In 1905, Sun Yatsen founded what became the Chinese Nationalist Party, or Guomindang. Plots and rebellions were organized by other groups. The Manchu government steadily lost control of the country. In 1911, a powerful general, Yuan Shikai, gave his support to a nationalist rebellion. Manchu authority collapsed, and a republic was declared.

This Chinese woodcut of 1902 shows Boxer rebels storming and taking a mountain fortress in Tianjin in northwest China.

# WOMEN'S SUFFRAGE 1848–1928

**During the 1800s and early 1900s, men and women in countries around the world were waging a campaign for women's suffrage—the basic right of women to vote.**

With her daughter, Christabel, Emmeline Pankhurst (1858–1928) founded the Women's Social and Political Union in 1903 and campaigned for women's rights in Britain.

With Lucretia Mott, Elizabeth Cady Stanton (1815–1902) organized the first women's rights convention in the United States in 1848. She went on to help found the National Woman Suffrage Association in 1869. The foundations of women's suffrage were laid in the face of fierce opposition.

During the early 1800s, only men who owned property could vote. The poor, women, and slaves were excluded. There were groups demanding reforms but only to extend the vote to all men. In the mid-1800s, some people began to say that everyone should be able to vote.

On July 20, 1848, a large group of men and women met in Seneca Falls, New York. The two organizers, Elizabeth Cady Stanton and Lucretia Mott, had met some years earlier while campaigning against slavery. But the fight for women's rights became their life's work. Improvements came in many small steps. In 1869, the Wyoming Territory gave women the right to hold public office. The same year, Susan B. Anthony and Elizabeth Cady Stanton founded the National Woman Suffrage Association. In 1872, another organization even nominated a woman to run for president. The campaign gained support in the 1900s. In 1920, the 19th Amendment granted voting rights to women.

The English suffragette Emmeline Pankhurst is arrested in 1914. Unlike the moderate suffragists, the suffragettes took radical direct action. They suffered imprisonment and were force-fed if they went on hunger strike.

New Zealand had been the first country to grant women voting rights in 1893. Finland was the first country in Europe to do so in 1906. In Britain, voting rights for women came in two stages: in 1918, for those over 30, and in 1928, for those over 21 (the same age as for men).

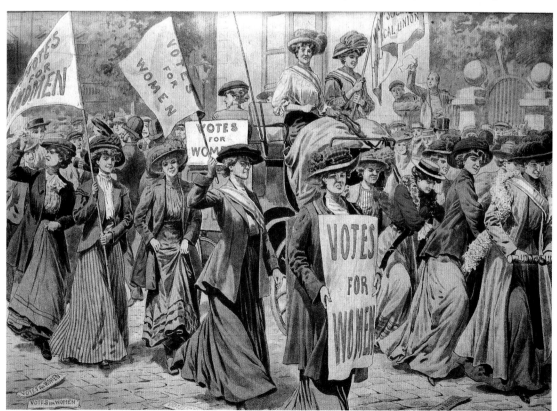

▶ Marches and protests became increasingly common. In Britain, the moderate suffragists were shocked by the violent direct action often taken by members of the Women's Social and Political Union (WSPU).

353

# AUSTRALIA 1788–1913

**The indigenous inhabitants of Australia faced a growing threat to their way of life, as white settlers encroached ever farther into their territories.**

Indigenous Australians led a way of life based around tribal territories and customs. Although the spread of white settlements destroyed much of this, they still kept a strong cultural identity.

During the 1800s, the new nation of Australia was created. More than 174,000 convicts had been shipped from Britain to Australia, mainly to Sydney, to serve their sentence in work gangs, for periods varying from a few years to life. Transportation to the colonies, which had begun in the reign of Elizabeth I, was an extension of the older punishment of banishment, and it did not end until 1868.

For many convicts, Britain held only bitter memories, so many of them chose to settle in Australia after their release. Early settlements were founded along the coast, but explorers gradually opened up the interior. They were followed by pioneers looking for grazing land for the ever-growing flocks of sheep.

As the wool industry grew, so did the demand for land. Many drove their sheep beyond the official settlement limits, earning themselves the name "squatters." Though they were later granted grazing rights, the name stuck. These early farmers gradually spread into the interior, acquiring land as they went. But eventually they came into conflict with the Indigenous Australians.

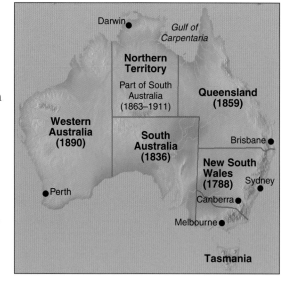

The colonies were granted self-government by 1890. New South Wales originally occupied all of eastern Australia, but was eventually divided.

## FIRST AUSTRALIANS

Australia's first inhabitants arrived from Southeast Asia 50,000 years earlier. They lived in nomadic groups, traveling around their territories, hunting with spears and boomerangs, fishing from canoes, and gathering fruit and vegetables. They had no written language, but passed on valuable knowledge by word of mouth and in song.

When the British settled in Australia, indigenous culture was threatened and their land was taken over by squatters. In the late 1700s, there were more than 300,000 to 1 million First Australians. Many were killed or driven off their land by settlers, and the population fell to under 45,000.

▲ Robert O'Hara Burke (1820–61) and William Wills (1834–61) were the first white men to cross Australia. Their expedition set out with 18 men in 1860 to travel north from Melbourne to the Gulf of Carpentaria. On the way back, they suffered from starvation and exhaustion. Only one man survived.

▶ This is Point Nepean Quarantine Station, in Victoria, built in 1852. Many emigrants spent their first weeks in a quarantine station to stop them spreading diseases to the local population.

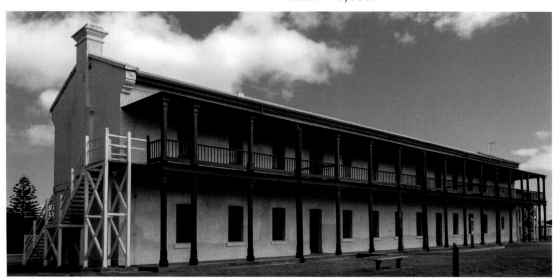

In Van Diemen's Land, later renamed Tasmania, the indigenous population was completely wiped out by the 1870s. Some had perished from European diseases, and white settlers had murdered the rest.

## THE GOLD RUSH

In 1851, many people rushed to Australia at the news that gold had been found in New South Wales and Victoria. This event became known as the Gold Rush. Melbourne, the capital of Victoria, became a wealthy city, and Australia's population more than doubled. In 1854, gold miners at the Eureka Stockade rebelled against their colonial rulers, and put on pressure for reform and self-government.

## GROWING UNREST

Squatter settlement also created problems when the immigrants and ex-convicts demanded that land be made available for farms. Many failed to gain land because of opposition from existing squatters. At the same time, a sense of nationalism was growing. Britain had granted self-government to all her colonies by the 1890s, and the leaders of the colonies had come to realize that some form of union was needed.

None of the Australian colonies were willing to give up their individual independence, so in 1890, after fierce arguments, the colonies agreed to unite in a federation. The Commonwealth of Australia was proclaimed on the first day of 1901, and the city of Canberra was chosen as the federal capital.

▲ In 1851, thousands of people from many countries moved to Australia after they heard that gold had been found in New South Wales and Victoria.

▶ Ned Kelly (1855–1880) and his gang of bushrangers roamed the country staging holdups and bank raids. Kelly, who often wore homemade armor, was hanged in 1880.

### KEY DATES

| | |
|---|---|
| 1797 | Sheep ranching introduced to Australia |
| 1836 | City of Adelaide founded |
| 1851 | Gold Rush starts in New South Wales |
| 1854 | Rebellion of gold miners at Eureka stockade |
| 1855 | Van Diemen's Land renamed Tasmania |
| 1860 | Burke and Wills set out to cross Australia |
| 1868 | Britain stops sending convicts to Australia |
| 1880 | The outlaw Ned Kelly is captured and hanged |
| 1901 | Commonwealth of Australia declared |

## SHEEP RANCHES

Introduced to Australia in 1797, sheep ranching became the major agricultural activity in the country. Because the land was often far from fertile, enormous areas of pasture were needed to keep the sheep healthy and well fed. This meant that more and more land was taken from the indigenous population.

# THE BALKAN WARS 1821–1913

**The Balkan states in the southeastern corner of Europe had long been an area of turmoil. As the Ottoman Empire shrank, they wanted independence.**

Peter I (1844–1921) was elected king of Serbia in 1903. He was exiled to Greece in 1916, but he returned in 1918 and was proclaimed king of the Serbs, Croats, and Slovenes.

The decline of the Ottoman Empire led to demands from the Balkan states for independence. There was also a rise in nationalism, which was encouraged by both Russia and Austria–Hungary, who did not want to see the other increase its influence in the region.

Britain and Germany supported Austria–Hungary, because they wanted to stop Russia from gaining access to any more ice-free ports in the Mediterranean or Black seas. Greece was the first to rebel, declaring independence as early as 1829. In 1878, Serbia, Montenegro, and Romania also became independent and Bulgaria gained self-government. Austria–Hungary occupied the Ottoman territory of Bosnia–Herzegovina in 1908, so that it would not fall under the growing power of the

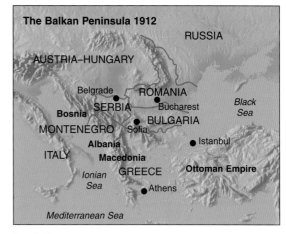

The Balkans had long been a turbulent area. The power of the Ottoman Empire was fading, and Russian power was growing. Austria–Hungary was trying to hold its own.

Serbian nationalists in the region. Albania and Macedonia remained under Ottoman control. When Italy attacked the Turkish-held territory of Tripoli (Libya) in 1912, it showed how weak Turkey was militarily. The Treaty of Ouchy gave Tripoli to Italy.

▲ In 1906, Ferdinand I (1861–1948) proclaimed Bulgaria independent from the Ottoman Empire and became king. In 1912, his country joined the Balkan League against Turkey.

▶ The Ottoman Turks were defeated by the Balkan League in 1912, because they were also fighting the Italians in North Africa. The Young Turks movement was also battling against the ways of the old regime.

## FIRST BALKAN WAR

In March 1912, Serbia and Bulgaria made a secret treaty to join forces to attack Turkey and divide the Ottoman territory between themselves. The Balkan League of Serbia, Bulgaria, Greece, and Montenegro was formed in October. By the end of the month they were all at war with Turkey.

The First Balkan War ended in 1913 with the signing of the Treaty of London, after what appeared to the rest of the world as the easy defeat of the Turks. In many ways, the First Balkan War merely served to increase the rivalries of the Balkan states. Serbia and Greece gained territory in Macedonia, while Bulgaria extended its territory to the Aegean Sea.

## SECOND BALKAN WAR

Albania had declared itself an independent Muslim principality in December 1912. Austria–Hungary supported Albanian independencein order to stop Serbia expanding to the Adriatic. The peace settlement led to disagreements among the victors. Bulgaria had gained far more territory than Serbia, which wanted more in Macedonia. Its three former allies combined against Bulgaria.

The Second Balkan War broke out in June 1913, when Bulgaria declared war on Serbia and Greece. Romania and Turkey fought against Bulgaria. The Bulgarians were surrounded and overpowered. In August, the Treaty of Bucharest was signed. Macedonia was divided between Greece and Serbia, and Romania gained some of Bulgaria. This settlement greatly increased the size of Serbia. Count Otto von Bismarck had declared, before either of the Balkan Wars, that the next major European war would be caused "by some foolish thing in the Balkans." He words proved to be correct.

▲ In November 1912, during the First Balkan War, the Bulgarian army captured Kirk-Kilisse from Turkish forces. The Bulgarians were allied with Greece, Serbia, and Montenegro.

▲ In this cartoon of the time, the Balkan countries were seen by Europe as a boiling pot of troubles.

During the Second Balkan War (June–August 1913), Bulgarian forces bombarded the Turkish town of Adrianopolis (now known as Edirne).

357

# THE ARTS 1836–1913

For all the arts, the period between 1836 and 1913 was a time of change and experiment. Painting and music in particular developed and flourished.

Glass shaded lamps by the Handel Company and Tiffany Studios were in the popular art nouveau style of the 1890s and 1900s.

In the late 1800s, the French impressionists such as Claude Monet, Auguste Renoir, and Edgar Degas developed spontaneous styles, filling their canvases with bold strokes of color in an attempt to capture the fleeting effects of light. In England, a group of artists, poets, and writers called the Pre-Raphaelites rejected the position of Raphael as the ultimate master of painting.

In European literature, more and more novels were being written for a growing number of readers. Romantic adventure stories were written by novelists such as Sir Walter Scott—*Ivanhoe*—and Jules Verne—*20,000 Leagues Under the Sea*. The wretched life of the poor in the cities was described with great skill by Charles Dickens in novels such as *Oliver Twist*. William Thackeray evoked an image of country and town living among the middle and upper classes in *Vanity Fair*, and Elizabeth Gaskell depicted life in the new manufacturing cities of the north in books such as *North and South*.

▲ Mark Twain, the pen name of Samuel Langhorne Clemens (1835–1910), was a writer and humorist who wrote *The Adventures of Tom Sawyer*.

▼ This is a scene from *David Copperfield* by Charles Dickens (1812–1870). Dickens's writing entertained and enlightened his readers about social problems.

This American daguerreotype (early photograph) is from about 1855. In 1888, George Eastman's Kodak box camera made photography available for everyone.

Wagner developed a new form of grand opera, and the Russian ballet changed ideas about dance. Beethoven's dramatic and expressive music had opened the way for the romantic period with composers such as Schubert, Mendelssohn, Schumann, Chopin, Berlioz, Verdi, Brahms, and Tchaikovsky producing works full of passion and drama.

▼ Giuseppe Verdi (1813–1901) was one of the greatest Italian composers of opera. His works include *Rigoletto*, *Il Trovatore* and *La Traviata*.

▲ "Dante's Dream" was painted by Dante Gabriel Rossetti (1828–1882), an English artist and poet who helped form the Pre-Raphaelite Brotherhood.

▶ Johann Strauss the Younger (1825–1899) toured Europe and the United States with his own orchestra. He was famous for his waltzes, such as *The Blue Danube*.

Drama became more realistic with plays by Ibsen, Chekhov, and George Bernard Shaw. In 1877, the British-born American photographer Eadweard Muybridge created the first motion picture sequences, and by the early 1900s, an entirely new form of performing art had appeared: the movies. Hollywood, in California, soon became the center of moviemaking.

▶ This bronze sculpture, *The Thinker*, by Auguste Rodin (1840–1917) went on show in France in 1904. His figures were expressive, conveying the power of emotion.

▼ Claude Monet (1840–1926) was the leader of the impressionists. He frequently worked outside and painted landscapes and scenes of simple middle-class life.

# ARCHITECTURE 1836–1913

**Architecture during the late 1800s reflected a new freedom of expression and a willingness to use modern technology.**

The style of architecture used for a building can depend on several factors. One consideration is that of the materials available to the builders. Another is the purpose to which the building is to be put. Equally important is the imagination of the architects and their clients. The main feature of architecture in Europe and North America during the 1800s was a willingness to use all the great styles of the past, from ancient Greece to the 1700s. Sometimes, very different styles were used in the same building.

Later in the century, a new kind of architecture developed. It was based on the use of steel to form the framework, or "skeleton," of a building. Since the walls did not have to support their own weight, buildings could be higher. Steel-framed skyscrapers were first made practical in the United States by the elevator, invented in 1852 by Elisha Otis (1811–1861). In 1884, William Le Baron Jenney (1832–1907) built the world's first skyscraper in Chicago. At ten stories, it would not be a skyscraper today, but its metal-frame structure set a new trend.

The Statue of Liberty, in New York Harbor, was a gift from France in 1884. It is made from copper sheets on an iron framework, designed by Gustave Eiffel. The statue—the work of sculptor Frédéric Bartholdi—rises 307 ft. (93.5m) from the bottom of the pedestal to the tip of the torch, and weighs 254 tons. A famous poem by American writer Emma Lazarus is on a plaque at its base.

▲ The Eiffel Tower, named after its designer, Gustave Eiffel (1832–1923), was built for the Paris Exhibition of 1889. It is 989 ft. (300 m) high, made from iron, and held together by 2.5 million rivets.

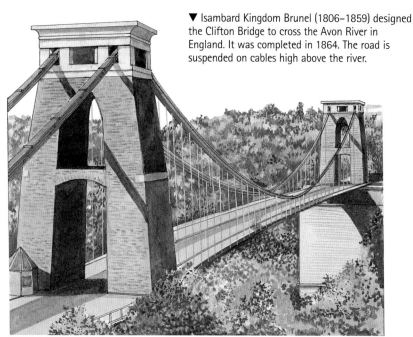

▼ Isambard Kingdom Brunel (1806–1859) designed the Clifton Bridge to cross the Avon River in England. It was completed in 1864. The road is suspended on cables high above the river.

As towns and cities became more and more densely populated, it was vital that services such as fresh water and removal of sewage were adequate. New water pipes were built under cities, and when cast-iron pipes became available it became easier to build drains. As engineering knowledge improved, it was also possible to built bridges that spanned ever greater distances.

◀ Opera became very popular during the 1800s, and many elegant opera houses were built. This opera house is at Manaus, in the Brazilian rain forest. The town was very rich for a short time thanks to profits from the local rubber industry.

## NEW TECHNOLOGY

The architecture of the late 1800s was adapted to make use of the discoveries of engineers and the availability of iron and steel. In addition to skyscrapers, the use of steel frames also made possible structures such as the Eiffel Tower in Paris, built for the great exhibition of 1889, and the Statue of Liberty in New York Harbor, a gift and symbol of friendship from the people of France to the people of the United States to celebrate the centennial of the Declaration of Independence.

The railroad age brought with it many new opportunities for architects and builders. Railroad stations, symbolizing the wealth of the new industrial age, were built in cities around the world. These grand edifices combined the new

▶ The ten-story steel-framed Home Insurance Building in Chicago is often described as the first skyscraper. After a fire destroyed most of the original city in 1871, the price of building land increased—if buildings were taller they needed less land.

technologies of iron and steel with styles from bygone periods.

However, the use of reinforced concrete in the early 1900s brought about a major change in architecture. Building design began to become simpler and less decorative. This "modern" style was to develop significantly after the end of WorldWar I.

▲ During the 1800s in Europe and the United States, the prosperous middle classes lived in imposing townhouses set in quiet, tree-lined streets.

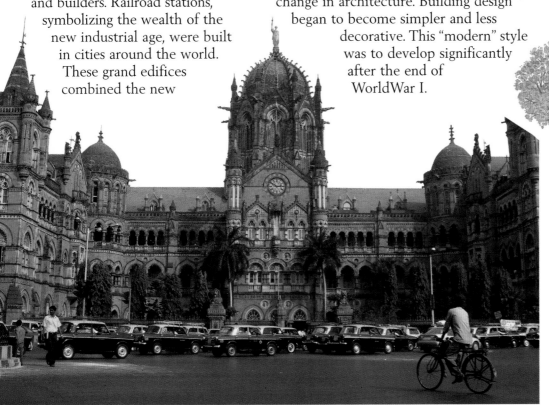

◀ The main railroad station in Bombay was opened in 1866. It was built in a mixture of the European Gothic and Renaissance styles, but the domes are Indian.

# SCIENCE AND TECHNOLOGY 1836–1913

**Technological progress continued at an ever-increasing pace. Major developments in communications and transportation were to change the world forever.**

Industry continued to develop, with new inventions, new products, and factories producing new types of goods. In 1850, coal and steam engines still provided the power for machinery, but by the early 1900s, electricity and oil were being used instead. In 1859, Edwin L. Drake found substantial reserves of oil at a depth of only 69 ft. (22m) in Oil Creek, Pennsylvania. Oil was to provide the fuel for the internal combustion engine. This, in turn, led to the invention of the first automobiles.

The German engineer Gottlieb Daimler invented the high-speed internal combustion engine in 1887. This was to prove convincingly better than the steam engines that had been used previously. In the United States, Frank and Charles Duryea produced their first vehicles in 1892, and Henry Ford made his first experimental car in 1893. Oil products also played a large role in the new chemical industry. They made possible the development of a huge range of materials such as plastics, detergents, fertilizers, paints, dyes, nylon, artificial rubber, and explosives.

▲ The telephone was invented by Alexander Graham Bell in 1875. The first public telephone exchange opened in Pittsburgh, in 1877.

▲ An American, Whitcomb Judson, invented the zipper in 1891. The first one, called a clasp locker, looked like the hooks and eyes that it replaced.

▲ The daguerreotype camera appeared in 1838. It was not until 1888 that George Eastman made photography available to all with the first roll film camera, the Kodak box.

The first bicycles were uncomfortable and dangerous. The "penny farthing" was invented by James Starley in the early 1870s, and had solid tires and no brakes.

The Scottish-born American inventor Alexander Graham Bell invented the telephone, and the first public exchange opened in Pittsburgh in 1877. That same year, prolific inventor Thomas Alva Edison produced the phonograph. This enabled sound to be recorded and played back on a foil-coated cylinder.

In 1879, Edison demonstrated the

Henry Ford (1863–1947) began producing cars like this Model T in 1908, using an assembly line. By 1914, his factory was producing a car every 90 minutes. During 19 years in production, around 15 million Model Ts were sold.

◄ Balloons were used for observation in the American Civil War. One of the observers was a retired German army officer named Zeppelin. He was an inventor of airships, which are sometimes called Zeppelins after him. Airships were more useful than balloons, because they could move under their own power.

▼ Wilbur and Orville Wright used gliders to test their experiments in controlled airplane flight. They made the first powered flight on December 17, 1903, at Kitty Hawk, North Carolina.

electric lightbulb, and in 1882, the world's first large-scale electric power station, designed and installed by Edison, was completed in New York City. The kinetoscope, used to produce moving pictures, was invented in 1891, again by Edison, and he was able to synchronize this with his phonograph to produce the first talking motion pictures in 1913.

▲ Thomas Edison was a pioneer of the electric lightbulb. In 1880, his system was first used to light a steamship.

▼ An early radio, called a wireless, had glass tubes. No one knew that radio waves existed until German scientist Heinrich Hertz (1857–1894) proved it in 1888, by transmitting and receiving them in his laboratory.

## WHEN IT HAPPENED
**1837** Samuel Morse invents Morse Code
**1856** Bessemer converter for steel invented
**1859** First oil well drilled in Pennsylvania
**1867** Nobel invents dynamite
**1868** Frenchman Georges Leclanché invents the dry-cell battery
**1869** Mendeleyev devises periodic table
**1875** First telephone call made by Bell
**1877** Nikolaus Otto patents four-stroke internal combustion engine
**1877** First public telephone exchange
**1882** First hydroelectric power plant uses water to generate electricity
**1885** First automobiles built in Germany
**1887** Dunlop invents pneumatic tire
**1896** Marconi invents first radio system
**1903** First powered and controlled flight by the Wright brothers
**1909** Leo Baekeland invents the first plastic, Bakelite

Scientists believed that all things were made up of atoms. Proof was provided by Ernest Rutherford's discovery of the atomic nucleus in 1911.

# THE WORLD AT WAR

## 1914–1949

In the years from 1914 to 1949, the world went through a period of rapid, intense, and painful change. The Great War, the "war to end all wars," was followed by a massive worldwide influenza epidemic. The 1917 Bolshevik Revolution made Russia the world's first socialist state. Then came the Great Depression, a collapse of capitalism that led to mass unemployment worldwide. This, followed by World War II, meant that European world dominance was replaced by that of the United States and the Soviet Union.

▲ World War I saw the first widespread use of aerial warfare. These early airplanes were used to spy on enemy positions and drop bombs.

◀ Malta was at the center of the battle to control the Mediterranean during World War II. The island was a base for the British Navy, and Germany and Italy fought with U.S. and British forces to seize the island.

# THE START OF WORLD WAR I 1914

The assassination of Archduke Franz Ferdinand, heir to the Austro–Hungarian Empire, in Sarajevo in June 1914, triggered the bloodiest conflict in human history.

Jealous of Britain's trade and colonies, Germany—which already had the world's largest army—had begun to build up its navy. Kaiser Wilhelm II's ambition to acquire more colonies overseas, along with his aggressive foreign policy, worried other European countries. In the years leading up to 1914, Britain and Germany competed to build bigger and better ships for their navies. The rivalry of other European countries over trade, colonies, and military power had also been growing, and the European powers had grouped together in defensive alliances.

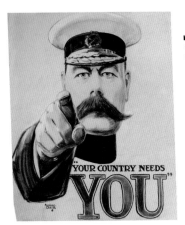

▲ A British recruiting poster at the start of World War I featured the War Minister, Lord Kitchener.

▲ Under Kaiser Wilhelm II (1859–1941), Germany built a battle fleet to rival Britain's navy.

## DEFENSIVE ALLIANCES

The main alliance was the Triple Alliance: Germany, Italy, and Austria–Hungary. An attack on any one country would bring its allies to its defense. The purpose of the alliance was to block Russian aggression in the Balkans (mainly the European areas of the old Ottoman Empire).

The Triple Entente, between Britain, France, and Russia, was not a military alliance, but its members had agreed to cooperate against German aggression.

The assassination of Archduke Franz Ferdinand in Sarajevo in 1914 triggered a series of political crises that dragged the world into a terrible war.

## HOW THE WAR BEGAN

The war began when a Serbian terrorist, Gavrilo Princip, assassinated the heir to the Austro–Hungarian Empire, Archduke Franz Ferdinand, and his wife in Sarajevo on June 28, 1914. This led Austria to declare war on Serbia on July 28. Russia's Czar Nicholas II mobilized his country's troops to defend Serbia from Austria. In return, Germany declared war on Russia on August 1. Russian armies were defeated by the Germans at Tannenberg and in the Battle of the Masurian Lakes. To the south, the Austro–Hungarian armies were defeated by the Russians in September.

## A WAR ON TWO FRONTS

Germany had always dreaded a war on two fronts, so it put the Schlieffen Plan into operation. Drawn up by General von Schlieffen, the plan aimed to defeat France in six weeks, so that Germany could concentrate its forces against Russia.

On August 3, Germany declared war on Russia's ally, France. When the German army marched into neutral Belgium to attack the French from the north, they were faced with determined Belgian resistance. This slowed down their advance and allowed the French, under General Joffré, time to reorganize their forces.

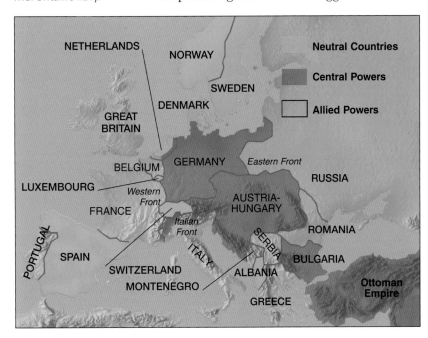

◄ In 1914, Europe was divided in two. Britain, France, and Russia, known as the Allies, combined to fight the Central Powers, comprising Germany, Austria–Hungary, and its allies. Fighting took place simultaneously on an eastern front and a western front.

## GERMANY INVADES FRANCE

The British then acted on the Treaty of London (1839), in which they had agreed to protect Belgian neutrality. It was on these grounds that Britain declared war on Germany on August 4. Britain went to Belgium's defense and sent the 100,000-strong British Expeditionary Force to France to help slow the German advance at Mons and Charleroi.

However, in the face of a determined German advance, Joffré retreated until he was behind the Marne River. Here, the French forces halted the Germans on September 8. Both sides then took up defensive positions and within three months, a line of trenches was dug from the English Channel to the Swiss frontier.

During the war, Britain, France, and Russia were known as the Allies, or Allied Powers. Germany, Italy, Austria–Hungary, and their allies were known as the Central Powers. Both sides raced to produce more and more deadly weapons, such as poison gas. They thought that by using these weapons they would shorten the war, but it lasted for four years and was the bloodiest conflict in human history. It has been estimated that the war cost the United States alone over $20 billion. The total number of men killed or wounded amounted to about 30 million.

THE DAILY MAIL, WEDNESDAY, AUGUST 5, 1914.

# GREAT BRITAIN DECLARES WAR ON GERMANY.

## SUMMARY REJECTION OF BRITISH ULTIMATUM.

The following announcement was issued at the Foreign Office at 12.15 a.m.:—

"Owing to the summary rejection by the German Government of the request made by His Majesty's Government for assurances that the neutrality of Belgium would be respected, His Majesty's Ambassador in Berlin has received his passports, and His Majesty's Government has declared to the German Government that a state of war exists between Great Britain and Germany as from 11 p.m. on August 4."

Huge crowds in Whitehall and Trafalgar Square greeted the news with round after round of cheers.

11 p.m. London time is midnight Berlin time, the hour at

| KEY DATES | |
|---|---|
| June 28 | Archduke Franz Ferdinand assassinated in Sarajevo by a Serbian terrorist |
| July 28 | Austria declares war on Serbia; Russia mobilizes its troops to defend Serbia |
| Aug. 1 | Germany declares war on Russia |
| Aug. 3 | Germany declares war on France |
| Aug. 4 | Germany invades Belgium; Britain declares war on Germany |
| Sept. 8 | German advance on Paris stopped at the Marne River |

◄ Shock headlines from August 1914 announce that Great Britain has declared war on Germany.

▲ The French army had the difficult task of defending hundreds of miles of frontier against the enemy.

▲ The German army was the largest and best trained in the world.

▲ In 1914, Britain had the smallest army, but it consisted of professional career soldiers.

◄ Across Europe, eager volunteers rushed to join up at army recruiting offices. Patriotic feelings ran high. Few people believed that the war would last longer than a few months.

# BATTLES OF WORLD WAR I 1914–1917

**In a series of horrific battles along the Western Front, millions of lives were lost to gain only a few miles. The land war soon reached a stalemate.**

Gas masks were introduced in World War I to protect the troops against poison gas attacks by the enemy.

During World War I, fighting took place in several areas. The Western Front was between Germany and northern France, and the Eastern Front between Germany and the Russian forces. There was also fighting at sea and in the Middle East, where the Allied Powers attacked the Ottoman Empire. In Africa, British and French troops attacked German colonies.

On the Western Front, French and British troops, together with thousands of men from the British Empire, occupied a network of deep trenches from September 1914. Facing them, across a few hundred yards of ground known as "no man's land," were trenches occupied by the Germans. Millions of men were killed on the Western Front in battles including Ypres, Verdun, and the Somme. One of the worst was the Third Battle of Ypres, or Passchendaele, in 1917. The troops had to wade through mud up to waist level. In 102 days, the Allies advanced just five miles at a cost of 400,000 lives.

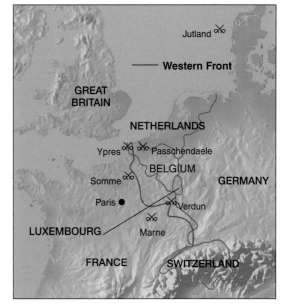

The Western Front stretched across Belgium and northeastern France. Millions of soldiers were killed in battles along it between 1914 and 1918.

For four years, the Western Front did not move more than 20 mi. (32km) in any direction. Barbed wire and machine-gun and artillery defenses made attack futile. Tanks, first used in 1916, could crush barbed wire or machine guns, but were unreliable. Aircraft were more successful, and were used to spot enemy troops, target shells, and drop bombs. The Eastern Front ran from the Baltic to the Black Sea and also had lines of trenches, to which the Russians retreated in September 1914.

▲ Only 12 years after the Wright brothers made their pioneering flight in North Carolina, aircraft were being used in warfare. Although control of the air was not a deciding factor in World War I, the war led to many advances in flight technology.

▶ In September 1914, the German advance toward Paris was stopped short of the capital when the Allies precariously held the line of the Marne River. The French government fled to Bordeaux. The Allied line held, and in their great counterattack, known as the First Battle of the Marne—regarded as one of the decisive battles of the war—the Allies drove the Germans back to the line of the Aisne River.

The war along the Western Front was fought from trenches guarded by barbed wire and machine guns. The conditions were appalling, with knee-deep mud, constant shelling, sniping, and raids. The battles of the Somme and Verdun in France in 1916 cost over two million casualties, but neither side was able to advance more than a few hundred yards.

Invented by two British scientists, Tritton and Wilson, the first tanks were used in the Battle of the Somme in 1916. These vehicles, fitted with machine guns, terrified the German soldiers, but suffered from too many mechanical failures to be fully effective.

## THE WAR AT SEA

There were only two significant sea battles in World War I. The first, in 1914, was when a German fleet was destroyed by the Royal Navy off the Falkland Islands. In 1916, the Battle of Jutland took place and both Germany and Britain claimed victory. However, the German fleet did not leave the port of Kiel again until the end of the war, when it surrendered to the Allies.

German submarines, called U-boats, attacked ships bound for Britain and France. U-boats sank hundreds of Allied ships, nearly crippling Britain. When the U.S.S. *Housatonic* was sunk in 1917, the United States declared war on Germany.

Jutland was the major sea battle of World War I. Although the German fleet inflicted far more serious losses than they sustained, Britain and Germany both claimed victory. After the battle, on May 31, 1916, the German fleet escaped in darkness and returned to port, where they remained for the rest of the war.

## DISASTER AT GALLIPOLI

Turkish officer

Australian private

During 1915, in an attempt to assist the Russians on the Eastern Front, Allied forces bombarded Turkish forts guarding the Dardanelles. Allied troops, including ANZAC forces from Australia and New Zealand, then landed at Gallipoli to try to capture the strategic positions overlooking the narrow straits. But the Allied powers grossly underestimated the strength of the Turkish forces. Almost 15 percent of Australian deaths in the war came from this battle.

# IRELAND: CIVIL UNREST 1916–1923

**Irish frustration at home rule being first granted, and then delayed by World War I, led to rebellion and civil war. Southern Ireland became self-governing in 1921.**

James Connolly (1868–1916) led the Irish Citizen Army. After the Easter Rising, he was shot in jail, even though he was already mortally wounded.

▲ On Easter Monday, April 24, 1916, the Republicans made their headquarters inside Dublin General Post Office. Fighting went on for a week. The Republicans surrendered on April 29. The British army fired heavy guns at the building, and it caught fire.

▶ Armed members of the Irish Citizen Army, founded by James Connolly and others, position themselves on the roof of Dublin's Liberty Hall. Connolly and other leaders of the Easter Rising were executed by the British.

Many Irish people wanted home rule, and a Home Rule Bill was approved by the British Parliament in 1912. This would have become law, and given Ireland its own parliament to deal with domestic affairs, but it was suspended when war broke out in 1914.

In the north, Protestants opposed home rule because they would be a minority in a Catholic country. Some people (Republicans) wanted Ireland to be an independent republic. Many supported a political party called Sinn Féin ("We alone"). Some belonged to the Irish Volunteers, the Irish Republican Brotherhood, or the Irish Citizen Army.

On Easter Monday 1916, members of the Irish Volunteers and the Irish Citizen Army, led by Patrick Pearse and James Connolly, took control of public buildings in Dublin. This event became known as the Easter Rising. From their headquarters in the General Post Office, Pearse and Connolly declared a republic, but were soon defeated by the British army. In the 1918 election, Sinn Féin won 73 of the 105 Irish seats in the British Parliament.

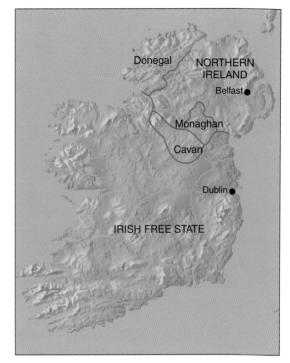

The Anglo-Irish Treaty of 1921 made southern Ireland into a self-governing country. In 1949, it became a republic, completely independent of Britain.

Sinn Féin set up their own parliament, the Dáil Eireann, and declared Ireland to be an independent republic in 1919. This led to war between the Irish Republican Army (IRA) and the Royal Irish Constabulary (RIC). Armed police, the Black-and-Tans, were sent to support the RIC. The fighting continued until 1921.

◄ Michael Collins (1890–1922), center, took part in the 1916 Easter Rising. He was imprisoned by the British. He became leader of Sinn Féin and head of intelligence in the Irish Volunteers. He negotiated the peace treaty with Britain in 1921. He became head of the provisional government in 1922, but was killed in an ambush that same year, as shown in this illustration from a French newspaper.

▲ Éamon de Valera (1882–1975) was born in the United States. He was arrested and imprisoned by the British for his part in the 1916 Easter Rising. In 1926, he founded the Fianna Fáil ("Soldiers of Destiny") Party. Between 1937 and 1959, he served as prime minister of Ireland three times. He then became president until 1973.

## THE ANGLO–IRISH TREATY

The British government wanted to divide Ireland into two countries, with six of the counties of Ulster, in the north, separate from the rest. Under the 1920 Government of Ireland Act, both countries would have some self-government. The six Ulster counties had a Protestant majority, who did not want to be ruled from Dublin. They agreed to the act and formed the new state of Northern Ireland. The Dáil Eireann, led by Éamon de Valera, opposed the act because they wanted complete independence for all Ireland.

In an attempt to bring peace to the country, the Anglo–Irish Treaty of 1921 made southern Ireland into a dominion of Great Britain. Called the Irish Free State, it was established in 1922. But this action led to civil war. On one side were the Free Staters who agreed to the treaty's terms. On the other side were the Republicans.

The civil war lasted until 1923, when de Valera ordered the Republicans to stop fighting. In 1926, he founded a new political party, called Fianna Fáil. In the general election of 1932, he defeated the Free Staters. The new constitution of 1937 changed southern Ireland's name to Eire, but it stayed within the British Commonwealth. It became independent and left the Commonwealth in 1949.

### KEY DATES

| | |
|---|---|
| 1916 | Easter Rising in Dublin is crushed by the British after a week |
| 1918 | In elections, Sinn Féin wins 73 of the 105 Irish seats in the British Parliament |
| 1919 | Sinn Féin declares Ireland independent—this leads to civil war |
| 1922 | Southern Ireland, known as the Irish Free State, becomes a self-governing dominion of Britain |
| 1923 | Civil war ends |
| 1926 | Fianna Fáil Party founded |
| 1937 | New constitution renames southern Ireland Eire |

▼ Both the Free Staters and the Republicans were well supplied with weapons during the civil war. This gun belonged to the Free Staters and was used in County Limerick.

# RUSSIA 1917–1924

**After years of rule by a corrupt and inept government, the people of Russia rose against the czar and his advisers and seized power in November 1917.**

▲ Czar Nicholas II (1868–1918) was forced to abdicate in 1917. He and his family were then imprisoned and killed by the Bolsheviks in 1918.

▲ Grigori Rasputin (1871–1916) was adviser to Czar Nicholas II and his wife Alexandra. They thought he was a holy man who could make their sick son better. But he was hated by the people of Russia.

Following the defeat of Russia by Japan in 1904, there were workers' strikes and revolts throughout Russia. The new czar, Nicholas II, issued a declaration promising civil rights and a national government, called the Duma. The Duma did not keep its promises. Elections were rigged so that reformers were kept out of government. Opponents of the government were arrested, and the leaders fled. But the Russian people thought that the czar was out of touch with the population and that his advisers were corrupt. The government, which had not been very efficient in peacetime, was even less effective during World War I. Soldiers who thought that they would be sent to fight in the war began to question their loyalty to their country.

Food and fuel were in short supply,

In July 1917, troops of the provisional Russian government machine-gunned workers and soldiers in Petrograd (St Petersburg). Kerensky became chief minister, but was overthrown by the Bolsheviks that November.

and many people in the cities began to starve. The economy was on the way to collapse. In March 1917, riots broke out in the capital, St. Petersburg, which had been renamed Petrograd at the start of World War I. Rioting crowds were usually broken up by troops, but this time they refused to obey their orders. When the troops joined the rioters, the czar abdicated, and his advisers resigned. A temporary government was set up, led by Prince George Lvov.

▼ Armed workers and Bolshevik-led soldiers and sailors attacked the Winter Palace in Petrograd on November 7, 1917. Although it was the headquarters of the czar's government, it was not well defended and was soon in Bolshevik hands.

ПРИЗРАК БРОДИТ ПО ЕВРОПЕ, ПРИЗРАК КОММУНИЗМА

◀ Vladimir Lenin (1870–1924) became a Marxist in 1887 after his brother was executed for trying to assassinate the czar.

▲ Leon Trotsky (1879–1940) was the most influential person after Lenin in the revolution. During the Russian Civil War, he led the Red Army to victory. He hoped to become president after Lenin's death, but lost to Stalin.

## THE BOLSHEVIKS SEIZE POWER

The government found it difficult to carry on with the war. Alexander Kerensky succeeded Prince Lvov as chief minister. After the March revolution, the Bolshevik Party was still determined to seize power. In April, their leader, Vladimir Lenin, returned from exile.

The Bolsheviks in Petrograd wanted Russia to become a communist state. After struggling with the government, the Bolsheviks, led by Lenin, seized power in November 1917. In March 1918, the new government signed the Treaty of Brest-Litovsk which made peace with Germany. It moved the capital from Petrograd to Moscow, broke up the large estates, and gave the farmland to the peasants. Control of factories was given to workers. Banks were taken into state control, and Church property was seized.

The White Russians (anticommunists) opposed these moves and, in 1918, the Russian Civil War broke out. The White Russians were finally defeated by the Bolshevik Red Army in 1922. By this time, around 100,000 people had been killed and two million had emigrated. That year, the country's name was changed to the Union of Soviet Socialist Republics (U.S.S.R.), or Soviet Union. Lenin led the U.S.S.R. until his death in 1924, when a new power struggle began between Leon Trotsky and Josef Stalin. Stalin won and dominated Soviet politics until 1953.

▲ Josef Stalin (1879–1953) joined the Bolshevik Party in 1903. In 1922, Stalin became general secretary of the Communist Party and in 1924, leader of the U.S.S.R.

▶ When Josef Stalin became leader of the U.S.S.R. in 1924 he carried out the Great Purge—millions of people were arrested and murdered. He decided to strip farmers of their land in order to reorganize farming into larger state-owned units called collectives. His orders were brutally carried out by the army and secret police. Villages were burned and the villagers killed or evicted.

# WORLD WAR I: THE AFTERMATH 1918–1923

**Germany, freed from Russia, launched an assault on the Western Front in 1918. Newly arrived U.S. troops helped stop the attack and Germany asked for peace.**

World War I involved whole populations. Women went to work to produce armaments and keep industries going while the men were at war.

The arrival of American troops in Europe in 1917 meant that the Allies could launch fresh attacks on the Western Front. In 1918, Russia withdrew from the war, so German soldiers were no longer needed on the Eastern Front. By 1918, more than 3.5 million German soldiers were fighting on the Western Front. In March, they broke through the trenches and advanced toward Paris. The French counterattacked in July, and in August, British tanks broke the German line at Amiens. As the United States poured troops into France, the Germans retreated.

The fighting in World War I left many areas of Belgium and northeastern France devastated. Cities such as Ypres, in northwestern Belgium, were left in ruins.

By October, the fighting was nearing the German border and a naval blockade was causing starvation in Germany. Early on the morning of November 11, Germany signed an armistice. Kaiser Wilhelm II abdicated, and at 11 o'clock, fighting in World War I ended. Almost 10 million people had been killed and over 20 million wounded. Most were young men, and their loss changed the social structure of several countries. As a result, many women gained more equality and freedom than they had had before the war. In many places, they also gained the right to vote.

▶ German submarines, or U-boats, attacked ships on the surface by firing torpedoes at them from under the water. They were so successful in attacking Allied ships that Britain came close to defeat in 1917.

▶ On January 31, 1917 the Germans announced to the world that they would begin unrestricted submarine warfare. This threatened U.S. ships. In February, U-boats sank a U.S. ship, the *Housatonic*. President Wilson cut off diplomatic relations with Germany, and on April 6, the United States declared war. The arrival of American troops in Europe tipped the balance in 1918 when the Germans launched a major, final attack on the Western Front.

## THE TREATY OF VERSAILLES

World War I was formally ended by the Paris Peace Conference, which was held between 1919 and 1920. All the nations that had been involved in the war (except Germany) met to draw up a peace agreement, but the United States, Britain, France, and Italy led the process. Five separate treaties were proposed.

The most important was the Treaty of Versailles, which punished Germany for its part in World War I. Vast amounts of reparations (compensation) were to be given to the Allies. The size of Germany was reduced and seven million people were removed from German rule. Germany had to surrender all its overseas colonies and reduce its army to 100,000 men. The German economy collapsed and this led to hyperinflation. Other nations also suffered as they tried to pay back money they had borrowed during the war. This led to political and economic upheaval.

Further strife was caused by the redrawing of international boundaries in Europe following the collapse of the German, Austro–Hungarian, Russian, and Ottoman (Turkish) empires.

### THE LEAGUE OF NATIONS

The League of Nations was also set up at the Paris Peace Conference. Its aim was to help keep world peace, settling disputes by discussion and agreement, but it failed. The problem was that it had little power because, although it had been drafted by President Wilson, the United States refused to join. There were still rivalries among the 53 members. These weakened the League and reduced its power, so by the late 1930s, few countries took any notice of it.

The Treaty of Versailles was signed on June 28, 1919. It declared that Germany's rulers were solely responsible for the outbreak of war, and so Germany had to make reparations (pay money) to the Allies.

## HYPERINFLATION

German industry was totally destroyed in the war and the country was unable to repay the reparations demanded by the Allies in the Treaty of Versailles. The Germans regarded the Treaty as unjust and indefensible. One of the outcomes was that the German economy was hit by hyperinflation in the 1920s. Hyperinflation is fast inflation that causes the value of money to drop very quickly. Firms now needed carts full of banknotes just to pay their staff a week's wages.

After the Paris Peace Conference (1919–1920), Germany gave back lands to France and Belgium. The Hapsburg monarchy was ended, and Poland, Czechoslovakia, Hungary, and Yugoslavia all became new states.

◄ Because of hyperinflation, this million mark note issued in Germany during the 1920s was worth virtually nothing.

# THE RISE OF FASCISM 1922–1939

**The political philosophy known as fascism became popular in many European countries during the 1930s. To many, it offered a way out of economic decline.**

▲ Benito Mussolini (1883–1945) became the fascist dictator of Italy in 1922.

▼ Italians make the fascist salute during a procession led by Mussolini in 1942.

Fascist ideas gained support after World War I. The first fascist government appeared in Italy in 1922. The term "fascism" comes from the Latin *fasces*— a bundle of rods with an ax that was a symbol of power in ancient Rome. Fascism was based on the idea that a nation would only succeed through disciplined, ruthless action and a determined will. To many people, it offered a way out of economic decline.

Fascists believed that achieving a worthwhile aim made any action they took acceptable. Schools, religion, newspapers, and the arts and sciences were expected to serve the nation. Military power and a secret police organization supported the fascist governments. Fascists believed that their race was superior to others. They opposed communism and encouraged national pride and racism (prejudice against other races). In Germany, this hatred was directed especially at Jews and gypsies.

## ITALY AND BENITO MUSSOLINI

In Italy, the Fascist Party was founded by Benito Mussolini in 1919, when economic depression and the threat posed by the communists helped its rise to power. In 1928–1929 he imposed one-party government.

To avenge a humiliating defeat in 1896, Mussolini's army invaded Abyssinia (Ethiopia) in 1935–1936. Britain, France, and other countries condemned the invasion. So, Italy, keen to become a major power, then formed an alliance with Germany. They became known as the Axis Powers. In May 1939, Mussolini and the German fascist dictator, Adolf Hitler, agreed a military treaty—the Pact of Steel. Mussolini's leadership led Italy to defeat in World War II, and he was dismissed and imprisoned by King Victor Emmanuel in 1943. He was later released by German soldiers and set up fascist rule in the north of the country. In April 1945, he was captured and executed by Italian partisans.

## GERMANY AND ADOLF HITLER

The terms of the Versailles Treaty were harsh on Germany, and the economic recession of the early 1930s saw large-scale unemployment in the country. The fragile Weimar Republic was under threat from the communists and Adolf Hitler's National Socialist German Workers' Party (known as Nazis). Hitler promised to end unemployment and poverty, and to build the country into a great state after its humiliation in World War I. Amid political turmoil and violence, President Hindenburg appointed Hitler as chancellor in January 1933. As *Führer* (leader), Hitler crushed all opposition, and ordered the murder of millions of Jews, gypsies, and others. In 1939, he led Germany into World War II, but killed himself when faced with defeat.

## THE SPREAD OF FASCISM

In other countries, economic difficulties and the threat of communism in the postwar period led to the establishment of many fascist governments. In Spain, the army leader, General Miguel Primo de Rivera, took power in 1923, and ruled until 1930. In 1933, his son José Antonio formed the fascist Falange Party.

To avenge Italy's humiliating defeat in 1896, Mussolini sent his army to invade Abyssinia. In 1936, Italian troops under General Badoglio victoriously entered the capital, Addis Ababa. The invasion led to a worldwide outcry and Italy's withdrawal from the League of Nations.

The Falangists supported General Francisco Franco's nationalist forces during the Spanish Civil War (1936–1939). With the support of Germany and Italy, they took power in 1939. Franco ruled as dictator until his death in 1975.

Fascism also won support in Portugal, Austria, the Balkan states, and South America in the years before World War II. Juan Perón ruled Argentina with his wife Eva in the 1940s and 1950s. Antonio Salazar was dictator of Portugal from 1932 to 1968. In England, former Cabinet minister Sir Oswald Mosley founded the Britsh Union of Fascists in 1931, during a period of economic depression and mass unemployment. His public meetings were known for the violence between his supporters and his opponents.

### KEY DATES

| | |
|---|---|
| 1919 | Italian Fascist Party founded by Mussolini |
| 1922 | Mussolini becomes prime minister of Italy |
| 1923 | Primo de Rivera takes power in Spain |
| 1928 | Mussolini becomes dictator of Italy |
| 1933 | José Antonio Primo de Rivera forms Spanish Falange Party; Hitler appointed chancellor of Germany |
| 1936 | Italian troops invade Abyssinia |
| 1939 | General Franco becomes dictator of Spain; World War II begins |

◀ Sir Oswald Mosley (1896–1980) resigned from Ramsay MacDonald's Labour government in 1931 to form the British Union of Fascists. The party stirred up anti-Semitism, especially in the East End of London, where many Jewish people lived.

▲ This antifascist poster showing Hitler threatening the world was issued in 1936 by Gruppo DAS, an antifascist group in Spain.

▲ José Antonio Primo de Rivera (1903–1936) founded the Spanish Falange nationalist movement in 1933.

▲ Adolf Hitler rose from obscurity to found the National Socialist German Workers' Party. During political unrest in 1933, he was appointed chancellor.

# U.S.A. BETWEEN THE WARS 1919–1941

**After World War, I the United States went back to its isolationism. The booming economy of the 1920s was followed by the Depression of the 1930s.**

Warren Harding (1865–1923) was elected 29th president in 1920. His health was affected when several cabinet members were involved in an oil scandal. He died suddenly while still in office.

▲ Al Capone (1899–1947) was born in Brooklyn. From 1925, he led Chicago's South Side Gang, and dominated the city's criminal underworld. He was finally jailed for tax evasion in 1931.

▶ Charles Lindbergh (1902–1974) made the first solo nonstop flight across the Atlantic in 1927. He became a hero to people around the world.

Before the outbreak of war in Europe, the United States had a policy of isolationism. This meant that the country only became involved in world affairs when it was necessary for self-defense. The United States was physically cut off from most of the world, preoccupied with its own affairs, and preferred to stay out of entangling alliances.

When World War I broke out, most Americans wanted to stay neutral. Between 1914–1917, President Wilson tried to mediate between the warring European countries. The United States did not enter the war until 1917, after its ships were attacked by German U-boats.

After World War I, the desire for isolationism grew stronger. The country had seen what happened in Europe because of alliances. Also, people were alarmed by what was happening in Russia. The Senate voted not to join the League of Nations—President Wilson's brainchild. By the early 1920s, the U.S. economy was coming out of its postwar slump, and industrial production began to grow.

In Chicago, gangs fought each other to gain control of illegal saloons called speakeasies. This scene depicts the murder of gangster John Dillinger in Chicago in 1934.

In 1920, newly-elected president Warren Harding promised "a return to normalcy." This meant not getting involved with other countries and strengthening law and order—including a ban on alcohol. This ban led to a lack of respect for the law and a growth of violence.

## PROHIBITION AND GANGSTERS

Before World War I, the Women's Christian Temperance Union and other pressure groups fought for Prohibition. They argued that alcohol is a dangerous drug that destroys family life and leads to crime. In 1920, their efforts led to the 18th Amendment to the Constitution. This banned the manufacture, sale, and transportation of alcoholic beverages in the United States. Many thought this would reduce crime, but the opposite happened. Gangsters set up illegal saloons called speakeasies, where they sold bootleg, or illegal liquor. Warfare between competing gangs became commonplace, and corruption in law enforcement agencies was rife. When it became clear that Prohibition was not working, the 21st Amendment was passed, and Prohibition ended in 1933.

## BOOM AND BUST

Following World War I, the United States withdrew from the world stage and continued its policy of isolationism into the 1930s. The country even put restrictions on immigration. During the economic boom of the 1920s, the United States became the first country in which millions of people drove cars, listened to radio, and enjoyed movies. It was a time when the arts flourished. The motion picture industry was growing. The New York skyline kept changing as more new buildings were added. But in 1929, the Roaring Twenties—the Jazz Age—ended in total economic collapse. A new president, Franklin Delano Roosevelt, would have to use all his skills to rebuild his country and restore his people's faith.

## THE END OF ISOLATIONISM

Roosevelt continued his country's isolationist policies after war broke out in Europe in 1939. But these policies ended abruptly when the Japanese attacked the U.S. Pacific Fleet at Pearl Harbor on December 7, 1941. President Roosevelt described December 7 as "a date which will live in infamy." The following day, Congress declared war on Japan, and the United States entered World War II. Isolationism had ended.

▲ Kid Ory and his Original Creole Jazz Band perform in the 1920s. Jazz developed around 1900 in New Orleans. By the 1920s, the music was called Dixieland, and soon, Chicago, St. Louis, and New York were the centers of jazz.

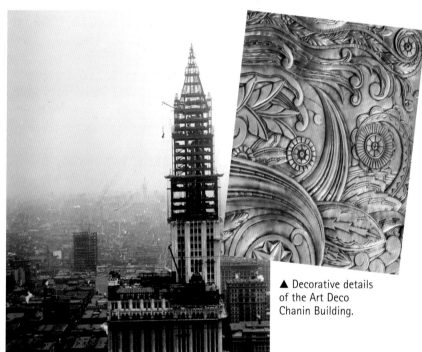

▲ Decorative details of the Art Deco Chanin Building.

▲ Skyscrapers only became possible when Elisha Otis developed the elevator, and steel girders began to be used in construction in the late 1800s. In New York, the Woolworth Building, designed in 1913 by architect Cass Gilbert, was for a time the tallest building in the world.

◄ The police enforce Prohibition by pouring illegal liquor down the drains of New York City in about 1921.

## KEY DATES

| | |
|---|---|
| 1917 | The United States enters World War I |
| 1918 | World War I ends |
| 1919 | The Senate votes not to join League of Nations |
| 1920 | Warren Harding becomes 29th president; 18th Amendment introduced—Prohibition era begins |
| 1925 | Al Capone becomes leader of Chicago's South Side Gang |
| 1929 | Wall Street Crash and start of Great Depression |
| 1931 | The gangster Al Capone is jailed for tax evasion |
| 1933 | 18th Amendment repealed—Prohibition ends |
| 1941 | Japanese attack Pearl Harbor; The United States enters World War II |

# CHINA 1911–1935

**Following the fall of the Manchus in 1911, and the founding of the Republic of China, the country soon became embroiled in a long-running civil war.**

When the Chinese nationalist leader, Sun Yatsen (1866–1925) died, he was buried in this tomb on Zijin Mountain, just east of Nanjing.

Opposition to the rule of the Manchus eventually led to the 1911 Chinese Revolution and their downfall. The revolutionary leader Sun Yatsen was named provisional president. The Republic of China was founded on February 12, 1912 with the official abdication of the imperial government. Sun Yatsen's presidency did not last long—he resigned because of lack of support just three days later. China was then ruled by the military leader Yuan Shikai until his death in 1916, when the political situation in the country began to disintegrate.

The followers of Yuan Shikai set up a government in Beijing, and Sun Yatsen's Guomindang (nationalist) Party formed a rival government in Canton. For the next ten years, the country was embroiled in civil war. Student demonstrations against the terms of the Treaty of Versailles in 1919, when Japan took over German colonies in China, eventually led to the founding of the Chinese Communist Party in 1921. With help from the Russians, Sun Yatsen reorganized the Guomindang Party and allowed Communist Party members to join. When Sun Yatsen died in 1925, leadership of China and the Guomindang Party passed to Jiang Jieshi.

## CHINESE CIVIL WAR

In 1926, Jiang Jieshi launched an expedition against the warlords in the north who wanted to overthrow the nationalist government. He was helped in this by the Chinese Communist Party. Together, they defeated the warlords. But in 1927, the Communist–Guomindang alliance ended and the two sides started fighting each other. This fighting became known as the Chinese Civil War. Jiang Jieshi set up his capital in Nanjing (Nanking). Later that year, the nationalists drove the communists out of Shanghai and into the Jiangxi hills. The nationalists claimed to have united China, but they still did not have control of the country.

▲ Jiang Jieshi (Chiang Kai-shek) (1887–1975) took control of the Guomindang Party in 1926. In 1927, he set up the nationalist government in Nanjing. After fighting against the Japanese invasion, he was ousted by the communists and fled to Taiwan (Formosa), where he established the Republic of China.

▶ Nationalist forces defending an area near Shanghai against the communist army in 1927.

380

## THE LONG MARCH

In October 1933, the Chinese nationalist leader Jiang Jieshi launched a massive attack against the communists in Jiangxi, southern China. In October 1934, 100,000 communists left Jiangxi and set out on what has become known as the Long March. Led by Mao Zedong, they traveled for nearly 6,300 mi. (10,000km) to northern China. They endured terrible conditions, cold, and hunger during the long journey. Only one fifth of them reached their destination.
The inset picture (right) shows Mao Zedong with Zhou Enlai during the Long March.

### THE RISE OF MAO ZEDONG

In 1931, taking advantage of the turmoil within China, the Japanese occupied Manchuria and set up the puppet state of Manchukuo in 1932. Meanwhile, the communists had set up a rival government (the Jiangxi Soviet) in southern China in 1931. In the same year, Mao Zedong became chairman of the Jiangxi Soviet. The communists built up their forces in Jiangxi and withstood four attempts by the Guomindang to oust them. In October 1933, Jiang Jieshi launched a massive attack against the communists with the intention of exterminating them. The communists resisted for a year, then in October 1934, 100,000 of them left Jiangxi and set out on the Long March.

### THE LONG MARCH

Mao Zedong led the Long March for almost 6,300 mi. (10,000km) until they reached Yan'an in Shaanxi Province in northern China. It took them until October 1935, and only about 20,000 of the original 100,000 marchers survived to reach their destination. The Long March established Mao Zedong as leader of the Chinese communists.

### KEY DATES

| | |
|---|---|
| 1911 | Chinese Revolution, end of the Manchus |
| 1912 | Republic of China is founded |
| 1921 | Chinese Communist Party founded |
| 1925 | Sun Yatsen dies |
| 1926 | Jiang Jieshi takes control of Guomindang (nationalist) Party |
| 1927 | Chinese Civil War starts |
| 1931 | Japanese occupy Manchuria |

▲ During the Long March of 1934–1935, the communists fled from nationalist forces in Jiangxi, winding through southern and western China, and finally reaching Yan'an in Shaanxi Province. Here, Mao Zedong emerged as the leader of the communists.

Mao Zedong (1893–1976) became involved with the Chinese Communist Party in 1919, and in 1931 became chairman of the Jiangxi Soviet. During 1934–1935, he led the Long March. In 1949, he proclaimed the People's Republic of China.

# THE GREAT DEPRESSION 1929–1939

**After World War I the U.S. economy saw rapid growth. The Wall Street Crash of 1929 brought an abrupt end to this and led to worldwide depression.**

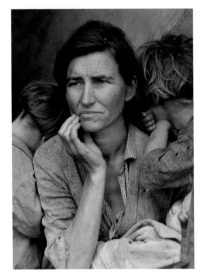

During the Depression of the 1930s, thousands of poverty-stricken American families fled the East Coast and rural farming areas to search for work in the West, especially in California.

▼ In October 1936, 200 men from Jarrow in northeast England marched to London with a petition. A major shipyard had closed down and caused unemployment to soar.

The Great Depression came at the end of a period of economic turbulence. In 1919, the Treaty of Versailles forced Germany to pay a lot of compensation to the Allies. Many Germans lost all their savings as the value of their money plummeted. In Britain, France, and the United States, industry struggled to adjust to peacetime trade. Millions of soldiers came home and looked for jobs, but there were none. Trade unions called on workers to strike against employers who imposed wage cuts. Food prices fell so low that many farmers were ruined and forced to give up their land.

During the 1920s, the U.S. economy grew at a tremendous rate. This was due to the continued development of industry and manufacturing. The growth was also encouraged by the economic policies of presidents Harding and Coolidge. Stock market share prices had been forced up beyond their real value by reckless speculators.

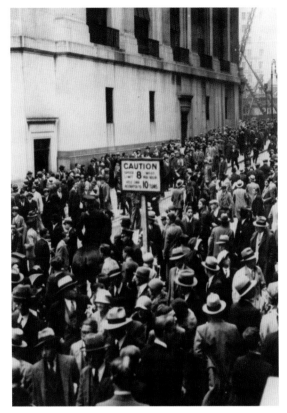

On October 29, 1929, the Wall Street Crash caused panic on the streets of New York. Share prices dropped so fast that many people lost all their money.

### THE WALL STREET CRASH

In October 1929, people began to panic and sell their shares rapidly. On a single day, almost 13 million shares were sold on the New York Stock Exchange. This started the crisis known as the Wall Street Crash. It soon affected the whole world.

Many people lost all their money. Banks and businesses closed. Unemployment began to rise. By 1933, the worst year of the Depression, there were 12 million people unemployed in the United States alone. Those who still had jobs saw their salaries halved, and more than 85,000 businesses went under. President Hoover arranged for federal loans to banks and businesses, but refused to give anything directly to the unemployed. People lost all faith in him as a leader.

The situation was made worse by a drought on the Great Plains. The soil turned to dust in many places and blew away in the wind, leading to crop failure on a massive scale.

## THE DUST BOWL

Because of a long drought in the 1930s, the soil in the southern Great Plains of the United States became very dry. A series of terrible dust storms swept across the area, which became known as the Dust Bowl. By 1933, hundreds of millions of tons of topsoil had been carried off by the winds, destroying the land. Faced with ruin, thousands of families fled the Dust Bowl looking for work in California and elsewhere.

▲ Franklin D. Roosevelt (1882–1945) was elected governor of New York in 1928. In 1932, he was elected president, and in 1933, he introduced the New Deal to combat the problems caused by the Depression.

## ROOSEVELT'S NEW DEAL

For the first two years of the Depression, President Hoover and the federal government took little direct action, believing that the economy would recover naturally. Franklin D. Roosevelt was elected president in 1932, and in 1933, he introduced the New Deal to combat the problems caused by the Depression. This was a set of laws designed to ease the worst of the poverty, provide support for the banks, and protect people's savings. Farm prices were subsidized, a minimum wage was introduced, and a huge construction program was started to create employment. The New Deal helped considerably, but it was not until 1939, when the outbreak of World War II gave an enormous boost to heavy industry, that the Depression came to an end.

▶ In the U.S.S.R., Josef Stalin proved to be a ruthless and dictatorial leader. In 1928–1933 he introduced the *kolkhoz* or collective farm (right) as part of his economic planning. However, in order to overcome opposition from the richest peasant farmers, he resorted to executions and imprisonment in Siberia. These actions disrupted agricultural production and led to a terrible famine.

## GLOBAL DEPRESSION

The Wall Street Crash led to the collapse of the system of international loans that handled war reparations. This affected Europe and North America directly. Other regions were also badly hit since much of their economies relied on selling food and raw materials to Europe and North America. As these markets collapsed, many people around the world lost their jobs. As a result, unrest increased, and nationalism grew in many countries.

▲ Under Roosevelt's New Deal many unemployed people were given work on government projects. Here, young members of the Civilian Conservation Corps (CCC) lift seedlings from the ground in Oregon for the Forest Service.

383

# WEIMAR AND HITLER 1919–1939

**Adolf Hitler took advantage of the economic and social turmoil in Germany in the 1920s to promote fascism. He seized power in 1933.**

▲ Field Marshal von Hindenburg (1847–1934) was president of the German Republic. At his death, the chancellor Adolf Hitler became *Führer* of Germany.

Following Germany's defeat in 1918, Kaiser Wilhelm II abdicated and fled to the Netherlands. Germany became a republic, and its new government ruled from Weimar, instead of Berlin. From 1919 to 1933, Germany was known as the Weimar Republic. Following elections in January 1919, Friedrich Ebert, a socialist, became its first president. Under his leadership, the Weimar Republic accepted the harsh terms of the Treaty of Versailles. In 1922–1923, the Republic survived several attempts to bring it down, first by the Bolsheviks, then by financial pressure, and finally through an attempted political revolution led by an unknown Austrian fascist named Adolf Hitler.

Ebert died in 1925 and was succeeded by Field Marshal Paul von Hindenburg, who was by then 78 years old. Germany joined the League of Nations in 1926. However, the worldwide Depression of the early 1930s led to massive social and financial problems in Germany.

## THE NUREMBERG RALLIES

German soldiers parade with the Standards of Victory at a Nazi Party rally in Nuremberg in 1933. The Nazi propaganda techniques of the 1930s were successfully used to create enormous public support for Hitler. His policies were popular because they promised to make Germany powerful.

## THE RISE OF ADOLF HITLER

The next presidential election was in 1932, when Germany was in economic crisis, with sky-high inflation and unemployment. Hindenburg was elected as president again, with Adolf Hitler, by then the leader of the National Socialist German Workers' (Nazi) Party, in second place. By using intimidation and violence started by Hitler's followers, the Nazi Party won the most seats in the Reichstag (German parliament). Hindenburg reluctantly appointed Hitler as chancellor in January 1933.

When the Reichstag was burned down in February, Hitler brought in emergency powers and called for new elections. By April 1933, he had gained absolute power in Germany and established a single-party government. As a result, Germany withdrew from the League of Nations.

On the "Night of the Long Knives" in June 1934, Hitler had many of his rivals killed. When Hindenburg died in August, Hitler was appointed *Führer* (leader) of the Third Reich (German Empire). He set out to avenge the humiliation brought on Germany by the Treaty of Versailles and to make Germany a powerful empire.

▲ Adolf Hitler (1889–1945) was born in Austria. In World War I, he served in the German army and won the Iron Cross. Hitler became leader of the Nazi Party in 1920.

## THE RISE OF ANTI-SEMITISM

Blaming the Jews and the labor unions for Germany's problems, Hitler and his Nazi Party started persecuting them. The Nuremberg Laws of 1935 deprived Jews of their German citizenship and banned them from marrying non-Jews. Many Jews were forced to live in ghettos and to wear a yellow star to show that they were Jewish.

On *Kristallnacht* ("Night of Broken Glass") in November 1938, Nazi mobs attacked Jewish property and synagogues all across Germany. Around 30,000 Jews were arrested—the start of a full-scale massacre of Jews in Germany. During the next seven years, six million Jews from many areas of Europe were murdered as part of Hitler's plan to exterminate the Jewish population.

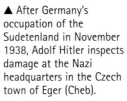

▲ After Germany's occupation of the Sudetenland in November 1938, Adolf Hitler inspects damage at the Nazi headquarters in the Czech town of Eger (Cheb).

▲ The deliberate burning of the Reichstag building in Berlin on February 27, 1933, was an excuse for Adolf Hitler to bring in emergency powers and call for new elections.

## GERMAN MILITARY EXPANSION

In 1935, Germany abolished its agreement to the armament restrictions imposed by the 1919 Treaty of Versailles. In 1936, its forces entered the Rhineland, an area of Germany that had been demilitarized at the end of World War I. Germany entered into alliances with fascist Italy and the military rulers of Japan. German forces also became involved in the Spanish Civil War, where they supported the fascists, led by General Francisco Franco.

▲ In Hitler's Germany, most Jews were forced to wear a yellow star to show that they were Jewish.

### KEY DATES

| 1919 | Friedrich Ebert becomes first president of German Republic |
| 1921 | Adolf Hitler becomes leader of Nazi Party |
| 1925 | Ebert dies; Hindenberg becomes president |
| 1933 | Hitler is appointed chancellor |
| 1934 | Hindenberg dies, and Hitler becomes Führer; The "Night of the Long Knives" takes place |
| 1935 | Jews deprived of German citizenship |
| 1936 | German forces enter demilitarized Rhineland; Germany forms alliances with Italy and Japan |
| 1938 | Germany annexes Austria and the Sudetenland |
| 1939 | Germany annexes Czechoslovakia and invades Poland—World War II starts |

▶ When Hitler came to power, he used every means to destroy opposition. This included the imposition of state censorship of newspapers, books, and radio. In support of this, students and members of the Nazi Party threw banned literature into a bonfire in Berlin in May 1933.

# THE SPANISH CIVIL WAR 1936–1939

**The Spanish Civil War was a battle between two opposing ideologies—fascism and socialism. Fascism won—to be followed by 36 years of dictatorial rule.**

Francisco Franco (1892–1975) led the rebellion against the republican government in 1936. From 1939 until his death, he ruled Spain as dictator.

Before World War I, Spain sent military expeditions to strengthen its position in northern Morocco. In 1921, the Spanish forces were defeated by the Berber leader, Abd el-Krim, and it was not until 1927 that Spain was able to subdue the Berbers. In 1923, a military defeat in Morocco led to a fascist military dictatorship in Spain, headed by General Primo de Rivera.

Primo de Rivera ruled Spain until he fell from power in 1930. In the following year, King Alfonso XIII gave in to the demand for elections. The Republican Party won, and the monarchy was overthrown. During the following years, the government survived revolts in Asturias and Catalonia, and a new Popular Front government was elected in February 1936.

The new government under the presidency of Manuel Azana included members of the Socialist Workers' Party and the Communist Party. With their support, it opposed the power of the Roman Catholic Church in Spanish affairs. The Church was supported by the army and by the fascists.

Both men and women took part in the civil war. These republicans are shown raising their fists in a photograph from 1938. The U.S.S.R. and the International Brigade of volunteers helped the republicans.

### FASCISM VERSUS SOCIALISM

On July 17 1936, army generals in Morocco, in North Africa, began a rebellion. Led by General Francisco Franco, and supported by the nationalists, or Falange Party, they invaded Spain. They had the support of the fascist governments of Italy and Germany. The rebellion led to a bitter civil war. By the end of 1936, the nationalists controlled most of western and southern Spain.

▲ This poster by the General Union of Workers (UGT) translates as "Peasants! The revolution is as necessary as the shoots on the vine."

► The Nationalists were supported by the fascist governments of Italy and Germany. This photograph shows nationalist troops just north of Madrid in January 1939.

## BATTLEGROUND OF BELIEFS

The republicans, supported by the Soviet Union, held the urban areas in the north and east, including the cities of Barcelona, Bilbao, Madrid, and Valencia. The nationalists captured Bilbao in 1937. In support of the nationalists, German dive-bombers attacked the Basque town of Guernica on April 27 of that year and killed hundreds of civilians. This was the first time that unrestricted aerial bombing was used in wartime against civilians, and marked a turning point in modern warfare.

The Spanish Civil War was a battleground between the beliefs of fascism and socialism. People from many countries, supporting one side or the other, volunteered to travel to Spain to fight because of their political ideals.

Some 750,000 people were killed in the war before government forces surrendered Barcelona in January 1939, and Madrid in March, to the nationalists. General Franco was declared "Caudillo of the Realm and Head of State."

Franco banned any opposition to the Falange Party, restored power to the Roman Catholic Church and took Spain out of the League of Nations. Although sympathetic to Hitler, he kept Spain neutral during World War II. Franco ruled Spain until his death in 1975, when the monarchy and democracy were restored.

▲ General Franco's troops are shown in battle with the republicans in the streets of Madrid during 1936. The surrender of Madrid by the republicans in March 1939 marked the end of the civil war.

▼ A turning point in modern warfare was the unrestricted aerial bombing of civilians in the town of Guernica by German aircraft in 1937.

387

# CHINA AND JAPAN AT WAR 1931–1945

**While the Chinese communists and nationalists were fighting a bitter civil war, Japan's expansionist policies and military strength were being felt in the region.**

▲ This American cartoon shows the League of Nations and Uncle Sam watching the fight between Japan and China. The 1931 invasion of Manchuria was the first true test of the League of Nations, of which Japan was a member and the United States was not.

▼ A truck full of Japanese soldiers awaits orders in 1933. The Chinese nationalist government announced that it would not negotiate directly with Japan, but would mobilize troops in its defense.

By 1905, the Japanese had defeated both China and Russia and taken control of Korea and Taiwan (Formosa), becoming the strongest military nation in the region. With the help of foreign expertise, industry expanded rapidly in Japan from 1900 to 1925. Industrial investment depended on heavy taxes levied on peasants. However, the industries, especially silk production, depended largely on foreign markets. During the Depression, these markets collapsed and many Japanese factories came to a halt. Faced with a growing population and weak political leadership, the military began to expand Japan's influence over its neighbors.

To keep control of the resource-rich region of Manchuria, in northeast China, the Japanese occupied the city of Mukden in 1931. In 1932, they set up a puppet state ruled for them by the last Chinese emperor, Puyi.

At the same time, China was ready to try to reclaim Manchuria, which Japan had dominated since 1905. An explosion on the south Manchurian railroad in 1931 led the Japanese to occupy the city of Mukden (Shenyang) in Manchuria. There they set up a puppet state called Manchukuo in 1932. Officially, it was ruled by Puyi, the last Chinese emperor, but in fact, the Japanese army was in control.

388

## JAPAN INVADES CHINA

During 1935–1936, Inner Mongolia came largely under Japanese influence. In China, civil war between the nationalists and the communists continued. Jiang Jieshi, leader of the nationalists, was captured by the communists in 1936. He was released when he agreed to stop fighting them and join the fight against the Japanese. The two sides became unwilling allies when Japan launched a full-scale invasion of China in 1937.

The better-equipped Japanese forces attacked Chinese cities, including Tianjin, Beijing, and Shanghai. Their massacre of over 100,000 Chinese in Nanjing (Nanking) came to be known as "the Rape of Nanking." Despite Chinese resistance, Japan controlled most of eastern China by 1938, and had installed puppet governments in Beijing and Nanjing. Jiang Jieshi and his nationalist government moved to Sichuan, where they received military supplies from the United States and Britain.

Meanwhile, Mao Zedong's communists still controlled much of northwest China. When the Japanese tried to advance westward in 1939, they were stopped by the Soviet army. The Chinese–Japanese War lasted until 1945, when Japan surrendered in World War II.

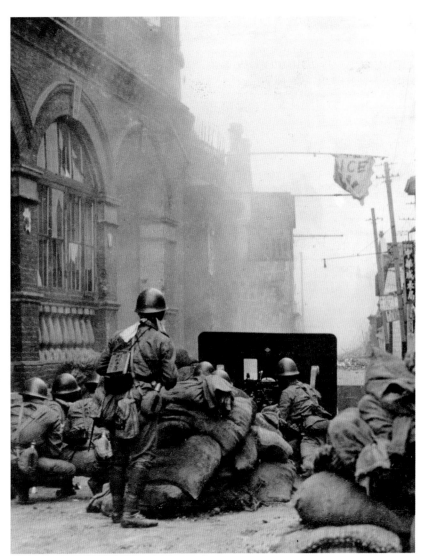

▲ Following the takeover of Manchuria, Japan launched a full-scale attack on China. In 1937, the better-equipped Japanese troops fought a long and bloody battle against the Chinese nationalist army, in Shanghai (above). They went on to take Nanjing, massacring many thousands of civilians.

▼ Thousands of civilians were killed when Japanese forces attacked the city of Shanghai in 1937. This photograph shows the terrible scenes of carnage at Shanghai station following the Japanese attack.

▲ During the reign of Emperor Hirohito (1901–1989), Japan had an aggressive policy toward its neighbors. After World War II, Japan became a strong industrial nation. Hirohito's death ended the longest reign in Japanese history.

▲ Following its occupation of Manchuria, Japan invaded eastern China, attacking Tianjin, Beijing, Shanghai, and Nanjing. By 1938, they occupied most of eastern China.

# GERMAN EXPANSION 1938–1939

**Hoping to avoid another war, Britain and France tolerated Hitler's expansionist policies, and allowed Germany to annex Austria and Czechoslovakia.**

After the signing of the Munich Agreement in September 1938, Britain's prime minister, Neville Chamberlain, declared, "I believe it is peace for our time."

German troops marched into Vienna in 1938. Hitler wanted to unite all German-speaking peoples into a Greater Germany, an important part of his vision of the third German Empire, or Third Reich.

▲ Artur von Seyss-Inquart (1892–1946), the leader of the Austrian Nazis, was a member of the Austrian government. He invited the Germans to occupy his country and make it a part of the Third Reich. The annnexation of Austria in March 1938 brought little criticism from Britain or France.

▶ German troops entered Prague in April 1939. To appease the Nazis, Czechoslovakia was forced to return the Sudetenland to Germany in 1938. However, this failed to appease Hitler, and German forces invaded Czechoslovakia on March 15, 1939.

One of Adolf Hitler's ambitions was to unite Germany and Austria. This union had been forbidden by the Treaty of Versailles in 1919, because France and other countries thought it would make Germany too powerful. By the early 1930s, however, many people in Germany and Austria wanted their countries to unite. In 1934, an attempted Nazi coup in Austria failed. In 1938, Hitler met with the Austrian chancellor, Kurt von Schuschnigg, and made new demands. With chaos and German troops threatening his country, Schuschnigg resigned in favor of Artur von Seyss-Inquart, leader of the Austrian Nazis. He invited German troops to occupy Austria, and the union, or *Anschluss*, of the two countries was formally announced on March 13, 1938.

Hitler also wanted to reclaim areas of Europe given to other states by the Treaty of Versailles. One of these was areas was Czechoslovakia's Sudetenland. The Munich Agreement of 1938 was signed as an attempt to keep peace in Europe.

This agreement gave the Sudetenland to Germany. This was seen as a reasonable concession to Hitler—a policy known as appeasement. But it was not enough for Hitler. He broke the agreement, and seized all of Czechoslovakia in March 1939.

390

# THE START OF WORLD WAR II 1939

**Hitler's confidence grew after years of appeasement by the rest of Europe. But his invasion of Poland led Britain and France to declare war on Germany.**

Winston Churchill (1874–1965) became British prime minister in 1940 and led Britain during World War II.

Messerschmitt Me 109

Supermarine Spitfire

▲ Between July and October 1940, the German air force (*Luftwaffe*) bombed British cities and attacked Britain's Royal Air Force (RAF). During these attacks, the RAF destroyed 1,733 Luftwaffe planes, while the RAF lost 915. By October 31, the British had won the Battle of Britain.

▶ On May 10, 1940, German forces invaded Netherlands and Belgium. British troops were sent to France in an unsuccessful attempt to halt the German advance. They were forced to retreat to the French port of Dunkirk. Between May 29 and June 4, 335,000 British and Allied troops were evacuated safely back to England from the beaches around Dunkirk.

The three Axis Powers, Germany, Italy, and Japan, all wanted more territory. After his invasion of Czechoslovakia, Hitler did not expect any international military action against his plans to expand farther. To counter any military threat to the east of Germany, he signed a nonagression pact, the Molotov–Ribbentrop Pact, with the Soviet Union in August 1939. The two countries secretly agreed to divide eastern Europe. Despite appeals from the United States, Britain and the Vatican, and feeling secure from any military threat, Hitler invaded Poland on September 1, 1939. Britain and France declared war on Germany two days later. Troops from the Soviet Union, which had signed the nonaggression pact with Germany, then invaded Poland from the east. Poland was divided between Germany and the U.S.S.R. In April 1940, German troops invaded Denmark and Norway, and in May, they invaded Belgium, the Netherlands, and France.

German forces attack the poorly equipped Polish army near the Vistula River in September 1939. Much of western Poland was taken into the Third Reich and many of its people were deported to Germany as forced labor.

In June, Italy declared war on the Allies. British troops sent to France were forced to retreat to Dunkirk, where hundreds of thousands of them were evacuated to Britain. With most of Europe under fascist control, Hitler planned to invade Britain. In July 1940, the *Luftwaffe* (German air force) started to attack targets in Britain. The United States remained in isolation.

# WAR IN THE WEST 1939–1945

**After German successes in Europe and North Africa, Allied victories at El Alamein and Stalingrad were a turning point in the war and led to Germany's defeat.**

▲ Erwin Rommel (1891–1944) was a leader of the German armored units. In North Africa, his tanks showed their superiority over the aging British machines.

▲ Bernard Montgomery (1887–1976) led the British forces in North Africa and Europe. The victory of his Eighth Army at El Alamein was a major turning point in the war.

▲ Georgy Zhukov (1896–1974) commanded the Soviet Red Army in their struggle against the German invaders.

▲ Dwight D. Eisenhower (1890–1969) was Supreme Allied Commander during the war and was elected president in 1952.

The Battle of Britain lasted until October 31, 1940, and forced Hitler to abandon his plan to invade Britain. Instead, he turned his attention to bombing Britain's industry, cities, and shipyards. This lasted until May 1941, but failed to break the morale of Britain, which received substantial supplies and equipment from the United States.

## GERMAN ADVANCES

Meanwhile, the Italians had invaded Greece and North Africa. British forces defeated the Italians in North Africa, but in April 1941, Hitler's troops occupied Greece and Yugoslavia to assist Mussolini's army. The Germans drove the British out of Greece and sent a large force, under General Rommel, to North Africa. His superior forces succeeded in driving the British back to Egypt.

In June 1941, encouraged by military successes in the West, and to capture oil supplies, Hitler's armies launched a massive attack on Russia. The Germans drove the Russian army back as far as Leningrad, Moscow, and Kiev. However, during the harsh Soviet winter they lost a large part of their recently gained territory.

Pilots of the British RAF "scramble" for a sortie against incoming German planes in July 1940. In this Battle of Britain, the outnumbered British prevented the German *Luftwaffe* from winning superiority in the air.

## THE TIDE TURNS AGAINST GERMANY

In August 1941, British prime minister Winston Churchill, and U.S. president Franklin D. Roosevelt, signed the Atlantic Charter—a declaration of freedom for all people. In December, the United States entered the war after a Japanese attack on Pearl Harbor. Meanwhile, Allied troops were sent to Africa to fend off Rommel's advance on Egypt. In November 1942, the Allies won the decisive battle of El Alamein against the Germans and the Italians. To the east, the Russians launched a counterattack against German forces at Stalingrad, forcing them to retreat. These two Allied victories marked the turning point of the war in the West.

▼ A German mortar detachment moves off in support of the infantry during the Battle of Stalingrad. In November 1942, the Russians launched a surprise counterattack on the German forces attacking the city, and forced them to retreat.

By 1941, Germany had conquered most of Europe apart from Britain, and was expanding into North Africa. From June 1940, Vichy France was ruled from the town of Vichy by Marshal Pétain as a puppet of the Germans.

▲ A prisoner recovers after the liberation of the Buchenwald concentration camp by U.S. troops in 1945. The camp had been used for slave labor. Other camps, such as Treblinka in occupied Poland, were used for mass-murder. The Nazis targeted Jews, Slavs, Roma, communists, democrats, homosexuals, and people with disabilities.

Throughout 1942 and 1943, German U-boats attacked ships carrying supplies to Britain. In 1943, Britain and the United States started bombing German industry and cities. In July, British and U.S. forces landed in Sicily, and by September they had invaded Italy. This brought about the downfall of Mussolini and the surrender of Italy.

▲ When France fell in 1940, General Charles de Gaulle became the leader of the Free French. He served as president of France in 1945 and 1959–1969.

## FINAL DEFEAT OF GERMANY

In the east, Russian troops were slowly driving back the Germans. A second front was opened on D-Day, June 6, 1944, with the Allied invasion of Normandy, France. The Germans launched a counteroffensive but had to retreat in January 1945. By March 1945, the Allies had crossed the Rhine and the Soviets had reached Berlin. Hitler killed himself on April 30. On May 7, Germany surrendered unconditionally.

## THE HOLOCAUST

Germany's defeat revealed the true horror of the most extreme example of genocide in history—12 million people had been exterminated by the Nazis. Around half were Jewish. The killing had begun in 1939, when Poland's Jews were forced to move into ghettos. Around 500,000 people died of sickness or starvation. As the Nazis pushed into Russia, they rounded up and shot almost two million Jews. From 1942 to 1944, the Nazis murdered millions more in specially-built death camps.

On D-Day (June 6, 1944), Allied forces landed on the coast of Normandy: 1,200 warships and 4,100 landing craft put 132,500 men ashore, and 10,000 aircraft attacked German positions. The D-Day landings allowed Allied troops to drive the Germans out of France.

393

# WAR IN THE PACIFIC 1941–1945

**The Japanese attack on Pearl Harbor catapulted the United States into World War II. After initial success, the Japanese were slowly driven back to their country.**

Admiral Yamamoto Isoroku (1884–1943) planned Japan's attack on Pearl Harbor. In April 1943, while flying to inspect Japanese forces in the Solomon Islands, his route was located by Allied codebreakers who were listening to Japanese radio signals. He was killed when American fighters shot his plane down.

Since September 1940, Japan had allied itself with Germany and Italy, but had not been involved in the fighting. After Japan's invasion of China in 1937, it had come under increasing pressure from the United States to withdraw its forces from that country. The war in the Pacific began on December 7, 1941, when Japanese aircraft from six aircraft carriers launched an unprovoked attack on the U.S. naval base at Pearl Harbor, Hawaii. More than 2,400 U.S. soldiers and sailors were killed and 18 major naval vessels were destroyed or severely damaged. The Japanese lost fewer than 100 men. Japanese forces invaded Thailand on the same day. On the following day, Congress declared war on Japan. Germany and Italy then declared war on the United States.

The U.S. battleships *Tennessee* and *West Virginia* on fire after the Japanese attack on Pearl Harbor on December 7, 1941. In the attack, 18 major U.S. ships, including eight battleships, were destroyed or severely damaged.

## JAPANESE KAMIKAZE PILOTS

Kamikaze means "divine wind," a reference to a heaven-sent gale that scattered the ships of a Mongol invasion fleet in 1281. Toward the end of the war in the Pacific, there was no shortage of Japanese pilots who volunteered to die for their emperor by diving their aircraft, laden with bombs, straight into an Allied ship. More than half of the 2,900 kamikaze attacks were launched during the defense of the island of Okinawa. The plane used most often in kamikaze attacks was the Zero fighter, because large numbers of them were available.

▼ Kamikaze attacks were first mounted by the Japanese Imperial Navy on October 25, 1944, during the Battle of Leyte Gulf. During the war, around 300 Allied ships were hit by kamikaze attacks.

▲ Kamikaze pilots often performed rituals before takeoff, and wore a special scarf.

On December 10, 1941, the British battleship *Prince of Wales* and the battle cruiser *Repulse* were sunk in the Gulf of Siam by Japanese aircraft. With American and British fleets severely damaged, the Japanese now thought that they had complete control of the Pacific. Within five months, their forces had overrun Burma, Hong Kong, Singapore, Malaya, the Dutch East Indies (Indonesia), Thailand, and the Philippines. They also invaded New Guinea and threatened the north coast of Australia. With most of its own troops and equipment helping the Allies in Europe, Australia had to turn to the United States for protection.

## JAPANESE LOSSES AT SEA

Not all of the U.S. fleet had been sunk at Pearl Harbor. Three American aircraft carriers were at sea at the time of the attack and they were soon joined by two new carriers. Japanese hopes of further expansion in the Pacific were stopped in 1942 in two major sea battles.

The Battle of the Coral Sea (May 4–8) was the first in naval history in which opposing ships were out of each other's sight during the fighting. It was fought by aircraft launched from aircraft carriers. There was no clear winner, but the battle did halt Japanese plans to invade Australia. In June, the Japanese planned to invade the small but strategic island of Midway and the Aleutian Islands. But first they had to destroy American aircraft based on Midway. However, the United States had cracked the Japanese radio codes and were prepared for the attack.

In the Battle of Midway (June 4–6) the Japanese navy was so severely damaged by U.S. carrier-borne aircraft that it retreated. Midway was a decisive victory for the United States and a turning point in the war. With the Japanese advance halted, the task of recapturing territory began.

Over the following three years, U.S. forces regained the Gilbert, Marshall, Caroline, and Mariana islands. From there, they could bomb Japanese cities and industry. In September 1944, U.S. forces began to retake the Philippines, while the British Fourth Army began to reconquer Burma. After fierce fighting, U.S. forces took the Japanese islands of Okinawa and Iwo Jima in early 1945.

▲ After their victory at Midway, U.S. forces took the island of Guadalcanal in August 1942. Following in their footsteps, New Zealand troops come ashore at Guadalcanal Bay in November 1943.

▼ Dislodging the Japanese from the jungles of Burma was a difficult task. In the early stages of the war, a small British force under General Wingate (standing on the left), known as the Chindits, operated many miles behind Japanese lines.

### KEY DATES

| | |
|---|---|
| 1941 | December 7—Japan attacks American Pacific Fleet in Pearl Harbor, Hawaii; United States declares war on Japan; Japanese sink British warships in Gulf of Siam |
| 1942 | Japanese overrun Hong Kong, Burma, Thailand, Singapore, Malaya, Dutch East Indies, and the Philippines; Battles of Coral Sea, Midway, and Guadalcanal |
| 1944 | Battle of Leyte Gulf; U.S. forces recapture the Philippines |
| 1945 | U.S. Air Force takes Okinawa and Iwo Jima; American air force drops atomic bombs on Hiroshima and Nagasaki; Japan surrenders on August 14 |

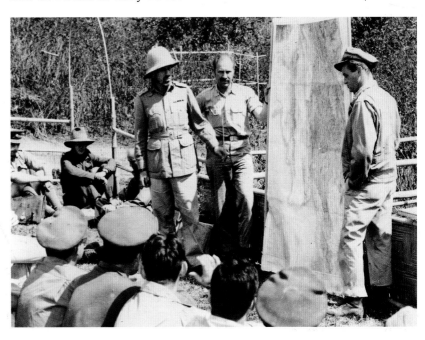

# PEACE IN THE PACIFIC 1945–1948

**With U.S. forces on their doorstep, the Japanese were prepared to fight to the bitter end. The dropping of atomic bombs forced them into surrender.**

Japanese representatives wait to sign the formal statement of surrender with General Douglas MacArthur (1880–1964) on the deck of the U.S. battleship *Missouri* on September 2, 1945.

In the taking of the island of Okinawa, more than 100,000 Japanese and 12,000 American soldiers were killed. After these enormous losses, Allied commanders were fearful of the deaths that might result if they invaded the Japanese mainland. They knew that the Japanese would fight to their last drop of blood to defend their country, and estimated that up to a million Allied soldiers would die in the invasion.

In the United States, Roosevelt had been elected to his third term of office as president in 1944. Meanwhile, amid great secrecy, American scientists had been developing a new and terrible weapon— the atomic bomb. Roosevelt died in office on April 12, 1945, and his successor, Harry S. Truman, made the decision to drop the new atomic bomb on Japan.

## JAPANESE SURRENDER

At the end of July 1945, the Allies gave Japan an ultimatum, threatening complete destruction if Japan did not surrender. Japan gave no signs of surrendering, so an atomic bomb was dropped on Hiroshima on August 6, 1945. It killed about 130,000 people. Three days later a second atomic bomb was dropped on the city of Nagasaki and caused up to 750,000 deaths. Thousands more died later from injuries and radiation sickness. The use of the bombs finally forced the Japanese to surrender on August 14.

World War II ended when the Japanese formally surrendered on September 2, 1945. More than two million Japanese had been killed in World War II, 100 of their cities were destroyed by bombing, and industrial production had practically ceased. It took ten years for Japanese industry to regain its prewar levels.

## THE BOMBING OF HIROSHIMA

The development of the atomic bomb by American scientists had been kept secret. Two atomic bombs were used in war. The five-ton "Little Boy" was dropped on Hiroshima (below) by an American B-29 Superfortress, the *Enola Gay* on August 6, 1945. Three days later a second atomic bomb, "Fat Man" was dropped from another Superfortress, the *Bockstar*, to destroy the city of Nagasaki.

▼ The Boeing B-29 Superfortress was the largest bomber used in World War II.

# THE UNITED NATIONS 1945–1948

**At the end of World War II, the victorious Allied powers divided Germany into four zones. The United Nations was created to keep international peace.**

On April 25, 1945, the United Nations was formally set up at a conference in San Francisco. It was meant to keep world peace and solve problems by international cooperation.

Following the Yalta Conference, the division of Germany was confirmed by the "Big Three" Allied powers at the Potsdam Conference. By this time, Roosevelt had died and been replaced by Harry S. Truman as president. Britain was represented by Clement Attlee. Germany also lost some of its territory to Poland and the U.S.S.R. Countries conquered by Germany and Japan regained their former status. The influence of the Soviet Union increased when Bulgaria, Hungary, Poland, Romania, Czechoslovakia, Yugoslavia, and eastern Germany became communist states. The Truman Doctrine promised American aid to all free peoples that were threatened by communism, while the Marshall Plan provided help for economic recovery.

At the Yalta Conference in February 1945, the "Big Three" Allied powers, represented by their leaders, Churchill (Britain), Roosevelt (U.S.), and Stalin (U.S.S.R.), decided to divide Germany into four zones after the war.

### THE UNITED NATIONS

The term "United Nations" (UN) was first used in January 1942 when the Atlantic Charter was signed by the Allies. In the Charter, they agreed to fight the Axis countries and not make any separate peace agreements. The UN was planned to be stronger than the League of Nations had been. It had a powerful Security Council to decide what should be done if disputes broke out. Members were to contribute arms and personnel to UN peacekeeping missions. In 1948, the UN issued a Universal Declaration of Human Rights.

▲ The Potsdam conference of 1945 made it possible to bring Nazi war criminals to justice, at trials held in Berlin and Nuremberg. At the International Military Tribunal held in Nuremberg in 1945–1946, 22 surviving Nazi leaders were in the dock. Eleven were sentenced to death. Three were acquitted and seven were jailed, three of them for life. On December 10, 1945 the new United Nations organization adopted the Universal Declaration of Human Rights, at Nuremberg.

▶ On June 25, 1948, the Soviet Union set up a blockade around Berlin to try to force France, Britain, and the United States to give up their rights to the western part of Berlin. To feed the population, Britain and the United States flew supplies into the city for 15 months until the blockade was lifted.

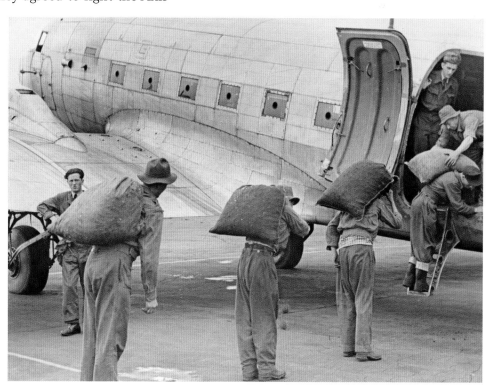

# ITALY AND THE BALKANS 1943–1949

**After World War II, Italy became a republic, Greece suffered from a three-year civil war, and Tito became head of a communist government in Yugoslavia.**

▲ Alcide de Gasperi (1881–1954) organized the Christian Democratic party. He became prime minister of Italy in 1945.

▲ During World War II, Josip Broz Tito (1892–1980) organized resistance to the German occupation of Yugoslavia. In 1953, he became president.

▲ The Yugoslavian coat of arms showed the red star of communism and six torches symbolizing the six republics: Bosnia-Herzegovina, Croatia, Macedonia, Montenegro, Serbia, and Slovenia.

After its surrender to the Allies in 1943, Italy had two governments. In the south, the king, Victor Emmanuel, and his prime minister Badoglio ruled with Allied support. In the north, the Germans rescued Mussolini from prison and set up a fascist Italian state. This lasted until April 1945, when Mussolini was shot by Italian resistance fighters. After that, the king and his new prime minister, Alcide de Gasperi, ruled all of Italy. In May 1946, the king abdicated in favor of his son, who became Umberto II. A month later, a national referendum voted for a republic, and the royal family left the country.

During the German occupation of Greece, the communists built up a powerful armed force. After the war, they hoped to make Greece a communist state. In 1946, a royalist government was elected, which returned King George II to the throne. The communists began to revolt and civil war broke out. Under the Truman Doctrine, the United States gave large amounts of aid to the army, which

Yugoslav partisan fighters photographed in about 1944, during World War II. The communist partisans fought fiercely against the Nazis and their Croatian fascist allies.

supported the king. Fighting lasted until the communists were defeated in 1949.

Yugoslavia was formed at the end of World War I from Montenegro, Croatia, Serbia, Slovenia, and Bosnia–Herzegovina, and ruled by King Alexander I. The country was occupied by the Germans in World War II, and the king fled to London. Resistance to the Germans was organized by Chetniks (Serbian nationalists) and communist partisans, but the two groups ended up fighting each other. After World War II, the partisan leader Tito became head of a communist government.

## THE GREEK CIVIL WAR

Following the restoration of the Greek king to the throne in September 1946, a full-scale civil war was started by the communists. Massive military and economic aid poured in from the United States to support the royalists. The communists proclaimed a provisional government in the north in 1947. The civil war lasted until October 16, 1949. During the three-year war, more than 50,000 people were killed and over half a million Greeks were made homeless.

# INDIAN INDEPENDENCE 1945–1947

**The Indian people had resisted British rule since the 1800s. In 1947, Britain partitioned India and gave independence to the Hindus and Muslims.**

Jawaharlal Nehru (1889–1964) was imprisoned for civil disobedience in 1921. In 1928, he became leader of the Indian National Congress Party, and in 1947, became the first prime minister of an independent India.

▲ Mohandas K Gandhi (1869–1948) studied law in England, then worked in South Africa. He returned to India in 1914 and was jailed for his nonviolent resistance to the British authorities. He was assassinated by a Hindu extremist in 1948.

After World War I, Britain promised India a major role in governing itself, in return for the support India had given during the war. In 1919, the Government of India Act was passed. This allowed the election of Indian ministers to an Indian parliament, but the British governors still held the real power. Indians felt that the Act did not go far enough.

There was a campaign of civil disobedience and noncooperation with the British by members of the Indian Congress Party. Guided in their campaign by Mahatma Gandhi, they encouraged the boycott of British goods, the nonpayment of taxes, and passive, or nonviolent, resistance to the British.

In 1945, the British government decided to grant India independence within the Commonwealth. The situation was complicated because India contained two major religious groups, Hindus and Muslims. There were fewer Muslims than Hindus, but the Muslims would not agree to any government that would put them under Hindu rule. As independence came closer, the pressure grew for a separate state for Indian Muslims.

After partition, both parts of Pakistan were governed from Karachi, and India was governed from New Delhi. East Pakistan broke away and became the separate state of Bangladesh in 1971.

After riots broke out and many people were killed, the British finally agreed to partition (divide) India. The mainly Muslim northeast and northwest of India became the independent country of Pakistan on August 14, 1947. Muhammad Ali Jinnah became the first governor-general. The next day, the remaining area became independent India with Jawaharlal Nehru as its first prime minister.

▶ In the large-scale migrations that followed partition, more than a million people were killed. This photograph shows a train crowded with refugees in 1947.

# ISRAEL 1948–1949

**Growing demands for a separate Jewish state and the flood of refugees from Europe forced the British to withdraw from Palestine. Israel became a reality.**

David Ben-Gurion (1886–1973) was born in Poland. As a young man he went to live in Palestine and in 1930 became leader of the Mapai Party. In 1948, he declared the State of Israel and became its first prime minister.

Until the end of World War I, Palestine was part of the Ottoman Empire. It was inhabited by Arabs and a growing number of Jews, some of whom wanted a Jewish homeland. When the Ottoman Empire collapsed, Palestine was ruled by Britain under a 1922 League of Nations' mandate. In 1917, the Balfour Declaration had promised British support for a Jewish homeland in Palestine, with specific protection for the rights of non-Jewish Palestinians. As problems grew in Europe, Jewish immigration increased.

Between 1922 and 1939, the Jewish population in Palestine had risen from 83,000 to 445,000. Tel Aviv had become a Jewish city with a population of 150,000. The Arabs resented this and fighting often broke out between the two groups. After 1945, Jewish immigration increased again. Under pressure from the Arabs, Britain restricted the number of new settlers allowed. Jewish terrorists then began to attack both the Arabs and the British.

The new State of Israel was surrounded by Arab states. On May 14, 1948, the Arab League of Lebanon, Syria, Iraq, Jordan, and Egypt declared war on Israel and attacked it. They were defeated and Israel increased its territory.

A secret Jewish army called *Haganah* (self-defense) was formed in 1920. More extreme groups were later formed, notably Irgun and the Stern Gang. Both groups thought that Britain had betrayed the Zionist cause—to establish a Jewish state in Palestine—and took part in a violent terrorist campaign against the Arabs and the British. Jewish leaders such as Chaim Weizmann and David Ben-Gurion took a more peaceful approach.

▲ One result of the hostility between the Arabs and Jews in 1948 was the migration of nearly one million Arabs from Palestine. They left their homes and became refugees because they were afraid of the action Israel might take after the war with the Arab League.

▶ After World War II, the number of Jewish refugees from Europe trying to enter Palestine became a problem for the British. In October 1947, the ship *Jewish State* arrived at the port of Haifa with 2,000 illegal Jewish immigrants aboard.

By June 1945, an enormous number of Jewish refugees, displaced by the war in Europe, were clamoring to live in Palestine. Despite British efforts to stop them, the number of refugees entering the country continued to increase. The United States put pressure on Britain to allow the admission of 100,000 refugees, but Britain refused. It soon found itself involved in a full-scale war with Jewish terrorist organizations.

## THE NEW STATE OF ISRAEL

Unwilling to be caught up in another bloody and costly war, Britain took the matter to the United Nations. In 1947, the UN voted to divide Palestine into two states. One would be Jewish and the other one Arab. Jerusalem, which was sacred to Jews, Muslims, and Christians, would be international. The Jews agreed to this, but the Arabs did not.

On May 14, 1948, Britain gave up its mandate to rule Palestine and withdrew its troops. On the same day, the Jews, led by Mapai Party leader David Ben-Gurion, proclaimed the State of Israel, and its legitimacy was immediately recognized by the governments of the United States and the Soviet Union.

▲ Haganah fighters in Tel Aviv, less than two weeks before Israel declared independence.

Israel was immediately attacked by the surrounding Arab League states of Lebanon, Syria, Iraq, Jordan, and Egypt. Israel defeated them and increased its territory by a quarter. Nearly one million Palestinian refugees, afraid of Jewish rule, fled to neighboring Arab countries. The United Nations negotiated a cease-fire in 1949, but conflicts between Israel and its Arab neighbors continue to this day.

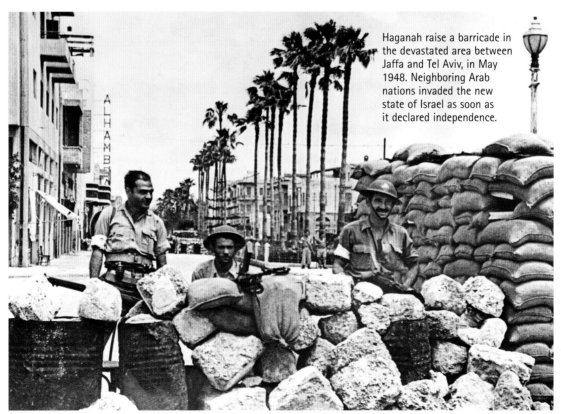

Haganah raise a barricade in the devastated area between Jaffa and Tel Aviv, in May 1948. Neighboring Arab nations invaded the new state of Israel as soon as it declared independence.

▲ The Israeli flag was raised at Eilat on the Gulf of Aqaba in 1949. It is the southernmost point in Israel, and its only port on the Red Sea.

# BRITISH COMMONWEALTH 1914–1949

**In 1931, the countries that formed the British Empire joined together to form the Commonwealth. Over the next 60 years many were given their independence.**

During both World Wars, soldiers from all corners of the British Empire and Commonwealth, as well as those from other African colonies, fought on the British side.

The relationship between Britain and parts of its empire had begun to change by the beginning of the 1900s. Some of the larger countries were made independent as dominions. They were completely self-governing, but they maintained strong links with Britain—the "mother country." Dominions retained the British Crown (king or queen) as the symbolic head of state. Each dominion had a lieutenant governor, a native resident of that country, who represented the Crown.

In the 1920s, the dominions asked for a clear definition of their status. In the 1931 Statute of Westminster dominions were defined as "autonomous (self-ruling) communities within the British Empire, equal in status…united by a common allegiance to the Crown and freely associated as members of the British Commonwealth of Nations." After this, the name British Commonwealth of Nations was used instead of British Empire. Many colonies started to clamor for independence.

▼ Commonwealth leaders in the garden of 10 Downing Street, London, while attending the Conference of Commonwealth Prime Ministers in October 1948.

## INDEPENDENT MEMBERS OF THE COMMONWEALTH

| | |
|---|---|
| Antigua and Barbuda 1981 | Namibia 1990 |
| Australia 1901 | Nauru 1968 |
| Bahamas 1973 | New Zealand 1907 |
| Bangladesh 1972 | Nigeria 1960 |
| Barbados 1966 | Pakistan 1947 |
| Belize 1981 | Papua New Guinea 1975 |
| Botswana 1966 | Rwanda 2009 |
| Brunei 1984 | St. Kitts-Nevis 1983 |
| Cameroon 1995 | St. Lucia 1979 |
| Canada 1931 | St. Vincent and the |
| Cyprus 1960 | Grenadines 1979 |
| Dominica 1978 | Seychelles 1976 |
| (Fiji suspended——2009) | Sierra Leone 1961 |
| Gambia 1965 | Singapore 1965 |
| Ghana 1957 | Solomon Islands 1978 |
| Grenada 1974 | South Africa 1994 |
| Guyana 1966 | Sri Lanka (Ceylon) 1948 |
| India 1947 | Swaziland 1968 |
| Jamaica 1962 | Tanzania 1961 |
| Kenya 1963 | Tonga 1970 |
| Kiribati 1979 | Trinidad and Tobago 1962 |
| Lesotho 1966 | Tuvalu 1978 |
| Malawi 1964 | Uganda 1962 |
| Malaysia 1957 | United Kingdom 1931 |
| Maldives 1965 | Vanuatu 1980 |
| Malta 1964 | Zambia 1964 |
| Mauritius 1968 | (Zimbabwe – suspended |
| Mozambique 1995 | 1980) |

In 1932, the dominions received better terms for trading with Britain than countries outside the Commonwealth. Canada, Australia, New Zealand, and South Africa had all become dominions before World War I. The Irish Free State also became a dominion in 1921. The first three colonies to gain independence after World War II were India (1947), Ceylon (1948), and Burma (now Myanmar, 1948). India and Ceylon (now Sri Lanka) stayed in the Commonwealth, but Burma did not join, and the Republic of Ireland left in 1949.

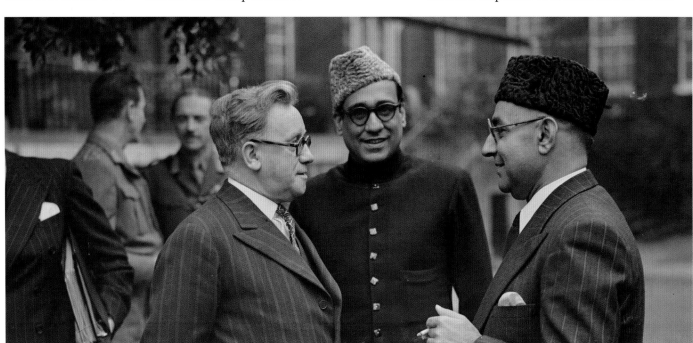

# COMMUNIST CHINA 1945–1949

**After the defeat of Japan in 1945, the Chinese nationalists and communists resumed their civil war. In 1949, the People's Republic of China was declared.**

The communists introduced collective farming to China. This meant that all the land, buildings, and machinery belonged to the community. Committees in each village decided what to grow. One improvement was that they replaced their oxen with tractors, which they called "Iron Oxen."

In 1936, the Chinese nationalist leader, Jiang Jieshi, was forced to make an alliance with the Communist Party to fight against the Japanese in Manchuria. This alliance lasted until 1945 and brought China into World War II on the Allies' side. While the Chinese were fighting the Japanese, Britain and the United States gave them aid. After the defeat of Japan in 1945, the alliance collapsed and civil war broke out in 1946. The nationalists were weak and divided, but Mao Zedong's communists had the support of the people. The communists also had a large army, and by January 1949 they had taken Tianjin and Beijing (Peking). From there they moved southward, pushing the nationalists onto the island of Taiwan (Formosa), which became known as the Republic of China. It held a seat in the United Nations until 1971. The communist People's Republic of China was declared on October 1, 1949, but many countries refused to recognize it.

The People's Republic of China came into being on October 1, 1949. In the coming years, the Chinese communist leader Mao Zedong introduced reforms in the countryside in order to gain the support of the people. This 1949 poster shows the Chinese people uniting in support of Mao Zedong.

Large posters of Communist Party leaders formed the backdrop to speeches at a meeting of the Communist Party in Shanghai. When they took power in 1949, the communists soon moved to control the press and nationalized industries.

# THE ARTS 1914–1949

## The prewar drift away from traditional art forms in music, painting, and sculpture led to further experimentation and expression after World War I.

During and after World War I, new styles of art appeared. Dadaism, founded in Switzerland in 1915, soon influenced the American Man Ray and the French Marcel Duchamp. Their work was designed to shock, and to question established art forms. Surrealism was born out of the Dadaist movement. Surrealists, such as the Spanish Salvador Dali and the Belgian René Magritte, produced paintings that seemed to reflect dreams and the subconscious mind.

▲ Charlie Chaplin (1889–1977) became the most successful Hollywood comedian of the silent movie era. At the height of his fame in the 1920s, he was known and loved throughout the world for his portrayal of the "Little Tramp" in films such as *The Gold Rush* (1925).

The onset of World War II led many European Surrealists to work in New York. Abstract art evolved before World War I in Germany, Holland, and Russia—artists grouped shapes and colors in patterns rather than painting objects in a realistic way. The American Georgia O'Keefe, the Dutch Piet Mondrian, and the Spanish Joan Miró were among the earliest abstract artists. Abstract expressionism started in the United States in the 1940s, and painters include Jackson Pollock, who developed a style using splashes of color, and Mark Rothko, who painted large areas of solid color. They were to influence European art in the 1950s.

### MUSIC AND BALLET

Classical music was also going through a formative period of change and experimentation. There were many notable composers during this period. The Austrian Arnold Schoenberg explored music in an abstract way. In Russia, Igor Stravinsky was composing lively music for ballet, and in Hungary the composer Béla Bartók was heavily influenced by his country's folk music. In the United States, Charles Ives composed a uniquely

▲ Vaslav Nijinsky (1890–1950) studied ballet in St. Petersburg, then joined the Ballets Russes company. In 1912, he electrified Paris audiences with his interpretation of the title role in *The Afternoon of a Faun* by the French composer Claude Debussy (1862–1918).

▶ Showgirl and actress Mary Eaton (1901–48) appeared on New York's Broadway in the Ziegfeld Follies revues. As a reaction to the horrors of World War I, young people tried to live life to the full and they loved to shock their elders. The U.S. gave birth to the Roaring Twenties. In Europe, Berlin was the center of a wild nightclub culture.

▲ The Dutch painter Piet Mondrian (1872–1944) was caught up in the whirl of artistic innovation that shook Paris in the first half of the twentieth century. His paintings were reduced to the essentials of color and form. He composed geometrical, abstract paintings for the rest of his life.

▲ The American composer George Gershwin (1898–1937) was born to Russian immigrant parents in New York. He incorporated elements of jazz and blues into his music. Among his works are *Rhapsody in Blue* and the opera *Porgy and Bess*.

American style of classical music.

Western popular music was dominated by the United States. The folk music of Black artists evolved into what became known as jazz—the Roaring Twenties are also called the Jazz Age. By the mid-1930s, big band music was popular, and U.S. bandleaders like Glenn Miller were well known throughout the world.

## THE MOVIES

By 1920, Hollywood was the movie capital of the world. In 1927, *The Jazz Singer* was the first movie with sound. Moviemakers began to use color in the early 1930s, and had perfected it by the time *Gone With the Wind* was released in 1939. Movies reflect history. During the Depression, musicals cheered people up; in wartime, stories of courage and oppression stirred patriotism.

▼ The Spanish artist Salvador Dali (1904–1989), was a surrealist painter who also designed jewelry. In his paintings, he tried to show a different reality—that of dreams and the subconscious mind.

◄ Judy Garland (1922–1969) is still known all over the world for her portrayal of Dorothy in *The Wizard of Oz* (1939). The movie, made by the Metro-Goldwyn-Mayer studios, was one of the first to be made in color.

▼ This jeweled watch was designed by Salvador Dali in the 1920s.

# ARCHITECTURE 1914–1949

After World War I, developments in building design and construction in Europe and the United States became known as the "International Style."

In 1914, two styles of architecture were being developed in the West. The Art Nouveau style, based on natural forms, had flowing lines. Other architects' designs were based purely on function. This modern style, which became known as the International Style, used steel, glass, and reinforced concrete.

The Bauhaus school of art and design, created in 1919 by Walter Gropius, moved from Weimar to this building in Dessau in 1925. Its staff included world-famous painters such as Paul Klee and Wassily Kandinsky.

## EUROPEAN DEVELOPMENTS

The trend toward more modern, functional design was led by architects such as Jacobus Oud and Gerrit Rietveld of Holland's de Stijl movement, Mies van der Rohe in Germany, and Le Corbusier in France, each with his own unique style. In Germany, Walter Gropius founded the Bauhaus school of design in 1919. The Nazis closed it in 1933, and in 1938, Gropius became professor of architecture at Harvard. In 1937, Mies van der Rohe had become professor of architecture in Chicago. This led to a new exchange of ideas.

The Moorish influence on Spanish architecture can be seen in the tower of the Bacardi Building in Havana, Cuba. The building, with a terracotta design, was built in 1931.

## AMERICAN STYLE

Frank Lloyd Wright designed buildings that were in harmony with the landscape. His early "Prairie style" of two-storied buildings was admired in Japan and Europe. In the 1930s, he was joined by architects escaping persecution. In 1936, he built his most famous house, "Fallingwater," which was suspended over a waterfall. A shortage of space in cities led to the construction of skyscrapers. New York's 102-story Empire State Building, completed in 1931, was the tallest building in the world.

◄ Built in the Art Nouveau style, the Einstein Tower in Potsdam, Germany, was designed after World War I by Erich Mendelsohn. This was the workshop in which Albert Einstein tested his theory of relativity.

▲ The architect Le Corbusier was born in Switzerland, but worked in France. This apartment block in Berlin, Germany, is an example of his use of reinforced concrete during the 1930s.

◀ The Darwin Martin House in Buffalo, New York, was designed by the U.S. architect Frank Lloyd Wright (1867–1959) and built in 1903–1905. It is a design of great simplicity and harmony. Wright's masterpieces included the Fallingwater residence (1935) and New York's landmark Guggenheim museum (1959).

## WORLD WAR II AND AFTER

The onset of World War II halted building development in Europe. But in South America, particularly in Brazil, the International Style and the work of Le Corbusier was influencing building design.

By 1945, in the capital cities of Europe, over 40 million new homes were needed to replace those destroyed in the war. The rapid building of new houses became a priority. In the United States, new prosperity saw many people buying homes, often for the first time. New suburbs and large housing tracts sprang up across the country.

▼ The Golden Gate suspension bridge in San Francisco, was completed in 1937. Its main span is 8,979 ft. (2,737m) long and its twin bridge towers are 745 ft. (227m) above sea level.

▲ The Chrysler Building in New York was designed by architect William van Alen and completed in 1930. It is a classic example of the Art Deco style that influenced building design between 1925 and 1939.

# SCIENCE AND TECHNOLOGY 1914–1949

**Between the two world wars, scientists developed many weapons of mass destruction. However, their work also led to new discoveries that had peaceful uses.**

World War I saw the first use of chemical warfare and the first use of tanks on the battlefield. Aircraft were used for observation, aerial combat, and bombing. By World War II, scientists had developed weapons that were far more sophisticated. Aircraft could fly faster and carry more bombs. In 1940, the radar system was developed to locate distant objects such as enemy aircraft. In 1934, the physicist Enrico Fermi found that a chain reaction of nuclear fission could be achieved using uranium. This led to the Manhattan Project in 1941, in which scientists developed the atomic bomb at Los Alamos. Developments in atomic physics also led to the discovery of the most accurate method of measuring time.

▲ After World War I, new, innovative equipment made domestic chores easier. The first electrically driven washing machines appeared in 1914.

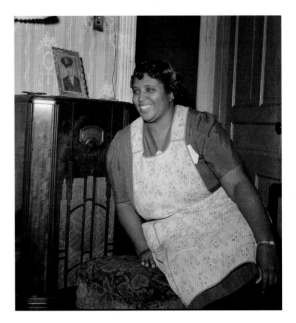

Until the invention of transistors in 1948, radios used tubes and were built into large polished wooden cabinets, such as this 1925 set. Transistors allowed miniaturization in all forms of electronics.

## SCIENCE FOR PEACE

The development of plastics and synthetic fibers in the 1930s meant that many consumer goods and clothes could be mass produced at prices that people could afford. Major advances were made in the development of computers. Early computers filled whole rooms and needed large amounts of electricity to handle a small amount of data. In 1948, the transistor was developed by the Bell Telephone Company. This brought about a revolution in electronics and led to the building of smaller and more powerful computers.

▲ John Logie Baird (1888–1946) invented an early television system. In 1926, he transmitted the first pictures of a moving object. His system was soon replaced by one developed by Russian-born U.S. scientist Vladimir Zworykin (1889–1982). The world's first high-definition public television service was started by the BBC, in England, in 1936.

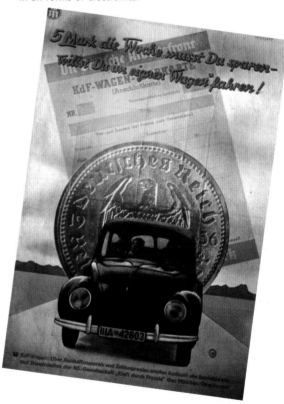

▲ Ferdinand Porsche (1875–1951) wanted to produce a car that people could afford. His Volkswagen was first planned in 1934 and first mass-produced in 1938.

◄ Back in 1937, this all-metal Douglas transport carried 12 passengers for Transcontinental and Western Air—later known as TWA.

▲ Penicillin was discovered by Alexander Fleming in 1928. He saw that a mold in his laboratory killed the bacteria around it. It was not until the 1940s that penicillin was made stable enough for use in medicine.

Cures and prevention methods were found for diseases that had killed thousands. As a result of warfare, many advances were made in the treatment of injuries. Peacetime advances included the discovery of insulin in 1921, by the Canadians Dr. Frederick Banting and Dr. Charles Best, and the Scottish Dr. John Macleod. In 1937, the first blood bank opened in the United States; plasma was first used in 1940.

The introduction of mass-production meant that cars could be sold at affordable prices. Military aircraft were redesigned to carry civilians, and by the 1930s, commercial airlines flew passengers to most parts of the world.

▲ In 1943, the first completely electronic computer was developed in England. Known as Colossus, it successfully decoded top-secret messages sent by the Germans on their Enigma machines.

▶ The first nylon products appeared in 1939. This is an advertisement for American nylon stockings from the 1940s.

▶ A mushroom cloud rising after the explosion of an atomic bomb. In August 1945, the United States dropped atomic bombs on the Japanese cities of Hiroshima and Nagasaki. This forced the Japanese to surrender.

Albert Einstein (1879–1955) won the Nobel Prize for Physics in 1921. His work led to the development of the atomic bomb. After the war, he fought to control the use of nuclear weapons.

## WHEN IT HAPPENED

**1915** The sonar system is developed to detect submarines under water
**1919** Ernest Rutherford splits the atom
**1922** BCG tuberculosis vaccine used in France
**1926** First liquid-fuel rocket launched in the U.S.A.
**1928** Penicillin discovered by Alexander Fleming
**1937** Frank Whittle designs first jet engine
**1938** Lazlo Biro introduces first ballpoint pen
**1939** First nylon stockings sold in the U.S.A.
**1940** Radar system developed
**1941** Scientists develop atomic bomb in the U.S.A.
**1944** Jet-engined fighter planes first used in battle by Britain and Germany
**1948** Atomic clock invented

# TIMES OF CHANGE

## 1950–1999

After World War II, there were hopes for peace in western Europe and North America, but the Cold War created ongoing tensions between capitalist countries and their communist rivals. Colonies won independence, but often failed to escape unrest and poverty. This was the age of jets, cars and space rockets, televisions and computers, and environmental pollution and population growth. The youth of the 1950s and 60s rejected tradition and explored new forms of music, spiritual values, or radical politics, with growing demands for civil rights and social justice. By the 1990s, business had become globalized and dominated by market forces rather than social welfare ideals.

▲ The Cold War "arms race" was based on giant aircraft carriers, fighter jets and bombers, submarines, and nuclear missiles.

◀ The U.S. Space Shuttle *Discovery* blasts off from the Kennedy Space Center at the beginning of its 21st spaceflight in July 1995.

411

# THE COLD WAR 1945–1989

**After the end of World War II, tensions between East and West and the buildup of nuclear weapons almost brought the world to the brink of war.**

▲ A year before the 1962 Cuban missile crisis, the two superpower leaders met for the first time—U.S.S.R.'s Nikita Khrushchev (1894–1971), on the left, and U.S. President John F. Kennedy (1917–63).

The U.S.S.R. and the United States fought as allies in World War II. But in 1945, these two superpowers became rivals and then enemies. This division became known as the Cold War, a conflict largely without any actual fighting. Both countries made threats and built up their armed forces and weapons. Each side also accumulated an enormous stockpile of nuclear weapons. The idea was to hold a kind of balance in which neither side would want to start a real war.

Friendly contacts ceased. The U.S.S.R. became shut off from the world. The great British statesman Sir Winston Churchill described the frontier between East and West as the "Iron Curtain" in a speech at Fulton, Missouri on March 5, 1946.

The Cold War dominated world politics for many years. On one side, the United States became the leader of NATO (North Atlantic Treaty Organization), a military alliance of Western nations providing collective defense against the communist powers. On the other side, the U.S.S.R. led the Warsaw Pact, a military alliance of East European states that backed communism.

Because of the serious threat of nuclear war between East and West during the 1960s, many Americans built fallout shelters in their backyards.

## BERLIN: A DIVIDED CITY

In 1945, the United States, France, and Britain took control of West Germany. The U.S.S.R. controlled East Germany. The capital, Berlin, inside East Germany, was also divided. In 1948, the Soviets closed all access to West Berlin. The Western powers brought in supplies by air, until the blockade was lifted in 1949. From 1949 to 1958, three million people escaped from East to West Berlin. In 1961, East Germany closed off this escape route by building the Berlin Wall across the city. It crossed tram lines and roads and created an area on either side known as No Man's Land.

▲ The Berlin Wall, built in 1961 to divide East and West Berlin, finally "fell" in November 1989.

▶ By 1955, most European states had joined rival alliances. Warsaw Pact countries supported the U.S.S.R. Members of NATO backed the U.S.A.

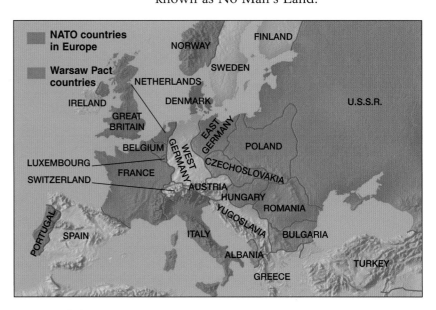

NATO countries in Europe

Warsaw Pact countries

NORWAY FINLAND SWEDEN NETHERLANDS IRELAND DENMARK U.S.S.R. GREAT BRITAIN EAST GERMANY POLAND BELGIUM WEST GERMANY CZECHOSLOVAKIA LUXEMBOURG FRANCE AUSTRIA SWITZERLAND HUNGARY ROMANIA YUGOSLAVIA PORTUGAL ITALY BULGARIA SPAIN ALBANIA TURKEY GREECE

## CUBAN MISSILE CRISIS

Although the United States and the U.S.S.R. never fought, they came close. The world held its breath for a week in October 1962. President John F. Kennedy received Air Force photographs showing that the Soviet Union was building missile launch sites in Cuba. From there, the nuclear missiles could reach and destroy many U.S. cities. On October 22, the president ordered a naval blockade of Cuba. The United States made plans to invade Cuba, and the world braced itself for nuclear war. Finally, on October 28, Nikita Khrushchev, the Soviet leader, backed down and agreed to remove the missiles and destroy the Cuban launch sites. The crisis was over.

## THE END OF THE COLD WAR

In the 1980s, the Soviet leader Mikhail Gorbachev introduced political and economic reforms. He and the U.S. president, Ronald Reagan, abolished medium-range nuclear missiles. In 1989, the U.S.S.R. allowed the communist countries of eastern Europe to elect democratic governments, and in 1991, the Soviet Union itself broke up into 15 independent republics. The Cold War was over, but the expansion of NATO from 1999 and authoritarian governance in Russia led to a renewal of tensions with the West in the next century.

◀ Francis Gary Powers (1929–1977) was the pilot of an American U-2 spy plane that was shot down over Russian territory in 1960. He was released in exchange for the imprisoned Soviet spymaster Rudolf Abel (1903–1971).

▼ Czech students tried to stop Soviet tanks in Prague, in August 1968. The U.S.S.R. feared that independent actions by Warsaw Pact members might weaken its power, so it moved into Czechoslovakia.

▶ During the Cold War, many people campaigned against the arms race and the spread of nuclear weapons.

◀ Here, supporters of the Campaign for Nuclear Disarmament (CND) march through London in 1983 to demonstrate against the deployment of Cruise and Trident nuclear missiles on British soil.

# SPACE RACE 1957–1999

**The space age began in 1957 when the U.S.S.R. launched *Sputnik I*. In 2000, the first crew of the International Space Station set up home in space.**

In the run-up to the *Apollo* flights, the American Gemini program was designed to teach astronauts how to cope with space travel. In November 1966, "Buzz" Aldrin carried out three space walks high up over Earth.

The development of German rocket technology during World War II helped scientists realize that one day it might be possible for people to travel in space. At the end of the war, both the U.S. and the U.S.S.R. obtained German rocket equipment and expertise and started work—but the U.S. was surprised when, in 1957, the Soviets sent the first artificial satellite into orbit. This triggered a "space race" between the U.S. and the U.S.S.R., with a human moon landing as the ultimate goal. Both sides felt that winning the race would increase their prestige. They also hoped that space science would help them develop new, more powerful weapons.

Soon both sides were investing enormous amounts of time and money in space science. The U.S.S.R. achieved another first in 1961, when Yuri Gagarin became the first person in space. Other notable achievements by both countries included probes sent to the Moon, Venus, and Mars, further manned flights, space walks, and the launch of communication satellites.

The *Apollo* spaceflights enabled the United States to win the space race by landing men on the Moon. Between July 1969 and

December 1972, the U.S. successfully carried out six of these missions.

After the Cold War, the two superpowers scaled down their space programs. In 1993, they agreed to work together to develop the International Space Station—the first parts of which were launched into orbit in 1998. The ISS received its first resident crew in 2000.

▲ *Sputnik 1* was launched by U.S.S.R. on October 4, 1957. The satellite was used to broadcast a radio signal and orbited Earth for three months.

▲ On April 12, 1961, cosmonaut Yuri Gagarin (1934-68) of the U.S.S.R., above, became the first person to orbit the Earth. Two years later, he was followed by the first woman cosmonaut, Valentina Tereshkova (b.1937).

## MAN ON THE MOON

In 1961, President John F. Kennedy said that his scientists would send a man to the Moon by 1970. In fact, the first manned Moon landing took place on July 20, 1969. The crew of the *Apollo 11* mission consisted of Neil Armstrong, the first man to set foot on the Moon, Edwin "Buzz" Aldrin, who was the second man to walk on the lunar surface, and Michael Collins, who remained in orbit in the command and service module. Armstrong described his first step on the Moon as "one small step for [a] man and one giant leap for mankind."

◀ *Apollo 11* was launched from Kennedy Space Center, Florida, on July 16, 1969. The first manned landing on the Moon was just three days later.

## SPACE SHUTTLES

The U.S.A.'s National Aeronautics and Space Administration (NASA) developed a reusable space vehicle, the space shuttle, which could be launched by a rocket and return to Earth like a plane. The launch of the first shuttle in 1981 marked a new phase in space exploration. It could be used to launch and repair satellites in Earth orbit or to carry crew and cargo to and from the ISS. In 1986, the *Challenger* shuttle broke up on launch, with the loss of all seven crew members. Another fatal accident would destroy the *Columbia* shuttle in 2003, and the program was halted in 2011.

▲ In the 1960s–70s, Mars was targeted by Soviet and U.S. space programs. In 1997, the U.S. *Mars Pathfinder* landed a small rover called *Sojourner* on the surface (above).

▲ Since 1998, the International Space Station has been in orbit around the Earth. The ISS is supported by the space agencies of the U.S.A., Canada, Russia, Europe, and Japan.

## EXPLORING DEEP SPACE

Exploration of the other planets in our Solar System was carried out by uncrewed space probes, landers, and rovers. The Soviet *Venera* program (1961–84) targeted Venus. In 1977, the U.S.A. launched its two *Voyager* missions, which flew by Jupiter and Saturn. *Voyager 2* was then redirected to fly by Uranus and Neptune. Both continued to transmit valuable data as they sped away into interstellar space.

Another U.S. spacecraft that performed beyond all expectation was the Hubble Space Telescope, launched in 1990. This craft enabled scientists to produce images of objects billions of light years away, and provide information about the Universe. The HST was serviced and repaired by space shuttle astronauts from 1993 onward.

▶ U.S. space shuttle *Endeavour* climbs away from the launch site on June 21, 1993.

# CHINA 1949–1999

**In 1949, the Communist Party under Mao Zedong came to power and reshaped battle-weary China. Political strife was followed by economic transformation.**

After Mao's death in 1976, Deng Xiaoping opened up trade with capitalist countries. Chinese factories (above) were soon exporting electronic equipment around the world.

▼ Mao Zedong sought to solve the problem of food shortages in China by the creation of collective farms. Nevertheless, China continued to suffer periods of extreme food shortages.

The Communist Party came to power in China in 1949. Their leader, Mao Zedong, became chairman of the new People's Republic of China. Civil war and the war with Japan had left the land poor and many people were starving. Roads, railroads, schools, and hospitals could not meet the people's needs. Many in the new government believed that they should follow the example of the Communists in Russia. Mao did not agree with the move to industrialization, instead believing in a peasant economy. He launched his Great Leap Forward experiment in 1958, which redistributed land to giant communes of peasants to encourage development via agriculture. This failed, and Mao lost much of his influence, but in 1966, he started the Cultural Revolution. With the help of students and the People's Liberation Army, he overthrew the party leaders.

Mao transformed China. Collective farms

To reduce the growth rate of China's enormous population, in 1980 the Chinese government introduced the one-child policy, limiting families to one child each.

grew basic foods, and industry produced more iron and steel. "Barefoot doctors" provided medical care to people in the countryside, and children learned to read and write. Mao wrote *The Thoughts of Chairman Mao*. It was required reading, and everyone carried a copy with them wherever they went—even the simplest peasants were able to quote from it.

▲ This picture of a lone student standing in the path of the army's tanks was seen on television all around the world.

## TIANANMEN SQUARE

On May 4, 1989, around 100,000 students and workers marched to Tiananmen Square in Beijing and demanded political reform. The government declared martial law on May 20, and on June 3–4, the People's Liberation Army and its tanks moved in to end the protest. It is believed that more than 3,000 protesters were killed and another 10,000 injured, although actual figures may never be known. Western nations were shocked by the brutality used by the Chinese government to deal with the students, and strong diplomatic protests were made. Many cultural and social aspects of Chinese life were becoming increasingly relaxed when compared with the strict controls of the Mao era, but the Chinese Communist Party did not relax its grip on power or allow democratic reform.

## CIVIL RIGHTS

In the early 1960s, educated people were beginning to criticize communism. Mao feared opposition to his own extreme form of communism, and decided to take drastic action. During the Cultural Revolution, many of Mao's political opponents were executed, scholars were imprisoned and tortured, families were split up, and millions of people died from famine.

## ECONOMIC GROWTH

Following Mao Zedong's death in 1976, his rivals gained power and opened up the Chinese economy, encouraging foreign trade and investment. The Communist Party remained in power, even though the economic model was now state-controlled capitalism rather than the Maoist form of communism. Huge new cities were developed at speed, such as Shenzhen on the Pearl River. Rural workers migrated into the cities to seek work.

## POPULATION GROWTH

China's soaring population growth was targeted by a drastic policy limiting the number of children permitted by law in certain areas to two and then one. The single-child policy was effective, but led to many social problems. It was amended and then, in 2015, finally dropped.

▼ A firework display was held to mark the return of Hong Kong to China in 1997—the official end of Britain's 99-year lease on the territory. This agreement, which promised "one country, two systems," would be challenged in the next century.

# COMMON MARKETS 1950–1999

**In the 1950s and 60s, new international economic alliances were formed, which largely replaced pre-war national and colonial trading arrangements.**

On the European Union flag of 1993, the stars represent 15 European nations who were members at that time. The organization had an ambitious program of monetary union and a degree of political integration.

During World War II, economists agreed that national trading tariffs and barriers had contributed to the economic instability that led to war. The Bretton Woods Agreement, which came into force in 1946, standardized the rules for international finance for the first time, linking currencies to the value of gold. In 1947, 23 countries signed up to a General Agreement on Tariffs and Trade (GATT). In 1995, this was replaced by the World Trade Organization (WTO), which now regulated 96 percent of world trade.

### EUROPE UNITES

Exhausted by the war, European nations decided to build a peaceful future by creating a single market for their goods, starting with a European Coal and Steel Community in 1951. They went on to form a common market called the European Economic Community (EEC) in 1957. An alternative trading bloc called the European Free Trade Association (EFTA) was set up in 1960. The U.K. left EFTA to join the EEC in 1973 and this decision was validated by a referendum in 1975. In 1993, now with 12 member states, the EEC became the European Union (EU) and by 1995, there were 15 EU nations.

▼ The European Parliament is directly elected from EU member nations. It meets in Strasbourg, France, (below) and also in Brussels, Belgium.

The Organization for Economic Cooperation and Development (OECD) was created in 1961 in order to research and promote economic progress.

### TRADING ALLIANCES

In 1969, the Association of Southeast Asian Nations (ASEAN) was set up. Canada and the U.S.A. founded the North American Free Trade Association (NAFTA) in 1988, and after 1994, this was extended to include Mexico. Another forum called the Asia-Pacific Economic Cooperation was founded in 1989.

In Asia, there were the Asia-Pacific Economic Co-operation Group (APEC) and the Association of Southeast Asian Nations (ASEAN). The North American Free Trade Agreement (NAFTA), originally the United States and Canada, now included Mexico. The Group of Eight, or G-8, was a group of major countries that met to monitor the world economic situation. The European Union (EU) was the successor of the European Economic Community (EEC) of the 1950s. It is made up of 27 members from across Europe and forms a significant world trading-bloc. Many of the EU members share a single currency—the euro.

The collapse of the Soviet Union in the early 1990s meant that the former communist countries had to adapt to the new post-Soviet realities. Many of the former countries of the "Eastern Bloc" have accepted membership in the EU, a development that raised tensions with Russia who tends to see these nations as part of its sphere of influence.

# WORLD ECONOMICS 1950–1999

**Throughout the second half of the 20th century, the U.S.A. had the world's biggest economy. Asian economies grew rapidly through business expansion.**

▲ In the 1990s, the European Union drew up plans for a new currency, the Euro. It came into circulation on January 1, 1999, and the first notes and coins appeared three years later.

During the 1950s and 60s, living standards rose rapidly in western Europe and North America, while developing countries remained poor. Defeated Germany revived its economy thanks to migrant labor, in what became known an "economic miracle." Japan's manufacturing industries also recovered after the war. Industry ran on "fossil" fuels such as oil and gas, which brought immense wealth to regions such as the Middle East.

## THE STATE VS MARKET FORCES

In much of northwestern Europe, social democratic governments sought to improve social equality through national insurance, welfare benefits, state-owned healthcare and utilities, and social housing. These operated alongside private enterprise. Many workers joined trade unions.

From the 1980s, governments in the U.S.A. and the U.K. privatized their state-owned enterprises. They reduced the role of the state and challenged the power of trade unions. Many western countries moved manufacture to low-wage economies overseas and focused more on service industries and banking.

Oil, known as "black gold," fired up the global economy, but it also damaged the environment and resulted in wars and political unrest.

There were many shocks to the world economy. In the 1970s and 80s, the oil exporting nations (OPEC) repeatedly raised the price of oil, resulting in inflation and debt. In 1987, there was a major stock market crash. The introduction of market forces into the Russian economy after the end of the Cold War was chaotic, and privatization of state assets made a few individuals immensely rich. The rapid expansion of business in countries such as South Korea and Singapore gave them the nickname of "Asian Tiger" economies.

▼ Panic trading on the floor of the New York Stock Exchange in 1987. The world's stock markets all suffered a dramatic fall in share prices at that time.

# EAST ASIAN WARS 1950–1999

**Japan's defeat and the collapse of colonial rule led to fighting among political rivals. The superpowers took sides, based on economic interest or Cold War strategy.**

In 1950, many nations in the East had not yet recovered from Japanese invasions during World War II. People needed peace and stability, but many countries were soon at war. These wars caused further damage to people, cities, and land. Eastern countries wanted to be free of distant European powers. The old colonial masters (France, Britain, and the Netherlands) wanted to hold on to these potentially rich lands.

Fighting broke out in Vietnam and its neighbors Laos, Thailand, and Cambodia, and in Indonesia, Malaysia, Burma, and the Philippines. These wars were often complicated by political differences between rival groups seeking independence. The situation became even more dangerous when the Soviet Union, China, and the U.S. joined in, offering money, weapons, or technical advice to these rival groups.

The French tried to restore colonial rule in Indochina, but were resisted by the Viet Minh, an alliance of communists and nationalists who defeated the French at Dien Bien Phu in 1954.

### THE KOREAN WAR

The Korean War began when communist North Korea attacked South Korea in June 1950. The United Nations quickly authorized its members to aid South Korea. The United States, along with 16 other countries, began sending troops. Within two months, North Korean troops had captured most of South Korea. In September, UN forces mounted a massive land, sea, and air assault at Inchon, near Seoul. The UN troops recaptured most of South Korea and advanced into the North. By November 1950, they had reached the North Korean border with China. Chinese troops then entered the fighting and forced the UN forces to retreat south. A cease-fire ended the war in July 1953.

Knocked out, a tank of the United Nations forces in Korea, in May 1951. Korea has remained divided into two countries since 1953.

▼ Fighting between rival political groups flared up in many parts of Asia between 1946 and 1988. After Japan's defeat in World War II and the collapse of European colonial power, Asia became very unstable.

British colonial troops go on patrol in Malaya in 1950. They were fighting the communist Malayan National Liberation Army (MNLA).

420

▲ Ho-Chi Minh (1892–1969) was a founder member of the French Communist Party. As a revolutionary Vietnamese leader, he led the struggle against French colonial rule and American-supported South Vietnam.

◄ During the war in Vietnam (1964–1975), large areas of the country were devastated. Many civilians were killed and injured. Others were made homeless, and fled as refugees to neighboring lands. Peace finally came in 1976 when Vietnam was united.

## WAR IN VIETNAM

After the French were defeated by Vietnamese communists in 1954, the country was temporarily divided into North and South. Planned elections for the country did not take place, and the communists in the North started giving aid to South Vietnamese communists, the Viet Cong, to help them overthrow the government of Ngo Dinh Diem.

In 1965, the United States sent the first troops to help the South—by 1969, there were over half a million U.S. troops in Vietnam. After Richard Nixon became president in 1969, he began to withdraw troops. A cease-fire was signed in 1973, and the remaining American soldiers returned home. During the war more than 57,000 Americans were killed or missing in action.

## CIVIL WAR IN CAMBODIA

In Cambodia, a guerrilla army, the Khmer Rouge, was led by Pol Pot. They sought to overthrow the government of Lon Nol. The Khmer Rouge took over Cambodia in 1975 and Pol Pot became Prime Minister. His regime of terror was overthrown in 1979 by Vietnamese troops.

▲ After Richard Nixon (1913–1994) became president in 1969, he began to withdraw U.S. troops from Vietnam. In 1973, a cease-fire was signed and all U.S. troops were withdrawn.

◄ In Cambodia, Pol Pot (1926–1998) was the leader of the Khmer Rouge guerrillas. They fought a long civil war, beginning in 1963, and took over the country in 1975. Over the following three years, it is estimated that between two and four million people were executed or died of famine and disease.

| KEY DATES | |
|---|---|
| 1950 | North Korean forces invade South Korea |
| 1953 | Cease-fire in Korea |
| 1954 | Vietnamese communists defeat the French |
| 1962 | Military coup in Burma ends democratic rule |
| 1963 | Civil war starts in Cambodia |
| 1965 | First U.S. troops land in Vietnam |
| 1969 | Richard Nixon becomes president |
| 1973 | All U.S. troops withdrawn from Vietnam |
| 1975 | Pol Pot takes over Cambodia |
| 1979 | Pol Pot deposed by Vietnamese forces |
| 1993 | First free elections in Cambodia for 20 years |

# CIVIL RIGHTS 1950–1999

**Civil rights are the basic freedoms and rights of people within a community. They are guaranteed by laws and customs that give everyone fair treatment.**

Ku Klax Klan members gather around a burning cross. This race hate organization was re-formed in the United States. in the 1950s. It harrassed, intimidated, and murdered black Americans and other minorities.

The idea of civil rights in the West dates back to the writings of ancient Greek and Roman philosophers, and to the ideas of Judaism and Christianity. In some countries, civil rights are protected by a written constitution. In the United States and in other democratic countries, such as Britain, they consist of laws and customs built up over hundreds of years. Civil rights mean that people must be treated fairly and equally, no matter what their gender, religion, or ethnic origin. They are allowed freedom to express what they believe in speech or in the media. They also have the right to organize a political party, to have a fair trial, and to vote in elections. However, many oppressive regimes still abuse their power and ignore civil rights.

During 1989, Chinese students demonstrated in Beijing, demanding democracy in their country. The government sent in the army and thousands of students were killed.

Many rights have been won only after a long and painful struggle. During the 1950s and 1960s, Martin Luther King, Jr. led the civil rights campaign to win equality for black Americans, but many still campaign for these rights today.

In the 1950s and early 1960s, many southern U.S. states still practiced racial segregation, on buses, in restaurants and in public spaces. Signs like this one were all too common.

## MARTIN LUTHER KING

The Reverend Martin Luther King, Jr. (1929–1968) was a Baptist minister and the main leader of the U.S. civil rights movement of the 1950s and 1960s. On August 28, 1963, he led a march on Washington, D.C., where he gave a famous speech that began "I have a dream." His dream was of a future in which his country lived by the ideals of freedom and liberty on which it had been founded. On April 4, 1968, he was shot dead by James Earl Ray. Every year, the third Monday in January is designated a federal legal public holiday in his honor.

## CIVIL RIGHTS ABUSES

In South Africa, Nelson Mandela was sent to prison in 1962 for opposing apartheid (the separation of whites and nonwhites). Many governments and people from all over the world campaigned to end apartheid by holding demonstrations. They boycotted goods from South Africa and stopped all sports links. F.W. de Klerk became president in 1989, and started to dismantle apartheid. Mandela was released in 1990, when apartheid was abolished. In 1994, he was elected as South Africa's first black president.

In 1976, Argentina was taken over by a military *junta* (ruling group). They suppressed opposition by arresting thousands of people and holding them in prison without trial. Between 20,000 and 30,000 people were never seen again by their families. They became known as *los desaparecidos*, or "the disappeared ones." Similar brutality was used by the military regime led by General Pinochet in Chile between 1973 and 1990.

## PROTECTING CIVIL RIGHTS

International bodies, such as the United Nations and the European Court of Human Rights, protect civil rights. Other organizations, such as Amnesty International, campaign on behalf of people who are persecuted. However, some governments continue to ban civil rights. Dictators and single-party nations deny rights to their people because they do not want their own power threatened.

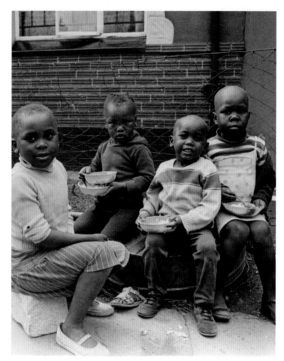

▲ In 1973 the democratically elected government of Chile was overthrown in a military coup led by General Augusto Pinochet. Many ordinary citizens were arrested and many were never seen again.

◀ In the South African city of Johannesburg in the 1980s, many black people and people of color were moved into slums and shantytowns to make more room for white people's homes.

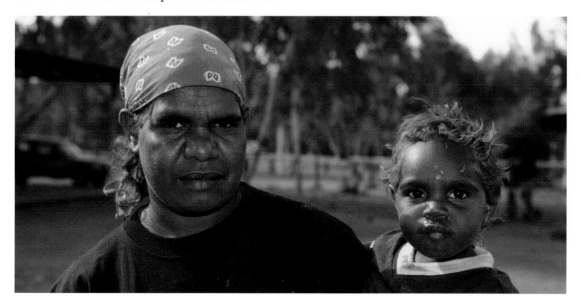

When European settlers first arrived in Australia in the 1700s and 1800s, the Indigenous Australians the original inhabitants of the land—were driven off their traditional hunting grounds. Many also died from diseases brought in by the settlers. It was not until 1967 that the Australian government recognized Indigenous Australians as citizens if the country in which they had lived for 50,000 years.

# TERRORISM 1952–1999

**Terrorism is the attempt to achieve political change through fear, by threatening or committing often indiscriminate acts of violence.**

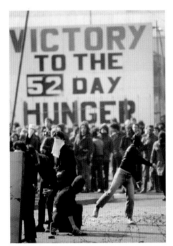

During 1981, some members of the Provisional Irish Republican Army (IRA) who were serving prison sentences in Northern Ireland for terrorist offences went on hunger strike. When one of them died, there was rioting.

▼ In 1988, an American jumbo jet was blown up by a bomb in midair over the Scottish town of Lockerbie, killing 270 people. In 2001, a Libyan spy was convicted of this terrorist act.

The term "terrorism" dates back to the French Revolution, when it referred to acts of terror committed by a state against its citizens. Terrorism committed by individuals or small groups against the state became common in the late 19th century.

Even when the cause was just, the use of terror as a tactic raised fundamental questions of morality. The Indian campaigner Mohandas K. Gandhi had called for complete non-violence, but was assassinated by a terrorist in 1948. Some campaigners rejected terror because its use was counterproductive, as it lost sympathy for their cause instead of gaining support. Some terrorists pointed out that those they targeted also engaged in state terror, such as torture or imprisonment without a trial.

### VICTIMS OF TERROR

The second half of the 20th century saw an increase in terrorist attacks. These included bombings, shootings, kidnappings, and hijackings. Many of those seeking freedom from colonial rule engaged in terror campaigns. Sometimes,

In April 1995, a bomb destroyed the Murrah Federal Building in Oklahoma City, and killed 168 people. The bomber, Timothy McVeigh, thought the federal government had too much control over people's lives.

the supporters of colonialism themselves carried out terrorist attacks, such as the right-wing OAS (Organization Armée Secrète), which caused 2,000 deaths in France and in Algeria from 1961 to 1962.

A historical dispute over Northern Ireland erupted into a cycle of violence known as "The Troubles," from the 1960s to 1998. Acts of terror were carried out in the island of Ireland and in the United Kingdom by Republican paramilitaries such as the Provisional IRA and by various Loyalist opponents. During this period, 3,532 people were killed.

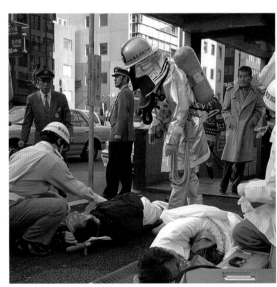

▲ In 1995, a Japanese doomsday cult called Aum Shinrikyo released deadly sarin gas on the Tokyo metro, killing 14 passengers and injuring 5,500.

# HELPING HANDS 1950–1999

**Non-governmental organizations (NGOs) played an important part in easing world humanitarian and environmental problems from the 1950s onward.**

▲ The 1985 Live Aid concert, in aid of Ethiopian famine victims, showed that the world was watching and that ordinary people cared and were full of goodwill.

▼ Central Africa experienced strife in the 1990s, with civil war and genocide. Hundreds of thousands of refugees fled fighting and violence. Here, an injured man is cared for by a Red Cross worker during the Rwandan civil war in 1994.

NGOs included campaigning groups, charities, trusts, non-profit companies and volunteers, and religious organizations. Some dealt with problems within a country, such as homelessness or poverty. Others acted internationally, working alongside United Nations agencies to help the victims of natural disasters such as earthquakes, and also of war or disease.

The Oxford Committee for Famine Relief, founded in England in 1942, later became known as Oxfam and grew into a huge international alliance tackling poverty. Médicins Sans Frontières (Doctors without Borders) was set up in France in 1971 to deal with victims of famine, warfare, and disease, and also became active around the world.

## AFRICAN EXPERIENCES

As the world became more globally connected, many ordinary people in the developed countries wished to lend a helping hand. One trigger for their concerns was a series of devastating famines in sub-Saharan Africa. These were often the result of warfare, civil unrest, or by-products of international Cold War politics. The Biafran War in Nigeria from 1967–70 resulted in perhaps a million deaths from starvation. In the 1970s and 80s, there were severe famines in Somalia and Ethiopia. A rock concert called Live Aid was held in London, U.K., and Philadelphia, in 1985. It was broadcast around the world and raised US$127 million for famine relief in Ethiopia.

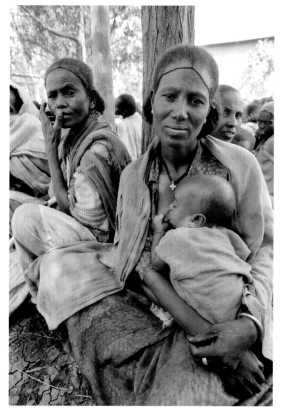

Ethiopia suffered from drought and famine for many years. Between 1977 and 2003, the combination of civil war and famine killed millions of Ethiopians.

Such support was wonderful, but it tended to broadcast a stereotypical view of Africa as always being needy and indebted to the developed world. As such, much of the world ignored the ongoing resilience, energy and inventiveness found all over the African continent. Today's NGOs look for ongoing sustainable support of local skills and enterprise.

▲ Foreign aid does more than supply food in emergencies or crises. Here, we see the results of a project to provide clean water for a community in Kenya. Projects like this help to improve the health of local people.

425

# NEW NATIONS 1950–1999

**Following centuries of rule by colonial powers, many nations gained independence—often achieved through war and terrorism as well as peaceful means.**

▲ Independence was granted to Ghana (formerly the Gold Coast) by Britain in 1957. The Duchess of Kent represented the British queen at the ceremony in the capital, Accra. In the following years, the country suffered from government corruption and military coups.

After World War II, the leaders of many European-ruled colonial countries felt the growing pressure from their people for independence from their foreign control. The days of colonial rule were rapidly coming to an end. During the 1950s and 1960s, many peoples in Africa and southeast Asia fought for their independence. Their people believed that they had a right to own and control their own countries. Many of these independence movements were led by men and women of courage and vision. They were frequently imprisoned before they eventually gained power.

When European colonists refused to give up power, independence groups resorted to fighting. The Mau Mau rebels in Kenya committed acts of terrorism, which were suppressed with internment, torture and hangings. Kenya finally became independent in 1963.

▲ The Federation of Malaya became independent from Britain in 1957. In 1963, it was expanded and renamed Malaysia. However, Singapore broke away as an independent city-state in 1965.

## NEW BORDERS

The creation of independent nations often raised new problems. When Pakistan became independent in 1947, it was made up of two parts, East and West, separated by 1,370 mi. (2,204km). After a bitter war in 1971, the East later broke away from the West, forming a new nation called Bangladesh.

In Africa, old colonial borders had often been agreed by European powers with little regard for ethnic groupings. This resulted in many disputes over power and territory, such as the Biafran War with Nigeria in 1967. There was ongoing strife in Somalia, and Eritrea broke away from Ethiopia in 1993 after a long conflict.

▼ A parade celebrates the independence of Cameroon from France in 1960. In 1961, its neighboring colony, the British Cameroons, voted to divide. The north joined Nigeria and the south merged with Cameroon.

▼ Crowds celebrate the independence of Jamaica in 1962. Many other Caribbean islands followed, but plans for a single independent "West Indian Federation" failed.

## AFTER INDEPENDENCE

Many new nations struggled with a colonial legacy of poor infrastructure, lack of training and resources. Some retained trading or financial links with former colonial powers. There were new regional groupings, such as the Organization of African Unity (OAU), established in 1963. New political ideas came from leaders such as Tanzania's Julius Nyerere, but the world's rich nations still held the real power. New countries could not develop without becoming overburdened with debt, and this instability increased corruption and military coups.

## AFTER THE COLD WAR

Maps of Eastern Europe and Central Asia also needed redrawing after the collapse of the U.S.S.R. in 1991. On the Baltic coast, in Eastern Europe and Central Asia, 13 new states broke away. Countries that had been under Soviet influence during the Cold War also re-emerged, with Czechoslovakia splitting to form the Czech Republic and Slovakia in 1993.

During 1991 to 1992, the Balkan nation of Yugoslavia also broke up as Slovenia, Bosnia-Herzogovina, Macedonia (now North Macedonia), and Croatia declared independence. Devastating civil wars tore the region apart, adding Serbia, Montenegro, and Kosovo to the list of new nations.

◀ Turkmenistan, on the eastern coast of the Caspian Sea, became a republic of the U.S.S.R. in 1925. Following the break-up of the Soviet Union in 1991, this mainly Muslim country declared independence and joined the Commonwealth of Independent States (CIS), consisting of 12 of the 15 former Soviet republics.

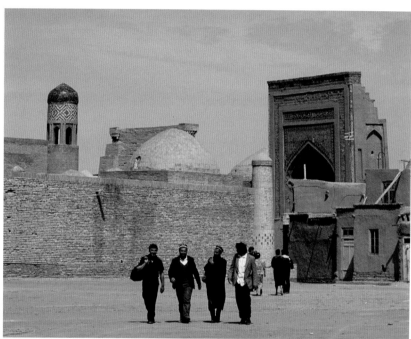

▶ Estonia regained its independence in 1991, having been occupied by the U.S.S.R. since 1940.

▲ After the break-up of the U.S.S.R. in 1991, the Muslim state of Uzbekistan became independent and joined the Commonwealth of Independent States (CIS).

◀ Bosnia and Herzegovina became part of what was to be known as Yugoslavia at the end of World War I. Nationalist feeling grew after the death of President Tito in 1980. Independence was declared in 1992, against the wishes of the Serbian population, and a bitter civil war broke out. Thousands of people died, while others lost their homes and became refugees. In Bosnia and Herzegovina, the capital city of Sarajevo was under siege between 1992 and 1995, during which time thousands of its citizens lost their lives.

# MIDDLE EASTERN WARS 1956–1999

**Following the formation of the State of Israel in 1948, there have been many tensions in the Middle East that have led to bitter disputes and even war.**

The Six-Day War took place between June 5–10, 1967. In a surprise attack, Israeli bombers destroyed Egyptian planes, and then sent in troops to capture the Egyptian soldiers left in Sinai.

The lands around Jerusalem have long been believed by the Jewish people to be their traditional home. After World War II, many Jewish refugees settled in Palestine, although the area was occupied by Arab peoples. The State of Israel was formed in 1948, and fighting broke out with neighboring Arab countries and continued on and off for many years.

In 1956, Egypt took over control of the Suez Canal, which was owned by Britain and France. Because it felt threatened, Israel invaded Egyptian territory in the Sinai, and Britain and France attacked the canal area. There was international disapproval, and the United States and U.S.S.R. both called for a cease-fire. UN troops moved in to keep the peace after the withdrawal of Israeli, British, and French troops.

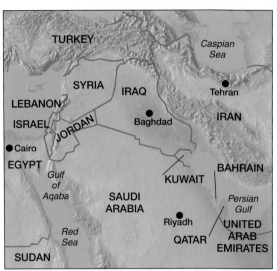

Since 1948 there have been many conflicts between Israel on the one side and the Palestinians and other Arab peoples on the other. Large areas of territory are disputed.

Tensions continued to grow in the 1960s between Israel and the Arab countries of Egypt, Jordan, and Syria. They were aided by several other Arab countries including Iraq, Kuwait, Saudi Arabia, Algeria, and Sudan. Both sides were hostile and unwilling to negotiate their differences. Both sides were also busy getting their troops ready for a possible armed conflict. In May 1967, Egypt closed the Gulf of Aqaba to Israeli shipping.

▼ The Yom Kippur War started in 1973 when Egypt and Syria launched a surprise attack on Israel after it refused to give up land captured during the Six-Day War.

◀ In 1980, Iraq invaded Iran. The two countries fought a long and bitter war. It did not end until August 1988, and cost the lives of over a million soldiers, and almost two million wounded.

▲ Saddam Hussein (1937–2006) was the leader of Iraq from 1979–2003. He fought a costly war against Iran (1980–1988) and invaded Kuwait in August 1990. In 2003 a U.S.-led military campaign overthrew him. He was executed in 2006.

## SIX-DAY WAR

In June 1967, the Israeli air force launched a surprise air attack on the Arab forces' air bases, which took them completely out of action. They then swiftly moved their army to occupy the Gaza Strip and parts of the Sinai. They also pushed their border with Jordan back and captured the Golan Heights from Syria.

## IRAQI AGRESSION

In 1979, the Shah of Iran was deposed and replaced by Islamic fundamentalist Shiite Muslims led by the Ayatollah Khomeini. Tension between Iran and Iraq finally resulted in Iraq's invasion of the oil-rich Iranian territory of Khuzistan in 1980. Iraq feared the power of the new Iranian government set up by the Ayatollah Khomeini. When the war ended in 1988, neither country had made any gains but the cost was enormous—over a million dead, and nearly two million injured.

Rivalries within the Arab world have often been caused by the region's oil deposits. In 1990, Iraq invaded Kuwait to improve its sea access. The UN Security Council demanded that Iraq immediately withdraw its troops. When Saddam Hussein refused, a multinational force led by the United States forced him to withdraw. Retreating Iraqis caused huge ecological damage because they set fire to most of Kuwait's oil wells.

The U.S.-led coalition advanced into Iraq, but did not pursue the enemy further. This Gulf War was over. However, the seeds were sown for a long series of new wars and extreme terrorist campaigns that raged across the whole Middle East region like wildfire from the start of the 21st century.

▼ Burning Kuwaiti oil wells blacken the sky as Iraqi troops withdraw from Kuwait in 1991. Oil brought great wealth to the Middle East, but also wars between nations.

| KEY DATES | |
|---|---|
| 1948 | Independent State of Israel declared; fighting with Arab neighbors erupts |
| 1956 | Suez Crisis |
| 1964 | Palestinian Liberation Organization (PLO) founded in Lebanon |
| 1967 | Six-Day War between Israel and Egypt |
| 1973 | Yom Kippur War in Israel |
| 1979 | Shah of Iran deposed |
| 1980 | Iraq invades Iran |
| 1982 | Israel invades Lebanon to attack the PLO |
| 1988 | Iran-Iraq War ends |
| 1990 | Iraq invades Kuwait |
| 1991 | Iraq forced out of Kuwait |

# THE ENVIRONMENT 1950–1999

**Unlike any other species on Earth, humankind has the power to destroy the world. A new concern for the planet dawned in the 1960s.**

In the second half of the 20th century, some people began to realize that the Earth was in grave danger, threatened with pollution and over-exploitation through ignorance and greed.

A book by U.S. naturalist Rachel Carson caused a sensation in 1962. Her book *Silent Spring* showed the damage done to animal species and the overuse of pesticides. It led to the banning of DDT (an insecticide) in the United States and many other countries, and signaled the beginnings of "green" politics and international campaigning organizations. Friends of the Earth was founded in 1969 and Greenpeace in 1971.

Some scientists had been aware of risks to the atmosphere from industrial gases as early as the 1800s, but in the 1960s and 70s, the fossil fuel industries played down or denied the dangers. Car exhausts and factories were pumping fumes into the air. Some of these gases were mixing with clouds to form acid rain, which killed plants and forests. In many cities, such as Los Angeles, the air quality became so poor that choking smog hung in the air, causing serious breathing problems and premature death.

On the night of 24 March 1989, the *Exxon Valdez*, a 984-foot (300-m.) long oil tanker, ran aground in Prince William Sound, Alaska. The ship leaked more than 35,000 ton of toxic petroleum over the next two days and was the biggest oil spill in American history, destroying wildlife and causing a major clean-up operation.

▼ Cities such as São Paulo in Brazil suffer from dangerous levels of air pollution from motor vehicles and industry.

Resistance to environmental campaigns was sometimes extreme. In 1985, a Greenpeace ship, the *Rainbow Warrior*, was preparing to monitor the effects of French nuclear weapon tests on Pacific islands. The ship was blown up by French government agents while anchored in Auckland, New Zealand, killing a member of the crew.

## PROBLEMS AND PROTECTION

Environmental problems were piling up— overfishing, whaling, logging, mining, habitat destruction. There were accidents at nuclear reactors at Three-Mile Island, U.S.A., in 1979, and Chernobyl, U.S.S.R., in 1986. There were explosions at chemical plants, and oil spills at sea.

In the 1970s, scientists working in Antarctica found that the ozone layer above them was becoming thinner. This part of the Earth's atmosphere is vital for life on Earth, because it blocks much of Sun's harmful ultraviolet radiation. It was being damaged by CFCs, chemicals used in refrigeration and aerosol cans. The use of CFCs was phased out by international treaties from 1987.

Governments passed new laws and brought in regulations to protect the environment. Schools began to teach new generations how to care for the planet. However, many scientists worried that these actions might be too little and too late.

## EARTH SUMMITS

The United Nations held international conferences on the environment in Stockholm in 1972 and Nairobi in 1984, but many politicians were sceptical or not prepared to put their own country's interests at a disadvantage. Poor countries often complained that the rich countries had already developed their industries at the expense of the environment in the past, but now were asking them to hold

▲ Huge tracts of the tropical rain forests in South America were being destroyed so that local farmers could graze cattle.

back. In 1992, the Rio de Janeiro Earth Summit considered toxic pollutants, water use, transportation, biodiversity, renewable energy, and climate change. The scale of the crisis was at last being recognized.

▲ In 1951, the world's population was about 2.6 bilion. By 1999, it was nearly 6.1 billion. The ever-growing impact on the environment was huge.

## RENEWABLE ENERGY

The 20th century was chiefly powered by fossil fuels—coal, oil, or gas. Hydrolectric power also played its part, with the Hoover Dam dating from 1936. Energy that was clean and sustainable or "renewable" was developed in the 1970s, using wind and sun to generate electricity.

▼ Wind farms with arrays of turbines were developed in the U.S.A. and Denmark. At first, they were criticized as unreliable, they became ever cheaper and more dependable in the next century.

▶ Solar panels, powered by the sun, became another renewable energy source.

# WORKING FOR PEACE 1950–1999

**The United Nations grew rapidly after its founding in 1945. It began with 50 member states and by 1999 had 185. Its aim was a more peaceful world.**

The civil war in Lebanon between Christians and a Muslim-PLO alliance during 1975–76 caused much destruction and bloodshed. United Nations forces were sent in as a peacekeeping force.

▲ The United Nations flag shows a map of the world on blue (a color of peace) and olive branches (a symbol of peace).

The most powerful nations in the UN formed a Security Council. This originally had five permanent members, each of which had the power of veto (the right to block a proposal). In addition, there were six non-permanent members, elected from the General Assembly. The total was increased to 15 in 1965. The Republic of China (Taiwan) was replaced by the People's Republic (Communist China) in 1971. The existence of a Security Council was a realistic way of keeping the "superpowers" on board, but it meant that disagreements could paralyse effective action, especially during the Cold War stand-offs. There were calls for reforms to reflect the changing world we live in.

The wider aim of the UN was to develop international cooperation in human rights, economics, cultur, and medicine. Its overriding aim was to maintain international peace and security, but this was harder to achieve.

▼ Indian soldiers on border patrol after border clashes over disputed territory in Kashmir during the Indo-Pakistan conflict of 1965

## TROUBLE SPOTS

During the second half of the 20th century, local and regional wars simmered without end. There were conflicts over colonialism, territory, religion, ideology, and ethnicity. There were also military coups, battles for power, and wars over resources, such as oil. Some places were ongoing "trouble spots," repeatedly making headlines in the news. The danger of smaller conflicts was that they could drag in larger, more powerful nations. Another concern was the possible spread of nuclear weapons. In 1970, the UN's Non-Proliferation Treaty (NPT) to prevent the spread of nuclear weapons came into force. However, India, Pakistan, Israel, and North Korea are not part of the NPT, and all except Israel have declared nuclear weapon development.

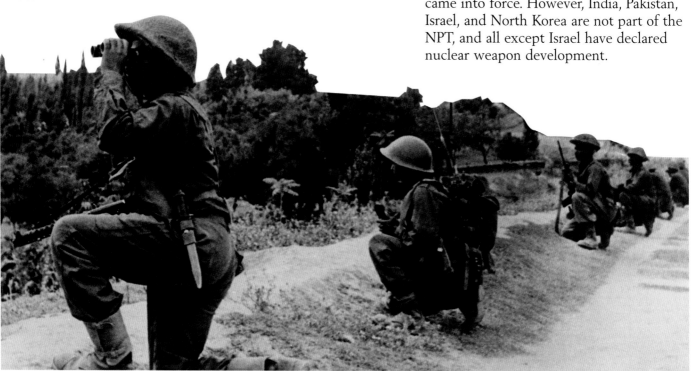

## UN PEACEMAKERS

The UN made a massive military intervention in the Korean War (1950–53) but failed to prevent major conflicts such as the Vietnam War (1955–75). From the Suez Crisis of 1956 onward, UN task forces helped keep the peace in many trouble spots around the world.

UN task forces were international, recruited from the armed forces of member nations, and serving under the UN flag, wearing blue berets or helmets. Their tasks included prevention of conflict, and monitoring ceasefires and peace treaties. They had many successes, and their work was recognized by the award of a Nobel Peace Prize in 1988.

## CONTINENTAL CONFLICTS

Between 1950 and 1999 there was trouble right across Asia. UN peacemakers served in Cyprus, Lebanon, Yemen, Kuwait, Afghanistan, Tajikistan, Kashmir, Cambodia, East Timor, and Western New Guinea (Papua).

In Africa, there were many bitter wars of liberation from the colonial powers, and Cold War rivalries stoked conflict too. UN peacemakers were active in Congo, Angola, Mozambique, Somalia, the Central African Republic, Western Sahara, Liberia, and Sierra Leone. A catastrophic failure occurred in Rwanda 1994 when UN forces failed to prevent a genocide in which perhaps a million people died.

In Europe, the 1990s saw some of the worst fighting since World War II, following the break-up of Yugoslavia. UN peacekeepers were deployed in Croatia, Bosnia-Herzegovina, and Kosovo. In 1995, a terrible massacre of Bosnian Muslim civilians took place at Srebrenica and the UN troops on the ground failed to defend them. Serbian war leaders were later convicted of war crimes.

In Central and South America, this period was marked by military coups and often brutal dictatorships, by revolutions, guerrilla campaigns and United States interventions. UN forces were deployed in El Salvador, Guatemala, and Haiti.

▲ In 1995, the UN sent a peacekeeping force to Rwanda after the death of President Habyarimana led to the Hutu people murdering around half a million Tutsi people.

◄ During the 1990s, Britain used its significant naval presence to support UN peacekeeping and humanitarian missions in many parts of the world.

▼ French armored cars as part of the United Nations Protection Force (UNPROFOR) in Sarajevo in 1994. The series of conflicts in the former Yugoslavia in the 1990s tested the UN to the limit. Tragically, UN troops failed to prevent the massacre of Muslim Bosnians by soldiers of the Serb Republic in 1995.

# APARTHEID SOUTH AFRICA 1948–1994

**South Africa was the last baston of imperialist, white minority rule in Africa. The release of Nelson Mandela from prison in 1990 signalled the end of this era.**

Frederick W. de Klerk (1936–2021) became president of South Africa in 1989 after P. W. Botha resigned because of his health. He worked toward ending apartheid.

Through most of the 20th century, South Africa was racially segregated and governed by white settlers, whether they were Afrikaners or "Boers" (of Dutch origin) or British. The white supremacist National Party was elected to power in 1948 and brought in harsh regulations affecting all aspects of everyday life. They called this system *apartheid*, meaning separation.

Society was strictly divided according to whether you were white, of mixed race, Asian, or black. Marriage between these groups was banned, and housing and work options decreed by the law. Millions of black families were evicted from their homes and forced to live in designated areas called bantustans.

Apartheid was condemned by the United Nations, and South Africa was expelled from the Commonwealth. There were international protests, but the South African government retained the sympathy and support of many conservative politicians in other countries.

South African Desmond Tutu (1931–2021), an Anglican Archbishop, was awarded the 1984 Nobel Peace Prize for his campaign against the racial segregation of apartheid.

## RESISTANCE AND REFORM

After a violent uprising in a township called Sharpeville in 1960, anti-apartheid political parties were banned. The oldest of these was the African National Congress (ANC), founded in 1912. Activists were imprisoned and tortured. The Rivonia trial of 11 activists in 1963–64 is remembered for the three-hour speech calling for democracy from a defendant called Nelson Mandela. He remained in prison for 27 years.

Minor reforms to apartheid were introduced during the premiership and then presidency (1978–84) of P.W. Botha.

▲ Nelson Rolihlahla Mandela (1918–2013) shared the Nobel Peace Prize with F. W. de Klerk in 1993 for their work in ending apartheid.

▶ Under apartheid, many black South Africans were moved out of cities and forced to live in shabby and crowded conditions in shanty towns on the outskirts. Their movement was severely restricted.

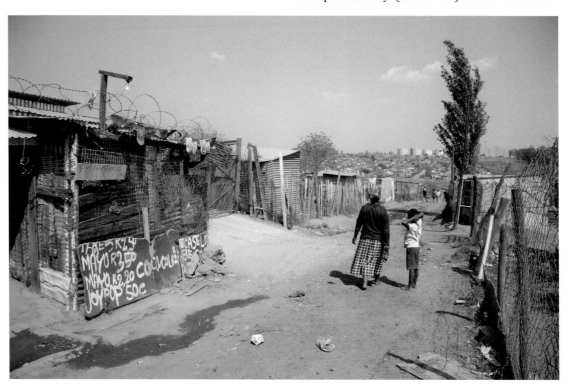

President (1989–94) F. W. de Klerk, under pressure of international sanctions and fear of civil war, took the final steps toward dismantling apartheid and introducing democracy. Nelson Mandela was released from prison in 1990, to worldwide acclaim.

In 1992, de Klerk organized a whites-only referendum that asked whether they would like to end apartheid. Two-thirds of the votes were in favor of ending apartheid.

The first free election, in which black people could also vote, was held in South Africa in April 1994. The ANC won a decisive victory and their leader, Nelson Mandela, became the first Black president of South Africa when de Klerk handed over power to him in May. Mandela focused on a programme of rebuilding South Africa as a "rainbow nation," through a Truth and Reconciliation Commission.

## POST-APARTHEID

A great victory for equality had been won, but under Mandela's successors, South Africa still had many problems to solve, including poverty, inequality, corruption, land ownership, increasing crime rates, and health, especially the impact of the AIDS pandemic.

▲ The modern city of Johannesburg is the financial center of South Africa and lies in the area known as Witwatersrand, at the heart of the gold mining area.

▲ Supporters of Nelson Mandela celebrate the triumph of the African National Congress after the first free elections in South Africa in 1994. The ANC were clear winners and Nelson Mandela became president. He led the country until he retired in 1999.

◀ Post-apartheid South Africa still faced many problems. At this demonstration, protestors from the Landless People's Movement called for more land to be transferred to black ownership.

435

# SCIENCE AND TECHNOLOGY 1950–1999

**The second half of the 1900s was a period of rapid development in science and technology. The arrival of the computer age revolutionized people's lives.**

Scientists and business people were able to develop the discoveries made earlier in the century and put them to practical use. Industry and business realized that there were enormous financial benefits to be made by working with universities and other academic centers and a great deal of important research was done in partnership between the two.

Since lasers were invented in the early 1960s, they have been used for a wide range of tasks, including eye surgery, construction work, mapping, and weapon guidance systems.

▲ The "double helix" structure of the DNA molecule was discovered in 1953 by Francis Crick and James Watson (above), from the X-ray research of Rosalind Franklin. It carries the blueprint for all of an organism's cells, along with the instructions that control their activities.

▶ Manufacturers first introduced robotics to the car assembly line in Detroit, in 1961. By 1990 most repetitive tasks were being done by computer-controlled robots. They were more efficient, but reduced the human workforce.

## ELECTRONICS

The most important breakthrough was the silicon chip, a tiny electronic component that could be cheaply mass-produced. It replaced old, bulky, and fragile pieces of equipment, and allowed much smaller, but more powerful, electronic machines to be built. Microprocessors—complex circuits fitted on a single chip—became widely used in all electrical devices ranging from computers and space rockets to robots and telephones. The silicon chip changed life radically in the late 1900s.

The silicon chip microprocessor, developed in the United States in 1971, caused a technological revolution. The chips were printed with tiny electronic circuits so that computers could process and store information.

## THE COMPUTER AGE

The developments in electronics also led to a revolution in communications. Copy and fax machines meant that office workers could handle vast amounts of information more quickly than ever before. They could also communicate rapidly with other people around the world. As the means of communications improved, information became more freely available. By the end of the 1900s, anyone with a personal computer and a telephone line could contact millions of other people around the world in an instant using the Internet.

In industry, electronics also brought about a new industrial revolution. By the 1990s, most aspects of the manufacturing process in a wide range of industries were computer controlled. Repetitive tasks on assembly lines were carried out by electronic machines or robots. Stock control, distribution, and administrative systems also came under the control of computer technology.

## MEDICAL BREAKTHROUGHS

First developed in the 1960s, lasers were used in surgery to burn away diseased tissue and perform delicate eye operations. In the 1950s, American and British scientists discovered the structure of DNA, the basic building blocks from which living cells are made. This knowledge led eventually to the production of new drugs by genetic engineering, which helped cure serious diseases. The discovery of DNA means that many genetic illnesses, passed down through families, will be curable.

Genetic engineering also raised the possibility of creating new or improved strains of plants and animals, resistant to disease. This technology has helped to feed people in poorer countries by increasing the amount that the land can support.

◀ The Hubble Space Telescope was launched into orbit by the U.S. space shuttle *Discovery* in April 1990. It allowed scientists to capture images of objects billions of light years away in space.

▲ Engineers check a satellite. The first communication satellite was launched in 1960. The introduction, in 1964, of geosynchronous satellites, which remain over the same place on Earth, meant that any two places on Earth could be linked almost instantly.

## THE WORLD WIDE WEB

The World Wide Web (WWW) was invented in 1989 by Tim Berners-Lee. Its original aim was to share data between scientists at different institutions around the world via the internet. This involved three new coding processes: HTML (HyperText Markup Language), URL (Uniform Resource Location, and HTTP (HyperText Transfer Protocol). The success of the web was made possible by small, affordable personal computers, developed from the 1970s onward, but the reliance of the internet on telephone lines made it very slow. That would change with the development of broadband connection from the 2000s. Instant access to web information was enabled by the development of search engines in the 1990s. The digital age would soon revolutionize almost every aspect of our daily lives and activities.

▼ This is the computer used by Tim Berners-Lee to develop the World Wide Web.

# ART AND ARCHITECTURE 1950–1999

**After World War II, there was a burst of creative energy that often confronted conventional forms of expression.**

▲ Art goes pop. Screenprints of film star Marilyn Monroe by Andy Warhol (1928–87) are hung for exhibition at the British Museum, U.K., in 2017.

▲ This Irish postage stamp commemorates Samuel Beckett (1906–89). Beckett wrote in both English and French. His plays had a dark sense of humor, but showed human existence as bleak and absurd.

▶The Beatles (Ringo Starr, George Harrison, Paul McCartney, and John Lennon) were a pop group from Liverpool, U.K.. Between 1960 and 1970, their fresh sound, creativity, and high energy made them the most famous band in the world. They came to symbolize their generation and the spirit of the 60s.

The visual arts and the performing arts went through many radical experiments in literature, art, photography, theater, cinema, music, and dance. Television, sound recording, and electronics offered new technologies and possibilities.

### WHAT IS ART?
New York City now challenged Paris, France, as the center of the visual arts. The paint-splattered canvasses of Jackson Pollock (1912–56) contrasted with the flat fields of color favored by Mark Rothko (1903–70). Both artists could be described as "abstract expressionists." The 1960s saw the rise of pop art, in the jokey comic-style paintings of Roy Lichtenstein (1923–97) and the prints of movie stars and soup cans by Andy Warhol (1928–97). The period of art after 1970 is often called "post-modern." It saw the visual arts blending with performance in "happenings," "conceptual" art, installations and interaction with landscapes or buildings.

▲ Bob Marley (1945-81) was a singer, musician, and inspired songwriter. He made reggae and other kinds of Jamaican music popular around the world.

### MUSIC REVOLUTIONS
Jazz music went through many experimental styles, from Cool to Hard Bop, Free Jazz, and Fusion. In the mid 1950s, a new style of popular music from the United States took the teenage world by storm—rock'n'roll. This style borrowed from blues and country music, and the 1960s and 70s saw an outpouring of creative new sounds from London to Jamaica, from Latin America to Africa.

## CONCRETE, STEEL, AND GLASS

In Europe, many buildings had been destroyed by bombing and post-war architects were determined to build for a new age. Some "modernist" architects were inspired by French-Swiss architect and city planner Le Corbusier (1887–1965) or by German-American Mies van der Rohe (1886–1969). Geometrical shapes in concrete, steel, and glass pleased designers, but residential city tower blocks did not always make for good community living. Some more controversial examples became known as "brutalist."

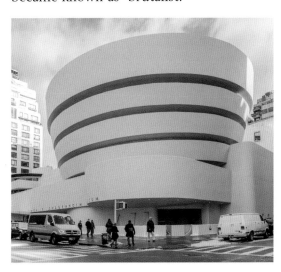

▲ The Guggenheim museum of art in New York City, moved into this iconic building in 1959. It was designed by the architect Frank Lloyd Wright (1867–1959).

◀ The Bank of China Tower in Hong Kong, China, is more than 1171 ft (357m.) high. It opened in 1990.

▲Berlin's New National Gallery (1968) was designed by Mies van der Rohe (1886–1969).

## CITY ICONS

Some public buildings became iconic city landmarks, such as the Guggenheim museum of modern art in New York City (1959), designed by Frank Lloyd Wright, or Australia's Sydney Opera House (1973), originally designed by Danish architect Jørn Utzon. The high-tech Pompidou Centre in Paris (Richard Rogers, 1977) caused a stir because it was inside out, with all its pipe work and structure displayed on the outside of the building.

City landmarks of the 1990s and 2000s were often designed for novelty, with strange shapes. In the next century, the tallest skyscrapers were built in Asia rather than the United States.

▲ Radical designs for the Sydney Opera House initially caused controversy, but it soon became one of the world's most admired buildings, and a symbol of modern Austraila.

◀ The Pompidou Centre, with its exterior in bright, bold primary colors, contrasts sharply with the classical stonework of central Paris.

# A NEW MILLENNIUM

## 2000 – PRESENT

In 2000, the United Nations' Millennium Declaration set out goals for tackling poverty, inequality, hunger, health, education, and the environment. By 2015, much progress had been made, but other problems were pressing. The climate was in crisis, wars and terrorism were continuing in many parts of the world, and there were economic troubles. A global pandemic struck in 2019 and effective vaccines were developed with great speed. This was an age of rapid medical, scientific, and technological advances. New digital platforms transformed the ways in which we communicate, learn, do business, and enjoy ourselves.

▲ Fireworks light up the sky at the Beijing Olympics in 2008. China was now challenging the United States as the world's biggest economy.

◀ As soon as the COVID-19 pandemic took hold, the race was on to produce vaccines. Mass vaccinations and boosters against the virus took place from 2020.

# A CROWDED PLANET 2000 – PRESENT

**In 2000, the world population stood at 6.1 billion. By 2020, it had reached 7.8 billion, with about 81 million babies being born every year.**

▲ A longer life expectancy means an increase in the number of elderly citizens in need of care and medical support.

▲ By 2021, the population density in Bangladesh was 3,277 people per mi², which presented major problems in public transport, drainage, sanitation, pollution, clean water supply, and public health.

During the 20th century, advances in medicine and public health caused the global birth rate—and life expectancy at birth—to rise dramatically. This was often referred to as a "population explosion."

By the 21st century, the numbers were still rising, but at the same time the rate of that growth was falling steadily. The United Nations (UN) predicts a world population of around 9.7 billion by 2050 and 10.9 billion by 2100. By that time, the growth rate could be as little as 0.1 percent each year.

## RISKS AND RESOURCES

Does the world have enough resources to cope? Is there room on the planet for so many people? Can we grow enough food to feed everyone? These questions predated the new millennium by many years. However, it acquired a new urgency because of problems caused by climate change.

Drought and the spread of deserts will lead to a crisis in the supply of water for drinking and farming. Flooding, rising sea levels, or wildfires can destroy precious crops. Other unknown risk factors that could affect population levels in the future include pandemics and wars over resources. The planet can produce enough food to feed the world, but this requires a radical global reform of land use, farming methods and crops, and an end to the vast amounts of food wasted in richer countries.

In 2021, the Greater Tokyo area (Japan's Capital Region) was home to about 38 million people. More than half of the world's population now lived in towns and cities, and it was predicted that by 2050 that proportion might exceed two-thirds.

## PLANNING FOR THE FUTURE

Kofi Annan, Secretary-General of the UN from 1997 to 2006, realized that there could be no sustainable development without stable population figures, but how could these be achieved? Family planning services, contraception, and legal abortion rights had been available since the 20th century, although these were challenged on religious or ethical grounds in some regions. Targeted taxation could also be used by governments to discourage larger families.

In China, legal limitations of the number of children, a "one-child policy," had been partially introduced in 1979 as China's population reached 1 billion. However, this created social problems and human rights issues. An ageing population and low birth rate meant that the workforce was growing smaller. In 2013, China relaxed the rules so some couples could have a second child if one parent was an only child. In 2015, the policy was abolished altogether.

Overall, the areas of the world with the highest predicted population increases are the least developed, and eliminating poverty is crucial to reducing population growth. Improved infant mortality rates, along with health, education, and the social and economic empowerment of young women remain the best route to stable population levels.

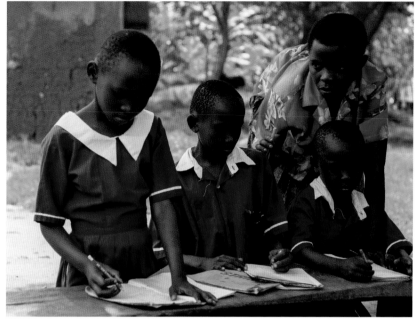

▲ Ugandan pupils hard at work. Education and employment opportunities for young women in developing countries help reduce the size of families.

◄ Farm buildings in the Russian countryside lie abandoned. During the 2000s, the rural population in Russia deserted the land and poured into Moscow, the capital and economic powerhouse of the nation. This process is called urbanization.

Children playing football in Niger. This country has one of the world's highest birth rates of an average of seven children born per woman in 2016.

# THE CLIMATE CRISIS 2000–PRESENT

**Many human activities, including transportation, industry, and agriculture, pump carbon dioxide, methane, and other gases into the atmosphere. There they trap heat around the planet, affecting our climate.**

▲ Wildfires have always been a risk in warm regions such as Australia (above) and California, but in the 2020s they raged on an unprecedented scale. They compounded the crisis by emitting even more carbon dioxide into the atmosphere.

▼ The decline of Arctic sea ice will contribute to rising sea levels. Polar bears roam far over sea ice to find food—the less sea ice there is, the smaller the area they can live and hunt in.

The scientific effects of this process had been predicted as long ago as the nineteenth century, and data emerging through the twentieth century supported this theory. However, the industries producing high-carbon "fossil fuels" such as coal, oil, and natural gas questioned the data and encouraged scepticism about human-induced climate change. Many conservative politicians refused to consider taking effective action.

## EARLY WARNINGS

In 2001, the third report of the I.P.C.C. (Intergovernmental Panel on Climate Change} warned that a change in climate like none since the last Ice Age was very likely. In the same year, the U.S. National Academy of Sciences noted a major shift of scientific opinion toward recognition of the problem. Even so, the U.S. government refused to sign the 2005 Kyoto Protocol on climate change. The violence of tropical storms seemed to be increasing. Could disasters such as Hurricane Katrina, which in 2005 struck New Orleans with the loss of over 18,000 lives, have been made worse by climate change?

▲ In 2019, Jair Bolsonaro became Brazilian president. He denied there was a climate crisis, and opened up one of the world's most precious environmental assets, the vast Amazon rain forest, to loggers, miners, and farmers. In his first two years in office, 10,000 square miles (25,900 km²) were destroyed.

## THE PARIS AGREEMENT

The Paris Agreement of 2015 was signed by 196 parties who pledged to tackle climate change and aim to keep the temperature increase at 2°C below pre-industrial levels (preferably 1.5°C). The U.S. pulled out of the accord in 2020, but it signed up again in 2021. Plans included reduction of emissions, increased use of ever cheaper renewable energy sources, planting more trees, and preventing destruction of forests—trees absorb carbon dioxide and give out oxygen. The practice of "carbon trading" (the buying and selling of quotas for carbon emissions) was to be reviewed.

◄ The regular United Nations Climate Change Conferences, also known as COPs (Conferences Of Parties who had signed up to the agreements), coordinate global policy.

▲ School strikes for the climate took place around the globe, urged on by Swedish teenage activist Greta Thunberg (b.2003).

## TIPPING POINTS

Some environmentalists feared that the measures of the Paris Agreement were too little and too late, and were not being implemented. By the 2020s, scientists were increasingly confident in linking extreme climate events to human-induced global heating. The Greenland and the Antarctic ice sheets were melting rapidly. Terrible wildfires were ravaging California, Australia, Greece, and even the Siberian Arctic. Record high temperatures were measured in Canada and Europe. Severe flooding wrought havoc in Germany and China. There were even fears that the circulation of currents in the Atlantic Ocean was breaking down, potentially a catastrophe with global impact.

There could be no quick fixes. Even at current temperatures the problems could persist for centuries. However, immediate action was essential to prevent the climate crisis becoming even worse.

Scientists suspected that the extreme rainstorms which caused flooding in Germany and Belgium in 2021, with the loss of 226 lives, were linked to the climate crisis.

▲ Extinction Rebellion, founded in 2018, is one of many climate protest groups. It engages in nonviolent direct action, including street theater (above).

▲ Surveying the damage caused by tornadoes in Kentucky, in December 2021. Warmer winter weather means more tornadoes strike the region.

445

# ENVIRONMENTAL THREATS 2000–PRESENT

**The natural world was coming under increasing threat from humans. By the twenty first century, the loss of wild habitats and the pollution of air, land, and water were endangering many species.**

Life on Earth has evolved to form networks—complex patterns of interaction in which each species (including humans) depends on others, through food chains or shaping the natural environment. If links in those chains and networks are broken, the results may be catastrophic.

▲ A young orangutan is rescued after its home—tropical forest in Sumatra, Indonesia—is cut down to make way for palm oil plantations. Palm oil is used in the manufacture of shampoo, toothpaste, cookies, and chocolate.

▼ Microplastics are tiny beads of plastic less than 0.2 in. (5mm) across. Nanoplastics are even smaller. They may come from industrial processes, car tires, synthetic clothing, or larger plastic items that have broken up.

## PROBLEMS WITH PLASTICS

Technological innovations and the increase in human population led to pollution of the planet on a vast scale. Tiny particles of plastic—unrecyclable "microplastics"—could now be found on top of Mount Everest and in the deepest parts of the Pacific Ocean, in the air, and in drinking water. They were present in the bodies of fish—and in humans. Garbage dumps towered above crowded makeshift housing in many cities around the world. Plastic bottles and toxic factory waste choked the life out of once clean rivers, from India to Indonesia.

Garbage collected from the streets from the city of Kathmandu, Nepal, overflows into the Bhagmati river.

## INDUSTRIAL DISASTERS

In 2010, the largest ocean oil spill in history occurred off the coast of Louisiana, when the BP-operated Deepwater Horizon oil rig exploded during a blowout. Every type of habitat in the Gulf of Mexico was contaminated with oil, and populations of marine creatures such as dolphins and turtles were devastated. In 2011, following an earthquake and tsunami, cooling systems failed in three nuclear reactors at Fukushima in Japan. There was partial meltdown and a series of explosions. Water, land, and crops were irradiated and tens of thousands of people had to be evacuated from the area.

▲ The Fukushima nuclear disaster that took place in Japan 2011 was a stark reminder of the long-term dangers of radioactivity to the environment.

446

## HABITATS LOST OR POISONED

The survival of many animal species has been threatened by a loss of wild habitats, caused by the spread of cities, tourist developments, intensive farming, and illegal logging. Overfishing and hunting also threatened the future of many species. Nitrates from agricultural fertilizers were poisoning rivers. Pesticides were killing off not only harmful insects, but also the useful ones that pollinate the crops we need to feed us.

## BIODIVERSITY OR EXTINCTION?

In the first two decades of the century, many governments and non-governmental organizations worked hard to protect the environment. They promoted biodiversity (the vast variety of life forms on the planet) but it was an uphill struggle. In 2021, 16,306 animal speices were officially classed as "endangered," threatened with extinction. Many scientists feared that we had already entered a new age of mass extinctions, like the one that eradicated dinosaurs 66 million years ago.

## REWILDING

From the 1960s, environmentalists explored the possibilities of putting human expansion into reverse gear by allowing certain areas to return to their original state. In the twenty first century, "rewilding" projects were carried out in many parts of the world: farmland and pasture were reforested and drained land was allowed to revert to wetland. Key species of wild animals such as wolves, bears, beavers, and eagles were reintroduced to areas where they had become locally extinct. Isolated animal populations were joined up by wildlife corridors, so that animals could migrate or breed more easily.

Northern white rhinoceroses were declared extinct in the wild in 2008. Only two survive in captivity, a mother and daughter, cared for by rangers in their Kenyan home. Rhinos are hunted for their horn, which is valued as a traditional medicine and a status symbol in some countries.

◄ Neonicotinoids are a group of insecticides used in farming. They are toxic to honeybees. They were banned in Europe in 2018 but are still often permitted. Humans depend on the pollination of plants by insects for their survival.

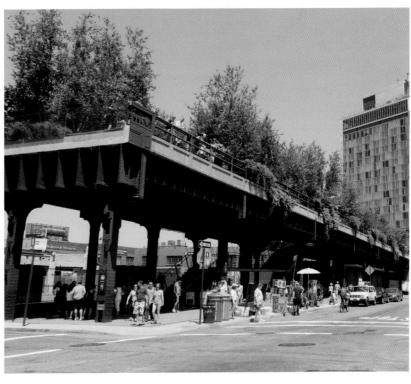

► In 2009, a new park opened in New York City, on a former railroad line. Called the High Line, the 1.45-mile (2.33-km) long park has been created to be a green space in the city with more than 500 plants and trees. It was one of the earliest rewilding projects in an urban area.

447

# A GLOBAL ECONOMY 2000–PRESENT

**At the start of the new millennium, world trade was becoming increasingly interconnected. This process was called globalization.**

▲ A worker locating products in one of the giant warehouses owned by the multinational e-commerce giant Amazon.

▼ Textile workers in Bangladesh complain about health and safety conditions in 2015.

Globalization aimed to boost international trade, building on improved communications and the impact of the internet on financial dealing and commerce. Companies from one nation could now operate in many countries at once, and many were set up as single "transnational" corporations. The economic model was free market capitalism, in which goods, services, and money could move between countries with fewer regulations and tariffs (taxes on imports). Critics of globalization pointed out that it often benefited richer countries at the expense of poorer nations, where labor and raw materials were cheaper.

Instant connectivity between markets and traders around the world has boosted economic globalization.

### THE CRASH OF 2007–2008

Globalization also meant that if there was an economic crisis, the troubles risked being spread around the world much more quickly. In 2007–2008, the failure of financial controls in the U.S. led to a housing crisis and then the collapse of major banks, triggering national economic disasters in many countries, including Iceland and Greece. This recession was the worst since the Great Depression of the 1930s. Many governments responded by reducing public spending and freezing wages. This policy, referred to as "austerity," caused widespread hardship and resentment even in the richest countries.

রানা প্লাজা ট্রাজেডির-২ বছর
রানা প্লাজা ট্রাজেডির-২ বছর

**ENSURE WORK PLACE SAFETY**

**WORKER'S ARE NOT CHEAP LABOR**

সম্মিলিত গার্মেন্টস শ্রমিক ফেডারেশন
সম্মিলিত গার্মেন্টস শ্রমিক ফেডারেশন

▲ A riot police officer in Athens, Greece. In 2008, Greece was badly affected by the global recession. Despite high taxes with lower wages, many people despaired and there were riots on the streets of Athens.

## TARIFFS OR FREE TRADE?

In 2016, Donald Trump was elected President of the United States. To try to protect American industries from competition outside the U.S., he imposed tariffs on certain goods imported from Europe and China. The danger of such "protectionist" policies is that they can grow into a "trade war" and increase political instability. China had developed its economy remarkably quickly and was challenging the U.S. as the world's leading economic power. Also in 2016, voters in a U.K. "Brexit" referendum narrowly voted to leave the EU, despite its tariff-free trade and vast single market, which was portrayed as diluting national identity and sovereignty. However, the U.K. still sought to join trading groups outside the EU. The U.K. withdrawal had a major impact on its economy and employment. At the same time, the global COVID-19 pandemic in 2020 disrupted global supply chains and international movement of freight.

## TAX AVOIDANCE

Some of the world's biggest transnational corporations were now being criticized for not paying a fair share of tax across all the countries where they operated. International finance made increasing of use of "tax havens"—jurisdictions with low or zero taxation rates and sometimes offering high levels of secrecy.

Despite criticism from many different political viewpoints, globalization remains a powerful force in the world.

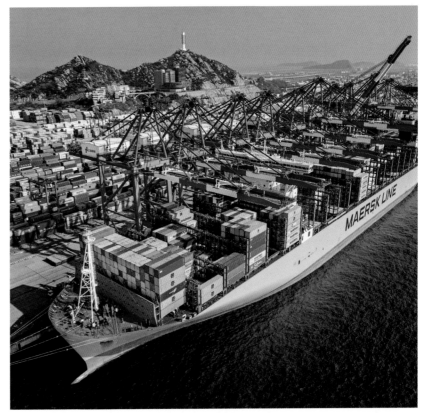

▲ A giant ship is loaded in Shanghai, China, the world's biggest and busiest container port.

▼ In 2012, campaign group U.K. Uncut marched to let people know that Starbucks hadn't paid any corporation tax for three years. The tax loophole meant the company was not doing anything illegal by not paying the tax.

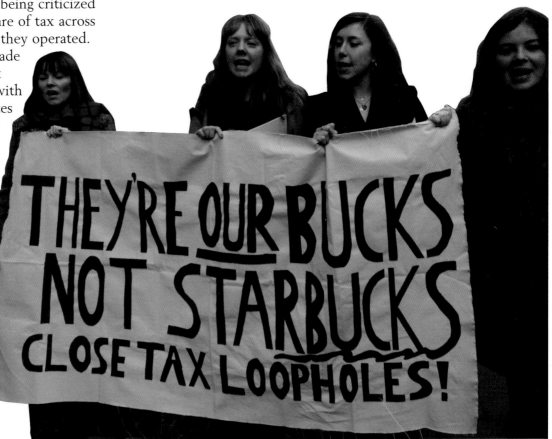

# WAR AND TERROR 2000–PRESENT

**When the Cold War ended in 1991, there was talk of a "peace dividend," with money spent on the arms race being diverted to more peaceful projects. It was not to be.**

The "9/11" attacks on the United States in 2001 killed 2,996 people. The terrorists were from Saudi Arabia, UAE, Lebanon, and Egypt.

Warfare was now often an ongoing conflict between a coalition of powerful nations and groups of insurgents or terrorists using different tactics. This uneven balance was called "asymmetric" warfare. The use of unmanned military drones, operated from a distant country, was by now a common feature of combat.

### 9/11 AND WAR IN AFGHANISTAN
On September 11, 2001 ("9/11"), there were four coordinated and devastating terrorist attacks on the United States, carried out by an organization called Al-Qaeda. The attacks had been planned from a base in Afghanistan. Following 9/11, a U.S.-led international coalition invaded Afghanistan and with local help drove the ruling Taliban faction from power. The war in Afghanistan and the occupation continued until the U.S. withdrew suddenly in 2021, prompting a rapid collapse of the Afghan government and the return to power of the Taliban.

▲ Coalition bombers attack Baghdad in 2003. The first phase of the U.S.-led invasion of Iraq may have killed more than 6,600 civilians.

### THE IRAQ WAR
Also following 9/11, U.S. President George W Bush declared a "War on Terror" on September 16, 2001. He declared that the dictator of oil-rich Iraq, Saddam Hussein (1937–2006), had weapons of mass destruction—a claim that proved to be untrue. Bush was supported by an international coalition that included the U.K. Troops invaded Iraq in March 2003 and Bush declared "Mission Accomplished" on May 1, but the war was only just beginning. It spilled over into insurgencies, battles, strife between Shia and Sunni Muslims, and acts of terror. The U.S. finally withdrew its forces in 2011. However, savage asymmetric warfare continued across the region with terrorist forces known as Islamic State (ISIS or Daesh) seizing territory in Iraq and Syria until 2017.

▲ In the years after 2002, 780 Muslims were flown in chains to a U.S. prison camp at Guantanamo Bay, on the island of Cuba. Indefinite detention without due process of law or trial, as well as prisoner abuse, led to worldwide protests.

## ACROSS THE MIDDLE EAST

The Israel–Palestine conflict led to repeated Israeli bombings of Gaza between 2008 and 2021. A series of revolts against authoritarian governments across the Arab world began in Tunisia in 2010. Most of these "Arab Spring" uprisings had failed by 2012, but in Syria and in Yemen they led to long-lasting conflicts backed by a complex network of regional and global alliances.

The Syrian civil war set out to challenge the authoritarian rule of president Bashir al-Assad and the Syrian army. The rebels included a number of different groups, some of them mutually hostile, and divided by religious, political, and ethnic factions. Assad was supported by Iran and Russia, and Turkey and the U.S. aided some of the rebel armies but not others. Syrian cities were bombed into rubble.

## GLOBAL SECURITY FEARS

By the 2020s, tensions were increasing between the U.S. and China, amid fears of a new Cold War. A new military pact for the Pacific region was set up in 2021 by Australia, the U.K. and the U.S. (AUKUS) to counter China's growing power. Meanwhile tensions between Russia and NATO were being ratcheted up along the borders of Eastern Europe. The proliferation of nuclear weapons was back on the agenda, with North Korea testing new missiles.

▲ Homs was the center of opposition to the government in Syria. Hundreds of people were killed and thousands stranded without basic supplies when government forces laid seige to the city. The seige lasted two years, from 2012–2014, and the Old City was ruined.

▶ There was division in independent Ukraine, formerly part of the Soviet Union, when pro-Russian groups in the east of the country clashed with the pro-Western government. In 2014, Russian president Vladimir Putin illegally annexed the Crimea region of Ukraine and in 2022 ordered a full-scale invasion of the whole country.

More hopefully, a new global ban accord, the Treaty on the Prohibition of Nuclear Weapons, was opened for nations to sign at the UN in 2021.

▲ U.S. President Donald Trump meets with North Korea's Kim Jong-Un in 2019. He was the first sitting president to meet a North Korean leader while in office.

▲ Children being taught in a camp for displaced people in Darfur. Africa suffered numerous conflicts in the 2000s. From 2003, rebel groups from the Darfur region of Sudan fought the central government. In return, government-backed militias killed hundreds of thousands of civilians and more than two million people were displaced.

# POLITICS AND PROTEST 2000–PRESENT

**Ideals of internationalism and democracy faced many challenges in the second decade of the new century, with increasingly divisive politics and authoritarian leadership in many lands.**

▲ Donald Trump's presidency was to place U.S. interests, as he saw them, above international diplomacy. He used social media and rallies to whip up popular support.

During the free market economics popular at the start of the twenty first century, liberal parties relied on political management skills rather than deeply held convictions. The presentation of policies (or "spin") became all important. In the U.K., Tony Blair had rebranded the Labour Party as "New Labour" and appealed to more middle-class voters, as had Bill Clinton's Democrats in the U.S.

## DEPRIVED COMMUNITIES

The moving of industries to low-wage economies overseas led to a weakening of trade union power in Europe and North America. Votes shifted to the right. The global economic crash of 2007–2008 was paid for by policies of "austerity," cutting public spending and social welfare. This hit poor and working-class communities the hardest. A protest movement called Occupy began in Wall Street, New York City's financial center, in 2011 and soon spread to 82 countries around the world.

▲ By 2020-2021, more than 2.5 million U.K. citizens were using "food banks"—donations of free food by charities.

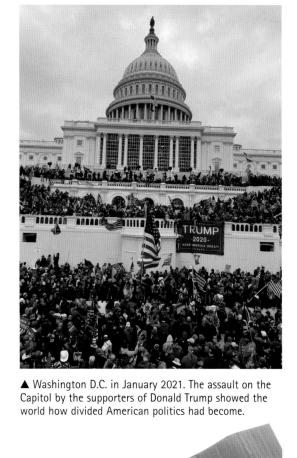

▲ Washington D.C. in January 2021. The assault on the Capitol by the supporters of Donald Trump showed the world how divided American politics had become.

A "United for a Global Change" protest in Valencia, Spain, in 2011.

## DIVIDE AND RULE

Populist politicians, many of them billionaires themselves, claimed that the abandoned and disadvantaged voters had been robbed by "liberal elites." Nations and international alliances became increasingly divided. In 2014, Narendra Modi won the Indian election for the Hindu nationalists. In 2016, Donald Trump won the presidential election in the U.S. on an "America First" ticket, and in a U.K. referendum, voters narrowly chose to leave the European Union (EU). Social media became ever more influential in elections, and at the same time open to influence from other countries.

Many people argued that political "spin" had turned into outright lying and cheap abuse. Far-right and fascist protests were appearing in many parts of the world. The results of the 2020 U.S. election were not accepted by Donald Trump. In January 2021, his followers stormed the Capitol in Washington D.C., despite the law courts rejecting Trump's claim that the election had been "stolen." Five people died and 128 police officers were injured.

Many world leaders could now be described as authoritarian, from Vladimir Putin in Russia to Xi Jinping in China.

▼ Belarussians protest against the government after the election in August 2020 in the city of Minsk.

▲ Angela Merkel, a German conservative, served as Chancellor from 2005–2021 and was a force for stability across the EU. Emmanuel Macron, the youngest president in French history, saw off a far-right challenge in the 2017 election, but many of his economic reforms were unpopular.

▲ New Zealand's Labour prime minister Jacinda Ardern went against the global trend by encouraging politics of unity rather than division.

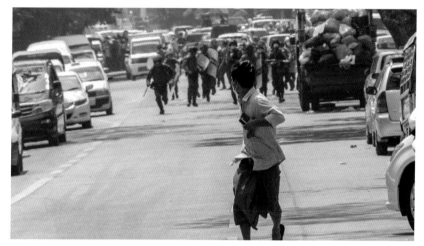

Mass protests disputing the reelection of Alexander Lukashenko in the Belarus election of 2020 were brutally suppressed, as were demonstrations in Myanmar after a military coup in 2021.

▲ Myanmar in 2021. Pro-democracy protestors showed extraordinary courage in many parts of the world.

# CALLS FOR EQUALITY 2000–PRESENT

**Equality and social justice are essential for the wellbeing of every human on the planet. They were declared important goals for the new millennium.**

A "Pride" march in Budapest in 2019 protests against an anti-LGBT (Lesbian, Gay, Bisexual, and Transgender) campaign led by the Hungarian government.

Equality issues have affected every aspect of life since 2000, including poverty or wealth, working opportunities, access to education, health, food, housing, political representation, and legal rights. Discrimination has been experienced by people because of their skin color, ethnicity, their sex, sexuality or gender, their faith or lack of faith, and their social class or caste.

A child plays football in a street in Rio de Janeiro, Brazil. At the current rate of progress, it will take Black Brazilians until 2089 to catch up with the wages of White Brazilians.

▼ In 2021, a report showed that only 75 percent of children worldwide in poorer households attended primary school. The huge wealth gap between the world's rich and poor countries is reflected in their provision of public education.

## ECONOMIC INEQUALITY

By 2018, nearly half of the world's population was now living on less than $5.50 a day. The World Bank defined extreme poverty as living on less than $1.90 a day. The most extreme poverty affected those regions suffering from conflict, natural disasters, or climate extremes. Economic inequality existed at relative levels between regions and nations, within nations, within organizations, and between individuals. It affected more women and children than men, and it denied access to healthcare and schooling for millions of people.

Poverty levels declined around the world from 2000 until 2020.

China in particular made great advances in tackling extreme rural poverty. In 2020, there was a setback globally as the COVID-19 pandemic caused economic disruption, which made the rich considerably richer and the poor even poorer. Even as extreme poverty declined, the gap between the richest and poorest grew ever wider. The get-rich-quick society of the 2000s created many billionaires, but taxation was low and, in many cases, avoided. By 2020, the world's wealthiest one percent owned more than twice as much as 6.9 billion people combined.

In 2021, only 22 women in the world were heads of state or government. One of them was Icelandic prime minister Katrin Jakobsdóttir, elected in 2017.

◀ A worker in a mobile phone care center in Nairobi, Kenya. The 22 richest men had more wealth between them than all the women in Africa.

## WOMEN'S RIGHTS

Women's rights had come a long way since the 1960s, but there was still a struggle for equal pay and recognition, even in the most progressive countries. Child marriage or trafficking into forced labor or sex slavery was increasing in many places and, in 2018, more than a billion women worldwide lacked legal protection against domestic violence.

In 2020, the World Economic Forum's Gender Gap Report stated that women globally would not have equality at least another century. Under-representation of women in the workplace was a key problem—in 2019, only around one quarter of parliamentary positions worldwide were filled by women.

## BLACK LIVES MATTER

There were growing demands for Western societies to re-examine their history regarding colonialism and slavery and its portrayal in public monuments. Racism still blighted many societies. From 2012 onward, following shootings of young Black Americans in the U.S., protests grew, often under the banner "Black Lives Matter." In 2020, the murder of an unarmed Black American named George Floyd by a police officer in Minneapolis during an arrest, sparked protests across the United States and around the world.

▼ "Taking the knee" before a sporting fixture began with Colin Kaepernick (right), a football player, in 2016, in protest against racial injustice. The practice soon spread around the world.

▲ Black Lives Matter demonstrators march in New York on June 16, 2020, holding an image of George Floyd who was killed by a police officer in May 2020.

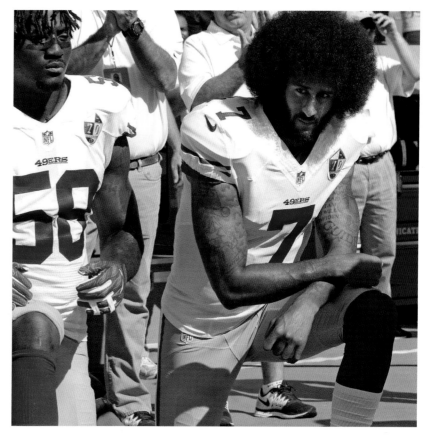

455

# MIGRANTS AND REFUGEES 2000–PRESENT

**Ongoing war, persecution, poverty, changing climate, and natural disasters caused many people to flee their homes in the twenty first century.**

▲ Desperate migrants and refugees from the conflict in Syria walk towards Greece along the Turkey–Greece border in 2020.

▼ Makeshift migrant camps grew up at bottlenecks around the coastlines of Europe. This is the Moria camp on the Greek island of Lesvos in 2019.

Throughout history, humans have been on the move, seeking a safe place to settle and raise a family in peace. In 2020, there were 82.4 million people around the world who had been forcibly displaced from their homes, according to the United Nations. Many remained homeless in their own countries, while others were refugees who had fled abroad.

## SAFE HAVENS

The greatest number of refugees worldwide were from Syria, Palestine, South Sudan, Afghanistan, Venezuela, and Myanmar. Most refugees found shelter in neighboring (mostly developing) countries, although news media often focused instead on those trying to enter richer countries. Of those fleeing the horrors of the war in Syria, 3.6 million sought refuge in Turkey, 944,000 in Lebanon, 676,000 in Jordan, and 532,000 in Germany.

▲ Berliners welcomed refugees to Germany in 2014. However, in the same year, the right-wing AfD party won seats in the EU parliamentary elections with an anti-migration message.

The rights of refugees to seek asylum— a safe haven from persecution and conflict—are supposed to be protected under international law, and all migrants have the right to be treated humanely. However, in reality migrants are often refused entry at borders or are treated with hostility by governments and police.

## DANGEROUS JOURNEYS

Desperate migrants have often been exploited by smugglers to whom money is paid for passage to another country. Some routes are controlled by criminal gangs, especially those to the U.S. through Latin America.

In 2021, more than 4,000 migrants were recorded as dead or missing in transit. Many people risk their lives crossing rivers or open sea in unsuitable boats. The most dangerous sea route is to Europe across the Mediterranean. Fortunately, many good people have saved lives at sea and welcomed incomers into their country. On just one day—May 23, 2017—workers for the Save the Children charity rescued more than 1,600 migrants in the Mediterranean.

## POLITICAL HOSTILITY

Migration fueled political tensions and divisions as the new century moved forward. In 2012, the U.K. Home Secretary (and future Prime Minister) Theresa May announced that, "The aim is to create, here in Britain, a really hostile environment for illegal immigrants."

▲ Open Arms (a Spanish non-governmental search-and-rescue organization) approaches a boat full of migrants off the coast of Italy on May 6, 2017.

Although the United States was a country founded by migrants and refugees from religious persecution and war, President Donald Trump boasted in his 2016 election campaign that he would seal off the U.S. southern border with "a big, beautiful wall." Australia detained would-be migrants on offshore islands under harsh conditions.

The challenge is to set up clear and humane international procedures. The twenty-first-century refugee crisis will continue if the causes are not understood and dealt with. Causes are many and include wars, extreme climate change, political and religious oppression, poverty, and crime.

▲ This Christian Cross is made from planks of a boat wrecked off Lampedusa, Italy, in 2013, when 311 refugees from Eritrea and Somalia drowned as they tried to cross to Italy from Libya. The islanders saved the lives of 155 others.

▼ President Trump stands before a section of wall along the southern border of the U.S. in 2020. During his 2016 election campaign, he promised to build the wall to keep out migrants fleeing poverty, political oppression, and gang violence in Central America.

▼ Migrants who have crossed from Mexico into the United States are held at an overcrowded detention center in Texas, 2019.

# MEDICAL CHALLENGES 2000–PRESENT

**Medical advances in the early twenty first century have been truly amazing. They were put to the test when the world faced the reality of a global pandemic, COVID-19, in 2019.**

The revolution in information technology was transforming medical research and practice. There were also great advances in scanning and imaging, in carrying out surgery using microscopes and miniature robotics, and 3D printing was applied to medical uses such as making implants, models, and prosthetics.

### MEDICAL ADVANCES IN GENETICS

In 2003, an international scientific project completed most of the mapping of the human genome, unlocking many secrets of our DNA. By identifying certain parts of the gene, doctors are making progress in understanding many diseases, identifying cancers, and researching new drugs. However, being able to identify genes also raised new ethical debates about inheritance and the medical manipulation of genes.

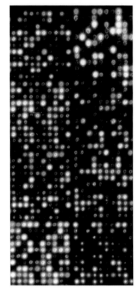

▲ The Human Genome project had unlocked many of the secrets of DNA by 2003. This is a microarray, part of a DNA sequence set in a grid pattern for genetic testing.

▲ Intrusive surgery has been reduced by microscopic and robotic technology. This da Vinci surgical robot has several robotic arms that are controlled remotely by a surgeon.

### PUBLIC HEALTH ISSUES

Health was improved by successful campaigns against smoking, however obesity and related illnesses such as Type 2 diabetes increased in developed countries. There were no known cures for HIV/AIDS, but treatments now allowed people who had the virus to live long lives in good health. The deadly Ebola virus, first identified in 1976, reappeared many times, with a major outbreak in west Africa from 2013–2016. In 2002, a virus named SARS (Severe Acute Respiratory Syndrome), transferred from wild bats, broke out in China and spread to neighboring countries then around the world through air travel. SARS infected more than 8,000 people in 29 countries and killed 774. Outbreaks were contained and the World Health Organization (WHO) declared that it had been contained by July 5, 2003.

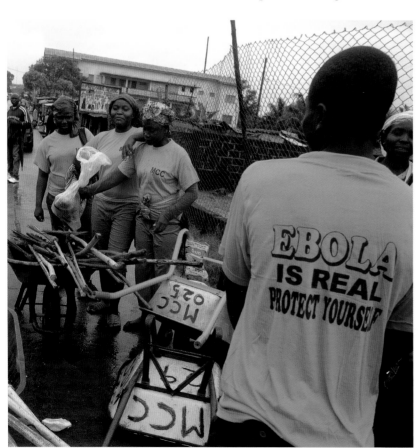

◀ City workers wear T-shirts warning of Ebola in Monrovia, Liberia in September 2014. By March 2016, 11,310 Ebola deaths had been reported in Guinea, Liberia, and Sierra Leone.

## COVID-19

SARS was a "coronavirus" similar to MERS, which appeared in Saudi Arabia in 2012, and to a new virus that first appeared in China in November 2019—COVID-19. By November 2021, 258 million cases of COVID-19 had been recorded worldwide, with more than 5 million deaths. At this point, the pandemic—in particular, a highly infectious strain called the Delta variant—was still raging. The pressure on health services, hospitals and care homes was in many cases overwhelming. The need for enough protective wear for doctors and nurses was a major logistical problem. Lockdowns, social distancing, tracking and tracing, mask wearing, and testing affected every aspect of daily life, limiting travel, tourism, education, work, entertainment, and social gatherings. Some people suffered from chronic symptoms (called "long COVID") and some experienced stress and mental health problems.

Vaccines for COVID-19 were developed in less than a year, a record-breaking achievement. During the pandemic, healthcare staff worked tirelessly, risking their lives in intensive care units. Some world leaders downplayed the risks or placed their own national or political interests above those of others. However, no country would be safe until all countries were safe, yet by September 2021 only 2 percent of vaccines worldwide had been administered in Africa.

▲ A COVID intensive care unit required effective personal protection equipment and long hours of hard work under very difficult conditions.

◄ An illustration of the COVID-19 virus. The original virus went through many mutations after 2019. It will remain with us for many more years.

◄ Effective COVID vaccines were produced with remarkable speed, however, the international roll out varied greatly and favored the world's richer nations.

▼ To help prevent the spread of the virus, people were told to keep 6 ft. (2m) apart and wear face masks.

# NEW VIEWS OF SPACE 2000–PRESENT

**The first two decades of the new millennium saw many remarkable discoveries in astronomy and far-reaching discoveries about the Universe beyond our Solar System.**

▲ Liu Yang became the first Chinese woman in space as part of the 2012 Shenzhou 9 mission, in which a crewed spacecraft docked with the Tiangong-1 experimental space station (2011–2018).

▼ In this photograph taken by Perseverance on Mars on April 25, 2021, a helicopter named Ingenuity hovers near the center of the image. It performed the first powered, controlled flight on Mars.

The focus of human-crewed missions in space over the last 20 years has been the International Space Station, which is expected to operate as it is until 2024 or 2028. It may then be used for commercial low-orbit projects, or replaced by other stations, such as one on the Moon. Space exploration has been left to uncrewed spacecraft since the Moon landings between 1969 and 1972, but the dream of humans setting foot on Mars has never gone away. By 2021, six rovers had successfully landed on Mars to gather crucial data—five of them American and one Chinese. Both the United States and China are planning to send humans to Mars in the 2030s.

## CHANGING PRIORITIES

Space has become a more international endeavor. China joined the U.S. and Russia in the top space league in 2003, but in all, citizens of 41 countries have now been astronauts. Another change has been the rise of private companies, such as the American entrepreneur Elon Musk's SpaceX taking over from national space agencies for missions and research.

▲ An Atlas V rocket is launched in July 2020, kicking off the Mars 2020 mission. Its rover, Perseverance, was landed safely on Mars in February 2021.

There is great interest in the commercialization of space, with visions of future mining missions to other planets or space tourism. There are also worrying scenarios for the militarization of space, with the founding of the United States Space Force (USSF) as a branch of the armed forces in 2019. This new branch of the military supports U.S. space missions, and protects national security and communication equipment, especially U.S. satellites in space.

◀ China's first Mars rover Zhurong posed for a selfie with its landing platform (right). Zhurong started exploring the planet's surface from May 22, 2021.

## OVERCROWDED ORBITS

Our planet increasingly depends on artificial satellites in Earth orbit for its day-to-day survival. They monitor the climate and weather, and they enable broadcasting and Global Positioning Systems (GPS). By April 2021, the UN calculated that there were 7,389 satellites circling the planet. An estimated 3,000 of these are no longer active.

There is also a large amount of debris known as "space junk" in orbit, which poses a risk of collisions. According to the European Space Agency, only about 24 percent of known orbiting objects are satellites. Other debris includes large objects discarded during space missions such as spent upper stages of rockets to tiny fragments of wire and dust. Active satellites have to be maneuvred around space junk to avoid collisions and damage. By 2021, collisions had destroyed only two satellites.

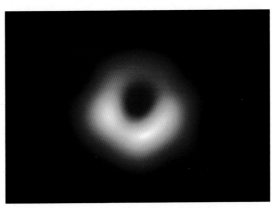

◀ The first ever photo of a supermassive black hole, in the galaxy Messier 87, was taken in 2019 by the Event Horizon ground array of radio telescopes.

▲ A 3D illustration of the James Webb Space Telescope (JWST), launched in December 2021. It is an infrared device that will succeed the Hubble Space Telescope.

| KEY DATES | |
|---|---|
| 2001 | First spacecraft to land on an asteroid (Eros) NEAR—U.S. |
| 2004 | First orbit of Saturn, Cassini-Huygens—U.S., European Space Agency (ESA) |
| 2008 | Discovery of ice on the Moon—India |
| 2009 | First space telescope survey of Milky Way to search for Earthlike plants, Kepler Mission—U.S. |
| 2010 | Asteroid samples returned to Earth, Hayabusa—Japan |
| 2011 | First orbit of Mercury, Messenger—U.S. |
| 2014 | First spacecraft to land on a comet, Philae—ESA |
| 2015 | First fly-past of Pluto, New Horizons—U.S. |
| 2019 | First soft landing on the far side of the Moon—China |

# SCIENCE AND TECHNOLOGY 2000–PRESENT

**Technological advances in the world of computing and IT (information technology) transformed our everyday lives in the twenty first century.**

Contactless payments started in 2018. Soon people were paying for goods not just with bank cards, but with apps on smartphones and smartwatches.

The innovations affected the way we communicated, worked, shopped, banked our money, read books, watched film and television, followed the news, listened to music, took photographs, and filed information. Short-range wireless communication came with Bluetooth in 2000. The year 2003 brought Skype, an app (short for "application") that could match chat with video from a webcam (short for "web camera"). Later joined by Zoom and many others, these video conferencing apps enabled people to keep in touch, work, and learn during the COVID-19 virus lockdowns of 2020–2021. The age of social media began and tens of millions of people around the world were connected through sites such as Facebook and Twitter. In 2007, the Apple iPhone was released—this smartphone with a touchscreen display brought together an internet browser, a multimedia player and a telephone in one compact device.

The humanoid robot Asimo (Advanced Step in Innovative Mobility) was developed by Honda in Japan. It made its debut in 2020.

The revolution in communications technology defined the new century. Online teaching in schools and universities became essential during the COVID-19 pandemic.

## ARTIFICAL INTELLIGENCE

New technologies fed into each other. Robotics had proved its value in auto-assembly and other factory work, and in carrying out dangerous tasks where people would be at risk. Driverless ("autonomous") vehicles were developed in the interests of road safety.

In Japan, humanoid robots were built that could interact with humans, and, in 2010, the Apple iPhone 4 introduced Siri, a personalized search engine with voice recognition; Amazon's Alexa followed in 2014. These electronic assistants interacted with other devices in the home to wake you up, turn on the heating, make your coffee, and give you a weather forecast. Such connectivity of devices is called the "Internet of things."

# GREEN TECHNOLOGIES

The need to reduce carbon emissions in transport, industry, power generation, and agriculture because of climate change, was a powerful motive for technological innovation. In 2016, an aircraft called Solar Impulse 2 became the first to fly around the world powered only by the sun. In 2017, a train fueled by hydrogen was operating in Germany. In 2021, plans were developed to make "green" steel using hydrogen instead of coal. By the 2020s, many countries were planning to phase out gasoline and diesel vehicles in favor of electric ones. Power stations running on coal were shut down as renewable power from wind farms and solar panels became cheaper and cheaper. The key to success in these technologies was in efficient storage of energy in the form of batteries.

▲ The new dependence on batteries required the metal lithium—the extraction of which creates environmental problems. In the Salar de Atacama, Chile, lithium is extracted from salt.
This process requires a lot of water in a water-scarce part of the country.

An electric car recharges its batteries. The age of fossil fuels was at last coming to an end.

## PARTICLE PHYSICS

In 2012, scientists working at CERN (the European Organization for Nuclear Research) confirmed the existence of a subatomic particle named the Higgs boson. This breakthrough in our understanding of matter was made possible by the Large Hadron Collider (LHC) program, with the help of more than 10,000 scientists worldwide.

▶ The yellow lines in this illustration show the paths of particles after a collision in the Large Hadron Collider.

# ART AND ARCHITECTURE 2000–PRESENT

In the twenty first century, the boundaries of art continued to expand, taking in high art and popular art, installations, performance, and public art, alongside more traditional arts and crafts.

The digital revolution encouraged exploration of new electronic media. There was a globalization of the art world, with greater international awareness and exchange between galleries and artists around the world. Music, television, and cinema thrived, despite streaming changing the way in which they were delivered to the public. Music and drama could now be accessed and played back over over a wide range of devices from smartphones to laptops and smart TVs. A single live theatre event could reach a nationwde audiece.

Live performances and exhibitions of art faced serious disruption from the COVID-19 pandemic in 2020–2021 as theaters, galleries, and festivals were shut down for public health reasons. Book publishing expanded its reach into the electronic world, but the days of paper and print proved to be far from over.

In the city of Oslo, Norway, people were encouraged to walk, cycle, and use public transport, rather than use cars, making the city streets safer and less polluted.

## NEW BUILDS

In architecture, new materials and structures were explored, making the most of computer modeling to produce strikingly original sculptural shapes. Some architects preferred simplicity or were inspired by traditional materials and designs. Concerns for the environment encouraged innovation, with buildings designed to conserve energy and generate their own power.

The economic decline of the main street shops in the age of online shopping posed new challenges for town planning. Ideas on how to create a welcoming environment where people could spend time together and shop were considered.

The Shanghai Tower in China, completed in 2015, captures rainwater and stores it for use in the building. Its 270 wind turbines generate electricity to light the tower at night.

▼ The paintings of French-born American artist Nicole Eisenman on show at the Whitechapel Gallery, London, U.K., in 2020. This was one of the many exhibitions disrupted when galleries had to close during the COVID-19 pandemic.

# READY
# REFERENCE

## 40,000 B.C.—present

# READY REFERENCE

## ANCIENT EGYPTIAN DYNASTIES

| PERIOD | DYNASTY | DATES (B.C.) | PRINCIPAL PHARAOHS |
|---|---|---|---|
| Early Dynastic | 1–3 | c.2925–2575 | Menes (Aha) |
| | | | Zoser (Djoser) |
| Old Kingdom | 4–7/8 | c.2575–2130 | Khufu (Cheops) |
| First Intermediate Period | 9–11 | c.2130–2040 | |
| Middle Kingdom | 11–14 | c.2040–1600 | Mentuhotep II |
| Second Intermediate Period | 15–17 | 1630–1540 | Hyksos kings rule lower Egypt |
| | | | Ahmose reunites Egypt |
| New Kingdom | 18–20 | 1550–1070 | Amenhotep I–III |
| | | | Thutmose I–IV |
| | | | Queen Hatshepsut |
| | | | Akhenaten (Amenhotep IV) |
| | | | Tutankhamun |
| | | | Ramesses I–XI |
| Third Intermediate Period | 21–25 | 1070–656 | Sheshonq I |
| | | | Rule of Nubians |
| Late Period | 25–31 | 664–332 | Psammatichus I |
| | | | Rule of Persians (D. 27 and 31) |
| | | | Nectanebo II |
| | | | Conquest of Alexander the Great |

## CHINESE DYNASTIES

| DYNASTY | DATE | DETAILS |
|---|---|---|
| Xia | c.2100–1600 B.C. | Legendary founder, Yu the Great |
| Shang | c.1600–1050 B.C. | Yellow river civilization |
| Zhou | c.1050–256 B.C. | |
| Qin | 221–206 B.C. | Shi Huangdi, first emperor of unified China |
| Early Han | 206 B.C.–A.D. 9 | Emperor Wu Di also rules Korea and southern China |
| Hsin | A.D. 9–25 | Wang Mang takes power |
| Later Han | 25–220 | Han rule restored |
| The Three Kingdoms | 220–280 | China breaks into three kingdoms – the Wei, Shu and Wu |
| Western Jin | 265–317 | |
| Eastern Jin | 317–420 | |
| Southern dynasties | 420–589 | |
| Sui | 589–618 | Grand Canal completed |
| Tang | 618–907 | Golden age of culture; includes reign of Emperor T'ai Tsung the Great |
| The five dynasties and ten kingdoms | 907–960 | Period of civil wars |
| Liao | 907–1125 | Part of northern China ruled by Khitan Mongols |
| Song | 960–1279 | Dynasty rules parts of China only |
| Northern Song | 960–1127 | |
| Western Hsia | 990–1227 | |
| Chin | 1115–1234 | |
| Southern Song | 1127–1279 | |
| Yuan (Mongol) | 1279–1368 | All China ruled by the Mongols led by Kublai Khan |
| Ming | 1368–1644 | Fine pottery, voyages of exploration |
| Qing (Manchu) | 1644–1911 | Manchu rule, foreign incursions, the Boxer Rebellion |
| Republic of China | 1911–1949 | Government set up under Sun Yat-sen, followed by disunity and the warlord era |
| People's Republic of China | 1949– | Mao Zedong is first chairman of Communist Party |

# ROMAN RULERS

## KINGS OF ROME

| | | | |
|---|---|---|---|
| Romulus | 753–716 B.C. | Tarquinios Priscus | 616–579 |
| Numa Pompilius | 716–673 B.C. | Servius Tullius | 579–534 |
| Tullus Hostilius | 673–640 B.C. | Tarquinius Superbus | 534–509 |
| Ancus Martius | 640–616 B.C. | | |

## THE REPUBLIC OF ROME — **509–27** B.C.

| | | | |
|---|---|---|---|
| Dictatorship of Sulla | 82–78 B.C. | Dictatorship of Julius Caesar | 45–44 |
| First Triumvirate | 60–53 B.C. | Second Triumvirate | 43–27 |
| (Julius Caesar, Pompey and Crassus) | | (Octavian, Mark Anthony and Marcus | |
| Dictatorship of Pompey | 52–47 B.C. | Lepidus) | |

## EMPERORS OF THE ROMAN EMPIRE

| | | | |
|---|---|---|---|
| Augustus (previously Octavian) | 27 B.C.–A.D. 14 | Gallus and Hostilianus (Volusianus) | 251–253 |
| Tiberius I | A.D. 14–37 | Aemilianus | 253 |
| Caligula (Gaius Caesar) | 37–41 | Valerian and Gallienus | 253–260 |
| Claudius I | 41–54 | Gallienus | 253–268 |
| Nero | 54–68 | Claudius II (Gothicus) | 268–270 |
| Galba | 68–69 | Quintillus | 269–270 |
| Otho | 69 | Aurelianus | 270–275 |
| Vitellius | 69 | Tacitus | 275–276 |
| Vespasian | 69–79 | Florianus | 276 |
| Titus | 79–81 | Probus | 276–282 |
| Domitian | 81–96 | Carus | 282–283 |
| Nerva | 96–98 | Carinus and Numerianus | 283–284 |
| Trajan | 98–117 | Diocletian (divides empire) | 284–305 |
| Hadrian | 117–138 | Maximilian (jointly) | 286–305 |
| Antoninus Pius | 138–161 | Constantius I | 305–306 |
| Marcus Aurelius | 161–180 | Severus | 306–307 |
| Lucius Verus (jointly) | 161–169 | Licinius (jointly) | 308–324 |
| Commodus | 177–192 | Constantine I (reunites empire) | 312–337 |
| Pertinax | 193 | Constantine II (jointly) | 337–340 |
| Didius Julianus | 193 | Constans (jointly) | 337–350 |
| Septimus Severus | 193–211 | Constantius II (jointly) | 337–361 |
| Caracalla | 198–217 | Magnentius (jointly) | 350–353 |
| Geta (jointly) | 209–212 | Julian (the Apostate) | 361–363 |
| Macrinus | 217–218 | Jovianus | 363–364 |
| Elagabulus (Heliogabalus) | 218–222 | Valentinian I (rules West) | 364–375 |
| Alexander Severus | 222–235 | Valens (rules East) | 364–378 |
| Maximinius I (the Thracian) | 235–238 | Gratian (rules West) | 375–383 |
| Gordian I | 238 | Magnus Maximus (usurper in West) | 383–388 |
| Gordian II | 238 | Valentinian II (rules West) | 375–392 |
| Balbinus and Pupienus Maximus | 238 | Eugenius (usurper in West) | 392–394 |
| Gordian III | 238–244 | Theodosius I (the Great) | 379–395 |
| Philip (the Arab) | 244–249 | (rules East, then unites East and West) | |
| Decius | 249–251 | | |

## EMPERORS OF THE EASTERN ROMAN EMPIRE

| | | | |
|---|---|---|---|
| Arcadius | 395–408 | Leo II | 474 |
| Theodosius II | 408–450 | Zeno | 474–491 |
| Marcian | 450–457 | Anastasius | 491–518 |
| Leo I | 457–474 | | |

## EMPERORS OF THE WESTERN ROMAN EMPIRE

| | | | |
|---|---|---|---|
| Honorius | 395–423 | Majorian | 457–461 |
| Maximus | 410–411 | Severus III | 461–467 |
| Constantius III | 421 | Anthemius | 467–472 |
| John | 423–425 | Olybrius | 472 |
| Valentinian III | 425–455 | Glycerius | 473–474 |
| Petronius Maximus | 455 | Julius Nepos | 474–475 |
| Avitus | 455–456 | Romulus Augustus | 475–476 |

# POPES OF THE ROMAN CATHOLIC CHURCH (999–present)

The head of the Roman Catholic Church is chosen by the cardinals of the Church. Occasionally rival popes have been elected in opposition to the chosen pope; the rivals are known as anti-popes (A.P.). There were many other popes before these, the first pope was St Peter in A.D. 42.

| | | | | | |
|---|---|---|---|---|---|
| Sylvester II | 999 | Celestine III | 1191 | Paul III | 1534 |
| John XVII | 1003 | Innocent III | 1198 | Julius III | 1550 |
| John XVIII | 1004 | Honorius III | 1216 | Marcellus II | 1555 |
| Sergius IV | 1009 | Gregory IX | 1227 | Paul IV | 1555 |
| Benedict VIII | 1012 | Celestine IV | 1241 | Pius IV | 1559 |
| Gregory (A.P.) | 1012 | Innocent IV | 1243 | St Pius V | 1566 |
| John XIX | 1024 | Alexander IV | 1254 | Gregory XIII | 1572 |
| Benedict IX | 1032 | Urban IV | 1261 | Sixtus V | 1585 |
| Sylvester III | 1045 | Clement IV | 1265 | Urban VII | 1590 |
| Benedict IX | 1045 | Blessed Gregory X | 1271 | Gregory XIV | 1590 |
| Gregory VI | 1045 | Blessed Innocent V | 1276 | Innocent IX | 1591 |
| Clement II | 1046 | Adrian V | 1276 | Clement VIII | 1592 |
| Benedict IX | 1047 | John XXI | 1276 | Leo XI | 1605 |
| Damasus II | 1048 | Nicholas III | 1277 | Paul V | 1605 |
| St Leo IX | 1049 | Martin IV | 1281 | Gregory XV | 1621 |
| Victor II | 1055 | Honorius IV | 1285 | Urban VIII | 1623 |
| Stephen IX (X) | 1057 | Nicholas IV | 1288 | Innocent X | 1644 |
| Benedict X (A.P.) | 1058 | St Celestine V | 1294 | Alexander VII | 1655 |
| Nicholas II | 1059 | Boniface VIII | 1294 | Clement IX | 1667 |
| Alexander II | 1061 | Blessed Benedict XI | 1303 | Clement X | 1670 |
| Honorius II (A.P.) | 1061 | Clement V | 1305 | Blessed Innocent XI | 1676 |
| St Gregory VII | 1073 | John XXII | 1316 | Alexander VIII | 1689 |
| Clement III (A.P.) | 1080 | Nicholas V (A.P.) | 1328 | Innocent XII | 1691 |
| Blessed Victor III | 1087 | Benedict XII | 1334 | Clement XI | 1700 |
| Blessed Urban II | 1088 | Clement VI | 1342 | Innocent XIII | 1721 |
| Paschal II | 1099 | Innocent VI | 1352 | Benedict XIII | 1724 |
| Theodorie (A.P.) | 1100 | Blessed Urban V | 1362 | Clement XII | 1730 |
| Albert (A.P.) | 1102 | Gregory XI | 1370 | Benedict XIV | 1740 |
| Sylvester IV (A.P.) | 1105 | Urban VI | 1378 | Clement XIII | 1758 |
| Gelasius II | 1118 | Clement VII (A.P.) | 1378 | Clement XIV | 1769 |
| Gregory VIII (A.P.) | 1118 | Boniface IX | 1389 | Pius VI | 1775 |
| Callistus II | 1119 | Benedict XIII (A.P.) | 1394 | Pius VII | 1800 |
| Honorius II | 1124 | Innocent VII | 1404 | Leo XII | 1823 |
| Celestine II (A.P.) | 1124 | Gregory XII | 1406 | Pius VIII | 1829 |
| Innocent II | 1130 | Alexander V (A.P.) | 1409 | Gregory XVI | 1831 |
| Anacletus II (A.P.) | 1130 | John XXIII | 1410 | Pius IX | 1846 |
| Victor IV (A.P.) | 1138 | Martin V | 1417 | Leo XIII | 1878 |
| Celestine II | 1143 | Eugene IV | 1431 | St Pius X | 1903 |
| Lucius II | 1144 | Felix V (A.P.) | 1439 | Benedict XV | 1914 |
| Blessed Eugene III | 1145 | Nicholas V | 1447 | Pius XI | 1922 |
| Anastasius IV | 1153 | Callistus III | 1455 | Pius XII | 1939 |
| Adrian IV | 1154 | Pius II | 1458 | John XXIII | 1958 |
| Alexander III | 1159 | Paul II | 1464 | Paul VI | 1963 |
| Victor IV (A.P.) | 1159 | Sixtus IV | 1471 | John Paul I | 1978 |
| Paschal III (A.P.) | 1164 | Innocent VIII | 1484 | John Paul II | 1978 |
| Callistus III (A.P.) | 1168 | Alexander VI | 1492 | Benedict XVI | 2005 |
| Innocent III (A.P.) | 1179 | Pius III | 1503 | Francis | 2013 |
| Lucius III | 1181 | Julius II | 1503 | | |
| Urban III | 1185 | Leo X | 1513 | | |
| Clement III | 1187 | Adrian VI | 1522 | | |
| Gregory VIII | 1187 | Clement VII | 1523 | | |

# RULERS OF ENGLAND

**SAXONS**

| | | | |
|---|---|---|---|
| Egbert | 829–839 | Edred | 946–955 |
| Ethelwulf | 839–858 | Edwy | 955–959 |
| Ethelbald | 858–860 | Edgar | 959–975 |
| Ethelbert | 860–865 | Edward the Martyr | 975–978 |
| Ethelred I | 865–871 | Ethelred II, the Unready | 978–1016 |
| Alfred the Great | 871–899 | Sweyn Forkbeard | 1013–1014 |
| Edward the Elder | 899–924 | Ethelred II, the Unready (restored) | 1014–1016 |
| Athelstan | 924–939 | Edmund Ironside | 1016 |
| Edmund | 939–946 | | |

**DANES**

| | | | |
|---|---|---|---|
| Canute | 1016–1035 | Harthacanute | 1040–1042 |
| Harold I Harefoot | 1035–1040 | | |

**SAXONS**

| | | | |
|---|---|---|---|
| Edward the Confessor | 1042–1066 | Harold II | 1066 |

**HOUSE OF NORMANDY**

| | | | |
|---|---|---|---|
| William I, the Conqueror | 1066–1087 | Henry I | 1100–1135 |
| William II | 1087–1100 | Stephen | 1135–1154 |

**HOUSE OF PLANTAGENET**

| | | | |
|---|---|---|---|
| Henry II | 1154–1189 | Edward I | 1272–1307 |
| Richard I, the Lionheart | 1189–1199 | Edward II | 1307–1327 |
| John | 1199–1216 | Edward III | 1327–1377 |
| Henry III | 1216–1272 | Richard II | 1377–1399 |

**HOUSE OF LANCASTER**

| | | | |
|---|---|---|---|
| Henry IV | 1399–1413 | Henry VI | 1422–1461 |
| Henry V | 1413–1422 | | |

**HOUSE OF YORK**

| | | | |
|---|---|---|---|
| Edward IV | 1461–1483 | Richard III | 1483–1485 |
| Edward V | 1483 | | |

**HOUSE OF TUDOR**

| | | | |
|---|---|---|---|
| Henry VII | 1485–1509 | Mary I | 1553–1558 |
| Henry VIII | 1509–1547 | Elizabeth I | 1558–1603 |
| Edward VI | 1547–1553 | | |

# RULERS OF SCOTLAND

| | | | |
|---|---|---|---|
| Malcolm II | 1005–1034 | Malcolm IV | 1153–1165 |
| Duncan I | 1034–1040 | William the Lion | 1165–1214 |
| Macbeth (usurper) | 1040–1057 | Alexander II | 1214–1249 |
| Malcolm III (Cranmore) | 1057–1093 | Alexander III | 1249–1286 |
| Donald Bane | 1093–1094 | Margaret of Norway | 1286–1290 |
| Duncan II | 1094 | (Interregnum | 1290–1291) |
| Donald Bane (restored) | 1094–1097 | John Balliol | 1292–1296 |
| Edgar | 1097–1107 | (Interregnum | 1296–1306) |
| Alexander I | 1107–1124 | Robert I, the Bruce | 1306–1329 |
| David I | 1124–1153 | David II | 1329–1371 |

**HOUSE OF STUART**

| | | | |
|---|---|---|---|
| | | James III | 1460–1488 |
| Robert II | 1371–1390 | James IV | 1488–1513 |
| Robert III | 1390–1406 | James V | 1513–1542 |
| James I | 1406–1437 | Mary, Queen of Scots | 1542–1567 |
| James II | 1437–1460 | James VI (I of Great Britain) | 1567–1625 |

# RULERS OF ENGLAND AND SCOTLAND

**HOUSE OF STUART**

| | | | |
|---|---|---|---|
| James I | 1603–1625 | Charles I | 1625–1649 |

| | |
|---|---|
| **COMMONWEALTH** | **1649–1653** |
| **PROTECTORATE** | **1653–1660** |

| | | | |
|---|---|---|---|
| Oliver Cromwell | 1653–1658 | Richard Cromwell | 1658–1659 |

**HOUSE OF STUART**

| | | | |
|---|---|---|---|
| Charles II | 1660–1685 | William III (jointly) | 1689–1702 |
| James II | 1685–1688 | Anne | 1702–1714 |
| Mary II (jointly) | 1689–1694 | | |

# RULERS OF GREAT BRITAIN

**HOUSE OF HANOVER**

| | | | |
|---|---|---|---|
| George I | 1714–1727 | George IV | 1820–1830 |
| George II | 1727–1760 | William IV | 1830–1837 |
| George III | 1760–1820 | Victoria | 1837–1901 |

**HOUSE OF SAXE–COBURG**

| | |
|---|---|
| Edward VII | 1901–1910 |

**HOUSE OF WINDSOR**

| | | | |
|---|---|---|---|
| George V | 1910–1936 | George VI | 1936–1952 |
| Edward VIII | 1936 | Elizabeth II | 1952– |

# PRIME MINISTERS OF GREAT BRITAIN

| | IN OFFICE | PARTY |
|---|---|---|
| Sir Robert Walpole | 1721–1742 | Whig |
| Earl of Wilmington | 1742–1743 | Whig |
| Henry Pelham | 1743–1754 | Whig |
| Duke of Newcastle | 1754–1756 | Whig |
| Duke of Devonshire | 1756–1757 | Whig |
| Duke of Newcastle | 1757–1762 | Whig |
| Earl of Bute | 1762–1763 | Tory |
| George Grenville | 1763–1765 | Whig |
| Marquess of Rockingham | 1765–1766 | Whig |
| William Pitt the Elder (Earl of Chatham) | 1766–1768 | Whig |
| Duke of Grafton | 1768–1770 | Whig |
| Lord North | 1770–1782 | Tory |
| Marquess of Rockingham | 1782 | Whig |
| Earl of Shelburne | 1782–1783 | Whig |
| Duke of Portland | 1783 | Coalition |
| William Pitt the Younger | 1783–1801 | Tory |
| Henry Addington | 1801–1804 | Tory |
| William Pitt the Younger | 1804–1806 | Tory |
| Lord Grenville | 1806–1807 | Whig |
| Duke of Portland | 1807–1809 | Tory |
| Spencer Perceval | 1809–1812 | Tory |
| Earl of Liverpool | 1812–1827 | Tory |
| George Canning | 1827 | Tory |
| Viscount Goderich | 1827–1828 | Tory |
| Duke of Wellington | 1828–1830 | Tory |
| Earl Grey | 1830–1834 | Whig |
| Viscount Melbourne | 1834 | Whig |
| Sir Robert Peel | 1834–1835 | Tory |
| Viscount Melbourne | 1835–1841 | Whig |
| Sir Robert Peel | 1841–1846 | Tory |
| Lord John Russell | 1846–1852 | Whig |

| | | |
|---|---|---|
| Earl of Derby | 1852 | Tory |
| Earl of Aberdeen | 1852–1855 | Peelite |
| Viscount Palmerston | 1855–1858 | Liberal |
| Earl of Derby | 1858–1859 | Conservative |
| Viscount Palmerston | 1859–1865 | Liberal |
| Earl Russell | 1865–1866 | Liberal |
| Earl of Derby | 1866–1868 | Conservative |
| Benjamin Disraeli | 1868 | Conservative |
| William Gladstone | 1868–1874 | Liberal |
| Benjamin Disraeli | 1874–1880 | Conservative |
| William Gladstone | 1880–1885 | Liberal |
| Marquess of Salisbury | 1885–1886 | Conservative |
| William Gladstone | 1886 | Liberal |
| Marquess of Salisbury | 1886–1892 | Conservative |
| William Gladstone | 1892–1894 | Liberal |
| Earl of Rosebery | 1894–1895 | Liberal |
| Marquess of Salisbury | 1895–1902 | Conservative |
| Arthur Balfour | 1902–1905 | Conservative |
| Sir Henry Campbell-Bannerman | 1905–1908 | Liberal |
| Herbert Asquith | 1908–1915 | Liberal |
| Herbert Asquith | 1915–1916 | Coalition |
| David Lloyd George | 1916–1922 | Coalition |
| Andrew Bonar Law | 1922–1923 | Conservative |
| Stanley Baldwin | 1923–1924 | Conservative |
| James Ramsay MacDonald | 1924 | Labour |
| Stanley Baldwin | 1924–1929 | Conservative |
| James Ramsay MacDonald | 1929–1931 | Labour |
| James Ramsay MacDonald | 1931–1935 | National Coalition |
| Stanley Baldwin | 1935–1937 | National Coalition |
| Neville Chamberlain | 1937–1940 | National Coalition |
| Winston Churchill | 1940–1945 | Coalition |
| Winston Churchill | 1945 | Conservative |
| Clement Atlee | 1945–1951 | Labour |
| Sir Winston Churchill | 1951–1955 | Conservative |
| Sir Anthony Eden | 1955–1957 | Conservative |
| Harold Macmillan | 1957–1963 | Conservative |
| Sir Alec Douglas-Home | 1963–1964 | Conservative |
| Harold Wilson | 1964–1970 | Labour |
| Edward Heath | 1970–1974 | Conservative |
| Harold Wilson | 1974–1976 | Labour |
| James Callaghan | 1976–1979 | Labour |
| Margaret Thatcher | 1979–1990 | Conservative |
| John Major | 1990–1997 | Conservative |
| Tony Blair | 1997–2007 | Labour |
| Gordon Brown | 2007–2010 | Labour |
| David Cameron | 2010–2016 | Conservative-Liberal Democrat Coalition |
| Theresa May | 2016–2019 | Conservative |
| Boris Johnson | 2019– | Conservative |

# HOLY ROMAN EMPERORS

Dates given are period of reign

| | | | |
|---|---|---|---|
| Charlemagne | 800–814 | Louis II | 855–875 |
| Louis I (the Pious) | 814–840 | Charles II | 875–877 |
| Lothair I | 843–855 | Charles III | 881–891 |

**HOUSE OF SPOLETO**

| | | | |
|---|---|---|---|
| Guy | 891–894 | Lambert | 894–898 |

**CAROLINGIAN DYNASTY**

Arnulf

| | | | |
|---|---|---|---|
| | 896–899 | Louis III | 901–905 |

**HOUSE OF FRANCONIA**

| | |
|---|---|
| Conrad I | 911–918 |

## CAROLINGIAN DYNASTY

| | | | |
|---|---|---|---|
| Berengar | 915–924 | | |

## SAXON DYNASTY

| | | | |
|---|---|---|---|
| Henry I | 919-936 | Otto III | 983–1002 |
| Otto I, the Great | 936–973 | Henry II | 1002–1024 |
| Otto II | 973–983 | | |

## FRANCONIAN DYNASTY

| | | | |
|---|---|---|---|
| Conrad II | 1024–1039 | Henry V | 1106–1125 |
| Henry III | 1039–1056 | Lothair III, Duke of Saxony | 1125–1137 |
| Henry IV | 1056–1106 | | |

## HOHENSTAUFEN DYNASTY

| | | | |
|---|---|---|---|
| Conrad III | 1138–1152 | Otto IV of Brunswick | 1198–1214 |
| Frederick I, Barbarossa | 1152–1190 | Frederick II | 1212–1250 |
| Henry VI | 1190–1197 | Conrad IV | 1250–1254 |
| Philip of Swabia | 1197–1208 | | |

## INTERREGNUM

| | | | |
|---|---|---|---|
| Electors gain power | 1254–1273 | | |

## TRANSITION PERIOD

| | | | |
|---|---|---|---|
| Rudolf I of Habsburg | 1273–1292 | Frederick of Austria (co-regent) | 1314–1326 |
| Adolf of Nassau | 1292–1298 | Charles IV, of Luxembourg | 1347–1378 |
| Albert I, King of Germany | 1298–1308 | Wenceslas of Luxembourg | 1378–1400 |
| Henry VII of Luxembourg | 1308–1314 | Rupert, Duke of Palatine | 1400–1410 |
| Louis IV of Bavaria (co-regent) | 1314–1347 | Sigismund of Luxembourg | 1410–1437 |

## HABSBURG DYNASTY

| | | | |
|---|---|---|---|
| Albert II | 1437–1439 | Leopold I | 1658–1705 |
| Frederick III | 1452–1493 | Joseph I | 1705–1711 |
| Maximilian I | 1493–1519 | Charles VI | 1711–1740 |
| Charles V, King of Spain | 1519–1556 | War of the Austrian Succession | 1740–1748 |
| Ferdinand I | 1558–1564 | Charles VII of Bavaria | 1742–1745 |
| Maximilian II | 1564–1576 | Francis I of Lorraine | 1745–1765 |
| Rudolf II | 1576–1612 | Joseph II | 1765–1790 |
| Matthias | 1612–1619 | Leopold II | 1790–1792 |
| Ferdinand II | 1619–1637 | Francis II | 1792–1806 |
| Ferdinand III | 1637–1657 | | |

# HABSBURG EMPERORS OF AUSTRIA

| | | | |
|---|---|---|---|
| Francis II | 1804–1835 | Francis Joseph | 1848–1916 |
| Ferdinand | 1835–1848 | Charles | 1916–1918 |

# HOHENZOLLERN EMPERORS OF GERMANY

| | | | |
|---|---|---|---|
| William I (of Prussia) | 1871–1888 | William II | 1888–1918 |
| Frederick III | 1888 | | |

# RULERS OF GERMANY

## WEIMAR REPUBLIC

| | | | |
|---|---|---|---|
| Friedrich Ebert | 1919–1925 | Paul von Hindenburg | 1925–1934 |

## THIRD REICH

| | |
|---|---|
| Adolf Hitler | 1934–1945 |

## POST WORLD WAR II

| | |
|---|---|
| Germany under Allied control | 1945–1949 |

# CHANCELLORS OF THE FEDERAL REPUBLIC OF GERMANY (WEST GERMANY)

| | | | |
|---|---|---|---|
| Konrad Adenauer | 1949–1963 | Willy Brandt | 1969–1974 |
| Dr Ludwig Erhard | 1963–1966 | Helmut Schmidt | 1974–1982 |
| Kurt George Kiesinger | 1966–1969 | Helmut Kohl | 1982–1990 |

# CHAIRMEN OF THE DEMOCRATIC REPUBLIC OF GERMANY (EAST GERMANY)

| | | | |
|---|---|---|---|
| Walter Ulbricht | 1949–1971 | Egon Krenz | 1989–1990 |
| Erich Honecker | 1971–1989 | | |

# CHANCELLORS OF REUNITED GERMANY

| | | | |
|---|---|---|---|
| Helmut Kohl | 1990–1998 | Angela Merkel | 2005–2021 |
| Gerhard Schroder | 1998–2005 | Olaf Scholz | 2021– |

# RULERS OF FRANCE

## THE CAROLINGIANS

| | | | |
|---|---|---|---|
| Charles II, the Bald | 843–877 | Robert | 922–923 |
| Louis II | 877–879 | Rudolph | 923–936 |
| Louis III | 879–882 | Louis IV | 936–954 |
| Charles III | 884–887 | Lothair | 954–986 |
| Eudes | 888–898 | Louis V | 986–987 |
| Charles III | 898–922 | | |

## THE CAPETS

| | | | |
|---|---|---|---|
| Hugh Capet | 987–996 | Louis VIII | 1223–1226 |
| Robert II, the Pious | 996–1031 | Louis IX | 1226–1270 |
| Henry I | 1031–1060 | Philip III | 1270–1285 |
| Philip I | 1060–1108 | Philip IV | 1285–1314 |
| Louis VI | 1108–1137 | Louis X | 1314–1316 |
| Louis VII | 1137–1180 | Philip V | 1316–1322 |
| Philip II | 1180–1223 | Charles IV | 1322–1328 |

## HOUSE OF VALOIS

| | | | |
|---|---|---|---|
| Philip VI | 1328–1350 | Louis XII | 1498–1515 |
| John II | 1350–1364 | Francis I | 1515–1547 |
| Charles V | 1364–1380 | Henry II | 1547–1559 |
| Charles VI | 1380–1422 | Francis II | 1559–1560 |
| Charles VII | 1422–1461 | Charles IX | 1560–1574 |
| Louis XI | 1461–1483 | Henry III | 1574–1589 |
| Charles VIII | 1483–1498 | | |

## HOUSE OF BOURBON

| | | | |
|---|---|---|---|
| Henry IV, of Navarre | 1589–1610 | Louis XV | 1715–1774 |
| Louis XIII | 1610–1643 | Louis XVI | 1774–1793 |
| Louis XIV | 1643–1715 | Louis XVII | 1793–1795 |

## THE FIRST REPUBLIC AND FIRST EMPIRE

| | | | |
|---|---|---|---|
| Napoleon Bonaparte (first consul) | 1799–1804 | Napoleon I (emperor) | 1804–1814 |

## RESTORATION OF MONARCHY

| | | | |
|---|---|---|---|
| Louis XVIII | 1814–1824 | Louis-Philippe | 1830–1848 |
| Charles X | 1824–1830 | | |

## SECOND REPUBLIC

| | | | |
|---|---|---|---|
| Louis Napoleon Bonaparte (president) | 1848–1852 | Napoleon III (emperor) | 1852–1870 |

## THIRD REPUBLIC

| | | | |
|---|---|---|---|
| Louis Adolphe Thiers | 1871–1873 | Raymond Poincaré | 1913–1920 |
| Marshal Patrice de MacMahon | 1873–1879 | Paul Deschanel | 1920 |
| Paul Grévy | 1879–1887 | Alexandre Millerand | 1920–1924 |
| Marie Carnot | 1887–1894 | Gaston Doumergue | 1924–1931 |
| Jean Casimir-Périer | 1894–1895 | Paul Doumer | 1931–1932 |
| François Faure | 1895–1899 | Albert Lebrun | 1932–1940 |
| Émile Loubet | 1899–1906 | Vichy government (under Germans) | 1940–1944 |
| Armand C. Fallières | 1906–1913 | Provisional government | 1944–1946 |

## FOURTH REPUBLIC

| | | | |
|---|---|---|---|
| Vincent Auriol | 1947–1954 | René Coty | 1954–1959 |

## FIFTH REPUBLIC

| | | | |
|---|---|---|---|
| Charles de Gaulle | 1959–1969 | Jacques Chirac | 1995–2007 |
| Georges Pompidou | 1969–1974 | Nicolas Sarkozy | 2007–2012 |
| Valéry Giscard d'Estaing | 1974–1981 | François Hollande | 2012–2017 |
| François Mitterrand | 1981–1995 | Emmanuel Macron | 2017– |

# RULERS OF SPAIN

## HABSBURG DYNASTY

| | | | |
|---|---|---|---|
| Charles I (V of Germany) | 1516–1556 | Philip IV | 1621–1665 |
| Philip II | 1556–1598 | Charles II | 1665–1700 |
| Philip III | 1598–1621 | | |

## BOURBON DYNASTY

| | | | |
|---|---|---|---|
| Philip V | 1700–1724 | Charles IV | 1788–1808 |
| Louis I | 1724 | Ferdinand VII | 1808 |
| Philip V (restored) | 1724–1746 | Joseph Bonaparte | 1808–1814 |
| Ferdinand VI | 1746–1759 | Ferdinand VII | 1814–1833 |
| Charles III | 1759–1788 | Isabella II | 1833–1868 |

## OTHER MONARCHS

| | |
|---|---|
| Amadeus of Savoy | 1870–1873 |

## FIRST REPUBLIC

**1873–1874**

## RESTORATION OF MONARCHY

| | | | |
|---|---|---|---|
| Alfonso XII | 1874–1885 | Alfonso XIII | 1886–1931 |
| General Miguel Primo de Rivera (dictator) | 1923–1930 | | |

## SECOND REPUBLIC

| | | | |
|---|---|---|---|
| Niceto Alcalá Zamora | 1931–1936 | General Francisco Franco | 1939–1975 |
| Manuel Azaña | 1936–1939 | | |

## RESTORATION OF MONARCHY

| | | | |
|---|---|---|---|
| Juan Carlos I | 1975–2014 | King Felipe VI | 2014– |

## PRIME MINISTERS

| | | | |
|---|---|---|---|
| Admiral Luis Blanco | 1973 | Jose Maria Aznar | 1996–2004 |
| Carlos Navarro | 1973–1976 | Jose Luis Rodriguez Zapatero | 2004–2011 |
| Adolfo Suárez | 1976–1982 | Felipe Mariano Rajoy | 2011–2016 |
| González Márquez | 1982–1996 | Pendro Sanchez | 2018– |

# PERIODS OF JAPAN

| PERIOD | DATE | DETAILS |
|---|---|---|
| Yamato | c.300–592 | |
| Asaka | 592–710 | Empress Suiko (592–628) |
| | | Emperor Temmu (673–686) |
| Nara | 710–794 | Emperor Kammu (781–806) |
| Heian | 794–1185 | Japan ruled from Heian (now called Kyoto) |
| Fujiwara | 858–1160 | Fujiwara clan rules |
| Taira | 1159–1185 | Taira clan take control |

| | | | |
|---|---|---|---|
| Kamakura | 1185–1333 | Minamoto Yoritomo defeats Taira clan and becomes shogun in 1192 | |
| Namboku | 1334–1392 | End of shogun rule in 1333; Emperor Godaigo rules alone 1333–1339; imperial line splits into northern and southern courts | |
| Ashikaga | 1338–1573 | Ashikaga Takauji becomes shogun in 1338 | |
| Muromachi | 1392–1573 | Two rival courts are unified | |
| Sengoku | 1467–1600 | Emperor Gonara (1527–1557) | |
| Momoyama | 1573–1603 | Oda Nobunaga, a *daimyo* (baron), deposes the shogun and becomes dictator to 1582 | |
| Edo | 1603–1867 | Ieyasu Tokugawa becomes shogun in 1603; Tokugawa shoguns rule until 1867 | |
| Meiji | 1868–1912 | Emperor Mutsuhito, Meiji Restoration; he ends the shogunate and modernizes Japan | |
| Taisho | 1912–1926 | Emperor Yoshihito | |
| Showa | 1926–1989 | Emperor Hirohito | |
| Heisei | 1989–2019 | Emperor Akihito | |
| Reiwa | 2019– | Emperor Naruhito | |

# TSARS OF RUSSIA

| | | | |
|---|---|---|---|
| Ivan III, the Great, ruler of Russia | 1462–1505 | Catherine I | 1725–1727 |
| Vasili, ruler of Russia | 1505–1533 | Peter II | 1727–1730 |
| Ivan IV, the Terrible, first tsar | 1533–1584 | Anna | 1730–1740 |
| Fyodor I | 1584–1598 | Ivan VI | 1740–1741 |
| Boris Godunov | 1598–1605 | Elizabeth | 1741–1762 |
| Fyodor II | 1605 | Peter III | 1762 |
| Demetrius | 1605–1606 | Catherine II, the Great | 1762–1796 |
| Basil (IV) Shuiski | 1606–1610 | Paul I | 1796–1801 |
| (Interregnum | 1610–1613 | Alexander I | 1801–1825 |
| Michael Romanov | 1613–1645 | Nicholas I | 1825–1855 |
| Alexis | 1645–1676 | Alexander II | 1855–1881 |
| Fyodor III | 1676–1682 | Alexander III | 1881–1894 |
| Ivan V and Peter I, the Great, joint rulers | 1682–1689 | Nicholas II | 1894–1917 |
| Peter I | 1689–1725 | | |

# EFFECTIVE RULERS OF THE UNION OF SOVIET SOCIALIST REPUBLICS

| | | | |
|---|---|---|---|
| Vladimir Lenin | 1917–1924 | Leonid Brezhnev | 1964–1982 |
| Joseph Stalin | 1924–1953 | Yuri Andropov | 1982–1984 |
| Georgy Malenkov | 1953 | Konstantin Chernenko | 1984–1985 |
| Nikita Khrushchev | 1953–1964 | Mikhail Gorbachov | 1985–1991 |

# PRESIDENTS OF RUSSIA

| | | | |
|---|---|---|---|
| Boris Yeltsin | 1991–2000 | Dmitry Medvedev | 2008–2012 |
| Vladimir Putin | 2000–2008 | Vladimir Putin | 2012– |

# PRESIDENTS OF THE UNITED STATES OF AMERICA

| | | |
|---|---|---|
| George Washington | 1789–1797 | None |
| John Adams | 1797–1801 | Federalist |
| Thomas Jefferson | 1801–1809 | Democratic-Republican |
| James Madison | 1809–1817 | Democratic-Republican |
| James Monroe | 1817–1825 | Democratic-Republican |
| John Quincy Adams | 1825–1829 | Democratic-Republican |
| Andrew Jackson | 1829–1837 | Democrat |
| Martin Van Buren | 1837–1841 | Democrat |
| William H. Harrison | 1841 | Whig |
| John Tyler | 1841–1845 | Whig |
| James K. Polk | 1845–1849 | Democrat |
| Zachary Taylor | 1849–1850 | Whig |
| Millard Fillmore | 1850–1853 | Whig |
| Franklin Pierce | 1853–1857 | Democrat |
| James Buchanan | 1857–1861 | Democrat |

| Abraham Lincoln | 1861–1865 | Republican |
|---|---|---|
| Andrew Johnson | 1865–1869 | National Union |
| Ulysses S. Grant | 1869–1877 | Republican |
| Rutherford B. Hayes | 1877–1881 | Republican |
| James Garfield | 1881 | Republican |
| Chester Arthur | 1881–1885 | Republican |
| Grover Cleveland | 1885–1889 | Democrat |
| Benjamin Harrison | 1889–1893 | Republican |
| Grover Cleveland | 1893–1897 | Democrat |
| William McKinley | 1897–1901 | Republican |
| Theodore Roosevelt | 1901–1909 | Republican |
| William Taft | 1909–1913 | Republican |
| Woodrow Wilson | 1913–1921 | Democrat |
| Warren Harding | 1921–1923 | Republican |
| Calvin Coolidge | 1923–1929 | Republican |
| Herbert Hoover | 1929–1933 | Republican |
| Franklin D. Roosevelt | 1933–1945 | Democrat |
| Harry S. Truman | 1945–1953 | Democrat |
| Dwight Eisenhower | 1953–1961 | Republican |
| John F. Kennedy | 1961–1963 | Democrat |
| Lyndon Johnson | 1963–1969 | Democrat |
| Richard Nixon | 1969–1974 | Republican |
| Gerald Ford | 1974–1977 | Republican |
| Jimmy Carter | 1977–1981 | Democrat |
| Ronald Reagan | 1981–1989 | Republican |
| George Bush | 1989–1993 | Republican |
| Bill Clinton | 1993–2001 | Democrat |
| George W. Bush | 2001–2009 | Republican |
| Barack Obama | 2009–2017 | Democrat |
| Donald Trump | 2017–2021 | Republican |
| Joe Biden | 2021– | Democrat |

## PRIME MINISTERS OF CANADA

| | | | |
|---|---|---|---|
| Sir John Macdonald | 1867–1873 | William King | 1935–1948 |
| Alexander Mackenzie | 1873–1878 | Louis St Laurent | 1948–1957 |
| Sir John Macdonald | 1878–1891 | John Diefenbaker | 1957–1963 |
| Sir John Abbott | 1891–1892 | Lester Pearson | 1963–1968 |
| Sir John Thompson | 1892–1894 | Pierre Trudeau | 1968–1979 |
| Sir Mackenzie Bowell | 1894–1896 | Charles (Joe) Clark | 1979–1980 |
| Sir Charles Tupper | 1896 | Pierre Trudeau | 1980–1984 |
| Sir Wilfrid Laurier | 1896–1911 | John Turner | 1984 |
| Sir Robert Borden | 1911–1920 | Brian Mulroney | 1984–1993 |
| Arthur Meighen | 1920–1921 | Kim Campbell | 1993 |
| William King | 1921–1926 | Jean Chrétien | 1993–2003 |
| Arthur Meighen | 1926 | Paul Martin | 2003–2006 |
| William King | 1926–1930 | Stephen Harper | 2006–2015 |
| Richard Bennett | 1930–1935 | Justin Trudeau | 2015– |

## PRIME MINISTERS OF AUSTRALIA

| | | | |
|---|---|---|---|
| Sir Edmund Barton | 1901–1903 | Francis Forde | 1945 |
| Alfred Deakin | 1903–1904 | Joseph Chifley | 1945–1949 |
| John Watson | 1904 | Sir Robert Menzies | 1949–1966 |
| Sir George Reid | 1904–1905 | Harold Holt | 1966–1967 |
| Alfred Deakin | 1905–1908 | Sir John McEwen | 1967–1968 |
| Andrew Fisher | 1908–1909 | John Gorton | 1968–1971 |
| Alfred Deakin | 1909–1910 | William McMahon | 1971–1972 |
| Andrew Fisher | 1910–1913 | Edward Gough Whitlam | 1972–1975 |
| Sir Joseph Cook | 1913–1914 | John Fraser | 1975–1983 |
| Andrew Fisher | 1914–1915 | Robert Hawke | 1983–1991 |
| William Hughes | 1915–1923 | Paul Keating | 1991–1996 |
| Stanley Bruce | 1923–1929 | John Howard | 1996–2007 |
| James Scullin | 1929–1932 | Kevin Rudd | 2007–2010 |
| Joseph Lyons | 1932–1939 | Julia Gillard | 2010–2013 |

| | | | |
|---|---|---|---|
| Sir Earle Page | 1939 | Tony Abbott | 2013–2015 |
| Sir Robert Menzies | 1939–1941 | Malcolm Turnbull | 2015–2018 |
| Sir Arthur Fadden | 1941 | Scott Morrison | 2018– |
| John Curtin | 1941–1945 | | |

# PRIME MINISTERS OF NEW ZEALAND

| | | | |
|---|---|---|---|
| Sir Joseph Ward | 1906–1912 | Norman Kirk | 1972–1974 |
| Thomas MacKenzie | 1912–1915 | Hugh Watt | 1974 |
| William Massey | 1915–1925 | Wallace (Bill) Rowling | 1974–1975 |
| Sir Francis Bell | 1925 | Robert Muldoon | 1975–1984 |
| Joseph Coates | 1925–1928 | David Lange | 1984–1989 |
| Sir Joseph Ward | 1928–1930 | Geoffrey Palmer | 1989–1990 |
| George Forbes | 1930–1935 | Michael Moore | 1990 |
| Michael Savage | 1935–1940 | James Bolger | 1990–1997 |
| Peter Fraser | 1940–1949 | Jenny Shipley | 1997–1999 |
| Sir Sidney Holland | 1949–1957 | Helen Clark | 1999–2008 |
| Keith Holyoake | 1957 | John Key | 2008–2016 |
| Sir Walter Nash | 1957–1960 | Bill English | 2016–2017 |
| Keith Holyoake | 1960–1972 | Jacinda Ardern | 2017– |
| Sir John Marshall | 1972 | | |

# PRESIDENTS OF THE REPUBLIC OF ITALY

| | | | |
|---|---|---|---|
| Alcide de Gasperi (acting head of state) | 1946 | Amintore Fanfani | 1978 |
| Enrico de Nicola (provisional president) | 1946–1948 | Alessandro Pemini | 1978–1985 |
| Luigi Einaudi | 1948–1955 | Francesco Cossiga | 1985–1992 |
| Giovanni Gronchi | 1955–1962 | Oscar Luigi Scalfaro | 1992–1999 |
| Antonio Segni | 1962–1964 | Carlo Ciampi | 1999–2006 |
| Giuseppe Saragat | 1964–1971 | Giorgio Napolitano | 2006–2015 |
| Giovanni Leone | 1971–1978 | Sergio Mattarella | 2015– |

## PRIME MINISTERS

| | | | |
|---|---|---|---|
| Alcide de Gasperi | 1946–1953 | Armintore Fanfani | 1982–1983 |
| Guiseppe Pella | 1953–1954 | Bettino Craxi | 1983–1987 |
| Amintore Fanfani | 1954 | Giovanni Goria | 1987–1988 |
| Mario Scelba | 1954–1955 | Luigi Ciriaco de Mita | 1988–1989 |
| Antonio Segni | 1955–1957 | Giulio Andreotti | 1989–1992 |
| Adone Zoli | 1957–1958 | Giuliano Amato | 1992–1993 |
| Amintore Fanfani | 1958–1959 | Carlo Azegho Ciampi | 1993–1994 |
| Antonio Segni | 1959–1960 | Silvio Berlusconi | 1994 |
| Fernando Tambroni | 1960 | Lamberto Dini | 1995–1996 |
| Amintore Fanfani | 1960–1963 | Romano Prodi | 1996–1998 |
| Giovanni Leone | 1963 | Massimo D'Alema | 1998–2001 |
| Aldo Moro | 1963–1968 | Silvio Berlusconi | 2001–2006 |
| Giovanni Leone | 1968 | Romano Prodi | 2006–2008 |
| Mariano Rumor | 1968–1970 | Silvio Berlusconi | 2008–2011 |
| Emilio Colombo | 1970–1972 | Mario Monti | 2011–2013 |
| Mariano Rumor | 1973–1974 | Enrico Letta | 2013–2014 |
| Aldo Moro | 1974–1976 | Matteo Renzi | 2014–2016 |
| Giulio Andreotti | 1976–1979 | Paolo Gentiloni | 2016–2018 |
| Francesco Cossiga | 1979–1980 | Giuseppe Conte | 2018–2021 |
| Arnaldo Forlani | 1980–1981 | Mario Draghi | 2021– |
| Giovanni Spadolini | 1981–1982 | | |

# PRESIDENTS OF THE REPUBLIC OF INDIA

| | | | |
|---|---|---|---|
| Dr Rajendra Prasad | 1949–1962 | Neelam Reddy | 1977–1982 |
| Dr Sarvepalli Radhakrishnan | 1962–1967 | Giani Zail Singh | 1982–1987 |
| Dr Zakir Hussain | 1967–1969 | Ramaswamy Venkataraman | 1987–1992 |
| Varahagiri Giri | 1969–1974 | Shankar Dayal Sharma | 1992–1997 |
| Fakhruddin Ahmed | 1974–1977 | K. R. Narayanan | 1997–2002 |
| Basappa Jatti | 1977 | Abdul Kalam | 2002–2007 |
| | | Pratibha Patil | 2007–2012 |
| | | Pranab Mukherjee | 2012–2017 |

| | | Ram Nath Kovind | 2017– |

## PRIME MINISTERS

| | | | |
|---|---|---|---|
| Jawaharlal Nehru | 1947–1964 | Rajiv Gandhi | 1984–1989 |
| Gulzarilal Nanda | 1964 | V. P. Singh | 1989–1990 |
| Lal Shastri | 1964–1966 | Chandra Shekhar | 1990–1991 |
| Gulzarilal Nanda | 1966 | P. V. Narasimha Rao | 1991–1996 |
| Indira Gandhi | 1966–1977 | Atal Bihari Vajpayee | 1996 |
| Shri Moraji Desai | 1977–1979 | H. D. Deve Gowda | 1996–1997 |
| Charan Singh | 1979–1980 | I. K. Gujral | 1997 |
| Indira Gandhi | 1980–1984 | Atal Bihari Vajpayee | 1997–2004 |
| | | Dr. Manmohan Singh | 2004–2014 |
| | | Narendra Modi | 2014– |

# MAJOR WARS

| DATE | NAME OF WAR | WARRING PARTIES |
|---|---|---|
| c.1250 BC | Trojan wars | Myceneans v. Trojans |
| 431–404 BC | Peloponnesian War | Athens v. Sparta |
| 264–146 BC | Punic Wars | Rome v. Carthage |
| 1096–1099 | First Crusade | |
| 1147–1149 | Second Crusade | Saracens v. Christians over Palestine |
| 1189–1192 | Third Crusade | |
| 1202–1204 | Fourth Crusade | |
| 1337–1453 | Hundred Years' War | England v. France |
| 1455–1485 | Wars of the Roses | House of York v. House of Lancaster |
| 1562–1598 | French Wars of Religion | Huguenots v. Catholics |
| 1642–1648 | English Civil War | Cavaliers v. Roundheads |
| 1618–1648 | Thirty Years' War | Catholic League (Germany, Austria, Spain) v. Denmark, Sweden, France |
| 1689–1697 | War of League of Augsburg | France v. the League, England and the Netherlands |
| 1700 | Great Northern War | Sweden v. Russia, Denmark, Poland, Holland |
| 1701–1713 | War of Spanish Succession | Spain, France and Bavaria v. England, Holland, Austrian empire and Portugal |
| 1730–1738 | War of Polish Succession | Russia, Poland v. France |
| 1740–1748 | War of Austrian Succession | Austria, Britain v. Prussia, Bavaria, France, Spain |
| 1756–1763 | Seven Years' War | Britain and Prussia v. France, Austria, and Russia |
| 1775–1783 | American Revolutionary War | American colonies v. Britain |
| 1793–1815 | Napoleonic wars | France v. Britain, Austria, Sweden, Russia, and Prussia |
| 1821–1829 | Greek War of Independence | Greece v. Ottoman Turkey |
| 1846–1848 | Mexican-American War | Mexico v. U.S.A. |
| 1854–1856 | Crimean War | Russia v. Britain, France and Turkey |
| 1859 | War for Italian Independence | France, Piedmont-Sardinia v. Austria |
| 1861–1865 | American Civil War | Confederates v. Unionists |
| 1866 | Austro-Prussian War | Prussia v. Austria |
| 1870 | Franco-Prussian War | France v. Prussia |
| 1894–1895 | Chinese-Japanese War | China v. Japan |
| 1899–1902 | Boer War | Britain v. Boers (Dutch) in South Africa |
| 1904–1905 | Russo-Japanese War | Russia v. Japan |
| 1914–1918 | World War I | Germany and Austria-Hungary v. France, Russia, Britain, and other nations |
| 1918–1921 | Russian Civil War | Bolsheviks v. White Russians |
| 1931–1933 | Chinese-Japanese War | Japan v. China |
| 1936–1939 | Spanish Civil War | Nationalists (Franco) v. Republicans |
| 1939–1945 | World War II | Britain, France, U.S.S.R., U.S.A. and other nations v. Germany, Italy, Japan |
| 1950–1953 | Korean War | North Korea v. South Korea |
| 1967 | Six-Day War | Israel v. Arab states |
| 1964–1973 | Vietnam War | North Vietnam v. South Vietnam and U.S.A. |
| 1980–1988 | Iran-Iraq War | Iran v. Iraq |
| 1982 | Falklands War | United Kingdom v. Argentina |
| 1991 | Gulf War | Iraq v. combined international forces |
| 2001–2021 | Afghanistan War | Combined international forces v. the Taliban in Afghanistan |
| 2003–2011 | Iraq War | United States and international coalition forces v. Iraq |
| 2011–present | Syrian Civil War | Syrian government with Russian support vs rebel groups with Turkish, Saudi, U.S., U.K., and French support |
| 2014–present | Yemeni Civil War | Cabinet of Yemen with Saudi coalition support v. Supreme Political Council and Houthi movement |

# INDEX

485

302–3, 307, 308, 310, 316
Napoleon III, Emperor 327, 340, 341
Napoleonic Wars 302–3, 309, 310, 348
Nara period 81
Narva, Battle of 264
NASA (National Aeronautics and Space Administration) 415
Naseby, Battle of 246
Nasmyth, James 321
nationalism
  Balkan 356
  European 326
  fascism and 376
  Indonesian 346
  Irish 261, 344
Nationalists (Spain) 386, 387
Nato (North Atlantic Treaty Organization) 412, 413, 451
Navarra/Navarre 191, 215
navigation 226
Nazca culture 123
Nazi Party 377, 384–5, 390, 397, 406
Neanderthals (Homo neanderthalis) 5
Nebuchadnezzar of Babylon 23, 34, 35
Nefertiti, Queen 24
Nehru, Jawaharlal 399
Nelson, Admiral Horatio 302, 303
Neoclassicism 313, 314
Neolithic period 6
Neptune 415
Nero, Emperor 63
Nestorian church 69
Netherlands
  art and architecture 268, 269
  Austrian War of Succession 274
  colonies and empire 235, 245, 256, 259, 266, 267, 290, 420
  Dutch independence 218–19, 243
  East India Company 244, 245
  new constitution 327
  Reformation 205
  Renaissance 192
  slave trade 304
  and South Africa 323
  and Southeast Asia 296–7, 346, 347
  Spanish rule 205, 212, 218, 219
  trade with Japan 296
  World War II 391
New Deal 383
New England 220, 234, 235, 266, 284
New France 285
New Granada 308
New Guinea 84, 395, 433
New Holland 294
New Kingdom (Egypt) 24–5
New Mexico 267
New Model Army 246
New Netherland 245
New Orleans 379, 444
New South Wales 329, 355
New World 225
New York 235, 266, 360, 361, 363, 379, 407, 439
New Zealand
  1792–1907 328–9
  as British dominion 349, 402
  explorers and settlers 294, 295, 328, 329
  politics 453
  Polynesians 84
  prime ministers 477

women's suffrage 353
  World War I 369
  World War II 395
Newcomen, Thomas 278, 279
Newfoundland 197, 234, 235
Newton, Isaac 254, 255, 270, 271, 288
Ngo Dinh Diem 421
Nicene Creed 69
Nicephorus, Emperor 106
Nicholas II, Tsar 366, 372
Niger 443
Niger River 29, 156, 198
Nigeria 259, 291, 342
  Bantu expansion 56
  Benin Kingdom 158
  Biafran War 425, 426
  Nok culture 29, 91
Night of the Long Knives 384, 385
Nightingale, Florence 330
Nijinsky, Vaslav 404
Nile, River 8
Nineveh 20, 21, 35
Nixon, Richard 421
Nizam al-Mulk 129
Nobel, Alfred 363
Nobunaga, Oda 222, 223
Nok culture 29, 56, 91
nomadic peoples 5, 6, 162, 163
non-governmental organizations (NGOs) 425, 447
Non-Proliferation Treaty 432
Nördlingen, Battle of 237, 239
Normandy, Allied invasion of 393
Normans 95, 117, 121, 125, 126–7, 135, 147
North Africa
  Arab invasions 101
  Greek colonies 48
  Ottomans 206, 253, 290
  Romans 61
  World War II 392
  see also countries by name
North America
  500 B.C.–AD500 72
  500–1200 122
  500–1492 104–5
  1460–1600 220–1
  1675–1791 284–5
  colonial 1600–1700 266–7
  European settlers 221, 234–5, 245
  explorers 197, 220
  slavery 266
  Spanish empire 211, 242, 267
  Vikings 125
  see also countries by name
North American Free Trade Association (NAFTA) 418
North German Confederation 341
North Korea 420, 421, 432, 451
North Macedonia 427
North Vietnam 421
Northern Ireland 424
Northwest Ordinance Act (U.S.) 311
Norway
  Great Northern War 264
  Vikings 124
  World War II 391
Nostradamus 227
Nova Scotia 284
Novgorod 216
Nubia 9, 28, 29
nuclear disasters 430, 446
nuclear fission 408
nuclear weapons 395, 396,

408, 409, 412, 413, 432
Nur Jahan 209, 251
Nuremberg Laws 385
Nuremberg rallies 384
Nuremberg Trials 397
Nyamwezi Empire 290
Nyere, Julius 427
nylon 409

O
Oba Eware the Great of Benin 158
obesity 458
Occupy 452
Oceania
  exploration 294–5
  see also countries by name
Ochterlony, Sir David 306
O'Connell, Daniel 344, 345
Octavian see Augustus
Odoacer, King of Italy 78
Ogodai Khan 162
oil 362, 363, 419
oil spills 430, 446
O'Keefe, Georgia 404
Okinawa, Battle of 395, 396
Old Testament 22, 23
Olmecs 30, 40, 72, 73
Oman 290
Omdurman, Battle of 343
one-child policy 416, 417, 443
Onin civil war 149
OPEC 419
opera 358, 361
opium 286, 287
Opium Wars 324–5
oracle bones 16
Organization of African Unity (OAU) 427
Organization for Economic Cooperation and Development (OECD) 418
Orléans, Siege of 169
Osei Tutu, King of Asante 259
Osman I, Sultan 206
Osman II, Sultan 252
Ostrogoths 79, 86
Otis, Elisha 360
Ottakar II of Bohemia 115
Ottawa tribe 284
Otto I, Emperor 114, 118, 119
Otto, Nikolaus 363
Ottoman Empire
  1453–1600 206–7, 226
  1602–1783 252–3
  Balkan Wars 356–7
  collapse of 375, 400
  Crimean War 330–1
  decline of 290
  and Moghuls 208
  and Russian expansion 262, 293
  and Safavid Persia 199
  and Seljuk Turks 128
  takes over Byzantine Empire 94, 95, 174, 175
  World War I 368, 369
  see also Turkey
Ouchy, Treaty of 356, 357
Oud, Jacobus 406
Oudh 280
Oxenstierna, Axel 236
Oxfam 425
Oyo 259, 290
ozone layer 430

P
Pachacutec 165
Pachacuti 188, 189
Pacific Ocean
  exploration 197, 294
  microplastics 446
  Polynesians 84–5
  World War II 394–5

Pact of Steel 376
Paine, Thomas 288
Pakistan
  East and West 426
  formation of 399
  and India 432
  nuclear weapons 432
Palaeolithic period 5
Palestine 21, 22, 24, 94, 330
  Crusades 140–1
  foundation of Israel 400, 401
  Muslim conquest 100, 101
  refugees 456
  Romans 57, 61
Palestine Liberation Organization (PLO) 429
Palladio, Andrea 224
Palmerston, Henry Temple, 3rd Viscount 324
Panama 308
pandemics 442
Pankhurst, Christabel 353
Pankhurst, Emmeline 353
Papacy 119, 127, 200, 338, 339, 468
Papal States 252, 338, 339
papermaking 90, 91, 137, 182
Papineau, Louis 337
Papua 433
papyrus 8, 87
Paracelsus 227
Paranthropus 4
Paris 170, 300, 326, 360, 361, 439
  Siege of (1870) 341
  Treaty of (1763) 285
  Treaty of (1783) 299
  Treaty of (1856) 331
Paris Agreement 444, 445
Paris Peace Conference (1919–20) 375
Parnell, Charles Stewart 345
Parni tribe 70
Parseeism see Zoroastrianism
Parthenon 88
Parthians 61, 70–1, 76
particle physics 463
partition of India 399
Pasargadae 38
Pascal, Blaise 255
Passchendaele, Battle of 368
patricians 58, 59, 60, 62
Patrick, St 146, 147
Paul, the apostle 68, 69
Paul III, Pope 205
Pawnee 350
peacekeeping, UN 432–3
Pearl Harbor 379, 392, 394, 395
Pearse, Patrick 370
Peloponnesian War 49, 52
penal colonies 295, 349, 354, 355
Penang 296, 346
penicillin 409
Peninsular Wars 303
Penn, William 266
Pennsylvania 267
People's Charter 326, 327
People's Liberation Army 416
People's Republic of China 381, 403, 416, 432
Pepin, King of the Franks 108
Pepys, Samuel 255
Pericles 50
periodic table 363
Perón, Juan 377
Perry, Commodore Matthew 332
Perry, Oliver 311
Persepolis 38, 39
Persia
  Abbasids 110, 128
  Alexander the Great 35, 52

# ACKNOWLEDGMENTS

**The publishers wish to thank the following for their contributions:**

**Photographs** (*t* = top; *b* = bottom; *m* = middle; *l* = left; *r* = right)

Cover front: Andrew Holt / Alamy Stock Photo; flap front WitR/Shutterstock; flap back sedmak/iStock,; cover back Attila Kisbenedek/Getty Images, TacioPhilip/iStock, Dotted Yeti/Shutterstock, FloridaStock/Shutterstock, Per Grunditz/Shutterstock, Corona Borealis Studio/Shutterstock; page i ; ii-iii ; vb and 441 robertharding/Alamy Stock Photo; vii ; viii ; 2 Michael Ochs Archives/Stringer/Getty Images; 12 and 13 AlexelA/Shutterstock; 14 Anna Pakutina/Shutterstock; 15t Starcevic/iStock, 15ml, 101, 371l Leemage/Getty Images; 16, 17, 249m Shan_shan/Shutterstock; 18tl Lefteris_/iStock, 18bl marketa1982/Shutterstock, 18br Izabela Miszczak/Shutterstock; 19, 33, 137, 147, 277m, 312, 348tr, 393m Print Collector/Getty Images; 23t Historic Images/Alamy Stock Photo, 23m, 32, 133tl, 138, 153b, 202tl, 269tr, 321bl, 332br, 341b, 343t, 348tl, 349m, 355tr, 381mr, 394tr, 397tl, 397tr, 403tl, 416b, 421tl, 426tl World History Archive/Alamy Stock Photo; 26 JossK/Shutterstock; 27 Lars Fortuin/Shutterstock; 28 guenterguni/iStock; 30 Barna Tanko/Shutterstock; 34 Stephane de Sakutin/Stringer/Getty Images; 37 Art Collection 3/Alamy Stock Photo; 38t Leonid Andronov/Shutterstock, 38b Sompol/Shutterstock; 39ml, 277t Colin Waters/Alamy Stock Photo, 39b Borna_Mirahmadian/Shutterstock; 40 The Natural History Museum/Alamy Stock Photo; 41 coddy/iStock, 41b Terence Kerr/Alamy Stock Photo; 43 Jule_Berlin/Shutterstock; 46 zoom-zoom/iStock; 52 Simone Crespiatico/iStock; 53 saiko3p/Shutterstock; 57t Kimmo Keskinen/Shutterstock; Orlov Sergei/Shutterstock; 69 Lex20/iStock; 72, 120r, 191tr, 209, 233, 247m, 294ml, 322ml, 323bl, 324tr, 327tr, 327bl, 329bl, 330tl, 337br, 375br, 376b, 382bl, 385tl, 391b, 395br, 413t, 420tl, 437tm Granger Historical Picture Archive/Alamy Stock Photo; 74 RealityImages/Shutterstock; 75t paul prescott/Shutterstock; 77 Vladimir Korostyshevskiy/Shutterstock; 79t Kayihan Bolukbasi/Shutterstock, 79b, 384cl Roger Viollet Collection/Getty Images; 81 EvergreenPlanet/Shutterstock; 89tl JetKat/Shutterstock, 89tr dwatanabe/iStock; 92 Mardox/Alamy Stock Photo; 93, 94mr, 109, 121t, 225, 339tl, 373mr, 381r DEA Picture Library/Getty Images; 94b Niday Picture Library/Alamy Stock Photo; 95tm clamon/iStock, 95b AGF/Getty Images; 97tr, 332tr, 395tr, 396tl Universal History Archive/Getty; 102, 103t, 238ml, 243b 245b, 307, 313t, 331tr, 357tr, 385mr, 387b, 387b Album/Alamy Stock Photo; 103bl, 103br, 153t, 208, 329tr, 340b, 347b, 379m The Picture Art Collection/Alamy Stock Photo; 105 Don Miller/iStock; 107tl Bolot/iStock, 107tr Coprid/iStock, 107b, 397ml,426bl ITAR-TASS News Agency/Alamy Stock Photo; 108, 219b, 293, 338tr, 364, 377bl DEA/A. Dagli Orti/Getty Images; 112 junce/iStock; 113 Krunja/Shutterstock; 114mr Millionstock/Shutterstock, 114b Iryna_Rasko/iStock; 115t, 191tl, 191tl, 203, 241b, 252t, 252b, 253t, 259t, 339b DEA/G. Dagli Orti/Getty Images, 115b kyrien/iStock; 119 no_limit_pictures/iStock; 120l Marissa Tabbada/iStock; 121m Traveller70/Shutterstock; 123t TacioPhilip/iStock, 123b JordiStock/iStock; 126 jorisvo/Shutterstock; 129t leshiy985/Shutterstock, 129m HSBortecin/Shutterstock; 130b, 173m Sepia Times/Getty Images; 131tl, 264tl, 288tr, 358tr Artokoloro/Alamy Stock Photo, 131tr ART Collection/Alamy Stock Photo; 133tr sedmak/iStock; 135 cassinga/iStock; 144, 156b, 305tm, 346ml, 372tr, 414cl, 436ml, 461mt Science History Images/Alamy Stock Photo; 146, 198tl North Wind Picture Archives/Alamy Stock Photo; 152 Lifestyle Pictures/Alamy Stock Photo; 154 Ivy Close Images/Alamy Stock Photo; 155, 178t, 219, 272 Heritage Images/Getty Images; 156m The History Collection/Alamy Stock Photo; 157 Joel Carillet/iStock; 159 evenfh/Shutterstock; 161 littlewormy/iStock; 169, 368bm, 428tl Photo 12/Getty Images; 172 Chefmd/iStock; 173b Barney Burstein/Getty Images; 175t bogdb/iStock, 175b Faraways/Shutterstock; 176 Sean Yuan/Shutterstock; 177 Marc Witte/Shutterstock; 178t, 198b, 202tr, 236ml, 289b, 335tr, 343b, 367tm Heritage Images Partnership Ltd/Getty Images, 178b clodio/iStock; 179 Brian Maudsley/Shutterstock; 181 ShaikhMeraj/Shutterstock; 184 Oleg Golovnev/Shutterstock; 191b Universal Art Archive/Alamy Stock Photo; 192, 269b classicpaintings/Alamy Stock Photo, 239b IgorGolovniov/Shutterstock, 239b, 377tm Imagno Contributor/Getty Images; 241tr Svintage Archive/Alamy Stock Photo; 242tl, 288b, 324tl, 330ml, 358tl, 359tl, 372ml, 373tr, 373tl, 391tl, 399ml, 406tr IanDagnall Computing/Alamy Stock Photo, 242b mistervlad/Shutterstock; 243t, 359br Prisma Archivo/Alamy Stock Photo; 244bl, 260t, 281b, 309t, 333tr, 344tr, 353tr, 370br, 405bl, 409tl Pictorial Press Ltd/Alamy Stock Photo, 244br Werner Forman/Getty Images; 244t, 274 DEA/M./Seemuller/Getty Images; 248, 287t, 291t, 325br, 352br, 376tl CPA Media Pte Ltd/Alamy Stock Photo; 249t HelloRF Zcool/Shutterstock; 253b DEA/G./Nimatallah/Getty Images; 255 Peter van Evert/Alamy Stock Photo; 258tr Marzolino/Shutterstock; 259m, 392br De Agostini Picture Library/Getty Images; 260b Hulton Archive/Stringer/Getty Images; 264ml, 292tr, 336bl, 344cl, 350tml, 350bml, 358ml, 359bl, 384b, 398tr, 402tl, 404m, 412tr, 415br, 420tr, 422tl, 422mr, 429br, 450bl Everett Collection/Shutterstock; 268br Shchipkova Elena/Shutterstock; 270, 397tl, 403tr agefotostock/Alamy Stock Image; 275 Claire Fraser Photography/Shutterstock; 276l FLHC50/Alamy Stock Image, 276b HeritagePics/Alamy Stock Image; 279, 287b duncan 1890/iStock; 282 Icom Images/Alamy Stock Image; 285, 346br, 383mr, 383br, 388tl Bettmann/Getty Images; 289t, 331m Lebrecht Music & Arts/Alamy Stock Image; 291b DEA/ICAS94/Getty Images; 295, 329mr, 332tl, 336tr, 337tr, 342tl, 374tr, 375bm, 386ml Chronicle/Alamy Stock Photo; 296ml Olemac/Shutterstock, 296b MCLA Collection/Alamy Stock Image; 297, 385tr Historical Picture Archive/Getty Images; 311 Keith Lance/iStock; 313t Gewgoat/iStock Photo, 313b Photo Josse/Leemage/Getty Images; 314 Colin Burdett/Shutterstock; 321br, 349b The History Emporium/Alamy Stock Photo; 322br MPI/Stringer/Getty Images; 324b History_docu_photo/Alamy Stock Photo; 325t Picture Now/Alamy Stock Photo; 325br Really Easy Star/Alamy Stock Photo; 328tl Morphart Creation/Shutterstock; 328b Lakeview Images/Alamy Stock Photo; 341t Falkensteinfoto/Alamy Stock Photo; 349t Royal Geographical Society/Getty Images; 353br, 377tr Photo 12/Getty Images; 354b Michiru Maeda/Shutterstock; 357br FLHC A33/Alamy Stock Photo; 358bl 19th era/Alamy Stock Photo, 358br Lanmas/Alamy Stock Photo; 361bl Photo Provider Network; 363br OSweetNature/Shutterstock; 366tl KGPA Ltd/Alamy Stock Photo, 366ml, 386tr, 389tr, 389bm, 398bl ullstein bild Dtl/Getty Images; 367bm akg-images/Alamy Stock Photo; 369br De Luan/Alamy Stock Photo; 372tl John Frost/Alamy Stock Photo; 373tl, 374tl, 390tl Shawshots/Alamy Stock Photo; 375tr Fine Art/Getty Images; 377br Elzbieta Sekowska/Shutterstock; 378ml PhotoQuest/Getty Images; 378bm General Photographic Agency/Stringer/Getty Images; 379tr JP Jazz Archive/Getty Images, 379bl GraphicaArtis/Getty Images, 379mr Patti McConville/Alamy Stock Photo; 380b, 389bl Topical Press Agency/Stringer/Getty Images; 382tl American Photo Archive/Alamy Stock Photo, 382tr RBM Vintage Images/Alamy Stock Photo; 384tl Estate of Emil Bieber/Klaus Niermann/Getty Images; 385mr Azoor Photo/Alamy Stock Photo; 386br TT News Agency; 387t SeM/Getty Images; 388tr, 390br, 412bl Sueddeutshe Zeitung Photo/Alamy Stock Photo, 388b, 408bl Underwood Archives/Getty Images; 390m Keystone/Staff/Getty Images; 392tr Hulton Deutsch/Getty Images; 393tr Galerie Bilderwelt/Getty Images; 394mr, 418tr, 428b Keystone Press/Alamy Stock Photo; 396b Prisma by Dukas Presseagentur GmbH/Alamy Stock Photo; 397br FPG/Staff/Getty Images; 399br, 400br Matteo Omied/Alamy Stock Photo; 401t GEO/Handout/Getty Images, 401bl Stringer/Getty Images; 402b, 426br Fox Photos/Stringer/Getty Images; 404tr Alpha Historica/Alamy Stock Photo; 405tl Peter Barritt/Alamy Stock Photo, 405tl Peter Barritt/Alamy Stock Photo, 405bm Georgi Stoyanov/Alamy Stock Photo, 405br Reporters Associes/Getty Images; 406bl, 455tl Agencja Fotograficzna Caro/Alamy Stock Photo, 406br Martine De Flander/Alamy Stock Photo; 407tl BDP/Alamy Stock Photo, 407cr Mishella/Shutterstock, 407b Dasha R/Shutterstock; 408tr Tennie Harris Archive/Carnegie Museum of Art/Getty Images, 408ml Science & Society Picture Library/Getty Images, UniversalImagesGroup/Getty Images; 409mr f8 archive/Alamy Stock Photo, 409bl Bachrach/Getty Images; 410, 415ml Artsiom P/Shutterstock; 412tl Getty Images; 413m CTK/Alamy Stock Photo, 413bl Brian Harris/Alamy Stock Photo, M&N/Alamy Stock Photo; 414tl intueri/Shutterstock, 414tr, 461mb Dotted Yeti/Shutterstock, 414bl NASA Archive/Alamy Stock Photo; 415tr NASA Image Collection/Alamy Stock Photo; 416tl humprhey/Shutterstock, 416tr Barry Lewis/Alamy Stock Photo; 417tl Euters/Alamy Stock Photo, 417mr, 422tr, 456tr, DPA Picture Alliance/Alamy Stock Photo, 417br Top Photo Corporation/Alamy Stock Photo; 418tl ImageFlow/Shutterstock, 418b Maykova Galina/Shutterstock; 419tr, 435mr Tom Stoddart Archive/Getty Images, 419tl Markus Mainka/Shutterstock, 419b ClassicStock/Alamy Stock Photo; 420br Haywood Magee/Getty Images; 421bm Roland Neveu/Getty Images; 422b Dom Slike/Alamy Stock Photo; 423t Asar Studios/Alamy Stock Photo, 423m Bernard Bisson/Getty Images, 423b Russotwins/Alamy Stock Photo; 424tl Michel Philippot/Getty Images, 424tr ZUMA Press Inc./Alamy Stock Photo, 424bl Bryn Colton/Getty Images, 424br The Asahi Shimbun/Getty Images; 425tl Georges De Keerle/Getty Images, 425tr Neil Cooper/Alamy Stock Photo, 425bl David Turnley/Getty Images, 425br robertharding/Alamy Stock Photo; 426tr Central Press/Getty Images, 426bl AFP/Getty Images; 427m Buddy Mays/Alamy Stock Photo, 427bl Alexey Stiop/Alamy Stock Photo, 427br TASS/Getty Images; 429t peter jordan/Alamy Stock Photo, 429tr Vladimir Mijailovic/Shutterstock; 430tr Patrick Riviere/Staff/Getty Images, 430tr Nelson Antoine/Shutterstock; 431tl Dylan Garcia Travel Images/Alamy Stock Photo, 431tr MikeDotta/Shutterstock, 431bl Luis A/Shutterstock, 431br MireXa/Getty Images; 432tl Peter Probst/Alamy Stock Photo, 432b Keystone-France/Getty Images, 432br Christine Osborne Pictures433tr POOL/Getty Images ; 433br Johnny Saunderson/Alamy Stock Photo, 433tr POOL/Getty Images; 434tl David Levenson/Getty Images, 434tr Bride Lane Library/Popperfoto/Getty Images, 434bl Mark Reinstein/Shutterstock, 434ml yuzu2020/Shutterstock; 435tr Greg da Silva/Shutterstock, 435br Alexander Joe/Staff/Getty Images; 436tl, 437b, 464b PA Images/Alamy Stock Photo, 436tr Grechanyuk Aleksandr/Alamy Stock Photo, 436bc RicAguiar/Getty Images; 437tr Gado Images/Alamy Stock Photo; 438tl Malcolm Park Editorial/Alamy Stock Photo, 438tr Pete Still/Getty Images, 438m, 462tr Catwalker/Shutterstock, 438b Fiona Adams/Getty Images; 439tm Daniel Fung/Shutterstock, 439l Tinnaporn Sathapornnanont/Shutterstock, 439bm myphotobank.au/Shutterstock, 439tr andersphoto/Shutterstock, 439b Luciano Mortula – LGM/Shutterstock; 440 Pradit_Ph/iStock, 442b fotoVoyager/iStock, 442tr Tarzan9280/iStock, 442tl, 454tl FG Trade/iStock; 443t Neil Thomas/Getty Images, 443m nikvasil6/Shutterstock; 443b Daniel_Berehulak/Staff/Getty Images; 444mr bear_productions/Shutterstock, 444tl Andrea Izzotti/Alamy Stock Photo, 444tr Tarcisio Schnaider/iStock, 444b FloridaStock/Shutterstock; 445tl rafapress/Shutterstock, 445bl James Pearce/Alamy Stock Photo, 445tr Per Grunditz/Shutterstock, 445br DOD Photo/Alamy Stock Photo; 446tl, 448bl Future Publishinh/Getty, 446tr Frank Bienewald/Getty Images, 446bl Tunatura/iStock, 446br DigitalGlobe/Getty images; 447t The Washington Post/Getty Images, 447m Daniel Prudek/Shutterstock, 447b Clarence Holmes Photography/Alamy Stock Photo; 448tl Geoffrey Robinson/Alamy Stock Photo, 448tr Ulrich Baumgarten/Getty Images, 448br Kostas Koutsaftikis/Shutterstock; 449tr Sky_Blue/iStock, 449br Jenny Matthews/Getty Images; 450tl Spencer Platt/Staff/Getty Images, 450tr Daily Mirror Gulf coverage/Getty Images; 451tr Olivier Bourgeois/Alamy Stock Photo, 451br Majority World/Getty Images, 451m, 455tr, 460tl Reuters/Alamy Stock Photo, 451bl UPI/Alamy Stock Photo; 452b Lalocracio/iStock, 452tl Grindstone Media Group/Shutterstock, 452tl Matt Cardy/Getty Images, 452tm, 457tr Anadolu Agency/Getty Images; 453tm Frederic Legrand – Comeo/Shutterstock, 453tr photocosmos1/Shutterstock, 453mr SOPA Images/Getty Images, 453b Pavel Stasevich/Alamy Stock Photo, 455br Sipa US/Alamy Stock Photo, 455tr Attila Kisbenedek/Getty Images, 455bl Richard Levine/Alamy Stock Photo, 455b FatCamera/iStock; 456tl Ozan Kose/Getty Images, 456b Dimitris Tosidis/Shutterstock; 457mr Darren Staples/Getty Images, 457bl Handout/Getty Images, 457br Saul Loeb/Getty Images; 458tr, 460tr, 461t Xinhua/Alamy Stock Photo, 458tl Deco/Alamy Stock Photo, 458bl Dominique Faget/Getty Images; 458mt Corona Borealis Studio/Shutterstock, 459t Alexandros Michailidis/Shutterstock, 459b Sabrina Bracher/iStock, 459mb Manoej Paateel/Shutterstock; 460b NASA/JPL-Caltech; 462tl ljubaphoto/iStock, 462bl insta_photos/Shutterstock; 463t Avalon/Construction Photography/Alamy Stock Photo, 463mr 3alexd/iStock, 463b Master_Andrii/shutterstockl; 464tr Anouchka/iStock./ Bride Lane / Popperfoto; 463 t iStock / MDA, m Getty / Walter Dhaladha, b Getty / Alexander Joe; 464 tl Getty / Mario Tama, b Corbis / Reuters.